Accounting Information Systems

Eleventh Edition

George H. Bodnar

William S. Hopwood

Florida Atlantic University

PEARSON

Boston   Columbus   Indianapolis   New York   San Francisco   Upper Saddle River   Amsterdam
Cape Town   Dubai   London   Madrid   Milan   Munich   Paris   Montreal   Toronto   Delhi   Mexico City
Sao Paulo   Sydney   Hong Kong   Seoul   Singapore   Taipei   Tokyo

Editorial Director: Sally Yagan
Editor in Chief: Donna Battista
AVP/Executive Editor: Stephanie Wall
Editorial Project Managers: Christina Rumbaugh, Nicole Sam
Editorial Assistants: Jane Avery, Lauren Zanedis
Director of Marketing: Maggie Moylan Leen
Marketing Assistants: Ian Gold, Kimberly Lovato
Project Manager: Renata Butera
Operations Specialist: Renata Butera

Creative Art Director: Jayne Conte
Cover Designer: Anthony Gemmellaro
Manager, Rights and Permissions: Hessa Albader
Cover Art: Getty Images, Inc.
Full-Service Project Management: Abinaya Rajendran
Composition: Integra Software Services, Pvt., Ltd.
Printer/Binder: R.R. Donnelley/Willard
Cover Printer: Lehigh-Phoenix Color
Text Font: 10/12 Times LT Std Roman

Credits and acknowledgments borrowed from other sources and reproduced, with permission, in this textbook appear on appropriate page within text.

Library of Congress Cataloging-in-Publication Data
Bodnar, George H.
    Accounting information systems/George H. Bodnar, William S. Hopwood.—11th ed.
       p. cm.
    ISBN-13: 978-0-13-287193-8
    ISBN-10: 0-13-287193-9
    1. Accounting—Data processing.   2. Information storage and retrieval systems—Accounting.
I. Hopwood, William   S. II. Title.
HF5679.B59 2013
657.0285—dc23
                                                        2011037960

10 9 8 7 6 5 4 3 2 1

PEARSON

ISBN 10:   0-13-287193-9
ISBN 13: 978-0-13-287193-8

Dedication

To my wife Donna

—George H. Bodnar

Dedicated to all the great people I work with in the Florida
Atlantic University School of Accounting

—William S. Hopwood

Contents

Chapter 10   The Production Business Process   349

PART III   Systems Development   381

Chapter 11   Systems Planning, Analysis, and Design   381

Preface

The eleventh edition of *Accounting Information Systems* continues to stress electronic commerce, database management, and systems development, all applied within the context of business processes, transaction cycles, and internal control. Detailed presentation of business processes and internal control is central to the topical organization. The business process chapters are traditionally oriented in presentation but at times rely on SAP™ ERP to extend the presentation to contemporary information systems. However, these chapters do not require the instructor to possess technical expertise in SAP™ ERP. The detailed presentation of internal controls in these chapters is consistent with all technological incarnations of accounting information systems.

The text contains an extensive CPA examination problem collection pertaining to business processes and internal controls, with complete answers and explanations in The Instructor's Resource and Solutions Manual. Our extensive CPA problem collection is drawn from the same pool of CPA examination questions that continue to serve as the cornerstone of the coverage of internal control provided by professional CPA Examination Review courses. The text also contains an assortment of CMA exam and CIA exam questions.

The textbook's core coverage continues to include business processes, transaction cycles, and internal controls. These topics have been central to this textbook since its original publication in 1980. The passage of the Sarbanes–Oxley Act is a testament to the continuing importance of these topics. An understanding of business processes is fundamental to contemporary auditing, and professional and legal considerations relating to an organization's internal control processes. Every business process is subject to loss exposures. Management should develop detailed control objectives for each business process. Such control objectives provide a basis for analysis and the risk-based audit of an organization's internal control processes as well as a basis for managing the loss exposures that are associated with an organization's dependence on information systems.

The eleventh edition presents "successive refinement" of the topical additions that were new in the tenth edition. These included discussion of various information systems reference models, enterprise architecture, Business Process Modeling Notation (BPMN), international standards for information security, integration of BPMN into our business process chapters, and an in-depth discussion of COBIT. Chapter 3 "eBusiness and eCommerce" has been streamlined to eliminate unnecessary technical details. All chapters have been edited to improve clarity of presentation and readability.

The eleventh edition features an entirely new chapter titled "Fraud Examination and Fraud Management." This chapter complements our presentation of internal controls and business processes by providing a vehicle to observe the effects of inadequate internal controls. The discussion of fraud investigations provides a step-by-step analysis of the processes required to prove that fraud has occurred. The objective is to teach students how to detect fraud, to conduct fraud investigations, and to appreciate that internal control, like the proverbial ounce of prevention, is worth a pound of cure. The chapter's discussion of the variety of methods used by employees to commit fraud reinforces the textbook's presentation of internal controls by providing scenarios in which the student can appreciate the value of specific controls in preventing specific types of fraud.

Learning Aids

Each chapter contains the following instructional aids:

- Learning Objectives
- Cases in Point in Text Boxes
- Glossary
- Annotated Webliography
- Chapter Quiz
- Review Problem

to top-level management accordingly consist largely of aggregated and summarized items such as total quarterly sales by product line or division. Middle managers need more detail, such as daily or weekly sales by product line, because their scope of control is narrower. Lower-level managers typically receive information relevant only to their particular subunit, such as the total sales of Department A. Personnel in the lower levels of an organization, such as clerks processing payroll or sales transaction data, constantly interact with the detailed transaction data.

The production of useful information is constrained by the environment of an AIS and the cost–benefit structure inherent in users' decisions. The uncertainty of the environment in which information is developed and presented means that estimates and judgments must be made. No information system can ignore the practicality of presenting information. If information costs more to provide than it is worth to the user, it is not practical to provide this information.

From an organization's viewpoint, a distinction might be drawn between two broad classes of accounting information: mandatory and discretionary. Various government agencies, private agencies, and legislation set statutory requirements for record keeping and reports. Reports, for example, are required for federal and state income taxes, and Social Security taxes, and by the Securities and Exchange Commission (SEC), Federal Trade Commission, and the like. In addition, certain basic accounting functions are essential to normal business activity. Payroll and accounts receivable are prime examples. These functions must be performed in any organization if the organization is to survive. Budgetary systems, responsibility accounting systems, and specific reports for internal management are examples of discretionary information. Conceptually, information should satisfy a cost–benefit criterion. Although the criterion theoretically applies to all the outputs of an AIS, the typical organization does not have control over all its information requirements. In meeting mandatory information requirements, the primary consideration is minimizing costs while meeting minimum standards of reliability and usefulness. When the provision of information is discretionary, the primary consideration is that the benefits obtained exceed the costs of production.

Information Systems

The term *information system* suggests the use of information technology (IT) in an organization to provide information to users. A *computer-based* information system is a collection of computer hardware and software designed to transform data into useful information. As indicated in Figure 1.3, one might distinguish several types of computer-based information systems.

DATA PROCESSING   **Electronic data processing (EDP)** is the use of IT to perform an organization's transaction-oriented data processing. EDP is a fundamental AIS application in every organization. Data concerning sales transactions, purchase transactions, cash receipts and cash payments transactions, and all other financial transactions that an organization undertakes must be accurately recorded, processed, and stored if the organization is to be sustainable. As

INFORMATION SYSTEMS
Electronic Data Processing System (EDP)
Data Processing System (DP)
Management Information System (MIS)
Decision Support System (DSS)
Expert System (ES)
Executive Information System (EIS)
Accounting Information System (AIS)

FIGURE 1.3

Types of Information Systems

computer technology has become commonplace, the term **data processing (DP)** has come to have the same meaning as EDP.

MANAGEMENT INFORMATION SYSTEMS   **Management information systems (MIS)** describes the use of IT to provide decision-oriented information to managers. An MIS provides a wide variety of information beyond that which is associated with DP in organizations. An MIS recognizes that managers within an organization use and require information in decision making and that computer-based information systems can assist in providing information to managers.

DECISION SUPPORT SYSTEMS   In a **decision support system (DSS)**, data are processed into a decision-making format for the end user. A DSS requires the use of decision models and specialized databases and differs significantly from a DP system. A DSS is directed at serving ad hoc, specific, non-routine information requests by management. DP systems serve routine, recurring, general information needs. A DSS is designed for specific types of decisions for specific users. A familiar example is the use of spreadsheet software to perform what-if analyses of operating or budget data, such as sales forecasting by marketing personnel.

EXPERT SYSTEMS   An **expert system (ES)** is a knowledge-based information system that uses its knowledge about a specific application area to act as an expert consultant to end users. Like DSS, an ES requires the use of decision models and specialized databases. Unlike DSS, an ES also requires the development of a knowledge base—the special knowledge that an expert possesses in the decision area—and an inference engine—the process by which the expert makes a decision. An ES attempts to replicate the decisions that would be made by an expert human decision maker in the same decision situation. An ES differs from a DSS in that a DSS assists a user in making a decision, whereas an ES makes the decision.

 CASE IN POINT

Federal National Mortgage Association (FNMA or "Fannie Mae") uses the Mavent Expert System (*www.mavent.com*) to review if loans are in compliance with the many lending-related government regulations, including those included in the Truth in Lending Act (TILA).

EXECUTIVE INFORMATION SYSTEMS   An **executive information system (EIS)** is tailored to the strategic information needs of top-level management. Much of the information used by top-level management comes from sources other than an organization's information systems. Examples are meetings, memos, television, periodicals, and social activities. Some information must be processed by the organization's information systems; however, an EIS provides top-level management with easy access to selective information that has been processed by the organization's information systems. This selective information concerns the key factors that top-level management has identified as being critical to the organization's success. Actual versus projected market share for product groups and budget versus actual profit and loss data for divisions might be key success factors for a top-level executive.

ACCOUNTING INFORMATION SYSTEMS   Analogous to the preceding definitions, we might define an AIS as a computer-based system designed to transform accounting data into information. However, we use the term *accounting information system* more broadly to include the use of IT, transaction processing cycles, and the development of information systems.

Accounting Information Systems and Application Architecture

AISs and IT are strongly intertwined. The fundamental benefits of IT are automation, information organization, and communication.

- **Automation.** In the AIS, automation not only means replacing humans with machines, it means performing work that would otherwise be impossible with humans alone. For example, computers make it possible for very large companies to produce complicated accounting reports on demand, a feat that was once impossible due to the extensive human processing requirements. The result is a move away from periodic financial reporting to real-time financial reporting via the Web.
- **Information organization.** Automated recording of transactions plus direct-access storage devices (DASDs) and database technology make it possible to record, store, and organize larger amounts of data than would otherwise be possible manually. For example, Walmart's data warehouse stores nearly a billion new records each day. The company reportedly applies sophisticated data mining techniques for retrieving data from its massive database.
- **Communication.** Communication technologies are a key component in the development of AISs. For example, Covisint (*www.covisint.com*, a subsidiary of Compuware) used electronic data interchange (EDI) technologies to develop a common Internet-based collaborative platform that permits the U.S. automobile industry to electronically coordinate and conduct their procurement activities with over 30,000 parts suppliers. This has permitted automakers and suppliers to work together as extended enterprises.

The confluence of changes in automation, information organization, and communications has profoundly affected the development of the typical organization's application architecture. **Applications architecture** involves the process of ensuring the suite of organization's applications work together as a composite application according to the goals and objectives of the organization.

EVOLUTION OF APPLICATIONS ARCHITECTURE   The earliest AIS application architecture focused on automating the traditional accounting cycle (i.e., the process that begins with recording transactions and ends with producing the financial statements). Eventually, software engineers shifted their attention to finding new ways to use computers to enhance functional planning and control within the organization. Several other types of functional information systems were developed.

A **customer relation management (CRM)** system manages all contacts with customers. Customers typically contact several different departments in the organization. Such departments may include, for example, sales, service, billing, support, and quality control. In a typical CRM system, all these departments record their contacts with customers in a common CRM database. IT technology allows this database to be very efficiently accessed and shared by all the involved departments.

A **supply chain management (SCM)** system encompasses the planning and management of all activities involved in sourcing, procurement, conversion, and logistics management. It also includes collaboration with suppliers in the extended enterprise. An **extended enterprise** is a group of loosely connected companies that work together to maximize the value of their economic outputs. Expressed in more tangible terms, this means manufacturers and suppliers work together to meet market demand while minimizing inventories.

SCM systems received considerable attention by developers. The result was **Material Requirements Planning (MRP)** software that assisted management in managing inventories and scheduling production. It wasn't long before MRP evolved into **MRP II (Manufacturing Resource Planning II)**, which added new capabilities such as integration with the financial accounting system, financial planning, and the ability to do extensive simulations of production-related activities.

MRP and MRP II paved the way for **computer-integrated manufacturing (CIM)** and **flexible manufacturing systems (FMSs)**. In CIM, computers take control of the entire manufacturing process, and in FMSs, computers not only control production processes but can also be reprogrammed so that the same processes can produce entirely different products.

CASE IN POINT

Chrysler's Sterling Heights Assembly Plant employs flexible manufacturing techniques that permit the production of several different models in the same plant at the same time. The plant's body shop uses over 750 different robots. Only the robots' "hands" need to be changed in switching the production from one model to another.

ENTERPRISE RESOURCE PLANNING (ERP) MRP, MRP II, CIM, and FMSs represented much more than innovation in the organization's application architecture. The new software capabilities plus the ability to rapidly process, organize, and communicate data helped to enable significant developments in related management science disciplines of logistics, process control, demand forecasting, queuing theory, and so on. Several process improvement methods emerged from these disciplines, such as just-in-time (JIT) manufacturing, lean manufacturing, and Six Sigma. These in turn were accompanied by various related international standards such as ISA-95, which includes various models for enterprise–control system integration. Today, a wide range of international standards apply not only to manufacturing companies but also to a variety of processes in many different types of organizations. ISO 9001 is a quality-management standard published by the International Standards Organization, *www.iso.org*. It is widely credited for promoting the process management approach. The process management approach involves the application of knowledge, skills, tools, techniques, and systems to manage and improve processes within the organization in a way that meets customers' needs and maximizes profitability.

However, these different systems tended to evolve as separate loosely coupled systems, with each system having its own database. In some cases, one functional system database would store the same data items that were stored in the databases of one or more other functional areas. This would result in unnecessary duplication. An equally important problem stemmed from different functional-area databases attempting to share information with each other. Differences in formats and standards made inter-database sharing a complicated and expensive data conversion process. To make things worse, simply updating the software for one functional database could necessitate the re-engineering of the conversion process before that database could again exchange data with other databases.

Enterprise resource planning (ERP) emerged as the solution to too-loosely connected functional information systems. ERP involves combining the various functional information systems under the umbrella of a single software package and a single database. Figure 1.4 shows a typical ERP view of a company, organized by various tightly integrated functional information systems: Human Resource Management, Operations, Services, Financial, and Governance. The Operations grouping includes the SCM system, and the Financial grouping includes financial and management accounting, as well as financial supply chain management (i.e., the flow of money and financial transactions).

Figure 1.4 is based on the organization within the SAP ERP™ system. It shows one way to view the organization's information systems. An alternate view, for example, might collapse

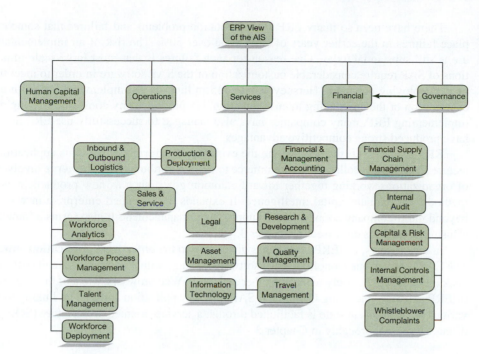

FIGURE 1.4

ERP Functional Systems View of a Typical Manufacturing Company

Services, Financial, and Governance into a single "Organization Infrastructure" process. This would leave three major groupings: Human Resources, Operations, and Infrastructure. Still another approach would be to view the organization in terms of primary versus secondary value chain activities, as discussed below.

ERP has evolved not just as a concept but as software. SAP (*www.sap.com*), for example, develops and markets comprehensive ERP solutions for small, medium-size, and large organizations. Such one-program-fits-all software is based on "best practices," which imply that at least some companies can improve their processes by conforming them to the way the software works. There are also industry-specific versions of software.

ERP has been a blessing and a curse. In theory, companies can benefit from "throwing away" their various functional system software packages and replacing them all with a single software solution. But in practice, many companies find it extremely painful (and costly) to make the switch. In many cases, companies have spent many millions of dollars to implement ERP, only to end up with doubtful net improvements. Many famous cases abound. For example, when the Hershey Company implemented SAP, it ran into problems with its inventory system and was unable to ship chocolates as planned for the Halloween holiday. This resulted in a 19% drop in Hershey's third quarter earnings, which Hershey blamed on "computer problems." Many other well-know companies have suffered ERP implementation problems to varying degrees. Those with such problems include Apple Computer, Boeing, Dow Chemical, Dell Computer, Waste Management, and Whirlpool.

 CASE IN POINT

FoxMeyer Drug, a pharmaceutical distributor in Texas, collapsed after a problematic SAP ERP implementation. The bankruptcy trustees then sued SAP and Andersen Consulting (the accounting firm that helped with the implementation) for $500 million.

There have been so many ERP implementation problems and failures that some estimates place failures in the earlier years of ERP to be over 50%. The risk of an implementation failure is still substantial today. One reason for such failures is that most large-scale implementations of SAP require considerable customization of the SAP software in order to meet the needs of the deploying company. Hershey spent $115 million on its implementation, with a significant portion of the costs going to customization. Despite the many companies having problems implementing ERP, many companies have also managed to successfully use ERP in ways that have produced strong competitive advantages.

ERP II represents the next step in the evolution of information systems applications architecture. ERP II adds collaborative commerce to ERP. **Collaborative commerce** involves groups of organizations working together toward common goals, such as new products, new process methods, and human capital intelligence. It expands the extended enterprise in ways that go beyond multi-company cooperation in supply chain management. It also forms a foundation for eBusiness, which is discussed in Chapter 3.

In recent years, the ERP system has given way to the **enterprise application suite (EAS)**. The EAS replaces one monolithic ERP software package with a group (i.e., a suite) of individual packages that work closely with each other and run in Web browsers. Most of the large providers of ERP software, including Oracle and SAP, market application suites. The linking together of various applications in suite is facilitated through a service-oriented architecture (SOA). SOA is discussed more thoroughly in Chapter 3.

Business Processes

All financially related activities of the organization can be viewed as part of various business processes. A **business process** is an interrelated set of tasks that involve data, organizational units, and a logical time sequence. Business processes are always triggered by some economic event, and all have clearly defined starting and ending points. For example, the customer order management process might be triggered by the receipt of a customer purchase order; the process might begin with the creation of a sales order, and it might end with the collection of the customer's payment on accounts receivable.

A key characteristic of business processes is that they are not necessarily limited to a single functional area of the information system or the organization chart. For example, a sales process can span various departments in the organization chart, such as sales, inventory, shipping, and credit checking. Of course, how any given process is defined is simply a matter of convenience. One could just as easily define a sales process as only the act of entering the customer's order.

Business Process Reference Models

Since most organizations experience similar types of economic events and activities, it is possible to define general basic business processes. These include the following:

1. Procurement (purchasing, ordering, soliciting bids, etc.)
2. Inbound sales logistics (inventory, control, returns to supplier, etc.)
3. Manufacturing (production) operations (machining, assembly, packaging, etc.)
4. Outbound sales logistics (sales order processing, collection, shipping, delivery, etc.)
5. Sales/Service (sales, installation, repair, post-sales support, etc.)
6. Marketing (advertising, promotion, etc.)
7. Human Resources/Human Capital Management (hiring, training, etc.)
8. Accounting (financial accounting, management accounting, reporting, etc.)
9. Finance (collections, payments, financing, etc.)
10. Research and Technology Development
11. Governance (corporate governance, IT governance, strategic management, etc.)

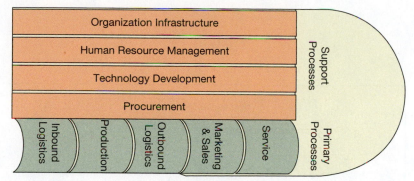

FIGURE 1.5

**The Porter Value
Chain Model**

The 11 basic business processes can be organized and grouped together according to various reference models, depending on the desired emphasis. Some key business process reference models include the ERP functional model, the value chain model, the supply chain model, the operational processes model, and the transaction cycle model. Each of these reference models is discussed.

THE ERP FUNCTIONAL MODEL   The ERP functional model was presented in Figure 1.4. The focus in this model is on different ERP or EAS components. This model is of primary interest to ERP/EAS development.

THE VALUE CHAIN MODEL   The **value chain** (Figure 1.5) is the chain of activities (i.e., processes) performed by the company that add value to the product. Defining business processes in terms of the value chain is popular because the value chain provides a simple and effective way of viewing the company's activities in a manner suited to analyzing its competitive advantages. The value chain breaks activities down into components that can be individually optimized in terms of the company's goals and strategies. This model is of primary interest to managers and process engineers in optimizing the value change as part of the organization's business strategies and goals.

Primary business processes involve activities that directly add value to the company's products, and **supporting business processes** involve activities that indirectly add value and support the primary processes. The primary processes include inbound logistics, production, outbound logistics, sales and marketing, and service. The supporting processes include firm infrastructure (accounting, finance, governance), technology development, human resource development, and procurement.

Collectively, the primary and supporting business processes comprise the entire value chain of activities. Both the primary and supporting business processes can be further subdivided into many subprocesses. For example, outbound sales logistics can be divided into order entry, credit checking, and so on. Subdividing processes is a helpful tool for the systems person and the accountant because it makes it possible to focus on clearly defined, specific areas of the enormous set of the company's activities.

 CASE IN POINT

Many companies use VCML (Value Chain Markup Language), a type of XML (Extensible Markup Language) used to electronically collaborate in eBusiness transactions. VCML is promoted by Vitria® (*www.vitria.com*), a company that specializes in business process management. The VCML language facilitates business-to-business (B2B) commerce throughout the extended value chain, which includes both manufacturers and their suppliers. VCML complements standards for EDI, such as eBusiness XML (ebXML).

FIGURE 1.6

**The Operations
Process Model**

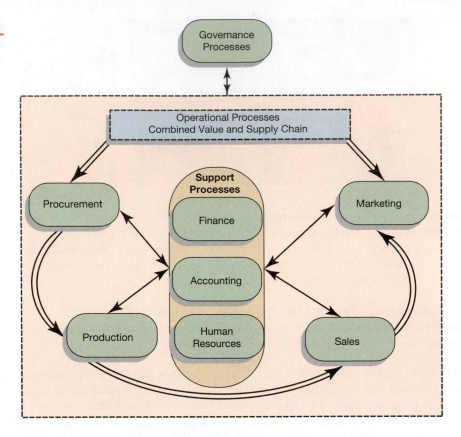

THE SUPPLY CHAIN MODEL   The supply chain reference model focuses on the movement of goods. In this model, the supply chain processes include inbound logistics, production, outbound logistics, sales, and service. This model differs from the primary value chain in that it includes procurement and excludes marketing. This model is of primary interest to those interested in optimizing the supply chain.

THE OPERATIONS PROCESS MODEL   The operations process model (Figure 1.6) differs from the value chain and supply chain models in that it includes all processes in the organization. The **operations process model** places all the organization's processes into three groups: operational processes, supporting processes, and governance processes. Operational processes include both the value chain and supply chain activities (procurement, inbound logistics, production, outbound logistics, sales and service, and marketing). Supporting processes include finance and accounting, technology, and human resources. Governance processes include corporate governance, strategic management, and IT governance.

THE TRANSACTION CYCLE MODEL   The transaction cycle model is the same as the operations process model except that six operational processes, plus accounting and finance, are combined into three operational processes called operational transaction cycles:

- **Revenue cycle.** Events related to the distribution of goods and services to other entities and the collection of related payments. This includes the outbound logistics (e.g., shipping), sales and service, and marketing, plus supporting finance and accounting.
- **Expenditure cycle.** Events related to the acquisition of goods and services from other entities and the settlement of related obligations. This includes procurement, inbound logistics, and supporting finance and accounting.
- **Production cycle.** Events related to the transformation of resources into goods and services—production, plus supporting finance and accounting.

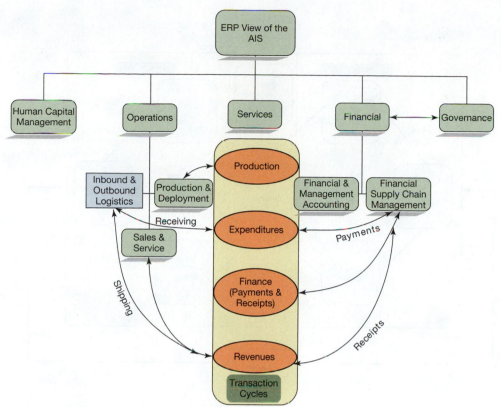

FIGURE 1.7

Transaction Cycles versus the ERP View of the Company

   Transaction processing cycles, being business processes, may span of one or more application systems or functional area, as is depicted in Figure 1.7. An **application system** processes logically related transactions. An organization's revenue cycle might commonly include application systems involving customer order entry, billing, accounts receivable, and sales reporting. An expenditure cycle might commonly include application systems involving vendor selection and requisitioning, purchasing, accounts payable, and payroll. A production cycle might include application systems involving production control and reporting, product costing, inventory control, and property accounting. The transaction processing cycles are called "cycles" because when viewed together, they involve chains of activities that repeat over and over again. This can be seen in Figure 1.8, which combines all the transaction cycles for a nonmanufacturing sales company. Note that the combined process begins with cash and ends with cash. Also note the repetition in all three cycles and the supporting roles played by accounting and finance.

   Defining business processes in terms of transaction cycles is popular with accountants, because transaction cycles provide a convenient way for auditors to trace transactions as they flow through the system. (Tracing transactions is an important tool that auditors routinely rely on in verifying the accuracy of account balances.) Transaction cycles also provide auditors and internal accounts a convenient way to verify that controls are in place and functioning as transactions flow through the system.

   As defined here, the operational transaction cycles include finance activities and financial reporting activities. However, one might also define finance and financial reporting as transaction cycles. The basic functions of an organization's **finance cycle** include the collection and disbursement of cash. They may also include application systems concerned with cash management and control, debt management, and the administration of employee benefit plans. The **financial reporting cycle** obtains accounting and operating data from the other cycles and processes these data in such a manner that financial reports may be prepared. The preparation of financial reports

FIGURE 1.8

Transaction Cycles Are Repetitive

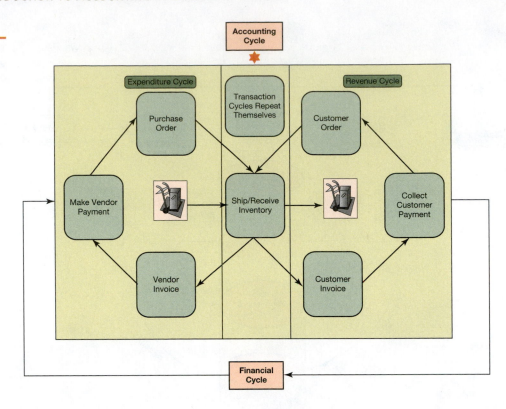

in accordance with generally accepted accounting principles requires many valuation and adjusting entries that do not directly result from operating transactions. Depreciation and currency translation are two common examples. Such activities are part of an organization's financial reporting cycle.

Internal Control Process

Perhaps the most important aspect of an AIS is the role it plays in an organization's **internal control process**. The term *internal control process* suggests actions taken within an organization to regulate and direct the activities of the organization.

Much information needed by management to control finances and operations comes from the AIS. One of management's major responsibilities is stewardship. Management must protect the resources of an organization against possible losses ranging from embezzlement to careless use of supplies or productive materials, unwarranted extension of credit, failure to purchase from the lowest-cost supplier, inefficient workers, and outright theft.

Control ensures that management policies and directives are properly adhered to. Management is far removed from the scene of operations in a large organization, and personal supervision of employees is impossible. As a substitute, management must rely on various control techniques to implement its decisions and goals and to regulate the activities for which it has ultimate responsibility. Control extends over a wide range of activities, such as the maintenance of inventory quantities, the consumption of supplies in production and administration, and the payment of bills within allowed discount periods. Good internal control is a key factor in the effective management of an organization.

ELEMENTS OF INTERNAL CONTROL PROCESS Internal control is a process designed to provide reasonable assurance regarding the achievement of objectives in (1) reliability of financial reporting, (2) effectiveness and efficiency of operations, and (3) compliance with applicable laws and regulations. An organization's internal control process consists of five elements: the control environment, risk assessment, control activities, information and communication, and monitoring. These elements are defined and discussed in Chapter 4. The present discussion seeks only to introduce the notion of internal control. The concept of internal control structure is based on two major premises: management's responsibility and reasonable assurance.

Internal control should require the establishment of responsibilities within an organization. A specific person should be responsible for each task or job function. The reason is twofold: Responsibilities must be clearly assigned in order to delineate problem areas and direct attention to them, and once employees have a clear understanding of the scope of their responsibilities, they tend to work harder toward controlling these responsibilities.

Internal control also calls for the maintenance of adequate records in an effort to control assets and analyze the assignment of responsibility. Good documentation means that records should be maintained by all parties involved in a transaction. Accordingly, all records should allow cross-referencing from one area of responsibility to another. Along this same line, responsibilities for related transactions should be divided. In the process, one area of responsibility will provide a check on the other, and vice versa. The people responsible for the custody of assets should not be responsible for recording the assets in the books of record. Employees are less likely to misappropriate or waste assets if they realize that others are recording their use. This does not mean that work should be duplicated, although in many cases some duplication is unavoidable. Ideally, a task can be so divided as to make job functions natural checks on each other.

For example, the inventory records maintained by an inventory application system establish accountability over goods in a store. Periodic physical inventory counts will reveal shortages or errors that may creep into the records, and the knowledge that the results of their activities will be compared gives the stock clerks and the inventory clerk an incentive to work carefully. The stock clerks will watch the accuracy of receiving room counts as goods are transferred to their custody because the receiving records will be the basis for charging the inventory records for the goods the stock clerks must account for.

SEGREGATION OF ACCOUNTING FUNCTIONS   Of primary importance is the segregation of duties so that no individual or department controls the accounting records relating to its own operation. A common violation of this principle is the delegation of both accounting and financial responsibilities to the same individual or department. Both the accounting and finance functions are concerned primarily with money, so "logical" thinking places both responsibilities under one person. The financing function of a business is just as much an operating responsibility as the manufacturing or sales function. Recognizing this fact suggests the need for segregation of the accounting and finance functions.

A common approach is to delegate the accounting function to a controller or similar office and the finance function to a treasurer. Typically, the controller and treasurer are top-management officials functioning on an equal plane with other executives who report directly to the president. The organization chart in Figure 1.9 illustrates such an arrangement.

The accounting function involves several subfunctions. In a small business, the controller is likely to handle these personally, but in a large concern, the duties ordinarily are delegated to staff assistants or department heads.

Figure 1.9 shows several normal staff positions that commonly report to the controller. The budgeting function involves the preparation of operating budgets, capital expenditure budgets, and the related forecasts and analyses used by management in planning and controlling the operations of the organization. The tax planning function concerns the administration of tax reporting and the analysis of transactions that have significant tax consequences for the organization. The accounting manager supervises the routine operating functions of the accounting department, such as posting the general ledger and preparing financial reports.

The treasurer is responsible for the finances of the business. He or she arranges to obtain the funds necessary to finance operations and is charged with securing any required funds under the best terms commensurate with the needs of the business. In addition, the treasurer is responsible for the liquid assets of the business—cash, receivables, and investments. Records of these assets are maintained under the controller in order to obtain the desired segregation of accounting and operations. Under the treasurer is the credit manager, who is responsible for credit and collections, even though the original charge to accounts receivable and the accounting for receivables are both handled by the accounting department. Cash collections on these receivables are placed in the custody of a cashier, who is also responsible to the treasurer. Accountability over the cashier is established through the accounts receivable records and the general ledger record of cash. The credit to receivables that relieves the credit manager of responsibility when cash is received on an account is offset by the debit to cash that charges the cashier with the collected funds.

INTERNAL AUDIT FUNCTION   Recognizing the need for and complexity of adequate internal control in a large organization has led to the evolution of internal auditing as a control over all other internal controls. Internal audit is charged with monitoring and assessing compliance with organizational policies and procedures.

Internal audit is an independent appraisal activity within an organization. The organizational level of the internal audit function must be high enough to enable it to operate independently. Figure 1.9 shows the director of internal audit at the vice-presidential level. This placement of internal audit responsibilities is now common in large organizations because it enhances the independence of internal audit, although historically most internal audit functions have subject to the authority of the controller or other chief accounting officer. Whatever its organizational status, the internal audit function must be segregated from the accounting function and must have neither responsibility nor authority for any operating activity.

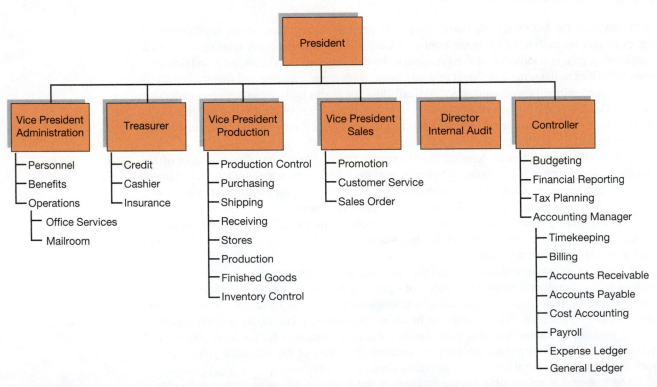

FIGURE 1.9

Organization Chart

Accounting and Information Technology

The term *accounting information system* includes the use of IT to provide information to users. Computers are used in all types of information systems. IT includes computers, but it also includes other technologies used to process information. Technologies such as machine-readable bar codes, scanning devices, communications protocols, and standards such as ANSI X.12 are essential to quick-response systems.

The Information System Function

Every organization that uses computers to process transactional data has an information system function. The **information system function** is responsible for DP. DP is a fundamental AIS application in every organization. The information system function in organizations has evolved from simple organizational structures involving few people to complex structures involving many qualified specialists.

ORGANIZATIONAL LOCATION   Figure 1.10 shows the head of the information systems function titled as **chief information officer (CIO)** and an advisory group called a *steering committee*. Each of these functions represents a common response to the issues related to the organizational placement of responsibility for the overall information system function. The location of the information system function in the organizational structure is important as computer applications have become common and essential in all parts of an organization. As computer applications have crossed functions and the information system function's budget has increased in size, there has been a trend toward elevating the information system function in the organization. The CIO typically reports to the organization's vice-presidential level or is in a position at the vice-presidential level. However, some information system departments still report to a senior

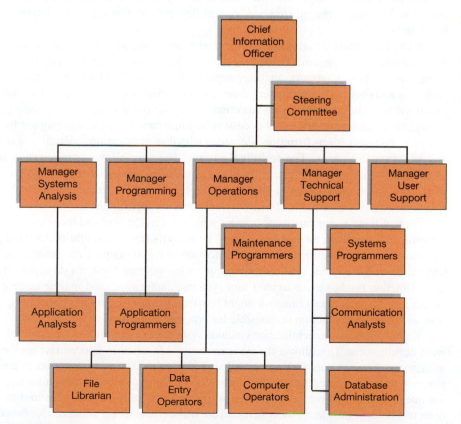

FIGURE 1.10

Functional Organization Structure of an Information Systems Department

financial officer such as the controller. This is often true in small firms and among relatively new users.

CASE IN POINT

Linda Dillman was voted several times by *Fortune* magazine (*www.fortune.com*) as one of the 50 most influential women in the United States. She served as CIO for Wal-Mart Stores, Inc. She was subsequently promoted to the position of Executive Vice-President of Benefits and Risk Management.

Regardless of the organizational location of the information system function, a **steering committee** or other advisory group is the means by which managers of other areas can influence the policies, budget, and planning of information services. A steering committee consists of high-level members of user functions such as manufacturing and marketing, as well as the head of the information system function and several of his or her staff. The steering committee meets periodically to set and review important policy, budget, and project decisions relating to information systems. Because the members are consumers of the product of the information system, a steering committee provides user feedback in controlling the information system function. A member of the internal audit function also might participate on the steering committee, or the audit function might advise and review the information system function through a different channel.

FUNCTIONAL SPECIALIZATIONS   The most prevalent information system departmental structure is the assignment of responsibilities and duties by area of technical specialization, that is, function. The larger the information system department, the more specialized functions are likely to be.

A large information systems department with functional organization is shown in Figure 1.10. The department is organized into five major functions: systems analysis, programming, operations, technical support, and user support. The **analysis function** focuses on identifying problems and projects for computer processing and designing systems to satisfy these problems' requirements. The **programming function** is responsible for the design, coding, testing, and debugging of computer programs necessary to implement the system designed by the analysis function. The **operations function** is charged with data preparation, operation of the equipment, and system maintenance. The **technical support function** allows specialization in areas such as operating systems and software, data management and database design, and communications technology. The **user support function** services end users, much as the technical support function services personnel of the information systems department.

Each of these major functions may be subdivided as the size and technical sophistication of the information system function increase. The analysis function might be factored into specialties concerning the identification of user information requirements (information analyst) and the translation of these needs into computer application systems (systems designer). The programming function might be subdivided into systems, application, and maintenance programming specialties. The operations function might be subdivided into computer operations, data preparation, and a librarian function responsible for program and data files.

Technical support specializations include systems programming, which concentrates on software development. This allows the systems analysis function to concentrate on identifying user information requirements and conceptual system design. Data administration as a technical support function coordinates data storage and use among system users and assumes responsibility for the integrity of the corporate database. Communication analysts specialize in data communications technology, the means by which data are transferred among networks for processing.

Specializations within the technical support function can vary greatly depending on the information system environment. This is true for the analysis, programming, operations, and user support functions as well. For example, note that in Figure 1.10 maintenance programmers report to the manager of operations rather than to the manager of programming. Assigning several maintenance programmers to the operations function often occurs in organizations that depend heavily on their computer-based information systems. The large number of programs makes maintenance a continuous activity and one on which the operation function becomes highly dependent.

The manager of the user support function works with the CIO to plan the supply of computing services to end users. The user support function often becomes an information center. An **information center** is a support facility for end users in an organization. It assists users in developing their own computer processing applications. An information center might provide users with equipment and software, as well as with consulting support. In many organizations, the information center helps end users evaluate personal computer (PC) hardware and software for their particular computing requirements. The user support function might also serve as a place where users can make comments and suggestions concerning the operation of the information systems department.

Although the functional form of organization is prevalent, a common variation is to structure the analysis and programming functions by project. In **project organization**, analysts and programmers are assigned to specific application projects and work together to complete a project under the direction of a project leader. Project organization focuses responsibility for application projects on a single group, unlike functional organization, in which responsibility for a specific project is spread across different functional areas.

End-User Computing

In information systems terminology, an *end user* is an organizational function other than the information system function that requires computer data processing. The sales or marketing function is an end user that requires computer processing for sales reports, market analyses, sales projections, sales budgets, and so forth. The accounting function is an end user that requires computer processing support for posting of journals and preparation of reports.

End-user computing (EUC) is the hands-on use of computers by end users. Functional end users do their own information processing activities with hardware, software, and professional resources provided by the organization. A common EUC application is information retrieval from the organization's database using the query language feature of database management systems (DBMS). For example, using a networked PC a user might access accounts receivable data from a company's centralized database, manipulate them, and then print a report. The end user has bypassed direct use of information systems specialists by developing his or her own data processing application and then directly implementing it with the query language interface. This direct, hands-on use of computers by users to perform functions that previously had to be performed by information systems specialists is the distinguishing feature of EUC (Figure 1.11). Prior to EUC capabilities, the end user would have had to specify his or her processing request to the organization's information systems department and then await the outcome. If the request was denied or delayed, the user might perform the task manually, if possible.

Cloud Computing

Cloud computing describes the increasing trend for data processing capabilities to be provided as a service via the Internet. In this context, *cloud* is simply a synonym for the Internet, and **cloud computing** is the use of cloud-based data processing services and data storage.

A Web browser and an Internet connection are the only physical items that are absolutely required for a user of cloud computing. But cloud computing differs from "cruising the Internet" in that cloud computing is used for data processing—inputting data which is processed into output. Thus, data processing and data storage capability have to be provided and maintained by the

FIGURE 1.11

Data Processing for the End User

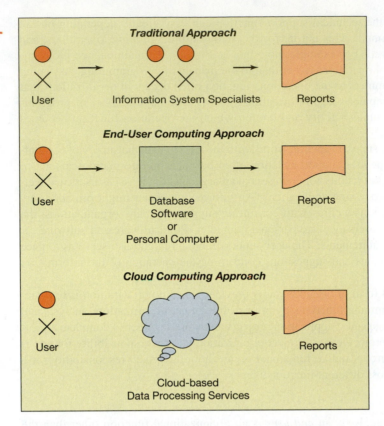

Traditional Approach

User → Information System Specialists → Reports

End-User Computing Approach

User → Database Software or Personal Computer → Reports

Cloud Computing Approach

User → Cloud-based Data Processing Services → Reports

provider of cloud computing services. The essence of cloud computing is that data storage is in "the cloud." Thus, as Figure 1.12 illustrates, users can access their data anytime and anywhere as long as they can access the Internet.

PCs give end users processing power, but data storage is physically onsite, and controlled either by the user or the IT function. Data storage is totally off-site with cloud computing. There are many fixed costs associated with the maintenance of an IT function, such as salaries of personnel, costs of data processing equipment and data storage equipment, and facility costs. Cloud computing avoids such costs by outsourcing data processing services. The end user requires only an input/output device to access the cloud. Cloud computing costs may be entirely incurred on a usage basis, with no fixed costs at all.

FIGURE 1.12

Cloud Computing

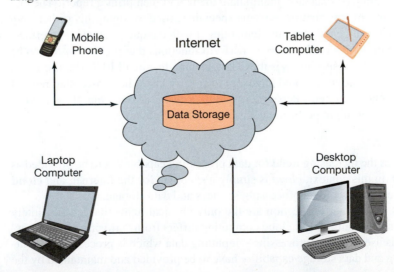

Mobile Phone

Internet

Tablet Computer

Data Storage

Laptop Computer

Desktop Computer

Quick-Response Technology

The term *quick-response system* is seemingly self-explanatory. Certainly, such systems are "quick" and "responsive." But much more is implied in the quick-response concept. Quick-response systems are essential to the **total quality performance (TQP)** movement in business. TQP (also called **TQM—total quality management**) is a philosophy that one should *do the right thing right the first time*. TQP requires high-quality production, operational efficiency, and continuous improvement in operations. TQP emphasizes customer satisfaction to the point of customer obsession. In the extremely competitive environment of the business world, TQP is a strategy for survival.

Several technologies interact to make quick-response systems feasible. Hardware and software standardization and the movement toward open systems have made the interconnection of computer systems easier. EDI is essential to quick-response systems. Although EDI is essential to the "quick" in quick-response systems, it alone is not sufficient. Electronic payment processing and universal product code (UPC) bar code identification of products and scanning technology, such as point-of-sale (POS) retail terminals, are other essential technologies. The scanning of a UPC bar code by POS technology at the checkout counter of a retail store is the initial event in a chain of events that ends with the item, *the right item*, being quickly replenished in the store's inventory so that it can be sold again (Figure 1.13). This is critical in retailing, where fads (i.e., customer demand for certain products) can and do change rapidly. What sold last year, last month, or maybe even last week may no longer be what the customer wants today.

Radio frequency identification (RFID) is another technology important to quick-response systems. RFID tags are very small tags that are placed on or in objects for which tracking is desired. RFID tags can be active, passive, or semi-passive. Active RFID tags use battery power to transmit to a nearby receiver a radio signal containing digital identifying and other information. Passive RFID tags do not contain an internal battery to power transmitting the radio signal. Instead, they use the minute amount of power that comes from a signal emitted by a transmitter. Semi-passive RFID tags work like passive tags in that their transmitting power comes from a signal emitted by a transmitter, but they use battery to power their internal chips. Generally speaking, active tags transmit to farther distances than do passive tags. The transmission distance may be anywhere from a few inches to hundreds of feet, depending on the type of tag and the environment it operates in.

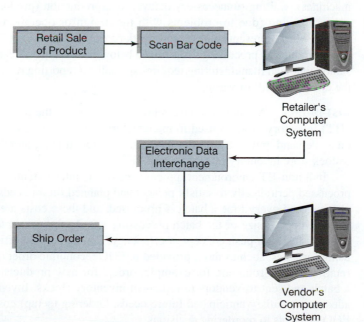

FIGURE 1.13

Chain of Events in a Quick-Response Sales System

Mobile Camera Phone → QR code with URL → YourProduct.com (Web Site)

RFID tags are used for a wide variety of applications. For example, Walmart and the U.S. Department of Defense have mandated that their suppliers attach RFID tags to shipments. At the time of its manufacturing, each RFID tag is assigned a unique code. The tag can also be assigned other information, such as UPC data. In total, the information transmitted from the tag assists companies in optimizing the supply chains. Other applications include passports, bus and rail passes, library-book tracking, livestock and pet tracking, and hospital patient tracking.

A **QR code** (*Quick-Response* code) is a two-dimensional barcode (Figure 1.14). These are used for identifying and tracking parts in manufacturing, but have also become commonplace in commercial applications aimed at mobile phone users. QR codes are read by scanning them with a mobile phone camera. The QR reader application in the mobile phone then takes whatever action is indicated by the code. Typically this opens a Web site, displays a video, or displays text. QR codes are embedded in advertising, such as magazines ads or in-store displays, and provide a convenient way to direct customers to a Web site where they can obtain additional information or promotional items such as discount coupons.

There are several iPhone® and Android® phone apps that use the phone's built-in camera to scan barcodes. The apps then automatically run Internet searches using services such as Google Products® to find the best price for a scanned item in the local area.

LEAN MANUFACTURING **Lean manufacturing (or lean production)** is a general class of production improvement principles that are based on the Toyota Production System. The main focus in lean manufacturing is eliminating waste and improving the smoothness of the production flow. The original system defined three major categories of waste—muda, muri, and mura. There are seven types of waste included in muda: transportation (unnecessary moving of products), inventory (not processed), motion (the unnecessary moving of people, equipment, or machines), waiting (unnecessary delays), overproduction (producing more than is demanded), overprocessing (due to problems with the design or operation of tool and equipment), and defects. Muri represents unnecessary work or wasted effort. Finally, mura represents unevenness in the production process. JIT (discussed below) is one type of lean manufacturing. From an AIS standpoint, lean manufacturing requires specialized reporting regarding the costs associated with the different kinds of waste.

JUST-IN-TIME A quick-response retail sales system is the retailing equivalent of **just-in-time** **(JIT)** inventory systems used in manufacturing. Purchase orders for inventory items are made on a "demand–pull" basis rather than a fixed-interval (e.g., monthly or weekly) "push" basis to restock store inventory levels.

In a non-JIT environment, process activity is intermittent. Batches of similar products are processed periodically to satisfy present and planned future needs. Setup activity costs are usually incurred every time a batch is processed, and these costs are typically the same regardless of the proposed size of the batch processing run. As the word *planned* indicates, a batch environment fosters a push concept of efficiency. Economic (i.e., efficient) batch size is derived by using formulas, such as those provided in EOQ (economic order quantity) models. In a non–JIT retail sales environment, for example, orders for new products are processed periodically as a batch and sent to vendors to replenish inventory stocks. Inventory stocks are kept at levels adequate to satisfy anticipated future needs. Ordering (setup) costs are minimized by applying EOQ concepts to reordering decisions.

A JIT environment is a continuous-flow environment rather than a batch-process environment. A JIT environment requires operation of a process on a continuous basis to minimize or totally eliminate inventories. JIT also advocates the elimination of waste in the manufacturing process and stresses continuous improvement in operation. JIT is similar in concept to TQM and is considered by many to be an essential aspect of TQM.

In a JIT environment, process activities occur under a pull concept. Activity (i.e., ordering new product) occurs only when it is needed to satisfy customer demand. Customer demand, as evidenced by current sales, pulls orders from the reordering process; in effect, demand causes orders to be placed to vendors. Orders to vendors are placed on the basis of actual sales to quickly replenish stocks of items that are selling. Current sales demand pulls (i.e., automatically generates) orders for inventory. Retailers can order on the basis of current buying trends.

WEB COMMERCE   Sales via the World Wide Web are an integral part of the economy. Such sales provide many benefits to both consumers and merchants. For consumers, some of the benefits are as follows:

1. There is no waiting in line for a salesperson or product information.
2. Through intelligent Web-based software, customers can find fast answers to complicated questions relating to the merchant's products.
3. Web-based transactions are normally encrypted, which provides enhanced security.

Benefits to merchants include

1. Cost savings through automated ordering.
2. Automatic electronic encoding of transaction data.
3. Low overhead. The entire Internet store can exist on a single desktop computer.
4. Worldwide availability of company's products.
5. The ability to rapidly update and disseminate new product or pricing information.

A central concern for anyone buying via the Web is security and privacy. For this reason, the American Institute of Public Accountants sponsors the **Web Trust** seal of approval that specially trained Certified Public Accountants (CPA) award to Web sites that meet the criteria.

ELECTRONIC DATA INTERCHANGE   **Electronic data interchange (EDI)** is the direct computer-to-computer exchange of business documents via a communications network (Figure 1.15). EDI differs from electronic mail in that electronic mail messages are created and interpreted by humans (person to person), whereas EDI messages are created and interpreted by computers. Public EDI-related standards, in particular **ANSI X.12** (an EDI standard that works mostly over value-added networks), **AS2** (which facilitates sending secure EDI and other messages via the Internet), and **ebXML** (eBusiness XML, a relatively new but important EDI standard for the Internet) have had great impact on the development of quick-response systems. Public EDI standards provide a common architecture for data interchange and thus eliminate costly and error-prone cross-referencing of codes by parties to an EDI transaction.

An EDI link between a retailer's computer system and a vendor's computer system eliminates paperwork and allows near-instantaneous placing and processing of purchase orders, facilitating quick-response shipment. The vendor might also invoice the retailer using EDI. In some cases, electronic funds transfer (EFT) payment might be made by the retailer to the vendor's account. All these events, including the picking of the order from the vendor's inventory, might take place without any human intervention.

EXTENSIBLE BUSINESS REPORTING LANGUAGE   **Extensible Business Reporting Language (XBRL)** is a language that facilitates the exchange of financial statements over the Internet. The SEC financial reporting requirements represent a good example of the application of XBRL. The SEC permits companies to file their financial reports electronically in XBRL format. Reports

FIGURE 1.15

Electronic Data
Interchange (EDI)

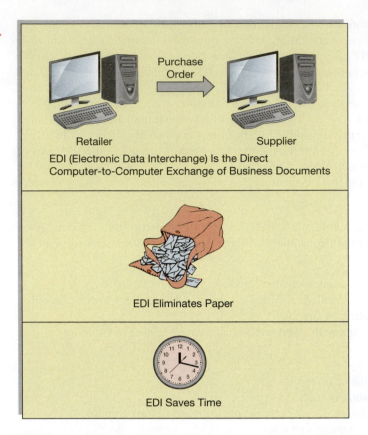

Retailer   Supplier

EDI (Electronic Data Interchange) Is the Direct
Computer-to-Computer Exchange of Business Documents

EDI Eliminates Paper

EDI Saves Time

filed this way become available publicly on the SEC's Web site within only minutes of their being submitted to the SEC.

○ CASE IN POINT

EDGAR® Online®, Inc. (*www.edgar-online.com*), publishes I-Metrix™, a software package for accessing the EDGAR® Online®'s database of over 11,000 financial reports in XBRL format. I-Metrix™ integrates with Microsoft Office and Web browsers. This software supports filtering against EDGAR Online's XBRL database of over 7,000 elements, based on a wide range of filtering criteria, including standard and custom financial ratios.

ELECTRONIC PAYMENT SYSTEMS   **Electronic funds transfer (EFT)** systems are electronic payment systems in which processing and communication are primarily or totally electronic. EFT systems provide electronic movement of funds between organizations based on customer instructions. Banks can interface with corporate EDI applications.

The banking and financial industry uses FedWire, Clearing House Interbank Payment System (CHIPS), and Clearing House Automated Payment System (CHAPS). FedWire is an electronic payment and communications system. Banks holding reserve accounts with the U.S. Federal Reserve Bank use FedWire to transfer funds among themselves. CHIPS is an automated clearinghouse system used for the clearing of Eurodollar payments between U.S. and non-U.S. financial institutions. CHAPS provides same-day settlement of sterling funds transfer and is used primarily by the major UK clearing banks and the Bank of England.

Retail EFT systems include the telephone wire transfers and telephone payment systems, preauthorized payment systems, POS applications, and automated teller machines (ATMs). Telephone wire transfer is the oldest form of funds movement and is primarily a manual system. Telephone payment systems, often referred to as *pay-by-phone applications*, are similar to wire transfers in that the telephone is the primary medium for data communications. In pay-by-phone systems, customers can call their bank and direct payments to merchants via a Touch-Tone phone. Preauthorized payment systems are used when both the creditor and the customer hold accounts at one bank. Preauthorized payment systems allow automatic payment of recurring items with no manual intervention. POS systems allow the electronic approval and debiting of customer accounts at the merchant's site. POS systems can have a direct telecommunications interface with the credit and debit card databases, thus eliminating the courier costs of physically transporting receipts and totals. ATMs perform banking transaction tasks rapidly with reduced manual intervention. ATMs connect to computer networks that process financial transactions and, in the case of shared networks, provide settlement clearing functions with other banks. Common customer uses for ATMs include depositing or withdrawing cash, transferring funds from one account to another, and making payments.

The Accountant and Systems Development

The term *accounting information system* includes system development activities that an accountant or auditor might expect to encounter professionally. Accountants may undertake systems development activities either internally for their company or externally as consultants. Systems development activities are often encountered by internal and external auditors during reviews of information systems controls conducted as part of an audit.

The Nature of Systems Development

A systems development project ordinarily consists of three general phases: systems analysis, systems design, and systems implementation. Systems analysis involves formulating and evaluating solutions to systems problems. The emphasis of systems analysis is on the objectives of the entire system under consideration. Basic to this is an analysis of trade-offs between system objectives. The general objectives of systems analysis can be summarized as follows:

- To improve the quality of information
- To improve internal control
- To minimize cost, where appropriate

These objectives are interrelated and often conflicting. Trade-offs often must be made between such qualities as economy and usefulness or between simplicity and a realistic but complex system. Frequently, the only method of evaluating such trade-offs is subjective because the factors involved defy quantification.

Systems design is the process of specifying the details of the solution selected by the systems analysis process. Systems design includes the evaluation of the relative effectiveness and efficiency of alternative system designs in light of the overall system requirements. Systems implementation is the process of placing the revised or newly designed procedures and methods into operation. Systems implementation includes testing the solution prior to implementation, documenting the solution, and reviewing the system when it actually begins operation to verify that the system functions according to the design specifications.

The **systems approach** is a general procedure for the administration of a systems project. Its purpose is to assist in the orderly development of effective systems. The systems approach can be viewed as a process that consists of six steps:

1. Statement of system objective(s)
2. Creation of alternatives

3. Systems analysis
4. Systems design
5. Systems implementation
6. Systems evaluation

The systems approach, like a system itself, is composed of subsystems. Thus each step in the process can itself be subjected to the systems approach. For example, the first step requires that the system objective(s) be stated. Solving this problem by the systems approach involves all six steps. A defined systems objective is the purpose being pursued. To achieve this purpose, alternatives can be created. The system might, for example, seek objective A, B, or C or some combination of them. These alternative objectives can then be analyzed, and the one that seems most suitable can be designed, implemented, and evaluated.

Executing each subsequent step in the systems approach also can be viewed as a process that involves all six steps. Figure 1.16 illustrates this with respect to the system design step. Top-down design with successive refinement is the essence of a systems approach to problem solving. Each successive refinement adds a finer level of detail to system plans, and a top-down approach to successive refinement structures this process in an orderly fashion.

Business Process Blueprinting

With business process **blueprinting**, the company uses generic or industry standard stock blueprints rather than designing its own system. The same approach is often taken by builders in planned housing communities. The builder works with the home buyer in selecting a set of

FIGURE 1.16

The Systems Approach to Design

Define Objectives of Design	Develop simple, clear, and precise specifications for effective and efficient systems implementation
Plan Alternative Possible Designs	Develop alternative design plans that meet design objectives
Analyze Alternative Possible Designs	This includes a. Separating plans into logical parts b. Evaluating the relative effectiveness and efficiency of alternatives against system output requirements c. Using a team approach in many cases d. Selecting the best alternative to form a design strategy
Develop Detailed Design Specifications	They should include a. Enough detail to serve as the basis for the implementation process b. Identification of system inputs c. Identification of system outputs d. Strategies for producing system outputs
Document Design Specifications	This should include specifications for every input and output data element and all circumstances for their uses
Evaluate Design Specifications	This involves testing for the desired output of the design process (specification of an effective and efficient design). The evaluation of the design should consider whether it is a. Developed according to the systems approach model b. Based on effective systems strategy produced by a careful and detailed systems analysis c. Effective, efficient, simple, clear, easy to build, easy to change, and easy to test or evaluate

blueprints from a large book of blueprints. The selected set of blueprints is then adapted according to the buyer's specific needs.

Many companies prefer blueprinting because they find it more cost-effective than designing their own system from the ground up. In many cases, blueprinting can save the company from having to reinvent the wheel, and the company can be free to focus more of its efforts on the processes that are key to its strategic goals and objectives.

One company that has pioneered the blueprinting approach is SAP. This company has developed a large knowledge base of many thousands of business processes that customers can readily adapt to their own needs. This approach has become increasingly popular in recent years.

It must be emphasized that blueprinting is no cure-all and virtually any problem that occurs without blueprinting can occur with blueprinting. Also, blueprinting can cost as much as or even more than the more traditional alternative.

Behavioral Considerations in Systems Development

Management, users, and systems personnel are necessarily involved in the design and subsequent operation of an information system. Typically, a design group or project team consisting of users, analysts, and management representatives is formed to identify needs, develop technical specifications, and implement a new system.

Technical, organizational, and project management problems are encountered in the implementation of an information system. A new information system creates new work relationships among existing personnel, changes in job content, and perhaps a change in the formal organizational structure. The related technical, behavioral, situational, and personnel factors should all be considered. Failure to do so may lead to the output of the system not being used, even if the system itself is technically sound. Furthermore, users' cooperation is continually required to operate the system (provide inputs, verify outputs) after its implementation.

The user cooperation needed to operate the system successfully should be ensured during the design of a system, not afterward. Most accounting applications are routine. To ensure adherence to production schedules, ongoing relationships between users and information system personnel are important. Schedules for inputs, reports, and other items are usually the responsibility of the systems group, but to implement and maintain these schedules, cooperation is required from users.

A philosophy of **user-oriented** design fosters a set of attitudes and an approach to systems development that consciously considers the organizational context. Users should be involved in the design of applications. Careful attention to output, both in quantity and format, in the design phase will prevent users having to rework data or request new reports once the system is in operation. Outputs should be directed toward decisions; users must understand the nature and purpose of outputs to be able to use them. Personnel training should be included in the design phase, not initiated after the system is installed. Finally, the system must be prepared to accept and make changes after operation begins. Users will usually request changes; anticipation of this possibility and the other factors mentioned is essential to a user-oriented philosophy of systems design.

Green IT: Designing for Sustainability

Sustainability is related to the environmental effects of business operations. The term **green IT** has come to denote utilization of IT resources in an environmentally responsible manner. There are several aspects that may be addressed during the design of new systems.

ENERGY USAGE   IT uses electrical energy to power its own operations and also requires significant quantities of energy for air-conditioning and cooling the buildings that house the equipment and personnel that are required for the system. The data centers—which house the IT equipment that powers the Internet, stores vast quantities of information, and makes possible the communications systems that are the backbone of the global economy—use large quantities of energy. Designing green data centers—centers that are designed to be energy efficient in both design structure and operation—can lower utility bills, reduce energy use, and minimize environmental impact. Green data centers use energy-efficient cooling technologies, energy-efficient equipment, and energy-efficient building designs to reduce their environmental footprint.

Virtualization is one approach to increasing the efficiency of IT operations. It involves consolidation of operations to reduce the physical numbers of devices used to power an IT system. Within a data center, multiple workloads might be placed on the same server, allowing for fewer physical servers, thus lowering the electricity and cooling requirements of the data center. Similar strategies might be applied to other aspects of IT system operations, such as PCs and storage devices.

E-WASTE E-waste is IT and other electronic products that are at or near the end of their useful life. Large quantities of e-waste have been discarded and are in landfills, and some of this waste is toxic and hazardous to the environment and human health. E-waste is one of the fastest growing segments of the global waste stream. Green IT is concerned with reducing e-waste through recycling and other approaches. Some IT products might be refurbished and reused rather than discarded. In addition to traditional concern for price, efficiency, and performance, system design should include consideration of what will happen to system components at the end of their useful lives with the goal of keeping reusable and potentially toxic materials out of the waste stream.

Summary

An accounting information system is a collection of resources designed to transform data into information. This information is communicated to a wide variety of decision makers. We use the term *accounting information system* broadly to include transaction processing cycles, the use of IT, and the development of information systems.

Most organizations experience similar types of economic events. These events generate activities that correspond to the value chain and can be grouped into five primary business processes (inbound logistics, production, outbound logistics, sales and marketing, and service) and into four support business processes (procurement, technology development, organization and human resource management, and firm infrastructure). An internal control structure consists of the policies and procedures established to provide reasonable assurance that specific organizational objectives will be achieved. Transaction business processes offer a systemic framework for the analysis and design of information systems in that there is a similar objective for each of the various business processes. This objective is to be an integral part of an organization's internal control structure.

The information system function is responsible for DP. The organizational structure and location of a large information systems department with functional organization were discussed, and common functions within the department were described. The direct, hands-on use of computers by end users to perform their own DP is known as end-user computing. Cloud computing describes the increasing trend for data processing capabilities to be provided as a service via the Internet. Three technologies interact to make quick-response systems feasible. These technologies are EDI, UPC bar code identification, and scanning technology, such as POS retail terminals. JIT, RFID, and EFT are also relevant to quick-response systems.

A systems development project ordinarily consists of three general phases: systems analysis, systems design, and systems implementation. The systems approach is a general procedure for the administration of a systems project. Its purpose is to assist in the orderly development of effective systems. Technical, organizational, and project management problems are encountered in the implementation of an information system. A philosophy of user-oriented design fosters a set of attitudes and an approach to systems development that consciously considers the organizational context.

Glossary

accounting information system (AIS) is a collection of resources, such as people and equipment, designed to transform financial and other data into information. This information is communicated to a wide variety of decision makers.

analysis function focuses on identifying problems and projects for computer processing and designing systems to satisfy these problems' requirements.

ANSI X.12 a widely recognized standard for EDI. This standard is slowly giving way to ebXML.

applications architecture involves the process of ensuring the suite of organization's applications work together as a composite application according to the goals and objectives of the organization.

application system processes logically related transactions.

AS2   a protocol for securely exchanging messages over the Internet. The messages can contain EDI data or any other type of data. As such, AS2 is not an EDI standard per se but rather a standard that facilitates the use of EDI.

blueprinting   the practice of adapting off-the-shelf system designs to suit an individual company's needs.

business process   an interrelated set of tasks that involve data, organizational units, and a logical time sequence.

chief information officer (CIO)   has overall responsibility for the information system function.

cloud computing   the use of Internet-based data processing services and data storage.

collaborative commerce   groups of organizations working together toward common goals, such as new products, new process methods, human capital intelligence, and so on.

computer-integrated manufacturing (CIM)   computers control the production processes.

customer relation management (CRM)   a system that manages all contacts with customers.

data processing (DP)   the use of computers to perform an organization's transaction-oriented data processing.

decision support system (DSS)   data are processed into a decision-making format for the end user.

eBusiness XML (ebXML)   a set of standards that enables enterprises of any size, in any global region, to conduct electronic business using the Internet.

electronic data interchange (EDI)   the direct computer-to-computer exchange of business documents via a communications network.

electronic data processing (EDP)   synonym for data processing.

electronic funds transfer (EFT)   payment systems in which processing and communication are primarily or totally electronic.

end-user computing (EUC)   the direct, hands-on use of computers by end users to perform their own DP.

enterprise application suite (EAS)   replaces one monolithic ERP software package with a group (i.e., a suite) of individual packages that work closely with each other and run in Web browsers.

enterprise resource planning (ERP)   the combining of the various functional information systems under the umbrella of a single software package and a single database.

enterprise resource planning II (ERP II)   ERP plus collaborative commerce.

executive information system (EIS)   an MIS tailored to the strategic information needs of top management.

expenditure cycle   events related to the acquisition of goods and services from other entities and the settlement of related obligations.

expert system (ES)   a knowledge-based information system that uses its knowledge about a specific application area to act as an expert consultant to end users.

extended enterprise   a group of loosely connected companies that work together to maximize the value of their economic outputs.

Extensible Business Reporting Language (XBRL)   a universal formatting language for exchanging business documents via the Internet.

finance cycle   events related to the acquisition and management of capital funds, including cash.

financial reporting cycle   obtains accounting and operating data from the other cycles and processes these data in order that financial statements can be prepared.

flexible manufacturing systems (FMSs)   in FMSs, computers not only control production processes but can also be reprogrammed so that the same processes can produce entirely different products.

green IT   the use of power-saving methods (such as virtualization) to reduce the use of energy in IT applications.

information center   a support facility for the computer users in an organization.

information system function   responsible for DP and information systems in an organization.

internal control process   a process designed to provide reasonable assurance regarding the achievement of objectives in (a) reliability of financial reporting, (b) effectiveness and efficiency of operations, and (c) compliance with applicable laws and regulations.

just-in-time (JIT)   a continuous flow environment that seeks to minimize or totally eliminate inventories.

lean manufacturing (or lean production)   a general class of production improvement principles that stem from Toyota. The principles involve eliminating waste and smoothing and balancing production flows. JIT is a well-known form of lean production principles.

management information system (MIS)   the use of computers to provide decision-oriented information to managers.

material requirements planning (MRP)   software that assisted management in managing inventories and scheduling production.

manufacturing resource planning II (MRP II)   MRP with added capabilities such as integration with the financial accounting system, financial planning, and the ability to do extensive simulations of production-related activities.

operations function   charged with data preparation, operation of the data processing equipment, and system maintenance.

operations process model   a business process reference model that groups an organization's processes into three groups: operational (procurement, production, sales marketing), support (accounting, finance, human resources), and governance (all governance functions).

primary business process   involves inbound logistics, production, outbound logistics, sales and marketing, and service.

production cycle   events related to the transformation of resources into goods and services.

programming function   responsible for the design, coding, testing, and debugging of computer programs.

project organization   organization of analysts and programmers by application projects rather than by organizational function.

QR (Quick Response) code   a two-dimensional barcode used for identification and also for providing links to Web sites, videos, and text.

radio frequency identification (RFID)   the technology of placing small tags in or on objects. The tags emit radio signals containing digital information regarding the object.

revenue cycle   events related to the distribution of goods and services to other entities and the collection of related payments.

steering committee   an advisory group consisting of high-level members of user functions that influences the policies, budget, and planning of information services.

supporting business process   mainly the nonoperational parts of the value chain.

systems approach   a general procedure for the administration of a systems project.

supply chain management (SCM)   encompasses the planning and management of all activities involved in sourcing, procurement, conversion, and logistics management activities. It also includes collaboration with suppliers in the extended enterprise.

technical support function   specialists in areas of IT expertise such as software, data management, and database design.

total quality management (TQM)   synonym for TQP.

total quality performance (TQP)   a philosophy that one should do the right thing right the first time.

transaction processing cycle   consists of one or more application systems. The four basic transaction cycles are revenues, expenditures, production, and finance. The financial accounting system represents a fifth transaction cycle.

user-oriented   a philosophy of design that fosters a set of attitudes and an approach to systems development that consciously considers organizational context.

user support function   services and supports end users and EUC.

value chain   the sequence of activities (processes) by which a company adds value to its product. The value chain is a way of viewing the company's activities in a manner suited to analyzing competitive advantages.

Web Trust   a seal of approval given to Web sites by CPA indicating that certain standards of privacy and security have been met.

Webliography

www.ebxml.org
The main Web site for eBusiness XML (ebXML). According to the Web site, "ebXML enables enterprises of any size, in any global region, to conduct business using the Internet." This site is hosted by the Organization for the Advancement of Structured Information Standards, a nonprofit open standards for the global information society.

www.wal-mart-edi.com
An independent supplier of EDI and RFID systems targeted to Walmart suppliers.

www.scdigest.com
A Web site devoted to supply chain management.

www.isaca.org
Organization devoted to providing professional certifications, standards, and guidance relating to accounting and information

systems. ISACA provides the following professional certifications: The Certified Information Systems Auditor (CISA), The Certified Information Security Manager (CISM), and The IT Governance Certification (CGEIT).

www.misti.com
A private company devoted to education, training, and certifications for IS professionals.

infotech.aicpa.org
The Information Technology Center for the American Institute of Certified Public Accountants (AICPA). Click on the Resources tab for information on a wide range of IT topics relevant to AIS. Some topics include XBRL, IT governance, and security and audit control. Information is also available for specific technologies such as RFID.

Chapter Quiz

Answers to the Chapter Quiz appear on page 34.

1. The term (_____) describes the use of computer technology to provide decision-oriented information to managers.
   a. DP
   b. EDP
   c. ES
   d. MIS

2. The text groups economic events into how many basic business processes?

   a. one
   b. four
   c. six
   d. eleven

3. Which of the following indicates a satisfactory situation from the viewpoint of good internal control?
   a. The cashier reports to the treasurer.
   b. Payroll accounting reports to the controller.
   c. Both of the above indicate an unsatisfactory situation.
   d. Both of the above indicate a satisfactory situation.

4. The statement "Amounts due to vendors should be accurately and promptly classified, summarized, and reported" might serve as a control objective in which of the following transaction cycles?
   a. revenue cycle
   b. expenditure cycle
   c. production cycle
   d. finance cycle

5. Which of the following information system functions is generally responsible for the design, coding, and debugging of computer programs?
   a. technical support
   b. programming
   c. operations
   d. systems analysis

6. Which of the following information system functions focuses on the identification of problems and projects for computer processing?
   a. user support
   b. programming
   c. operations
   d. systems analysis

7. Which of the following is a general term that is used to describe the use of electronic technology for business documents?
   a. telecommuting
   b. information system
   c. office automation
   d. EDI

8. (_____) is the direct computer-to-computer exchange of business documents via a communications network.
   a. EDI
   b. EFTr
   c. telecommuting
   d. e-mail

9. The three general phases of analysis, design, and implementation are part of a (_____).
   a. system development study
   b. systems approach
   c. ES
   d. DSS

10. (_____) is the first step in the systems approach.
   a. systems design
   b. stating objectives
   c. systems analysis
   d. systems evaluation

Review Questions

1. What is an AIS?
2. What groups need the outputs of an AIS?
3. Identify and describe several types of computer-based information systems.
4. Identify the common operating cycles of business activity.
5. Characterize an organization's internal control structure.
6. Distinguish between a controller and a treasurer.
7. Describe the purpose of the internal audit function.
8. Characterize the organizational structure of the information system function.
9. Identify several functions that may be specialized areas of expertise in an information system department.
10. How does project organization differ from functional organization in an information system department?
11. What is the purpose of a steering committee?
12. Describe blueprinting.
13. Give an example of EUC.
14. Identify several components of quick-response technology.
15. How does EDI differ from e-mail?
16. Identify several components of CIM.
17. List the six steps in the systems approach.
18. What is meant by user-oriented systems design?

Discussion Questions and Problems

19. "A credit sale is not a complete transaction." Discuss.
20. Discuss factors that should be considered in the organizational location of the internal audit function.
21. Apply the systems approach to the following objectives:
   a. to improve the quality of an AIS
   b. to improve the image of a university
   c. to better the competition
22. Identify several accounting-related decisions that you feel might be made by the following personnel. Do the information needs of these positions differ?
   a. president of a company
   b. controller
   c. accounting manager

23. Discuss briefly the importance in systems design of good communication among systems analysts, management, and systems operating personnel.

24. The AIS of an organization may be simple or it may be massive and complex. AISs are designed and implemented not only to maintain the ledger balances from which financial statements and reports are prepared but also to produce other types of management and operating information that are essential to the operation of a business. Regardless of how large and complex—or how simple—an organization's AIS is, accountants, auditors, and other parties are required to study the internal controls periodically. Without such studies, it would be impractical or impossible in many cases to acquire a detailed knowledge of the processing procedures that affect all types of transactions. Simplification is not only acceptable but is both desirable and necessary.

Business processes can be used to simplify this task. Although all entities differ, they experience similar economic events, which can be classified into one of the nine business processes discussed in the chapter. Each process should be an integral part of an organization's internal control structure.

Required

In periodic studies of the internal controls in an organization's AIS, accountants and auditors often develop control objectives for each major business process. The control objectives provide a basis for analysis. The accountants or auditors collect information to determine the extent to which control objectives are being achieved in each of the organization's major business processes.

Each of the following statements is a control objective relating to a particular business process. Identify the relevant business process.

a. Vendors should be authorized in accordance with management's criteria.

b. The prices and terms of goods and services provided should be authorized in accordance with management's criteria.

c. All shipments of goods and services provided should result in a billing to the customer.

d. Customers should be authorized in accordance with management's criteria.

e. Employees should be hired in accordance with management's criteria.

f. The production plan should be authorized in accordance with management's criteria.

g. The amounts and timing of debt transactions should be authorized in accordance with management's criteria.

h. Compensation rates and payroll deductions should be authorized in accordance with management's criteria.

i. Amounts due to vendors should be accurately and promptly classified, summarized, and reported.

j. Cost of goods manufactured should be accurately and promptly classified, summarized, and reported.

k. Billings to customers should be accurately and promptly classified, summarized, and reported.

l. Access to cash and securities should be permitted only in accordance with management's criteria.

m. Access to personnel, payroll, and disbursement records should be permitted only in accordance with management's criteria.

25. The Red Wine Company manufactures wine coolers. The company began operations several years ago and has experienced rapid sales growth. The company is organized by business function, with vice-presidents for manufacturing, marketing, finance, accounting, and general administration. The firm operates a computer network, which supports a variety of applications for manufacturing, marketing, finance, accounting, and general administration. The manager of information systems (IS) reports to the vice-president of general administration.

The company's rapid growth has strained the firm's computer resources, and the number of complaints concerning inadequate support and service from IS has increased dramatically in the past year. The vice-presidents for both manufacturing and marketing have taken their complaints about IS directly to the company president. Citing inadequate IS support of the online computer applications relating to inventory control and shipment information, manufacturing and marketing have requested that the firm purchase a computer that would be used exclusively to support these systems. The president is somewhat perplexed by this request because she recently received a request from the vice-president of general administration to fund a significant upgrading of the firm's mainframe computer system. The president is also aware that the finance and accounting divisions have recently began using cloud computer services for several tasks and are planning to request funds for additional cloud computing applications in their next budget submissions. The president realizes the importance of adequate computer resources to the firm's operations, but given the recent complaints about IS support and these seemingly contradictory requests for additional computer hardware and cloud computing services, she has begun to wonder whether there is sufficient control and adequate planning for the acquisition and use of computer resources at the Red Wine Company. The president thinks forming a steering committee might help solve these problems.

Required

What is a steering committee? Discuss the role of a steering committee in planning for the acquisition and use of computer resources at the Red Wine Company.

26. *Robinson Industries: Organization of the EDP Function*[1]

Introduction

Robinson Industries is a loosely knit conglomerate that offers centralized data processing services to its affiliated companies. To improve the attractiveness of its services, the data processing department this past year introduced online services. Several affiliates have become or are becoming users of this service. It has resulted in a reorganization of the data processing department that concerned Mat Dossey, the senior on the audit. Dick Goth, the semi-senior on the engagement, reported that the client had not prepared a new organization chart but agreed to see what he could find out. His report is as follows:

[1]Prepared by Frederick L. Neumann, Richard J. Boland, and Jeffrey Johnson; funded by The Touche Ross Foundation Aid to Accounting Education Program.

Data Processing Department Organization

The data processing department now consists of 25 people reporting to the president through the director of data processing. In addition to these data processing department employees, key committees perform important roles, as do the internal and external auditors for the company. The internal auditors now report operationally to the board of directors and functionally to the president.

Committees

Selected functions of key committees that are important to the management and control of the data processing department are described briefly in the following:

Data Processing Committee This committee, composed of three members of the board of directors, meets as required to review and evaluate major changes in the data processing area and to review approval of pricing of all services offered. Their responsibilities also include a review of major agreements with hardware and software vendors.

Audit Committee In its oversight of the audit function, this committee of the board of directors is directly concerned with the quality of the records and reports processed by the department and the controls employed.

User Groups These groups consist of representatives from online users within a specific geographic area. They meet periodically throughout the year to discuss common areas of interest, possible enhancements, and current problems related to the online system. The results of these group meetings are reported directly to the data processing department through a user advisory committee.

Data Processing Department

Data processing department management consists of five managers who report to the director through an assistant director. The department management meets weekly to review the status of projects, customer service levels, and any problems. Weekly status reports are then prepared and distributed to each level of line management. Formal meetings with Robinson's president are held quarterly or more often if required, to review future plans and past performance.

The following describes the sections within the department under the direction of each of the five managers.

Online Services

Online Technical Staff This staff conducts all user training, conversions, and parameter definitions necessary to set up a new user. Training classes are conducted at the data processing center. Conversion assistance is provided to the user prior to the initiation of online services. If conversion programs are required, these are defined by the online services section to the online analyst programmers for program preparation. During the first month after conversion of a new user, calls are directed to online services; thereafter, user calls are directed to the user liaison section.

Applications Coordinator This person is responsible for coordinating the approval of user and data processing department project requests, assisting in the requirements definition of a systems maintenance project, monitoring ongoing projects, and approving project test results.

Operations

Data Communications Coordinator This person monitors all service levels and response time related to the communications network and terminals. The coordinator receives all user calls regarding communications problems. The coordinator logs all calls, identifies the nature of the problem, and reports the status of the problems until they are corrected.

Computer Operators This section consists of operators, supervisors, and librarians who execute, review, and service the daily computer production runs, special computer runs, and program compilations and tests. The operations are scheduled on a 24-hour basis for 6 days a week. Shift supervisors review all online operations and prepare written documentation of each problem encountered.

Scheduler This person is responsible for setting up the computer job runs and adjusting them for online special requests.

User Liaison This staff consists of four people who receive, log, and report all questions of potential problems, other than communications problems, by online users. User input is obtained through telephone calls, letters, and online messages over the communications network and notes from user committee meetings.

Online Reports Control This staff is responsible for the distribution of all hard copy output to all users. Microfiche are sent directly to users from the outside processing vendor. Logs are maintained where appropriate to control distribution and to reconcile items such as check numbers and dividend totals.

Systems and Programming

Online Analyst Programmers This staff is responsible for all the applications and system software programming required for the online system. Systems analysis and programming consist primarily of maintenance to existing computer programs, correction of problems, and enhancements to the current applications.

In-House Analyst Programmer This staff is responsible for all applications and system software programming not online.

Research and Development

This staff evaluates and conducts preliminary investigations into new applications such as electronic funds transfers.

Marketing

This staff responds to requests for information regarding the services provided by the data processing department. Once a user signs an online service agreement as a new user, that member is turned over to online services for training and conversion.

Required

Based on Dick Goth's report, prepare an organization chart of the data processing department and of its relationships to the rest of the organization affecting it.

27. The Fishco Company is a regional fish distributor that sells fish to restaurants in southern Florida. It purchases all its fish from small boats at the local docks, and it pays only with cash.

    To simplify its operations, Fishco takes orders only via its Web site. All orders are delivered by a third-party contractor, and all sales are made on account. This very simple system allows the entire business to be operated only by Mr. and Mrs. Fishco. Mrs. Fishco does the Web programming, answers the telephone, and provides replacement fish when a customer is dissatisfied. Mr. Fishco does everything else, including all accounting and the handling of collections.

Required

   a. Identify all the major business processes for Fishco.
   b. Specify which business processes are probably the most important to Fishco's strategic goals and objectives.
   c. How would Fishco's business processes change if it became larger and more complicated?
   d. How would Fishco's major business processes change if it began selling shrimp in addition to fish?

28. Assume that the GreenLeaf Tea Company has decided to focus its information system development efforts on its procurement business process. At present, GreenLeaf purchases all its tea directly from tea-leaf farms, but soon it has plans to begin purchasing at spot market prices offered on overseas commodity exchanges.

Required

   a. Generate a rough sketch of GreenLeaf's procurement process.
   b. Indicate changes in the purchasing process that might occur as a result of GreenLeaf's move to purchase in the spot market.
   c. Identify at least four subprocesses for the procurement process.

29. All business processes have at least three common components: a starting point, an ending point, and a triggering event. For each business process below, give all three components.
   a. customer order management process
   b. inventory management process
   c. product delivery management process
   d. production order process
   e. payroll process

30. Luxdale is a large Internet-only vitamin store that sells retail to the public. Over the years, the business has grown steadily to the point that it now processes 15,000 orders per day from sales worldwide.

Recently, Luxdale has run into a serious problem through no fault of its own. Only 1 week ago all the major financial newspapers carried a story about one of Luxdale's major competitors, HealthVite. The problem was that some consumer organization discovered that HealthVite had sold its entire mailing list, along with telephone numbers, to SlabM, a company that sells burial insurance. SlabM then launched a highly aggressive telephone campaign and called every one of HealthVite's customers with offers for discount burial insurance. To make things worse, the salespersons made all the calls around the evening meal hour, a time that most people are in their homes but most likely to be angered by a call from a salesperson.

HealthVite's customers were furious, and the whole affair made all the television talk shows, with many people complaining that one should never trust Internet-based companies with their personal information. Sales for HealthVite dried up overnight, and the CEO quickly resigned before the creditors began moving the armies of lawyers and accountants.

The problem for Luxdale was that its sales suddenly dropped 50%, even though it was in no way affiliated with HealthVite. Robert Baker, the CEO for Luxdale, held a series of press conferences to assure its customers and the public that his company was an innocent casualty, but the more he talked to the press, the worse the problems grew. In general, the press was very hostile, and the overall atmosphere in the industry became one of mistrust and recriminations.

Required

   a. Was Luxdale in any way responsible for its problems?
   b. What things could Luxdale have done before the problem arose to protect itself?
   c. What things could Luxdale have done after the problem arose to protect itself?

31. RoundSoft produces and markets an accounting system for small retail business. The system contains all the usual modules, such as those for accounts receivables, payables, inventory, payroll, general ledger, and so on. In addition, the RoundSoft system includes special modules for sales analysis and prediction.

    The core logic for the sales analysis and prediction modules is based on a patented artificial intelligence technique that is so effective that the system can predict actual sales, by product, up to 6 months in advance with an accuracy rate exceeding 98%. There exists no other product this effective in the industry. As a result, RoundSoft enjoys robust sales and has grown 10,000% in the previous 2 years.

    The main problem facing RoundSoft is its accounting system. The volume of sales orders from authorized resellers has grown so large that the accounting system can no longer handle all the transactions in a timely manner. Software deliveries and installations are backed up by a full 3 weeks, and many angry customers are seeking other software solutions to their accounting problems. If something is not done soon, RoundSoft's reputation will likely be damaged seriously and a permanent loss of market share may follow.

Barbara Conta is RoundSoft's controller, and she is presently considering various options. Her assistant, Bob Blake, argues that RoundSoft needs to develop a completely new accounting system from the ground up. Blake's arguments in favor of his position include the following:

a. The present accounting system was designed for a company one-tenth the company's present size. It is nearly impossible to adapt such a system to the present environment.

b. The original accounting system did not include modules to record contracts for installations of the software. Over time, RoundSoft has found it very profitable to install and service installations for large regional companies. To accommodate this growing line of business, Round-Soft developed a separate software system for processing these transactions. Keeping a separate system has caused many problems, however, and has complicated the end-of-quarter process of producing financial statements.

Barbara Conta, however, has a great deal of experience in systems development and knows how painful it can be to develop an entirely new system. Recognizing Blake's arguments, she is seriously considering the option of developing the new system based on a blueprint from SysQuick, a national systems consultant that specializes in business systems blueprinting.

The salesperson from SysQuick claims that by using their blueprint method an entire new system can be implemented for RoundSoft in only 4 weeks for only a quarter of the cost required to develop a new system from the ground up. However, Bob Blake is skeptical about using a stock blueprint. "No two systems are alike," he said. "How can you just take a stock system and force it on our company? Something is bound to go wrong."

Barbara Conta is very worried about the decision. She knows that a bad decision could seriously damage her entire career. After all, who wants to hire a controller who managed the development of a failed system? On the other hand, a good decision would put her in a position to become the controller for one of the many large, sought-after high-tech companies in her area, with a salary twice as large as her present salary.

Required

a. Describe arguments both for and against the blueprint option.

32. Fancy Ropa operates a national chain of retail clothing stores. The company's main corporate offices are in Saint Louis, with warehouses in Houston and Miami. It also has offices in the Republic of Panama and Los Angeles, which coordinate the company's import operations.

Fancy Ropa runs a central accounting system from its Houston offices. The retail stores throughout the United States transmit daily sales and inventory data to Houston via ANSI X.12 software installed at all sites. Payroll for all company employees is outsourced to Automatic Data Processing, Inc (ADP). Human resource management is handled through the Miami office using a software package called MyHRC Manager. Some human resource data is stored both in the ADP system and in the MyHRC.

Fancy Ropa's warehouse and distribution manager tracks the movement of all incoming shipments using various spreadsheets. The two main warehouses maintain their own inventory records in local databases.

At the end of every week, all stores relay expense reports via e-mail to the central office. Payments for local-store and corporate expenses are made by the treasurer using the electronic bill-pay system attached to the company's bank account in Houston.

Karen Falda, Fancy Ropa's CEO, recently toured all the company's offices and warehouses, and also many of its retail stores. Her trip was precipitated by her gut feeling that things weren't going well for the company. Many regional store managers were complaining of long delays in receiving new shipments of clothes and about receiving identical items that were being sold for a lot less at Walmart stores.

Karen Falda's visits to the warehouses revealed large storage areas with thousands of unmarked crates and boxes. The warehouse managers couldn't explain what type of clothing was in the boxes and crates or how long the boxes and crates had been sitting in their present locations. But it looked like they had been there for quite some time, as they were covered in dust.

Karen met with Ken Marsten, Fancy Ropa's controller and chief technology officer, regarding the problem. "We just can't compete given our current software applications architecture," he said. She agreed with him, but neither had any ideas for improving the situation.

Required

a. Explain how Fancy Ropa might have gotten in its present situation.

b. Explain Fancy Ropa's software problem.

c. Make a recommendation for a solution to the software problem.

Web Research Assignments

33. You are the accountant for a mid-sized manufacturing company. Your boss has asked you to explain some of the most important technologies affecting accounting.

Required

a. Visit the Information Technology Center Web for the American Institute of Public Accountants (infotech.aicpa. org) and find the current list of "top technology initiatives." (These initiatives are often listed under the site's Resources tab, but you might need to search the site to find them.)

b. For your boss, write a brief summary of the AICPA's current 10 technologies.

c. Do a Google search and provide a brief update on the general status of the AICPA's number 1 technology.

34. Assume you are a controller for a regional chain of restaurants. You are discussing with your CEO the idea of going public, and you have explained to your boss that going public will require that your company put all of its internal controls in order. But your boss majored in Marketing and knows almost nothing about internal controls.

Required

a. Visit the Web for the American Institute of Public Accountants (*www.aicpa.org*) and find the *Journal of Accountancy*. (Hint: it can sometimes be found under "Magazines and Newsletters.")

b. Search the archives and find an article that explains some basic things about internal control. Summarize the article in 500 words or less.

Answers to Chapter Quiz

1. d   **2.** d   **3.** d   **4.** b   **5.** b   **6.** d   **7.** d   **8.** a   **9.** a   **10.** b

Systems Techniques and Documentation

Learning Objectives

Careful study of this chapter will enable you to:

- Characterize the use of systems techniques by auditors and systems development personnel.
- Describe the use of flowcharting techniques in the analysis and documentation of information processing systems.
- Illustrate the preparation of an analytic flowchart for a business process.
- Define and illustrate a variety of common systems techniques, including HIPO charts, logical data flow diagrams, business process diagrams, and resource utilization analysis.

Users of Systems Techniques

Systems techniques are tools used in the analysis, design, and documentation of system and subsystem relationships. They are largely graphic (pictorial) in nature. Systems techniques are essential to both internal and external auditors and are indispensable to systems personnel in the development of information systems. Systems techniques are also used by accountants who do systems work, either internally for their company or externally as consultants.

Use of Systems Techniques in Auditing

Most audits are divided into two basic components. The first component, usually called the *interim audit*, has the objective of establishing the degree to which the organization's internal control structure can be relied on. This usually requires some type of compliance testing. The purpose of compliance testing is to confirm the existence, assess the effectiveness, and check the continuity of operation of internal controls on which reliance is to be placed.

The second component of an audit, usually called the *financial statement audit*, involves substantive testing. Substantive testing is the direct verification of financial statement figures, placing such reliance on internal control as the results of the interim audit warrant. For example, substantive testing of cash would involve direct confirmation of bank balances. Substantive testing of receivables would involve direct confirmation of balances with customers. Both compliance testing and substantive testing might be undertaken by both internal and external auditors.

INTERNAL CONTROL EVALUATION As indicated earlier, auditors are often involved in the evaluation of internal controls. As such, auditors typically are concerned with the flow of processing and distribution of documents within an application system. Because segregation and division of duties is an important aspect of internal control, the auditor needs techniques that structure the system to distribute documents and divide processing duties among personnel and/ or departments. Analytic flowcharts, document flowcharts, and forms distribution charts may be used by auditors to analyze distribution of documents. These charts are organized into columns to group the processing functions performed by each entity. Several other system techniques, such as questionnaires and matrix methods, might also be used to evaluate internal controls.

COMPLIANCE TESTING   Auditors undertake compliance testing to confirm the existence, assess the effectiveness, and check the continuity of internal controls. When these controls to be tested are components of an organization's information system, the auditor must also consider the technology employed by the information system. This requires understanding the systems techniques commonly used to document information systems, such as input–process–output (IPO) and hierarchy plus input–process–output (HIPO) charts, program flowcharts, logical data flow diagrams (DFDs), branching and decision tables, and matrix methods. Auditors will encounter these techniques frequently as they review systems documentation. This is why familiarity with such techniques is desirable. However, auditors usually have little need to prepare such instruments in the course of an audit because these techniques are useful primarily in planning or designing a system. The usual focus of an audit is to review an existing system rather than to design a new system.

WORKING PAPERS   Working papers are the records kept by an auditor of the procedures and tests applied, the information obtained, and the conclusions drawn during an audit. The auditor is required by professional standards to maintain working papers, and these constitute the principal record of work done.

Auditors use systems techniques to document and analyze the content of working papers. Internal control questionnaires, analytic flowcharts, and system flowcharts appear frequently in working papers because they are commonly used by auditors in the evaluation of internal controls. DFDs, HIPO charts, program flowcharts, branching and decision tables, and matrix methods might appear in working papers if they are part of the documentation of a system that is being reviewed.

Use of Systems Techniques in Systems Development

A systems development project generally consists of three phases: systems analysis, systems design, and systems implementation. Systems development personnel include systems analysts, systems designers, and programmers. Systems analysis involves formulating and evaluating solutions to systems problems. Systems design is the process of specifying the details of the solution selected by the systems analysis process. Systems design includes the evaluation of the relative effectiveness and efficiency of alternative system designs in light of the overall system requirements. Systems implementation is the process of placing the revised or newly designed procedures and methods into operation. Systems implementation includes testing the solution prior to implementation, documenting the solution, and reviewing the system when it actually begins operation to verify that the system functions according to the design specifications.

SYSTEMS ANALYSIS   Much of a systems analyst's job involves collecting and organizing facts, using interviewing techniques, questionnaires, document reviews, and observation. Formal techniques for organizing facts include work measurement analysis, work distribution analysis, and other matrix techniques. Information flow analysis is also an important part of systems analysis. Many systems techniques are useful for this kind of analysis. DFDs and analytic flowcharts can be helpful in giving an overall picture of transaction processing within the organization.

SYSTEMS DESIGN   Systems design must formulate a blueprint for a completed system. Just as an artist needs special tools for painting, the designer needs certain tools to assist in the design process. These include techniques such as input/output (matrix) analysis, systems flowcharting, and DFDs. Many design problems concern information systems design, such as forms design for input documents, and database design. IPO and HIPO charts, program flowcharts, branching and decision tables, and other systems techniques are used extensively in documenting information systems design.

SYSTEMS IMPLEMENTATION Systems implementation involves actually carrying out the design plan. Typical activities include selecting and training personnel, installing new computer equipment, detailed systems design, writing and testing computer programs, system testing, standards development, documentation, and file conversion.

Documentation is one of the most important parts of systems implementation. Computer programs in particular should be documented adequately. Systems techniques such as program flowcharts and decision tables serve as documentation tools as well as tools used for analysis by programmers. Good documentation, a result of the use of systems techniques in analysis and design, assists in training new employees and generally assists in ensuring that systems design specifications are met.

CASE IN POINT

Underestimating the time necessary for documentation can lead to an unrealistic expectation of the benefits and return on investment that will result from the implementation of an enterprise resources planning (ERP) system.

Use of Systems Techniques by Sarbanes–Oxley Act Compliance Participants

System documentation is the underpinning support of the internal control and process documentation requirements that have been set by the Sarbanes–Oxley Act (SOX). Section 404 of SOX requires that annual filings of publicly traded companies include a statement of management's responsibility for establishing and maintaining an adequate internal control structure and procedures for financial reporting and an assessment of the effectiveness of the company's internal control structure and financial reporting procedures. An organization's external auditors must attest to and report on management's assessment of internal controls.

CASE IN POINT

The Bedfordshire and Hertfordshire Strategic Health Authority prepared a diagram titled "Flowchart for Fraud & Corruption Referrals" that outlines the response plan if there is suspicion of fraud at the authority level.

Organizations of all sizes are using systems documentation to understand their information systems and the attendant internal controls, data flows, and information flows related to key business processes that must be examined under SOX. Many different participants, such as management, auditors, accountants, information systems personnel, and SEC personnel, are involved in the preparation and/or review of the internal control and process documentation requirements that have been set by the Act. All of these participants must be able to interpret and/or prepare systems documentation to fulfill their respective compliance responsibilities under SOX. Many organizations use specially designed application software packages that strive to automate SOX compliance requirements and facilitate continuous updating of business process documentation. SOX necessitates that every participant in the compliance process possess an ability to read and interpret systems documentation that is attendant to an effective and ongoing compliance program.

CASE IN POINT

Robert Half Management Resources, an international provider of senior-level accounting and finance professionals, describes the responsibilities for a position as a SOX analyst to include responsibility for documentation, testing, remediation, flowcharting, and narratives.

Systems Techniques

Flowcharts are probably the most commonly used systems technique. A **flowchart** is a symbolic diagram that shows the data flow and sequence of operations in a system.

Flowcharting Symbols

Flowcharts are used by both auditors and systems personnel. Flowcharts became widespread when business data processing was computerized, giving rise to the need for standard symbols and usage conventions. In the United States, this need was filled largely by the publication of *American National Standard Flowchart Symbols and Their Usage in Information Processing*. ANSI X3.5-1970 is still a basic source for standard symbols and usage conventions.

ANSI X3.5 defines four groups of flowchart symbols—basic symbols, specialized input/output symbols, specialized process symbols, and additional symbols. It also defines the shape of each symbol but not the size and illustrates conventions governing the use of symbols.

The **basic symbols** (Figure 2.1) include the input/output symbol, the process symbol, the flowline symbol, and the annotation (comment) symbol. These correspond to the basic data processing functions and can always be used to represent these functions. A specialized symbol may be used in place of a basic symbol to give additional information.

The input/output symbol represents an input/output (I/O) function, that is, making data available for processing (input) or recording processed information (output). For example, a keyboard or magnetic disk may be used to input data for processing; the processed data may be output to paper or to another magnetic disk. The process symbol represents any kind of processing function, for example, executing a defined operation or group of operations resulting in a change of value, form, or location of information, or determines which of several flow directions is to be followed.

The flowline symbol is used to link other symbols. Flowlines indicate the sequence of available information and executable operations. Flowlines may cross or form a junction. A crossing of flowlines means that they have no logical relation. A junction of flowlines occurs when two or more flowlines join with one outgoing flowline. Every flowline entering or leaving a junction should have arrowheads near the junction point.

FIGURE 2.1

Basic Symbols

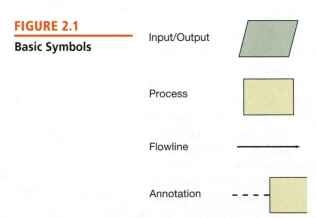

Input/Output

Process

Flowline

Annotation

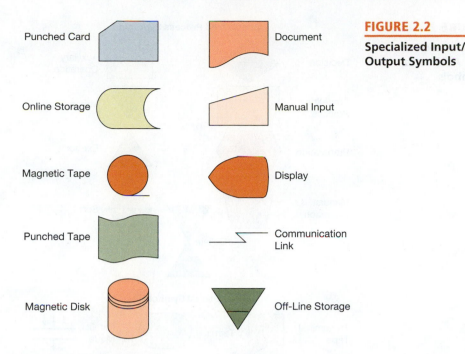

FIGURE 2.2

**Specialized Input/
Output Symbols**

The annotation (comment) symbol represents the addition of descriptive comments or explanatory notes as clarification. The broken (dashed) line is connected to any symbol where the annotation is meaningful by extending the broken line in whatever fashion is appropriate. A brace (connected to a symbol by a broken line) may also be used to indicate an annotation or comment.

Specialized input/output symbols (Figure 2.2) may represent the I/O function and, in addition, denote the medium on which the information is recorded or the manner of handling the information, or both. If no special symbol exists, the basic input/output symbol is used.

The punched card symbol represents an I/O function in which the medium is punched cards, including mark-sense cards, stub cards, deck of cards, and file of cards. The online storage symbol represents an I/O function using any type of online storage, for example, magnetic disk or optical disk. The magnetic tape symbol, the punched tape symbol, the magnetic drum symbol, the magnetic disk symbol, and the document symbol each represent an I/O function using a particular medium.

The manual input symbol represents an input function in which the information is entered manually at the time of processing, for example, by means of online keyboards, switch settings, or touch screens. The display symbol represents an I/O function in which the information is displayed for human use at the time of processing by means of video devices, console printers, plotters, and so forth. The communication link symbol represents a function in which information is transmitted by a telecommunications link. The off-line storage symbol represents the function of storing information off-line, regardless of the medium on which the information is recorded.

Specialized process symbols (Figure 2.3) may represent the processing function and, in addition, identify the specific type of operation to be performed on the information. If no specialized symbol exists, the basic process symbol is used.

The decision symbol represents a decision or switching type of operation that determines which of a number of alternative paths is to be followed. The predefined process symbol represents a named procedure consisting of one or more operations or program steps that are not specified within this set of flowcharts. The preparation symbol represents modification of an instruction or group of instructions that change the program itself, for example, to set a switch, modify an index register, or initialize a routine.

FIGURE 2.3

Specialized Process and Additional Symbols

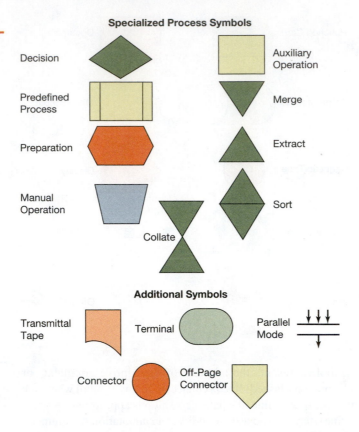

The manual operation symbol represents any off-line process geared to the speed of a human being without using mechanical aid. The auxiliary operation symbol represents an off-line operation performed on equipment not under direct control of the central processing unit. The merge, extract, sort, and collate symbols may each be used to represent the associated specific type of processing function.

The **additional symbols** (see Figure 2.3) may be used to clarify a flowchart or to make the flowcharting of a complete process more convenient. The connector symbol represents an exit to or an entry from another part of the flowchart. A set of two connectors is used to represent a continued flow direction when the flow is broken by any space or stylistic limitation. The terminal symbol represents a terminal point in a flowchart; for example, start, stop, halt, or interrupt. The parallel mode symbol represents the beginning or end of two or more simultaneous operations. The off-page connector symbol is not in the ANSI X3.5 standard but is used commonly to represent an exit to or entry from another page of a flowchart. The transmittal tape symbol is commonly used to represent a manually prepared batch control total.

 CASE IN POINT

BreezeTree Software cites regulatory and quality management requirements as one of the top five reasons to use flowcharts. Many organizations are subject to international certification requirements such as ISO 9000 for quality management systems. In these cases, flowcharts are not only useful but in certain clauses they are actually mandated.

Symbol Use in Flowcharting

Symbols are used in a flowchart to represent the functions of information or other type of system. Flow direction is represented by lines drawn between symbols. Normal direction of flow is from left to right and from top to bottom. When the flow direction is not left to right or top to bottom, open arrowheads should be placed on flowlines to show that direction is reversed. To increase clarity, open arrowheads can be placed on normal-direction flowlines. When flowlines are broken by page limits, connector symbols should be used to indicate the break. When flow is bidirectional, it can be shown by either single or double lines, but open arrowheads should be used to indicate both normal-direction flow and reverse-direction flow.

Figure 2.4 contains four illustrations that correctly use symbols, flowlines, arrowheads, and the connector symbol. In the first illustration, notice that the document symbol is used for an invoice, which is shown as input to a manual operation symbol. The text inside the manual operation symbol indicates that the invoice is to be reviewed and approved. The approved invoice is output from this process. Because the direction of flow is normal in this illustration (left to right and top to bottom), no arrowheads are necessary.

The second illustration is a different flowchart for the same process of approving an invoice. In this case, the reverse flow of the approved invoice is indicated with arrowheads.

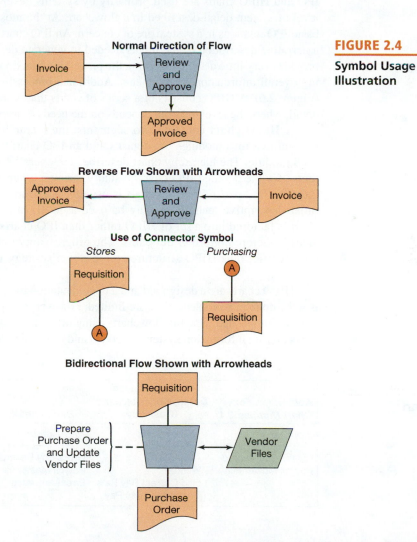

FIGURE 2.4

Symbol Usage Illustration

The third illustration shows how the connector symbol is used to flowchart the transmission of a requisition from the stores department to the purchasing department. Instead of a flowline, the connector symbol is used to indicate this transmission.

The fourth illustration shows the manual preparation of a purchase order. The document symbol is used to represent the requisition, which is shown as input to a manual operation symbol. Notice that the annotation (comment) symbol is used to indicate operations that are manual. The annotation symbol is used here because all the text necessary for a complete description will not fit within the manual operation symbol.

The basic input/output symbol is used to represent vendor files. Assuming that the files were on paper or cards, it would be correct to represent the vendor files with the document symbol. It is always correct to use the basic input/output symbol for any input or output regardless of its physical form. Notice that arrowheads are used to indicate the bidirectional (both normal and reverse) flow between the manual operation and the vendor files. This indicates that the vendor files are both used in the operation and modified (updated) by the operation. The document symbol is used to represent the purchase order that is output from the manual operation.

IPO and HIPO Charts

IPO and HIPO charts are used primarily by systems development personnel to distinguish the level of system detail described in a flowchart. At the most general level of analysis, only the basic IPO relations in a system are of concern. An IPO chart (Figure 2.5) may be used to provide a narrative description of the inputs needed to generate desired system outputs. An **IPO chart** provides very little detail concerning the processing function but is a useful technique for analyzing overall information requirements. Additional processing detail is provided by HIPO charts (Figure 2.6). A HIPO consists of a series of charts that represent systems at increasing levels of detail, where the level of detail depends on the needs of users.

A **HIPO chart** contains two segments: the hierarchy chart that factors the processing task into various modules or subtasks and an IPO chart to describe the IPO requirements of each module. The hierarchy chart describes the overall system and provides a "table of contents" for the detailed IPO charts, usually through a numbering scheme, as shown in Figure 2.6. The IPO part of a HIPO chart is usually in narrative form, as shown in Figure 2.5, but other descriptive techniques may be used as well. In a complex system, the initial HIPO chart is factored into a set of HIPO rather than IPO charts, and then each separate sub-HIPO chart is factored into IPO diagrams. The progression of charts is always from the general to the specific; thus HIPO structures a top-down strategy in structured systems analysis and design.

HIPO charts are a design aid and a documentation tool. They are useful for identifying what is to be done in a problem; they are limited, however, for specifying how or when processing is to be accomplished. Graphic flowcharts using the symbols discussed previously are better suited to specifying information system functions and processing logic.

FIGURE 2.5

IPO Chart

Author: Mr. Foxx Chart Number: 3.1	System: Payroll Description: Calculate Gross Pay	Date: 6/9/0X
Input	Process	Output
Payroll Job Record Payroll Master File	Accumulate Hours Worked Find Correct Pay Rate Compute Gross Pay	Gross Pay Records Payroll Master File Error Messages

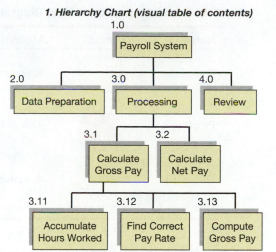

FIGURE 2.6

HIPO Illustration

Each numbered module would be detailed in an IPO chart.

Systems and Program Flowcharts

Systems flowcharts are used by both auditors and systems personnel. A **systems flowchart** identifies the overall or broad flow of operations in a system. A systems flowchart shows where inputs originate, the sequence and mode (manual or machine) of processing, and the disposition of outputs. The focus of systems flowcharting is on media and processing functions rather than the detailed logic of individual processing functions.

Program flowcharts are used primarily by systems development personnel. A **program flowchart** (also called a **block flowchart**) is more detailed with regard to individual processing functions than a systems flowchart. Each of the processing functions depicted in a systems flowchart is further detailed in a program flowchart, similar to the successive layering of IPO charts in HIPO charts.

Systems flowcharts are associated with the analysis phase of a systems project and program flowcharts with the design phase. A program flowchart is the design step between overall system design and coding the system for computer processing.

Logical Data Flow Diagrams

Logical data flow diagrams or **data flow diagrams** (both abbreviated as **DFD**) are used primarily by systems development personnel in systems analysis. A systems analyst often acts as the communication link between a user who desires some type of computer-based processing and the programmers/systems support staff who will actually prepare the physical design of a system to satisfy the user's need. Explicit documentation of the user–systems analyst interface is a major systems-development-control concern. DFDs are used by systems analysts to document the logical design of a system that meets user requirements. The DFD provides the user with a picture of the systems analyst's conception of the user's problem.

The emphasis here is on the word *logical*. The intent of using DFDs is to clearly separate the logical process of systems analysis from the physical process of systems design. The systems

TABLE 2.1   Logical Data Flow Diagram Symbols

Name	Symbol	Meaning
Terminator		Represents sources and destinations of data
Process		Task or function being done
Data store		A repository of data
Data flow	⟶	Communication channel

analyst provides a logical description to the systems designer/programmer, who then designs the physical specifications.

Table 2.1 illustrates the DFD symbols that will be used in this book. Although the symbology of DFDs is simple, a complete standardization of usage does not exist. This, of course, is also the case with traditional flowcharting symbols.

There are four DFD symbols. The *terminator* is used to indicate a source or a destination of data. The *process* indicates a process that transforms data. The *data store* is used to indicate a store of data. The *data flow* is used to indicate a flow of data. Although these terms and symbols are representative, many variations exist.

Note here the similarity between the four DFD symbols and the four basic flowcharting symbols, which can be used to prepare any type of flowchart. Although a DFD could reasonably be drawn with the four basic flowcharting symbols, the DFD symbols serve two purposes. The first is to emphasize the analysis of data flows. The second is to emphasize logical rather than physical design. Many of the traditional flowcharting symbols represent data processing operations or physical media. The use of such symbols by a systems analyst necessarily causes a blurring of the separation of logical analysis from physical design. This is not quite true if only the four basic flowcharting symbols are used. Nevertheless, this reasoning is the major argument offered by those who support the use of DFDs.

Logical Data Flow Diagrams and Structured Analysis

This section illustrates the construction of DFDs and their role in structured systems analysis. As indicated earlier, structured systems analysis is characterized by top-down design and successive refinement. We will illustrate these ideas in the context of a payroll application system.

Figure 2.7 shows a DFD for a top-level view of a payroll system that is a very general description of the system. Payroll data supplied by timekeeping are processed against a store or file of payroll data to generate paychecks for employees. The arrowhead flowlines indicate the

FIGURE 2.7

DFD for Payroll Processing

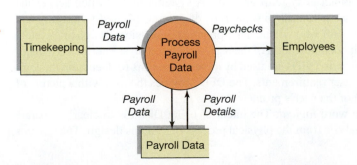

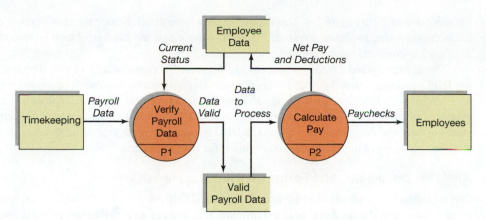

FIGURE 2.8

Expansion of the DFD of Payroll Processing

flow of data. Notice that the store of payroll data is both used in the payroll process (the flowline payroll details) and updated by the payroll process (the flowline payroll data).

Several points about the construction of a DFD as illustrated in Figure 2.7 can be made:

- The DFD should consist solely of DFD symbols.
- Each symbol in the DFD, including each arrowhead flowline, should be labeled.
- The flow of logic should be clear, with all sources and destinations of data indicated on the DFD.

Successive refinement of the payroll DFD in Figure 2.7 is required to attain a more meaningful description of the system. Figure 2.8 illustrates an *expansion* of the initial payroll DFD to incorporate more detail. Note that the source and destination are the same as in Figure 2.7. However, a new store—employee data—has been added, and the process payroll data in Figure 2.8 has been factored into two processes: "verify payroll data" and "calculate pay." Each of these processes has been numbered so that it may be referenced easily.

When the analyst is satisfied that all major modules have been identified, structured analysis proceeds with successive refinement of each of the major processing modules. Figure 2.9 illustrates

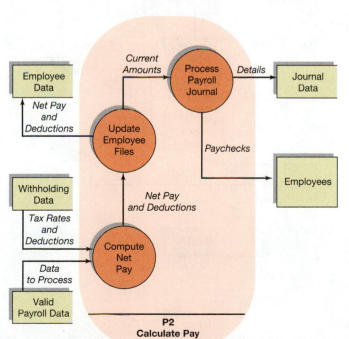

FIGURE 2.9

Explosion of Process P2

the *explosion* of P2 in Figure 2.8. This explosion adds more detail. Notice the new stores of data and the new processing modules. Explosion of each of these new modules may then be undertaken as necessary to complete the description of the system.

The expansion and explosion process just described is conceptually identical to that used in the HIPO charts discussed earlier in this chapter. Expansion and explosion of modules generate a hierarchical collection of processing modules that is very useful in providing a description of a proposed or existing system. An important aspect of DFDs, however, is that they concentrate on stores of data and decision logic. When the DFD is complete, the systems analyst can proceed to analyze the stores of data identified as required for the application.

Analytic, Document, and Forms Distribution Flowcharts

Often, auditors are concerned more with the flow and distribution of documents in an application system than with the mode of processing, particularly when evaluating the internal controls in an existing or proposed system. Because the segregation and division of duties is an important element of internal control, the auditor needs techniques that structure the system to distribute processing duties among personnel and/or departments.

Analytic flowcharts, document flowcharts, and forms distribution charts may be used to analyze the distribution of documents in a system. These charts are organized into columns to group the processing functions performed by each entity. Flowcharting across the separate columns, which represent the entities in the system, is an effective way to evaluate segregation of duties. This form of flowcharting also highlights the interfaces between entities. These interfaces—such as sending a document from one department to another—are important control points in an application system.

An **analytic flowchart** (Figure 2.10) is similar to a systems flowchart in level of detail and technique. The flow of processing is depicted using symbols connected with flowlines. An

FIGURE 2.10

Analytic Flowchart

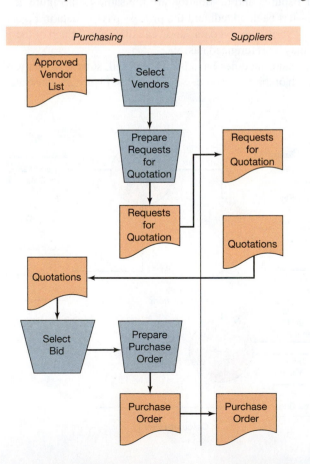

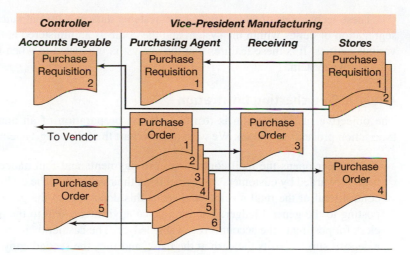

FIGURE 2.11

Document Flowchart

analytic flowchart identifies all significant processing in an application, emphasizing processing tasks that apply controls. Note the organization of the chart by columns. All the activities of the purchasing department are collected in one column so titled.

A **document flowchart** (Figure 2.11) is similar in format to an analytic flowchart but contains less detail about the processing functions of each entity shown on the chart. Strictly speaking, the only symbol used in a document flowchart is the document symbol. However, other symbols may be used as necessary for clarity. The intent is to take each document used in an application system and identify its points of origin, distribution, and ultimate disposition. Comments should be added as necessary to clarify the illustration. Each document symbol generally represents a batch of documents rather than a single document.

Closely related to the document flowchart is the **forms distribution chart** (Figure 2.12). A forms distribution chart illustrates the distribution of multiple-copy forms within an organization. The emphasis is on who gets what forms rather than on how these forms are processed. Forms may be represented by symbols, reduced photos of the forms themselves, or simply word descriptions. The form is pictured or designated on the left side of the chart and usually progresses horizontally through the various columns allotted to organizational units. Analysis may be directed toward eliminating unnecessary copies, unnecessary filing of copies, unauthorized distribution, and so on.

Purchasing	Inventory	Payables	Production	Accounting
Purchase Order Copy				
1	1			1 ▽
2		2		2 ▽
3				3 ▽
4			4	
5			▽	
▽				

FIGURE 2.12

Forms Distribution Chart for a Purchase Order

These techniques structure application-systems data in a format suitable for analyzing the segregation of duties within the system and the controls administered at the interfaces between various entities. It is these features that the analyst is interested in when reviewing the internal controls in a system.

Analytic Flowcharting Illustration

The objective of this section is to illustrate the preparation of an analytic flowchart for a transaction processing system. We wish to flowchart the following system:

> The cashier opens the mail containing cash payments and remittance advices that have been forwarded by customers as payments on their accounts. The cashier prepares a batch control total of the mail receipts and sends this document to the general ledger clerk for posting to the general ledger. The remittance advices are sent to the accounts receivable clerk for posting to the accounts receivable ledger. The cashier then prepares two copies of a deposit slip, deposits the cash at the bank, and files the second copy of the deposit slip, which has been validated at the bank, by date.
>
> The general ledger clerk posts the batch control total to the general ledger and then files the batch control total by date. The accounts receivable clerk posts the remittance advices to the accounts receivable ledger and then files the remittance advices by date.

PLANNING THE FLOWCHART   First, the necessary resources must be obtained. An appropriate software application is required when using a computer. If the chart is to be drawn on paper, then a flowcharting template and suitable instruments are necessary. It is then necessary to select which type of flowchart should be drawn, determined by the intended purpose of the flowchart. Here we draw an analytic flowchart.

SYMBOL SELECTION   After determining which type of chart is required, it is necessary to determine which symbols will be used in chart construction. ANSI X3.5 standard symbols, as discussed and illustrated in this chapter, are recommended, but in some cases organizations have their own symbol definitions, which should then be used.

Figure 2.13 illustrates several flowchart symbols commonly used in preparing analytic flowcharts that depict manual processing operations. All the symbols illustrated in Figure 2.13 have been defined in this chapter and are reproduced here to emphasize their importance in preparing analytic flowcharts. Auditors and accountants frequently prepare such flowcharts for the purpose of analyzing internal controls in a system.

Figure 2.13 contains the basic flowcharting symbols—manual process, transmittal tape, document, terminal, connector, and off-line storage. Note the letter *A* inside the off-line storage symbol indicates the manner in which documents are filed. *A* indicates that documents are filed alphabetically. *N* indicates that documents are filed by number. *D* indicates that documents are filed by date.

SYSTEM ANALYSIS   In preparing any type of flowchart, it is important to carefully review the material to be charted to obtain a good understanding of the description of the system. In preparing an analytic flowchart, it is necessary to determine what entities will be represented as separate columns—usually only entities for which some detailed processing activities are described. Analyzing the system to be charted here reveals three such entities: the cashier, the general ledger clerk, and the accounts receivable clerk. Because no processing activities are described for the other two entities—customers and the bank—they will be represented in ways discussed below.

The next step in the analysis is to identify the documents involved in the system. There are six such documents: cash payments, remittance advices, batch control total, deposit slip, general ledger, and accounts receivable ledger. Each of these should appear in the flowchart as appropriate.

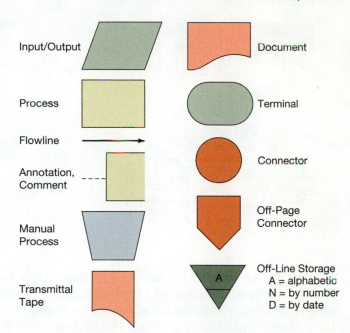

FIGURE 2.13

Symbols for Flowcharting Manual Procedures

DRAWING THE FLOWCHART   Our intent here is to chart the flow of documents in the system using appropriate flowchart symbols, flowlines, and style. The first step described is opening mail that contains cash payments and remittance advices by the cashier. This is a manual operation and may be charted as in Figure 2.14. The terminal symbol is used to indicate the source of the mail (customers). It also indicates the starting point in the flowchart. The mail is represented by a document symbol. The basic input/output symbol could also be used here. The manual operation symbol is used to represent the "open mail" process. The basic process symbol could also be used to represent this process. In both cases, a specialized symbol was selected because it clearly describes the system. For the same reason, the special document symbol is used to represent the cash payments and remittance advices. Although cash payments (cash and/or checks) are not documents in the same sense as remittance advices, they are important in this transaction processing system and should be clearly identified in the flowchart. Flowlines are used to indicate the flow of action. This portion of the flowchart would be placed in a column labeled "Cashier" because the cashier is performing this process.

The next step described is the preparation of a batch control total of the mail receipts. This also is a manual operation and may be charted as in Figure 2.15. The manual operation system is used to represent the "prepare batch control total" process, and the document symbol is used to represent the cash payments and the remittance advices. The document symbol has also been selected to represent the batch control total. The transmittal tape symbol shown in Figure 2.13 could also be used to represent the batch control total. This portion of the flowchart would also be placed in the column labeled "Cashier" because it is a continuation of the flowchart of the cashier's activities.

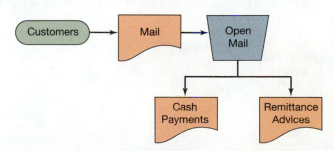

FIGURE 2.14

Open-Mail Portion of an Analytic Flowchart

FIGURE 2.15

**Prepare Batch
Control Total Portion
of an Analytic
Flowchart**

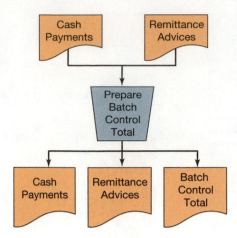

SANDWICH RULE   Notice the similarity of construction between the two portions of the flowchart that have been described. In both cases, inputs (documents) flow into a process symbol and outputs (documents) flow out of the process symbol. Every process symbol should have its inputs and outputs clearly specified. This has been called the **sandwich rule:** Every process symbol should be "sandwiched" between an input symbol and an output symbol.

USING THE CONNECTOR SYMBOL   The cashier forwards the batch control total to the general ledger clerk and the remittance advices to the accounts receivable clerk. This may be flowcharted as in Figure 2.16. Connector symbols are used here to eliminate long flowlines. The matching connector symbols appear in the columns for the general ledger clerk and the accounts receivable clerk in the complete flowchart, which is shown in Figure 2.18.

   Using connector symbols is a question of style that affects the overall appearance and clarity of a flowchart. One important advantage connector symbols have over long flowlines that cross over columns of a flowchart is that they add flexibility by making a flowchart modular. Notice that the absence of long flowlines crossing over columns of the flowchart in Figure 2.18 makes it possible to add or move columns without affecting the logical clarity or actual physical construction of the flowchart, or erasing and redrawing flowlines. This feature is especially useful when making changes to an existing flowchart.

ENTITY-COLUMN RELATIONS   The cashier prepares two copies of a deposit slip, deposits the cash at the bank, and files the second copy of the deposit slip, which has been validated by the bank, by date. This may be charted as in Figure 2.17. The manual operation system is used to represent the "prepare deposit slip" process, and the document symbol is used to represent the cash payments and the deposit slips. This portion of the flowchart is also placed in the "Cashier" column because it is a continuation of the flowchart of the cashier's activities.

   The bank is a separate entity, yet the process of depositing the cash payments at the bank is shown as a manual operation in the "Cashier" column of the flowchart. The bank could be shown as a separate column, and the flow of the deposit slip to and from the bank could be charted. The

FIGURE 2.16

**Use of a Connector
Symbol**

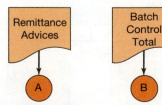

FIGURE 2.17

Cashier Activities Flowchart

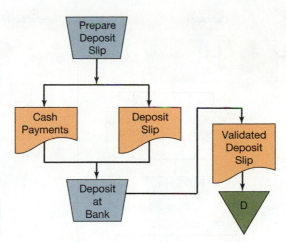

method shown was chosen because the narrative description being charted does not contain any discussion of processing at the bank. This is a question of style that affects the overall appearance and clarity of the flowchart. This same point is true for customers, who are also separate entities. The terminal symbol rather than a separate column was used to indicate the source of the mail (customers) because the narrative description being charted does not contain any discussion of customer processing.

Because the narrative contains a description of the processing by the general ledger clerk and the accounts receivable clerk, both these entities are shown as separate columns. The charting of the manual processing activities performed by the general ledger clerk and the accounts receivable clerk is very similar to that of the cashier's activities. The completed flowchart is shown in Figure 2.18. Notice that the basic input/output symbol has been used to represent the general ledger and the accounts receivable ledger. The document symbol or off-line storage (file) symbol could be used in either case. The basic input/output symbol has been used to emphasize that it is always correct to represent input or output with this symbol.

The preceding points have been discussed to emphasize that many choices must be made when preparing a flowchart. The result should be clear in appearance and should effectively convey the functioning of the system. Five general guidelines are as follows:

1. Analyze the system to identify entities and documents.
2. Select the symbols to be used in accordance with the general guidelines described in this chapter.
3. Sketch a rough first draft of the system to organize the entity columns and flow of documents.
4. Review the sketch for major omissions or errors.
5. Finalize the flowchart, making sure that comments are added as necessary to clarify the flowchart.

⬤ **CASE IN POINT**

The Trane Company, a $3 billion developer of heating, ventilation, and air-conditioning systems, was able to cut 30% off of its systems development process using an object-oriented development tool that is based on the Unified Modeling Language (UML).

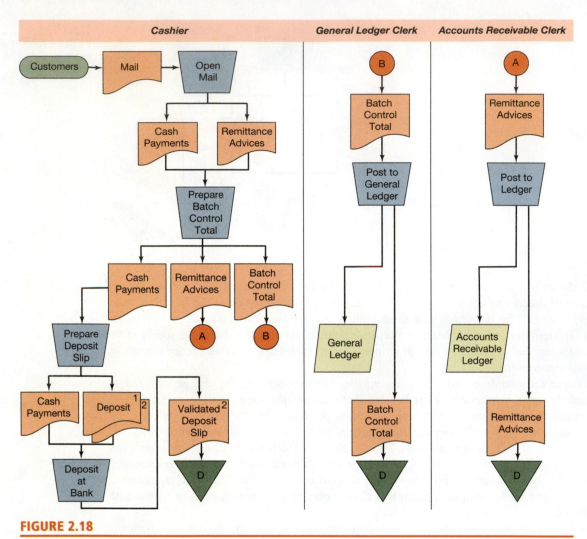

FIGURE 2.18

Analytic Flowchart Illustration

Unified Modeling Language™ (UML®)

UML® is a registered trademark of the Object Management Group (OMG™), which is an international, open membership, not-for-profit computer industry consortium. OMG task forces develop standards pertaining to the development and implementation of information systems and other technologies. UML is also an international standard (ISO/IEC 19501) supported by the International Organization for Standardization (ISO).

UML is a technology that assists in the specification, visualization, and documentation of models developed to structure and design software systems. UML is an embodiment of successful practices that have proven to be successful in the modeling of large software systems. UML uses a variety of graphical techniques to model different aspects and views of software development projects at various levels of abstraction. UML can also be used to model business processes and other nonsoftware systems as well. There are a variety of UML-based tools available from vendors in the systems development market. These tools are typically software applications that are used to design, publish, store, and manipulate UML diagrams that are attendant to the design of software in accordance with the UML open-standards published by OMG.

UML is a very broad collection of modeling tools. In addition to techniques used to model the specifics of software development, UML includes techniques that are the functional equivalent of DFD, document flowcharting, and analytic flowcharting. UML version 2.4 defines more than a dozen types of diagrams, divided into two categories: *structure diagrams* and *behavior diagrams*. Structure diagrams illustrate the static structure of the system and its components on different abstraction and implementation levels and how they are related to each other. The elements in a structure diagram represent the meaningful concepts of a system, and may include abstract, real world, and implementation concepts. Structure diagrams include the class diagram and the object diagram, among others. Behavior diagrams model the dynamic behavior between the objects in the system; that is, how the system changes over time. Behavior diagrams include the use case diagram, activity diagram, state machine diagram, and the interaction diagram. There are several types of interaction diagram.

The type of a diagram is defined by the primary graphical symbols shown on it. The UML specification does not preclude mixing of different kinds of diagrams. Thus, the boundaries between the various kinds of diagrams are not strictly enforced. However, some UML software tools do restrict the set of available graphical elements which could be used when working on a specific type of diagram.

UML is predominately a software systems development technology. Thus, detailed descriptions of all of the types of diagrams are beyond the scope of this textbook. Hence, we shall discuss use case diagrams and activity diagrams, as these two types can be used to model business processes at the overview level.

Use case diagrams describe what a system does from the standpoint of an external observer. Using UML terminology, use case diagrams display the relationship among actors and use cases. A use case is a statement of a single task or goal. An actor is who or what initiates the events involved in that task. Consider the most basic description of a sales processing system from the viewpoint of a customer. The customer uses the sales system to search the company's inventory for product information, to place orders, and to access customer support. Figure 2.19 illustrates a UML use case diagram for this overall level of abstraction of the system. In UML, actors are stick figures. Use cases are ovals. Communications are lines that link actors to use cases. Use case diagrams are useful in determining features and requirements, and in establishing communication between developers and clients concerning these features and requirements. Successive refinement will often lead to new use cases as system development proceeds.

Activity diagrams model the flow of activities involved in a single process, showing how these activities depend on one another. Symbols are used to represent activity flow, and activities are connected with lines. In UML, rounded rectangles indicate events. Continuous lines with arrows are used to show the sequence of events. The document symbol is used to represent documents and reports. Dotted lines with arrows are used to represent the flow of information between events. A small filled-in circle indicates the start of an activity and a small bull's eye (i.e., two concentric circles) is used to represent the end of the activity. The diamond-shaped decision symbol is used as such in UML to represent branching situations. Guard expressions

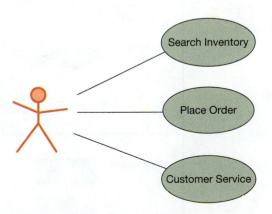

FIGURE 2.19

Basic Features of UML Use Case Diagram

(words enclosed in [ ]) label the transitions coming out of a branch. A transition may fork into two or more parallel activities. The fork and the subsequent join of the threads coming out of the fork appear in a UML activity diagram as solid bars.

When used to model business processes, the graphical techniques used in UML to prepare activity diagrams can result in diagrams that are very similar to analytic flowcharts. The essential feature of analytic flowcharting is the grouping of activities prepared by a single entity in columns. In UML terminology, this technique is called dividing the chart into object "swimlanes" that determine which object is responsible for which activity. Figure 2.20 illustrates a UML activity diagram with swimlanes used to group the activities performed by the customer and the sales office. The event "place order" is the start of the process. An order—represented by the document symbol—is sent from the customer to the sales office. A dotted line is used for this flow of information. Disposition of documents is not usually indicated in UML. The sales office receives the order, and then checks as to whether it is from a new or established customer. This is shown with a decision symbol and the two guard expressions [established] and [new customer]. New customers are entitled to a discount on their first order. The two guard expressions are joined—illustrated by the solid bar—and the order is processed. This is the end of the activities shown in the diagram. A professional who can read and interpret an analytic flowchart will most likely also be able to read and interpret a UML activity diagram that has been prepared to model the same business process.

◯ CASE IN POINT

The programmers at Sammy Studios, Inc., an interactive entertainment company that creates and distributes video games, use business graphics software on a weekly basis to create UML diagrams for video games.

Business Process Diagrams

The **business process diagram (BPD)** is a graphical representation of a business process. It focuses on the sequence of activities that constitute a business process, and also on the related

FIGURE 2.20

UML Activity Diagram

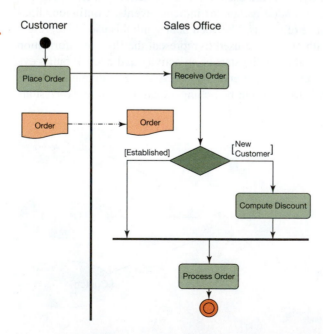

business logic that guides that sequence of activities. A variety of graphical techniques may be used to prepare a BPD.

Business Process Modeling and Notation (BPMN) is a widely accepted standard for modeling business processes using BPDs. Similar to UML, BPMN is a computer industry specification standard developed and supported by the OMG, a nonprofit computer industry consortium. BPMN is similar to UML but differs in that BPMN is a process-oriented approach to modeling whereas UML is an object-oriented approach. Where BPMN has a focus on business processes, UML has a focus on software design. Thus, BPMN and UML are not competing notations but rather are different views of a business process.

The choice of shapes and icons used for graphical elements is a key element of BPMN. The intent is to create a standard visual language that all process modelers will recognize and understand. The ability to provide both a simple tool for modeling business processes as well as a powerful tool that can be used to model the details of complex processes stems from the organization of the graphical aspects of BPMN into a small set of specific categories. This organization enables a user to readily recognize the basic types of elements in any BPD. Additional features within the basic categories of elements provide the capability to model the details of complex processes without dramatically changing the basic look and feel of the BPD.

CASE IN POINT

The Object Management Group/Business Process Management Initiative Charter states, in part, that "Business Process Modeling Notation (BPMN) will provide businesses with the capability of understanding their internal business procedures in a graphical notation and will give organizations the ability to communicate these procedures in a standard manner."

The five basic categories of elements are flow objects, data, connecting objects, swimlanes, and artifacts. Flow objects are the main graphical elements. There are three flow objects: events, activities, and gateways. There are four data elements: data objects, data inputs, data outputs, and data stores. There are four connecting objects: sequence flow, message flow, associations, and data associations. There are two types of swimlanes: pools and lanes. Artifacts, most commonly the annotation symbol, are used to provide additional information but do not affect the basic sequence or message flow of a business process and are thus optional in the construction of a BPD. These concepts will be illustrated with examples.

The most common basic symbols are shown in Figure 2.21. The task symbol represents tasks or activities. Task symbols represent the work that is performed in a process. The sequence

Symbol	Symbol Name	Description	Usage
	Task Symbol	Rounded Rectangle	Represents Tasks/Activities
	Sequence Flow Symbol	Solid Arrow	Represents Flow
	Gateway Symbol	Diamond	Represents Decisions that Affect the Flow
	Event Symbol	Circle	Represents Different Types of Events
	Data Object	Icon	Data Objects Provide Information about What Activities Require to be Performed and/or What they Produce

FIGURE 2.21

BPMN Basic Symbols

flow symbol represents flow. Sequence flow symbols are used to show the order in which activities will be performed in a process. The gateway symbol represents decisions that affect the flow. A gateway symbol is used to model the divergence and convergence of sequence flows in a process. Gateways will determine branching, forking, merging, and joining of flows in a process. The event symbol represents events. The most common events are "start" and "end." The data object symbol provides information about what activities require to be performed and/or what they produce. BPMN defines the shape of each symbol but not the size.

The extended BPMN modeling elements specify an extensive list of concepts that could be depicted through business process modeling notation. For example, there are many different types of gateways and event relations. Figure 2.22 shows several decision gateways. Figure 2.23 shows several merge gateways.

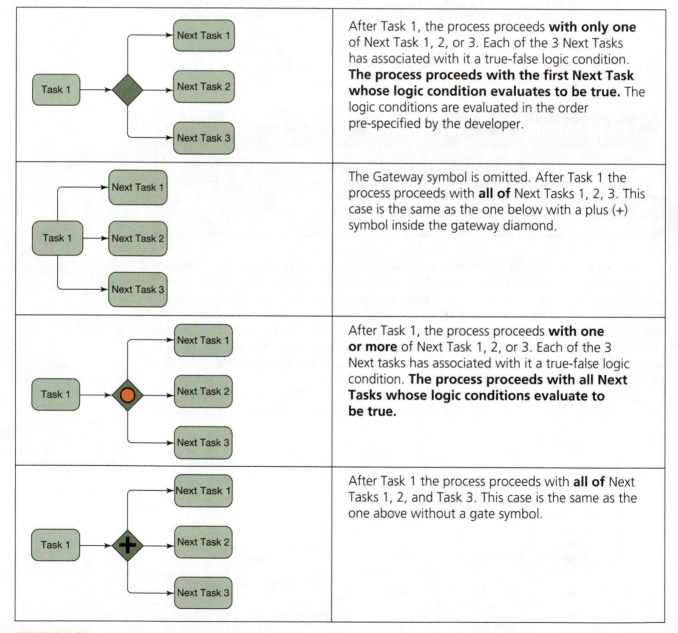

Task 1 → ◆ → Next Task 1 / Next Task 2 / Next Task 3	After Task 1, the process proceeds **with only one** of Next Task 1, 2, or 3. Each of the 3 Next Tasks has associated with it a true-false logic condition. **The process proceeds with the first Next Task whose logic condition evaluates to be true.** The logic conditions are evaluated in the order pre-specified by the developer.
Task 1 → Next Task 1 / Next Task 2 / Next Task 3	The Gateway symbol is omitted. After Task 1 the process proceeds with **all of** Next Tasks 1, 2, 3. This case is the same as the one below with a plus (+) symbol inside the gateway diamond.
Task 1 → ◉ → Next Task 1 / Next Task 2 / Next Task 3	After Task 1, the process proceeds **with one or more** of Next Task 1, 2, or 3. Each of the 3 Next tasks has associated with it a true-false logic condition. **The process proceeds with all Next Tasks whose logic conditions evaluate to be true.**
Task 1 → ✚ → Next Task 1 / Next Task 2 / Next Task 3	After Task 1 the process proceeds with **all of** Next Tasks 1, 2, and Task 3. This case is the same as the one above without a gate symbol.

FIGURE 2.22

BPMN Decision Gateways

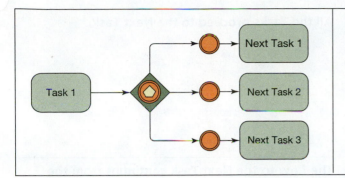

After Task 1, the process proceeds **with one or more** of Next Task 1, 2, or 3. Each of the 3 Next Tasks has associated with it an event. **The process proceeds with the Next Task whose event occurs first.**

FIGURE 2.22

Continued

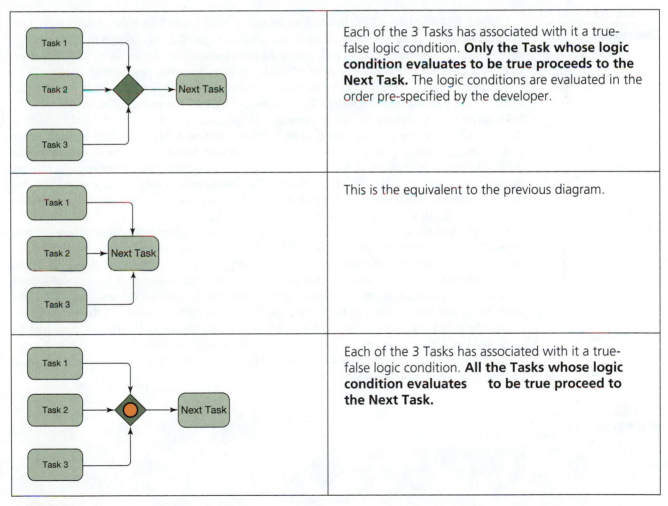

Each of the 3 Tasks has associated with it a true-false logic condition. **Only the Task whose logic condition evaluates to be true proceeds to the Next Task.** The logic conditions are evaluated in the order pre-specified by the developer.

This is the equivalent to the previous diagram.

Each of the 3 Tasks has associated with it a true-false logic condition. **All the Tasks whose logic condition evaluates   to be true proceed to the Next Task.**

FIGURE 2.23

BPMN Merge Gateways

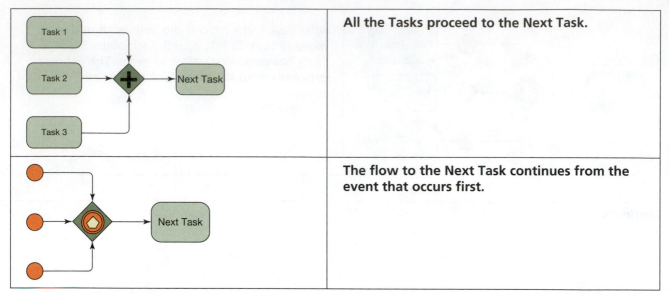

	All the Tasks proceed to the Next Task.
	The flow to the Next Task continues from the event that occurs first.

FIGURE 2.23

Continued

Figure 2.24 illustrates a BPD in which a customer's credit is checked. If the credit is good, then the order is processed; otherwise the customer is contacted. Figure 2.25 illustrates a BPD for processing an approved customer order. As indicated by the plus symbol inside the decision gateway symbol, processing proceeds with both of the actions "pull goods from inventory" and "e-mail customer."

Figure 2.26 shows the use of the annotation symbol, which is a bracket, attached to the start event symbol with a dotted line. Dotted lines are used to indicate association. The annotation symbol is an artifact that is used to include comments in a diagram. A "Timer Start Event" is used to start the task of mailing the customer a monthly billing statement. The start event is diagrammed with the event symbol, a circle; and the timer indication is included as a symbol contained within the event symbol. As illustrated, the annotation symbol is associated to the timer event to provide the comment "wait until the first of the month." The task symbol is used to diagram the activity, and flow concludes with an end event symbol. The end event symbol is diagrammed as a thick-line circle to distinguish it from a start event.

BPMN uses the concept of "swimlanes" to partition and organize activities. There are two types of swimlanes: pools and lanes. A pool is a rectangular box that represents a participant, an entity such as a customer, or a business process participant such as a credit function. A pool can be a "black box" in that no internal details are represented in the diagram. A pool can also have internal details, which may be organized with subswimlanes that are called lanes. Lanes are vertical or horizontal lines that extend to the entire pool. Lanes in BPMD function in the same manner as swimlanes in UML. For example, a pool representing a business process in a company may be portioned into two lanes, such as sales and shipping, to group their respective activities in the diagram. These concepts are illustrated in Figure 2.27, which shows three different pools: payment gateway, company, and customer.

FIGURE 2.24

BPMN Example 1

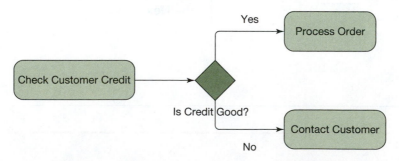

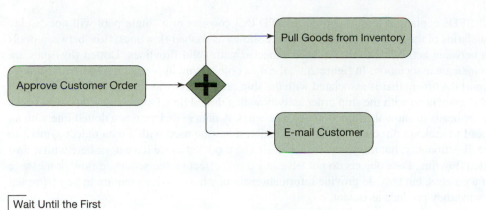

FIGURE 2.25

BPMN Example 2

FIGURE 2.26

BPMN Example 3

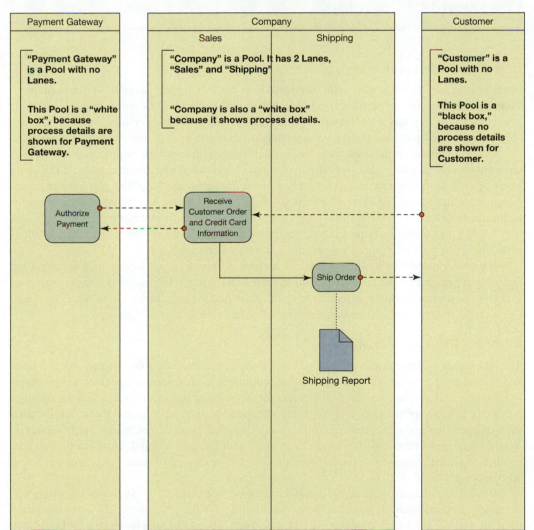

FIGURE 2.27

BPMN Swimlanes Example

All BPDs contain at least one pool. A BPD that consists of a single pool will not display the boundaries of the pool. Messages, which are shown as dashed flowlines, flow between pools but not between activities. Activities are connected with solid flowlines. Dotted flowlines are used to indicate association. In figure 2.27, the data object symbol is used to represent the shipping report document that is associated with the ship order activity as an output. The data object symbol is associated with the ship order activity with a dotted line. Optionally, dotted lines may have arrowheads to show the direction of association. A data association is a dotted line with an arrowhead to indicate direction. A data association might be used with a data object symbol to indicate directionality, but this association can also be modeled as we have done here with a simple dotted flowline. Data objects do not have any direct effect on the sequence flow or message flow of a process, but they do provide information about what activities require to be performed and/or what they produce as output.

CASE IN POINT

The BPMN 2.0 Poster provides an overview over the constructs in BPMN 2.0. The poster was created by the "Berliner BPM-Offensive" and is available for download for free (www.bpmb.de/images/BPMN2_0_Poster_EN.pdf).

Narrative Techniques

Narrative techniques are often useful, particularly in the fact-finding stage of systems analysis. Interviews are useful for familiarizing the analyst with individual decision makers and their problems. In-depth interviews allow the systems analyst to establish a personal working relationship with the manager. Structured interviews might be used to answer a specific set of questions.

Open-ended questionnaires are a fact-gathering technique where people provide written answers to general rather than specific questions. Open-ended questionnaires serve the same purpose as in-depth interviews, asking very general questions such as, "Do you have any suggestions for improving the system? Please explain." Closed-ended questionnaires are a useful technique for gathering answers to a large number of questions. They require considerably less time on the part of the systems analyst. Such questionnaires are very effective in many situations, including for collecting information about internal control.

Narrative techniques include document reviews. Often, a large number of documents are available for review by the analyst or auditor, such as flowcharts, organization charts, procedure manuals, operation manuals, reference manuals, and historical records. These documents can assist the analyst or auditor in gaining an overall understanding of the organization.

Resource Utilization Analysis

The techniques we have discussed assume an existing or proposed flow or structure of operations and do not directly address the question of system resource utilization requirements. For example, assume that you had prepared flowcharts for a particular procedure, identified the changes necessary to accomplish the task at hand, and obtained approval to prepare (design) the detailed plan of operation and/or to implement the newly designed procedure. Clearly, further analysis would be required to match the resources at hand with the task at hand. How many clerks or machines will be required to process the data? What type or size of machine is required? And who gets what task?

Resource utilization analysis must always be considered by systems development personnel in implementing systems. Auditors should consider resource utilization when they plan an audit. Tasks such as assigning staff to particular audit functions can be facilitated with systems techniques. Thus systems techniques for resource utilization analysis may be used by both auditors and systems personnel.

WORK MEASUREMENT   Work measurement is based on a simple premise: Quantitative measurement is essential to the design of efficient procedures. **Work measurement** includes the variety of techniques used to model, measure, or estimate clerical or other activities in a production framework. In an accounting framework, work measurement is similar to the concept employed in standard cost systems. The essential ingredient is the development of a standard, a yardstick, that may be used to gauge the efficiency of the actual operation.

Work measurement involves four basic steps:

1. Identify the tasks.
2. Obtain time estimates for performing the tasks using time and motion studies, test runs, historical data, or some other source.
3. Adjust the time estimates for idle time and similar considerations.
4. Analyze requirements based on these data.

The following are general examples of Step 4:

$$\left(\frac{\text{Average time}}{\text{unit}} + \frac{\text{idle time}}{\text{unit}} \right) \times \text{average volume} = \text{total task time}$$

$$\frac{\text{Total time available}}{\text{total task time}} = \text{capacity utilization}$$

To illustrate the general idea, consider the following excerpt from an actual systems analysis:

Our desire to evaluate the relative costs associated with various operating configurations for the CVU Unit led to the programming of a computational model of the CVU operation. The model is essentially a personnel cost model. A constant volume is passed through the CVU operation under certain assumptions as to operating configuration. Costs are accumulated and reported. Costs are calculated in terms of the work hours needed to perform a given operation. A standard computation would appear as follows:

$$Y = C\left(\frac{X}{R} \right)$$

where

X = volume to be processed
R = processing rate (volume/hour)
C = average hourly personnel cost for this processing rate
Y = resulting cost

This standard includes operations such as counting, bundle and strap counts, verification, and destruction. In most cases, certain fixed costs are added, such as the cost of observers. Since several days are used in processing a given lot, the assumption of a constant volume allows us to calculate the cost per lot. The constant volume used is the average daily volume for the preceding year.

Work measurement techniques have two major areas of application in systems work. The first is in evaluating the technical feasibility or technical requirements of a system design. Examples of this are determining the number of magnetic disks needed to store a specific number of documents, the size of computer system necessary to process a proposed work load, and the number of clerks necessary to input data.

The second major area of application is in performance evaluation of system-related tasks such as computer programming and project development. Performance evaluation requires the definition of performance standards in terms of some directly measurable criterion such as "number of lines coded" or "hours of project work," so that actual performance may be quantified and evaluated with respect to managerial expectations for the task.

 CASE IN POINT

The Institute of Management Services, a body in the United Kingdom concerned with the promotion, practice, and development of the range of methodologies and techniques for the improvement of productivity and quality, notes that the results obtained from work measurement are commonly used as the basis of the planning and scheduling of work, manpower planning, work balancing in team work, costing, labor performance measurement, and financial incentives.

WORK DISTRIBUTION ANALYSIS   After the operational characteristics of a system have been identified and selected through some form of work measurement, a **work distribution analysis** must be undertaken to assign specific tasks to employees. This analysis may take several forms, but conceptually the problem may be represented as a matrix. Table 2.2 illustrates a work distribution table.

A work distribution analysis requires detailed information about the functions and responsibilities of all employees involved in the analysis. A task list is used to record each separate item of work performed by an individual and the average number of hours spent on each task per week. The detail of tasks considered depends on the level of work measurement analysis. Table 2.2 shows the assignment of several tasks (left-hand column). Each employee (or department, and so on) is represented by a column; the work assignments are spread across the table. The method of assignment should be rational; that is, employee qualifications, internal control, scheduling, timing of events, and so forth, should be considered. The method of assignment is the choice of the analyst. Formal techniques using mathematical programming or similar algorithms may be found in management science and industrial engineering literature.

Decision Analysis Techniques

BRANCHING AND DECISION TABLES   Branching and decision tables are used primarily by systems development personnel. The decision logic required in a computer program is usually too complex to use a standard decision flowcharting symbol. In such cases, a **branching table** may be used to depict a decision function. The table is composed of a statement of the decision to be made, a list of the conditions that can occur, and the path to be followed for each condition. The "Go to" section contains either an inconnector (connector symbol) reference or a single flowline exiting to another symbol. Examples of branching table formats are shown in Figure 2.28.

TABLE 2.2 **Sample Work Distribution Table**

Task	Estimated Hours per Day	Assignment to Employees Lola	Dale	Neil
Open mail	2	1	1	0
Sort advices	6	2	2	2
Batch control	2	0	0	2
File advices	8	4	4	0

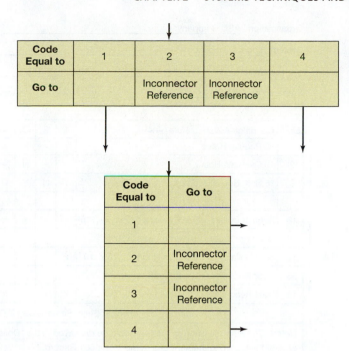

FIGURE 2.28

**Branching Table
Formats**

A **decision table** is a tabular representation of a decision-making process (Figure 2.29). It is similar to a branching table but more complex in that it incorporates multiple decision criteria. Decision tables are constructed on an IF–THEN premise and appear as a two-dimensional matrix in general form. The table is divided into four areas: the condition stub, the condition entries, the action stub, and the action entries. Conditions are listed on horizontal rows in the condition stub area and are read as "IF Condition 1 and Condition 2…and Condition *N*, THEN Action 1, Action 2, Action *N*." Rules are numbered horizontally across the top of the table and represent the logical combinations of condition entries and action entries that constitute the decision process. There is one vertical row for each combination.

An example of a decision table is shown in Figure 2.30. As the figure shows, condition entries are usually limited to *Y* (for "true"), *N* (for "false"), or — (for "not applicable"). Action entries are listed as applicable or not applicable—the presence or absence of an *x* in Figure 2.30. The interpretation of Rule 1 in Figure 2.30 is "IF Conditions 1, 2, and 3 are *Y*, then take Actions 10, 11, 12, and 14." The other rules are interpreted in the same manner.

The type of decision table just discussed is called a *limited-entry table* because condition and action entries are restricted to Y, N, or not applicable. An *extended-entry decision* table also might be used, where the entries indicate specific types of actions to be taken, specific conditions, or references to other decision tables. Decision tables might be used in lieu of program flowcharts to analyze and document the logic of an application program. The tabular structure of a decision table is an important advantage compared with graphic flowcharts as the complexity of a decision process increases.

Table Title		Rules				
		1	2	3	· · ·	N
If:	Condition Stub	Condition Entry				
Then:	Action Stub	Action Entry				

FIGURE 2.29

**Decision Table
Format**

FIGURE 2.30

Decision Table

| Organization | ABC Company | | Page | 1 | of | 1 |

System Labor Distribution Project No. 123

Program Name Labor Dist. Print No. LD01 Revision Date 3/26

Prepared by W. Smith Date 2/26 Approved by J. Jones

	Line	Condition Action Rule →	1	2	3	4	5	6	7	8		
IF {	1	15 Regular Hours	Y	–	–	–	N					
	2	15 Overtime Hours	Y	–	N	–	Y	–	N			
	3	15 Shift Bonus Hours	Y	N	Y	N	Y	N	Y	N		
THEN {	10	Regular Dollars = Reg. Hours x (Hourly + .115)	x	x	x	x						
	11	Overtime Dollars = Overtime Hrs. 150%	x	x								
	12	Shift Dollars = Shift Bonus Hours = $10 x .10	x		x							
	13	Error No Shift or OT without Reg. Hours					x	x	x			
	14	Next Record	x	x	x	x	x	x	x			

Go to - F (Function); R (Rule, Same Table); T (Table)

Notes: The error message at line 13 should be displayed in the "Dollars" area of the report, to the right of a dump of the 501 Record.

Condition Entries ("If") { Y = True   N = False   – = Not applicable

Action Entry x = Take Action ("Then")

MATRIX METHODS Matrix methods are used by both auditors and systems personnel. A decision table is essentially a matrix presentation. Matrices and array forms of presentation have many uses in systems work because they are a convenient method for analyzing and displaying a large volume of data. The worksheets or spreadsheets used in accounting systems to spread or distribute account balances through different subclassifications or to facilitate the closing process are common examples of matrix techniques. The essential analytic feature of matrix techniques is the spreading of row entries through various column entries. This ensures that each row/column combination is explicitly analyzed and documented.

In an application control matrix, the row entries are controls, and the column entries are processing actions. This technique may be used systematically to evaluate the internal controls in an application system. In a data control matrix, the row entries are data elements and the column entries are forms or reports. Analysis may be directed to the elimination of redundant data on a set of forms or to the commonality of data on a set of reports.

Software for Systems Techniques

A variety of software tools can be used to create flowcharts and other graphical systems techniques. Preparing graphical documentation with software has many advantages over manual preparation. These advantages include legibility, enhanced formatting and presentation capabilities, and enhanced capabilities to revise and reproduce documentation. Specialized software tools are available for the preparation of specific graphical techniques such as flowcharts, DFDs, and UML charts. These tools might be individual stand-alone applications such as a flowcharting program or tools that are part of larger software applications that integrate the creation and manipulation of various types of systems documentation. These larger applications are generally known as CASE (Computer-Aided Software Engineering). In addition to specialized tools, general purpose word processing software and general purpose graphical/drawing software might also be used to create systems techniques.

MICROSOFT OFFICE® APPLICATIONS   Microsoft Visio® is a Microsoft Office® application that is targeted at the creation of flowcharts and other graphical diagrams. Microsoft PowerPoint® is a general presentation tool that contains specific drawing features that may be used to create flowcharts and other graphical diagrams. When the Drawing toolbar is visible, lines, arrows, rectangles, and ovals are shown as selections that allow one to "draw" these items by simply selecting them and then placing and sizing them on a drawing. Many more shapes are available under the AutoShapes menu. In particular, a flowchart submenu contains 28 specific flowchart symbols that can be used to draw flowcharts. These same drawing tools are also available in both Microsoft Word® and Microsoft Excel®, allowing either of these general software applications to be used to prepare graphical diagrams and flowcharts.

COMPUTER-AIDED SOFTWARE ENGINEERING   Computer-aided software engineering (CASE) is the process of using computer software technology that supports an automated engineering discipline for software development and maintenance. The term *CASE* is also used to refer to a particular product or a set of products that automate (at least in part) the process of building and maintaining software. CASE is intended to increase productivity; improve software quality through introduction of rigorous standards and analysis; and decrease the cost of developing, documenting, and maintaining software. CASE requires a highly structured approach to analysis, design, coding, testing, and maintenance of software. There is diversity in CASE tools from different vendors. The terms *Upper CASE* and *Front-end CASE* describe tools that are directed at the analysis and design stages of software systems development. The terms *Lower CASE* and *Back-end CASE* describe tools that are directed at the implementation stage. CASE diagramming tools provide automated support for drawing DFDs, structure charts, and other such graphics.

UML MODELING TOOLS   UML is a technology that assists in the specification, visualization, and documentation of models developed to structure and design software systems. UML is complex and thus the use of some type of software is essential. A variety of software tools to draw UML charts are available from vendors. Professional UML software is similar to CASE in its objectives and its potential benefits in that it integrates UML charts with other aspects of systems development, such as database design and code generation.

BPMN MODELING TOOLS   Business Process Modeling Notation (BPMN) is a graphical notation that depicts the steps in a business process. A variety of BPMN software tools are available from vendors. Some tools are available at no cost on the Internet. Many flowcharting software packages, such as Microsoft Visio®, have templates available that can be used to build diagrams that conform to the BPMN standards.

Summary

Systems techniques are used by both auditors and systems personnel as tools for analysis and documentation. Table 2.3 summarizes the many techniques described in this chapter and indicates the primary users of each technique. Systems techniques are necessary for a structured systems approach to the analysis and design of information systems. One popular and widely used systems technique is flowcharting. Several different types of flowcharts may be used, incorporating standard flowcharting symbols. Even though standard symbols are in widespread use, flowcharting is more art than science.

Many other systems techniques are used in addition to flowcharts. Logical DFDs are frequently used in systems analysis and design. DFDs may be used to successively refine the design of a system. Branching and decision tables, IPO and HIPO charts, UML, BPDs, and matrix methods are also used in systems analysis and design.

Techniques used in resource utilization analysis and decision analysis include flowcharts, DFDs, and other graphic techniques. Although very useful, these techniques do not consider system resource use. Work measurement techniques are necessary to address how much or how many resources will be required for the operation of a system.

TABLE 2.3   Primary Users of Systems Techniques

Analytic flowchart	Charts the flow of documents and processing between different entities, which are represented by separate columns in the chart	Auditor Systems analyst
Block flowchart	Synonym for program flowchart	Systems designer Programmer
Branching table	A tabular technique used to represent a decision function in a flowchart	Systems designer Programmer
Data flow diagram (DFD)	A charting technique used to document the logical design of a system	Systems analyst Systems designer
Decision table	Used to supplement or replace the preparation of flowcharts when there are a large number of alternative decision paths	Systems designer Programmer
Business process diagram (BPD)	A graphical representation of a business process	Auditor Systems analyst
Document flowchart	A flowchart of document flow in which the only symbol used is the document symbol	Auditor Systems analyst
Flowchart	A symbolic diagram that shows the data flow and sequence of operations in a system	Auditor Systems analyst Systems designer Programmer
Forms distribution chart	Illustrates the distribution of multiple-copy documents within an organization	Auditor Systems analyst Systems designer
HIPO chart (hierarchy plus input–process–output)	An organized collection of IPO charts	Systems analyst Systems designer
IPO chart (input–process–output)	Describes the inputs necessary to produce certain outputs, and generally provides very little detail concerning the required processing	Systems analyst Systems designer
Logical data flow diagram	Synonym for data flow diagram	Systems analyst Systems designer
Program flowchart	A flowchart indicating detailed processing functions	Systems designer Programmer
Systems flowchart	A pictorial or graphical representation of the overall flow of work, documents, and operations in an application system	Auditor Systems analyst Systems designer
Unified Modeling Language™ (UML®)	A technology that assists in the specification, visualization, and documentation of models developed to structure and design software systems.	Systems analyst Systems designer
Work measurement	Techniques used to measure activities in a production framework	Systems analyst Systems designer
Work distribution analysis	Techniques used to rationally assign work to entities	Auditor Systems analyst System designer

Glossary

additional symbols   a group of flowchart symbols in ANSI X3.5 consisting of miscellaneous symbols that make flowcharting more convenient.

analytic flowchart   charts the flow of documents and processing between different entities—which are represented by separate columns in the chart—in a system.

basic symbols   one of the four groups of flowchart symbols in ANSI X3.5, consisting of symbols that correspond to the basic data processing functions.

block flowchart   synonym for *program flowchart*.

branching table   a tabular technique used to represent a decision function in a flowchart.

business process diagram (BPD)   a graphical representation of a business process.

Business Process Modeling and Notation (BPMN)   widely accepted standard for modeling business processes in the form of BPDs.

data flow diagram (DFD)   a charting technique used to document the logical design of a system.

decision table   used to supplement or replace the preparation of flowcharts when there are a large number of alternative decision paths.

document flowchart   a flowchart of document flow in a system in which the only symbol used is the document symbol.

flowchart   a symbolic diagram that shows the data flow and sequence of operations in a system.

forms distribution chart   illustrates the distribution of multiple-copy documents within an organization.

HIPO (hierarchy plus input–process–output) chart   an organized collection of IPO charts.

IPO (input–process–output) chart   describes the inputs necessary to produce certain outputs and generally provides very little detail concerning the required processing.

logical data flow diagram   synonym for *data flow diagram*.

program flowchart   a flowchart indicating detailed processing functions.

sandwich rule   the flowcharting principle that every process symbol should be "sandwiched" between an input symbol and an output symbol.

specialized input/output symbols   a group of flowchart symbols in ANSI X3.5 consisting of symbols that may be used to represent I/O function and also the medium on which the information is recorded.

specialized process symbols   a group of flowchart symbols in ANSI X3.5 consisting of symbols that may be used to represent processing and, in addition, identify the specific type of operation to be performed.

systems flowchart   a pictorial or graphical representation of the overall flow of work, documents, and operations in an application system.

systems techniques   tools used in the analysis, design, and documentation of systems.

Unified Modeling Language™ (UML®)   a technology that assists in the specification, visualization, and documentation of models developed to structure and design software systems.

work distribution analysis   techniques used to rationally assign work to entities.

work measurement   techniques used to measure activities in a production framework.

Webliography

www.omg.org
The home page of the OMG, a not-for-profit computer industry specifications consortium whose members define and maintain the UML specification. OMG was originally founded by 11 organizations that included IBM, Hewlett-Packard, American Airlines, and Apple Computer. This consortium also maintains the BPMN.

www.bpmn.org
The home page of the OMG's Business Process Modeling Notation site.

www.bpmi.org
The home page of the Business Modeling & Integration (BMI) Domain Task Force (DTF). The BPMN standard is available for download at this site.

www.uml.org
The UML™ home page of the OMG.

portal.acm.org
A Web portal for the Association for Computing Machinery (ACM). This site contains the ACM Digital Collection, which includes many free-to-the-public and members-only articles on flowcharting.

www.wikipedia.com/wiki/Diagram
A comprehensive article on various types of diagrams. This article lists over 100 different types of diagrams, with links to many of the different diagram types.

Chapter Quiz

Answers to the Chapter Quiz appear on page 79

1. The group concerned with establishing standards for flow-chart symbols is (_____).
   a. ASCII
   b. EBCDIC
   c. ANSI
   d. AICPA

2. A pictorial or graphic representation of the overall flow of work, documents, and operations in an application system is shown in a(n) (_____).
   a. IPO chart
   b. forms distribution chart
   c. systems flowchart
   d. process chart

3. Which type of diagram emphasizes the physical description of a system?
   a. analytic flowchart
   b. DFD
   c. HIPO chart
   d. IPO chart

4. ANSI X3.5-1970—the information system flowcharting standard published by the American National Standards Institute—defines four groups of flowchart symbols and illustrates conventions regarding their use. Which of the following is *not* one of these groups?
   a. specialized input/output symbols
   b. specialized processing symbols
   c. branching and decision table symbols
   d. basic symbols

5. Structured systems analysis can best be referred to as (_____).
   a. a process of increasingly complex sets of controls
   b. a process of successive refinement
   c. a procedure for documenting process logic
   d. a statement of decision tables

6. An important omission from flowcharts and matrix techniques is (_____).
   a. the ability to represent decisions
   b. the ability to include internal control considerations
   c. the ability to incorporate error conditions
   d. the ability to specify systems resource requirements

7. Which of the following items would be most useful in analyzing the separation of duties and functions in an application system?
   a. document flowchart
   b. program flowchart
   c. HIPO chart
   d. source document

8. In the preparation of a DFD for a payroll processing application, which of the following symbols should be used to indicate the payroll data?
   a. terminator symbol
   b. data store symbol
   c. process symbol
   d. input/output symbol

9. In the preparation of an analytic flowchart for a payroll processing application, which of the following symbols could be used to indicate the payroll data?
   a. connector symbol
   b. decision symbol
   c. process symbol
   d. input/output symbol

10. In the preparation of an analytic flowchart, which of the following symbols should be used when flowlines are broken due to a page limitation?
    a. terminal symbol
    b. connector symbol
    c. manual operation symbol
    d. input/output symbol

Review Problem

This review problem involves a manual system. A service request form (two copies) is prepared in the production department. Copy 2 is forwarded to the repair and maintenance department. Copy 1 is filed in the production department.

In the repair and maintenance department, Copy 2 of the service request is used to manually prepare a four-part work order form. Copy 2 of the service request form is then filed in the repair and maintenance department. Copy 4 of the work order form is forwarded to the production department to acknowledge the service request. Copy 3 of the work order form is filed in the repair and maintenance department. Clerks in the repair and maintenance department manually record actual materials and supplies used and labor time required on Copies 1 and 2 of the work order. When the work order is completed, Copy 1 is filed in the repair and maintenance department, and Copy 2 is forwarded to the accounting department.

Clerks in the accounting department manually complete a detailed costing of Copy 2 of the work order and prepare a work order summary report (three copies). Copy 2 of the work order is filed in the accounting department. Copy 1 of the work order summary is forwarded to the production department. Copy 2 of the work order summary is forwarded to the repair and maintenance department. Copy 3 of the work order summary is filed in the accounting department.

Required

Prepare an analytic flowchart of the preceding procedures. (See Figure 2.31 for the solution.)

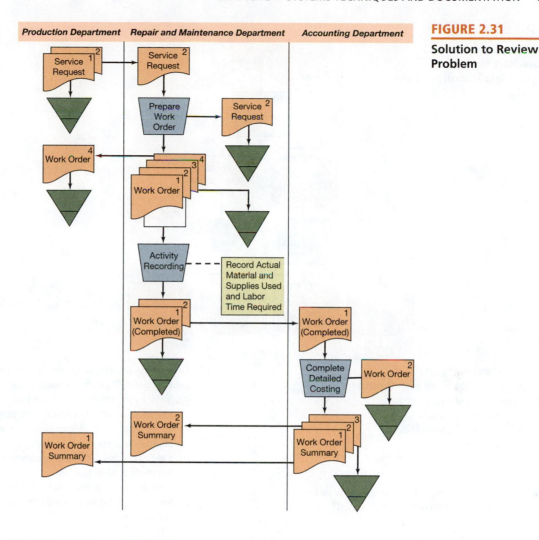

FIGURE 2.31

Solution to Review Problem

Review Questions

1. Define flowcharting.
2. List and draw the basic flowchart symbols.
3. Flowchart symbols represent what aspect of a system?
4. Distinguish between IPO and HIPO charts.
5. What is the difference between a systems flowchart and an analytic flowchart?
6. A DFD can be used to document what aspect of a system?
7. Why do auditors prepare analytic flowcharts of processing systems?

8. What important feature is common to analytic, document, and forms distribution charts?
9. Identify the symbols that are used to construct DFDs.
10. Is flowcharting useful in analyzing the resources required to implement a system?
11. Relate the concept of work measurement to the system implementation process.
12. Outline the steps involved in a work distribution analysis.

Discussion Questions and Problems

Questions 13 through 15 are based on the section of a system flowchart for a payroll application shown in Figure 2.32.

13. Symbol A could represent (_____).
    a. computation of gross pay
    b. input of payroll data

c. preparation of paychecks
d. verification of pay rates

14. Symbol B could represent (_____).
    a. computation of net pay
    b. separation of erroneous time cards

FIGURE 2.32

Section of a System Flowchart for a Payroll Application

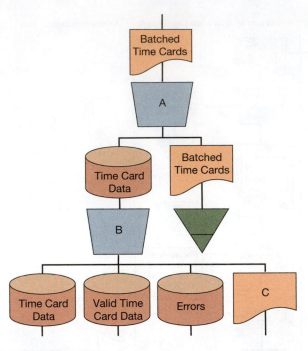

c. validation of payroll data
d. preparation of the payroll register

15. Symbol C could represent (_____).
   a. batched time cards
   b. unclaimed payroll checks
   c. erroneous time cards
   d. an error report

(*CPA*)

16. Which of the symbolic representations in Figure 2.33 indicates that a sales invoice has been filed?

(*CPA*)

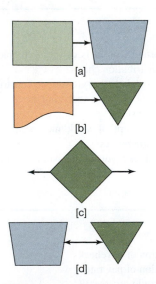

FIGURE 2.33

Symbolic Representations for Problem 16

17. During the review of an electronic data processing (EDP) internal control system, an auditor may review decision tables prepared by the client. A decision table is usually prepared by a client to supplement or replace the preparation of (_____).
   a. an internal control questionnaire when the number of alternative responses is large
   b. a narrative description of a system where transactions are not processed in batches
   c. flowcharts when the number of alternatives is large
   d. an internal control questionnaire not specifically designed for an EDP installation

(*CPA*)

18. Which of the symbolic representations in Figure 2.34 indicate that a file has been consulted?

(*CPA*)

19. The XYZ Company distributes three product lines to seven customers. Sales are recorded manually on invoices. Separate invoices are always used to record sales of product line number 1. Sales of the other two product lines are always recorded together on a single invoice.

   The manager would like to know the total daily sales of each product line in dollars and also the daily sales total for each product line sold to each customer.

   To develop this information manually, the manager will collect all the invoices at the end of each day. A separate worksheet will be used to record the daily sales total for each product line. Each worksheet will have seven columns with separate headings—one for each customer. The manager will record each day's sales totals on a separate line of each worksheet.

   Design a system with the specific steps necessary to develop and record the desired information from the daily batch of sales invoices.

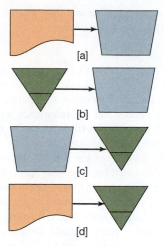

FIGURE 2.34

Symbolic Representations for Problem 18

20. The HRZ Company maintains a perpetual inventory system. Clerks in the accounting department post the data manually from receiving reports, materials requisition forms, copies of purchase orders, and other transactions, such as returns and adjustments to the inventory records. The source documents are filed by posting date. The inventory records are analyzed after each posting to determine if the item should be reordered. If an item needs to be reordered, a purchase requisition (one copy) is prepared and sent to the purchasing department. There, clerks select a vendor from a master vendor file, prepare a purchase order (four copies), and update the vendor file to reflect the order. The purchase order is approved and distributed as follows: original copy to the vendor; Copy 2 is filed numerically with the corresponding purchase requisition attached; Copy 3 is forwarded to the receiving department; Copy 4 is sent to the accounting department.

Required

a. Prepare an analytic flowchart of the preceding procedures.

b. Prepare a DFD of the preceding procedures.

21. As part of an audit engagement, you have been assigned the task of documenting the internal control system for the BrownSole Shoe Store. The business is operated by a single owner, who operates the store daily with only two additional employees who help out in everything, from stocking new shoes, to helping customers, to bill paying and accounting.

The owner, Marjorie Renalwald, is a very stubborn person with little business education. She very much needs a set of audited financial statements in order to obtain a loan, but at the same time she seems very irritable and not especially interested in working with you.

Your first experience with her was a 10:00 A.M. appointment with her the other day. You sat in the back of the store, in a small storage room, and waited for 1 hour while she talked on the telephone to her daughter in London. Then, after allowing you to ask her only one or two questions, she abruptly told you that she was late for a hair appointment.

Required

Describe the approach you will take in dealing with Marjorie Renalwald. Which systems techniques will you use, and what order will you use them in?

22. A systems analyst has asked you for advice concerning the construction of a DFD for the process of validating a user ID, which is input from a data terminal, to request access to a computer system. Criticize the DFD that has been prepared by the systems analyst (see Figure 2.35).

23. You are reviewing audit work papers containing a narrative description of the Tenney Corporation's factory payroll system. A portion of the narrative is as follows:

Factory employees punch time clock cards each day when entering or leaving the shop. At the end of each week, the timekeeping department collects the time cards and prepares duplicate batch control slips by department showing total hours and number of employees. The time cards and original batch control slips are sent to the payroll accounting section. The second copies of the batch control slips are filed by date.

In the payroll accounting section, payroll transaction records are input from the information on the time cards, and a batch total record for each batch is input from the batch control slip. These records are input to a magnetic disk. The time cards and batch control slips are then filed by batch for possible reference. The payroll transaction file is sent to data processing, where it is sorted by employee number within batch. Each batch is edited by a computer program, which checks the validity of employee number against a master employee disk file and the total hours and number of employees against the batch total record. A detailed

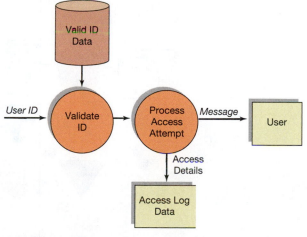

FIGURE 2.35

DFD for Problem 22

printout by batch and employee number is produced, which indicates batches that do not balance and invalid employee numbers. This printout is returned to payroll accounting to resolve all differences.

In searching for documentation you found a flowchart (Figure 2.36) of the payroll system, which included all appropriate symbols (American National Standards Institute) but was only partially labeled.

Required

a. Number your answer 1 through 16. Next to the corresponding number, supply the appropriate labeling (document name, process description, or file order) applicable to each numbered symbol on the flowchart.
b. Flowcharts are one of the aids an auditor may use to determine and evaluate a client's internal control system. List advantages of using flowcharts in this context.

(*CPA*)

24. Harvard Square Software Company uses a manual sales order processing system. Sales order forms (three copies) are prepared by the sales department and forwarded to the accounting department. In the accounting department, an invoice (three copies) and a shipping order (four copies) are prepared manually on the basis of the sales order. One copy each of the sales order, the invoice, and the shipping order is forwarded to the sales department. A copy of the sales order is attached to two copies of the shipping order and then forwarded to the shipping department. One copy of the invoice is forwarded to the customer. The remaining documents are attached to each other and then filed in the accounting department by sales order number.

Required

Prepare an analytic flowchart of the previous procedures.

25. Batches of customer payments on account are processed manually in the cashier's office. Clerks open the payments, separate the checks and the remittance advices, and prepare a batch control total (two copies) of the remittances. The checks are processed manually to prepare a deposit slip (two copies). Copy 1 of the deposit slip and the batch of checks are forwarded for deposit at the bank. Copy 2 of the deposit slip is verified with Copy 1 of the batch control total, attached to it, and then filed in the cashier's office by date. Copy 2 of the batch control total is forwarded to the general ledger department. The remittance advices are forwarded to the accounts receivable department.

Clerks in the accounts receivable department manually post the remittance advices to the accounts receivable ledger. The remittance advices are then filed in the accounts receivable department by customer number.

Required

Prepare an analytic flowchart of the previous procedures.

26. Production workers prepare materials requisition forms (four copies) and forward them to the production supervisor for approval. The materials requisition form is then forwarded to stores. In stores, the order is filled, and the materials requisition form is signed by a clerk. The clerk then returns Copy 1 of the materials requisition form along with the materials

---

FIGURE 2.36

Flowchart for Problem 23

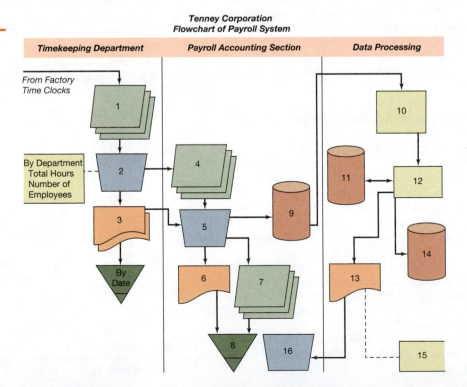

Tenney Corporation
Flowchart of Payroll System

to the production workers. Copy 2 of the materials requisition form is forwarded to the production supervisor. Copy 4 is forwarded to the cost accounting department. Copy 3 of the materials requisition form is used in stores to manually post the materials that were issued to the perpetual inventory records. Copy 3 is then filed in stores by number.

Required

Prepare an analytic flowchart of the previous procedures.

27. Collateral Deposit (Part 1).[1] (This case is continued as Problem 57 in Chapter 4.)

Dan Matt, a junior auditor for Kramp and Company, was assigned the responsibility of conducting a preliminary application review of a client bank's loan department operations.

Dan had completed his flowchart and explanation of the loan process and turned it over to his senior. He was writing up his assessment of the process from his notes when his senior interrupted and asked what happened to the collateral received on loans. Dan recognized the significance of this omission and agreed to check it out right away.

Collateral can be anything of value acceptable to the bank but is typically some type of security. Dan found that customers turn over any collateral to their loan officer, who prepares and signs the next in sequence in a prenumbered four-part form that describes the collateral and serves as a receipt. Each copy of the form is a different color to facilitate identification. The customer receives the original of the collateral receipt form, which is pink. The second, or white, copy of the form is sent directly to the collateral records clerk, who logs it in. The loan officer takes the blue, or third, copy to the vault custodian along with the collateral. The final, or yellow, copy is cancelled and discarded. The vault custodian compares the blue copy of the receipt with the collateral in the loan officer's presence. If they agree, the vault custodian signs the blue copy. The vault custodian then attaches a tag to the collateral and carries it and the blue copy of the collateral receipt to the vault attendant. The vault attendant also compares the description on the blue copy with the tagged collateral. If they match, the vault attendant opens the vault and jointly with the vault custodian deposits the collateral within. The vault attendant notes the location on the blue copy and signs it. The completed blue copy is then taken by the vault attendant to the collateral clerk. Until the blue copy is received, the collateral clerk keeps the unmatched white copy, filed numerically in a suspense file as a reminder for follow-up purposes.

On receiving the blue copy from the vault attendant, the collateral clerk compares it to the white copy previously received directly from the loan officer. If the blue and white copies match, the collateral clerk completes the entry in the collateral register in numerical order. The white copy and the blue copy of the collateral receipt are placed in a permanent file by name. Any differences are resolved with the loan officer's assistance.

List of Procedures

Customer

1. Brings in collateral to loan officer
2. Receives receipt for collateral

Loan Officer

3. Receives collateral from customer
4. Removes prenumbered four-part form from file
5. Completes form describing collateral and signs it
6. Gives pink copy to customer
7. Sends white copy to collateral clerk
8. Takes blue copy to vault custodian
9. Cancels and discards yellow copy
10. Takes collateral in sealed bag to vault custodian

Vault Custodian

11. Receives blue copy of collateral receipt from loan officer
12. Receives collateral from loan officer
13. Reads description and instructions regarding collateral on blue copy
14. Compares collateral with blue copy
15. Signs blue copy
16. Gives blue copy to vault attendant
17. Opens vault jointly with vault attendant
18. Deposits collateral in vault

Vault Attendant

19. Receives blue copy from vault custodian
20. Compares blue copy to collateral being deposited
21. Assists vault custodian in opening vault
22. Signs blue copy upon witnessing deposit of collateral
23. Takes blue copy to collateral clerk

Collateral Clerk

24. Receives white copy from loan officer
25. Makes entry in numerical sequence in logbook
26. Holds white copy until later receipt of blue copy
27. Matches blue copy when received to white copy and notes appropriate signatures
28. Records deposit of collateral in collateral register
29. Files collateral receipt copies in permanent file

Required

Prepare a flowchart of the collateral receipt process and cross-reference it to the list of procedures provided.

28. A partially completed charge sales systems flowchart is shown in Figure 2.37. The flowchart depicts the charge sales activities of the Bottom Manufacturing Corporation.

A customer's purchase order is received and a six-part sales order is prepared from it. The six copies are initially distributed as follows:

Copy 1: Billing copy—to billing department
Copy 2: Shipping copy—to shipping department

[1]Prepared by Frederick L. Neumann, Richard J. Boland, and Jeffrey Johnson; funded by the Touche Ross Foundation Aid to Accounting Education Program.

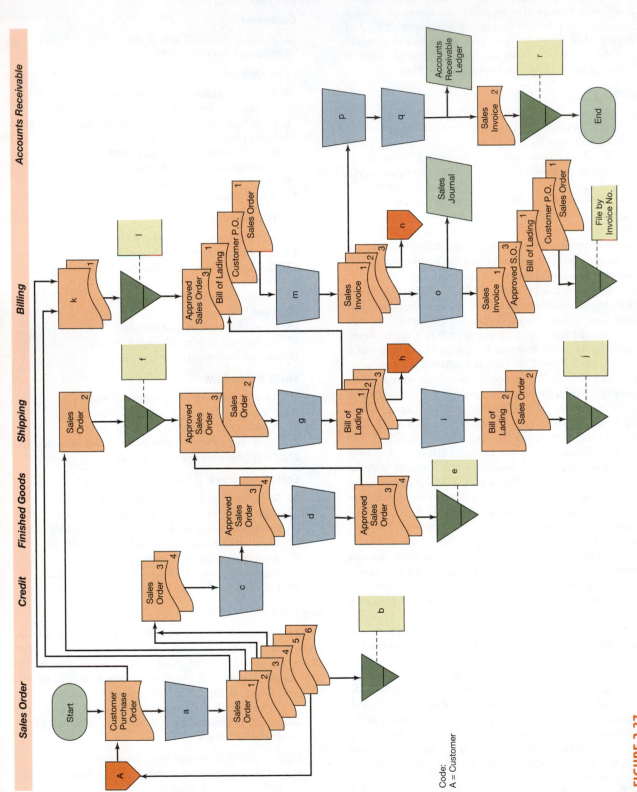

FIGURE 2.37

Flowchart for Problem 28

Copy 3: Credit copy—to credit department
Copy 4: Stock request copy—to credit department
Copy 5: Customer copy—to customer
Copy 6: Sales order copy—file in sales order department

When each copy of the sales order reaches the applicable department or destination, it calls for specific internal control procedures and related documents. Some of the procedures and related documents are indicated on the flowchart. Other procedures and documents are labeled letters *a* to *r*.

Required

List the procedures or the internal documents that are labeled letters *c* to *r* in the flowchart of Bottom Manufacturing Corporation's charge sales system.

Organize your answer as follows (an explanation of the letters *a* and *b*, which appear in the flowchart, is given):

Flowchart Symbol Letter	Procedures or Internal Document
a	Prepare six-part sales order
b	File by order number

(*CPA*)

29. Figure 2.38 illustrates a manual system for executing purchases and cash disbursements transactions.

Required

Indicate what each of the letters A through L represents.

(*CPA*)

30. An analyst wishes to prepare a decision table for purchase order procedures. First, there is a credit check of the customer. If credit is approved, the order is accepted. If the order calls for 0–25 units, there is no discount on the order. If the order calls for 26–55 units, it is eligible for a 5% discount; if more than 55 units are ordered, the discount is 10%.

Required

a. Prepare a limited-entry decision table.
b. Prepare an extended-entry decision table.

31. An analyst wishes to document credit card purchase authorization procedures in a decision table. A purchase under $50 is approved automatically. Purchases between $50 and $100 are given an authorization number. For purchases over $100, a "hold" is placed on the customer's account in addition to an authorization number being assigned to the purchase.

Required

a. Prepare a limited-entry decision table.
b. Prepare an extended-entry decision table.

32. Analyze the following data incident to machine posting of checks drawn by bank depositors:

Number of checks posted	570
Total elapsed minutes	480
Rest period minutes	20
Interruption and delay minutes	20

Develop a standard time per check. In terms of percentage, what is the rest and delay allowance?

33. The Big Plastic Company manufactures a variety of plastic utensils, employing approximately 400 factory workers. Supervisors are paid a salary for a 40-hour week but receive overtime for hours worked in excess of 40. Supervisors record hours worked on a weekly time card, clocking in and out at the beginning and end of each day.

Factory workers are paid on an hourly basis. Activity rates are assigned to the operation of various machines in the factory; a worker assigned to a machine is paid the higher of either the machine's activity rate or the standard hourly pay rate. Workers clock in and out of each assigned activity on a daily basis. Supervisors record the activity code and elapsed time for each entry on a machine operator's daily time card. Supervisors maintain a record of machine operator overtime. All workers must account for 8 hours a day and receive time-and-a-half for hours worked in excess of 8 hours per day.

A timekeeper collects time cards on a daily basis. Supervisors' time cards are collected at the end of each week. Time cards are compared to an authorized employee list, initialed by the timekeeper, and forwarded to the payroll department.

In the payroll department, a clerk verifies the timekeeper initials, batches the cards in groups of 40 or fewer cards, and prepares a prenumbered batch control form for each batch. This form contains total regular hours, overtime hours, date, and number of documents in the batch. The payroll clerk transcribes the contents of each batch control form onto an input batch control log to record and maintain control of each batch. The time cards are then submitted to the computer processing department, where they are key-transcribed, verified, and processed by a payroll system edit program to produce a detailed listing of the input items. At the end of the listing, control totals are printed for the valid and rejected items. If any item in a batch is rejected, then all items in the batch are rejected to maintain batch integrity. The payroll clerk corrects rejected items, prepares a new batch control form using the original batch number plus a suffix to identify the batch as a correction batch, and resubmits the batch to the computer processing department. This procedure is repeated throughout the week until all errors have been corrected.

The payroll is processed weekly to produce an updated payroll master file, employee checks, and payroll register. These reports are distributed to the payroll department, where a reconciliation with the input controls is performed.

Required

Flowchart the preceding payroll procedure.

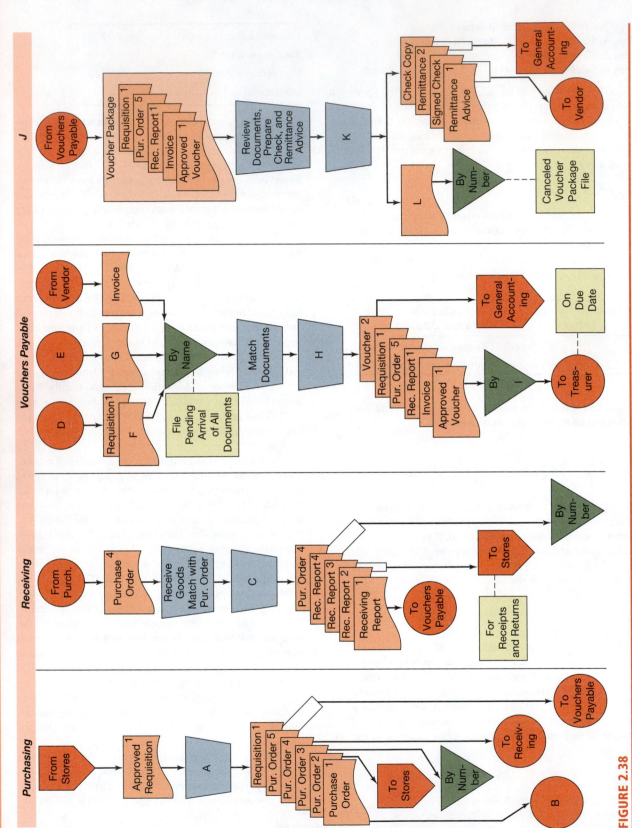

FIGURE 2.38

Flowchart for Problem 29

34. Prepare a program flowchart for the following application. This application calculates straight-line depreciation for a file of fixed assets. The fixed-asset file consists of the following record types:
    a. A header record, which contains the file ID number and a hash total of all the record ID (key) values.
    b. A record for each fixed asset. Each record contains the following fields: ID number, a location code, original cost, useful life in months, depreciation taken to date, and salvage value.

    The program should read each fixed-asset record, compute the amount of depreciation for the year (12 months), update the necessary fields, and write the updated record. End-of-job processing should print the number of assets processed, print the total depreciation computed, and verify the hash total for this run.

35. Modify the preceding problem to compute depreciation by the double-declining-balance method.

36. Microsoft Word®, Microsoft Excel®, and Microsoft PowerPoint® contain a Drawing toolbar that has an AutoShapes menu with a flowchart submenu that contains 28 specific flowchart symbols that can be used to draw flowcharts. Print each of these symbols along with its name. (To print a symbol, click it to select it, then place and size it on a document, pressing the left mouse button as you do so.)

37. Draw the following flowcharts as they appear in the textbook using the Drawing toolbar that contains Flowchart symbols as a submenu in the AutoShapes menu in Microsoft Word®, Microsoft Excel®, or Microsoft PowerPoint®. (To draw a symbol, click it to select it, then place and size it on a document, pressing the left mouse button as you do so.) When the Drawing toolbar is visible, lines and arrows are shown as selections that allow one to draw these items by simply selecting them and then placing and sizing them on a drawing.
    a. Figure 2.17
    b. Figure 2.18
    c. Figure 4.7

38. Match the following list of BPMN symbols to the letters A through I in Figure 2.39.
    1. Message flow
    2. Association
    3. Pool
    4. Event
    5. Lane
    6. Data object
    7. Gateway
    8. Activity
    9. Sequence flow

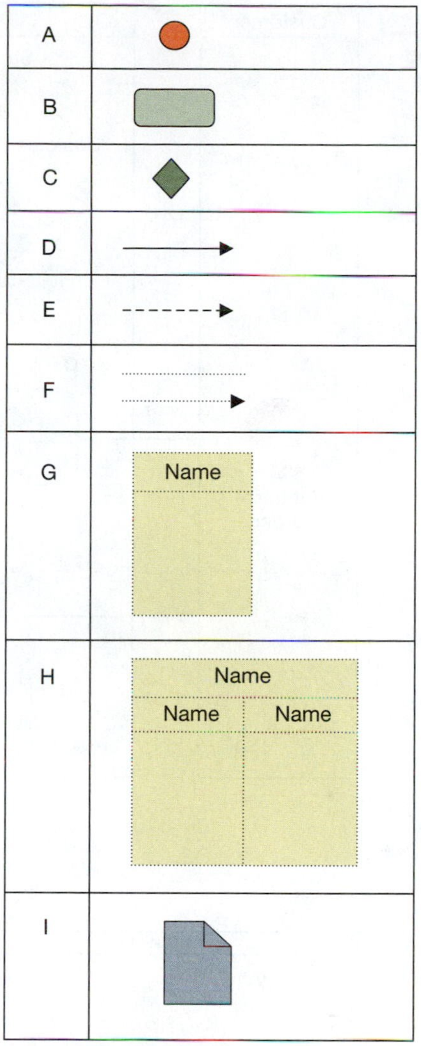

39. Figure 2.40 is an incorrectly prepared business process diagram (BPD).

Required

Identify errors in the use of symbols in the BPD in this figure.

40. Figure 2.41 is an incorrectly prepared business process diagram (BPD).

FIGURE 2.39

BPMN Symbol Quiz

Required

Identify errors in the use of symbols in the BPD in this figure.

41. The sales business process at Salt Company begins with credit approval. The bank center is contacted for credit authorization and notifies the sales department that credit has been approved. Once credit has been approved, the sales department prepares the order. The next event occurs when the shipping department ships the order. This is the end of the process.

Required

Prepare a business process diagram that includes the bank center activity as well as the sales department and shipping department activities within Salt Company.

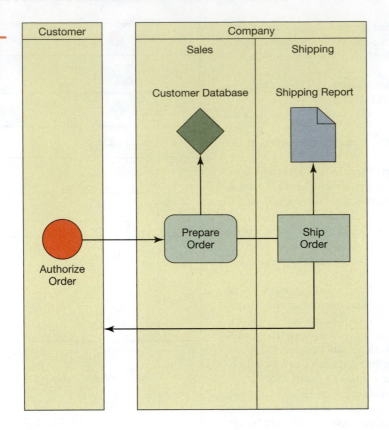

FIGURE 2.40

Incorrectly Prepared BPD for Problem 39

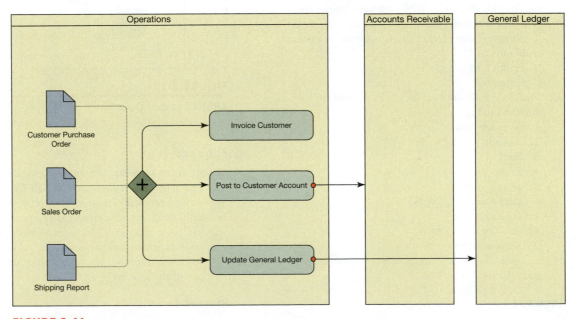

FIGURE 2.41

Incorrectly Prepared BPD for Problem 40

Web Research Assignments

42. Contrast and compare SmartDraw (*www.smartdraw.com*) and Business Process Visual Architect (*www.visual-paradigm.com*), two diagramming programs. Which is more suitable for BPD? Which is more flexible?

43. You work for the chief information officer in a large company. Your company develops most of its software in-house. Your boss is trying to decide whether you should use UML or BPMN, or both, to document your business processes. An important consideration will be using your diagrams as a starting point in software programming.

Required

a. Write a brief report that will help your boss make a decision

44. You are a recent accounting graduate who works in a small accounting firm along with several other recent graduates. Since you graduated with a perfect 4.0 grade point average, your firm's partner in charge has asked you to help prepare the other recent graduates to take the CPA exam.

Required

a. Write a brief report that explains what flowcharting-related knowledge and skills you and your colleagues will need to pass the CPA exam.

Answers to Chapter Quiz

1. c   **2.** c   **3.** a   **4.** c   **5.** b   **6.** d   **8.** b   **9.** d   **10.** b

eBusiness and eCommerce

Learning Objectives

Careful study of this chapter will enable you to:

- Explain what is meant by eBusiness, eCommerce, and Web Commerce.
- Describe enterprise architecture and its domains.
- Explain enterprise architecture frameworks and business process reference models.
- Describe various approaches to securing electronic financial transactions.
- Describe various eCommerce applications, including payment systems and Web stores.

Introduction: Electronic Business and Electronic Commerce

In the broadest sense, **electronic business (eBusiness)** refers to the use of information technologies in any aspect of the business or organization. **Electronic commerce (eCommerce)** is that part of eBusiness that directly involves the exchange of products and services among organizations and individuals. In other words, eCommerce is defined as the use of information technologies in the exchange of products and services among organizations and individuals. **Web Commerce** involves using information technologies in the exchange of products and services among individuals and organizations and over the World Wide Web and the Internet. Web Commerce is a type of eCommerce, and eCommerce is a type of eBusiness.

The Internet

The **Internet** is a global system of interconnected computer networks. Every computer on the Internet needs an **IP (Internet Protocol) address.** An IP address is a string of numbers separated by periods, such as 207.46.131.43. IP addresses are obtained from public organizations which manage and distribute them to the general public. Mnemonic alias names can usually be used instead of IP addresses. For example, the name www.microsoft.com might be used in place of 207.46.131.43. This name, www.microsoft.com, is called the **domain name,** which is simply an alias name that can be used in place of the IP number. Domain names and their corresponding IP addresses are registered in electronic "phone books" at many sites on the Internet. These electronic phone books are called **domain name servers (DNSs).**

Many companies have adapted Internet protocols for private, in-house communications networks. These self-contained, in-house networks are known as **intranets. Extranets** are private networks created when the intranets of two or more companies are linked together or when outsiders (such as customers or suppliers) are able to access a company's intranet.

Intranet Security Issues Intranets pose considerable security risks by potentially exposing the organization's sensitive information to everyone on the Internet. Many companies use combinations of hardware and software called *firewalls* to limit access from outsiders. **Firewalls** limit access to information on the company's private computers and servers from the rest of the world. Specifically, the only way an outsider can access information on the company's intranet is through a single point guarded by a firewall.

Client and Servers

The Internet has largely evolved around client–server technology. A **server** is a robot-type program that constantly runs and exchanges information with remote users. **Clients** are programs that access and exchange information with servers.

TYPES OF SERVERS   Various types of servers exist in support of eBusiness.

- **Mail servers** act as electronic mailboxes that hold incoming electronic mails until the user's client program requests it. They also serve as relay stations for outgoing mail, holding it until the intended recipient's mail server is able to receive it (Figure 3.1). The most common type of mail server on the Internet uses the POP protocol, and for this reason, it is often referred to as a POP server. Most POP servers are accessed by clients with an account name and password. The server hands over any new incoming mail to the client and then picks up outgoing mail.

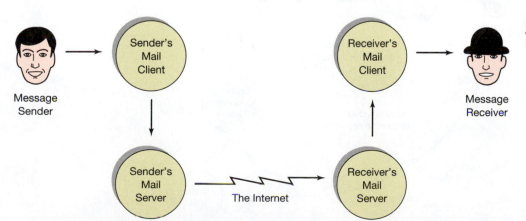

FIGURE 3.1

Mail Server

Message Sender — Sender's Mail Client — Sender's Mail Server — The Internet — Receiver's Mail Server — Receiver's Mail Client — Message Receiver

- **File servers** allow authorized clients to retrieve files from libraries of files. They exist mainly as repositories of files. The most common protocol for transferring files to and from file servers is called *file transfer protocol (FTP)*, and a file server that uses this protocol is called an **FTP server.**
- **Web servers** allow a user (client) to access documents and run computer programs that reside on remote computers. Web servers are the engines that run the World Wide Web, which consists of all the documents, files, and software on the Internet that are available through Web servers. The clients that access Web servers are called *Web browsers*. Microsoft Internet Explorer™ and Firefox™ are Web browsers. Web clients read and interpret **HTML** (hypertext markup language) and convert documents into a format that is easily readable by the user.
- **Commerce servers** are specialized types of Web servers with various commerce-related features (Figure 3.2). Commerce servers support various types of client and server authentication, and make it possible for the client to exchange information with programs and databases that reside on the server's computer. Commerce servers provide for enhanced security features and support electronic payment systems.
- **Application servers** and **database servers** make applications and data in databases available to remote clients. An "application" is a software program for some functional use such as for accounting, communications, or e-mail. A **database** is an organized collection of data that is structured to be useful to those who use it. Application and database servers often work together in a three-tiered architecture, as depicted in Figure 3.3. A **three-tiered application architecture** involves applications that contain three tiers (i.e., parts): the presentation tier, the logic tier, and the data tier. The presentation tier merely receives input from the user and displays output in response to the user's input. A typical presentation tier is the user's Web browser. The logic tier processes commands, evaluates logical decisions, and makes calculations. Finally, the data tier stores all data relevant to the application. In a Web environment, the three tiers are typically the Web browser, application server, and database.

FIGURE 3.2

Commerce Server

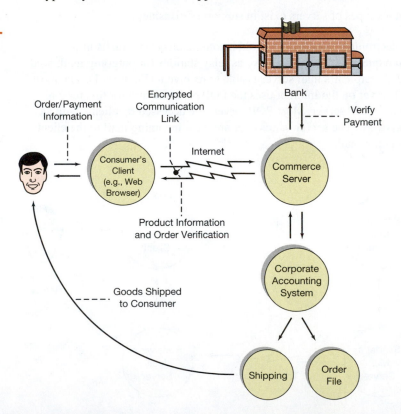

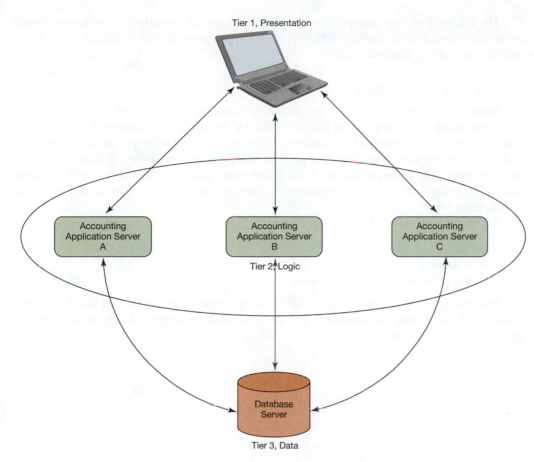

FIGURE 3.3

Three-Tiered Application– Database Architecture

Tier 1, Presentation

Accounting Application Server A

Accounting Application Server B

Accounting Application Server C

Tier 2, Logic

Database Server

Tier 3, Data

eBusiness and Enterprise Architecture

The **enterprise architecture (EA)** describes the joint structure and behavior of the enterprise and its information system. An EA should achieve the following objectives:

- The alignment of the organization's information technology planning and strategy with company's business goals
- The management of risks associated with the information system
- The optimal use of information system resources
- The flexibility to adapt to the information system to changing business models and management needs

EA falls within the functional area of IT governance, which in turn is a functional part of corporate governance. As such, like any management system, EAs must be planned, executed, monitored, controlled, and improved.

 CASE IN POINT

The state of Virginia documents its entire EA on-line through its Virginia Information Technology Agency's Web site (www.vita.virginia.gov).

The EA involves four enterprise architectural domains (i.e., broad views of the enterprise): the business architecture, the data architecture, the applications architecture, and the technical architecture. Each is discussed below.

The Business Architecture

The **business architecture** defines the human resources, processes, and infrastructure that a business needs to accomplish its business strategy. Business architectures are described in terms of **business domains,** which describe groups of business functions, business processes, and concepts for which management may be assigned responsibility. Business domains may correspond to the organization chart, but in many cases, architects may plan domains that significantly differ from the organization chart as a way of redefining or improving the organization.

Some of the specific components of the typical business architecture are as follows:

- Strategies, goals, objectives, general policies, business plan, plan of operations, organization structure
- Business processes, workflows, events

The business architecture is the primary architecture in the sense that the data, application, and technology architectures are all structured to support the business structure (Figure 3.4).

FIGURE 3.4

Development Is Top Down in the Enterprise Architecture

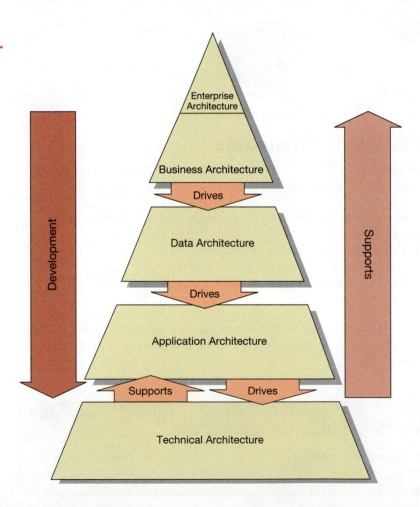

The Data Architecture

The **data architecture** defines the needed data, how it is to be stored, how it is to be processed, how it is to be utilized, and how it integrates with the other main architectural domains. The database is the primary concept in data architecture. Databases must be developed in support of the business architecture.

DATABASES   The **data model** determines how the database is structured, as well as the operations that can be performed on its data. **Structured Query Language (SQL)** is a technology used to define, access, and manipulate data in a relational database. The **relational data model** structures data in two-dimensional tables that resemble spreadsheets, with rows and columns. For example, an employee table might have one row per employee, with each column containing a different piece of data regarding the employee:

Simple Employee Table

Last Name	First Name	Employee ID	Position	Department
Doe	Jane	2132	Clerk	Shipping
Jones	John	3423	Maintenance	Production

Database design proceeds through three phases: conceptual, logical, and physical. The conceptual phase of data modeling basically sketches out the tables that are needed and how they relate to each other. For example, the design might call for tables called Customers and Orders. The relationships between these tables might be defined by saying that Customers have Orders, or that each order belongs to a customer. If each customer can have many orders, then we would say that the relationship between customer and orders invoices is one-to-many. In general, relationships may be one-to-many, one-to-one, or many-to-one, with one-to-many being the most commonly found relationship. After the relationships are sketched out, individual attributes for each table can be defined. The attributes represent the column items (e.g., in the example above, Last Name, First Name, Employee ID, Position, and Department).

Technically speaking, the conceptual phase does not involve defining tables. Rather, it defines more general concepts called *entities* (Figure 3.5), but in the relational model, entities and tables end up being the same thing. However, such may not be the case using non-relational data models.

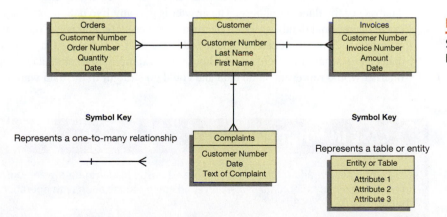

FIGURE 3.5

Simple Entity-Relationship Table

FIGURE 3.6

The Corporate
Information Factory

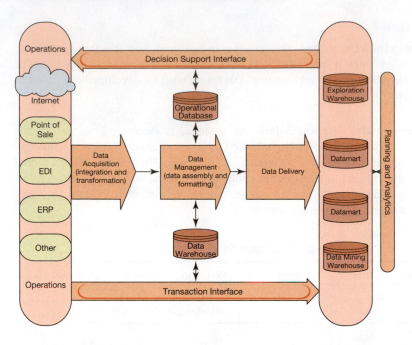

THE CORPORATE INFORMATION FACTORY The **Corporate Information Factory** provides a logical architecture for the EA. The architecture is based on data being acquired from business operations, transformed to support business management and business intelligence, and then delivered to management. This represents a three-part model, as depicted in Figure 3.6:

- Data acquisition—Data are acquired from various operations applications, including individual internal accounting systems, ERP systems, the Internet, electronic data interchange (EDI), and so on.
- Data management—After being acquired from various sources, data are integrated into databases and are also transformed and stored in operational databases and data warehouses. **Operational databases** store relatively current transaction data for quick access by management in support of tactical decision making. **Data warehouses** store enormous volumes of current and historical data for use in research and analysis. Data in operational databases are live and may be updated. On the other hand, data in data warehouses are static and not updated. When new data arrives to the data warehouse, it is simply appended to the existing data.

    The question sometimes arises with respect to which comes first, the operational database or the data warehouse. The answer is that any live data must first be entered in the operational database. Once the data becomes static and is no longer needed in the operational database, it can be transferred to the data warehouse. On the other hand, some data can go straight to the data warehouse. For example, market data collected from the Internet would represent static data and could go straight to the data warehouse.

 CASE IN POINT

Teradata (www.teradata.com, NYSE TD) is an industry leader in data warehousing technologies. The company's Teradata Server serves an entire organization with operational and warehouse data.

- Data delivery—Data is delivered to various data marts. **Data marts** contain subsets of the data contained in the operational database and data warehouse. These subsets of data are specially organized for use by specific functions or units in the organization. They are created, deleted, and modified according to users' needs. The frequency of their being updated is also determined by users' needs. The exploratory warehouse can contain any kind of data, but it is typically associated with "throwaway" data that is used for testing out new ideas for data storage and organization. For example, one vendor markets its exploratory warehouse as a place to prototype (i.e., to test) different ways to integrate diverse databases. The exploratory warehouse can also be used to do prototype analyses of data that the company possesses but does not want to keep permanently in the data warehouse. Finally, the **data mining warehouse** may contain copies of subsets of the data warehouse.

 CASE IN POINT

A convenience store clerk noticed that men often bought beer and diapers together. Data mining of the store receipts showed this to be true. The store began putting diapers next to the beer, and sales soared. The explanation was that when men stopped by to buy beer, their wives ask them to also pick up diapers for their babies.

Data in the data marts, exploratory warehouse, and data mining warehouses might be (and often are) stored in nonrelational databases. Relational databases work very well with typical transaction processing but their use in complex analysis is too slow and inefficient. Complex analysis, called **online analytical processing (OLAP),** works much better with tables that have more than two dimensions. OLAP's improvement in speed is substantial.

Data, Information, and End Users Various options exist for end users to access and manipulate data in the various data sources. A transactional interface is used for access and manipulation of data in the operational database. A decision support interface is used in conjunction with data mart and the data mining warehouse for sophisticated queries, complex analysis of many different data items, and research. The typical ERP or EAS (Enterprise Application Suite) will include both transactional and decision support interfaces. In addition, many third parties market decisions support interfaces that will integrate with ERP or EAS databases. Microstrategy™ (www.Microstrategy.com) and Crystal Reports™ are two examples. Crystal Reports™ is a product of Business Objects™, which is owned by SAP.

The Applications Architecture

The **applications architecture** defines the applications needed to run the business and how the applications communicate with each other through intranets or extranets and EDI. The focus is on the applications and how they work together to form a single composite application.

General options for applications are as follows:

- Use an ERP system or executive application suite that meets all the application software needs of the company.
- Use an ERP system or executive application suite in combination with other application software. The other software may be prepackaged or internally developed.
- Use some mixture of individual prepackaged and internally developed applications.

Some general options for sharing data between applications so that they work together are as follows (each is discussed below):

- Rely on the data sharing and integration that comes built in with ERPs and EASs.
- Use a service-oriented architecture (SOA).
- Use client–server technology that is built into applications to communicate between them.
- Use **middleware,** software specially designed to work in between two different applications.

ERP AND EAS ARCHITECTURES   A truly comprehensive ERP program is by definition a single program and may have little need to communicate with other programs inside the organization. With respect to communicating with applications outside the organization, it might include built-in interfaces needed to communicate via EDI or other means.

EASs typically have built-in SOAs that manage all inter-application communications, especially within the company. SOAs are explained in the discussion that follows.

SERVICE-ORIENTED ARCHITECTURE   **Service-oriented architecture (SOA)** is an applications architecture design framework that facilitates the development of application suites, which are groups of different applications that share information with each other using some common communications framework.

SOA services are independent software units of functionality. A service might, for example, create a certain type of report or locate a record in an inventory database. Regardless of a service's function, it operates as a self-contained software unit that does not depend on another service or application to function.

SOA services have the ability to communicate with each other, and when grouped together and orchestrated, they form working applications. **Orchestration** is the process of linking and sequencing services in order to make them work together. The task of orchestration is typically performed by a software engineer, although in theory services can be orchestrated by software.

SOA services cannot be of much use unless there is some standard that defines what a given service does and how it works. The SOA framework itself does not specify such a standard, but the common approach is to use the **Web Services Description Language (WSDL)** to describe services and the Simple Object Access Protocol (**SOAP**) for communication between services. SOA services constructed using WSDL and SOAP are called **Web services,** since they work over the Internet. WSDL and SOAP are called **Web service specifications.** SOA can be implemented with Web specifications other than WSDL/SOAP. However, the WSDL/SOAP combination is very popular. For example, Microsoft's Web services architecture is based on Windows Communications Foundation, which uses WSDL/SOAP.

BENEFITS OF SOA   In theory, SOA is advantageous in that it is possible to rapidly create new applications by selecting the needed services from a repository of services, and then orchestrating the selected services. The result is rapid development or applications with minimal costs.

The services to be orchestrated do not even need to come from the same source. Since service descriptions are standardized by WSDL, the application developer can choose services from multiple service providers that exist in multiple locations on the Internet. The existence of multiple sources for services enhances a second benefit of SOA: the ability to create applications that are fitted to the company's business architecture and not the other way around.

 CASE IN POINT

As important as SOA is, it is already being supplanted by "Web-oriented architecture." To find out more, enter "Web-oriented architecture" into one of the major Web search engines.

The major EASs integrate their applications using SOA. For example, SAP Business Application Suite™ uses Netweaver™, their proprietary SOA and the Web services platform to integrate individual SAP applications. As with many Web-service platforms, Netweaver™ uses WSDL/SOAP; hence custom-developed and third-party applications can easily connect to and communicate with SAP applications.

SAP Netweaver™ includes an enterprise services repository and registry. This repository/registry serves as a central catalog of SAP services, and describes and classifies the services so they can be easily referenced and accessed. Documenting all services in a single location using a common description language greatly simplifies the IT governance process.

MIDDLEWARE   Middleware refers to software that serves as a go-between for two applications, enabling communications between them that would otherwise be impossible. For example, a company that has an inventory application from one vendor and a general accounting application from another vendor might use middleware to enable a smooth, automatic transfer of inventory data from the inventory application to the general ledger in the accounting application. Middleware serves the following functions:

- Connecting the parts together in distributed applications. A **distributed application** is an application that has different services (which may be SOA services) located in different places. The different services can be anywhere on the local network or the Internet. Middleware may be used to connect the different services together so that they appear to operate as a single application.
- Connecting services and applications together even though they may individually reside on different types of hardware, use different operating systems, or use different communication protocols.
- Providing a standardized way that different services and applications can use to communicate with each other.
- Making services available to be used by more than one application. This avoids duplication.

A variety of middleware methods have been developed. Two of the most basic methods are the application programming interface and the database driver (also called *database connector* or *database adapter*). An **applications programming interface (API)** is a set of commands that a given piece of software makes available so that its functions and data can be accessed by other pieces of software. To provide an illustration, an accounting application might have a Web API that permits another program (or Web browser) to access the account balance for customer number 2341 using a HTML API command similar to this hypothetical example: http://www.wxyzwebsite.com?request=balance?customer_number=2341.

The following is another illustration, this time using the XML-based API for the Google Checkout Web shopping system. In this example, the API command causes order number 841171949013218 to be archived:

<?xml version="1.0" encoding="UTF-8"?>
<archive-order xmlns=http://checkout.google.com/schema/2google-order-
number="841171949013218"/>

A database connector (also called *database adapter* or *database driver*) works like a printer driver. When one purchases a new printer for her personal computer, she installs a "printer driver" for that printer, and the new printer is immediately available for use. For example, after installing the printer driver, all she needs to do before printing her word processing program is to select the new printer from one of the print menus. Further, if she has more than one printer attached to her computer, she can use the same menus to select whichever printer she wants to print to.

By making such a selection, she is simply telling her computer which printer driver to use. The printer driver thus serves the function of connecting the application (the word processing program) to the printer.

Database drivers work the same way with applications, except that instead of connecting applications to printers, they connect applications to databases. This means that a given application can connect to any database that has a suitable database driver. For example, an accounting application might connect to an Oracle database using an Oracle database driver, or alternatively connect to a MySQL™ database using a MySQL™ database driver. As long as a given database has an appropriate driver, the accounting application can connect to it.

In some organizations, especially smaller ones, APIs and database drivers might be all that is needed to completely integrate the applications. However, large organizations with many different applications that need to make many different types of connections require a more sophisticated solution. One such solution is the **enterprise service bus (ESB),** a middleware that serves as a central switchboard for communications between all enterprise services and applications. The typical ESB provides various functions such as the following:

- Database drivers for large numbers of databases
- APIs for legacy applications that do not work with database drivers
- The ability to communicate with different services or applications using different communication channels (e.g., HTML or SOAP), including e-mail
- The ability to transform and reformat data as it moves from one service or application to another
- Security features, such as the ability to ensure the integrity of transactions in the event of a power loss

In other words, the ESB serves as a universal translator between services and applications in the organization. The idea is for any enterprise or service or application to smoothly connect to any other enterprise service or application, regardless of where it is located, on what hardware or software it resides in, what program language it is developed in, what communication protocols it uses, or what type of database it uses.

The ESB has become the de facto standard for middleware in SOA in general and in EASs in particular. SAP's Netweaver™ is based on ESB architecture. Similarly, Oracle's application suite is based on Oracle Service Bus™. Finally, Microsoft provides ESB services through its application platform, which includes its .NET framework, Windows Server, and BizTalk Server.

The Technical Architecture

The technical architecture describes the structure and behavior of the IT infrastructure and defines standards, principles, procedures, and best practices to govern the IT architecture. Its scope includes, for example, hardware, hardware configuration, the network, network protocols, and software. The main function of the technical architecture is to support the business, data, and application architectures. The technical architecture can be broken down into eight technical domains:

- Applications—This domain includes setting standards for application development (design, compatibility, ease of use, engineering), application acquisition, application and development support platforms, and enterprise applications.
- Database—This domain includes specifications database methods (e.g., relational and OLAP) and data management (e.g., database design, data modeling, data backup and recovery, database administration, and enterprise database integration).
- Enterprise systems management—This domain includes IT support services (e.g., help-desks), IT services delivery (e.g., financial management, security management, IT workforce management, and other IT administrative functions that oversee the delivery of IT services), and operations (e.g., maintenance, repairs, job scheduling, and network administration).

- Information—This domain includes data warehouse design, reporting tools, and the general use of information to assist managers in decision making.
- Integration—This domain defines how the application architectures integrate (e.g., via an ESB and SOA).
- Network and telecommunications—This domain defines the LAN, network protocols and components, telephone communications, voice-over-IP communications, and video conferencing.
- Platform—This domain deals with choices of operating systems, hardware, servers, and communication frameworks.
- Security—This domain deals with physical and information security in the technology architecture.

Enterprise Architecture Frameworks

Various frameworks for enterprise architecture have been published that define systems for transforming (i.e., developing) EAs. The **Zachman Framework** is based on defining models applicable to a given organization. The models are defined by answering six basic questions (What, How, Where, Who, When, and Why) in relation to each of the six stakeholder groups (Planner, Owner, Designer, Builder, Implementer, and Worker). Carefully documenting each question–stakeholder combination leads to a complete understanding of the company and hence its EA. The Zachman Framework simply views the organization from the perspectives of the different stakeholders. For example, the answers to the Planner's questions define the scope of the enterprise and what is to be modeled. The answers to the Owner's questions define the business model.

Several other frameworks exist. The U.S. Government officially uses the *Federal Enterprise Architecture (FEA)*, a framework produced by the U.S. Office of Management and Budget. The U.S. Department of Defense uses the Department of Defense Architecture Framework. There are also commercial frameworks such as *The Open Group Architecture Framework (TOGAF)*, which is published by The Open Group (www.opengroup.org), an industry consortium devoted to computing infrastructure standards. Some of the organizations in the consortium include HP, IBM, NASA, and the U.S. Department of Defense.

Business Process Frameworks and Reference Models

While EA frameworks focus on transforming EAs, **business process frameworks** focus on transforming business processes (i.e., making them better). Of course, transforming business processes involves transforming the business architecture, which is likely to require related transformations in the other main architectures.

A **business process reference model** is a set of best practices for a given business process or group of processes. The typical business process framework is a combination of reference models plus guidance on planning, governance, and execution relating to the process or group of processes.

VALUE CHAIN FRAMEWORKS   eBusiness can be viewed in terms of using information technology in support of value chain activities. As discussed in Chapter 1, the value chain refers to a series of activities that add value to the product. The five primary value chain activities include inbound logistics, outbound logistics, manufacturing, marketing, and sales and service. Support activities include human resources, procurement, technology, and firm infrastructure.

The original nine-activity value chain model, as described in Chapter 1, was introduced in 1985 by Michael Porter and is often referred to as the *Porter Value Chain*. In the years that followed, managers and enterprise architects began to focus on value chain management.

This lead to value chain frameworks for process improvement. The *Business Process Transformation Framework,* published by the Value Chain Group, is an example. The heart of this framework is the **Value Reference Model**[SM], which depicts the value chain at four levels of abstraction: strategic, tactical, operational, and activities and actions. At each abstraction level, processes are defined for planning, governing, and executing. For example, the model defines the following execution process at the tactical level: market, research, develop, acquire, build, fulfill, support, sell, and brand.

SUPPLY CHAIN FRAMEWORKS   Coordinating and optimizing supply chain processes is an impossible task without sophisticated software. EASs normally include extensive supply-chain management capabilities. For example, SAP's EAS (SAP Business Suite™) includes SAP SCM™ (a comprehensive SCM system) that tightly integrates with SAP ERP™ (SAP's ERP System). SAP's EAS also includes other applications that tightly integrate with SAP ERP™: CRM (customer relations management), PLM (product lifecycle management), and SRM (supplier relations management).

EAS and ERP systems support all specific aspects of the value chain and information system, as well as all forms of eCommerce and Web Commerce. Such support extends not only to large businesses but to small ones too, as EAS vendors produce scaled-down versions of their large-enterprise software.

Various supply-chain management frameworks and reference models exist. The Global Supply Chain Forum, a member-based group hosted in the Ohio State University College of Business (fisher.osu.edu), publishes a comprehensive framework built on eight key business processes. Perhaps more widely known is the *Supply Chain Operation Reference (SCOR)* model developed by PRTM (www.prtm.com, a private management consulting firm) and endorsed by the Supply Chain Council (www.supply-chain.org). SCOR is a process reference model that is based on three "pillars" (process modeling, performance measures, and best practices) and five management processes (plan, source, make, deliver, and return).

eBusiness Architectures

A given eBusiness can be viewed as a particular EA, that is, a given set of specifications for the four architectural domains. These specifications will in turn depend on the enterprise's business model and related strategies. The **OsterwalderReference Model (ORM)** is a reference model for business models in general. The ORM defines the typical business model in terms of four major domains: infrastructure, offering, customers, and finance, all of which have a major impact on the extent to which a given organization engages in eBusiness:

- Infrastructure—This domain includes in part core competencies and capabilities and partner networks. This suggests, for example, that the enterprise will need core capabilities in electronic design interchange format if its partner networks depend on EDI.
- Offering—This domain includes the products and services offered by the firm. This suggests, for example, that a company selling its products over the Internet will at least in part need an Internet-capable technical architecture, accounting applications that integrate with the company's Web sites, and database that integrates well with Web servers.
- Customers—This domain includes in part target customers and product distribution channels. For example, if the company is a manufacturing company with a complex distribution channel, then a sophisticated SCM system would need to be part of the application architecture.
- Finance—This domain includes in part the ways in which customers can pay the company. For example, if the company sells products over eBay (www.ebay.com), it would need that its accounting applications integrate with PayPal™ (www.paypal.com), since eBay merchants routinely accept PayPal™ payments.

CASE IN POINT

Authorize.net (www.authorize.net), one of the largest credit card payment gateways, provides a developer support Web site (developer.authorize.net) that documents its APIs for use in integrating credit card payments into shopping carts and Web pages. Authorize.net is a product of Cybersource Corporation (www.cybersource.com, NASDAQ: CYBS), a world leader in eCommerce payment management.

Electronic Commerce Technologies

Electronic Payment Systems

Business has created demand for specialized types of payment systems. Several of these are discussed.

Electronic Bill Payment Systems In these types of systems, the payer sends electronic instructions to his or her bank. The instructions detail who is to be paid, when the payment is to be made, and the amount of the payment. The bank then makes the payment either electronically or by mail.

Credit and Debit Card Systems In these types of systems, the payer transmits a credit or debit card number to a secure server. A **secure server** is one in which the communications link between the client and server is protected by encryption. The payee then presents the card information to a bank for collection, probably through a secure credit payment gateway such as Authorize.net (www.authorize.net). All electronic card transactions are governed by the Payment Card Industry Data Security Standard (PCI DSS), a standard developed by the major credit card companies. The standard represents a security framework based on a dozen control objectives.

Payment Intermediaries This type of payee serves as an intermediary between a payer and a payee. PayPal™ is a good example. A user can login to her PayPal™ account, requesting that a payment be made to a given payee. PayPal™ first removes the fund from the payer's bank account, or charges the funds to the payer's credit or debit card. PayPal™ then credits the payee's PayPay™ account, less any collection fees. PayPal™ also provides invoicing and various other account services.

DIGITAL CASH Cryptographic techniques have given rise to whole new payment systems based on digital cash. **Digital cash** (or *e-cash* or *electronic money*) is typically created when a bank attaches its digital signature to a note promising to pay the bearer some amount of money. A **digital signature** is an encrypted, digested version of a document that can be used to verify the document's authorship and authenticity. In digitally signing a document, the author creates the encrypted, digested version using a secret password (a private key) that is only known to the author. The author also publishes a public key that anyone can use to decrypt the encrypted, digested version. The public key is only useful for decrypting and is not useful for encrypting the author's documents.

VIRTUAL CASH Most electronic cash systems are based on the concept of an electronic wallet. An **electronic wallet** is a computer program that keeps track of the various items of information associated with electronic money. The user acquires digital cash, which is then stored in the electronic wallet. Money is then received or spent by transferring it in or out of the wallet.

VIRTUAL CASH IN ELECTRONIC CARDS A **smart card** is a handheld electronic card that is used for payments. There are four types of cards: memory cards, shared-key cards, signature-transporting cards, and signature-creating cards.

  Memory cards contain microchips that are only capable of storing information. They also contain the hardware that provides PIN (personal identification number) access to the card's contents. Memory cards possess very weak security and should be used only for the simplest applications where the amount of money is small and security is not of much concern.

Shared-key cards overcome the weakness of memory cards by using encryption for all communications between the card and the cash register (or other point-of-payment device). Thus it is useless for an attacker to intercept and record communications between the card and the cash register.

Signature-transporting cards allow the user to spend digital cash. These cards are digitally signed by the card provider.

Signature-creating cards are similar to signature-transporting cards but are capable of generating their own digital signatures. This type of card might be used to write electronic "checks" that bear the digital signature of the cardholder.

The Internet Store

This section describes the typical Internet store and brings together many of the concepts discussed in this chapter.

A typical sales transaction follows the pattern described in Figure 3.7. The major functions performed in this diagram are discussed individually.

1. The customer uses a Web browser to access the merchant's Web site via the Internet. The Web browser may perform important functions, such as opening an encrypted communication session. If the browser is "wallet enabled," it might pass customer information to the Web site, including the name, address, and credit card information. Further, the browser might assist in authenticating both the customer and merchant to each other. This authentication typically would be completed via an exchange of digital certificates, with the assistance of a certificate server from a third-party digital certificate authority.

2. The merchant's on-line Web transaction server will perform several key functions. First, it will communicate with "shopping cart" software that will display current items available for

FIGURE 3.7

The Internet Store

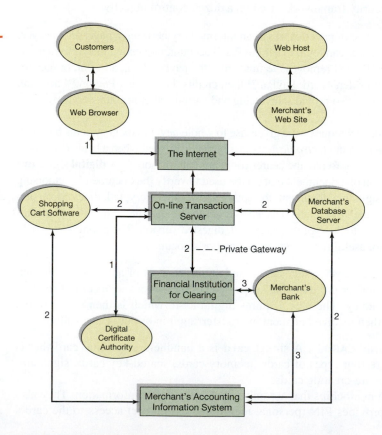

sale and current prices. It will also relay the customer payment information to a financial institution for clearing the transaction. The clearing institution might be any type of financial institution that processes electronic payments. Finally, the transaction server will send the purchase information to the merchant's database/accounting server for further processing and order fulfillment.

3. The financial institution that clears the payment will then electronically remit the funds, less any processing fees, to the merchant's bank. The merchant's bank in turn will send an electronic advice to the merchant's accounting system. The accounting software will reconcile sales transactions with bank receipts.

Note that the entire system is fully automated with no human intervention. Systems such as this can be set up in as little as 24 hours if the accounts with the financial institutions are already in place. Such rapid deployment can be accomplished by using turnkey storefront software solutions that are readily available for sale on the Internet. These solutions can be implemented even if one does not have a merchant account with a financial institution because there are companies who supply reseller agreements in which they collect funds using their own merchant accounts.

Trust in eCommerce: Privacy, Business Practices, and Transaction Integrity

Electronic commerce has opened up previously unthought-of problems with consumers' privacy. Most Web browsers support the use of **cookies,** small pieces of information that the electronic merchant can place on the user's computer. One problem with cookies is that any merchant who knows how can view and analyze all cookies on a user's computer, including those placed there by other merchants.

The result is that it is possible for a Web site to capture all of a person's cookies and immediately discover every other Web site that the user has visited and received a cookie from. Further, given a telephone number, address, or birth date, it might also be possible for a marketer to cross-reference the cookie information with additional information in public databases, such as driver's license information, court records, property records, and so on.

To complicate things even further, many Web merchants collect extensive amounts of information on their customers' private lives, such as income, number of children, and so on. In many cases, these merchants publish statements of what protections they provide for the privacy of information collected, but all too often such statements, when studied carefully, indicate that the merchants share the private information with others. Too often customers do not carefully read merchants' privacy statements.

Some of the adverse results of privacy problems include large volumes of spam (unsolicited e-mail), telephone solicitations, credit card fraud, and even identity theft. By some estimates, the rate of credit card fraud on the Internet is as high as 30%.

It is usually very much in the merchant's best interest to assure its customers that it will protect their privacy. This is usually accomplished by the merchant obtaining some third-party seal of approval, audit, or limited endorsement. One example of such a program is the American Institute of Certified Public Accountants' (AICPA) **Web Trust** attestation program, by which specially trained Certified Public Accountants (CPAs) provide a seal of assurance after a special audit. Assurances are made along three lines: information protection, business practice disclosure, and transaction integrity.

Regarding information protection, the CPA examines all important control, policies, and procedures relevant to protecting the customer's private information. Thus even a merchant with a strict privacy policy might not obtain the Web Trust seal if there are weak controls in place to ensure that the policy is enforced.

Business practice disclosure simply requires that the merchant adequately disclose its business practices.

Finally, transaction integrity involves proper user identification, validation, data accuracy, completeness, and timeliness, as well as complete disclosure of all terms relating to billing and shipping.

Summary

The Internet is a global system of interconnected computer networks. Each computer on the Internet is assigned a unique address called the IP number. Client–server technology serves as the backbone of business communications over the Internet. Mail servers, file servers, FTP servers, Web servers, and commerce servers were discussed.

The EA describes the joint structure and behavior of the enterprise and its information system. The EA falls within the functional area of IT governance and involves four enterprise architectural domains: the business architecture, the data architecture, the applications architecture, and the technical architecture. EA frameworks, such as the Zachman framework, define systems for developing EAs.

Business process frameworks focus on transforming business processes. Business process frameworks include business process reference models, which define best practices for a given business process or group of processes. There are also various frameworks and reference models for supply-chain management.

Digital cash is an important application of encryption technology. It is created when a bank digitally signs a financial note. Four types of smart cards were discussed: memory cards, shared-key cards, signature-transporting cards, and signature-creating cards. Various types of electronic payment systems exist on the Internet. These include traditional bill payment systems, debit and credit card systems, virtual cash systems, and intermediary payment systems.

Glossary

applications architecture   defines the applications required to run the business and how the applications communicate with each other through intranets, extranets and EDI.

application server   a server that supports remote access to one or more applications.

Applications Programming Interface (API)   a set of commands that a given piece of software makes available so that its functions and data can be accessed by other pieces of software.

blinded digital signature   a digital signature and a related digital cash that have been issued with blinding.

blinding   a technique in which a bank issues digital cash in such a way that it is unable to link the payer to the payee.

business architecture   one of the primary domains of the EA; it defines the human resources, processes, and infrastructure that a business needs to accomplish its business strategy.

business domains   describe groups of business functions, business processes, and concepts for which management responsibility may be assigned responsibility.

business process frameworks   focus on transforming business processes.

business process reference model   a set of best practices for a given business process or group of processes.

client   a program that accesses and exchanges information with a server.

commerce server   a specialized type of Web server with various commerce-related features.

cookies   small amounts of information placed on a user's computer by a Web site.

Corporate Information Factory   a logical architecture for the enterprise information system.

cryptanalysis   various techniques for analyzing encrypted messages for purposes of decoding them without legitimate authorization.

data architecture   one of the major domains of the EA; it defines the needed data, how it is to be stored, how it is to be processed, how it is to be utilized, and how it integrates with the other main architectural domains.

data marts   contain subsets of data in the operational database and data warehouse that are specially organized for use by specific functions or units in the organization.

data mining warehouse   contains copies of subsets of the data warehouse.

data model   determines how the database is structured, as well as the operations that can be performed on its data.

data warehouse   stores enormous volumes of current and historical data for use in research and analysis. New data is added to the data warehouse by appending only.

database   is an organized collection of data that is structured to be useful to those who use it.

database driver (also *database adapter* or *database connector*)   software that connects applications to databases.

database server   a server that supports remote access to one or more databases.

digital cash   money created when a bank attaches its digital signature to a note promising to pay the bearer some amount of money.

digital signature   an encrypted, digested version of a document that can be used to verify the document's authorship and authenticity.

distributed application   an application that has different services (which may be SOA services) located in different places.

domain name   an alias name that can be used in place of the IP address.

domain name server (DNS)   electronic phone book that associates domain names with IP addresses.

electronic business (eBusiness)   the use of information technologies in any aspect of the business or organization.

electronic commerce (eCommerce)   that part of eBusiness that directly involves the exchange of products and services among organizations and individuals.

electronic wallet   a computer program that keeps track of the various keys, digital certificates, and items of information associated with digital money.

enterprise architecture (EA)   describes the joint structure and behavior of the enterprise and its information system.

Enterprise Service Bus (ESB)   middleware that serves as a central switchboard for communications between all enterprise services and applications.

extranets   private networks created when the intranets of two or more companies are linked together or when outsiders are able to access a company's private intranet.

file server   allows authorized clients to retrieve files from libraries of files.

firewall   limits access to information on the company's servers from the rest of the world.

FTP server   a file server that uses the FTP, the most commonly used protocol for file servers.

HTML   Hypertext Markup Language, a protocol that specifies the format of documents on the World Wide Web.

Internet   a global system of interconnected computer networks.

intranet   a self-contained in-house Internet.

IP (Internet Protocol) address   address for an individual computer on the Internet.

mail server   an electronic mailbox that holds incoming electronic mails until the user's client program requests it.

memory card   a type of smart card that contains microchips only capable of storing information.

middleware   software specially designed to work in between two different applications, permitting them to exchange data with each other.

online analytical processing (OLAP)   a processing method for very large databases, normally used for research, analysis, and complicated reporting and not for transaction processing.

operational databases   databases that store relatively current transaction data for quick access by management in support of tactical decision making.

orchestration   the process of linking and sequencing service in order to make them work together.

Osterwalder Reference Model (ORM)   defines the typical business model in terms of four major domains: infrastructure, offering, customers, and finance.

relational data model   a data model that structures data in two-dimensional tables that resemble spreadsheets, with rows and columns.

secure server   a server in which the communications link between the client and server is protected by encryption.

server   a robot-type program that constantly runs on some computer and exchanges information with clients.

service-oriented architecture (SOA)   an applications architecture design framework that facilities the development of application suites.

shared-key card   a type of smart card that uses encryption for all communications between the card and the cash register (or other point-of-payment device).

signature-creating card   a type of smart card that is capable of generating its own digital signatures.

signature-transporting card   a type of smart card that stores digital cash.

smart card   an electronic card that is used for payments.

SOA services   independent software units of functionality.

SOAP   a protocol for communication between services.

Structured Query Language (SQL)   used to define, access, and manipulate data in a relational database.

three-tiered application architecture   applications that contain three tiers (i.e., parts), consisting of the presentation tier, the logic tier, and the data tier.

Value Reference Model^{SM}   a business process reference model that depicts the value chain at four levels of abstraction: strategic, tactical, operational, and activities and actions.

Web commerce   the use of information technologies in the exchange of products and services among individuals and organizations and over the World Wide Web and the Internet.

Web server   a server that allows a user (client) to access documents and run computer programs that reside on remote computers.

Web service   a service that is accessible via the Web.

Web service specifications   specifications for documenting Web services and how they communicate with each other.

Web Services Description Language (WSDL)   a language used to describe Web services in an SOA environment.

Web Trust   An AICPA-sponsored attestation program that provides assurances in three areas for on-line merchants: information protection, business practice disclosure, and transaction integrity.

Zachman Framework   an EA framework that is based on defining models applicable to a given organization.

Webliography

www.icann.org
The Web site of the organization that controls domain names for the Internet.

www.microstrategy.com
The Web site of Microstrategy, a company that provides data mining (business intelligence) software that works with a wide range of application databases. This site has some interesting articles on data mining.

www.businessobjects.com
The Web site of Business Objects, a company owned by SAP (www.sap.com). This company offers business intelligence (data mining) software for small, medium, and large businesses. The site is helpful for creating online demos.

java.sun.com/javaee
The Web page for Sun Microsystems, Inc. Java Platform Enterprise Edition™ (JEE). JEE is a widely used application server used for running Java™ applications. Java™ is a server-side scripting language that is used to develop many Rich Internet Applications.

webservices.xml.com
This Web site is rich in information about SOA and Web services.

www.oracle.com
The home page of Oracle Corporation. This site is rich in information about many SOA-oriented products, including Oracle E-Business Suite™, middleware, and data warehousing.

www.sonicsoftware.com
The home page of Progress Software's Sonic Software, including their industry leading enterprise service bus, Progress® Sonic ESB®. Drilling down through the site leads to the ESB adapters page, which reveals that the ESB has adapters for a very large number of adapter for applications and protocols.

www.zifa.com
The home page of The Zachman Institute for Framework Advancement. The Zachman framework is widely used as a Federal Enterprise Architecture framework.

www.opengroup.org
The home page of The Open Group. This site contains information on one of the most widely accepted FEA frameworks, TOGAF.

www.value-chain.org
The home page of the Value Chain Group, Inc. and their Business Process Transformation Framework published Value Reference Model^{SM}.

www.prtm.com
The home page of the SCOR model. PRTM is a private group of management consultants.

www.webtrust.org
Home of the WebTrust service. WebTrust is a family of assurance services targeted toward eCommerce-based system. It is backed by the American Institute of Certified Public Accountants.

Chapter Quiz

Answers to the Chapter Quiz appear on page 102.

1. Which best describes the functional area under which EA belongs?
   a. internal control
   b. information technology support services
   c. information technology governance
   d. none of the above

2. Which of the following statements best describes the business architecture's relation to other architectures?
   a. The business architecture supports all the other architectures.
   b. The data and technology architectures determine business architectures.
   c. The business architectures determine the data and technology architectures.
   d. None of the above correctly describes a relationship.

3. Which of the following is a correct statement?
   a. SQL would normally be used to access the data warehouse data.
   b. SQL would normally be used to access OLAP databases.
   c. OLAP would normally be used to access the operational database.
   d. none of the above.

4. SQL stands for (_____).
   a. Semantic Query Language
   b. Strong Query Language
   c. Simple Query Language
   d. Structured Query Language

5. Which of the following is a standard communications protocol in SOA?
   a. SOAP
   b. XML
   c. XBRL
   d. none of the above

6. Which of the following is not an example of middleware?
   a. database driver
   b. enterprise system bus
   c. AP
   d. all of the above

7. The Zachman Framework is an example of a (_____).
   a. process reference model
   b. process improvement model
   c. a supply chain framework
   d. none of the above
8. The main domains in the ORM are (_____).
   a. infrastructure, offering, customers, and finance
   b. technology, analysis, sales, and finance
   c. technology, offering, sales, and finance
   d. none of the above

9. PCI DSS is (_____).
   a. a communication specification for EDI
   b. a security standard for credit card processing
   c. a data specification standard for banking
   d. none of the above
10. Which of the following is not an EA framework?
   a. Zachman
   b. JAVA
   c. FEA
   d. TOGAF

Review Questions

1. Distinguish between intranets and extranets.
2. What is the main security risk inherent in any intranet.
3. Explain how addressing works on the Internet.
4. Summarize any differences between firewalls and proxy servers. In what situations would both be used?
5. How might EDI be implemented on a commerce server?
6. Define and describe several different types of servers used in electronic commerce.
7. Discuss one or two different types of hacker attacks that might be made against a commerce server.
8. What is the advantage of using a three-tier application architecture?
9. How does the value chain differ from the supply chain?
10. Would a small business ever need a data warehouse? Why or why not?
11. Give an example of where a small business might want to use an Application Programming Interface.
12. Why is XML needed when we already have HTML?

Discussion Questions and Problems

13. The Yacht Company in Chicago manages several divisions around the United States, including the Arco Division. Arco produces sailboats and spans a 100-acre site near the Port of Miami, in Miami, Florida. All of Arco's personal computers are presently linked together over a LAN. Specifically, sales records are kept on a personal computer at the dockside warehouse, and all other records are kept in the main building, where most of top management is also located. The only exception is payroll, which is kept on a personal computer in the maintenance building.

    Arco has recently hired Betty Brill, a new information systems manager. At her first staff meeting, Betty informed Brad Wilson, the controller, that she wanted to develop a virtual private network to link all the company's computers together. Brad's initial response was negative. He said the following:

    > Our present systems work fine. As it now stands, the sales and payroll departments are translating their accounting files into ASCII text and sending them over the Internet to the main building. When the text files arrive in the main building, we then run a program that converts them into a format compatible with our main computer system.

    Betty interrupted:

    > Brad, that's an archaic system. We're using all kinds of incompatible formats, and on top of that we're wasting a lot of effort by expressing mailing disks of our payroll files to Chicago every week so that they can handle the taxes and write the paychecks. What we really need is our own intranet with an outside link to the Internet. That will help us make the transition to compatible file formats. We can also set up a server so that the people in Chicago can access any of the accounting data any time they need them. There will be no need to send them disks all the time.

    Brad responded:

    > That's really dumb, Betty. Our present system works fine. But your plan will probably cost a lot of money, generate a lot of hassle, and it will even open us to potential hackers. The results could be a major disaster.

    Betty concluded her argument:

    > Brad, I don't appreciate your calling my ideas dumb. Yours are even dumber. You need to go back to school and learn about today's technology. Everyone is switching to intranets and wiring up to the Internet. When you get right down to it, we don't have any choice but to keep up with the times.
    >
    > What I suggest we do is put our entire accounting system on our own private Web site. This way any of us can access the system from either here or Chicago, and I'm not worried about hackers. We can require passwords to access anything on this Web.

Required

a. Select one side of the argument and defend your position.

b. Assume that Arco has decided to implement Betty's plan. What would be some important considerations relevant to the implementation?

14. The HZP Company operates in Chicago, where it designs and manufactures its own line of specialized women's clothing. The company maintains a Web presence and recently started accepting orders through a commerce server that it developed in-house. The problem is that the commerce server stores incoming orders in a format that is not consistent with the format used by the accounting system. In fact, the problem is so bad that all incoming data require a considerable amount of manual editing in a word processor before they can be read into the accounting system.

Required

Sketch out a general solution to HZP's problem.

15. Comway Corporation is a medium-sized shoe wholesaler whose sales territory includes Illinois, Michigan, and Indiana. Every day, the sales managers for these states collect orders from retail stores. They then use local Internet service providers to connect to the Internet and enter the order information. In each case, the sales manager uses a Web browser client to enter the information into a Web server dedicated to collecting orders.

    A problem has arisen recently with deliveries to some of Comway's retail customers. For example, one customer, Brown Shoe Store, complained that it never received delivery of a $6,000 order that it had recently made. In order to investigate the matter, Sandra Hill, Comway's controller, looked at the order files and concluded that the shoes were in fact shipped to a warehouse, several blocks from Brown Shoe Store. Brown, however, said that it had never authorized a shipment to anywhere but directly to its store.

    Puzzled, Sandra Hill checked with Brown's sales manager, who immediately produced a printed copy of the order. The sales manager had printed out the contents of the computer screen at the time he had entered the order, and sure enough, he had set the shipment up for normal delivery right at Brown's store.

    To further investigate, Sandra Hill checks the logs of the Web server used to collect orders from the sales managers. However, everything seemed in order, and it appeared the sales manager had used his proper password to access the Web server.

Required

Analyze the problem and make suggestions as to its possible cause. What additional information would you need to complete Sandra Hill's investigation? What additional security measure should be taken, if any?

16. ACE Company is a small start-up company that intends to publish electronic documents on the World Wide Web. It does not intend to engage in publishing any printed materials.

    Janet Thompson, the president of ACE, has decided that a Web commerce server will be set up to take all orders. The server will also be required to take payments and distribute documents to customers.

Required

Design and specify the requirements for the desired commerce server. Your design should include all relevant considerations, including the following:

a. information collected by the server

b. means for organizing electronic documents (Assume that ACE's catalog will consist of approximately 2,000 documents.)

c. security issues

d. payment methods

e. the overall structure of ACE's Web site and any necessary and related hyperlinks

17. For each of the following electronic payment systems, give an example of a company for which it might be applicable:

a. traditional electronic bill payment system

b. traditional credit card system

c. secure Electronic Transaction system

d. virtual cash system.

18. Ramco Company sells gift items and flowers through its Internet store. In the past, it has accepted traditional credit card payments through its secure commerce server. However, the company has recently decided to accept digital cash.

    The company's head of finance feels that digital cash would save the company a considerable amount of money in bank processing fees, as compared to credit card transactions. The only problem is that if digital cash is accepted, many customers may elect to pay with blinded digital notes.

    Ramco's vice-president of marketing is against accepting blinded digital cash because it will allow customers to order and pay with pseudonyms, that is, fake names designed to protect the customers' identities. The result is that the marketing department will not be able to build its usual database of information for customers paying with the blinded notes. That in turn will prevent marketing from soliciting those customers for repeat business.

    John Carlos, Ramco's controller, is more concerned about the potential for fraud. Specifically, he is concerned that the company may end up accepting counterfeit digital money. Furthermore, due to cost considerations, Ramco does not have the resources for online verification of each note of digital cash. He estimates that in most cases approximately 2 days will elapse before a note can be determined to be counterfeit. The problem is that flowers are normally shipped the same day the order is taken.

Required

Present the arguments for and against implementing the acceptance of digital cash. What changes might be made to make the system more workable?

19. Roadco Company has been hired to collect tolls for the Blue Ocean toll road. Robert Asphalt, the controller of Roadco, has been analyzing the situation and has come up with the following pieces of information:

a. During rush hour, commuters must presently wait in line for approximately 40 minutes at the main exit from the toll road.

b. Estimates show that during the rush hour 95% of all cars on the toll road are driven by regular commuters.

c. The technology is available for the inexpensive creation of electronic smart cards that are capable of radio-controlled communications directly with the toll booths.

Required

Design a smart card for collecting tolls from regular commuters. Your design should include the following:

a. procedures for issuing and accounting for cards
b. procedures for accounting for card usage
c. security measures
d. specifications for the types of smart cards to be used
e. procedures for communicating between the tollbooth and the central office

20. The following facts pertain to the eCommerce Web site for WCEComp, a personal computer manufacturer and seller.

Privacy Statement

a. All information collected on this Web site will be used only for legitimate business purposes. We do not give away or rent any information to third parties.

b. We will only contact you for legitimate business purposes, possibly from time to time, as needed. Please be 100% assured that all transactions between you and us are held in the strictest confidence.

Disclosure of Business Practices, Shipping, and Billing

a. All items will be shipped at the earliest possible date.
b. You are not required to accept items that you did not order.
c. All invoices are generated on the first day of the month.
d. In the event that you are accidentally billed twice for the same item, you will immediately be issued a refund.

Transaction Integrity

a. We thoroughly audit at least 10% of all transactions for accuracy and integrity. This ensures that our system is working properly.

b. All transactions are encrypted by the latest encryption standards.

Required

Evaluate these statements in terms of how well the stated policies promote customer trust and confidence in WCEComp's on-line business.

21. The Tinjin Company is in the process of developing a Web site to market fine linens. Some of the basic business considerations are as follows:

a. Tinjin is new and without much capital. Therefore, obtaining a merchant account from any of the major credit card companies seems unlikely.

b. Tinjin has a small storefront in the city, but business there is too slow to make enough money to survive. It is hoped that Internet sales will make the business a success.

c. The owners of Tinjin do not have enough capital to hire any professional consultants, but they have some basic knowledge of personal computers and the Internet.

Required

Draft a plan for a solution to Tinjin's problems described here.

a. Describe at least two options for Tinjin to set up its Web site.
b. Describe options for Tinjin to collect funds from customers.
c. What problems might Tinjin encounter in integrating its Web site with its accounting system?

22. Ramwood Company is a large distributor in the candy business with offices in Miami, Florida. The company accepts only very large orders from wholesalers, and the controller has a strict policy that orders will only be filled on the basis of an encrypted electronic purchase order from the customer.

Ramwood has recently had some serious problems with its Web site. The problem is that someone has spoofed its domain name and has been intercepting its business. In other words, many recent orders have gone to a competitor with offices in the Cayman Islands, who just happens to operate under a similar legal name, namely, Ramwood Candy.

The CEO checked with the company's outside attorney and found out that there was little that could be done about another company using a similar name, and given that the competitor was offshore it would even be difficult to do anything about the domain name spoofing.

The controller spent her nights without sleep, thinking about the problem. Finally, she concluded that they needed to add something to their Web site that the competitor could not counterfeit, some sort of token or something that the customer could look for to be assured that it was dealing with the real www.ramwoodcandy.com.

Required

a. How would you suggest that Ramwood solve its problem?
b. Design a complete system that can protect Ramwood from imposters.

23. WhiteFlowers4You sells flower arrangements over the Internet. Recently the company has been experimenting with accepting digital cash. At first, the introduction of digital cash brought an immediate 10% increase in sales, and everyone in the company was pleased.

Problems began to occur, however, with some of the digital cash notes received. In one day, a week ago, 20 notes, each denominated in the amount of $20, turned out to be counterfeit. The bad notes were received from different customers, but in each case, the flowers were being sent to someone as a gift. Further, in every case, the flowers were shipped the same day that the order was placed. It was not until the next day that the bank refused to pay the digital notes.

To make things worse, all the notes turned out to be blinded digital cash, so the bank could not provide any information on the maker. Further verification showed that in every case the customer had entered a false name, address, and telephone number. In short, there was no easy way to find out who had perpetrated the frauds.

The controller argued strongly for contacting the recipients of the flowers to ask questions about who had made the false purchases. But the CEO was against this, as she felt that to make an issue of it would produce bad customer relations and possibly bad press. The last thing the company needed was bad press.

While the controller and CEO were debating what to do, the treasurer popped in and said that they had just discovered another 120 bad notes for $20 from only the day before.

Required

a. What should WhiteFlowers4You do about its problem with bad digital notes? Design a solution to the problem.

b. Should the company contact the recipients of the fraudulent orders? Explain why they should or should not.

24. Tammy Wilson runs a small, independent shoe store in Pataxy, Georgia. At present, she has no employees besides herself, she purchases five brands of shoes from eight different wholesalers, and she grants revolving credit to many of the long-established families that regularly buy from her.

At present her cousin keeps all her accounting records in a paper notebook, but because of overflow traffic from a new nearby mall the business has grown so large that Tammy has decided to set up a computerized system. She wants the system to be able to grow as her business continues to grow. She is eventually planning to turn her store into a giant discount warehouse that will serve the entire region.

Required

Tammy has asked her other cousin, a software developer, to set up a custom accounting system based on a relational database.

a. Define the basic tables that will be initially required for the database.

b. Describe what data she might want to use to create a data warehouse.

c. What types of analyses might Tammy do on the data warehouse?

25. Tom Hinkerton of Miami, Florida, has decided to set up a high-tech street-corner lemonade stand. He wants to use a notebook computer to record all sales in real time, and he also wants to track his inventories of fresh lemons, bottled water, and sugar. Some things he wants from his system:

a. profit reports

b. sales tax reports for the state of Florida

c. any type of report that can help him improve his profits

Required

You have been hired as Tom's accountant.

a. Define EA for Tom's business.

b. Define a supply chain model for Tom's business.

Web Research Assignments

26. Assume you are an accounting consultant for a hardware store that wants to set up a Web store using osCommerce (www.oscommerce.com), the open-source shopping cart software. Your job is to advise the owner on how to set up the shopping cart and connect it to a merchant account for credit card processing.

Required

a. Describe the server requirements for osCommerce.

b. What steps would you need to take to make Authorize.net (www.authorize.net) work with osCommerce?

c. What steps would you need to take to the shopping cart PCI DSS compliant, assuming 100 transactions per month?

27. Nancy Belachi runs a small, high-quality private K-12 school in Watkins Glen, New York. About 25% of her 900 students are boarding students from all parts of the United States, Canada, and the rest of the world. Nancy's accountant has recently set up a basic student tracking system using Intuit Quickbase™ (quickbase.intuit.com), a Platform-as-a-Service (PaaS) database system. She now wants the capability to use the Web for new students to apply for admission and pay their fees, including the initial deposit fee, which is $500 for grades K-8, and $1,000 for grades 9–12. You have been hired to help her develop a new Web site enabled with the application and registration capabilities. You have decided to use the Ruby programming language (www.ruby-lang.org), an Apache (www.apache.org) Web server, and the Quickbase™ API to accomplish your task.

Required

a. What steps will be needed to complete the task?

b. You are considering using REST (Representational State Transfer) to communicate between your Web-based Ruby application and your Quickbase™ application. Explain how this would work. Is it consistent with the Quickbase™ API?

Answers to Chapter Quiz

1. c   **2.** c   **3.** d   **4.** d   **5.** a   **6.** b   **7.** d   **8.** a   **9.** b   **10.** b

Transaction Processing and the Internal Control Process

Learning Objectives

Careful study of this chapter will enable you to:

- Understand the nature of control exposures.
- Discuss the concept of the internal control process.
- Identify general and application processing controls.
- Discuss the behavioral assumptions inherent in traditional internal control practices.
- Describe the techniques used to analyze internal control systems.

The Necessity for Controls

Enterprise Risk Management

The basic responsibility of management in business entities is to provide value to the stakeholders. In carrying out this responsibility, management faces various opportunities and uncertainties. Selecting the best opportunities and managing uncertainties is part of the larger task of **enterprise risk management (ERM).**

The Committee of Sponsoring Organizations of the Treadway Commission (COSO, www.coso.org) is a voluntary, private organization made up from various influential professional accounting associations. COSO defines ERM as follows:

> Enterprise risk management is a process, effected by an entity's Board of Directors, management and other personnel, applied in strategy setting and across the enterprise, designed to identify potential events that may affect the entity, and manage risk to be within its risk appetite, to provide reasonable assurance regarding the achievement of entity objectives.

ERM contains eight components:

- Internal Environment—The overall culture, atmosphere, and tone of the organizations. The internal environment sets the backdrop for management's philosophy for seeking/avoiding risks, general approaches to dealing with risk, as well as entity-wide ethics.
- Objective Setting—Management's process for setting objectives in a way that is consistent with their "appetite" for risk.
- Event Identification—The process of identifying internal and external events that affect the entity's opportunities and risks as they relate to achieving management objectives.
- Risk Assessment—The process of analyzing risks, their likelihood of identified events, and their potential impact.
- Risk Response—The process of responding to risks and identified events. Responses may include avoiding, reducing, sharing, and accepting risks.

- Control Activities—The policies and procedures that are implemented to effect risk responses. These policies and procedures are typically referred to as "controls."
- Information and Communication—The overall flow of information as applied to managing risks in support of the other seven ERM components.
- Monitoring—The process of monitoring the entire ERM process. Changes are made to the process as needed.

 CASE IN POINT

The job of chief risk officer (CRO) became very popular in the wake of the Sarbanes–Oxley Act (SOX). In a large international company, the CRO is faced with the task of managing a wide range of different risks. Examples include internal fraud, foreign currency fluctuations, natural disasters, political instabilities, product liabilities, supply shortages, sudden shifts in consumer demand, and labor shortages.

Controls and Exposures

Controls are needed to reduce exposures to potential adverse events that are identified as part of the ERM process. An organization is subject to a variety of exposures that can have an adverse effect on its operations or even its very existence as a viable going concern. An **exposure** consists of the potential financial effect of an event multiplied by its probability of occurrence. The term **risk** is synonymous with *probability of occurrence*. Thus an exposure is a risk times its financial consequences.

Undesirable events such as floods or thefts are not themselves exposures. An organization's exposure to these types of events is the organization's potential financial loss times the probability of the occurrence of these events. Exposures do not arise simply due to a lack of controls. Controls tend to reduce exposures, but controls rarely affect the causes of exposures. Exposures are inherent in the operation of any organization and may result from a variety of causes (Figure 4.1).

Common Exposures

EXCESSIVE COSTS Excessive costs reduce profits. Every expenditure made by an organization is potentially excessive. Prices paid for goods purchased for use in the organization may be excessive.

FIGURE 4.1

Common Business Exposures

Paychecks may be distributed for work that was ineffective, inefficient, or both. Production may be inefficient, causing the purchase and use of excessive materials and labor. Excessive assets may be purchased. Excessive expenses for advertising and travel expense may be incurred. Bills or taxes may be paid late, causing penalty fees and interest expense to be incurred.

DEFICIENT REVENUES   Deficient revenues reduce profits. Bad debt expense on credit sales may be excessive. Sales may be shipped to customers but not recorded and thus not collected. Customers may be incorrectly billed for smaller amounts than they should be. Bills may be lost or incorrectly summarized as receivables. Sales may be returned or cancelled due to late shipment of orders, shipment of unacceptable quality, or incorrect shipment of items ordered. Excessive sales allowances may be incurred for similar reasons.

LOSS OF ASSETS   Assets may be lost due to theft, acts of violence, or natural disasters. An organization has custody of a large quantity of assets, all of which are subject to loss. Assets may be lost unintentionally. Cash, materials, or equipment may be accidentally misplaced or damaged by careless employees or even by careful employees. Cash, materials, or equipment also may be intentionally misplaced or damaged by employees, as well as by management.

INACCURATE ACCOUNTING   Accounting policies and procedures may be error-prone, inappropriate, or significantly different from those that are considered to be generally acceptable. Errors may include valuation, timing, or classification of transactions. Errors in record keeping may be unintentional or intentional. Errors can result in inaccurate information for management decisions and materially misleading financial statements.

BUSINESS INTERRUPTION   Business interruption may consist of a temporary suspension of operations or ultimately the termination of operations and end of the organization. Business interruption may result from excessive operating exposures, from physical acts of violence, or from natural disasters.

STATUTORY SANCTIONS   Statutory sanctions include any penalties that may arise from judicial or regulatory authorities who have jurisdiction over an organization and its operations. An organization must ensure that its activities comply with a variety of laws and regulations. Interruption of normal business operations might result as a penalty imposed by regulatory agencies when corporate crime has been committed.

COMPETITIVE DISADVANTAGE   Competitive disadvantage is the inability of an organization to remain viable in the marketplace. Competitive disadvantage might result from any combination of the previous exposures and might also result from ineffective management decisions.

FRAUD AND EMBEZZLEMENT   Fraud is the intentional perversion of truth in order to induce another to part with something of value or to surrender a legal right. Embezzlement occurs when assets are fraudulently appropriated to one's own use. Fraud and embezzlement may be perpetrated by outsiders against an organization or by insiders within the organization. Excessive costs, deficient revenues, loss of assets, inaccurate accounting, business interruption, statutory sanctions, and competitive disadvantage may all result from fraud and embezzlement.

Fraud and White-Collar Crime

The term **white-collar crime** describes a grouping of illegal activities that are differentiated from other illegal activities in that they occur as part of the occupation of the offender. White-collar crime occurs when assets are deceitfully diverted from proper use or are deceitfully misrepresented by an act or series of acts that are nonviolent in nature. White-collar crime often involves the entry of fictitious (i.e., fraudulent) transactions into an accounting system.

CASE IN POINT

When SOX was passed, President Bush created the Corporate Fraud Task Force (CFTF), headed by the deputy attorney general. The CFTF works with the U.S. Department of Justice and other agencies and focuses on regulatory enforcement and investigation and prosecution of corporate fraud.

The CFTF has been involved in many criminal prosecutions, including the one involving Martha Stewart, who was the CEO of Martha Stewart Living Omnimedia, Inc.

Three basic forms of theft occur in white-collar crime. Employee theft involves diversion of assets by an employee for personal gain. Employee–outsider theft involves diversion of assets by an employee in collusion with an outsider (i.e., nonemployee) for personal gain. Management fraud concerns diversion of assets or misrepresentation of assets by management. **Management fraud** may involve diversion or misrepresentation of assets from either employees or third-party outsiders, or both. Management is responsible for the establishment of controls in an organization and is thus not subject to these controls to the extent that other employees are. Irregularities by management are less likely to be detected than are irregularities committed by other employees.

CASE IN POINT

Research shows that revenue recognition fraud is the most common type of financial statement fraud. Revenue recognition fraud schemes may involve recognizing unearned revenues, recognizing revenues in the wrong period, and even recognizing fictitious revenues. The incidence of revenue recognition fraud is at least several times higher than that of any other type of financial statement fraud.

White-collar crime may result in fraudulent financial reporting. **Fraudulent financial reporting** is intentional or reckless conduct, whether by purposeful act or by omission, that results in materially misleading financial statements. Employees at any level of the organization might be involved. Fraudulent financial reporting might involve fictitious transactions processed by an accounting system, falsified valuation of assets such as inventories, or misapplication of accounting principles. No organization of any size is immune from the possibility that fraudulent financial reporting might occur.

Corporate crime is white-collar crime that benefits a company or organization, rather than the individuals who perpetrate the fraud. Such individuals may benefit indirectly. Examples of corporate crime include defense contract cost overages charged to the federal government by defense contractors, publicized charges for reimbursement for noncontract-related expenses by universities, and bidding improprieties at auctions for government securities by major brokerage firms.

The fascinating aspect of white-collar crime is that it often seems to be victimless. Crimes such as embezzlement, tax fraud, fraudulent financial statements, unemployment insurance fraud, and the like require some sort of procedural analysis (a physical examination and analysis of transaction records, documentation, inventories, etc.) as a prerequisite to discovering and proving that a crime has been committed. In one publicized case of corporate crime, a major brokerage firm was convicted of mail and wire fraud concerning bank deposits that it processed. During the investigation, most of the banks that had been victims of the fraud were surprised to learn that they had in fact been robbed. They were unaware of this until they were contacted by investigators, which was well after the crimes had occurred.

FORENSIC ACCOUNTING   Forensic accounting is concerned with the prevention and detection of fraud and white-collar crime. **Forensic accounting** is one of several terms that are used to describe the activities of persons who are concerned with preventing and detecting fraud. The terms *fraud examiner, fraud auditor*, and *loss prevention professional* are also descriptive of persons involved in this type of activity.

The Association of Certified Fraud Examiners (ACFE, www.acfe.com) is a professional organization that was established as a response to the increased concern for fraud in business and government. The mission of ACFE is to reduce the incidence of fraud and white-collar crime and to assist its membership in its detection and deterrence. ACFE provides bona fide qualifications for certified fraud examiners (CFEs) through administration of the Uniform CFE Examination. Certified fraud examiners have expertise to resolve allegations of fraud, obtain evidence, take statements and write reports, testify to findings, and assist in the prevention and detection of fraud and white-collar crime. Typical CFEs include fraud auditors and investigators, forensic accountants, public accountants, law enforcement personnel, loss prevention professionals, and academicians. All CFEs must exemplify high moral and ethical standards and must abide by a code of professional ethics.

Fraud examination draws on the fields of accounting, law, and criminology. A knowledge of accounting is necessary to understand the nature of fraudulent transactions. There are many legal aspects involved in fraud examination; thus, an understanding of related law is essential. The basics of criminology are essential to understand the behavior of criminals. Principles of legal investigation are also central to fraud examination. Fraud examiners must know how to legally gather evidence related to fraud—how to obtain documentation, interview witnesses, take lawful statements, and write unbiased reports. Fraud examination has to adhere to investigation standards acceptable to a court of law.

SERIOUSNESS OF FRAUD   Fraud is a serious problem that occurs to some extent in almost every large company. Frequent frauds include misappropriation of funds, check forgery, credit card fraud, false invoices, and theft. Other types of fraud include accounts receivable manipulation, false financial statements, diversion of service, phantom vendors, purchase for personal use, diversion of sales, unnecessary purchases, vandalism, and sabotage.

Internal controls are frequently the reason frauds are discovered. Internal auditor review and specific investigation by management are also important in discovering fraud. Poor internal controls are generally the primary reason that frauds occur. Collusion between employees and third parties and management override of controls are significant contributing factors in many cases. In a large percentage of cases, "red flags"—such as changes in an employee's lifestyle or spending habits—point to the possibility of fraud(s), but these red flags are too often either ignored or not acted on quickly enough by personnel or management.

Control Objectives and Transaction Cycles

Controls act to reduce exposures. The analysis of exposures in an organization is often related to the transaction cycle concept. Although no two organizations are identical, most organizations experience the same types of economic events. These events generate transactions that may be grouped according to four common cycles of business activity:

- **Revenue cycle:** Events related to the distribution of goods and services to other entities and the collection of related payments.
- **Expenditure cycle:** Events related to the acquisition of goods and services from other entities and the settlement of related obligations.
- **Production cycle:** Events related to the transformation of resources into goods and services.
- **Finance cycle:** Events related to the acquisition and management of capital funds, including cash.

FIGURE 4.2

Representative
Control Objectives

Representative Control Objectives	
Revenue Cycle	Customers should be authorized in accordance with management's criteria.
	The prices and terms of goods and services provided should be authorized in accordance with management's criteria.
	All shipments of goods and services provided should result in a billing to the customer.
	Billings to customers should be accurately and promptly classified, summarized, and reported.
Expenditure Cycle	Vendors should be authorized in accordance with management's criteria.
	Employees should be hired in accordance with management's criteria.
	Access to personnel, payroll, and disbursement records should be permitted only in accordance with management's criteria.
	Compensation rates and payroll deductions should be authorized in accordance with management's criteria.
	Amounts due to vendors should be accurately and promptly classified, summarized, and reported.
Production Cycle	The production plan should be authorized in accordance with management's criteria.
	Cost of goods manufactured should be accurately and promptly classified, summarized, and reported.
Finance Cycle	The amounts and timing of debt transactions should be authorized in accordance with management's criteria.
	Access to cash and securities should be permitted only in accordance with management's criteria.

Each transaction cycle will have exposures. Management should develop detailed control objectives for each transaction cycle. These control objectives provide a basis for analysis. Once control objectives have been stated, management may collect information to determine the extent to which control objectives are being achieved in each of the organization's transaction cycles.

Figure 4.2 lists representative control objectives for each transaction cycle. Control objectives such as those illustrated are drawn from the concept of an internal control structure. Management must first develop an internal control structure. This structure can then be applied to transaction cycles by developing specific control objectives for each cycle.

Components of the Internal Control Process

Internal control is a process—affected by an entity's Board of Directors, management, and other personnel—designed to provide reasonable assurance regarding the achievement of objectives in the following categories: (1) reliability of financial reporting, (2) effectiveness and efficiency of operations, and (3) compliance with applicable laws and regulations.

An organization's **internal control process** consists of five elements: the control environment, risk assessment, control activities, information and communication, and monitoring

FIGURE 4.3

Internal Control Structure

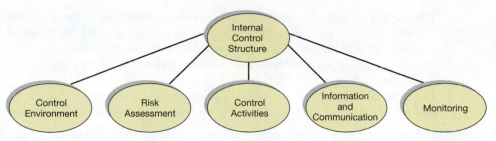

(Figure 4.3). The concept of internal control is based on two major premises: responsibility and reasonable assurance. Note that the five elements of the internal control process overlap with the eight components of ERM. This is because the internal control process is simply an application of ERM with an emphasis on the accounting information system.

The first premise, **responsibility,** has to do with management and the Board of Directors being responsible for establishing and maintaining the internal control process. While specific responsibilities for controls may be delegated to subordinates, final responsibility remains with management and the Board of Directors. External auditors, internal auditors, and other parties may be concerned directly with an organization's internal control process, but the ultimate responsibility for the control remains with management and the Board of Directors.

The second premise, **reasonable assurance,** has to do with the relative costs and benefits of controls. Prudent management should not spend more on controls than the benefits to be received from the controls. For example, suppose that purchasing a credit check report for new customers costs $35. The credit check would tend to reduce bad debt expense for new customers (i.e., reduce the probability or risk of its occurring) and thus would reduce the organization's exposure in this area. If sales to new customers average only $25, however, then the cost of this control would exceed its expected benefits. It would not be rational to implement this control.

Quite often, management's consideration of the relative costs and benefits of controls will necessarily be subjective in nature. It is often difficult to measure costs and benefits when intangible factors such as the reputation of the company or the morale effects of controls on employees are major considerations. Management must exercise its judgment to attain reasonable assurance that its control objectives are being met.

External Influences Concerning an Entity and Internal Control

Many organizations are subject to specific statutory requirements that are issued by judicial or regulatory authorities. An organization must ensure that its activities are in compliance with laws and regulations issued by those who have jurisdiction over it and its operations. The Securities and Exchange Commission (SEC) is active in the area of financial accounting, as is the Financial Accounting Standards Board (FASB). Laws, regulations, and pronouncements from such agencies are a major factor in an organization's internal control process.

The Federal Foreign Corrupt Practices Act of 1977 (FCPA) is a specific legal requirement that concerns many organizations. Failure to comply with this law could result in fines and imprisonment.

Section 102 of the FCPA requires all companies who are subject to the Securities Exchange Act of 1934 to

A. Make and keep books, records, and accounts, which, in reasonable detail, accurately and fairly reflect the transactions and dispositions of the assets of the issuer;

B. Devise and maintain a system of **internal accounting controls** sufficient to provide reasonable assurances that

1. Transactions are executed in accordance with management's general or specific authorization;

2. Transactions are recorded as necessary (i) to permit preparation of financial statements in conformity with generally accepted accounting principles or any other criteria applicable to such statements and (ii) to maintain accountability for assets;

3. Access to assets is permitted only in accordance with management's general or specific authorization;

4. The recorded accountability for assets is compared with the existing assets at reasonable intervals and appropriate action is taken with respect to any differences.

Noncompliance with these provisions could result in fines up to $10,000 for both the corporation and its officials along with 5 years' imprisonment for those executives involved.

CASE IN POINT

U.S. companies that make overseas acquisitions may take on unexpected risks of violating the Foreign Corrupt Practices Act (FCPA). Overseas companies may engage in many practices that are not illegal under local laws but are illegal under the FCPA. This means that acquiring a foreign company might immediately put a U.S. company in violation of the FCPA.

A section of the Omnibus Trade and Competitiveness Act of 1988 (OTCA) amends both the accounting and antibribery provisions of the FCPA. The FCPA requires registrants to keep records in "reasonable detail" and to maintain systems of internal accounting control that provide "reasonable assurances" that the specified goals are met. As originally passed, the act did not contain definitions of either *reasonable detail* or *reasonable assurances*. A new subsection added by the OTCA defines the terms *reasonable detail* and *reasonable assurances* to mean a level that would satisfy prudent officials in the conduct of their own affairs. Another amendment to the accounting provisions limits criminal liability to intentional actions taken to circumvent the internal accounting control systems or to falsify company records. The OTCA also includes several amendments that clarify or modify the antibribery provisions of the FCPA and increase penalties for violations of the antibribery provisions.

THE SARBANES–OXLEY ACT   For public companies, the Sarbanes–Oxley Act of 2002 (SOX) imposes certain requirements and restrictions on management, auditors, and company audit committees. Severe financial and criminal penalties may apply.

The act establishes the five-member Public Company Accounting Oversight Board (PCAOB), whose responsibilities are directed primarily toward regulating the conduct of auditors but with important implications for management in all publicly traded companies. SOX grants the PCAOB powers to make up rules and impose sanctions, subject to SEC review. Violations of PCAOB rules are deemed to be violations of the 1934 Securities Act.

SOX significantly increased criminal penalties for various types of white-collar crimes. It increases the maximum penalties for violations of the 1934 Securities Act from $1 million and 10 years in prison to $5 million and 20 years in prison. The maximum jail time for mail fraud is increased from 5 to 20 years. Similarly, the maximum jail time for violating the reporting and disclosure portions of the Employee Retirement Income Security Act of 1974 is increased from 1 to 10 years.

The act greatly expands the scope of laws relating to obstruction of justice. Under SOX, any acts of obstruction that are merely done in *contemplation of a future investigation* may subject the perpetrator to imprisonment for up to 20 years. (Prior to SOX, obstruction of justice was limited to ongoing investigations.) Under SOX, acts of obstruction include knowingly altering, destroying, or falsifying documents with the intent to impede, obstruct, or influence any federal investigation or bankruptcy proceeding. It is also illegal to attempt to improperly influence or impede an audit firm in the course of its duties.

Special provisions in the act provide whistleblower protection to employees who disclose private employer information in certain judicial proceedings involving claims of fraud against the company. Whistleblowers may collect attorneys' fees and damages from the company.

Restrictions on Nonaudit Services SOX severely restricts the nonaudit services that auditors can provide to their clients. Barred services include (1) bookkeeping or other services related to the accounting records or financial statements of the audit client, (2) financial information systems design and implementation, (3) appraisal or valuation services, fairness opinions, or contribution-in-kind reports, (4) actuarial services, (5) internal audit outsourcing services, (6) management functions or human resources, (7) broker or dealer, investment adviser, or investment banking services, (8) legal services and expert services unrelated to the audit, and (9) any other service that the board determines, by regulation, is impermissible.

Other nonaudit services are permissible with prior approval of the company's audit committee. Such prior approval is not required if the nonaudit services constitute less than 5% of the audit fees.

Role of the Audit Committee SOX legislates the importance of the audit committee. The company must maintain a properly funded audit committee (as part of the Board of Directors) that is composed of independent members who do not receive any compensation from the company (or its subsidiaries) for work other than service on the Board of Directors.

The auditor is required to report all audit-relevant information to this committee, and the audit committee has sole responsibility for selecting, hiring, and overseeing the auditor.

Conflicts of Interest The chief executive officer (CEO), controller, chief financial officer (CFO), chief accounting officer, or any other person in an equivalent position cannot have been employed by the company's audit firm during the 1-year period preceding the audit.

Corporate Responsibility for Financial Reports The CEO and CFO must prepare a statement to accompany the audit report to certify the "appropriateness of the financial statements and disclosures contained in the periodic report and that those financial statements and disclosures fairly present, in all material respects, the operations and financial condition of the issuer." An intentionally false certification may result in penalties as large as a $5 million fine and 20 years in prison.

Insider Trades During Pension Fund Blackout Periods Prohibited SOX prohibits the purchase or sale of stock by officers and directors and other insiders during blackout periods. Such blackout periods typically exist in pension plans, for example, at times when employees are not permitted to sell their shares in the company.

Prohibition on Personal Loans to Executives and Directors Companies are barred from lending money to directors or executive officers.

Code of Ethics Companies are required to disclose whether they have adopted a code of ethics for senior financial officers, and they must also disclose the contents of the code.

Management Assessment of Internal Controls Section 404 of SOX requires the annual report to contain an internal control report that (1) states the responsibility of management for establishing and maintaining an adequate internal control structure and procedures for financial reporting and (2) contains an assessment, as of the end of the company's fiscal year, of the effectiveness of the internal control structure and procedures of the company for financial reporting.

Compliance with Sox Section 404

SOX does not prescribe guidelines or safe harbor rules that a company can follow in order to be sure that it complies with Section 404 (Management Assessment of Internal Controls). Therefore, managers must look to various authoritative sources for guidance. Such guidance typically comes from information technology and security governance guidance and standards such as the following:

- **COSO Reports.** The most fundamental of these reports is "Internal Control—Integrated Framework." This is one of the oldest and most authoritative and fundamental documents setting forth a comprehensive framework for internal control processes. This document sets forth internal control as the five interrelated components that are used to describe internal control in this chapter: control environment, risk assessment, control activities, information and communication, and monitoring.
- Other important COSO reports include ERM—Integrated Framework, Internal Control over Financial Reporting—Guidance for Smaller Public Companies, and Guidance on Monitoring Internal Control Systems. The COSO reports are not detailed security standards but rather conceptual and practical frameworks that are helpful in developing internal control processes.
- **COBIT.** "Control Objectives for Information and related Technology" (**COBIT**) is published by the IT Governance Institute (ITGI™, www.itgi.org). COBIT is an international standard for best practices in IT management. The standard sets forth 34 high-level objectives categorized into four general "domains" that include Planning and Organization, Acquisition and Implementation, Delivery and Support, and Monitoring. The high-level objectives are broken down into 318 detailed control objectives. ITGI™ also publishes IT Control Objectives for Sarbanes–Oxley, which provides specific guidance relating to Sarbanes–Oxley compliance.
- **ISO 27002.** A standard published by the International Organization for Standardization (ISO, www.iso.org) and by the International Electrotechnical Commission. ISO 27002 is a widely accepted international standard for best practices in information security. The standard is organized into 11 general topics, 132 general security controls, and over 5,000 detailed security controls. As is with other ISO standards, company certification against the standard is available by independent certifying authorities.

  ISO 27002 is part of the ISO 27000 series of security-related standards. ISO also publishes ISO 15408, a standard for information security that is used for IT security evaluations. ISO 27002 is meant to be used in conjunction with ISO 27001, a related standard that sets forth best practices relating to the management of information security systems.
- **The U.S. Federal Sentencing Guidelines.** The U.S. Sentencing Commission (USSC, http://www.ussc.gov/) sets forth guidelines for sentencing individuals and organizations in relation to convictions of federal criminal statutes. These guidelines include rules for determining criminal sentences for organizations convicted of violating the criminal provisions of SOX. In general, the guidelines set forth standards that, when complied with, help to mitigate the punishment that organizations receive when convicted of criminal conduct. Specifically, Section 8B2.1 sets forth minimal criteria that organizations must meet in order to receive some leniency. These criteria involve the organization having systems in place to detect and prevent criminal activity; an ethics compliance program; adequate training, auditing, and monitoring; and due diligence in quickly dealing with and reporting problems.

CASE IN POINT

Many companies have complained about the costs of complying with SOX. Testing controls often constitutes the largest percentage of costs associated with compliance. Implementing strategies to automate the testing of controls often results in significant reductions in compliance costs.

The Impact of the Business Environment on Internal Control

Another important consideration is that an entity's internal control process will vary depending on the context of its size; organizational structure; ownership characteristics; methods of transmitting, processing, maintaining, and assessing information; legal and regulatory requirements; and the diversity and complexity of its operations.

For example, in small organizations, there may not be a large enough number of employees to achieve the same degree of separation of duties that might be expected in a large company. This situation can often be dealt with by involving the owner in various aspects of transactions, such as signing checks, approving invoices, and record keeping. Furthermore, procedure manuals, policy manuals, organization charts, and many other types of documentation, as well as complex policies and procedures, may prove infeasible for the small organization.

Control Environment

An organization's control environment, the first of the five components of internal control process, is the foundation of all other components of the control system. The **control environment** is the collective effect of various factors on establishing, enhancing, or mitigating the effectiveness of specific policies and procedures. In other words, the control environment sets the overall tone of the organization and influences the control consciousness of the employees.

Factors included in the control environment are as follows:

- Integrity and ethical values
- Commitment to competence
- Management philosophy and operating style
- Organizational structure
- Attention and direction provided by the Board of Directors and its committees
- Manner of assigning authority and responsibility
- Human resource policies and procedures

INTEGRITY AND ETHICAL VALUES   Potential ethical violations present a significant loss exposure for the corporation (Figure 4.4). Such exposures include the possibility of large fines or criminal prosecution against both the company and its executives. For example, the brokerage firm E. F. Hutton was fined $12 million when it pleaded guilty to allegations relating to wire and

FIGURE 4.4

Corporate Ethics Breaches

Corporate Ethics Breaches
Marketing executives of Anheuser-Busch were accused of taking kickbacks from a supplier, Hanely Wordwide, Inc. It was alleged that this supplier contributed $13,500 toward the purchase of a Porsche automobile by Anheuser-Busch's director of promotions.
Chrysler Corporation was charged in a 16-count indictment. The allegations stated executives of the company drove Chrysler automobiles with their odometers disconnected. The automobiles were then allegedly sold as new.
General Dynamics, a large defense contractor, was suspended from doing business for defrauding the Pentagon. Investigators alleged that General Dynamics was guilty of fraudulently billing the government.
General Electric and Rockwell were found guilty of fraudulently billing the federal government.
E. F. Hutton & Company pleaded guilty to 2,000 counts of mail and wire fraud.

mail fraud. In another case, Film Recovery Systems, which used cyanide to extract silver from film, was accused of knowingly creating a dangerous work environment that led to the death of an employee. Three of the company's executives were charged and convicted of murder. They were subsequently sentenced to 25 years in prison. In another case, Manville Corporation was driven into bankruptcy by problems relating to health hazards associated with asbestos, its primary product. Court testimony indicated that for years the company knew and intentionally overlooked severe damage to the health of company employees by asbestos.

Ethics and Corporate Culture Many companies have adopted ethics codes of conduct that specify guidelines for conducting business in an ethical manner. Similarly, many professional organizations, such as the American Institute of Certified Public Accountants, have adopted codes of conduct. The code of conduct is often written in legal-style language that focuses on laws that might be broken. Accordingly, such codes have been criticized sometimes as being devoid of general ethical values such as "diligently looking out for the safety of employees" or "always telling the truth when dealing with customers."

Many have argued that every corporation has its own corporate culture and that it is this corporate culture that either promotes or hinders ethical behavior. The corporate culture pertains to the general beliefs, practices, and attitudes of employees. It does not matter how good a code of conduct is if there are significant problems in the corporate culture. For example, some companies have an excessively inward focus. A company that focuses too much internally and not enough on the outside world is more likely to get into trouble. Examples of excessive internal focus would include overemphasis on sales quotas, making unreasonable deadlines, pleasing the boss, and so on. For example, if construction employees were told to either complete a building by a certain date or be fired, they might be tempted to cut corners and compromise safety. An excessive short-run focus also may be a problem. A company that focuses too much on the short run might be more inclined not to worry about the long-term consequences of its actions. In the case of Manville Company, the long-run health hazards of asbestos were overlooked to the point that the company was destroyed. Morale can be a problem. Unhappy employees can be dangerous. One such case involved a disgruntled employee of a company that produced an accounting software package. The employee made changes to the software that scrambled up the records of those companies who used the accounting system. Some companies have an excessively autocratic organizational structure. Highly autocratic managers are relatively unlikely to accept criticism, and the employees of such managers may fear pointing out ethics problems.

Producing a corporate culture supportive of ethical behavior can be difficult and certainly cannot be accomplished without education, training, and compliance. Some companies use seminars to educate and train their employees. Compliance is achieved by giving ethics a formal place in the organization chart. Each division should have an ethics director. The ethics director should be readily available to employees for consultations. All employees should be trained in how and when to contact the ethics director. Employees should be advised of penalties for ethics violations. The ethics director should be contacted whenever an employee observes an ethics violation or is ordered to commit an ethics violation, or whenever an employee needs advice on any problem involving ethics. Employees should be able to report problems anonymously. Some companies have "squeal systems" that reward employees for reporting ethical violations.

⬤ CASE IN POINT

Gannett Co., an international news and information company, provides all employees a toll-free voice mail number for reporting suspected ethics violations. Employees may also report by e-mail or postal mail to the company's outside law firm.

For any ethics program to work, the company should have a cultural audit of its culture and ethical behavior. Ethical problems can exist in many areas. Some of the areas that must be dealt with relate to safety, equal opportunity employment, sexual harassment, product and service quality, privacy, honesty in business dealings, conflicts of interest, and respect for intellectual property.

Ethical Considerations in Job Design Consider the following job description:

> The person who accepts the treasurer's position shall be entirely responsible for the company's securities transactions. The position entails keeping the supporting records, exclusive control over the safe deposit box, and complete discretion over buying and selling of securities.

Would you accept this job?

Many readers will recognize several violations of conventional internal control principles in the preceding job description. Is this job offering an invitation to fraud? That is, does the lack of conventional controls over the treasurer's duties constitute the equivalent of an invitation to steal? What is an organization's responsibility for the integrity of its employees?

These questions raise issues that should be considered in the design of business systems. The need for an adequate system of internal control can be viewed ethically as well as from the view of efficient management. The following quotation is representative of this often expressed view:

> I can recall a sizable industrial concern which was headed by a president who was perhaps more interested in his avocation of preaching than in running his business. Attempts to improve internal control in his corporation were constantly rebuffed because he believed that people were fundamentally honest, that his employees could be trusted, and therefore that there was no need for any system of checks and balances. The accountant became increasingly concerned with the company's exposure of its assets to possible defalcation. Finally, he went to the company president and said, "As a good Christian, you have a moral obligation to remove temptation from your employees!" This ethical appeal succeeded where an appeal to good business judgment alone failed, and the company's system of internal control was improved after all.[1]

Organizations should have sufficient controls to deter fraudulent actions, if only through reducing temptation by the threat of being caught. On the other hand, overly rigid controls hamper the actions and decisions of individuals, artificially limiting an employee's response to the variety of her or his task. Accountability and pressures for performance may boomerang. Rigid control systems may create or stimulate the types of actions that the controls were designed to prevent.

COMMITMENT TO COMPETENCE   Competence in employees is essential to the proper functioning of any process of internal control. In the final analysis, it is the quality and competence of the employees that ensure the ability to carry out the control process. No control process can function adequately without competent employees.

MANAGEMENT PHILOSOPHY AND OPERATING STYLE   Effective control in an organization begins with and ultimately rests with management philosophy. If management believes that controls are important, then it will see to it that effective control policies and procedures are implemented.

This control-conscious attitude will be communicated to subordinates through management's operating style. If, on the other hand, management pays only "lip service" to the

---

[1]"Business Ethics." *Review*. New York: Price Waterhouse, 1977.

need for controls, it is very likely that subordinates will sense management's true attitude and control objectives will not be achieved.

ORGANIZATIONAL STRUCTURE   An organization's structure is defined by the patterns of authority and responsibility that exist within the organization. The formal organization structure is often denoted by an organization chart, such as Figure 4.5. As shown, the billing function is directly responsible to the accounting manager. At the next higher level in the chart, the accounting manager is responsible to the controller. The controller is, in turn, responsible to the president.

An organization chart indicates the formal communication patterns within an organization. In Figure 4.5, for example, one would not normally expect the billing function to communicate the results of its operations to the vice-president of production. As indicated in the chart, billing is not directly responsible to the vice-president of production. An informal organization structure exists when regular communication patterns do not follow the lines indicated by the formal organization structure.

FUNCTIONS OF THE BOARD OF DIRECTORS AND ITS COMMITTEES   An organization's Board of Directors is the interface between the stockholders who own the organization and the organization's operating management. Stockholders exercise control over management through the functions of the Board of Directors and its committees. If the Board consists entirely of members of management, or if the Board meets infrequently, then stockholder control over operating management is likely to be weak or nonexistent.

Audit Committee   Typically, a Board of Directors delegates specific functions to various operating committees. All public companies whose stock is traded on the New York Stock Exchange are required to have an audit committee composed of outside directors. Many other companies also have audit committees.

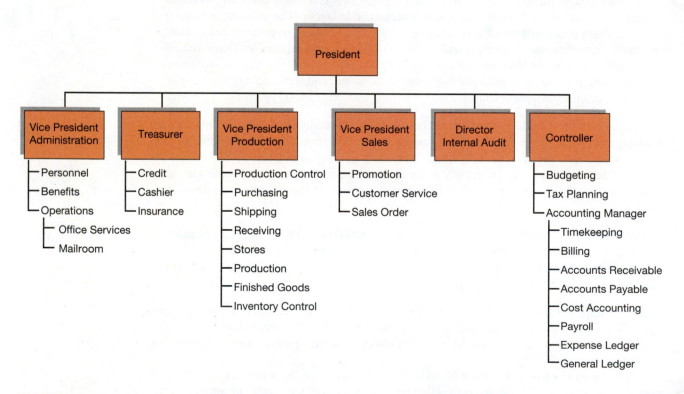

FIGURE 4.5

Organization Chart

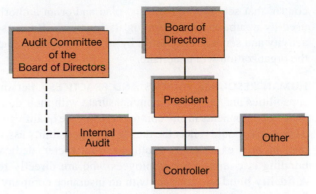

FIGURE 4.6
Audit Committee

The audit committee should be independent of an organization's management, composed primarily of outside members of the Board of Directors (Figure 4.6). The audit committee is usually charged with overall responsibility for the organization's financial reports, including compliance with existing laws and regulations. The audit committee nominates public accountants, discusses the scope and nature of audits with public accountants, and reviews and evaluates reports prepared by the organization's public accountants. Audit committees should be charged with reviewing management's reaction to public accountants' reports on the organization's internal control process.

To be effective, the audit committee must maintain communication with an organization's internal audit function as well as with the organization's external auditors (i.e., public accountants). As shown in Figure 4.6, an internal audit should report to the audit committee of the Board of Directors to maintain independence of internal auditing from other functions.

MANNER OF ASSIGNING AUTHORITY AND RESPONSIBILITY The methods of assigning authority and responsibility within an organization are indicative of management's philosophy and operating style. If only verbal or informal methods exist, control is likely to be weak or nonexistent.

A formal organization chart, a written document, is often used to indicate the overall assignment of authority and responsibility in an organization. The organization chart is often accompanied by formal job descriptions and statements of work assignments. Written memoranda, policy manuals, and procedure manuals are other common means used to formally assign authority and responsibility within an organization.

Budgeting Budgeting is the process of preparing budgets. Budgeting is a major management activity. Budgets are generally set for the entire organization as well as for each subunit. The budget for the entire organization is usually called the *master budget*. The master budget is often presented as a set of pro forma financial statements. Pro forma financial statements are forecasted statements—such as a balance sheet and income statement—that represent the predicted financial results of management's plan of operation for the coming budget period. The master budget is the accumulated result of all the detailed budgets that are prepared for the organizational subunits. Detailed operating budgets are prepared for subunits to evidence management's plan concerning operation of each subunit and to serve as the device by which management's plans are communicated to subunits. In addition to operating budgets, other types of budgets may be prepared as necessary to help management plan and control the activities of the firm. A common example is the capital expenditure budget, which is used to plan capital expenditures. Budgets are generally prepared on both a monthly and a yearly basis; frequently, a 5-year or 10-year long-term budget is prepared as well.

Budgeting data are used to plan and control the activities within a firm. Control is established by comparing the results of activity to the budget for each activity. A budget is a control that sets forth a financial plan and/or an authorized amount of resources that may be used by a subunit in performing its functions. Budgets are set in advance of organizational activity and serve as the control by which management authorizes the transactional activity that the organization will undertake.

HUMAN RESOURCE POLICIES AND PRACTICES   Personnel should be competent and have capabilities and/or training commensurate with their duties. In the final analysis, personnel are the key components in any control system. The qualifications established for each job position in a company should reflect the degree of responsibility associated with the position. Qualifications may include experience, intelligence, character, dedication, and leadership ability. Fidelity bonding is common for employees who are directly responsible for the custody of assets. A **fidelity bond** is a contract with an insurance company that provides a financial guarantee of the honesty of the individual who is named in the bond contract. The insurance company will usually investigate the background of a person who is to be bonded. Thus, fidelity bonding helps ensure that an organization is hiring reliable personnel.

Segregation of Duties Responsibility for specific tasks in an organization should be clearly designated by manuals, job descriptions, or other documentation. Effective **segregation of duties** depends to a considerable extent on the precise and detailed planning of all procedures and the careful assignment of functions to various people in the organization. The details of the procedures should be set forth in memoranda that also show explicit assignment of duties to individual departments or employees. Written procedures, instructions, and assignments of duties will prevent duplication of work, overlapping of functions, omission of important functions, misunderstandings, and other situations that might weaken the internal accounting controls. Such notes typically form the basis for a formal manual on procedures and policy.

Supervision   **Supervision** is the direct monitoring of personnel performance by an employee who is so charged. In addition to properly selecting and adequately training employees, proper supervision is necessary to ensure that duties are being carried out as assigned. Supervision becomes very important in a small firm or in other situations where segregation of duties is not possible.

Job Rotation and Forced Vacations   Job rotation and forced vacations allow employees to check or verify the operations of other employees by performing their duties for a period of time. Several advantages may be gained by these techniques.

Irregularities that may have been committed by an employee may be disclosed while the employee is on vacation and her or his duties are assumed by another employee. Job rotation allows more than one employee to become familiar with certain duties and procedures so that the replacement of employees in cases of emergency is less difficult. Job rotation frequently serves as a general check on the efficiency of the employee on vacation or who has been rotated to another job. Finally, job rotation broadens the training of the personnel in general.

 CASE IN POINT

A breakdown in the segregation of duties can occur even in large companies. An internal investigation in NEC, a multinational IT company, discovered that 10 employees were engaged in a scheme involving over $4 million in kickbacks from outside contractors. The fraud went undetected for a very long time because the same employees who made the orders also confirmed and validated them.

Dual Control   Closely related to direct supervision is the concept of **dual control**—the assignment of two individuals to perform the same work task in unison. The intent of dual control is not work reduction but work redundancy. Each individual is assumed to check the work of the other constantly. Responsibility for the custody of high-valued securities, for example, is frequently delegated to two or more people working in unison. Multiple control involves three or more people in unison. Dual or multiple control differs from supervision in that a supervisor is expected to supervise several people or operations simultaneously and, therefore, may effectively supervise a particular operation or employee less than 100% of the time. Dual control is essentially "dedicated" supervision; that is, one employee constantly checks the work of another, and vice versa.

Risk Assessment

Risk assessment, the second of the five components of internal control, is the process of identifying, analyzing, and managing risks that affect the company's objectives. Probably the most critical step in risk assessment is identifying the changing internal and external conditions and the related actions that may be necessary. Examples of risks relevant to the financial reporting process include changes in the organization's operating environment, changes in personnel, changes in the information system, new technology, major industry changes, new product lines, and new rules, laws, or accounting pronouncements.

Control Activities

Control activities, comprising the third component of internal control, are the policies and procedures established to help ensure that management directives are carried out. There are many potential control activities that may be used by organizations. These include accounting controls designed to provide reasonable assurance that the following specific control objectives are met for every significant application system within an organization:

- The plan of organization includes segregation of duties to reduce opportunities to allow any person to be in a position to both perpetrate and conceal errors or irregularities in the normal course of his or her duties.
- Procedures include the design and use of adequate documents and records to help ensure the proper recording of transactions and events.
- Access to assets is permitted only in accordance with management's authorization.
- Independent checks and reviews are made on the accountability of assets and performance.
- Information processing controls are applied to check the proper authorization, accuracy, and completeness of individual transactions.

Each of these specific control objectives is discussed in turn.

SEGREGATION OF DUTIES   Segregation of duties is necessary to reduce opportunities to allow any person to be in a position to both perpetrate and conceal errors or irregularities in the normal course of his or her duties. Segregation of duties is implemented by assigning to different people the responsibilities of authorizing transactions, recording transactions, and maintaining custody of assets. To achieve segregation of duties, the responsibilities of authorizing transactions, recording transactions, and maintaining custody of assets should be performed by independent functions.

Segregation of Authorization from Recording of Transactions   Segregation of authorization of transactions from recording of transactions reduces opportunities for errors and irregularities by establishing independent accountability for authorization functions. If each function in an organization kept its own records, there would be no accountability. There would be no basis for an independent reconciliation and analysis of a function's activities because there would be no assurances that all transactions have been recorded. In order to ensure unbiased information, record-keeping functions are usually centralized in a separate function headed by the controller.

For example, in a sales order application, the sales manager authorizes credit sales. A copy of the sales order form is sent to the warehouse to authorize the shipment of goods. If notice of the shipment is subsequently sent only to the sales manager, then the sales manager is accountable for his or her own performance. The sales manager is thus in a position to perpetrate errors and irregularities in the normal course of his or her duties. Perhaps he or she has authorized a shipment to a relative or friend. When notice of the shipment is received, the sales manager simply may destroy it or ignore it rather than forward it to billing for collection.

Segregation of Authorization from Custody of Assets Segregation of authorization of transactions from custody of assets reduces opportunities for errors and irregularities by establishing independent accountability for the use (custody) of assets. Authorization of activities is communicated to those who have custody of assets and simultaneously communicated to the record-keeping function (i.e., accounting). Those charged with the custody of assets subsequently communicate the results of activity (i.e., transactions) to the record-keeping function. Reconciliation of these data with the authorizations that were received from an independent function provides accountability for both the authorization and the subsequent use of assets.

For example, in a sales order application, the sales manager authorizes credit sales. A copy of the sales order form is sent to the warehouse to authorize the shipment of goods. Another copy of the sales order form is sent to accounting. Notice of the shipment is subsequently sent to accounting. Reconciliation of shipment data with the authorizations that were received from an independent function provides accountability for both the authorization and the subsequent use of assets. Notice of shipment without a matching authorization indicates unauthorized shipments. Notice of authorization without subsequent shipment indicates ineffectiveness or inefficiency in completing sales transactions.

Segregation of Recording Transactions from Custody of Assets Segregation of recording transactions from custody of assets reduces opportunities for errors and irregularities by establishing independent accountability for the use of assets. Authorization of activities is communicated to those who have custody of assets and simultaneously communicated to the record-keeping function (i.e., accounting). Those charged with the custody of assets subsequently communicate the results of activity (i.e., transactions) to the record-keeping function. Reconciliation of these data with the authorizations that were received from an independent function provides accountability for both the authorization and the subsequent use of assets.

If there is no segregation of duties between recording transactions from custody of assets, then those charged with the custody of assets are accountable for their own performance. There would be no basis for an independent reconciliation and analysis of a function's activities because there would be no assurances that all transactions have been recorded. The persons charged with the custody of assets are in a position to perpetrate errors and irregularities in the normal course of their duties by omitting records or falsifying entries into the records. In the preceding sales example, goods may be shipped by those who have custody of assets without authorization and without recording the shipment because there is no independent accountability for shipments.

ADEQUATE DOCUMENTS AND RECORDS   Procedures should include the design and use of adequate documents and records to help ensure the proper recording of transactions and events. Documents and records are the physical media used to store information. They may take many different forms, ranging from common paper documents such as sales orders and purchase orders to magnetic and optical storage media such as magnetic tape and optical disk.

Certain control practices are relevant to any type of documents and records. Items should be prenumbered in sequential order to facilitate accountability. Items should be easy to use and clearly understood by those who use them. Forms should provide specific space for the indication of necessary authorizations and approvals.

RESTRICTED ACCESS TO ASSETS   Access to assets should be permitted only in accordance with management's authorization. This requires adequate physical controls and safeguards over access to and use of assets and records, such as secured facilities and authorization for access to computer programs and data files.

It is well documented that physical theft and embezzlement are substantial threats to the solvency of business organizations. Physical controls are directed at reducing the opportunities for theft and embezzlement. Safeguarding of assets such as cash, securities, and inventory is accomplished by close supervision, physical protection devices, and segregation of duties. Common examples of physical controls include the following:

- Cash registers and lock boxes
- Locks, vaults, and limited-access areas
- Security forces
- Closed-circuit TV monitors
- Alarm systems

No physical control or safeguard in and of itself can protect assets; it is the procedures surrounding the use of physical controls that dictate whether or not the controls are effective. For example, every lock has a key; therefore, a lock is only as effective as is access to the key. TV monitors are effective only if they are being watched constantly or, alternatively, if personnel believe they are being watched. Limited-access areas are effective only if access is truly limited. The effectiveness of physical controls depends largely on the measures surrounding their use, not on the mere existence of the devices.

INDEPENDENT ACCOUNTABILITY CHECKS AND REVIEWS OF PERFORMANCE   The recorded accountability for assets should be compared with the existing assets at reasonable intervals and appropriate action taken with respect to any difference. This reconciliation function should be performed by someone who is independent of authorization, record keeping, and custody of the assets in question. Examples of independent checks on performance and proper valuation of recorded amounts include clerical checks, reconciliations, comparison of assets with recorded accountability, computer-programmed controls, management review of reports that summarize the detail of account balances (e.g., an aged trial balance of accounts receivable), and user review of computer-generated reports.

Budgets and general performance reviews are also an important means for assessing performance. These reviews are accomplished by comparing actual results with budgets, forecasts, standards, and prior-period performance.

INFORMATION PROCESSING CONTROLS   Information processing controls ensure the proper authorization, accuracy, and completeness of individual transactions.

Authorization limits the initiation of a transaction or performance of an activity to selected individuals. Authorization prevents unauthorized transactions and unauthorized activities. Proper authorization of transactions and activities is necessary if management is to obtain reasonable assurance that its control objectives are achieved.

Management's authorization may be general or specific in nature. Specific authorization pertains to individual transactions. Setting automatic reorder points for inventory items is an example of general authorization because no specific transaction is involved. Approval of a construction budget for a (specific) warehouse is an example of specific authorization. Establishment of general requirements to be met in determining customers' credit limits is an example of general authorization because no specific transaction (i.e., customer) is involved. Establishment of sales prices for products to be sold to any customer is another example of general authorization.

Approval is the acceptance of a transaction for processing after it is initiated. Approval comes after authorization and is used to detect unauthorized transactions and unauthorized activities. Approval is necessary to ensure that employees are operating within the realm of their authority.

Completeness and accuracy ensure the integrity of the data and information in the accounting system. Both completeness and accuracy are necessary to ensure a system whose information can be relied on. A wide range of transaction controls enhances completeness and reliability. Transaction controls are discussed later in a separate section.

Information and Communication

Information and communication comprise the fourth component of internal control. *Information* refers to the organization's **accounting system,** which consists of the methods and records established to identify, assemble, analyze, classify, record, and report the organization's transactions and to maintain accountability for the related assets and liabilities. The accounting system of an organization may be simple, or it may be complex. Many organizations have systems that are able to process huge numbers of various types of transactions. Information systems are designed and installed not only to produce the ledger balances from which financial statements are prepared but also to produce management control and operational information. Thus accounting systems and operational control are closely related in an organization.

DOCUMENTATION OF THE ACCOUNTING SYSTEM
Documentation of the accounting system is essential. Accounting procedures should be set forth in accounting procedure manuals so that policies and instructions may be known explicitly and applied uniformly. Well-designed forms should be used to report transactions. Subsidiary ledgers should be used to accumulate detailed information that is summarized in the general ledger. A chart of accounts containing detailed descriptions of the meanings and uses of accounts in the general ledger should be maintained and revised as necessary. A chart of accounts will aid in the consistent application of accounting policies, ensure proper recording of transactions, and facilitate the preparation of financial statements. Control accounts should be used extensively because they are a proof of accuracy between the account balances of duly segregated employees in a double-entry system of accounting.

DOUBLE-ENTRY SYSTEM OF ACCOUNTING
An accounting system should contain features that readily confirm or question the reliability of recorded data. Double-entry systems of accounting should not be underestimated as a device that will produce a balanced set of records. To conceal an irregularity under a double-entry system, it is necessary to omit from the accounts both sides of the transaction or to record entries offsetting the amount of the irregularity. Errors can be made under a double-entry system; however, the system alone will not prove omission, incorrect entry, or dishonesty.

Audit Trail The term *audit trail* originates with the concept of an external auditor who is asked to express an opinion on the financial statements of an organization. An **audit trail** exists if a financial total that appears in a general ledger account can be supported by evidence concerning all the individual transactions that comprise that total and vice versa. If an audit trail exists, the auditor can be confident that the accounting information system and related financial statements are very reliable—that is, the system and its outputs are accurate. If an audit trail does not exist, then the reliability of the accounting information system must be suspect.

 CASE IN POINT

The audit trail is also important in money laundering. The primary goal of the money launder is to hide or eliminate any audit trail that connects money in a legitimate financial institution to its original illegal source.

The audit trail concept is basic to the design and audit of an accounting information system and is relevant to internal auditors, management, systems analysts, and other parties involved in the operation of an accounting information system. An audit trail consists of the documentary evidence of the various control techniques that a transaction was subject to during its processing. Each transaction should be subjected to a set of control techniques that in total provides a sufficient degree of assurance that the transaction was processed accurately and reliably. The nature of the documentary evidence that comprises the audit trail will depend on the technology of the system and also on the design of the system. Audit trails do not have an independent existence—they are a consideration that must be included in the design of an accounting information system. That is particularly true in computer-based systems.

COMMUNICATION   Communication relates to providing a clear understanding regarding all policies and procedures relating to controls. Good communication requires effective oral communication, adequate procedure manuals, policy manuals, and other types of documentation.

Effective communication also requires an adequate upstream flow of information in the organization. Such information is used for performance reviews, exception reports, and so on.

Monitoring

Monitoring, the fifth component of internal control, involves the ongoing process of assessing the quality of internal controls over time and taking corrective actions when necessary to ensure the controls remain effective. The quality of controls might be adversely affected in various ways, including a lack of compliance, changing conditions, or even misunderstandings.

Monitoring is accomplished through ongoing activities, separate evaluations, or some combination of the two. Ongoing activities would include management supervisory activities and other actions that personnel might take to ensure an ongoing effective internal control process.

An internal audit function is common in large organizations to monitor and evaluate controls on an ongoing basis. The expanded span of control and the growth in the volume of transactions associated with large organizations were factors in the emergence of the internal audit function. The increased reliance on accounting data that is necessary in management of a large organization, coupled with the increased possibilities of defalcations and improperly maintained accounting records in a large organization, has created the need for continuous auditing. The objective of the internal audit function is to serve management by furnishing management with the results of analysis and appraisals of such activities and systems as

- The organization's information systems
- The organization's internal control structure
- The extent of compliance to operating policies, procedures, and plans
- The quality of performance by company personnel

As indicated, the scope of auditing activity undertaken by a modern internal audit function is broader than just the financial activities of the organization. The terms **management audit** and **operational audit** describe internal audit services to management that extend beyond the financial activities of the organization. The existence of an effective internal audit function does not substitute for the external auditor, although internal audit may be of assistance to the external auditor in arranging and accumulating audit evidence.

The internal audit function has no less of a need for independence than the external auditor, but the nature of independence is different. The external auditor must be independent of the organization, for his or her opinion is given to third parties (e.g., banks, stockholders). The internal auditor cannot be independent of the organization, but he or she must be independent from management of the activities being reviewed. This can be accomplished by having the internal audit function report to the organization's audit committee.

External auditors may participate in monitoring controls. For example, it is common practice for external auditors to provide lists of specific recommendations for management to improve internal control.

A MODEL FOR MONITORING   A report from COSO titled "Guidance on Monitoring Internal Control Systems" presents a three-phase model for monitoring:

1. **Establish foundation for monitoring**—The foundation is established by building the right tone from the top of the organization, setting in place an organization structure in which top management and the Board of Directors assume responsibility for monitoring, clarifying roles of competent and objective evaluators, and developing a baseline understanding of internal control effectiveness.
2. **Design and execute monitoring procedures that are based on risk**—The procedures are developed by prioritizing risks; by selecting meaningful, important controls commensurate with the identified risks; and by identifying direct and indirect relevant information that can be used to persuasively indicate whether the controls are effective as planned. The performance of the controls is then assessed using ongoing monitoring and separate evaluations. Separate evaluations tend to focus on issues that may be overlooked by the ongoing evaluations. If a given separate evaluation must be repeated frequently, it probably needs to be included as part of the ongoing monitoring.
3. **Assess and report the results**—Control problems should be reported to those responsible. The focus should be on what went wrong, the consequences of the problem, what role compensating controls may have played, and recommendations for changes in the related management and control processes.

Transaction Processing Controls

Transaction processing controls are procedures designed to ensure that elements of an organization's internal control process are implemented in the specific applications systems contained within each of an organization's transaction cycles. Transaction processing controls consist of general controls and application controls. **General controls** affect all transaction processing. **Application controls** are specific to individual applications.

General Controls

General controls concern the overall environment of transaction processing. General controls comprise the following:

- The plan of data processing organization
- General operating procedures
- Equipment control features
- Equipment and data-access controls

General controls are not a substitute for application controls. It is possible to have relatively strong general controls with relatively weak or nonexistent application controls. General controls thus may be seen as necessary but not sufficient for adequate control of transaction processing.

A plan of organization for data processing includes provision for segregation of duties within data processing and the organizational segregation of data processing from other operations. General operating procedures include written manuals and other documentation that specify procedures to be followed. Equipment control features are those that are installed in computers to identify incorrect data handling or erroneous operation of the equipment. Equipment and data-access controls involve procedures related to physical access to the computer system and data. There should be adequate procedures to protect equipment and data files from damage or theft.

THE PLAN OF DATA PROCESSING ORGANIZATION AND OPERATION

Segregation of Duties Responsibility for authorization, custody, and record keeping for handling and processing of transactions are separated.

> **Example:** The computer librarian maintains a depository of computer programs and documentation but does not have access to or authority to operate the computer processing equipment.

Segregation of Duties in Data Processing Computer data processing functions should be centralized. Computer data processing should have neither custody nor authority over any assets other than the data processing assets.

> **Example:** Departments that are responsible for the custody of inventories should not report to the vice-president of computer data processing.

It is also desirable to segregate the following personnel functions associated with computer processing within the data processing department.

- *Systems analysts.* Systems analysts are responsible for development of the general design of computer system applications. Systems analysts work with users to define their specific information requirements.
- *Programmers.* Computer programmers develop the programs that produce computer output. They design and code newly developed computer programs based on specifications provided by systems analysts.
- *Computer operators.* Computer operators operate the mainframe computer equipment. They should not have access to detailed program listings in order to maintain a segregation of functions between programming and operations.
- *Librarian.* The librarian function maintains a depository of computer programs and documentation. This function is responsible for the custody of information assets.
- *Data control clerks.* Data control clerks establish control over jobs and input data for processing. This includes consideration of the quality of input, the completeness of processing, and the reasonableness of output.

GENERAL OPERATING PROCEDURES

Definition of Responsibilities: Descriptions of tasks for each job function within a transaction processing system. Beginning and termination points for each job function should be clearly indicated, as should the relationship of job functions to each other.

Example: The computer operator has restricted access to programs and data files.

Reliability of Personnel: Personnel performing the processing may be relied on to function in a consistent manner.

Example: The supervisor of computer operations has a good attendance record and a good performance record.

Training of Personnel: Personnel are provided explicit instructions and tested on their under-standing before being assigned new duties.

Example: All new programmers attend a 5-day training seminar before beginning duties.

Competence of Personnel: Persons assigned to processing or supervisory roles in transaction processing systems have the technical knowledge necessary to perform their functions.

Example: The director of data processing is an MBA.

Rotation of Duties: Jobs assigned to people are rotated periodically at irregularly scheduled times, if possible, for key processing functions.

Example: Responsibility for the destruction of sensitive data is rotated among clerical personnel.

(Continued)

Forms Design: Forms are constructed to be self-explanatory, understandable, and concise and to gather all necessary information with a minimum of effort.

Example: The form to authorize a purchase has clear and concise instructions for each field in which data are to be entered.

Prenumbered Forms: Sequential numbers on individual forms are printed in advance to allow subsequent detection of loss or misplacement.

Example: Checks are prenumbered.

Preprinted Forms: Fixed elements of information are entered on forms in advance and sometimes in a format that permits direct machine processing to prevent errors in entry of repetitive data.

Example: MICR account encoding on checks and deposit tickets.

Simultaneous Preparation: The one-time recording of a transaction for all further processing, using multiple copies, as appropriate, to prevent transcription errors.

Example: A one-write system is used to prepare a receiving report form and receiving register simultaneously.

Turnaround Document: A computer-produced document that is intended for resubmission into the system.

Example: The part of a utility bill that the customer returns with payment.

Documentation: Written records for the purpose of providing communication.

Example: Standard journal entries communicate the accounting data to be supplied by various operating departments.

Labeling: The identification of transactions, files, or other items for control purposes.

Example: All computer files have an external label.

EQUIPMENT CONTROL FEATURES

Backup and Recovery: Backup consists of file equipment and procedures that are available if the originals are destroyed or out of service. Recovery is the ability to recreate master files using prior files and transactions.

Example: Master files and transaction files are maintained after the creation of an updated master file in case the current master file is corrupted.

Transaction Trail: The availability of a manual or machine-readable means for tracing the status and contents of an individual transaction record backward or forward and between output, processing, and source.

Example: A list of changes to online computer files is stored on magnetic tape to provide a transaction trail.

Error-Source Statistics: Accumulation of information on the type of error and origin. This is used to determine the nature of remedial efforts needed to reduce the number of errors.

Example: The data input supervisor collects and reviews statistics on input errors made by clerks.

EQUIPMENT AND DATA-ACCESS CONTROLS

Secure Custody: Information assets are provided security similar to tangible assets such as cash, negotiable securities, and the like.

Example: The general ledger master file is locked in a safe each night.

Dual Access/Dual Control: Two independent, simultaneous actions or conditions are required before processing is permitted.

Example: A safe deposit box for sensitive computer files requires two keys to open it.

Application Controls

Application controls are specific to individual applications. Application controls are categorized into input, processing, and output controls. These categories correspond to the basic steps in the data processing cycle.

INPUT CONTROLS   **Input controls** are designed to prevent or detect errors in the input stage of data processing. When computers are used for processing, the input stage involves the conversion of transaction data into a machine-readable format. Typical input controls include the following items:

Authorization: Limits the initiation of a transaction or performance of a process to selected individuals.

Example: Only the timekeeper may submit payroll hours data for processing.

Approval: The acceptance of a transaction for processing after it is initiated.

Example: An officer of the company approves the payroll before it is distributed to employees.

Formatted Input: Automatic spacing and format shifting of data fields during data input to a recording device.

Example: The computer automatically inserts commas into the numbers that are input by clerks using data terminals.

Endorsement: The marking of a form or document to direct or restrict its further processing.

Example: Checks are restrictively endorsed "Pay only to the order of ABC Company" immediately on receipt.

Cancellation: Identifies transaction documents in order to prevent their further or repeated use after they have performed their function.

Example: Marking bills as "paid" to prevent duplicate payment.

Exception Input: Processing proceeds in a predefined manner unless specific input transactions are received that indicate special processing with different values or in a different sequence.

Example: Overtime hours are input on special forms.

Passwords: The authorization to allow access to data or processing by providing a code or signal known only by authorized individuals.

Example: An automatic bank terminal requires that a user enter his or her password before processing is initiated.

Anticipation: The expectation of a given transaction or event at a particular time.

Example: Daily cash deposits are always made at 3:00 P.M.

Transmittal Document (Batch Control Ticket): The medium for communicating control totals over movement of data, particularly from source to processing point or between processing points.

Example: Daily cash deposits are accompanied by a deposit slip that indicates the total amount of the deposit.

Batch Serial Numbers (Batch Sequence): Batches of transaction documents are numbered consecutively and accounted for.

Example: Sales tickets are batched daily, numbered, and filed by date.

Control Register (Batch Control Log): A log or register indicating the disposition and control values of batches of transactions.

Example: A register is used to record the time and batch control number of express mail that is picked up by courier services.

Amount Control Total: Totals of homogeneous amounts for a group of transactions or records, usually dollars or quantities.

Example: Total net pay is an amount control total for a payroll processing application.

Document Control Total: A count of the number of individual documents.

Example: A count of the number of time cards is a document control total for a payroll application.

Line Control Count: A count of the number of lines of data on one or more documents.

Example: A count of the number of individual products sold (i.e., a line) on invoices is a line control count for a sales order application.

Hash Total: A meaningless total that is useful for control purposes only.

Example: Total department number of all paychecks processed is a meaningless total that is useful for control purposes only.

Batch Control (Batch Totals): Any type of control total or count applied to a specific number of transaction documents or to the transaction documents that arrive within a specific period of time.

Example: Total sales dollars is a batch control total for a billing application.

(Continued)

Visual Verification: The visual scanning of documents for general reasonableness and propriety.

Example: Clerks visually scan each invoice before submitting the document for further processing.

Sequence Checking: A verification of the alphanumeric sequence of the "key" field in items to be processed.

Example: Prenumbered checks are sorted in sequence for further processing.

Overflow Checks: A limit check on the capacity of a field, file, or device.

Example: The number 12345 cannot be entered into a four-digit, numeric field.

Format Check: Determination that data are entered in proper mode—numeric or alphabetic—in fields.

Example: Vendor number is checked to ensure that all characters in the field are numeric.

Completeness Check: A test that ensures that fields cannot be processed in a blank state.

Example: A voucher will not be processed if the "vendor number" field is blank.

Check Digit: A digit that is a function of the other digits within a record or number used for testing an accurate transcription.

Example: An account number contains a check digit that is validated during processing.

Reasonableness Test: Tests applied to various fields of data through comparison with other information available within the transaction or master records.

Example: A male patient should not be billed for services by the gynecology department of a hospital.

Limit Check: A test to ensure that only data within predetermined limits will be entered into and accepted by the system.

Example: A test ensures that rate per hour cannot be lower than the minimum set by law or higher than the maximum set by union contract.

Validity Check: The characters in a coded field are either matched to an acceptable set of values in a table or examined for a defined pattern of format, legitimate subcodes, or character values, using logic and arithmetic other than tables.

Example: All Social Security numbers should have nine numeric digits.

Readback: Immediate return of input information to the sender for comparison and approval.

Example: A computer echoes messages received from a data terminal back to the terminal for visual verification.

Dating: The recording of calendar dates for purposes of later comparison or expiration testing.

Example: Customer remittances are stamped with the date received.

Expiration: A limit check based on a comparison of current date with the date recorded on a transaction, record, or file.

Example: Checks to vendors are dated and marked "void after 60 days."

Key Verification: Reentry of transaction data with machine comparison of the initial entry to the second entry to detect errors.

Example: A second clerk keys payroll into a computer. The computer compares this input, character by character (i.e., key by key) to the initial input of the data by the first clerk and reports differences.

PROCESSING CONTROLS   **Processing controls** are designed to provide assurances that processing has occurred according to intended specifications and that no transactions have been lost or incorrectly inserted into the processing stream. Typical processing controls include the following items.

Mechanization: Consistency is provided by mechanical or electronic processing.

Example: Cash deposits are totaled by adding machine.

Standardization: Uniform, structured, and consistent procedures are developed for all processing.

Example: A chart of accounts documents the normal debits and credits to each account.

Default Option: The automatic use of a predefined value in situations where input transactions have certain values left blank.

Example: Salaried employees receive pay for 40 hours each week.

Batch Balancing: A comparison of the items or documents actually processed against a predetermined control total.

Example: The cashier batch balances deposit tickets to control totals of cash remittances.

Run-to-Run Totals: The use of output control totals resulting from one process as input control totals over subsequent processing. The control totals are used as links in a chain to tie one process to another in a sequence of processes over a period of time.

Example: Beginning accounts payable balance less payments plus net purchases should equal ending accounts payable balance.

Balancing: A test for equality between the values of two equivalent sets of items or one set of items and a control total. Any difference indicates an error.

Example: The balance of the accounts receivable subsidiary ledger should equal the balance of the general ledger control account.

Matching: Matching items with other items received from independent sources to control the processing of transactions.

Example: The accounts payable clerk matches vendor invoices to purchase orders and receiving reports.

Clearing Account: An amount that results from the processing of independent items of equivalent value. Net control value should equal zero.

Example: The imprest payroll checking account has a zero balance after all paychecks have been cashed.

Tickler File: A control file consisting of items sequenced by age for processing or follow-up purposes.

Example: Invoices are filed by due date.

Redundant Processing: A repetition of processing and an accompanying comparison of individual results for equality.

Example: A second payroll clerk computes the gross and net pay of each employee for comparison purposes.

Summary Processing: A redundant process using a summarized amount. This is compared for equality with a control total from the processing of the detailed items.

Example: Total overhead applied to production is recomputed by applying the overhead rate to the total amount of direct labor cost charged for all jobs.

Trailer Label: A record providing a control total for comparison with accumulated counts or values of records processed.

Example: The last record of an inventory file contains a record count of the number of records in the file.

Automated Error Correction: Automatic error correction of transactions or records that violate a detective control.

Example: A credit memo is automatically generated when customers overpay their account balances.

OUTPUT CONTROLS   **Output controls** are designed to check that input and processing resulted in valid output and that outputs are distributed properly. Typical output controls include the following items:

Reconciliation: An identification and analysis of differences between the values contained in two substantially identical files or between a detail file and a control total. Errors are identified according to the nature of the reconciling items rather than the existence of a difference between the balances.

Example: The bank reconciliation identifies service charges and fees on the monthly bank statement that have not yet been recorded in the company's accounts.

Aging: Identification of unprocessed or retained items in files according to their date, usually the transaction date. The aging classifies items according to various ranges of duties.

Example: The aging of accounts receivable balances to identify delinquent accounts.

Suspense File: A file containing unprocessed or partially processed items awaiting further action.

Example: A file of back-ordered items awaiting shipment to customers.

(Continued)

Suspense Account: A control total for items awaiting further processing.

Example: The total of the accounts receivable subsidiary ledger should equal the balance of the general ledger control account.

Periodic Audit: Periodic verification of a file or process to detect control problems.

Example: All customers are mailed monthly statements of account to confirm their balances.

Discrepancy Reports: A listing of items that have violated some detective control and require further investigation.

Example: A list of customer accounts that have exceeded their credit limit is sent to the credit manager for review.

Upstream Resubmission: The resubmission of corrected error transactions backwards (i.e., upstream) in the flow of transaction processing so that they pass through all or more of the detective controls that are exercised over normal transactions.

Example: Rejected transactions are resubmitted as a special batch as if they were new transactions.

CASE IN POINT

A batch control total was used to detect a bank employee's attempted fraud. The bank routinely accepted customers' monthly payments on behalf of the local electric company. A bank employee attempted to exploit this payment collection system by entering a credit to her electric account but without the supporting payment. The end-of-the-day batch control total showed that the total cash received was less than the total credits posted to customers' electric accounts. A review of the day's transactions directly led to her fraud.

Preventative, Detective, and Corrective Controls

Transaction processing controls may also be classified as being primarily preventative, detective, or corrective in nature. **Preventative controls** act to prevent errors and fraud before they happen. **Detective controls** act to uncover errors and fraud after they have occurred. **Corrective controls** act to correct errors.

Many detective controls apply to both the input and processing stages of transaction processing. An example is the batch control total procedures used in an insurance company. Each day's incoming premium payments (checks) are grouped into batches of 50 checks; a clerk totals and records the dollar amount of the 50 checks. Then the batches of checks are given to a data conversion operator, who keys the check data into the computer by batch. A printout of the batch totals from the computer is then compared with the totals recorded by the clerk. Discrepancies are immediately uncovered and traced back, usually to mistakes by either the clerk or operator or both. This control procedure affects both the input and processing steps and is illustrated in a manual system in Figure 4.7.

The general ledger clerk compares the totals at point A in the figure with the totals at point B. Notice how the concept of segregation of duties is employed. An output detective control is simply a procedure to compare output totals with the control totals generated at the input and processing steps.

Classification of the general and application controls discussed here as preventative, detective, or corrective in nature is shown in the application controls matrix in Figure 4.9.

Communicating the Objectives of Internal Control

Internal control must be seen not as a process unto itself but as part of a larger process. It must fit in or it may be totally ineffective or perhaps even harmful. One must not lose sight of what the purpose of internal control is.

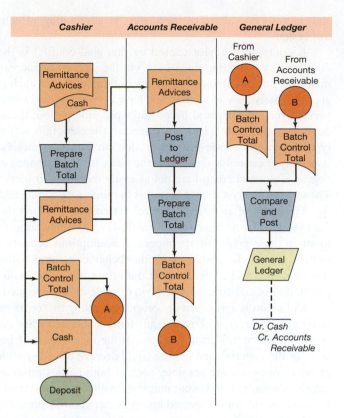

FIGURE 4.7

Batch Control Total Illustration

People are an essential element in every internal control process. People are not perfect; they commit errors of omission and commission. If people were perfect, internal control would be an unnecessary waste of resources. Internal control is people. An internal control process consists of people checking the work of other people. The principal function of internal control is to influence the behavior of people in a business system.

There is a paradox inherent in a system of internal control. Controls such as rules and procedures are imposed on people who ideally, from a more humanistic view, should be responsible for their own self-control and self-direction. This inconsistency must be dealt with in every organizational control system.

Management's job is to ensure the efficiency of operations. Thus behaviors and activities need to be organized and controlled so that the organization's goals are attained. A system of internal control does interfere to some extent with an individual's self-control. By promoting the interests and safeguarding the assets of the overall organization, however, a system of internal control is really protecting the interest and integrity of each individual employee who is a part of that organization.

The objectives of internal control must be seen as relevant to the individuals who will comprise the control system. The system must be designed such that each employee is convinced that controls are meant to prevent difficulties or crises in the operation of the organization that otherwise could affect him or her very personally.

Goals and Behavior Patterns

An information system has several goals; chief among them is productivity. Reliability of information and the safeguarding of assets are also important goals. These goals are at times contradictory. Productivity in an information system is often constrained by the consideration of reliability. Controls are redundant. They constrain productivity but increase the reliability of resulting outputs. This conflict between internal controls and productivity must be acknowledged and carefully considered by the analyst because it may influence the behavior of people in a control system.

A common behavior caused by this goal conflict is the omission of an internal control duty (such as counting documents) in the interest of increasing production. Consider a clerk manually posting invoices. If the clerk double-checks each posting, the number of postings is approximately 50% of what would have been performed without double-checking. If the clerk's performance is evaluated by postings per time period, there will be a temptation to omit the double-checking for at least some items if the clerk falls behind schedule. Internal control duties typically require a trade-off with production. The basic motivational problem is that productivity is usually measurable and forms the basis for performance evaluation, whereas reliability and degree of internal control are not as easily measured or incorporated into performance reviews. The systems analyst should keep this in mind in designing and evaluating internal controls.

The goals of an internal control system are achieved through the actions of the people in the system. The reliance on a formal plan of organization and related methods and measures to attain these goals entails important assumptions concerning collusion, reporting of irregularities, power relationships, and other behavior patterns within the organization. Organizational independence and segregation of duties are consistent with good internal control only if the probability of collusion between two or more duly segregated employees is low.

Collusion is agreement or conspiracy among two or more people to commit fraud. In a purchase procedure, control over acquisitions is obtained when duly segregated personnel from both receiving and stores acknowledge that the materials have been received by stores. Both must sign for the material, and neither could deceive the other without collusion or fraud. Of course, errors of omission are possible, such as both parties miscounting quantities. In fact, the same error (a shortage) could occur unintentionally as well as intentionally. However, if unintentional, the error would not be covered up, and other controls probably would uncover the discrepancy.

Justification for the assumption that the probability of collusion between two or more people will be low is found in the formal plan of organization. For one individual to suggest an irregularity to another person and be rejected would entail prohibitive costs to the first individual. He or she will be turned in by the second individual and hence lose his or her job or incur another punishment. This entails a related assumption that employees will always report irregularities to those higher up in the organization. This assumption, in turn, requires several others. One is that the formal plan of organization as denoted in procedures manuals and the like solely determines power relations in a system. A related assumption is that actions not specified by a system are dysfunctional or "wrong"—that is, deviations suggest irregularities that should be reported to those higher up.

 CASE IN POINT

Probably the most famous collusion fraud of all time involved Equity Funding Corporation of America, a nationally prominent financial conglomerate. As many as 100 company employees were involved in a scheme that included creating, maintaining, and selling fictitious insurance policies. The case was so famous that the story was retold in the movie *Billion Dollar Bubble*.

Numerous factors influence an individual's behavior in a control system. One important influence is the formal plan of organization and the related methods and measures employed by an organization. Other factors do exist, however. Groups and other sources of informal pressure bear on an individual's behavior and may at times mitigate the desired, formally planned relationships between people in the system. For example, an individual with lengthy service may convince a young coworker that the omission of a control step is okay and need not be reported, because "it's been done that way in the past."

A receiving clerk transferring goods to inventory may convince the inventory clerk just to sign and not waste time counting the items she or he is receiving. A clerk performing a bank reconciliation may not examine several checks in detail because it is near quitting time.

What might be called *people failure* is the source of all theft and fraud in a system and is a prime contributor to serious errors of the production type and other ineffectiveness and inefficiency. In cases of defalcations, "the procedures did not fail, the people did." The variety and complexity of human behavior and the value constraints (principles of just, humane, compassionate conduct) we work within combine to make the production of "people-proof" procedures infeasible. As long as people have access to valuables, there will be the possibility of theft, sabotage, and serious error. These possibilities are minimized when employees fully understand, accept, and internalize the objectives of the internal control system of which they are an essential element.

Analysis of Internal Control Processes

The analysis of an internal control process requires an understanding of the process both as it is designed and as it actually operates. The actual process may or may not conform to expectations. Documentation may be outdated, and the structure may be operating under new procedures. Procedures may have changed informally to adapt to circumstances not foreseen when the original system was designed and documented.

Internal control processes routinely collect information concerning fulfillment of duties, transfer of authority, approval, and verification. This documentation of internal control duties must be examined to evaluate the reliability of the system's operation.

Reliability depends on the people who administer internal control procedures. Designing an internal control process is only the first part of the problem; it is essential that internal control duties are actually performed as prescribed.

There are several reasons why internal control duties may not be administered. New employees or perhaps even experienced employees may not understand their duties. More common is the omission of an internal control duty (such as counting documents) in order to increase production.

Analytic Techniques

The **internal control questionnaire** is a common analytic technique used in internal control analysis. Internal control questionnaires traditionally have been a central element in an audit program; accordingly, questionnaires are a standard form in public accounting firms, internal audit departments, and other organizations that are regularly involved in reviews of internal controls. Questionnaires are available for the review of specific application areas as well as for special reviews such as computer center audits. At times, the analyst may design a questionnaire specifically for a particular audit, or she or he may modify a standard questionnaire to better suit the needs or nature of a particular audit. Questionnaires are usually designed so that an affirmative answer to a question indicates an adequate degree of internal control, and a negative answer indicates the need for further information or a potential weakness in the structure.

However, a negative answer does not always indicate a weakness because other controls may compensate for the omission identified by the negative response. Questionnaires are essentially checklists to ensure that a review does not omit an area of major importance. Figure 4.8 illustrates a portion of a questionnaire for sales and shipping procedures.

Questionnaires are only tools; the manner in which they are used is extremely important. The questionnaire should be filled in on the basis of actual observations and inquiries. But filling

FIGURE 4.8

**Portion of an
Internal Control
Questionnaire**

Sales and Shipping

1. Are sales orders adequately controlled?
2. Are all orders approved by the credit manager or department before shipment?
3. Is the credit department entirely independent of the sales department?
4. Are sales prices and credit terms based on approved standard price lists?
5. If so, are any deviations from standard approved
   a. by an officer?
   b. by another? Explain.
6. If not, are all sales prices and credit terms approved by the sales manager or in the sales department?
7. Are prenumbered shipping advices prepared for all goods shipped?
8. Are the quantities shown on the shipping advices double-checked in the shipping department?
9. Does the billing clerk or some other designated employee receive the shipping advices directly from the shipping department? (If so, identify this employee.)
10. Does this employee check the numerical sequence of shipping advices to assure that all are accounted for?

in the questionnaire is not the essence of the review. The essence of a review is the analyst's analysis of his or her findings. Questionnaires do serve as documentation that a review was undertaken; however, questionnaires are necessarily standardized and therefore are not equally applicable in all circumstances. Their use often must be supplemented with other forms of analysis, such as write-ups, flowcharts, or other charting techniques.

Analytic flowcharts might be used in internal control analysis, particularly if the analysis involves a computer system application. Flowcharting itself is not a form of structured analysis but rather a technique to organize data for analysis. An **application controls matrix** provides a structured form of analysis that is particularly relevant to internal control reviews of information systems. The rows of the matrix consist of various control techniques. The columns of the matrix consist of activities or data values in the system under review. The matrix organization provides a structured method for the systematic evaluation of each activity or data item with respect to each type of control activity listed in the rows. Figure 4.9 illustrates an application controls matrix that is preprinted with a comprehensive list of controls. An application controls matrix can be designed as needed in any specific situation by providing one's own list of controls as the rows of the matrix.

To use the matrix, the analyst identifies the activities or data items that should be subject to control and lists them as the columns of the matrix. A matrix can be used systematically to evaluate an analytic or other type of flowchart by listing the sequence of operations shown in the chart as the columns of the matrix. Each row/column contribution of control/activity or control/data items can then be evaluated systematically. The analyst might enter an X or other symbol in each row/column box where a control existed and/or was performed, leaving blank those combinations that were absent. Another technique would be to rate the strength or relative reliability of each present control/activity combination by assigning numbers or letters to indicate relative strength or reliability. A 1 might indicate highly reliable, a 3 reliable, a 5 functioning but not reliable, and so on.

 CASE IN POINT

External auditors routinely use analytical techniques as part of evaluating clients' internal controls. The results of the analytical review plus tests of compliance help the auditor determine the extent to which transactions and accounts need to be tested.

Transaction/Process → Control Feature ↓																	

Characteristics that Constitute Controls

PREVENTIVE CONTROLS

Reliability of personnel	Check digits	
Segregation of duties	Reasonableness	
Definition of responsibilities	Limit check	
Rotation of duties	Validity check	
Training of personnel	Read back	
Competence of personnel	Dating	
Secure custody	Expiration	
Dual access/dual controls	Keystroke verification	
Standardization	Approval	
Mechanization	Exception input	
Forms design	Default option	
Prenumbered forms	Labeling	
Precoded forms	**Completeness of Processing**	
Authorization	Run-to-run totals	
Endorsement	Balancing	
Cancellation	Reconciliation	
Simultaneous preparation	Aging	
Documentation	Suspense file	
Formatted input	Suspense account	
DETECTIVE CONTROLS	Matching	
Accountability of Input	Clearing account	
Anticipation	Tickler file	
Transmittal documents	Periodic audit	
Batch serial numbers	Activity log	
Control register	**Correctness of Processing**	
Completeness of Input	Redundant processing	
Amount control total	Summary processing	
Document control total	Sequence checking	
Line control count	Overflow checks	
Hash total	Scan before distribution	
Batch totals	Trailer label	
Batch balancing	**CORRECTIVE CONTROLS**	
Visual verification	Discrepancy reports	
Turnaround document	Transaction trail	
Passwords	Error source statistics	
Correctness of Input	Automatic error correction	
Format	Upstream resubmission	
Completeness check	Backup and recovery	

FIGURE 4.9

Application Controls Matrix

Internal Control and Compliance in Small Business and Small Public Companies

Although SOX compliance applies only to public companies, both public and private small companies face similar special needs in developing their internal control processes. When we think of public companies, we tend to think of large organizations such as Microsoft or General Motors, but some public companies are so small (i.e., "microcap" companies) that they have only a handful of employees.

The small business has no independent IT or internal audit department, and in many cases it is run by managers with no accounting education or financial expertise. Further, the small number of employees typically makes traditional segregation of duties next to impossible. Finally, there may be little or no separation between the owners and managers, generating increased opportunity for management override of internal control.

The COSO report, "Internal Control over Financial Reporting—Guidance for Smaller Public Companies," suggests various ways small public companies can compensate for their small size. The suggestions in this report apply to private small businesses as well:

- **Leadership Involvement.** Many small businesses are run by a single leader. This individual is typically familiar with all aspects of the business. The result is that the leader can actively oversee and be involved in all operations and the financial reporting process.
- **Effective Boards of Directors.** Smaller businesses are often relatively simple. This means that the members of the Board of Directors can develop substantial expertise in all areas of the business, effecting better oversight. Also, the informal nature of small businesses often facilitates better communications between members of the board and management.
- **Limited Segregation of Duties and Increased Focus on Monitoring.** Large companies can easily have separate departments for purchasing, inventory, billing, general accounting, receiving, sales, and so on. Such is typically not possible in the small business, where many functions often get collapsed into single individuals. Managers can compensate for the relative lack of segregation of duties by placing increased emphasis on monitoring. This can be accomplished by management's focusing more on observing employees, reviewing reports, investigating unusual transactions, and so on.
- **Compensating for Limitations in Information Technology.** Businesses without an IT department or IT expertise can rely on outside application service providers (ASPs) for the accounting, software, and IT needs. For example, a business might use the Web-based Microsoft Dynamics for their accounting system.

Another challenge facing small business is how to develop their internal control processes within limited budgets. In order to ensure strong internal control, large companies often spend millions of dollars on consultants and IT resources. On the other hand, small businesses often work with very tight budgets. Both small and large companies can gain cost efficiencies by using the following approaches:

- **Apply a Top-Down Risk Assessment (TDRA) Approach to Internal Control Assessment.** TDRA is defined by PCAOB Auditing Standard No. 5 as "An audit of internal control over financial reporting that is integrated with an audit of financial statements." The goal of TDRA is to determine the scope and required evidence necessary to adequately test and assess internal controls. Under TDRA, the scope and required evidence are determined by management, applying quantitative and qualitative risk factors in prioritizing controls to focus on. The idea is to focus on those controls that are most likely to be related to material misstatements of the financial statements.
- **Focus on Changes.** Financial items that have changed the most from one period to the next get special attention. For example, a 50% increase in accounts receivables over one quarter would likely deserve investigation.
- **Manage Reporting Objectives.** Considerable gains in efficiencies can be produced by giving the most attention to financial reporting objectives that are material to the financial statements.
- **Right-Size Documentation.** For SOX compliance, it is not only necessary to have adequate controls in place but also necessary to be able to demonstrate the existence of the controls through documentation. To this end, large companies often maintain extensive amounts of complicated documentation such as training manuals, procedure manuals, and flowcharts. Small companies can gain efficiencies by using informal documentation, such as notes and memos.

Illustration of an Internal Control Analysis

Many professional examinations, such as the Certificate in Public Accounting (CPA) examination and the Certified Internal Auditor (CIA) examination, test a candidate's knowledge of internal controls by requiring the candidate to evaluate potential control structure weaknesses that are evident in a narrative or graphic (flowchart) description of an application system. The candidate is usually required to do the control analysis solely on the basis of analytic reasoning. That is, questionnaires or other analytic aids, such as the application controls matrix discussed previously, are not provided for the candidate's use. In such a case, the candidate must carefully evaluate the described system and, with the professional definition of internal control structures as a reference, identify potential control weaknesses through analytical reasoning.

As an illustration, following is a CPA examination question in which one is expected to evaluate internal controls in the manner just described. The published unofficial answer immediately follows the question.

> The Art Appreciation Society operates a museum for the benefit and enjoyment of the community. During hours when the museum is open to the public, two clerks who are positioned at the entrance collect a five dollar admission fee from each nonmember patron. Members of the Art Appreciation Society are permitted to enter free of charge upon presentation of their membership cards.
>
> At the end of each day one of the clerks delivers the proceeds to the treasurer. The treasurer counts the cash in the presence of the clerk and places it in a safe. Each Friday afternoon the treasurer and one of the clerks deliver all cash held in the safe to the bank, and receive an authenticated deposit slip which provides the basis for the weekly entry in the cash receipts journal.
>
> The Board of Directors of the Art Appreciation Society has identified a need to improve their system of internal control over cash admission fees. The Board had determined that the cost of installing turnstiles, sales booths, or otherwise altering the physical layout of the museum will greatly exceed any benefits that may be derived. However, the Board has agreed that the sale of admission tickets must be an integral part of its improvement efforts.
>
> Smith has been asked by the Board of Directors of the Art Appreciation Society to review the internal control over cash admission fees and provide suggestions for improvement.

Required Indicate weaknesses in the existing system of internal control over cash admission fees, which Smith should identify, and recommend one improvement for each of the weaknesses identified.

Organize the answer as indicated in the following illustrative example:

Weaknesses	Recommended Improvements
1. There is no basis for establishing the documentation of the number of paying patrons.	1. Prenumbered admission tickets should be issued upon payment of the admission fee.

Unofficial Answer

Weaknesses	Recommended Improvements
1. There is no segregation of duties between persons responsible for collecting admission fees and persons responsible for authorizing admission.	1. One clerk (hereafter referred to as the collection clerk) should collect admission fees and issue prenumbered tickets. The other clerk (hereafter referred to as the admission clerk) should authorize admission upon receipt of the ticket or proof of membership.
2. An independent count of paying patrons is not made.	2. The admission clerk should retain a portion of the prenumbered admission ticket (admission ticket stub).

(Continued)

Weaknesses	Recommended Improvements
3. There is no proof of amounts collected by the clerks.	3. Admission ticket stubs should be reconciled with cash collected by the treasurer each day.
4. Cash receipts records are not promptly prepared.	4. The cash collections should be recorded by the collection clerk daily on a permanent record that will serve as the first record of accountability.
5. Cash receipts are not promptly deposited. Cash should not be left undeposited for a week.	5. Cash should be deposited at least once each day.
6. There is no proof of accuracy of amounts deposited.	6. Authenticated deposit slips should be compared with daily cash collection. Discrepancies should be recorded, promptly investigated, and resolved. In addition, the treasurer should establish a policy that includes an analytical review of cash collections.
7. There is no record of the internal accountability for cash.	7. The treasurer should issue a signed receipt for all proceeds received from the collection clerk. These receipts should be maintained and periodically checked against cash collection and deposit records.

(CPA)

Summary

Controls are needed to reduce exposures. An organization is subject to a variety of exposures that can have an adverse effect on its operations or even its very existence as a viable going concern. Many aspects of computer processing tend to significantly increase an organization's exposure to undesirable events. The analysis of exposures in an organization is often related to the transaction cycle concept. Management should develop detailed control objectives for each transaction cycle.

An entity's internal control process consists of the policies and procedures established to provide reasonable assurance that the following entity objectives will be achieved: (1) reliability of financial reporting, (2) effectiveness and efficiency of operations, and (3) compliance with applicable laws and regulations. An internal control process consists of five components: the control environment, risk assessment, control activities, information and communication, and monitoring. Controls can be classified as either general controls or application controls. A standard method of classifying application controls is by considering whether a given control applies to inputs, processing, or outputs. This chapter discussed and illustrated a variety of common control practices.

Ethical considerations must be addressed in the design of an internal control structure. People are an essential element in every internal control structure. It is important that the objectives of internal control be communicated and understood. The objectives of internal control must be seen as relevant to the individuals who will comprise the control system.

The analysis of an internal control structure requires an understanding of the structure both as it is designed and as it actually operates. The most common analytical technique used in internal control analysis is the internal control questionnaire. Analytic flowcharts are also useful in internal control analysis.

Glossary

accounting system   the methods and records established to identify, assemble, analyze, classify, record, and report the organization's transactions and to maintain accountability for the related assets and liabilities.

aging   identification of unprocessed or retained items in files according to their date, usually the transaction date.

amount control total   totals of homogeneous amounts for a group of transactions or records, usually dollars or quantities.

anticipation   the expectation of a given transaction or event at a particular time.

application controls   specific to individual applications.

application controls matrix   a structured form of analysis that utilizes a matrix of application controls.

approval   the acceptance of a transaction for processing after it is initiated.

audit committee   subcommittee of the Board of Directors that is charged with overall responsibility for the organization's financial reports.

audit trail   financial totals that appear in a general ledger account can be supported by evidence concerning all the individual transactions that comprise that total and vice versa.

authorization   limits the initiation of a transaction or performance of an activity to selected individuals.

batch control   any type of control total or count applied to a specific number of transaction documents or to the transaction documents that arrive within a specific period of time.

batch control log   synonym for control register.

batch control ticket   synonym for transmittal document.

batch sequence   synonym for batch serial numbers.

batch serial numbers   batches of transaction documents are numbered consecutively and accounted.

batch totals   synonym for batch control.

cancellation   identification of transaction documents in order to prevent their further or repeated use after they have performed their function.

clearing account   an amount that results from the processing of independent items of equivalent value. Net control value should equal zero.

COBIT   Control Objectives for Information and related Technology. COBIT is an international standard for best practices in IT published by the IT Governance Institute (www.itgi.org).

collusion   agreement or conspiracy among two or more people to commit fraud.

control activities   the policies and procedures in addition to the control environment and accounting system that management has established to provide reasonable assurance that specific entity objectives will be achieved.

control environment   the collective effect of various factors on establishing, enhancing, or mitigating the effectiveness of specific policies and procedures.

control register   a log or register indicating the disposition and control values of batches or transactions.

corporate crime   white-collar crime that benefits a company or organization, rather than the individuals who perpetrate the fraud.

corrective controls   act to correct errors.

detective controls   act to uncover errors and fraud after they have occurred.

document control total   a count of the number of individual documents.

dual control   the assignment of two individuals to perform the same work task in unison.

endorsement   the marking of a form or document so as to direct or restrict its further processing.

enterprise risk management (ERM)   a process effected by an entity designed to identify potential events that may affect the entity, to manage risk, and to provide reasonable assurance regarding the achievement of entity objectives.

exposure   the potential financial effect of an event multiplied by its probability of occurrence.

fidelity bond   a contract with an insurance company that provides a financial guarantee of the honesty of the individual who is named in the bond contract.

forensic accounting   an activity concerned with preventing and detecting fraud.

fraudulent financial reporting   intentional or reckless conduct, whether by purposeful act or omission, that results in materially misleading financial statements.

general controls   affect all transaction processing.

hash total   a meaningless total that is useful for control purposes only.

input controls   designed to prevent or detect errors in the input stage of data processing.

internal accounting control   the plan of organization and the procedures and records that are concerned with the safeguarding of assets and reliability of financial statements.

internal control process   the policies and procedures established to provide reasonable assurance that the following entity objectives will be achieved: (a) effectiveness and efficiency of operations, (b) reliability of financial reporting, and (c) compliance with applicable laws and regulations.

internal control questionnaire   a set of questions pertaining to internal controls in an application area.

ISO 27002   Code of practice for Information Security Management, published by the ISO (www.iso.org), and by the International Electrotechnical Commission. ISO 27002 is a widely accepted international standard for best practices in information security.

line control count   a count of the number of lines of data on one or more documents.

management audit   internal audit services to management that extend beyond the financial activities of the organization.

management fraud   diversion of assets or misrepresentation of assets by management.

operational audit   synonym for management audit.

output controls   designed to check that input and processing resulted in valid output and that outputs are properly distributed.

preventative controls   act to prevent errors and fraud before they happen.

processing controls   designed to provide assurances that processing has occurred according to intended specifications and that no transactions have been lost or incorrectly inserted into the processing stream.

reasonable assurance   principle that the costs of controls should not exceed their benefits.

responsibility   management and the Board of Directors are responsible for the internal control process.

risk   the probability of occurrence of an event.

run-to-run totals   the utilization of output control totals resulting from one process as input control totals over subsequent processing.

segregation of duties   responsibilities for authorization, custody, and record keeping for handling and processing of transactions are separated.

supervision   the direct monitoring of personnel performance by an employee who is so charged.

suspense account   a control total for items awaiting further processing.

suspense file   a file containing unprocessed or partially processed items awaiting further action.

tickler file   a control file consisting of items sequenced by age for processing or follow-up purposes.

transmittal document   the medium for communicating control totals over movement of data, particularly from source to processing point or between processing points.

upstream resubmission   the resubmission of corrected error transactions backward (i.e., upstream) in the flow of transaction processing so that they pass through all or more of the detective controls that are exercised over normal transactions.

white-collar crime   deceitful diversion of assets from proper use or deceitful misrepresentation of assets by an act or series of acts that are nonviolent in nature.

Webliography

www.acfe.com
The Association of Certified Fraud Examiners (ACFE) is a private organization that focuses on training and education related to the prevention, detection, deterrence, and investigation of fraud. The ACFE provides the Certified Fraud Examiner (CFE) certification to members who meet the examination, academic, and professional requirements.

www.coso.org
The Committee of Sponsoring Organizations of the Treadway Commission (COSO) is a voluntary private-sector organization that is dedicated to "guiding executive management and governance entities toward the establishment of more effective, efficient, and ethical business operations on a global basis."

Through its Web site, COSO makes available links to various guidance reports that have played a key role in the accounting world. These reports form an authoritative theoretical and practical framework for internal control.

www.isaca.org
This Web site strongly promotes the COBIT framework.

The Information Systems Audit and Control Association (ISACA) is a global organization composed of information governance, control, security, and audit professionals. ISACA publishes IS auditing and IS control standards that are widely respected and followed by accounting professionals everywhere.

ISACA provides a number of well-recognized professional certifications: Certified Information Systems Auditor (CISA), Certified Information Security Manager (CISM), and Certified in the Governance of Enterprise IT (CGEIT).

www.itgi.org
The IT Governance Institute (ITGI) calls itself a "research think tank" that is focused on being a leading authority in the area of IT governance. The ITGI publishes the COBIT framework and makes an online version of it available through its Web site.

www.iso.org
The International Organization for Standardization (ISO) refers to itself as "the world's largest developer and publisher of International Standards."

The ISO has published a number of standards relevant to internal control and information security, including the ISO 27000 family of standards relating to information security. Organizations sometimes look to these standards as helpful guidance in complying with the SOX.

www.justice.gov
Web site for the U.S. Department of Justice. Search for "Corporate Fraud Task Force" and "Significant Criminal Cases and Charging Documents."

www.ussc.gov
The U.S. Sentencing Commission (USSC) operates as an independent agency under the judicial branch of the U.S. government. The USSC publishes the Federal Sentencing Guideline Manual, which gives federal courts guidelines on sentencing individuals and organizations.

The USSCs federal sentencing guidelines for organizations includes specific ethics and compliance programs that organizations can put in place in order to mitigate the severity of sentencing they may receive in the event they are convicted of violating federal criminal laws.

www.pcaob.org
The Public Company Accounting Oversight Board (PCAOB) is a nonprofit private organization that operates under the supervision of the Securities and Exchange Commission (SEC) and exists for the purpose of overseeing and regulating auditors of public companies. The PCAOB was created by the SOX.

en.wikipedia.org/wiki/Sarbanes-Oxley_Act
The Sarbanes–Oxley Act (SOX) is a sweeping act of the U.S. Congress that, among many other things, requires company executives to "certify" internal controls in their annual reports. The act also requires external auditors to render an opinion on the internal controls of public companies that they audit.

www.sec.gov
According to the Securities and Exchange Commission (SEC), its mission is "to protect investors, maintain fair, orderly, and efficient markets, and facilitate capital formation."

The SEC oversees the PCAOB, and its enforcement division can initiate legal actions against companies that do not comply with the SOX or other securities-related acts.

Chapter Quiz

Answers to the Chapter Quiz appear on Page 149.

1. The potential negative financial effect of an event multiplied by its probability of occurrence is a(n) (_____).
   a. control
   b. exposure
   c. hazard
   d. risk

2. Fraud that benefits a company or organization, rather than the individual(s) who perpetrate the fraud, is known as (_____).
   a. white-collar crime
   b. corporate crime
   c. management fraud
   d. fraudulent financial reporting

3. The responsibility for establishing and maintaining an internal control structure rests with (_____).
   a. internal auditing
   b. the treasurer
   c. management
   d. the controller

4. Which of the following is an element of an internal control process?
   a. information and communication
   b. reasonable assurance
   c. internal audit function
   d. management control methods

5. Which of the following limits the initiation of a transaction or performance of an activity to selected individuals?
   a. authorization
   b. approval
   c. fidelity bond
   d. audit trail

6. Computer master files and transaction files are maintained after the creation of an updated master file in case the current master file is corrupted. This is an example of (_____).
   a. labeling procedures
   b. recovery procedures
   c. documentation procedures
   d. secure custody

7. Marking bills as "paid" to prevent duplicate payment is an example of (_____).
   a. cancellation
   b. backup
   c. approval
   d. endorsement

8. A meaningless total that is useful for control purposes only is called a(n) (_____).
   a. line control count
   b. hash total
   c. document control total
   d. amount control total

9. An imprest payroll checking account has a zero balance after all paychecks have been cashed. This type of control practice is an example of a(n) (_____).
   a. tickler file
   b. upstream resubmission
   c. redundant processing
   d. clearing account

10. Agreement or conspiracy among two or more people to commit fraud is known as (_____).
    a. dual control
    b. complicity
    c. intrigue
    d. collusion

Review Problem

The Fox Company, a client of your firm, has come to you with the following problem. It has three clerical employees who must perform the following functions:

a. maintain general ledger
b. maintain accounts payable ledger
c. maintain accounts receivable ledger
d. prepare checks for signature
e. maintain cash disbursements journal
f. issue credit memos on returns and allowances
g. reconcile the bank account
h. handle and deposit cash receipts

Assuming there is no problem as to the ability of any of the employees, the company requests that you assign these functions to the three employees to achieve the highest degree of internal control. Assume that these employees will perform no other accounting functions than the ones listed and that any accounting functions not listed will be performed by people other than these three employees.

a. State how you would distribute these functions among the three employees. Assume that with the exception of the nominal jobs of the bank reconciliation and the issuance of credits on returns and allowances, all functions require an equal amount of time.

b. List four possible unsatisfactory pairings of the listed functions.

(CPA)

Solution to Review Problem

Undesirable combinations are as follows:

1. Cash receipts and accounts receivable
2. Cash receipts and credit memos on sales returns and allowances
3. Cash disbursements and accounts payable

4. Cash receipts and bank reconciliation
5. Cash disbursements and bank reconciliation
6. Cash receipts and general ledger
7. Accounts receivable and credit memos on sales returns and allowances

Assignment of Functions

Employee no. 1:
a. maintain general ledger
f. issue credit memos on returns and allowances
g. reconcile bank account

Employee no. 2:
e. maintain cash disbursements journal

d. prepare checks for signature
h. handle and deposit cash receipts

Employee no. 3:
b. maintain accounts payable ledger
c. maintain accounts receivable ledger

Review Questions

1. Distinguish between risks and exposures.
2. Identify several common business exposures.
3. What is corporate crime?
4. What is management fraud?
5. What is forensic accounting?
6. List the basic elements of an internal control process.
7. Distinguish between general controls and applications controls.
8. Why are written procedures manuals considered to be controls?
9. Differentiate preventative, detective, and corrective controls. Give an example of each.
10. What is the purpose of a forced vacation policy?
11. What is batch control?
12. Why is collusion a problem in internal control design?
13. Why is it important that the purpose and nature of internal control be communicated to employees within an organization?
14. Discuss the following statement: "The procedures did not fail, the people did."
15. What role do physical security devices have in a system of internal control?
16. Why has the importance of the internal audit function continued to grow?
17. What are the functions of an audit committee?
18. Discuss the advantages and disadvantages of using a questionnaire or checklist in evaluating an internal control system.
19. Does filling out a questionnaire constitute an evaluation of internal controls?
20. What is an analytic flowchart? What is an application controls matrix?

Discussion Questions and Problems

21. Internal accounting controls are not designed to provide reasonable assurance that
    a. transactions are executed in accordance with management's authorization.
    b. irregularities will be eliminated.
    c. access to assets is permitted only in accordance with management's authorization.
    d. the recorded accountability for assets is compared with the existing assets at reasonable intervals.
    (CPA)

22. Internal control is a function of management, and effective control is based on the concept of charge and discharge of responsibility and duty. Which of the following is one of the overriding principles of internal control?
    a. Responsibility for accounting and financial duties should be assigned to one responsible officer.
    b. Responsibility for the performance of each duty must be fixed.
    c. Responsibility for the accounting duties must be borne by the audit committee of the company.

d. Responsibility for accounting activities and duties must be assigned only to employees who are bonded.

(CPA)

23. Effective internal control requires organizational independence of departments. Organizational independence would be impaired in which of the following situations?
    a. The internal auditors report to the audit committee of the Board of Directors.
    b. The controller reports to the vice-president of production.
    c. The payroll accounting department reports to the chief accountant.
    d. The cashier reports to the treasurer.

(CPA)

24. Transaction authorization within an organization may be either specific or general. An example of specific transaction authorization is the
    a. setting of automatic reorder points for material or merchandise.
    b. approval of a detailed construction budget for a warehouse.
    c. establishment of requirements to be met in determining a customer's credit limits.
    d. establishment of sales prices for products to be sold to any customer.

(CPA)

25. A system of internal accounting control normally would include procedures that are designed to provide reasonable assurance that
    a. employees act with integrity when performing their assigned tasks.
    b. transactions are executed in accordance with management's general or specific authorization.
    c. decision processes leading to management's authorization of transactions are sound.
    d. collusive activities would be detected by segregation of employee duties.

(CPA)

26. When considering internal control, an auditor must be aware of the concept of reasonable assurance that recognizes that
    a. the employment of competent personnel provides assurance that the objectives of internal control will be achieved.
    b. the establishment and maintenance of a system of internal control is an important responsibility of management, not of the auditor.
    c. the cost of internal control should not exceed the benefits expected to be derived from internal control.
    d. the segregation of incompatible functions is necessary to obtain assurance that the internal control is effective.

(CPA)

27. Which of the following elements of an entity's internal control structure includes the development of personnel manuals documenting employee promotion and training policies?
    a. control procedures.
    b. control environment.

c. information and communication.
d. quality control system.

(CPA adapted)

28. Which of the following statements about internal control structure is correct?
    a. A properly maintained internal control process reasonably ensures that collusion among employees cannot occur.
    b. The establishment and maintenance of the internal control structure is an important responsibility of the internal auditor.
    c. An exceptionally strong internal control structure is enough for the auditor to eliminate substantive tests on a significant account balance.
    d. The cost–benefit relationship is a primary criterion that should be considered in designing an internal control structure.

(CPA adapted)

29. Which of the following is not an element of an entity's internal control process?
    a. control risk.
    b. control activities.
    c. information and communication.
    d. the control environment.

(CPA adapted)

30. Employers bond employees who handle cash receipts because fidelity bonds reduce the possibility of employing dishonest individuals and
    a. protect employees who make unintentional errors from possible monetary damages resulting from their errors.
    b. deter dishonesty by making employees aware that insurance companies may investigate and prosecute dishonest acts.
    c. facilitate an independent monitoring of the receiving and depositing of cash receipts.
    d. force employees in positions of trust to take periodic vacations and rotate their assigned duties.

(CPA)

31. Proper segregation of functional responsibilities calls for separation of the
    a. authorization, approval, and execution functions.
    b. authorization, execution, and payment functions.
    c. receiving, shipping, and custodial functions.
    d. authorization, recording, and custodial functions.

(CPA)

32. A company holds bearer bonds as a short-term investment. Custody of these bonds and submission of coupons for interest payments normally is the responsibility of the
    a. treasury function.
    b. legal counsel.
    c. general accounting function.
    d. internal audit function.

(CPA)

33. Operating control of the check-signing machine normally should be the responsibility of the
    a. general accounting function.
    b. treasury function.
    c. legal counsel.
    d. internal audit function.

    (CPA)

34. Internal control over cash receipts is weakened when an employee who receives customer mail receipts also
    a. prepares initial cash receipts records.
    b. records credits to individual accounts receivable.
    c. prepares bank deposit slips for all mail receipts.
    d. maintains a petty cash fund.

    (CPA)

35. For good internal control, the monthly bank statements should be reconciled by someone under the direction of the
    a. credit manager.
    b. controller.
    c. cashier.
    d. treasurer.

    (CPA)

36. For good internal control, the person who should sign checks is the
    a. person preparing the checks.
    b. purchasing agent.
    c. accounts payable clerk.
    d. treasurer.

    (CPA)

37. For good internal control, the credit manager should be responsible to the
    a. sales manager.
    b. customer service manager.
    c. controller.
    d. treasurer.

    (CPA)

38. The authorization for write-off of accounts receivable should be the responsibility of the
    a. credit manager.
    b. controller.
    c. accounts receivable clerk.
    d. treasurer.

    (CPA)

39. In general, material irregularities perpetrated by which of the following are *most* difficult to detect?
    a. cashier
    b. controller
    c. internal auditor
    d. data entry clerk

    (CPA)

40. A well-designed system of internal control that is functioning effectively is most likely to detect an irregularity arising from
    a. the fraudulent action of several employees.
    b. the fraudulent action of an individual employee.

    c. informal deviations from the official organization chart.
    d. management fraud.

    (CPA)

41. To provide for the greatest degree of independence in performing internal auditing functions, an internal auditor most likely should report to the
    a. financial vice-president.
    b. corporate controller.
    c. Board of Directors.
    d. corporate stockholders.

    (CPA)

42. The use of fidelity bonds may indemnify a company from embezzlement losses. The use also
    a. reduces the company's need to obtain expensive business interruption insurance.
    b. protects employees who made unintentional errors from possible monetary damages resulting from such errors.
    c. allows the company to substitute the fidelity bonds for various parts of internal accounting control.
    d. reduces the possibility of employing people with dubious records in positions of trust.

    (CPA)

43. For good internal control, which of the following functions should *not* be the responsibility of the treasurer's department?
    a. data processing.
    b. handling of cash.
    c. custody of securities.
    d. establishment of credit policies.

    (CPA)

44. Which of the following sets of duties would ordinarily be considered basically incompatible in terms of good internal control?
    a. preparation of monthly statements to customers and maintenance of the accounts receivable subsidiary ledger.
    b. posting to the general ledger and approval of additions and terminations relating to the payroll.
    c. custody of unmailed signed checks and maintenance of expense subsidiary ledgers.
    d. collection of receipts on account and maintaining accounts receivable records.

    (CPA)

45. The Foreign Corrupt Practices Act requires that
    a. auditors engaged to examine the financial statements of publicly held companies report all illegal payments to the SEC.
    b. publicly held companies establish independent audit committees to monitor the effectiveness of their system of internal control.
    c. U.S. firms doing business abroad report sizable payments to non-U.S. citizens to the Justice Department.
    d. publicly held companies devise and maintain an adequate system of internal accounting control.

    (CPA)

46. Establishing and maintaining a system of internal accounting control is the primary responsibility of
   a. management and the Board of Directors.
   b. the internal auditor.
   c. the external auditor.
   d. a financial analyst.
   e. the data processing manager.

(CMA adapted)

47. A certain business receives all payments of account by check. Checks are always received, so an analyst wants to use the checks themselves as posting media to the accounts receivable ledger rather than have to prepare and process remittance advices. Discuss the conflict between productivity and reliability that is inherent here.

48. What duties should not normally be performed by the same individual in each of the following procedures?
   a. bad debt write-off.
   b. payroll preparation.
   c. sales returns.
   d. inventory purchases.

49. The internal auditing department was told that two employees were terminated for falsifying their time records. The two employees had altered overtime hours on their time cards after their supervisors had approved the hours actually worked.

   Several years ago, the company discontinued the use of time clocks. Since then, the plant supervisors have been responsible for manually posting the time cards and approving the hours for which their employees should be paid. The postings are usually entered in pencil by the supervisors or their secretaries. After the postings for the week are complete, the time cards are approved and placed in the mail racks outside the supervisors' offices for pickup by the timekeepers. Sometimes the timekeepers do not pick up the time cards promptly.

Required

Assuming the company does not wish to return to using time clocks, give *three* recommendations to prevent recurrence of the situation described. For each recommendation, indicate how it will deter fraudulent reporting of hours worked.

(IIA)

50. Discuss the purpose of the following questions that appear on an internal control questionnaire.
   a. Does the company have an organization chart?
   b. Are the duties of the principal accounting officer segregated from those of the treasurer?
   c. Are employees in positions of trust bonded?
   d. Are bank accounts reconciled regularly by the company?
   e. Does the company maintain a ledger of its fixed assets?
   f. Are journal entries approved by a responsible official?
   g. Are aging schedules of accounts receivable prepared periodically and reviewed by a responsible person?
   h. Does the company compare budgeted amounts with actual expenditures?
   i. Are trial balances of the accounts receivable ledgers prepared and reconciled regularly?
   j. Do the employees who maintain inventory records have physical access to the inventory?
   k. Are the inventory records adjusted to physical counts at least once a year?
   l. Are remittance advices that accompany receipts separated and given to the accounting department?
   m. Are costs and expenses under budgetary control?
   n. Is a postage meter used?
   o. Are monthly statements of account mailed to all customers?
   p. In reconciling bank accounts, do employees examine endorsements?
   q. Has the bank (or banks) been instructed not to cash checks payable to the company?

51. Mary's mother was dismayed. Her daughter had just been brought home by a city detective. Mary has been arrested at the bank where she had been working for three months.

   Mary's job had been in the cash receipts/payment processing operation. Her job was to operate a machine that would magnetically encode the amount of a customer's payment on the customer's remittance advice. Mary did not have access to the customer's payment. The amount that she was to encode was handwritten on each remittance advice. The magnetic encoding allowed the remittance advices to be processed by a computer.

   "I was only trying to help us, Mom," Mary explained. "with Dad laid off from the mill and all, I just figured that no one would notice if I took our utility bills in to work, encoded them with amounts as if payment had been made, and then inserted them with the other remittances I was working on. I didn't realize that my work was being checked. I guess I should have known better."

Required

Should Mary have known better? Does an organization, such as the bank where Mary worked, have any obligation to explain the control environment of a job to an employee?

52. The internal auditor of a manufacturer is reviewing order-entry and shipping procedures. Figure 4.10 represents the procedures in place. All documents used in the procedure are prenumbered. There are many undershipments on customers' orders, but goods not shipped are *not* automatically back-ordered.

Required

   a. Identify deficiencies and/or omissions in the control system for the order-entry and shipping functions.
   b. Suggest improvements in the control system to remove the deficiencies you noted.

Use the following format in responding to this question:
   a. Deficiency and/or omission
   b. Improvements suggested

(IIA)

53. The cashier of the Easy Company intercepted Customer A's check payable to the company in the amount of $500 and deposited it in a bank account that was part of the company petty cash fund, of which he was custodian. He then drew

FIGURE 4.10

Flowchart for
Problem 52

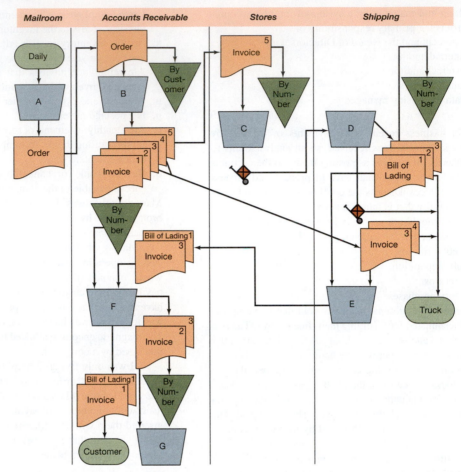

Explanatory Notes
A = Open Mail
B = Prepare Invoice from Customer Order and Distribute
C = Pick Goods to Extent Available and Forward to Shipping
D = Prepare Bill of Lading and Label Cartons for Shipment
E = Note Undershipments on Invoice #3 after Goods are Shipped
F = Complete Invoice Extensions Based on Actual Quantities Shipped
G = Post to Ledger and Prepare Daily Sales Journal
◆ = Handtruck–Goods Movement

a $500 check on the petty cash fund bank account payable to himself, signed it, and cashed it. At the end of the month while processing the monthly statements to customers, he changed the statement to Customer A so that it showed that A had received credit for the $500 check that had been intercepted. Ten days later, he made an entry in the cash received book that purported to record receipt of a remittance of $500 from Customer A, thus restoring A's account to its proper balance but overstating the cash in the bank. He covered the overstatement by omitting from the list of outstanding checks in the bank reconcilement two checks, the aggregate amount of which was $500.

List what you regard as five important deficiencies in the system of internal control in this situation, and state the proper remedy for each deficiency.

(CPA)

54. As the internal auditor for a large company, you have been asked to consult with the operating management of a new division that consists of a chain of video game arcades. Specifically, the management wants advice on the nature of accounting risks posed by the new operation and on the internal controls needed to reduce those risks. In reviewing the proposed video game arcade operation, you learn the following information.

The chain will consist of 40 locations, the most distant location being only 200 miles from the corporate offices. The 40 locations will be divided into two regions, each having a regional manager. Each location will contain an average of 35 machines, with some locations having as many as 60 machines and others having as few as 10 machines. Access to the game counter and coins in each machine will be by use of a master key.

To minimize cost, the management insists on minimizing the number of operating and accounting personnel. However, the management has agreed to hire sufficient maintenance personnel in-house to minimize downtime. The management also has agreed to provide a local manager for each operating location because of the cash nature of the business.

The management insists on daily collection and deposit of coins in a local bank by the resident manager. Validated deposit slips are to be mailed to the corporate offices. Bank statements will be mailed directly by the banks to corporate offices.

Required

The definition of internal accounting control addresses aspects of transaction execution, transaction recording, access to assets, and periodic comparisons of accountability. Based on these aspects and using the format that follows:

   a. Identify the risks for the major activities listed.
   b. Suggest internal accounting controls for the risks identified.

The required answer format is as shown:

Activity	Risk	Control
Transaction execution		
Transaction recording		
Access to assets		
Periodic comparisons of accountability		

(IIA)

55. The Luxnet division of the WSH Corporation publishes college textbooks. Luxnet employs about 20 senior editors, each of whom manages the production of several different textbooks.

In the production of a textbook, editors usually request several manuscript reviews from different college professors, with each professor being paid a fee for the service. Each senior editor is given a yearly budget that is to be spent for manuscript reviews.

Senior editors select professors whom they think will provide useful reviews. Requests for manuscript reviews are made by sending a letter that specifies the general terms and the fee to be paid. If the professor agrees to perform a review, a signed copy of the letter is returned to the editor. The editor then forwards the manuscript to the professor for review.

When the professor's review is received, the editor sends a memo to accounts payable indicating the account number charge, the professor's name and address, and the amount to be paid. Accounts payable prepares a check for the amount indicated and forwards it to the editor for delivery to the professor.

Required

   a. Identify deficiencies and/or weaknesses in the procedures described.
   b. Suggest an improvement to remove each weakness/deficiency you noted in part a.

Use the following format to answer this question.
   a. Deficiency/weakness
   b. Improvement suggested

56. You were recently appointed the internal auditor for a private college. Your first assignment is to appraise the adequacy and effectiveness of the student registration procedures. You have completed your preliminary survey. Based on your interviews and a walk-through of the student registration operation, you prepared an informal flowchart.

Required

Examine the following informal flowchart and list five internal control weaknesses (such as omission of certain steps or measures) in the student registration procedures.

Admission—Processing of Registrations

   a. Mailroom
      Opens all mail; prepares remittance advices and remittance listings.
      Sends copies of advices and listings to
      1. cashier (with cash and checks).
      2. accounts receivable clerk.
      3. general bookkeeper.
      Destroys other copies of advices and listings.

   b. Registration clerk
      Receives three copies of completed registration forms from students.
      Checks for counselor's or similar approval.
      Records appropriate fee from official class catalog.
      If completed properly, approves forms and sends student with registration forms to cashier.
      If not completed properly, returns forms to student for follow-up and reapplication.

   c. Cashier
      Collects funds or forwards two copies of registration forms to billing clerk.
      Records cash receipts in daily receipts record.
      Prepares and makes daily deposits.
      Forwards duplicate receipted deposit slips and daily receipt records to general bookkeeper.
      Destroys copies of daily receipts records.

   d. Billing clerk
      Receives two copies of registration form, prepares bill, and makes entries in registration (sales) journal.
      Forwards copies of billings and registration forms to accounts receivable clerk and copies of bill to general bookkeeper.

   e. Accounts receivable clerk
      Posts accounts receivable subsidiary ledger detailed accounts from remittance listings. Matches billings and registration forms and posts accounts receivable subsidiary ledger detailed accounts.

   f. General bookkeeper
      Journalizes and posts cash receipts and applicable registrations to general ledger. Enters registration (sales) journal data in general ledger.

(IIA)

57. Collateral Deposit (Part 2)[2]
    (This is a continuation of Problem 27 in Chapter 2.)

Required

Part 1 Prepare an analytic flowchart and cross-reference it to the list of procedures that accompanies Problem 27 in Chapter 2.

Part 2 Prepare an application controls matrix for the process using the form shown in Figure 4.9. Cross-reference the controls to the matrix using the appropriate numbers from the list of procedures.

Identify any apparent weaknesses noted in the description of the collateral receipt process.

58. Collateral Withdrawal

Dan Matt drew up a flowchart for the depositing of collateral (Problem 57) and turned it over to his senior. The senior inquired if collateral was only deposited and never withdrawn. Dan realized he had not followed the collateral process through to its completion. He still had to investigate the withdrawal of collateral that resulted when the loan was paid.

Dan found that the customer initiates the withdrawal of collateral by presenting the pink receipt copy to the loan officer. The loan officer forwards the customer's request for return of the collateral to the collateral clerk, who prepares a prenumbered, four-part withdrawal form. Each copy of the form is a different color to facilitate its distribution. The original (pink) copy of the request is sent back to the loan officer, the second (blue) copy is sent to the vault custodian, and the third (white) copy is filed by the collateral clerk with the deposit form. Again, the yellow or fourth copy is discarded. The vault custodian takes the blue copy of the request to the vault attendant, and together they remove the collateral and match it against the request. If they match, both the vault custodian and the vault attendant sign the blue copy of the request. If they are not in agreement, the vault custodian contacts the loan officer to iron out the discrepancy. The signed blue copy is sent back to the loan officer, accompanied by the collateral. The loan officer verifies that everything is proper and then signs the blue copy and turns over the collateral to the customer. The customer, after verifying that the collateral is correct, signs the pink copy of the request, which had been on file with the loan officer. Then both the blue and the pink copies are returned to the collateral clerk. The collateral clerk matches the two copies of the request to the white copy in his file. If they are all in agreement, he records the return of the collateral in his log, staples the copies together, and files them in the completed file by number.

Required

a. Prepare an analytic flowchart of the collateral withdrawal process using the description given in the case.
b. Prepare the application controls matrix for the process, using the form shown in Figure 4.9.

c. List any apparent weaknesses in the collateral withdrawal process as described.

59. The Whip-O Manufacturing Company manufactures neck braces for special orders. The firm hires 20 artisans who each work on a brace until completion. There are 8–10 operations performed on each custom brace, ranging from 1 to 6 hours each. At present, prescriptions and measurements are obtained from doctors by the sales representative. On receipt at the plant, the production agent prepares a production ticket and holds the information until an artisan is free.

Lists of materials needed for each job are compiled by the artisan and given to the production agent. The agent purchases the locally available items and orders the unavailable items from a medical supply catalog. Delivery of the ordered items usually takes less than a week.

When an employee finishes a job, he or she gives the brace, production ticket, and hours spent to the accountant, who adds the cost of materials and overhead and then calculates the price. The receivable is recorded, and the brace and invoice are sent to the sales representative for delivery.

Each week, the artisans turn in a time card to the general manager, who approves the cards and passes them to the accountant for payroll preparation and check distribution. The general manager has had several concerns:

a. Doctors persistently call inquiring about cost and delivery date, and little information is available.
b. Total time from receipt of order to delivery time seems excessive in most cases.
c. Payroll costs do not appear to be in control.

Required

a. Document in a flowchart the sales processing and payroll system.
b. List the weaknesses and suggestions for improvement concerned with the general manager's comments. (Use the format below; you should have *at least six*.)

Weakness Recommended Improvement

60. The following procedures relate to the sales-order system of the Tallahassee Sailboat Manufacturing Company.

All sales orders are received in the sales department. Customers deal directly with salespeople who write up specifications for custom-manufactured sailboats. Once an order is complete, it is sent to the production supervisor, who makes three additional copies of the sales order on the company's copying machine. The supervisor then numbers all four copies. Copy 1 is retained in an open file. Copy 2 is sent to the accountant. Copy 3 is returned to sales and is filed according to customer name. Copy 4 is attached to a job cost sheet for reference.

The accountant, on receiving her copy of the sales order, immediately checks the numerical sequence written in by the supervisor to ensure that it conforms to the company's scheme of prenumbering.

[2]Problems 57 and 58 were prepared by Frederick L. Neumann, Richard J. Boland, and Jeffrey Johnson; funded by the Touche Ross Foundation Aid to Accounting Education Program.

The job cost sheet is used to collect labor, material, and overhead costs. Materials are obtained from the stores supervisor, who reviews the specifications on the job cost sheet and estimates the materials required. He then pulls the appropriate materials and personally delivers them to the appropriate workers. He likes to do this personally because he feels that it minimizes errors and ensures that the workers do not enter the storeroom.

The company bills are based on the stage-of-completion method. When the supervisor feels that a job is half complete, he notifies the accountant, who then bills the customer for 50% of the agreed-upon price. When the job is complete, the same procedure is followed.

The president's secretary opens the mail and separates checks and their accompanying invoices. The checks are rubber-stamped for deposit only. They are immediately forwarded to the cashier, who deposits them first thing the following workday. A copy of the deposit receipt is then forwarded to the accountant as a remittance advice. The invoices are sent to the accountant, who enters the amount received in the special journal for accounts receivable. Once a month, she posts the journal entries to the accounts receivable subsidiary ledger and cash account. After posting to the control accounts, she makes up financial statements. These procedures are comprehensive and describe everything she does relating to sales and receipts.

Required

a. Prepare an analytic flowchart relating to the procedures discussed above.
b. Using a two-column approach, list internal control weaknesses and make suggestions for improvements.

61. Jayde, Inc., is a private, medium-sized manufacturing company with an office, a warehouse, and a distribution center in metropolitan Chicago. Jayde's accounting system currently comprises a hodgepodge of various software packages: a general ledger system (custom developed by a local software company), a Web-based inventory system, an off-the-shelf payroll system, and a different off-the-shelf accounts receivable/payable system.

Jane Spinner, Jayde's controller, is a minority shareholder who has been overseeing all accounting operations for the past 20 years. She pretty much has a complete picture of the accounting system in her head, but little system documentation exists except for the vendor-supplied user manuals relating to the various accounting software packages.

Required

Betty Brins, Jayde's CEO and primary shareholder, has decided that Jayde will go public. Your assignment is to write a memo relating to the issue of what Jayde needs to do in order to prepare for Sarbanes–Oxley compliance, as part of going public.

Web Research Assignments

62. Managers seeking to comply with SOX must be concerned with the external audit process. Such knowledge can help managers structure their systems so as to help minimize audit costs and maximize the chance of being in compliance with SOX.

You are an internal auditor in a large national manufacturing company. You have agreed to assist the controller of your company by writing a report relating to the process that auditors must follow under PCAOB Auditing Standard No. 5. (The PCAOB regulates the auditing profession as per the SOX.)

Required

Write a report that summarizes key process that the auditor must follow per PCAOB Auditing Standard No. 5. The PCAOB audit standards are available on the PCAOB Web site, *www.pcaob.org*. Specifically, address the following key audit issues:

a. The role of risk assessment in structuring the audit.
b. Scaling the audit.
c. Assessing the risk of fraud.
d. The top-down approach.

63. Fraud is a serious issue in almost all organizations. Assume that you are an outside consultant to a regional clothing retailer. You have agreed to write a brief report outlining ways to manage the risk of fraud. For assistance, visit anti-fraud.aicpa.org and use the Web search engines.

Required

Include the following topics in your report
a. how fraud is defined
b. the role of the audit committee oversight in fraud risk management
c. fraud risk assessment
d. fraud prevention, detection, and deterrence
e. fraud investigation and response

Answers to Chapter Quiz

1. b   **2.** b   **3.** c   **4.** a   **5.** a   **6.** b   **7.** a   **8.** b   **9.** d   **10.** d

Fraud Examination and Fraud Management

Learning Objectives

Careful study of this chapter will enable you to:

- Explain the steps in the fraud management process.
- Define the different types of evidence and explain the evidence collection process.
- Explain the interview process.
- Define the elements of a fraud report.
- Be familiar with the major aspects of expert testimony.
- Discuss how financial statement fraud occurs and how it might be prevented.
- Explain a variety of employee fraud schemes.
- Know how to apply computer science techniques to gather evidence from computers.

We use the terms **"fraud examination"** and **"fraud investigation"** interchangeably to refer to the application of accounting and other specialized skills to the prevention, detection, investigation, correction, and reporting of fraud. Fraud examination can apply to any type of fraud relating to an organization, including occupational fraud, vendor fraud, consumer fraud, fraudulent financial statements, and tax fraud. Fraud examination applies to various types of entities, including individuals, estates and trusts, and even governmental entities. Fraud against such entities can include things like bankruptcy fraud; divorce fraud; various types of scams, bribery, and kickbacks.

Fraud examination is a subspecialty of *forensic accounting*, an area within accounting that applies specialized skills to actual or potential legal matters. The term "forensic" simply refers to matters that are legal in nature—that is, matters that have the potential to invo lve civil or criminal courts.

Quite a wide range of specialized skills applies to forensic accountants and fraud investigators. Specialized techniques relating to the areas of fraud prevention, auditing, evidence gathering, interviewing and interrogating, computer forensics, forensic science, testifying in court, loss recovery, valuation, and fraud reporting are relevant. Certifications relating to fraud expertise include the Certified Fraud Examiner (offered by the Association of Certified Fraud Examiners, www.acfe.com) and the Certified in Financial Forensics credential (offered by the American Institute of Certified Public Accountants, www.aicpa.org).

The Fraud Management Process

Fraud management is a process that involves several closely related phases: prevention, detection, investigation, reporting, and litigation and recovery. Accountants specializing in fraud routinely perform services in all these phases of the fraud management process.

Fraud Prevention

At the most basic level, fraud prevention within the organization is a matter of good internal control. However, because of the ever-increasing complexity of information technologies, the application of internal control now requires specialized information security management systems (ISMS's). Such systems share three common objectives:

- *Confidentiality*. Data are available only to authorized persons.
- *Integrity*. Data are accurate and complete.
- *Availability*. Data are available when and where needed.

Fraud prevention is part of the Enterprise Risk Management (ERM) process. As such, prevention is never absolute but only relative to the risk appetite of the organization. Therefore, prevention is a matter of degree, so that careful cost–benefit analyses always result in ISMS's that retain some risk of fraud.

Optimal fraud prevention requires much more than simply implementing control checklists that contain items such as firewalls, anti-virus software, and so on. Rather, a systematic life-cycle approach is required that begins with threats and vulnerabilities and ends with implementing corresponding risk-based controls. The process is so complex that authoritative bodies have promulgated various standards and frameworks for ISMS.

The ISO 27000 family of standards is promulgated by the International Standards Organization. This group of standards includes lists of over 5,000 controls along with descriptions of processes for their as-applicable selection, customization, and adaptation to individual organizations. COBIT (Control Objectives for Information and Related Technology) is another well-known standard for ISMS development. This standard is based on 34 high-level objectives that are broken down into 318 detailed control objectives. COBIT provides guidance for all phases of the information security life cycle.

ISMS's are further discussed in Chapter 6 *Information Security*.

 CASE IN POINT

The International Register of ISMS Certificates (www.iso27001certificates.com) maintains a list of organizations that have gone through an accredited certification process for ISO 27001. Over 7,000 organizations are ISO 27001 certified, with more than half of them in Japan. A relatively small percent of them are in the United States. Organizations certified in the United States include, among others, the Federal Reserve Bank of New York, the University of Texas at Dallas, the World Bank, SAP America Inc., Unisys, and Xerox.

Fraud Detection

Fraud detection is part of the larger group of processes that include fraud prevention, investigation, correction, reporting, and recovery. None of these individual processes stands alone. The extent of resources devoted to one individual process affects the need to devote resources to the others. For example, better prevention can lead to less fraud, which in turn can result in fewer frauds being detected, which in turn can lead to fewer investigations, and so on.

Fraud detection involves identifying indicators of fraud that suggest a need for further investigation. Fraud indicators can be individual indicators (i.e., "red flags") or composite indicators. Red flags include events such as a mismatch in an inventory count, a cash register that doesn't balance, a suspicious invoice, and so on. Composite indicators are typically based on combining multiple individual indicators that when viewed one at a time might not signal possible fraud. Composite indicators are sometimes referred to as *risk scores*. **FICO®** (www.fico.com) is a well-known risk-score indicator that is used by banks and lenders in judging consumer credit applications. The FICO score is based on various factors that include payment history, credit utilization, length of credit history, and types of credit used. The higher the FICO score, the lower the credit risk.

CASE IN POINT

Running a Web search for "fraud indicators" produces sites with industry-specific fraud indicators. For example, an article on www.crimetime.com suggests insurance fraud indicators that include the following: a claim against a new policy, hand delivery of documents (in order to circumvent mail fraud charges), and familiarity with the claims process.

Data-driven fraud detection involves the formal analysis of large sets of data in search for fraud indicators. Such large sets of data include basic tips, incidents of internal control violations, security breaches, and pattern data. Pattern data tend to indicate fraud when various data items are considered jointly. Pattern data include but are not limited to risk scores. For example, an automobile insurance claim alone might seem normal. But the same claim might be viewed with suspicion if it occurs after a sudden large drop in the insured's credit score.

Various software packages and services exist to assist with fraud detection. Examples included Experian Detect™ (www.experian.com) for risk scoring of credit applications, and Approva One (www.approva.net) or ACL (www.acl.com) for continuous controls monitoring in organizations. It is also possible for an organization to build its own fraud-risk system using data mining software such as SAS Data Mining (www.sas.com), SAP BusinessObjects (www.sap.com), and the Microstrategy Business Intelligence Platform (www.microstrategy.com).

Fraud detection software and services sometimes use sophisticated statistical techniques such as Logistic Regression, decision trees, and time series analysis. There are also software detection systems (e.g., www.orgnet.com) that rely on social-networking analysis. One example of social-networking analysis involves mapping phone-call records to identify relationships between suspects and others. However, some frauds are best caught by random investigations, since there is always a possibility that the fraud detection system itself might be manipulated by the fraudster.

Content and text analysis and Benford analysis are also data-driven approaches. Content and text analysis analyze the content of documents (e.g., e-mail messages) and conversations to identify possible fraud indicators. The CIA and FBI use this approach to flag possible terrorist activities. **Benford Analysis** exploits an interesting pattern relating to the first digit of numbers appearing in a random data set. Specifically, the Number 1 is more likely to appear than the Number 2; the Number 2 is more likely to appear than the Number 3; the Number 3 is more likely to appear than the Number 4, and so on. The Number 1 is about 6 times more likely to appear in the first digit than the Number 9. This relationship can be used on items such as batches of invoice amounts to indicate possible falsifications or alterations.

Despite there being many excellent sophisticated fraud detection tools available, fraud is typically discovered in a variety of other ways, some of them quite unsophisticated. In general, roughly 25% of fraud in organizations is detected by accident. Another 35–50% or so is detected through tips and hotlines. The remainder of fraud within the organization is detected by internal and external auditors.

Given the incidence of fraud reported through tips and hotlines, it is important to set up phone numbers, e-mail address, and Web sites to collect tips. In all cases, tip-reporting systems should make clear the exact types of frauds or ethics violations that are of interest, and whether anonymity or confidentiality are promised. Anonymity assures the tipster that the tipster's identity will remain unknown, whereas confidentiality merely represents a promise to protect the name of the tipster, subject to state and federal laws.

Tips should be forwarded to a person who is reasonably independent from the rest of the company's operations. The internal auditor is a good candidate to receive tips, because he or she typically reports directly to the Board of Directors. The legal department, or outside legal counsel, is also a good choice in some cases.

OPTIMAL FRAUD DETECTION SYSTEMS   There are trade-offs between fraud prevention, fraud detection, and fraud investigation. Fraud detection is an imperfect process. Recall from the discussion above, that fraud detection involves identifying indicators that suggest the *possibility* of fraud. It's the "possibility" that introduces imperfection into the process. This is because fraud indicators require a follow-up investigation, which in some cases will uncover fraud and in other cases won't.

A *Type 1* error occurs when a fraud indicator falsely signals fraud. A *Type 2* error occurs when a fraud indicator fails to signal fraud. Type 1 errors result in unnecessary fraud investigations, whereas Type 2 errors result in frauds escaping detection. Given these two types of errors, an optimal fraud detection system will define the fraud indicator in such a way so as to "balance" the Type 1 and Type 2 costs. Doing so balances the total costs associated with the ISMS. The goal is to minimize Total Fraud Costs defined as follows:

$$\text{Total Fraud Costs} = \text{Costs of Prevention} + \text{Costs of Investigations}$$
$$+ \text{Costs of Detections} + \text{Costs of Losses}.$$

In some cases, investigation costs can be quite high. For example, an insurance fraud claim investigation might require a lot of time from a field investigator. So a fraud indicator that signals fraud too often, especially in cases in which small amounts of fraud are involved, might result in large investigation costs and relatively small savings from fraudulent claims.

Although minimizing total fraud costs might be a daunting task in some situations, there are cases in which it is an easily manageable process. For example, if the costs of prevention are determined by industry-standard internal controls and investigation costs are handled in a department whose costs are fixed, then the optimal solution is to set the fraud indicator so that it refers all the most likely cases of fraud to the investigation department. For example, if the investigation department can handle 100 cases a year, then the optimal solution would be to send exactly the 100 most-likely cases of fraud to the investigation department. Of course, if some possible cases are higher value than others, then the 100 highest-value cases could be referred for investigation. The value of each case can be computed as the value of the possible loss times the difference between one and the probability of a related Type 1 error. For example, if a given fraud's possible value is $1,000 and its related Type 1 error is .10, then it could be valued at $900 (i.e., [1–.10]*$1,000). Using this approach, the 100 fraud cases with the highest value would be referred to the investigation department.

Fraud Investigation Process

Fraud investigation is the process of systematically gathering and reviewing evidence for the purpose of documenting the presence or absence of fraud. There are four phases in the fraud investigation process (Figure 5.1):

1. The fraud engagement process. This phase begins with a fraud indicator and the investigator's first contact with the case, and ends with the launching of an investigation.
2. The evidence collection process. This phase includes various steps in which evidence is collected in support of the scope and objectives of the investigation.
3. The investigation reporting process. This phase involves documenting and summarizing the results of the fraud investigation.
4. The loss recovery process. This phase involves events such as enabling civil and criminal litigation, resolving tax issues, and collecting insurance.

FIGURE 5.1

The Fraud Investigation Process

The Engagement Process — This Ends with an Agreement that Defines the Scope and Objectives of the investigation

The Evidence Collection Process — Collect Physical, Document, Observation, and Interview Evidence

The Reporting Process — Report the Findings of the Investgation

The Loss Recovery Process — Repair Internal Control Weaknesses, Collect Insurance, Litigate

THE FRAUD ENGAGEMENT PROCESS At some point, the presence of a fraud indicator may trigger a need to consider a possible investigation. But before a possible investigation is launched, various steps must be followed. These steps are:

1. Create and review an incident report;
2. Conduct the initial notifications and evaluation;
3. Consider legal issues;
4. Evaluate the loss mitigation and recovery considerations;
5. Define the scope, objectives, and costs of the investigation; and
6. Create an engagement letter or memorandum.

Create and Review an Incident Report A fraud incident report can be anything from a red flag to a formal report written by a responsible person. But not all incident reports lead to fraud investigations; the initial facts must be weighed, and consideration may be given to other factors such as the cost of a possible investigation, the size of the potential loss, the effect of an investigation on employee morale, and so on.

The incident report can take on important legal significance. If the incident report is made by law enforcement, it may serve as the basis of a probable-cause justification that would be required to obtain subpoenas, search warrants, and even arrest warrants. If made by a company employee, the incident report may serve as evidence that any subsequent investigation is based on reasonable cause rather than, say, illegal discrimination or a violation of employee union rights.

A unified case file should be established if the incident report is followed by additional actions or information gathering. All information pertinent to the case should be included in this file, and access to the file should be restricted in such a way as to avoid tipping off any suspects or spreading negative rumors. It should be assumed the contents of the file will eventually end up in a court proceeding; so it should be maintained meticulously.

Conduct the Initial Notifications and Evaluation Responsible persons should conduct an evaluation of the incident report to decide whether an investigation is warranted. It is critical at this phase to avoid any degree of investigation by someone other than a trained investigator. Information gathering by nonprofessionals can spoil evidence or otherwise severely damage or compromise an investigation. What can happen is that in deciding whether an investigation is warranted, an untrained manager can begin gathering information, which is tantamount to investigation.

One of the worst things that can happen at this point is for someone to confront a suspect. Best investigation practices require a considerable amount of evidence-gathering work before a suspect is confronted, and even then there are right ways and wrong ways to confront suspects.

Once a decision is made to commence an investigation, appropriate individuals must be notified. Possible candidates to receive notifications include the CEO/owner, legal counsel, the loss management department, the internal auditor, insurers, and the Board of Directors. One person with sufficiently high authority should make the final decision on whether to proceed with an investigation.

Consider Legal Issues Before commencing with any investigation, possible legal issues should be considered. These include the rights of suspects under investigation, the possibility of conducting the investigation under attorney–client privilege, how to handle suspects during the investigation, the rights of investigating employers, to the extent to which a government entity might be involved in the investigation, and reporting obligations.

Suspects may be granted special rights via federal or state laws or regulations, employment contracts, and collective bargaining agreements. Review of such rights by legal counsel should be conducted as appropriate. Regarding attorney–client privilege, in some cases it may be advisable for an investigation to be conducted under the supervision of outside legal counsel. In many cases, this can place the work product of the investigation under the umbrella of attorney–client privilege. Regarding the handling of suspects during an investigation, consideration should be given as to whether there is sufficient justification to immediately fire a worker-suspect or place the worker on administrative leave either with or without pay. Regarding the rights of employers, consideration should be given to the employer's possible rights to search and seize evidence and to compel suspects or others to cooperate in an investigation. Regarding government entity involvement, to the extent that a government entity is involved in the investigation, the employee may have constitutional rights that limit the employer's powers of investigation. Failure to respect such rights could spoil a case against a suspect or even generate a lawsuit from the suspect. Finally, regarding reporting obligations, consideration should be given to any obligation to report the incident to law enforcement or government regulators.

Evaluate the Loss Mitigation and Recovery Considerations In many cases, the best approach is to immediately stop a recurring fraud or one that is in progress. But in some cases, the best approach might be to let the fraud continue in order to catch the fraudster in the act. Catching a fraudster in the act, say, by a video recording, may result in a quick confession and a complete unraveling of the fraud scheme. On the other hand, documenting and proving a fraud can easily take many months of work and cost large sums of money, even for investigations that might appear to be very simple at the beginning. Forensic investigations of financial records are often complicated by damaged or incomplete records, and by the need to rule out innocent explanations for apparent frauds.

In an organizational setting, funds missing from accounts may appear to be an obvious matter to managers. But what may be obvious to managers is likely to not at all be obvious to police or to juries, especially when there is a defense attorney challenging everything. For example, if there are missing funds and damaged or missing financial records, a skilled defense attorney could argue that if the records were correct the apparent fraud could be explained. Therefore, any investigation that is to be pursued through a court trial must rule out all innocent explanations for an apparent fraud. In addition to missing or damaged records, other possible explanations for the missing funds include, for example, possible computer errors, hacker intrusions, and losses spilling over from a previous period. Ruling out such explanations requires reverse proof, proof that the apparent fraud was not a result of something other than deliberate actions of the suspect.

Given the issues of damaged or incomplete records and the need for reverse proof, as well as the general complexity of developing a case based on sometimes obscure financial records, law enforcement officials will typically decline to prosecute fraud cases without a confession or incriminating video recording. Most law enforcement agencies do not have teams of forensic accountants at their disposal to build and prosecute financial fraud cases, except when they involve organized crime rings or high-profile suspects or organizations.

Consideration must also be given to any insurance coverage applicable to possible fraud losses, and any related requirements imposed on organizations. For example, insurance policies frequently require notifications of losses and steps to mitigate losses when they are suspected to exist.

Define the Scope, Objectives, and Costs of the Investigation

Define the Scope, Objectives, and Costs of the Investigation One might assume that the purpose of an investigation is simply to prove a fraudster's guilt. But there are other equally important issues to consider. These include stopping the fraud from continuing, identifying the loss for insurance and tax purposes, making an example of the fraudster, minimizing embarrassing disclosures in the press, and discovering weaknesses in the internal control system. The exact scope and extent of the investigation will depend on all of these factors, and will vary from one case to another. For example, if a suspect is no longer an employee, and the main objective is preventing more losses, the optimal decision might be to simply improve internal controls and not investigate at all. On the other hand, if the goal is to make an example of a fraudster, then it might be desirable to expend large amounts of money on an investigation even if the actual or potential loss is small.

If the main goal is to recover via an insurance claim, it might only be necessary to prove that a loss has occurred and not prove that a particular person is responsible. This is because insurance policies typically require proof of loss but not proof of a particular suspect's guilt.

If negative publicity is a consideration and no insurance is involved, it might be desirable to simply repair any internal control problems and estimate the loss for tax purposes. In many cases, fraud losses are deductible from income. Of course, giving a fraudster a pass might seem distasteful, but sometimes the best business decisions are not emotionally satisfying.

Create the Engagement Letter or Memorandum Various aspects of the investigation should be set forth in a letter or memorandum. These include the objectives and scope of the investigation, the methods to be used, the resources required, the responsibilities of the respective parties, the basis and methods to be used for charging fees (if any), and the means for resolving disputes (e.g., via arbitration), and if an outside investigator is involved.

The Evidence Collection Process

Evidence is anything (e.g., tangible objects, documents, and testimony) that relates to the truth or falsity of an assertion made in an investigation or legal proceeding. When well organized, evidence provides answers to the basic perennial questions asked by sleuths regarding a possible fraud: who, what, when, where, how, and why. That is, who did it; what did he do; when, where, how, and why did he do it.

The first question always asked is "what." If there's no fraud, then there's nothing to investigate. The widely accepted principle of **predication** requires investigations be started or continued only when there is a reasonable basis to do so. Without predication, there is no clear fraud to investigate, and the issue becomes one of either detection or simply fishing for fraud.

But if there is a reasonable basis to investigate, the investigator begins by forming a fraud theory. A fraud theory merely provides answers to the basic questions regarding who, what, when, where, how, and why. Once the investigator establishes a tentative fraud theory, he or she collects evidence that either supports or negates the theory. If the theory is confirmed with sufficient evidence, the investigation is concluded. If the theory is negated, he or she either ends the investigation or modifies the theory and continues to collect evidence until he or she ends the investigation with either a confirmed theory or a negated theory (Figure 5.2).

Regardless of how strongly a theory may be confirmed by the evidence, the investigator never "points the finger" at a suspect and declares that person guilty of fraud. Rather, the

FIGURE 5.2

Testing a Fraud Theory

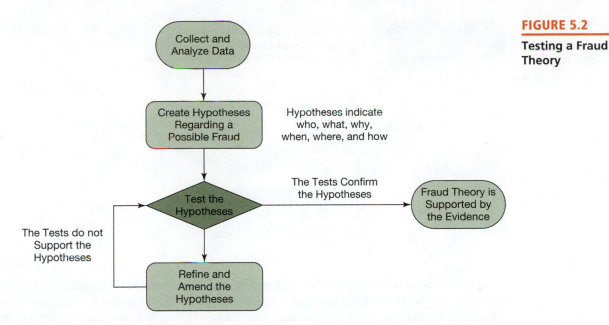

investigator merely summarizes and presents evidence as it appears. It is up to the courts and attorneys to interpret the evidence and make decisions regarding guilt. Guilt is a legal concept, and only courts have the power, legally speaking, to make determinations of guilt. The evidence itself may point to guilt, but the investigator should not attempt to go beyond what the evidence says in regards to possible guilt. For example, if the investigator records on video a bookkeeper stuffing money in his pockets, the appearance of guilt may be strong. But the investigator need not, and should not, interpret the actions of the suspect to suggest guilt. After all, a suspect in such a case might be entitled to argue in court that his boss told him to stuff the money in his pockets and carry it to the bank for deposit.

CASE IN POINT

An article by Jeff Windham in *Fraud Magazine* (www.fraud-magazine.com) cites two cases in which fraud investigators were sued by suspects regarding comments made by the investigators. In one case, the fraud investigator allegedly told a group of representatives of his client that in his opinion the suspect was a "crook." In another case, an investigator allegedly told someone that suspects were going to jail for what they had done.

In general, investigators collect three types of evidence: physical and document evidence, observation evidence, and interview evidence. *Physical and document evidence* include things like fingerprints, trace evidence, and forged or incriminating documents. In a courtroom setting, document evidence might also include things like charts and exhibits admitted into evidence as part of expert testimony. *Observation evidence* results from monitoring suspects. In some cases, when legally permissible, such evidence may include audio or video recordings of suspects' activities. *Interview evidence* includes the results of interviews, with the ultimate in interview evidence being a court-admissible signed confession.

Evidence is collected in a specific order. First, physical and document evidence is collected, then observations are conducted, and finally the interviews are conducted (Figure 5.3). This order is important because a careful review of the document evidence can provide important

FIGURE 5.3

**Evidence Is Collected
in a Specific Order**

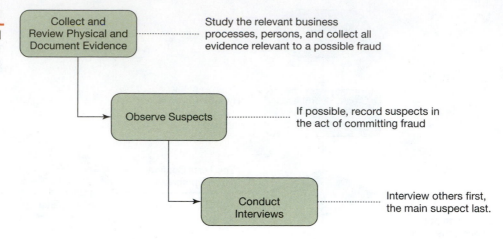

clues as to what to observe, and a thorough knowledge of the document evidence, coupled with observations, can provide the essential background often needed for conducting interviews. Carefully preparing for interviews not only helps the investigator to know what questions to ask but also provides the investigator with the knowledge needed to know when a suspect is lying. The interviewer will typically ask the suspect many questions before revealing what he or she knows. This approach prevents the suspect from concocting a story that conforms to the facts as the investigator knows them. For example, if the investigator secretly observed an employee entering the building late at nights, the suspect might be asked if he ever comes in to work after hours. In this case, the suspect might be more inclined to lie if he is unaware that his nighttime entries into the building were observed by the investigator. In this way, the investigator can get the suspect on record with a series of lies that can later be used to at least show a consciousness of guilt. Further, suspects might confess when confronted with strong evidence of their lying.

Interviews are conducted in a specific order. They begin with those furthest from the prime suspect and work their way toward the prime suspect. This approach assures that the investigator has the maximum amount of information when interviewing the prime suspect and it maximizes the chances of obtaining a confession.

PHYSICAL, DOCUMENT, AND OBSERVATION EVIDENCE   Physical evidence is typically collected at crime scenes by criminalists and then interpreted in court by forensic scientists. It includes things like fingerprints, DNA, and trace evidence (e.g., hair and fibers). Document evidence is typically collected by fraud investigators and includes a wide range of items such as personnel files, resumes, public records, tax returns, credit files, credit applications, vehicle records, bank records, and accounting records. In some cases, such records may be obtained via a subpoena or search warrant. A **subpoena** is an order from a government agency or officer of a court that compels the recipient, under penalty, to produce physical evidence, documents, or testimony. A **search warrant** is a court order that authorizes law enforcement officials to search for and seize evidence. To obtain a search warrant, law enforcement officials are typically required to first present to the court a sworn statement (an *affidavit*) that indicates probable cause that a crime has been committed. Subpoenas, on the other hand, are used in both civil and criminal investigations and proceedings, and may or may not require the signature of a judge, depending on the jurisdiction and circumstances.

In some cases, law enforcement agencies may issue "silent" subpoenas to obtain financial records. For example, a subpoena may be directed to a bank and order the production of account records belonging to the individual being targeted in the investigation. The individual will never even know that the bank has shared her account records with law enforcement.

In civil cases, and in criminal cases in which the subpoena isn't silent, the counter-party in the litigation will typically have knowledge of subpoenas issued in the case. This may permit the counter-party to fight in court to suppress the subpoena. Subpoenas can also be fought by third parties who receive them. They can even be ignored in some cases, such as with subpoenas for medical records whose privacy is protected by state or federal law.

The investigator may use various auditing and analytical techniques during the process of obtaining documentary evidence. Analytical procedures typically compare actual financial data to expected financial data. Examples include comparing current financial results to those of previous periods, current financial data with industry data, and current financial data with financial data predicted by statistical models. Such comparisons can help pinpoint areas in which fraud exists, which in turn can lead to discovering concrete documentary evidence of fraud. In general, fraud investigators use all types of fraud indicators in order to narrow down areas of possible fraud.

The investigator may also use a wide range of other audit techniques in uncovering fraud. These include techniques such as surprise counts of cash, inventories, or other assets; reconciliations; batch controls; totals; statistical sampling; ratio analyses; and tracing and vouching. **Tracing** involves beginning with a source document (e.g., a sales order) and following the related transaction through the entire accounting cycle (i.e., through the customer's account receivable, the cash account, the sales account, all the way into the financial statements). **Vouching** is the same as tracing but works in reverse: It begins with numbers in accounts and follows them backward to the source documents. In other words, vouching checks helps ensure that amounts posted to accounts are supported by valid source documents.

 CASE IN POINT

In one case, an auditor visited a client bank to conduct a routine surprise audit of the tellers. Almost as soon as the auditor began her work, one teller became afraid and stepped forward and began to confess to a fraud scheme that the auditor would have not discovered as part of her surprise audit.

Questioned Documents It is common for fraud investigators to encounter documents whose authenticity or authorship is in question. Such documents are called **questioned documents.** Documents can be questioned for a wide variety of reasons, including questionable signatures, missing data, incorrect or inconsistent data, document numbers out of sequence, and erasures. **Document examiners** specialize in analyzing questioned documents. They can detect document alterations by analysis of things like the paper, the ink, and typefaces. They can investigate authorship by comparing the signature or handwriting on a document to an *exemplar* (i.e., a handwriting sample) obtained from a person suspected of authoring or altering the document. This comparison can lead to the conclusion that the provider of the exemplar either did or did not author or alter the document.

 CASE IN POINT

Document examiners handle a wide range of case types. These include threatening letters identity theft, document forgeries, graffiti, altered contracts, and forged signatures. Many document examiners work with photocopies that can be submitted by e-mail. Many document examiners have Web sites with domain names that reflect their line of work. Examples include www.documentexaminerexpert.com, www.expertdocumentexaminer.com, www.documentexaminer.com, and www.handwritingexpertking.com.

Handwriting analysis is not a definitive science, and in court the handwriting expert is likely to couch expert opinions using qualifiers such as "likely." For example, the expert might say that the exemplar is a likely match to the handwriting in the questioned document.

Observation Observation involves the use of the senses to assess the behavior of persons and other activities such as business processes. Observational evidence can be the most powerful form of evidence. It can provide the "smoking gun" that juries need to reach a quick conviction. A jury can easily understand a video of a bookkeeper stuffing cash receipts in his pockets, whereas the same jury might have great difficulty understanding weeks and weeks of boring testimony regarding accounting procedures and arcane issues relating to embezzlement.

In law enforcement circles surreptitious observation is called **surveillance.** A wide range of surveillance techniques exist that include not only traditional ones such as audio or video recording but also newer, sophisticated electronic techniques. For example, with a court order law enforcement authorities can remotely activate the microphone in many modern cell phones and listen to conversations involving persons close to the phone. This technique can be used even when the phone is turned off! The only way to prevent this type of monitoring is to remove the phone's battery.

Invigilation is a commonly used observation technique. This involves observing a suspect's behavior before, during, and after an announced investigation. For example, assume that a suspected inventory supervisor has a habit of being the last employee to leave every day. But then when a fraud investigation is announced, the same employee leaves earlier every day and is no longer the last employee out. Finally, after the investigation appears to be complete, the same employee reverts to leaving late every day. Given this pattern of behavior, the investigator might want to focus on what the suspect does when working late.

The Interview Process Proper interviewing can either make or break an investigation. In some cases, managers or owners angry about fraud losses are eager to confront a suspect even before an investigation has begun. As mentioned previously, such confrontations can completely spoil investigations. On the other hand, a well-prepared interview conducted by a skilled interviewer can sometimes result in a confession that completely unwinds a complicated case.

The investigator should prepare for the interview by carefully studying all evidence collected to date, and also in organizational settings by studying items such as the employee's resume, job description, job functions, salary and benefits, promotions that may have been expected but not received, and performance evaluations. In addition, the investigator should build a *fraud-triangle profile* of the suspect that includes both work and personal data that may relate to the three sides of the fraud triangle: opportunity, pressure, and rationalization. Opportunity to commit fraud can often be identified by studying a suspect's job functions and relationships within the organization. Pressure can be identified by looking for signs of excessive debt or spending (which may be caused by things like drug or gambling addiction, large medical expenses, or an extravagant lifestyle). Rationalization is more difficult to access, but rationalizations can include things like, "I'm only borrowing the money," or "I need it more than they do."

Interviewing involves establishing rapport, asking questions, listening, and responding appropriately. All interviews begin in the same way, asking introductory and general information questions. *Introductory questions* seek to establish rapport, seek the interviewee's cooperation, and seek to observe the demeanor of suspects when they are asked non-sensitive and non-incriminating questions. The process of carefully observing suspects under such conditions is called **calibration.** *Informational questions* seek information relevant to the investigation. When asking informational questions, it is normal to ask a suspect if she knows the purpose of the interview, whom she believes committed the crime, and why.

After the initial introductory and informational questions, further questioning proceeds differently for suspects versus non-suspects. For suspects, the goal of the remainder of the interview is to seek a confession. For non-suspects, the goal is to simply conclude the interview in an orderly matter, which is done by asking concluding questions. *Concluding questions* focus on thanking the interviewee for his cooperation, confirming information provided by the interviewee as part of the interview, seeking any additional information that the interviewee may want to volunteer, and seeking the interviewee's continued cooperation in the future.

After the informational questions, the suspect is asked *assessment questions* that seek to assess his honesty. If he is honest and confesses, then the investigator simply documents the confession and proceeds to concluding questions. But if the suspect demonstrates deception, the investigator will commence with *admission seeking questions*, with an eye on obtaining a confession (Figure 5.4).

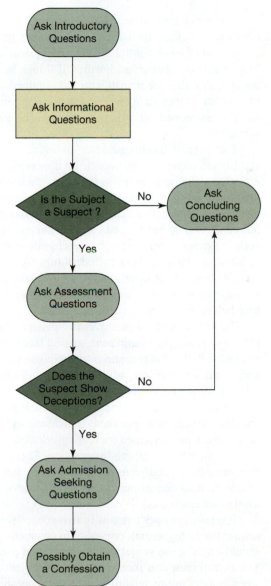

FIGURE 5.4

The Fraud Interview Process

CASE IN POINT

Polygraphs (also known as "lie detectors") may sometimes be used to detect dishonesty in fraud investigations. Although the polygraph can sometimes be used as a helpful investigative tool, it is generally without credibility in the scientific community and not admissible as evidence in courts. Nevertheless, the polygraph is used for screening employees in various government agencies, including the FBI and CIA.

There are many prominent cases in which a polygraph produced erroneous results with suspects. For example, the Gary Ridgway, "Green River Killer" passed a polygraph and then confessed nearly 20 years later to a string of murders.

There are many Web sites on the Internet that explain ways to beat the polygraph test.

There are various ways of assessing a suspect's honesty when asking informational and admission-seeking questions. At this point in the investigation, the investigator may be in possession of a substantial amount of physical, document, and observational evidence relating to the suspect's behavior. Further, if things have gone well the suspect will not be aware of the evidence that the investigator has obtained. As a result, the suspect may tell a series of lies to concoct a story in answer to the informational questions. In this case, the investigator can use the assessment questions to observe the suspect's behavior, mannerisms, and demeanor when lying.

But even if the investigator enters the interviews without already having obtained any significant physical, document, or observation evidence, the investigator can still employ effective techniques to assess the suspect's honesty. This is done by the investigator observing verbal and nonverbal cues exhibited by the suspect in response to assessment questions. Verbal cues can include things like evasiveness, hesitation, inconsistencies, and vagueness in answering questions. Nonverbal cues can include things like body language and eye movements. Regarding body language, a suspect may signal guilt or deception in various ways when presented with sensitive questions. These include things like sitting in a "fleeing position" with feet and face pointing toward the door, reaching for nearby objects, picking lint off clothes, scratching, and shifting positions. Sometimes suspects engage in such actions in order to give themselves more time before answering a question.

There are certain eye movement patterns that can suggest honesty or deception. The exact pattern depends on whether the suspect tends to respond more to audio, visual, or tactile stimuli. Individuals who respond more audio stimuli typically look down and to the left, or simply horizontally to the left, when recalling information. Such individuals will tend to look in a different direction when not telling the truth.

Visual-oriented individuals tend to look up and to the left or straight ahead, or both, when recalling information. For these individuals eye movements in other directions tend to indicate deception. Touch-oriented (or feeling-oriented) individuals tend to look downward or downward to the right when recalling information. These individuals also sometimes close or blink their eyes in cases of genuine recall. As with the other types of individuals, touch-oriented individuals tend to indicate deception when their eyes move in other directions when responding to sensitive assessment questions.

It is not necessary to know in advance, or even for certain, whether a suspect is more oriented toward the audio, visual, or tactile. In conducting the initial calibration process, the investigator should observe the subject's eye-movement patterns when answering non-sensitive questions. The investigator can then compare the subject's calibration patterns to the subject's patterns when responding to sensitive assessment questions. The investigator should also make similar before and after comparisons for body language and verbal cues.

Conducting Interviews Normally, interviews should not be recorded unless the subject matter is too complex for taking notes. But if the interview is to be recorded, permission should be obtained and properly documented in advance. On the other hand, taking brief notes is reasonable and effective, but even then notes should be brief so that the note-taking doesn't interfere with the interview.

Non-suspects can be interviewed anywhere that is convenient, but suspects should be interviewed in a neutral location that they are unfamiliar with. An unfamiliar location can interfere with a suspect's ability to recall previously rehearsed concocted answers to questions. Further, the suspect should be seated without any obstruction between him and the door to exit the room; the room temperature should be comfortable; and there should be no distractions for things like pictures, books, and memorabilia. The suspect should not be seated behind a desk or other object that obscures a view of his body, to make it easier for the investigator to observe his body language.

Getting a Confession After the suspect is on record with many lies, the investigator can get tough and confront the suspect with the evidence. But then the investigator needs to turn "soft" and help the suspect confess by assisting the suspect with a moral excuse for the fraud. For example, the investigator can say things like, "I understand that you were going to pay it back," or "I understand how your wife lost her job and how difficult it would have been for you to have to let your daughter drop out of college because of family money problems."

Once an oral confession is obtained, the investigator should immediately present the suspect with a written confession to sign. This can only happen if the investigator prepares the confession in advance of the interview. If the suspect has committed more than one crime, there should be a written confession for each one. The standard confession should include a statement of the acts committed; an acknowledgment that they were wrong; a place for the suspect to initial each page; a place for a witness to countersign; and paragraphs in which the suspect acknowledges signing freely and voluntarily, and with full understanding of the entire confession. A paragraph might be added to indicate that the suspect is contrite and cooperative.

The Fraud Report

The investigator prepares a report at the conclusion of an investigation. Reports are used for various purposes, such as to justify tax deductions for fraud losses, to justify firing an employee in possible litigation relating to the firing, to justify civil or criminal litigation relating to the fraud, to claim insurance for covered fraud losses, and to enable regulatory reporting (Figure 5.5).

The fraud report will typically contain sections that describe the client for whom the report was prepared, contain background information relating to the case (such as what triggered the investigation), an executive summary, the scope and objectives of the investigation, a description of the fraud investigation team and the methods used, and the findings and recommendations resulting from the investigation. As previously discussed, the report should never draw conclusions regarding a suspect's guilt. This important and necessary limitation is likely to disappoint managers and police who are looking for the report as probable cause to make an arrest, or as evidence that is strong enough in its own right to win a case in court. Expert analysis and testimony are normally required in addition to a report in order to make a case in a court.

Loss Recovery and Litigation

Loss recovery options include accepting the loss, collecting insurance if available, and pursuing the perpetrator in court. In many cases, simply accepting the loss is the preferred solution. This is simple and fast, avoids embarrassing publicity, and avoids costly litigation.

In some cases, the option of collecting insurance may be available. This requires the business to submit a proof of loss statement to the insurer. The problem is that the nature of the loss and its amount may not be known until the investigation is complete, making it difficult or impossible to immediately submit the required statement. Further, fraud investigations of

FIGURE 5.5

**Fraud Investigation
Reports Are Used for
Many Purposes**

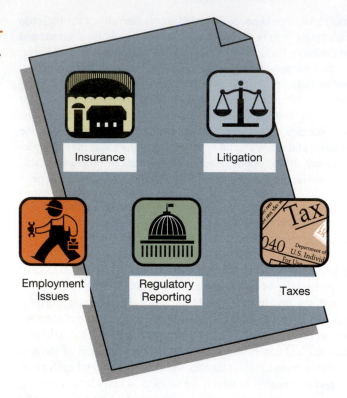

accounting records can often take many months, even in relatively small and simple cases. Even in a small business, because of the need for reverse proof, a simple investigation of cash receipts and bank accounts can easily cost over $100,000. The result is that the cost of the investigation may exceed the amount recovered from insurance, or the insurance payment may arrive so late that the company is bankrupt before it arrives. Still, insurance policies typically cover embezzlement losses, losses to valuable papers and records, lost income, and the costs of preparing the proof of loss. On the other hand, policies typically do not cover attorney's fees, and they tend to place strict limits on coverage for lost income.

Pursuing the perpetrator in civil court is often not helpful. The cost of pursuing a civil case can be very high, and in many cases perpetrators have no assets to be won in a court judgment. It is advisable to carefully investigate a perpetrator's assets before launching an expensive civil suit. Public records searches can be helpful, especially in locating real estate. But locating hidden assets can be a very difficult process and may be best handled by an investigator who specializes in collecting court judgments.

Criminal prosecution is sometimes an option. The advantage of criminal prosecution is that the case is pursued at the expense of the state; also, criminal courts frequently have the power to order restitution. The main problem is in getting the police to investigate and getting prosecutors to prosecute. Fraud cases frequently require extensive amounts of forensic accounting work and expert analysis and testimony. Such resources tend to be available to law enforcement agencies in very limited amounts. A signed confession or an incriminating video recording can be of a great help, as such things make it much easier for prosecutors to reach quick plea bargains with perpetrators.

Expert Testimony

Forensic accountants and fraud investigators can become involved in a variety of different types of court cases, including those relating to occupational fraud, divorces, bankruptcy, breach of contract suits, damage suits, civil loss recovery, and mergers and acquisitions. In general, forensic accounts can serve in such cases as either expert consultants or expert witnesses.

Expert consultants provide expert opinions and analyses to attorneys under the umbrella of attorney–client privilege. Expert consultants are not subject to discovery. **Discovery** is the process in which opposing parties can require each other and relevant parties to produce out-of-court evidence. Discovery may include compelling an expert witness to submit documents and answer questions in depositions made under oath. The main requirement to maintain the attorney–client privilege is that the expert consultant cannot testify or be expected to testify in court. On the other hand, the forensic accountant who expects to testify in court becomes an *expert witness* (as opposed to an expert consultant) and is fully subject to discovery.

Expert witnesses are granted special consideration in court proceedings. Normally, witnesses can only testify to "personal knowledge," to things they have personally experienced through their physical senses. Expert witnesses, on the other hand, are permitted to state opinions and conclusions based on facts admitted into evidence and other information on which they choose to reasonably rely.

 CASE IN POINT

Expert witnesses are available for almost every imaginable type of case. In addition to basic forensic accounting testimony, very specialized areas exist that include exotic things like automotive lamp filament analysis, plumbing failure analysis, and glass failure analysis. A comprehensive directory of expert consultants is available at www.experts.com.

Before a forensic accountant can be permitted to testify, he or she must first demonstrate expert qualifications. Expert qualifications include things like degrees, certifications, publications, training, and experience. Once qualified, the actual expert testimony must meet certain special standards that vary somewhat from one jurisdiction to another. The U.S. federal court system is governed by Rule 702, which permits those qualified as experts to present expert testimony in court if (1) the testimony is based upon sufficient facts or data, (2) the testimony is the product of reliable principles and methods, and (3) the witness has applied the principles and methods reliably to the facts of the case.

The key phrase in Rule 702 is "reliable principles and methods." In one decision, the Supreme Court set forth guidelines for determining what are reliable principles and methods: (1) The technique or theory has been subjected to scientific testing, (2) the technique or theory has been published in peer-reviewed scientific journals, (3) the error rate for the technique is reasonably estimated or known, and (4) the technique or theory is accepted in the relevant scientific community. Collectively these guidelines constitute what is widely referred to as the *Daubtest Test*, named after the Supreme Court case in which it originated. In a subsequent decision the court made this test mandatory for expert testimony in all federal courts, and indicated that the test should be applied strictly only to the extent that its strict application to a particular case is possible.

A different standard is applied in some state courts. The *Frey Test*, also named after a court case, only requires that the theory or method be generally accepted by the scientific community. Still, regardless of which standard applies, the forensic accountant must be prepared to defend the techniques used.

Fraud Schemes

Financial Statement Fraud

Financial statement fraud is the intentional misrepresentation (either by commission or omission) of any information included as part of a financial statement or report. Financial statement fraud differs from legal financial statement manipulation or *earnings management*. Earnings management refers to management acting within generally accounting principles (GAAP) to produce financial reports in a way that some might consider biased or unethical. This is quite different from fraud, which is always illegal (at least for public companies), and can never be justified by GAAP.

Managers can legally manipulate or manage financial statement numbers within GAAP by doing things such as assuming the longest possible lives of new assets for purposes of reducing annual depreciation and thus increasing current income. But not all manipulative or management-type behavior involves management actions that increase income. Sometimes managers write off large depreciable or amortizable assets in bad years, when their performance is going to look bad anyway, so that income will thereby look better in future years. Managers might also manipulate earnings through economic actions, by doing things like deferring maintenance of equipment in the current period to a future period, or by not replenishing inventories in the current period so that they eat into older, lower-priced inventory layers and thus reduce current cost of goods sold.

One can safely say that all financial statement fraud is unethical. Further, some would say that legal financial manipulation and earnings management are unethical, although most would agree that it is difficult to define bright lines regarding what is ethical and what is not ethical within the legitimate use of GAAP. Legal earnings management involves management taking GAAP-compliant accounting and/or legal economic actions within bad years to improve income. It also involves management taking similar actions in good years in order to reduce current income, thereby storing "extra income" for the future when it might be needed in bad years. Sometimes earnings management is called *cookie jar accounting,* because it involves storing "extra income" in a metaphorical accounting cookie jar in good years and pulling it out and using it in bad years.

 CASE IN POINT

> The "Great Salad Oil Scandal" was one of the most notorious financial statement frauds of all time. The 1960s-era Allied Crude Vegetable Oil Company managed to borrow substantial sums of money based on its inventories of salad oil. But in reality its large tanks of salad oil were filled mostly with water, with salad oil floating on top. When this deception was eventually uncovered, companies that included American Express and Bank of America suffered major consequential losses.

WHO COMMITS FINANCIAL STATEMENT FRAUD AND WHY   Generally, managers commit financial statement fraud either as a way of boosting financial performance or as a way of hiding theft, bribery, or other illegal activities. Managers may boost financial performance as a shortcut to getting ahead, thus artificially boosting share prices and opening up better business opportunities and sources of financing. Of course, managers might financially gain from such activities through increases in the value of shares they may hold, or through their receiving better performance evaluations.

We know from the Security and Exchange Commission's (SEC) published enforcement actions that financial statement fraud tends to occur most often in relatively small companies, in companies with downward trends in earnings, in companies with weak audit committees, in companies with weak governance structures (e.g., with Board members not sufficiently independent from management), or with anomalous situations like a change of auditor or an adverse audit opinion. In a large percentage of the cases, the CFO or the CEO is involved in the fraud, and it is not uncommon for the external auditor to be accused of participating in the fraud.

Managers who commit fraud run the risk of being criminally charged under a wide range of federal statutes, including those related to the Sarbanes–Oxley Act (SOX), the Foreign Corrupt Practices Act, wire fraud, mail fraud, conspiracy, racketeering, and money laundering. Potential jail sentences can reach into the hundreds of years. A manager accused of financial statement fraud may also be named in civil class–action suits, and SOX empowers the SEC to bar offenders of public companies from serving as corporate officers or directors.

HOW TO PREVENT FINANCIAL STATEMENT FRAUD Aside from good internal control and information security, the main road to honest financial statements is through good corporate governance. The main entities that contribute to corporate governance are the Board of Directors, the audit committee, the internal auditor, the CEO/CFO, the external auditor, and public oversight organizations. The likelihood of financial statement fraud is minimized to the extent that each of these entities does its job well.

The members of the Board of Directors must possess the appropriate business, industry, and financial competencies and be financially independent of the company except for their board-related compensations. The audit committee must possess appropriate accounting and systems skills, actively supervise the internal auditor, work with the external auditor, and investigate and follow up weaknesses or problems pointed out by internal auditors and external auditors. The CEO and CFO should be actively involved in the internal control processes of the company and should take very serious the development and implementation of ethics and internal control processes across the organization. The internal auditor should report directly to the audit committee and operate completely independent of the CEO, the CFO, and top management. The external auditor should be completely independent of the company, the members of its Board of Directors, and the top managers. Finally, public oversight bodies such as the SEC and the Public Company Accounting Oversight Board (PCAOB) should assure that external auditors do their job well.

Indicators of Financial Statement Fraud Various red flags signal possible financial statement fraud. These include weak internal controls; inadequate personnel-related practices; weak, sloppy, or irregular accounting practices; managers who are either weak or not competent; managers who place too much emphasis on short-run financial performance; managers who are excessively authoritarian; and of course, companies with weak or pressured earnings or cash flows, or with financial problems.

Financial Statement Fraud Schemes A report of the Committee of Sponsoring Organizations (COSO, www.coso.org) identified various categories of fraud schemes relevant to financial statement fraud. These include improper revenue recognition, overstatement of assets, understatement of expenses and liabilities, misappropriation of assets, inappropriate disclosures, and other miscellaneous techniques.

Roughly half of all financial statement frauds may involve overstating revenues. This is perhaps because there are so many ways revenues can be overstated. These methods include sham (i.e., fictitious) sales, premature revenue recognition (e.g., recognizing sales revenues before products are shipped), revenue recognition for sales subject to contingencies, extending the closing date for the sales account so as to include revenues for the next accounting period, misstating the percentage of completion, and channel stuffing. Channel stuffing involves end-of-the-period shipping of unwanted goods to customers in order to artificially boost revenue. The goods might be then returned in the next accounting period.

Regarding the overstatement of assets, almost any asset can be overstated. Required depreciation might be avoided, asset valuations can be inflated, bad-debt allowances can be understated, and so on. But the most common scheme is to overstate ending inventories, which boosts earnings when companies compute cost of goods sold as the difference between good available for sale and ending inventory. Management may also understate liabilities with the same effect.

Employee Fraud

In the United States, organizations lose billions of dollars a year as a result of frauds committed by their employees. Most of these frauds are never reported, and of those that are reported very few are prosecuted. It is too often the case that police and prosecutors just don't have the forensic accounting resources to investigate and prosecute frauds.

Most frauds within the organization are typically committed by employees who do not have a criminal record. Given the right financial pressures, opportunity, and rationalizations, normally honest employees may commit fraud. Financial pressures can come from things like large unpaid medical bills, gambling losses, or an extravagant lifestyle.

The corporate culture can play a major role in fostering employee dishonesty. Underpaid employees may steal to make up for what they think they deserve but do not get as wages. Excessive pressure by managers on subordinates can lead to their developing hostility against the company, thereby breeding resentment and a motive to steal. Corporate financial troubles can breed an atmosphere of chaos, thereby creating a lack of respect for internal control and thus creating related opportunities for employees to steal. Unscrupulous behavior from top management can lead to more of the same by subordinates. Problems with the corporate culture are likely to increase the risk of employee fraud regardless of how good the internal controls are.

REVENUE CYCLE FRAUD   Understanding different fraud schemes can help an investigator develop the most appropriate fraud theory given the evidence. A convenient way to classify employee fraud schemes is by the basic transaction cycles. This section discusses revenue cycle fraud.

The revenue cycle includes the collection of cash. Cash tends to be a favorite target for thieves. It is very light and occupies little space, it can be directly converted into other assets, and it usually cannot be identified as stolen property.

Cash Collection Fraud   Cash receipts, including those from checks, can be intercepted anytime beginning with their initial receipt up to and through the time they are deposited in the bank. **Sales skimming** schemes typically involve an employee pocketing cash but not recording its collection. The employee might give the customer a forged receipt or no receipt at all. Sales skimming schemes can be controlled through using prenumbered customer receipts, incentives for customers to report not receiving a receipt, and cash registers that clearly display the amounts involved in transactions.

A related scheme involves unapproved "moonlighting" using company resources. For example, an employee of a carpet-cleaning service might use company-cleaning equipment to create her own secret business on the side. This type of scheme can be avoided by limiting after-hours access to company resources.

Robbing the Cash Register   In situations where cash register receipts are not reconciled with sales receipts per each individual cash register, the employee is free to rob the cash register with impunity. The solution is to perform the reconciliations on a register-by-register basis and separately for each cashier shift.

Swapping Checks for Cash   This is a cash register fraud that involves removing cash from the cash register and replacing it with bogus checks. This scheme can be defeated by the video recording of cash register activities, and by using a point-of-sale check scanning device that connects to a service that verifies that the check is good, or at least is not fraudulent. Some such services can even convert point-of-sale checks into electronic payments.

Shortchanging the Customer   This is a fraud scheme in which a cashier uses distraction or deception in order to pocket part of the change due to the customer. For example, a cashier might simply return less change than due to a customer who is preoccupied with a crying baby or an incoming cell phone call. A cashier might also distract the customer by beginning to make change in the normal way, but in the middle of making change ask the customer to return some of the change in exchange for bills of a different denomination. These types of schemes can be foiled or detected by using video surveillance techniques to monitor cashiers. Cashiers should be trained in and required to follow strict procedures for making change.

Stealing Cash in the Mailroom Cash from customers might be received in the mail. In such situations, employees opening the mail can sometimes appropriate the incoming cash for their personal use. The solution to this situation is to have two employees together open each piece of mail backed up by video surveillance. Amounts received should be immediately recorded, with the completed remittance list being sent to the accounting function.

Stealing Cash in Transmission Anytime cash exchanges hands, some of it can get "lost." To prevent this, both parties in the exchange of cash should count the cash at the time of the exchange. They should also both sign a transmittal form acknowledging the exchange and send a copy to the accounting department. This process ensures that cash "leakages" can always be traced to one responsible person.

Lapping of Accounts Receivable This scheme requires that the bookkeeper for accounts receivable also handle incoming payments for customer accounts. The bookkeeper receives a payment from one customer, misappropriates the payment, and does not credit the customer's account. The bookkeeper then later covers the misappropriated payment by misappropriating a subsequent payment from a second customer. Next, the bookkeeper covers the second customer's payment by misappropriating a third customer's payment. This sequence of misappropriations continues on indefinitely. The solution to this problem is to segregate the bookkeeping and payment-handling functions.

Short Bank Deposits The person who makes bank deposits can fail to deposit all the funds. In an advanced version of this scheme, the person making the deposit may replace good checks for bogus ones, thus keeping the total of the deposit intact. These schemes can be foiled by a careful reconciliation between accounting deposit records and bank deposit records.

Noncustodial Theft of Cash In the presence of weak internal controls, losses of cash can arise as a result of theft involving individuals other than those charged with its custody. For example, a cash drawer left open can create an opportunity for theft from any nearby customer or employee.

Stolen blank company checks might be negotiated, resulting in unauthorized withdrawals from the company's bank account. Stolen checks from customers can be cashed using false or stolen identities. Stolen customer checks can also be "washed." **Check washing** involves using chemicals to remove a check's payment details and then adding new details for the payee, date, or amount of payment. An equally sophisticated scheme involves **check laundering,** which involves using a stolen customer check to make a payment on account. For example, a thief could use a stolen customer check in the amount of $100 to make a payment on his credit card account. Even though the credit card company is not named on the check as the payee, the bank processing the payment may process the payment anyway, mainly because in such cases banks do not always verify that the name of the payee on deposited checks matches the name on the bank account to which the deposit is to be applied. The best solution to check washing and laundering is good physical security over bank checks.

Accounts Receivable Fraud Aside from lapping, accounts receivable fraud involves improper account approvals, account credits, and improper write-offs. All these problems can be controlled by enforcing documentation for credit-related events, and by requiring that such events be reviewed and approved by an independent credit department.

EXPENDITURE CYCLE FRAUD Expenditure cycle frauds involve improper purchases, payments, and payroll-related payments and activities. The best general approach to avoiding improper purchases is to use a voucher system, in which purchase-related disbursements are made only upon review by the finance department of a complete voucher package: a purchase requisition, purchase order, vendor's invoice, and receiving report. Each document within the voucher package is reviewed and approved by an independent department.

Kickbacks and Bid Rigging Even with a good voucher system, various frauds can be perpetrated by a company purchasing agent. A dishonest purchasing agent might rig bids or take kickbacks on purchases made from vendors. In the case of *bid rigging* frauds, a dishonest purchasing agent might purchase from a friend or relative even though doing so is not in the best interest of the company. In the case of *kickback frauds,* a dishonest purchasing agent might accept secret payments or favors in exchange for favoring a particular vendor. The best way to foil bid rigging and kickback frauds is to have a multi-level review and approval process within the purchasing department for all bids and purchases. In addition, purchasing agents should be required to disclose any relationships with vendors that might pose a conflict of interest.

Theft of Petty Cash Petty cash may be misappropriated for personal expenditures. The best way to control this problem is to manage petty cash with an *imprest fund* accounting system. As discussed in Chapter 4, an imprest fund involves keeping a predetermined fixed amount of money in the petty cash box. As funds are expended they are replaced by cash receipts. Then, periodically the cash receipts are exchanged for an equal amount of cash, thereby restoring the cash box to the predetermined fixed amount. This procedure is accompanied by at least after-the-fact review and approval of all cash receipts. Of course, careful physical security must be maintained over the cash box, and one individual at a time must be held accountable for its custody.

Abuse of Company Credit Cards Company credit cards can be used for improper purchase of travel and entertainment and goods and services. The best way to prevent such frauds is to have careful after-the-fact review and approval of all credit card purchases. In addition, the credit cards themselves can have built-in restrictions that prevent them from even being accepted in unapproved industries. For example, a card might be restricted so that if it is presented for payment in the travel industry, the issuing bank will automatically decline the transaction.

Theft of Company Checks Employees can steal company checks and use them for unauthorized purchases. Checks that already contain payment details can be washed and then diverted for unapproved purposes. These types of schemes can be foiled by good physical security over checks, careful review of bank statements, and by using checks that cannot be easily altered. Check-printing inks are available that are resistant to washing or alterations.

Fraudulent Returns Employees can return properly purchased good in exchange for cash, and then convert the cash to personal use. This type of fraud is best controlled by maintaining individual custodial accountability for all assets.

Theft of Inventory and Other Assets Any asset can be misappropriated. The best way to prevent asset theft is through a combination of good physical security, periodic inventories, individual custodial responsibility, good record keeping, proper asset disposal management, and internal auditing.

Payroll Fraud Payroll fraud may involve improper hiring, improper changes to employee personnel files and pay rates, and improper work-related reporting. Regarding improper hiring, employees may hire unqualified friends or relatives, or add "phantom" (i.e., non-existent) employees to the payroll. Regarding improper changes to personnel files, employees can do things such as giving friends unauthorized pay raises. Regarding improper work-related reporting, employees can report work hours that they do not perform, fail to document absence from work, and even tamper with performance evaluations in their personnel files. Control over payroll frauds is obtained by maintaining personnel files in an independent personnel department, and requiring and documenting management and personnel review and approval for all personnel-related activities.

Other Types of Employee Fraud There is no end to the possible list of employee frauds. For example, employees can deliberately violate environmental laws, commit illegal discrimination, or commit illegal insider trading. Good internal control and a good corporate culture represent the company's defenses against all types of fraud.

PRODUCTION CYCLE FRAUD   Production cycle fraud can involve misappropriation of waste, scrap, and spoiled goods. Control over these items requires carefully defined policies, procedures, documentation, and approvals for the handling of all waste, scrap, and spoiled goods. Conflicts of interest must be avoided, such as in the case in which employees are permitted to keep for personal use (or either directly or indirectly benefit from) any of these items.

Vendor Fraud

Vendors can and frequently do defraud their buyers. However such frauds generally are not a problem unless the buyer has internal control weaknesses relating to purchasing. Several types of fraud are briefly described.

Short Shipments   The vendor ships fewer than the ordered amount of goods but bills for the amount ordered. This only works if the buyer does not conduct blind counts of the goods ordered.

Substandard or Defective Goods   The vendor can only get away with this scheme if the buyer does not properly inspect incoming goods, and/or trace returns from customers back to vendors.

Balance Due Billing   With this type of fraud the vendor simply bills the buyer for the balance due on account and not for specific invoices. Since payments on the vendor's account are applied to the balance and not to specific invoices, the buyer may have no easy way of knowing or proving that any particular invoice is paid or that the balance on account is correct. This lack of knowledge by the buyer, especially one with weak controls, can lead to the vendor padding the balance due.

Fraudulent Cost-Plus Billing   Sometimes vendors bill customers for the vendor's costs plus a markup. This can open the door to the vendor passing fictitious costs on to the buyer.

Computer Forensics

Computer forensics is the application of computer science to computer-related matters that might come before a court. Such matters can include almost any type of business transaction or entity, and almost any issue involved in, or potentially involved in, any civil or criminal investigation or litigation. Computers are everywhere and come in many forms that range from mobile devices to desktops to supercomputers. Even cars have computers in them; so there are an endless number of places where computer forensics can be applied.

The primary objectives of computer forensics include studying computers and computer networks in order to (1) identify perpetrators of crimes or undesirable behavior, (2) locate missing or hidden data, and (3) reconstruct damaged files and databases.

The following is a list of activities that are routinely used in computer forensics analysis:

- Content analysis—determining the content of computer files and electronic communications
- Comparison analysis—comparing the content of computer files in order to determine any differences between them
- Transaction analysis—investigating the source, date, time, and other details relating to changes in files or databases
- Data extraction—locating and extracting data of interest from computer storage devices
- Data recovery—recovering deleted or corrupted data from computer storage devices
- Format conversion—converting data from one format to another
- Keyword searching—searching large amounts of data for content of interest

- Location analysis—locating the source or destination of network-connected devices
- Password recovery—gaining access to files or communications that are encrypted or protected by passwords
- Computer program analysis—studying computer programs to understand and document the functions they perform and the steps in which their functions are executed

Evidence Gathering with Computers

The investigator should maintain meticulous working papers that document each step performed during evidence gathering. The investigator should avoid drawing summary conclusions in the working papers, keeping in mind that such conclusions could later be used in court to possibly impeach his credibility.

PRELIMINARY STEPS   In performing any investigation relating to computers, there are preliminary steps that should generally be followed. These include sizing up the situation, taking control of (and preserving) the evidence, and deciding the best approach to take in gathering evidence.

In sizing up the situation, the investigator should consider what fraud may have been committed (i.e., as part of a fraud theory), the sophistication of suspects, and the evidence that may be available. The investigator's consideration of these items will lead him to an understanding of what evidence needs to be collected and the best way to go about collecting it. For example, the fraud scheme may suggest that two employees, and hence two computers, are involved in the fraud. Based on this information, the investigator might seize both computers involved. The investigator might also seize centralized backup copies of the two computers and centrally stored copies of e-mail communications between the two employees.

The sophistication of suspects is important because sophisticated suspects sometimes put anti-forensic countermeasures in place. For example, in an extreme situation a terrorist could rig a computer to explode if tampered with. Therefore, the investigator must always consider possible anti-forensic measures as part of the investigation plan.

COLLECTING COMPUTER-RELATED EVIDENCE   In many situations computers contain evidence relevant to a fraud investigation. The investigator's job includes extracting and preserving such evidence for use in the investigation and possible legal proceedings. This may seem simple on the surface, but in practice it can be fraught with complexities that if ignored can lead to the data being either altered or destroyed.

One problem is with deleted files. The issue is that deleted files are not really deleted, at least not immediately. When a user deletes a file, the operating system simply deletes the file from the listing of available files on the computer. The data in the file still remain in the same place untouched. This is obviously true in operating systems that use a "recycle bin" for deleted files. In such systems, the user can simply visit the recycle bin and request that the file be un-deleted or restored to the same location and condition that it was before it was deleted.

But even after a file has been "completely" deleted and is no longer available in a recycle bin, its data still remain on the computer. After it is deleted, the space occupied by its data becomes part of the free storage available for storing other files. But its data still reside in that free space until the operating system stores another file there.

Operating systems perform many routine internal tasks that create and delete files. Examples of such tasks include anti-virus scanning, disk optimization, and memory management. Any of these tasks can at any time overwrite deleted-file data stored in free space. Further, any use of the computer by the investigator poses additional risks that deleted-file data will be overwritten and lost. For example, word-processing programs automatically create hidden backup copies of documents opened by users. Therefore, if an investigator opens a document in a word processor, the word processor might create a hidden backup copy of the document that just happens to get stored in the free space occupied by an important deleted file.

CASE IN POINT

Even after computer data is erased and overwritten by new data, it may still be possible to recover the erased data. When data on a hard drive is overwritten, traces of the original data may remain. Special techniques, such as magnetic-force microscopy and magnetic-force tunneling microscopy, exist to recover such data. To really make sure that erased data is not recoverable, it is necessary to overwrite it many times. The U.S. Department of Defense standard requires that each sector of erased data be overwritten seven times. Some experts recommend overwriting erased data as many as 35 times in order to be sure that it cannot be recovered.

PULL THE PLUG   Simply shutting down a computer in a normal way can also lead to data loss and therefore, evidence loss. When a computer is shut down, the operating system typically saves information regarding the state of the system at the time of the shutdown and performs various other file operations. For example, the operating system might save information regarding the arrangement of icons on a desktop. Therefore, in many cases the best way for an investigator to avoid the risk of data loss is to simply pull the plug on the computer. With a mobile device, this might mean cutting the power source by removing or disconnecting a battery.

Pulling the plug can also defeat certain anti-tampering techniques sometimes used by sophisticated fraudsters. In addition to the anti-tampering technique mentioned above (rigging the computer to explode if tampered with), sophisticated perpetrators can install password-protected software that will permanently erase data if the computer is tampered with in any way. Such software can also do other things like send out a secret e-mail message (one that leaves no trace), warning the perpetrator that an investigation is underway.

In summary, cutting the power to the computer is generally the best way to avoid data loss on a hard drive or solid-state storage device. Further, it avoids the possible problem of a court litigant later claiming that data recovered from the computer cannot be trusted because it was somehow altered by the investigator.

DON'T PULL THE PLUG   There is one major disadvantage to pulling the plug: In doing so any data stored in the computer's volatile memory will be immediately lost. This might mean that the investigator permanently loses access to documents or messages that have not yet been saved or sent. It can also mean losing access to encrypted files that might be viewable before the plug is pulled but never again afterwards. Losing access to encrypted files can be a serious issue, because there are many unbreakable publicly available encryption programs. In fact, the computer's entire main storage device can be encrypted, so that pulling the plug makes it impossible for the investigator to access any of the computer's data.

The decision as to whether to pull the plug must be made based on the situation, the fraud theory, the likelihood of anti-forensic countermeasures, and alternative sources of evidence that may be available if computer data is lost. If the situation is especially urgent, such as in stopping an imminent terrorist attack, the investigator may be more interested in immediately discovering what is on the computer rather than in taking it a forensic lab for analysis. On the other hand, for example, if the situation is not urgent and the investigator suspects anti-forensic measures, then pulling the plug might be the best alternative.

In some cases, it might be advisable to pull the plug but first run forensic analysis software (such as the Forensic Toolkit® published by www.accessdata.com). Such software can dump to an external storage device the contents of volatile memory and provide an analysis of running programs and processes. Such software can be installed and run from USB drives with minimal interference to the computer's files and internal environment.

DEVICE PROCESSING Once the power to the computer has been cut, the hard drive or solid-state storage device should be removed from the computer and placed in an evidence bag, with key pieces of information noted on the outside of the bag (e.g., the time, date, and the device's serial number). It is also beneficial to take photographs of both the computer and storage device, and of the area surrounding the computer. Numbered cards can be placed next to the storage device and computer to help better identify them. The numbers on the cards should be recorded and cross-referenced in the investigator's working papers along descriptions of the related items and with the related photographs. Once removed, the storage device is transferred to a lab or office for analysis. Changes in custody, as they become known to the investigator, should be noted on the outside of the evidence bag and in the investigator's notes.

The first step in the lab is to make one or more duplicate copies of the storage devices. The copying should be done by a system that includes special hardware to block the possibility of writing any data to the storage device under investigation.

CONTENT INVESTIGATION The next step is to investigate the contents of the storage device using forensic analysis software. Such software can provide many helpful functions:

1. Password cracking and decryption. Passwords can be easily cracked for most of the typical office-based software applications.
2. Steganography identification. This involves identifying images that contain hidden documents or data.
3. Large-volume searching for keyword phrases of interest to the investigator (using software like dtSearch® published by www.dtSearch.com).

DELETED OR CORRUPTED DATA RECOVERY Data from deleted or corrupted files can sometimes be recovered using software that permits the investigator to directly access data on the storage devices while bypassing the normal file system. On a hard drive this involves accessing disk sectors, the smallest units of data that computers use to physically store or retrieve data. Disk sectors in of themselves are completely unstructured blocks of data that are physically arranged on the disk in a semi-random fashion. The semi-random arrangement of sectors applies even to files that have not been deleted. This is because operating systems tend to store files in pieces, with one piece being stored in a group of adjacent sectors in one place on the hard drive, a second piece being stored in a group of adjacent sectors in a completely different place on the hard drive, and so on. Therefore, working at the sector level to recover a deleted file on a hard drive can involve first searching the hard drive to find the right pieces, and then assembling the pieces together into a file.

Location Analysis

In many cases, the investigator will seek to find the physical location associated with a computer device that is used to communicate over the Internet. This is normally accomplished through the IP (Internet Protocol) address, a unique number that is assigned to every device that communicates on the Internet.

IP addresses are normally issued to individuals and organizations through Internet service providers (ISPs). An IP address can be directly traced to the person or organization it is assigned to. This can be done by first checking to find out which ISP owns the IP address, and then by finding out from the ISP the name of the person or organization to which it has assigned the IP address. Obtaining the needed cooperation from the ISP may require an enforceable subpoena. Furthermore, it is also possible that the person or organization to which the IP is assigned has in turn assigned the IP to a particular person or employee.

In some cases, IP assignments can change over time. For this reason, IP assignments must be considered on particular dates and times relevant to the investigation. Sufficient records within the ISP and subsequent assignees may or may not exist to identify an IP assignee as needed.

Thus far, we have considered IPs as they are used on the Internet. These are more formally referred to as Wide Area Network (WAN) IPs. There are also Local Area Network (LAN) IPs, IPs that are used only within a given group or organization. LAN IPs are used as a way of multiple individuals sharing a WAN IP. Such sharing is accomplished within the group or organization via hardware devices. Only the WAN IP is visible on the Internet. Therefore, Internet communications with individuals sharing the same IP address can only be traced to that shared IP. Local IP addresses are visible only inside the group.

ISPs are reasonably likely to keep logs that record assignees of WAN IPs. But organizations typically do not keep similar logs regarding LAN IPs. The result is that it might be impossible to trace Internet communications to a specific individual within a group sharing a WAN IP. This is especially true in groups of individuals accessing the Internet through a wireless router. This is because, normally speaking, wireless routers dynamically assign local IPs to users as they connect to the Internet, and then reassign them to other users after the first users disconnect from the Internet and the others connect in their place.

In some organizations employees' IPs can be static, so that each employee always has the same local IP. But this might not help an investigator much, because, as mentioned above, many organizations do not record or retain log files that indicate which local IP does what on a given day and time. For example, a Web server log at Google.com might indicate that a user from a given IP ran a particular search on January 1, 2016 at 9:01 P.M. An investigator might trace this IP to a particular company, but the company might not have any records regarding which local IP connected to Google.com at the indicated date and time. Such records are normally kept inside of the network-sharing devices themselves, but often companies do not enable the logging features in these devices, and even if they do enable them, the devices might retain record of only the very most recent activities.

Even though there may be no company records regarding which particular local IP did what on a given date and time, similar information can sometimes be available on users' computers. For example, Web browsers typically maintain their own history records, so that it is possible to open the browser's history screen to see if there was a visit to Google.com at a given date and time.

E-mail messages can be a valuable source of IP-tracing information. This is because virtually all e-mail programs store with each message internal "header records" that keep a record of the IP address of the sender, the sender's e-mail provider, the recipient's e-mail provider, and the recipient. The investigator need to only look at the header records to find the IP address of the sender.

Documents can sometimes be traced by metadata contained in them. For example, word processing documents typically contain somewhat hidden data called "document properties" that contain the name, computer user name, or initials of the document's author. The word processing programs themselves contain functions for displaying the document properties. Such functions are normally very easy to use but may be unfamiliar to the average user. Document properties alone probably are not strong enough to serve as evidence of proof of authorship, but they may provide sufficient evidence to obtain a subpoena or search warrant, or to at least point the investigator in the right direction.

IP tracing is not a foolproof method. Hackers routinely use various services to hide their real IP addresses. They do this by connecting to the Internet through proxy servers. By running their communications through a proxy server, all their Internet communications are marked with the IP address of the proxy server and not their own server.

To be really secure in hiding their IP addresses, some hackers connect through proxy server chains (Figure 5.6). This involves first connecting to one proxy server, then from that proxy server connecting to a second proxy server, and so on. The IP address of the last proxy server in the chain becomes the user's WAN IP address. Moreover, the individual proxy servers in the chain might not maintain log files and may be spread all over the globe. The result is that the individual's true IP address cannot be discovered by an investigator. For example, if an individual connects to the Internet through a proxy chain and then sends an e-mail message, the e-mail message will show the sender's IP address being that of the last proxy server in the chain.

FIGURE 5.6

Proxy Server Attack

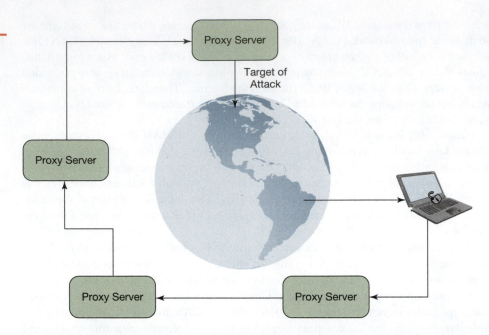

Further, if that proxy server does not maintain connection logs, it will be impossible to trace the user's connection backwards to the previous proxy server connection.

Password Cracking

There is plenty of commercial software that utilizes encryption schemes that, if used with a sufficiently long password or encryption key, cannot be broken by the typical investigator or law enforcement agency. But in many cases software programs rely on encryption schemes that contain vulnerabilities, and fraudsters often use weak passwords or encryption keys.

Cracking vulnerable programs, passwords, and encryption keys simply requires one of the many programs sold on the market for that purpose. The Forensic Toolkit® by Accessdata® is one example of a program marketed to crack passwords for a wide range of office-type applications. The Forensic Toolkit® can harness the simultaneous power of more than one computer to crack difficult passwords.

Users tend to use the same passwords over and over again, for many different services and purposes. So discovering a user's password for one service (e.g., webmail) can at the same time yield the user's password for a different services (e.g., an online bank account).

Surreptitious User Monitoring and Reporting

There are various commercial software programs that are virtually undetectable by most anti-malware products and yet can monitor and report on user activities. These programs typically work by reporting to a central server all user activities, including online chat conversations, incoming and outgoing e-mails, and Web visits. They can even record and report screen shots.

To access recorded data, the investigator logs in to the Web site that provides the service. From there it is possible to view all the user activity data. Data on the service may be stored for weeks or months, so that the investigator can view both current and previous activities.

Cell phone versions of this type of software are also available. Such software can record and report on all phone calls and text messages, and also any Internet activities relating to the phone's Internet functions. Of course, proper legal authority must exist in order to use these kinds of surreptitious monitoring, and one must have sufficient access to the target computer or mobile devices in order to install the monitoring and reporting software.

Summary

Fraud investigation refers to the application of accounting and other specialized skills to any type of fraud. Fraud management involves prevention, detection, investigation, reporting, and litigation and recovery. Accountants specializing in fraud routinely perform services in all these phases of the fraud management process. Fraud prevention within the organization requires good internal control.

Fraud detection involves identifying indicators of fraud that suggest a need for further investigation. Fraud indicators can be individual indicators or composite indicators. Various software packages and services exist to assist with fraud detection. Content and text analysis and Benford analysis are also useful in detecting fraud.

Fraud detection is an imperfect process. A Type 1 error occurs when a fraud indicator falsely signals fraud. A Type 2 error occurs when a fraud indicator fails to signal fraud. Total Fraud Costs were defined as Cost of Prevention + Costs of Investigations + Costs of Detections + Costs of Losses.

The fraud engagement process includes the following steps: (1) create and review an incident report, (2) conduct the initial notifications and evaluation, (3) consider legal issues, (4) evaluate the loss mitigation and recovery considerations, (5) define the scope, objectives, and costs of the investigation, (6) and create an engagement letter or memorandum. Fraud investigation involves collecting evidence. When well organized, evidence provides answers to the basic perennial questions asked by sleuths regarding a possible fraud: who, what, when, where, how, and why. The first question always asked is "what." If there's no fraud, then there's nothing to investigate.

Fraud theories are tested with evidence. Investigators collect three types of evidence: physical and document evidence, observation evidence, and interview evidence. The investigator may use various auditing and analytical techniques as part of the process of obtaining documentary evidence. The investigator may also use a wide range of other audit techniques in uncovering fraud, such as tracing and vouching. The investigator should build a fraud-triangle profile of the suspect that includes both work and personal data that may relate to the three sides of the fraud triangle: opportunity, pressure, and rationalization.

Interviewing techniques were discussed, emphasizing the types of questions that are used as well as how investigators might assess honesty by observing verbal and nonverbal cues exhibited by the suspect during interviewing.

At the conclusion of an investigation, the investigator prepares a report. The typical fraud report will contain sections that describe the client for whom the report was prepared, background information relating to the case, an executive summary, the scope and objectives of the investigation, a description of the fraud investigation team and the methods used, and the findings and recommendations resulting from the investigation. The report should never draw conclusions regarding a suspect's guilt.

Forensic accountants and fraud investigators sometimes serve as expert consultants and provide expert opinions and analyses to attorneys under the umbrella of attorney–client privilege. In this role, they are not subject to discovery. Forensic accountants and fraud investigators can also serve as expert witnesses. Expert witnesses are granted special consideration in court proceedings and are permitted to state opinions and conclusions based on facts admitted into evidence and other information on which they choose to reasonably rely.

Financial statement fraud involves the intentional misrepresentation of any information included as part of a financial statement or report. Financial statement fraud differs from legal financial statement manipulation or earnings management. Generally, managers commit financial statement fraud either as a way of boosting financial performance or as a way of hiding theft, bribery, or other illegal activities. The main road to honest financial statements is through good corporate governance.

Various financial statement fraud schemes were discussed, including improper revenue recognition, overstatement of assets, understatement of expenses and liabilities, misappropriation of assets, and inappropriate disclosures. Most employee frauds are never reported, and of those that are reported very few are prosecuted.

Employee fraud schemes were discussed in the context of transaction cycles. Revenue cycle fraud typically involves sales, accounts receivable, and inventory. Expenditure cycle frauds involve improper purchases, payments, and payroll-related payments and activities. Payroll fraud may involve improper hiring, improper changes to employee personnel files and pay rates, and improper work-related reporting. Production cycle fraud can involve misappropriation of waste, scrap, and spoiled goods. Vendor fraud might result in short shipments, substandard or defective goods, overpayment of balances due, or fraudulent cost-plus billing.

Computer forensics is the application of computer science to computer-related matters that might come before a court. The primary objectives of computer forensics include studying computers and computer networks in order to (1) identify perpetrators of crimes or undesirable behavior, (2) locate missing or hidden data, and (3) reconstruct damaged files and databases.

A variety of issues relating to obtaining and preserving evidence were discussed. These include problems with deleted files and whether or not to "pull the plug"—to cut power to a computer that potentially possesses evidence. The investigator might seek to find the physical location associated with a computer device that is used to communicate over the Internet. This is normally accomplished through analysis of the IP (Internet Protocol) address. IP tracing is not a foolproof method. Hackers routinely use various services to hide their real IP addresses. Cracking vulnerable programs, passwords, and encryption keys simply requires use of one of the many programs sold on the market for that purpose.

Glossary

Benford Analysis   a data analysis technique that is based on the distribution pattern of the first digit of numbers appearing in a random data set.

calibration   the process of carefully observing a suspect's behavior during introductory questioning.

check laundering   involves using a stolen customer check to make a payment on account.

check washing   using chemicals to remove a check's payment details and then adding new details for the payee, date, or amount of payment.

discovery   the process in which opposing parties can require each other and relevant parties to produce out-of-court evidence.

document examiners   people who specialize in analyzing questioned documents.

evidence   anything that relates to the truth or falsity of an assertion made in an investigation or legal proceeding.

FICO   a composite risk-score indicator that is based on various factors that include payment history, credit utilization, length of credit history, and types of credit used.

fraud examination   the application of accounting and other specialized skills to preventing, detecting, investigating, correcting, and reporting fraud.

fraud investigation   an occasional synonym for fraud examination

invigilation   an observation technique that involves observing a suspect's behavior before, during, and after an announced investigation.

observation   the use of the senses to assess the behavior of persons and other activities such as business processes.

predication   widely accepted principle that requires that investigations be started or continued only when there is a reasonable basis to do so.

questioned documents   document evidence whose authenticity or authorship is in question.

sales skimming   a scheme that typically involves an employee pocketing cash but not recording its collection.

search warrant   a court order that authorizes law enforcement to search for and seize evidence.

subpoena   an order from a government agency or officer of a court that compels the recipient, under penalty, to produce physical evidence, documents, or testimony.

surveillance   surreptitious observation.

tracing   following a source document that evidences a transaction through the entire accounting cycle.

vouching   selecting numbers in accounts and following them backward in the accounting cycle to the source documents.

Webliography

www.abfde.org
This is the home page of the American Board of Forensic Document Examiners (ABFDE). The ABFDE offers the Certification in Forensic Document Examination designation to those who meet the organization's qualifications and requirements.

www.acfe.org
This is the home page of the Association of Certified Fraud Examiners (ACFE). The ACFE is a worldwide organization devoted to anti-fraud training and education. The ACFE awards the Certified Fraud Examiner designation to those who meet the organization's qualifications and requirements.

www.endfraud.com
This is the home page of a Web site devoted to publishing summaries of class-action cases related to financial statement disclosure issue that can include fraud.

www.fbi.gov/scams-safety/fraud
A Federal Bureau of Investigation Web page devoted to information regarding common fraud scams.

www.iacis.com
This is the home page of the International Association of Computer Investigative Specialists (IACIS). The IACIS offers the Certified Forensic Computer Examiner designation to those who meet the organization's qualifications and requirements.

www.isfce.com
This is the home page of the International Society of Forensic Computer Examiners® (ISFCE). The ISFCE offers the Certified Computer Examiner designation to those who meet the organization's qualifications and requirements.

www.polygraph.org
This is the home page of the American Polygraph Association (APA). The APA establishes standards and ethical practices, and provides education in the polygraph field.

Chapter Quiz

1. Which of the following is one of the common objectives shared by information security management systems?
   a. Reliability
   b. Timeliness
   c. Integrity
   d. Accuracy

2. Which of the following is a risk-score indicator that is widely used by banks and lenders in judging consumer credit applications?
   a. FICO
   b. ISMS
   c. GAAP
   d. HIPO

3. Benford Analysis exploits an interesting pattern relating to the distribution of (_____) appearing in a random data set.
   a. the first digit of numbers
   b. duplicate numbers
   c. the last digit of numbers
   d. matching numbers

4. A (_____) error occurs when a fraud indicator signals fraud but fraud does not exist.
   a. Type 1
   b. Type 2
   c. Type 3
   d. Type 4

5. The principle of (_____) requires investigations be started or continued only when there is a reasonable basis to do so.
   a. reasonable assurance
   b. cost–benefit analysis
   c. exemplar
   d. predication

6. Which type of evidence should be collected first?
   a. spurious evidence
   b. physical and document evidence
   c. observation evidence
   d. interview evidence

7. Which of the following is an order from a government agency or officer of a court that compels the recipient, under penalty, to produce physical evidence, documents, or testimony?
   a. exemplar
   b. search warrant
   c. subpoena
   d. staying order

8. Which of the following is an observation technique that involves the observation of a suspect's behavior before, during, and after an announced fraud investigation?
   a. invigilation
   b. cracking
   c. surveillance
   d. calibration

9. Expert consultants are not subject to (_____).
   a. invigilation
   b. investigation
   c. discovery
   d. predication

10. Which of the following is most often involved in financial statement frauds?
    a. overstating expenses
    b. understating expenses
    c. overstating revenues
    d. understating revenues

Answers to the Chapter Quiz appear on page 186

Review Problem

An internal investigation of purchasing activities at the Red Bag Rental Company has uncovered several suspicious invoices for apparently unnecessary items that have somehow been ordered and paid for. The items cannot even be located and the sums of money involved are significant. The recurring nature of these suspicious purchases has led management to consider the possibility of a fraud investigation.

What steps should be followed before a possible investigation is launched?

Solution to Review Problem

The steps that should be followed are:
1. create and review an incident report,
2. conduct the initial notifications and evaluation,
3. consider legal issues,
4. evaluate the loss mitigation and recovery considerations,
5. define the scope, objectives, and costs of the investigation, and
6. create an engagement letter or memorandum.

Review Questions

1. Identify several certifications relating to fraud expertise.
2. Identify the six phases of the fraud management process.
3. Describe several of the data-driven approaches to fraud detection that were discussed in the chapter.
4. What formula can be used to describe total fraud costs in an organization?
5. Describe the four phases in the fraud investigation process.
6. Designate the steps that should be followed in a fraud engagement.
7. Discuss the relationship between "predication" and a "fraud theory."
8. Identify the three general types of evidence that might be collected during a fraud investigation.
9. Distinguish between a "subpoena" and a "search order." Which is more difficult to obtain?
10. Describe and give an example of "invigilation."
11. A fraud investigator might construct a "fraud-triangle" profile of a suspect that includes both work and personal data. Identify the three elements ("sides") of a fraud-triangle profile.
12. Proper interviewing can either make or break an investigation. Describe the types of questions that are used in the interviewing process.
13. How does the testimony of "expert witnesses" differ from the testimony of normal witnesses in court?
14. What is "financial statement fraud"? Identify several characteristics of companies that have been involved in financial statement fraud that have been identified in the published enforcement actions of the Security and Exchange Commission.
15. Describe several types of revenue cycle fraud.
16. Describe several types of expenditure cycle fraud.
17. What are the primary objectives of computer forensics?
18. How might an investigator obtain the physical location associated with a computer device that is used to communicate over the Internet?

Discussion Questions and Problems

19. Fraud detection involves (_____).
    a. Finding frauds
    b. Finding fraud indicators
    c. Finding the perpetrator
    d. None of the above
20. The pattern of numbers associated with Benford Analysis involves (_____).
    a. First digit numbers that are randomly distributed
    b. First digit numbers beginning with 1 being more likely to appear than those beginning with 8
    c. First digit numbers beginning with 8 being more likely to appear than those beginning with 1
    d. None of the above
21. A false positive signal by a fraud indicator is an example of a (_____).
    a. Type 1 error
    b. Type 2 error
    c. Either a Type 1 or Type 2 error
    d. All of the above
22. The main objective of a fraud investigation is to (_____).
    a. Prove that a given person has committed fraud
    b. Ensure that guilty persons are punished, regardless of their importance in the organization
    c. Systematically gather evidence for the purpose of documenting the presence or absence of fraud
    d. None of the above
23. Which of the following is true regarding fraud incident reports?
    a. They do not take on legal significance
    b. Once an incident report is made, an investigation is required
    c. They are of internal interest but never of interest to law enforcement
    d. None of the above
24. A bookkeeper embezzles $1,000 over a period of 2 years. He then quits his job, leaving the cash receipts and accounts receivable records in poor condition, with many incomplete records and missing source documents. In this case, filing a police report is likely to
    a. Spur a thorough police investigation
    b. Spur little or no investigation
    c. Spur an investigation if the assistance of a private, independent fraud investigator is offered
    d. None of the above
25. Which of the following questions should be asked first in a fraud investigation?
    a. Who
    b. What
    c. When
    d. How
26. Regarding the issue of a suspect's guilt, which of the following is the best answer?
    a. The fraud investigator should never state that a suspect is guilty.
    b. The fraud investigator should only state that a suspect is guilty if the suspect provides a proper confession.
    c. The fraud investigator can and should routinely provide an expert opinion regarding a suspect's guilt.
    d. The fraud investigator can and should provide an expert opinion regarding a suspect's guilt if such an opinion is justified by the evidence.

27. Seizing evidence in a suspect's home would typically require (_____).
    a. A normal subpoena
    b. A silent subpoena
    c. The approval of a law enforcement official
    d. None of the above
28. Handwriting analysis (_____).
    a. Can typically provide a definitive match between a sample and an exemplar
    b. Can typically provide a likely match between a sample and an exemplar
    c. Cannot typically provide any kind of match between a sample and an exemplar
    d. None of the above
29. Invigilation (_____).
    a. Can typically catch fraudsters in the act
    b. Can typically provide circumstantial evidence of a fraudsters' guilt
    c. Both a and b.
    d. None of the above
30. The main benefit of calibration in an interview is (_____).
    a. Confronting suspects so as to obtain a confession
    b. Establishing rapport with the interviewee
    c. Observing suspect's behavior in the presence of non-incriminating questions
    d. None of the above
31. What is the best order for interviews?
    a. Begin with suspects and end with non-suspects
    b. Begin with non-suspects and end with suspects
    c. Begin with non-suspects and end with non-suspects
    d. Begin with suspects and end with suspects
32. Accepting a fraud loss without punishment or recovery from the perpetrator is (_____).
    a. Never a good option because it sets a bad example
    b. Always a good option because pursing perpetrators is generally fruitless
    c. Is sometimes a good option in order to avoid embarrassing publicity
    d. None of the above
33. Expert consultants (_____).
    a. Are never subject to discovery
    b. Are always subject to discovery
    c. Are subject to discovery if they are expected to testify
    d. Are subject to discovery if they are not expected to testify
34. Manipulation or management of earnings by company officials is (_____).
    a. An act of financial statement fraud
    b. An act of financial statement fraud under the right circumstances
    c. Never an act of financial statement fraud
    d. Not an issue related to financial statement fraud
35. Financial statement fraud is more likely to occur in (_____).
    a. Small companies
    b. Medium-sized companies
    c. Large companies
    d. The size of the company doesn't matter

36. Roughly half of financial statement frauds involve the (_____) transaction cycle.
    a. Revenue
    b. Expenditure
    c. Production
    d. Finance
37. Check washing generally involves (_____).
    a. Fake checks printed by the perpetrator
    b. Fake checks purchased on the black market
    c. Paperless transactions
    d. None of the above
38. The type of fraud involving the receipt of substandard goods is typically (_____).
    a. Employee fraud
    b. Production fraud
    c. Vendor fraud
    d. None of the above
39. For most types of office-based software, passwords can (_____).
    a. Be cracked
    b. Be obtained from the manufacturer
    c. Not be cracked
    d. None of the above
40. Bob Marwell is the controller for the Wascoo waste management company in Chicago. Wascoo is a small company that collects waste products from offices that want a higher level of security for their waste products. To this end, all Wascoo waste collection trucks have built-in shredders and waste bins with locked doors to prevent unauthorized individuals from even seeing inside them.

    Bob supervises two bookkeepers and an assistant. The assistant collects the incoming customer payments on account and keeps her work segregated from the two bookkeepers. In reviewing the monthly bank reconciliations and cash receipts records, Bob notices that collections have dropped from the usual $250,000 per month to $195,000. Upon further investigation, he finds many strange and unexplainable entries into the cash receipts journal. He also finds that the bank deposit records are incomplete.

    It did not take Bob long to figure out that one of the two bookkeepers was in collusion with the assistant, and they had somehow embezzled about $55,000 over the last month. Bob went straight to the office of Barbara Enton, the CEO and sole owner of the company. "I want them to go to jail," she said. "I've got some really strong proof," he replied, handing her several deposit slips. "I found these deposit slips that were obviously forged, and my assistant's handwriting on them is obvious, since she writes in such a funny way. There's no way they are going to get out of this."

    Barbara stormed down to the assistant's office and neatly laid three of the forged deposit slips on the assistant's desk.

    "I hope you can explain these," said Barbara.

    "Explain what?" replied the assistant.

    "We've short $55,000 and your handwriting is on these forged deposit slips," said Barbara.

The assistant was silent for a moment and then said, "I'm calling my lawyer, and I'm going to sue you for embarrassing me like this." The assistant then stood up quietly and walked straight toward the front door of the building.

Required

What, if anything, should have been done differently in this situation?

41. Jan Merkle is a fraud investigator who was working alone for the first time on an assignment. In previous cases, she had always worked under one of the senior partners in her forensic accounting firm. But this time, she was alone.

The case was a fairly routine one. It involved an inventory clerk suspected of stealing books from the college bookstore that he was working in. According to the initial report, the suspect had bragged to coworkers about stealing large amounts of books, and he had been covering up his ongoing scheme by falsifying inventory count reports.

Unfortunately, someone had tipped off the suspect that Jan was going to perform a fraud examination, and so when she arrived she could not find any evidence of an ongoing fraud. Further, she had no way of proving that any of the inventory reports were false. So she decided to use invigilation. As a result, she announced that her investigation was complete and that she found no evidence of fraud. She also conducted her own count of all the books that she thought might be stolen and waited a few days to see if she could detect any more shortages.

When she did her next count of the books, she concluded that about $4,000 in books were unaccounted for, just as a result of activities for the last few days. She reported her findings to the store's owner. The owner immediately contacted her insurance company and opened a claim under her policy that covered employee theft.

After discussing the matter with the store owner, Jan set up hidden cameras in key places, hoping to catch the suspect in the act. But after 2 weeks she was still unable to prove anything. Further, over that time an additional $8,200 in books became unaccounted for. The owner then approached Jan and asked for a letter to her insurance company indicating that she had $12,200 in theft losses. Jan balked at the request, indicating that her investigation was not yet complete. But the owner begged her, indicating that the stolen books were all books that she would have returned to the publishers as unsold and for credits to her account. "If I don't get a quick payment from my insurance company, I'm going to be out of business."

Jan responded, "You know he's robbing you, and I know it too. But until I get some real proof, there's nothing I can do to help you with your insurance company."

Required

Assess Jan's response to the owner's request.

42. Tim Raven is an independent fraud investigator called to investigate an anonymous tip made on the tip line of the Wilson Fast automobile dealership. The tip reads as follows:

> I am an employee of the company, and I find it necessary to tell you what is going on right under your nose. You are being cheated on trade-ins for new cars. What's happening is that trade-ins are being overvalued, and you can be sure that at least one of your employees is personally benefiting from this.

The dealership is a large organization, with 11 sales persons, four sales managers, and four used car buyers. There are two shifts every day, and all these employees take turns operating on one shift versus the other. Any of the sales managers or car buyers can approve trade-in prices.

Required

a. Develop a fraud theory that fits with the reported tip.
b. Develop a plan for collecting evidence to test your fraud theory.

43. Launa Neta is a CPA, Certified Fraud Examiner, and the internal auditor for Remco Produce Distribution Company. A confidential tip from an employee in the central warehouse who serves the U.S. east coast has been referred to her. The tip was submitted through the company's Web site. It reads as follows:

> Something very strange is going on with two of the workers here in the warehouse. These guys are supposed to be working for $10 per hour, but both of them have recently purchased brand new Mercedes convertibles, and I saw one of them the other night at the high-stakes poker table when I was in Atlantic City. I don't know what they are up to, but I bet they are somehow robbing the company.

Required

a. Should this tip be investigated? What additional information, if any, should be used as a basis for the decision as to whether to investigate?
b. Formulate at least one fraud theory applicable to the reported tip.
c. What evidence would be needed to test your fraud theory?

44. The Westco Plumbing Services Company serves the Miami metropolitan area. It has 24 plumbers on staff, each with his or her own company truck. Each truck is fully equipped, and all plumbers take their trucks home at night, as Westco provides 24-hour emergency services. Barbara Westco is the company's controller. She has heard rumors that some of the plumbers are using the company trucks to conduct their own business on the side.

Required

a. Formulate a fraud theory relating to the rumors.
b. Formulate a plan for collecting evidence to test the fraud theory.

45. Maria Feliz is the controller for the Getmore Global Hedge Fund. Getmore manages over $100 billion in investments and has a wire-transfer department with eight employees. All outgoing wire transfers undergo a rigorous approval process. But despite this process, Bert Hemp, the internal auditor, recently discovered that a series of unauthorized outgoing transfers had taken place over the previous 6 months, with losses totally over $1 million. Maria immediately ordered an investigation upon hearing about the problem from Bert. Bert then logged in the accounting system to show Maria the transactions in question. But then, to his amazement, the transactions were no longer in the system. It was as if they had never taken place.

Maria followed up with the IT department to see if copies of the transactions could be recovered from backup files. But the IT department responded that there were no such transactions in any of the backup files, and there was nothing else they could do to help.

Bert then logged into the company's bank account used for the transfers and located the transactions in question. They were all transfers to a small private bank in the Grand Cayman.

It took Maria a lot of work, but she eventually found out that funds in Grand Cayman had been in the name of an anonymous Cook Island trust and had already been forwarded to a small private bank in Zimbabwe, Africa, which was unreachable by phone or e-mail. A government official in Zimbabwe explained that the money had probably already been passed on through several more countries and that trying to recover it was a waste of time. Even if the money were found, Maria would not be able to get her hands on it without opening legal cases in every country through which the money had passed. In fact, the entire chain of transfers would have been litigated and reversed, one country at a time, beginning with the last company in the chain. Moreover, each bank in the chain would probably fight the reversal, and the process couldn't be completed in 200 years.

Unfortunately for Maria, all employees in the wire transfer department shared a login to the bank's wire-transfer division. Therefore, the online bank records only showed that Getmore's login had been used to authorize the transfers. The records did not show which employee authorized the transfer.

"We're out of luck," Bert said to Maria. "We aren't going to recover a penny of this money." "I don't care," replied Maria. "Start an investigation and catch the person who did this." They both agreed that the thief was probably one of their eight wire-transfer employees. No one else would have had the knowledge to pull off such a crime.

Required

a. Develop a fraud theory for this case.
b. Develop a plan for gathering evidence testing your fraud theory.

46. Barbara Darko is an independent CPA and Certified Fraud Examiner hired by a joint task force of the SEC and the U.S. attorney's office to investigate a case of financial statement fraud. The case involves Great Burger, Inc., an international fast-food company. The company directly owns and runs some stores, and others are operated under franchising arrangements with local owners. It has operations is the United States and all parts of Latin America.

Barbara has heard from a reliable informant that Great Burger is a shell company for organized crime. Instead of just selling fast food, the company launders proceeds from illegal drug sales. She believes that the company reports drug revenues as fast-food sales, and engages in financial obfuscation through series of intercompany sales and transfers between its U.S. division and its foreign subsidiaries.

Required

a. Develop a fraud theory for this case.
b. Develop a plan for gathering evidence and testing your fraud theory.

47. The Squeaky Electrical Company store serves building contractors in all parts of Central Illinois. The company has one bookkeeper, Ester Ladrona, who is in charge of general bookkeeping, incoming payments on accounts from customers, payments to vendors, and also bank deposits. Tom Wilson, the company's owner knows that Ester's job functions involve a lack of a segregation of duties, but because of family politics in the family-run business, he has been forced to trust her.

Over the previous 12 months business has steadily grown. Tom has a really good feel for the business after having run it for over 20 years, and so he's always in close touch with the local economy and sales activity.

The problem is that despite his certainty that sales have been steadily improving, his sales reports from the bookkeeper has been showing steadily declines, to the tune of almost $10,000 per month. Monthly sales a year before were about $700,000 but have dropped below $600,000.

Tom is certain that Ester is somehow embezzling funds. So he contacts Liza Matadora, an independent forensic accountant who specializes in fraud investigation.

Required

a. Where should Liza begin her investigation? What might be a good initial fraud theory?
b. How should Liza go about gathering evidence?

48. Crako Premium Nutraciticals Company manufactures and sells a wide range of specialty health and beauty products. Crako only sells through its distributors, which it has located in all major regions of the United States.

What makes Crako successful is its excellent research division, which has buyers constantly roaming the globe in search of things like new kinds of skin crèmes, soaps, and cosmetics. The company even employs chemists with Ph.D.s for custom blending and testing ingredients in the company's labs.

Crako has been having a problem for the last 2 years. Every time Crako gets close to launching a new product, one particular competitor, always the same one, first launches the exact same product. Crako's CEO is convinced that the competitor is somehow stealing Crako's secrets, because recently the competitor launched a skin crème that Crako had been researching for 4 years. The formula for the cream requires exact proportions of rare natural ingredients from four different continents. It would be impossible for a competitor to produce a perfect copy of such a formula by chance.

Required

a. Formulate two alternative fraud theories to explain Crako's problem.

b. For each fraud theory, develop a plan for collecting evidence.

49. An internal control structure is an organizational plan to protect assets, ensure the integrity of accounting information, and promote operational efficiency. Indicate whether each of the following situations is satisfactory or unsatisfactory in a manufacturing company from the viewpoint of good internal control. If the situation is unsatisfactory, suggest an improvement.

a. Purchase requisitions are made verbally by departments to the purchasing agent.

b. The clerk who is responsible for maintaining raw material inventory records does not have access to the storeroom where the raw materials are kept.

c. All receiving operations related to shipments from vendors are handled by the clerks who are responsible for managing the storeroom where goods are kept.

d. Purchase orders are prepared by the clerks who are responsible for managing the storeroom where goods are kept.

e. Employees who are responsible for counting the shipments of goods received from vendors do not have access to the information concerning how many units were ordered from the vendor.

f. A periodic physical inventory is taken and reconciled to the materials inventory records by the same clerks who are responsible for managing the storeroom where goods are kept.

g. Purchase orders must be compared to receiving reports before a vendor can be paid.

h. Copies of purchase orders are sent to the personnel who originally requested the material.

i. A firm employs personnel whose only function is to move materials and supplies as needed by the production departments.

50. Identify an internal accounting control or procedure that would detect the following errors or omissions in a transaction processing system.

a. A nonprofit organization regularly receives unsolicited cash donations in the mail. Clerks opening the mail routinely steal a sizable percentage of the cash sent as donations.

b. Employees in the mailroom routinely mail their own—as well as their friends'—letters at the company's expense.

c. A clerk accidentally posts a customer payment of $35 as $53 to the customer's account in the receivables ledger.

d. A clerk purposefully posts a payment of $35 received from a close friend as $53 to the friend's account in the receivables ledger.

e. A customer receives a bill for an item that was ordered but never shipped.

f. A vendor sends a company a bill for 50 copies of a report when only 25 copies of the report were ordered and received.

g. A clerk sends a check to a vendor to pay an invoice. The same invoice was paid by a check drawn last week by a different clerk.

h. Certain workers in a factory routinely request more materials than are needed for a job, taking the excess materials home for personal use.

i. A customer orders an item, which is requisitioned and shipped. The customer is never billed for the shipment.

j. A shipment received from a vendor is accepted by an employee in the receiving department. The employee forwards a receiving report to payables so that the vendor will receive payment. The shipment, however, is taken home for personal use.

51. Listed are 12 internal control procedures and requirements for the expenditure cycle (purchasing, payroll, accounts payable, and cash disbursements) for a manufacturing enterprise. Next to the list of controls is a list of reasons for the various controls.

Required

List the numbers 1 through 12 and then match each procedure or requirement with the most appropriate reason for implementing the control. Each reason can be used only once.

Procedures and Requirements	Reasons for Controls
1. Duties between the cash payments and cash receipts functions are segregated.	a. Prevents people from processing phony payables and diverting the signed checks to themselves.
2. Signature plates are kept under lock and key.	b. Prevents payroll checks for excessive amounts from being cashed.
3. The accounting department matches invoices to receiving reports or special authorizations prior to payment.	c. Ensures that people writing checks cannot cover a temporary "borrowing" of cash.

(continued)

Procedures and Requirements	Reasons for Controls
4. All checks are mailed by someone other than the person making out the check.	d. Prevents the abstraction of cash receipts from being concealed by the recording of fictitious payments.
5. The accounting department matches invoices to copies of purchase orders.	e. Helps guard against checks being forged.
6. The blank stock of checks is kept under lock and key.	f. Prevents the fraudulent use of properly signed checks.
7. Imprest accounts are used for payroll.	g. Helps prevent temporary "borrowing" from established cash funds.
8. Bank reconciliations are to be accomplished by someone other than the one who writes checks and handles cash.	h. Helps prevent unauthorized changes to very important documents.
9. A check protector is used.	i. Prevents payment for goods and services not actually received.
10. Surprise counts of cash funds are conducted periodically.	j. Prevents payments for purchases that have not been properly authorized.
11. Orders can be placed with approved vendors only.	k. Assures that purchases are "arm's-length" transactions.
12. All purchases must be made by the purchasing department.	l. Prevents inappropriate purchases by unauthorized people.

52. The Morgan Department Store has approximately 1,000 customer accounts. Each month a special clerk opens the mail and prepares a remittance list of all monies received on account. The checks are then sent to a cashier for further processing. In addition, copies of the remittances are sent to accounting and data processing services. At the computer services office, an operator keys the remittances directly onto a disk file. The disk file is then used to update the accounts receivable master file. The computer operator has devised an interesting scheme for defrauding the company. The operator keys in approximately a $100 credit to a friend's account each month. The operator and the friend agree in advance about the amount to be keyed in. The friend will then make purchases exactly in this amount. Normally, the error entered into the system by this procedure would be detected by the batch control totals; however, the operator decreases the amount credited to a number of other accounts. In each case, the amount of the decrease is only $1 or $2. Because the error is very small, most customers let it go unnoticed. However, in a relatively small number of cases where they do detect the error, corrections are made on an authorized basis without further comment. For example, in the previous month, a total of $10 worth of corrections were made because of the complaints. However, these corrections were all processed semi-automatically by the system, and no one realized that it was part of a cover-up.

Required

What can be done to detect and prevent this problem relating to input manipulation?

53. West Manufacturing's computer division is quite large, consisting of over 200 employees. Relations among the employees within the company are quite good. Although the accounting department is a separate group, the accountants and computer people eat lunch together and socialize regularly. This has led to some problems. Recently, two accountants, a systems programmer, systems analyst, and computer operator worked together to divert the deposit of funds from the company's bank account to their individual personal accounts. The defalcation involved the forging of source documents by the accountants and cover-up by the systems programmers and operators. The systems analyst designed the entire scheme. The whole thing was discovered by accident when the accountant was forced to take time off from work for a surgical operation. The replacement accountant suspected that something was wrong when she noticed that a number of deposit slips were missing.

As it turns out, the total loss to the company was only a couple of thousand dollars. However, if it had not been for the accidental discovery by the temporary accountant, the fraud could have grown to the extent that it could have bankrupted the company.

Required

What could have been done to prevent the problem that occurred?

54. The Base Level National Bank of Washington, D.C., uses the financial module in its ERP system to process cash deposits made by its customers. The bank's ERP module for customer deposit accounting is a batch-processing system. Customers fill out a deposit slip when they deposit cash. The cashier validates the deposit slip, collects the cash, and then issues a dated receipt to the customer to evidence the deposit. The batches of deposit slips are processed overnight in a batch-processing run to update the customer account records.

Two different types of deposit slips might be used by a customer. One type is a blank-form deposit slip that the customer obtains at the bank. Typically, large quantities of blank-form deposit slips are left on counters in the bank's lobby for the customers' convenience. A blank-form deposit slip does not contain any pre-entered data. In particular, the customer or the cashier must manually enter the customer's account number on this form. The other type of deposit slip is contained in a customer's checkbook. In the case of a checkbook deposit slip, the customer's account number has already been entered on the form in computer-readable form. Each checkbook deposit slip contains the customer's account number in magnetic-ink character recognition (MICR) format to facilitate computer processing.

The two types of deposit slips look similar but are distinguishable. When batches of deposit slips are processed in the computer department, one of the first steps is to enter, using a special machine, both the customer's account number and the amount of the deposit in MICR format at the bottom of each deposit slip. MICR input is used because of the large volume of transactions. Because each checkbook–type slip already has the customer's account number in MICR, it is only necessary to MICR-encode the amount of the deposit. Both the customer's account number and the amount of the deposit must be MICR-encoded on the blank-form deposit slips.

Several months ago, Base Level National Bank was the victim of a clever fraud. It seems that some person entered the busy bank and left a stack of fraudulent blank deposit slips on one of the bank's counters. These deposit slips were exact duplicates of those normally placed on the counters, with one important difference. Each fraudulent blank deposit slip had been MICR-encoded with the account number of a checking account that apparently had been opened under a false name. Recall that the MICR-encoded account numbers are normally entered on the blank-form deposit slips after the deposit has been accepted by a cashier. During the day, the fraudulent deposit slips were used by many people making deposits at the bank. Most or all of these deposits were incorrectly credited to the fraudulent checking account in the overnight computer batch-processing run of the day's deposit slips. Within a few minutes of opening the next morning, this person returned to the bank, inquired as to his checking account balance, and withdrew 90% of the balance in cash. To date the identity of the person is unknown, and the cash, more than $150,000, has not been recovered.

Required

a. What factors contributed to the success of this clever fraud? What role did Base Level's computer system play in the perpetration of this fraud?

b. Suggest control procedures that could prevent the occurrence of this type of fraud.

Web Research Assignments

55. Research and write a brief report on the requirements to obtain the Certified Fraud Examiner designation.
56. Research and write a brief report on Graphology. Explain how graphology can be useful to fraud investigations.
57. One of the newest methods to assess honesty is "brain printing." Write a brief report that explains how brain printing might be applied to a fraud investigation.

58. False confessions are a serious issue in practice. Write a brief report that explains the issues surrounding false confessions and how they can relate to a fraud investigation.
59. Identity theft fraud rings are rampant. What is the internal organization structure like in an identity theft ring?
60. What recourse does one have if defrauded in an Internet scam?

Answers to Chapter Quiz

1. c   2. a   3. a   4. a   5. d   6. b   7. c   8. a   9. c   10. c

Information Security

Learning Objectives

Careful study of this chapter will enable you to:

- Describe general approaches to analyzing vulnerabilities and threats in information systems.
- Identify active and passive threats to information systems.
- Identify key aspects of an information security system.
- Discuss contingency planning and other disaster risk management practices.

An Overview of Information Security

Information security involves protecting information and information systems from unauthorized access, use, disclosure, disruption, modification, or destruction in order to provide—

Confidentiality: preserving authorized restrictions on access and disclosure, including means for protecting personal privacy and proprietary information

Integrity: guarding against improper information modification or destruction, and ensuring information nonrepudiation and authenticity

Availability: ensuring timely and reliable access to and use of information.

The term *computer security* is often used interchangeably with *information security*, but information security is a much broader concept in that it deals with the security of all information in the organization, regardless of whether it is computerized. For example, information security is concerned with paper documents and faxes, even though no computer may be involved. Computer security, then, is the application of information security to computerized information. This chapter focuses on the broader topic of information security.

The **information security management system (ISMS)** is an organizational internal control process that controls the special risks associated with information within the organization. Its objectives coincide with those of information security in general: to provide confidentiality, integrity, and availability of information. The ISMS typically has the basic elements of any information system, such as hardware, databases, procedures, and reports. For example, data concerning system usage and security violations might be collected in real time, stored in databases, and used to generate reports.

Given that the ISMS is an internal control process and manages risks, it is part of the larger enterprise risk management (ERM) process. ERM is the process by which management balances risks versus opportunities.

The Information Security Management System Life Cycle

The ISMS is an information system, so its development requires application of the life-cycle approach. Information security systems are developed by applying the established methods of systems analysis; design; implementation; and operation, evaluation, and control. The objective of each of these life-cycle phases is as follows:

Life-Cycle Phase	Objective
Systems analysis	Analyze system vulnerabilities in terms of relevant threats and their associated loss exposures.
Systems design	Design security measures and contingency plans to control the identified loss exposures.
Systems implementation	Implement the security measures as designed.
Systems operation, evaluation, and control	Operate the system and assess its effectiveness and efficiency. Make changes as circumstances require.

The objective of the first phase of the security system life cycle is to produce a vulnerability and threat analysis report. The objective of the second phase is to design a comprehensive set of risk-control measures, including both security measures to prevent losses and contingency plans to deal with losses should they occur. Collectively, all four phases are referred to as *information system risk management*. Information system risk management is the process of assessing and controlling information system risks.

International Standards for Information Security

The International Organization for Standardization (ISO, www.iso.org) promulgates the 27000 family of standards: ISO 27000, ISO 27001, ISO 27002, ISO 27003, ISO 27004, and ISO 27005. ISO 27000 includes ISMS-related vocabulary and definitions; ISO 27001 defines standards for building, operating, and maintaining ISMSs; ISO 27002 defines a code of best practices for ISMSs; and the remaining three standards (ISO 27003–05) provide guidance for implementation, measuring ISMS performance and general risk management with the ISMS.

ISO 27001 and ISO 27002 are the center of the ISO 27000 family of standards. Companies aspire to achieve the coveted "ISO 27001" certification. ISO 27002 comprises 132 general security controls organized under 11 topics and is further classified into over 5,000 detailed controls. The detailed controls are to be applied on a case-by-case basis, depending on the individual company's situation.

ISO 27001 involves a general ISMS development structure consistent with the life-cycle approach described above. However, instead of using the terms *systems analysis*, *design*, *implementation*, *operation*, *evaluation*, and *control*, ISO 27001 uses the terms *planning*, *doing*, *checking*, and *acting*. Planning corresponds to analysis and design, doing corresponds to implementation and operation, and checking and acting correspond to evaluation and control. In both schemes, the checking phase involves continuous monitoring and improvement of the ISMS.

There are several other guidelines regarding ISMS. COSO (Committee of Sponsoring Organizations of the Treadway Commission, www.coso.org) issued reports titled "Internal Control—Integrated Framework," "Enterprise Risk Management—Integrated Framework," and "Guidance on Monitoring Internal Control Systems." COBIT ("Control Objectives for Information and related Technology") is promulgated by the Information Systems Audit and Control Association (ISACA) and the IT Governance Institute (ITGI). COBIT, similar to the ISO 27000 series, provides a set of best practices for IT management. ISMS standards are discussed further later in this chapter.

The Information Security System in the Organization

If the information security system is to be effective, it must be managed by a chief security officer (CSO). This individual should report directly to the Board of Directors so as to maintain complete independence. A primary duty of the CSO should be to present reports to the Board of Directors for approval. These reports should cover each phase of the life cycle:

Life-Cycle Phase	Report to the Board of Directors
Systems analysis	A summary of all relevant loss exposures.
Systems design	Detailed plans for controlling and managing losses, including a complete security system budget.
Systems implementation, systems operation, evaluation, and control	Specifics on security system performance, including an itemization of losses and security breaches, an analysis of compliance, and costs of operating the security system.

Analyzing Vulnerabilities and Threats

There are two basic approaches to analyzing system vulnerabilities and threats. In the **quantitative approach to risk assessment,** each loss exposure is computed as the product of the cost of an individual loss times the likelihood of its occurrence. For example, assume that the likelihood of a loss can be represented by a risk factor between 0 and 1. Then a threat analysis report might look something like the one in Figure 6.1. In this example, data theft is the largest loss exposure, immediately followed by fraud and virus attacks (i.e., attacks that result from computer programs designed to sabotage important files). A significant benefit of an analysis such as this is that it often shows that the most likely threat to occur is not the threat with the largest loss exposure. For example, in Figure 6.1, the threat most likely to occur is equipment theft, but this threat represents one of the smallest loss exposures.

There are several difficulties in applying the quantitative approach to assessing loss exposures. First, identifying the relevant costs per loss and the associated likelihoods can be difficult. The relevant cost of a loss is the decrease in the company's profitability as a result of the loss's occurrence. But this cost can be difficult to estimate because it might involve estimating unpredictable business interruption costs or estimating the replacement cost of computers that can only be replaced by noncomparable newer models. Second, estimating the likelihood of a given failure requires predicting the future, which is particularly difficult in a rapidly changing technological environment. For example, many managers fail to foresee problems with computer viruses. Furthermore, in assessing the likelihood of intentional attacks on the system, one must estimate the costs and benefits of such attacks to potential perpetrators. This estimate, however, requires assumptions about perpetrators' risk preferences. For example, one perpetrator might be

THREAT ANALYSIS REPORT			
	Potential Loss ($)	Risk	Loss Exposure ($)
Data Theft	700,000,000	0.050	35,000,000
Fraud and Virus Attacks	1,200,000,000	0.025	30,000,000
Sabotage	2,500,000,000	0.010	25,000,000
File Alteration	400,000,000	0.050	20,000,000
Program Alteration	80,000,000	0.020	1,600,000
Equipment Theft	15,000,000	0.100	1,500,000
Natural Disaster	100,000,000	0.008	800,000

FIGURE 6.1

Threat Analysis Report

willing to undergo substantially larger risks than another for the same dollar gain. An extremely risk-seeking perpetrator will take very large risks for a small reward.

A second method of risk assessment for computer security is the **qualitative approach to risk assessment**. This approach lists out the system's vulnerabilities and threats, subjectively ranking them in order of their contribution to the company's total loss exposures. Both the qualitative and quantitative approaches are used in practice, and many companies mix the two methods. Regardless of the method used, any analysis must include loss exposures for at least the following areas:

- Business interruption
- Loss of software
- Loss of data
- Loss of hardware
- Loss of facilities
- Loss of service and personnel
- Loss of reputation

If the quantitative approach is used, costs might be estimated using replacement costs, service denial costs, third-party liability costs resulting from the company's inability to meet contracts, and business interruption costs.

Vulnerabilities and Threats

A **vulnerability** is a weakness in a system, and a **threat** is a potential exploitation of a vulnerability. There are two categories of threats: active and passive. **Active threats** include information systems fraud and computer sabotage, and **passive threats** include system faults, as well as natural disasters, such as earthquakes, floods, fires, and hurricanes. **System faults** represent component equipment failures such as disk failures and power outages.

The Seriousness of Information Systems Fraud

Computer-based crimes are part of the general problem of white-collar crime. The problem of white-collar crime is serious. Statistics have shown that corporate losses due to fraud and embezzlement exceed total losses due to bribery, burglary, and shoplifting by a wide margin. This might seem surprising because we seldom read about crimes such as embezzlement in the newspaper. This is so because, in the vast majority of cases, detected frauds are never brought to the attention of law enforcement officials because this would lead to public disclosure of internal control weaknesses. Managers tend to shy away from the adverse negative publicity that would result from public prosecution.

Information system security is an international problem. Accordingly, many countries have laws directed at computer security (see Figure 6.2). In the United States, various laws, regulations, and pronouncements address the problem of electronic crime. Most states have enacted specific criminal statutes directed against computer crimes. The Computer Fraud and Abuse Act of 1986 (as amended and enhanced by a subsequent series of "cybersecurity enhancement" acts) makes it a federal crime to knowingly and with intent fraudulently gain unauthorized access to data stored in the computers of financial institutions, computers owned or used by the federal government, or computers operating in interstate commerce. Trafficking in computer access passwords is also prohibited. In general, under the act, first offenders could be sentenced up to 20 years in prison.

The National Commission on Fraudulent Financial Reporting (Treadway Commission) linked management fraud to computer crime. Management fraud is deliberate fraud committed by managers with the intent of deceiving investors and creditors using materially misleading financial reports. This type of fraud is committed by those who are high enough in an organization to override accounting controls. Management might commit other types of errors or omissions

FIGURE 6.2

International
Computer Security
Laws

INTERNATIONAL COMPUTER SECURITY LAWS	
 Canada	Criminal Code 301.2(1), Unauthorized Use of Computers, sets criminal penalties of up to 10 years for fraudulent use of computer service or interception of computer signals or functions.
 Denmark	Criminal Code Section 263, Access to Another Person's Information, sets criminal penalties of up to 2 years for unlawful access to another person's data processing information or programs.
 Finland	Penal Provisions of the Personal Registers Act, 1987, Section 45, Personal Register Trespass, sets criminal penalties of up to 6 months for use of another individual's user code or fraudulent means to access personal data maintained with automated data processing.
 France	Law Number 88-19, Criminal Code, Chapter III, Article 462-2 through 9, sets criminal penalties of up to 3 years for unauthorized access to, falsification, modification, or deletion of data, or the use of such data from an automated data processing system.
 Switzerland	Criminal Code Section 147, Fraudulent Misuse of a Data Processing System, sets criminal penalties of up to 10 years for intentionally adding or deleting a data processing record for the intent of enrichment.

that potentially could defraud employees or investors, but the term *management fraud* generally refers to financial statement manipulations.

The Treadway Commission defined fraudulent financial reporting as intentional or reckless conduct, whether by act or omission, that results in materially misleading financial statements. The commission studied 456 lawsuits brought against auditors. Management fraud was found to be present in about half these cases. The commission noted that computer-based information systems multiply the potential for misusing or manipulating information, thus increasing the risk of fraudulent financial reporting.

Individuals Posing a Threat to the Information System

A successful attack on an information system requires access to hardware, sensitive data files, or critical programs. Three groups of individuals—systems personnel, users, and intruders and hackers—differ in their normal ability to access these things. Systems personnel often pose a potential threat because they are often given wide-ranging access privileges to sensitive data and programs. Users, on the other hand, are given much narrower access, but they still find ways to commit fraud. Intruders and hackers are given no access at all, but they are often highly determined individuals who are capable of inflicting great losses on the company.

COMPUTER AND INFORMATION SYSTEMS PERSONNEL Systems personnel include computer maintenance persons, programmers, operators, information systems administrative personnel, and data control clerks.

Computer Maintenance Persons Maintenance persons install hardware and software, repair hardware, and correct minor errors in software. In many cases, these individuals must have high-level security access to do their jobs. For example, an individual installing a new version of an accounting program is often given complete access to the file catalog containing the accounting system and its related data files. In some cases, such an individual might not even work for the company but rather for the vendor from whom the company bought the accounting software. In any case, maintenance persons typically possess the ability to illegally browse through and alter data and program files. Some maintenance persons may even be in the position to make undesirable modifications to the security portion of the operating system.

Programmers Systems programmers often write programs to modify and extend the network, network operating systems, workstations, and so on. Such individuals typically are given accounts with universal access to all the company's files. Application programmers might make undesirable modifications to existing programs or write new programs that do undesirable things.

Network Operators Individuals who oversee and monitor the immediate operation of the computer and communications network are called *network operators*. Typically, the operator is assigned a high level of security clearance, thus allowing him or her to secretly monitor all network communications (including individual users entering passwords), as well as access any file on the system.

Information Systems Administrative Personnel The systems supervisor is in a position of great trust. This person normally has access to security secrets, files, programs, and so on. Account administrators have the ability to create fictitious accounts or to give away passwords to existing accounts.

Data Control Clerks Those responsible for the manual and automated inputting of data into the computer are called *data control clerks*. These individuals are in the position to fraudulently manipulate the input data.

USERS Users are composed of heterogeneous groups of people and can be distinguished from the others because their functional area does not lie in data processing or information technology. Many users have access to sensitive data that they can disclose to competitors. In some cases, users may control important computer inputs such as credit memos, account credits, and so on.

INTRUDERS AND HACKERS Anyone who accesses equipment, electronic data, files, or any kind of privileged information without proper authorization is an intruder. Intruders who use electronic and other means to break into or attack information systems for fun, challenge, profit, revenge, or other nefarious motives are generically referred to as **hackers.** However, not all hackers are malicious. **White hat hackers** legitimately probe systems for weaknesses in order to help with security. **Black hat hackers** attack systems for illegitimate reasons. **Gray hat hackers** are white hat hackers who skirt along the edges of the law.

Social Engineering Many tend to think that hackers always possess significant technical prowess; the truth, however, is that many hackers rely heavily on social skills and other nontechnical means to carry out their exploits. In the context of information security, the term "**social engineering**" involves manipulating victims in order to trick them into divulging privileged information. Social engineering relies on human interaction rather than technical prowess and often involves tricking people into violating normal security procedures. Kevin Mitnick, an infamous hacker

FIGURE 6.3

Kevin Mitnick: Profile of a Notorious Hacker

When he was only 12, Kevin Mitnick began his hacking career by tricking the Los Angeles bus system into giving him free rides. His next major exploit was phone phreaking, which involves manipulating telephones into giving free long-distance calls. He later graduated to using social engineering methods to break into computers and systems of various large companies, including those of DEC, Motorola, Nokia, Sun Microsystems, and Fujitsu Siemens. His hacking career culminated in him becoming the most wanted computer criminal in the world and a 2-year chase by the FBI. He was finally caught when he broke into the personal computer of Tsutomu Shimomura, a computer security expert. The entire chase was documented in the book and movie *Takedown*

After serving a nearly 6-year sentence in solitary conferment, Mitnick started his own security consulting firm (www.kevinmitnick.com).

documented in the movie *Takedown*, claimed that he compromised computers using only social engineering to obtain user IDs and passwords (Figure 6.3).

Pretexting is a form of social engineering in which the perpetrator impersonates another person, typically in a phone call or electronic communication. This type of scheme has been used extensively to get unauthorized access to individuals' phone records, utility bills, and even banking records. The perpetrator typically answers various authenticating questions about her date of birth, mother's maiden name, and so on.

Many companies have implemented sophisticated identity verification systems to guard against pretexting. One system verifies the identities of its customers by asking them a series of personal questions based on information collected from public records. For example, a caller might be asked to indicate the color of a car he owned 3 years before, with the possible answers being red, blue, white, or gray.

However, even sophisticated public records–based systems can be defeated by someone willing to devote sufficient effort. Anyone can use services such as www.intelius.com to build an extensive public profile about an individual. The information in that profile can then be studied and memorized.

The U.S. Congress has passed various laws making certain types of pretexting a federal crime. The Telephone Records and Privacy Protection Act of 2006 makes it a federal felony for anyone other than law enforcement or intelligence officers to pretext phone records. Under this act, almost any type of fraud or deception in relation to obtaining another's phone records is punishable by up to 10 years in prison. In a similar vein, the Gramm–Leach–Bliley Act makes it a federal crime, with a maximum sentence of 10 years in prison, to pretext any kind of information that concerns a relation between a consumer and a financial institution.

Phishing is another form of social engineering. It differs from pretexting in that it aims to trick victims into giving passwords, money, or other valuable assets directly to the perpetrator. The Nigerian bank e-mail scam was of the earliest phishing scams. Perpetrators sent millions of e-mail messages that claimed to come from either a Nigerian government official or bank official or surviving spouse of a government official who needed help in transferring a large amount of funds out of the country. Victims who responded typically ended up sending the perpetrators money for transfer fees, taxes, and so on.

Phishing scams often involve the perpetrator sending large numbers of e-mail messages that appear to come from a bank or other financial institution. The messages contain links to perpetrator-controlled fake Web pages that are made to look exactly like the real Web pages they impersonate. After being directed to the phony Web pages, the victims enter their login information, which is then recorded by the phisher's Web site. The phisher then uses the victim's login information to access and steal money from the victim's account.

Phishing scams may also be conducted over the telephone. In one scam, the perpetrator uses a telephone call to persuade the victim to divulge her bank account number, which can then be used to withdraw money out of the customer's account. In another scam, the perpetrator surreptitiously watches while a customer in a department store makes a credit card purchase. The perpetrator uses a cell phone to pass to an accomplice the credit card number and the amount of the purchase. Then, at a later time, the perpetrator phones the victim and pretends to work for either the department store or the victim's credit card company. The perpetrator tells the victim that he is doing a security check to verify that victim in fact made the recent purchase. The perpetrator cites the item purchased along with the date, time, and amount of the transaction. The perpetrator's detailed knowledge of the transaction immediately convinces the victim that the perpetrator is authentic. The scam terminates in the perpetrator asking the victim for his credit card number to verify that he is in possession of the card.

 CASE IN POINT

> Phishing scams can be carried to extremes. In one case, the scammers placed a fake ATM machine in a mall. The machine recorded the card and pin numbers of everyone who tried to use it.

Malware The term **malware,** a contraction of the words "malicious" and "software," describes software that is malicious. Malware is hostile, intrusive, or annoying software that was specifically designed to be so by its creator. Obviously, malware is not obtained on purpose. Malware can be obtained in a variety of ways. A **Trojan horse** (or simply "trojan") describes malware that either is contained within benign software or is masquerading as benign software. A Trojan can be hidden in e-mail attachments, downloaded software, software on disk, software that runs in the Web browser, and so on. For example, the user might be tricked into visiting a Web page that contains a malicious ActiveX script. The user may then be tricked into saying "yes" when the Web browser asks the victim to approve or deny the script. ActiveX scripts can be especially dangerous because they potentially have access to all the data and programs on the victim's computer.

Malicious programs and scripts can compromise security in many ways. **Keyboard loggers** secretly record and transmit to the hacker all the victim's keystrokes. The keystrokes might contain login information that the victim uses to access her bank accounts. A **backdoor** (or trapdoor) is a method of covertly eluding normal authentication procedures while accessing a computer system. A backdoor might covertly be inserted into a program during its development or modification by a programmer, or the backdoor may arise from installing software that contains a Trojan. A Trojan backdoor might allow a hacker to remotely take control of the victim's computer. Once under the hacker's control, the computer is wide open so that the hacker can access all its software and data. Such control might also be used to access other computers on a network. In other cases, the target computers are turned into slave computers that serve as parts of botnets. A **botnet** is a collection of computers that are infected with malware and controlled by a hacker. A botnet might be used to conduct denial-of-service attacks against Web sites, e-mail servers, and distributed name servers. **Denial-of-service (DoS) attacks** involve flooding the victim with such enormous amounts of illegitimate network traffic that the victims become so overloaded that they can no longer process legitimate traffic. In some cases, DoS attacks have been used to extort money from their victims. In one case, one major online casino paid a "ransom" to stop a DoS attack only to find major damage to one of its servers after the attack stopped.

> ### ◯ CASE IN POINT
>
> Hacker sabotage has become a major issue for Web Commerce. Despite annual expenditures for electronic security that exceed $6 billion, successful hacker attacks on Web sites have increased steadily. Even the largest and most sophisticated organizations have suffered, and almost every day the financial press continues to report cases of hackers successfully hacking corporate Web sites.
>
> - Sony Corporation was the target of a large-scale, coordinated denial of service attack by a group called *Anonymous*. The attack caused a massive customer data breach that exceeded 100 million records.
> - One cyber gang hijacked the *New York Times* Web site for 3 hours. Other hackers have co-opted the Web sites of federal agencies such as the CIA, the FBI, NASA, and also the White House.
> - The Google search engine was shut down for several hours as a result of a distributed DoS attack.

Viruses, Spyware, Logic Bombs, and Worms Viruses, spyware, logic bombs, and worms are malware. **Viruses** are designed to replicate themselves and thus spread throughout a computer or a network. Some viruses are very destructive and wipe out critical data and files on the victim's computer. Other viruses are simple annoyances, such as browser hijackers that change the browser's home page. **Spyware** is covertly installed on a victim's computer and then collects and relays to the perpetrator personal information about the victim. There are many types of spyware programs. These include keyboard loggers, backdoors, browser hijackers that point to Web pages of products for sale, and adware. **Adware** is software that displays advertisements, typically in pop-up windows.

Hackers often trick victims into accepting malware by piggybacking them onto programs voluntarily installed by victims. For example, a hacker might entice victims into downloading and installing a free and beautiful screensaver that contains a hidden keyboard logger or backdoor. Hackers also trick victims into opening e-mail attachments that contain malware.

A logic bomb involves a dormant piece of code purposely designed to do damage. A "bomb" is inserted into a benign program for later activation by a specific event. A disgruntled programmer might design a logic bomb that sabotages the payroll files if his or her identification number is not processed during a payroll run (because he or she quit or was fired).

A **worm** is malware that silently spreads from one computer to another over a network. A worm is a type of virus that can spread without the intervention of any individual or server. The typical worm is spread by e-mail that contains a Trojan file attachment. It uses social engineering to trick victims into opening the attachment. For example, the MyDoom worm sent victims an e-mail and attachment that appeared to be a message that had been sent by the victim but returned to the sender because it was not deliverable to its destination. The typical subject line was something like "Mail Delivery System" or "Mail Transaction Failed." When the victim opened the attachment to gain information about the supposed nondelivered e-mail message, the worm's Trojan payload would surreptitiously send a copy of the MyDoom e-mail message to everyone in the victim's e-mail address book. The payload also placed program code in the victim's KaZaA folder, if one existed, that caused the victim's copy of KaZaA to spread MyDoom over the entire KaZaA peer-to-peer file-sharing network. The same payload also installed a backdoor that permitted its 1 million victim computers to be used in a distributed DoS attack against The SCO Group, Inc., a software company that sold variants of the Unix operating system. A **distributed DoS attack** is a DoS attack that is distributed over many different nodes on the Internet or other network.

CASES IN POINT

- A 'coordinated spam attack' resulted in sexually explicit images spreading on Facebook's member's pages. Facebook identified the hacker tactic as an exploit of a "self-XSS browser vulnerability."

Viruses can spread quickly through a company's computers, wreaking havoc.

- In one hospital, a virus destroyed nearly 40% of the patient records.
- The Melissa Macro virus attached itself to Microsoft Word files and spread over the Internet. It propagated itself by automatically sending out infected e-mail attachments to those in the user's e-mail address book. Recipients trusted the infected attachments because they appeared to come from someone they knew. The virus generated such a large volume of messages that it rapidly forced the shutdown of the e-mail servers for many large corporations.
- Robert Morris, Jr., a 22-year-old graduate student at Cornell University, developed a computer virus program that entered the Internet. The worm spread through the network very rapidly, temporarily disabling the operation of thousands of computers across the United States.

Direct Observation Hackers occasionally do not even need to use deception. **Shoulder surfing** involves the surreptitious direct observation of confidential information. This method of spying on others can be applied to many different nefarious ends. For example, it can be applied to obtain personal identification numbers at ATM machines, credit card numbers at checkout counters, passwords at point-of-sale (POS) terminals, and computer passwords at the office.

Dumpster diving involves sifting through garbage to find confidential information such as discarded bank statements, department store bills, utility bills, and tax returns. In cases not involving trespassing, dumpster diving might be completely legal, although the improper use of information obtained through dumpster diving is likely to be illegal.

Electronic Interception Much of the information processed by computers and telephones travels over wires, cables, and airwaves. Some information is transmitted only from one room to the next, and other information may be transmitted across the country via the Internet. These lines of communication are vulnerable to wiretapping and interception, which may be done with even inexpensive devices (e.g., a simple digital recorder and a short piece of wire to intercept wire-type transmissions) that are capable of performing the task without giving any clues that the wire is being tapped.

Cell phone calls can be intercepted using cloned cell phones. A **cloned cell phone** is an exact and illegitimate copy of another cell phone, including a copy of the internal SIM (subscriber identity module) chip if one exists. A cloned cell phone will intercept text messages sent to and from its legitimate counterpart phone. It will also intercept voice calls if it is near the same cell tower as the legitimate counterpart phone.

Piggybacking is the most sophisticated type of wiretapping. Piggybacking occurs when legitimate information is intercepted and fraudulent information is substituted in its place. Encryption is the best defense against electronic interception. Most financial institutions use SSL (secure socket layer) encryption to communicate with their clients through Web browsers. (Web pages that use SSL have URLs that begin with http://.) However, most e-mails are not encrypted and are easily subject to interception.

Exploits An **exploit** occurs when a hacker takes advantage of a bug, glitch, or other software or hardware vulnerability to access the software or hardware, or related data or other resources, in an unauthorized manner. Exploits against software require vulnerabilities in the software.

Such vulnerabilities might arise from improperly installed or improperly configured software or from unforeseen/neglected defects or deficiencies in the software. For example, the installation of many software packages involves the automatic creation of an administrator account with a default username and password. Failure to subsequently change the password for this account leaves it wide open to anyone with access to the login screen. Another common configuration-setup error involves incorrectly setting file-access permission on a Web server and by doing so making private data available to the entire Internet. Further, if the Web server is accidentally configured to grant Internet users the ability to write data and run programs/scripts in the same, any Internet user can upload programs to the insecure folder and then run them at will. Depending on the operating system setup, this could amount to giving the uploader unlimited access to all data stored on the computer that hosts the Web server.

There are many types of possible software vulnerabilities and related exploits. Some exploits depend on inputting abnormal data, data that the program is unable to handle in a proper manner. This causes the program to behave in a way that "crashes" at least part of the program's security or escalates the hacker's access privileges. A good example of this type of exploit is the buffer overflow. The buffer overflow exploit causes the target program to attempt to store more data in a given portion of computer memory than the program was designed to store. The result is that the excess data gets stored in an area of memory that is already being used to store the program's internal instructions. The instruction set then becomes gibberish and causes the program to crash. The crashed program then behaves in unexpected ways, which may include leaving critical data exposed or escalating the access privileges of the user.

Another common class of exploits involves **code injection.** Code injection involves tricking a computer program into accepting and running software supplied to a user. This is sometimes achieved by inputting specially crafted program code in place of data. This injected program code is crafted in such a way that the host program executes its instructions instead of processing it as data.

A common trick of hackers is to use a port scanner or **vulnerability scanner** to remotely scan networked computers, searching for responses on open ports connected to software that has a known vulnerability. Port scans typically are done by using PC-based software that accesses remote sites by their Internet protocol (IP) addresses. For example, at this writing, the main IP number for Google's search page is 72.14.207.99. Thus entering http://72.14.207.99/ into a Web browser takes one to the Google search page. This address can also be entered as http://72.14.207.99:80. The ":80" appended at the end represents the port number. Port 80 is the standard port for Web servers. Other standard port numbers include port 21 for file transfer protocol (FTP) servers, port 25 for e-mail servers, and port 531 for AOL instant messaging. In all, there are 65,535 ports for hackers to systematically scan in hopes of encountering a response from a port that contains a vulnerability that can be exploited.

When the hacker does find an "open port," she may encounter attached software that requires authentication. At that point, she might use a password-cracking tool, a piece of software that might try hundreds of thousands or even millions of passwords, in an attempt to guess the login password. Many server programs defend themselves against this type of attack by refusing to respond to a remote IP address after several failed attempts originating from that IP address.

Password attacks can be initiated in many contexts, such as Web logins and local-machine logins. A standard defense is to lock an account from further access by anyone after several failed attempts to access it.

CASE IN POINT

During the First Iraq War, many hackers broke into Web sites and modified the home pages to contain antiwar messages.

Some remotely accessible software might permit some level of access to the entire Internet. The Web server is a good example. One can normally access Web pages without any authentication. In some cases, the remote hacker may have many exploit opportunities beyond password cracking. For example, a hacker might discover an instant messaging program running on a remote port. He might then use a buffer flow attack to crack the program.

Browser exploits take advantage of vulnerabilities in Web browsers. Web browsers are inherently risky as they typically run programs called scripts. JavaScript and VBScript are the main browser scripting languages. In theory, browser-run programs using these languages are supposed to operate only within the browser environment and with no access to the general computer files and data. However, vulnerabilities in the Web browsers can create the possibility of exploits that escape the sandbox.

Most individuals set their browser security settings so as to automatically run JavaScript and VBScript programs without prompting the user. After all, programs written in JavaScript and VBScript are supposed to be safe because they only run in a sandbox. The result is that a victim need only visit a Web page that contains JavaScript or VBScript code that exploits some browser vulnerability. When this happens, the victim can end up with a malware program on her machine but with no idea of its presence.

The best defense against exploits is to use certified technicians to install and configure all hardware and software. Once software is properly installed and configured, all updates must be applied to the software in a timely manner. However, these measures are no guarantee against exploits. Even software that is tried and true changes with updates, thus creating new opportunities for vulnerabilities. There is no such thing as 100% safety in information security. One can only manage the risks.

Methods of Attack by Information Systems Personnel and Users

As discussed above, there are three groups of individuals that may attack information systems: information systems personnel, users, and hackers. We discuss here six methods that information systems personnel and users might use to perpetrate an information systems fraud (Figure 6.4). Of course, information systems personnel and users can also resort to the hacking methods discussed above.

INPUT MANIPULATION   In most cases of insider computer fraud, manipulation of input is the method used. This method requires the least amount of technical skill. One can alter input with almost no knowledge of how a computer system operates.

- A teller employed by Union Dime Bank was discovered skimming money from bank accounts. This was accomplished by inputting fraudulent entries for computer processing. The crime was uncovered after police raided a bookie the teller was frequenting and discovered that the teller was betting over $30,000 per week. The bank lost more than $1 million.

FIGURE 6.4

The Six Methods of Attack Favored by Systems Personnel and Users

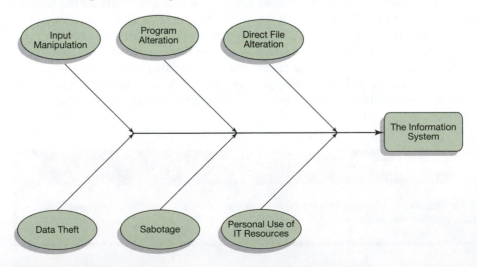

- The bank Morgan Guaranty accepted a fraudulent telex from the Central Bank of Nigeria. Twenty million dollars in funds were to be electronically transferred to three different banks. However, when an attempt was made to transfer funds to a recently opened $50 account in Santa Ana, California, the transfer was refused. This led to the discovery of the fraud, with no loss to Morgan Guaranty.
- In one case, four men who were involved in a complicated bank fraud scheme stole $1.3 million through manipulating deposit memos.
- In another case, not only did a woman steal $200 a month for 10 years by altering the input documents, she also paid herself an extra salary.
- The systems analyst in a department store purchased some items on his personal account, intercepted the documents, and lowered the prices.
- A data processing operator put flaws in some of the checks that were being processed. As a result of the errors, the checks were rejected by the computer and had to be processed manually. He then converted the checks to his own use.

PROGRAM ALTERATION Program alteration is one of the least common methods used by insiders to commit computer fraud. This is because program alteration requires programming skills that are possessed by only a limited number of people. Sometimes program developers place a backdoor in a program to ensure that they will always have access to it.

- Managers of Equity Funding Life Insurance Company created a program that generated over $100 million in fictitious insurance policies. The bogus policies were sold to other insurance companies, and the company's billing program was then altered to omit the billing of these policies. This was done by assigning fictitious policies to Department 99. When the computer came to a Department 99 policy, it would ignore the billing process.
- A programmer programmed the computer to ignore overdrafts in his account. He was caught when the computer broke down, and the records had to be processed manually.
- The data center manager of a brokerage firm stole $81,000 over several years based on a scheme relying on unauthorized program changes. He drew checks on his firm and then sent them to false accounts he had constructed.

DIRECT FILE ALTERATION In some cases, individuals find ways to bypass the normal process for inputting data into computerized information, and by doing so directly access and pilfer information from or alter computer files. Most accounting programs encrypt their files, thereby preventing direct access to them; however, in many cases, the encryption key (password) is weak, thus making it possible to easily crack the database. Program configuration files might not be encrypted even though the main database is encrypted. This opens a possible window of attack.

- One defrauder substituted his own version of a master file of accounts receivables for the real one.

DATA THEFT Theft of important data is a serious problem. In many highly competitive industries, both quantitative and qualitative information about one's competitors is constantly being sought.

The courts have long upheld that data stored in a company's computers are private and cannot be used without the company's permission. For example, in California, data theft can lead to conviction of violating a trade secret, punishable by a 10-year prison sentence. Similar trade secret laws apply in other states.

A considerable amount of information is transmitted between companies via the Internet. If not well encrypted, this information is vulnerable to theft while en route, where it may be intercepted or tapped. It can also be vulnerable to someone smuggling it out of the company via e-mail, perhaps in encrypted form so as to avoid detection. There are even encryption schemes that disguise the fact that the data is encrypted. For example, software that embeds and encrypts text in a graphics file such as a picture is readily available. To the unaware person, the picture would look like just another picture, and the person would have no way of knowing that it contains hidden text.

Critical data might also be smuggled out of the firm on removable media such as disks or small flash drives. Bulkier items such as thick reports can be smuggled out in the trash.

- The Encyclopaedia Britannica Company allegedly accused the computer operators on its night shift of copying nearly 3 million names from the computer file containing the company's most valued customer list. Employees were accused of selling the list to a direct mail advertiser. Encyclopaedia Britannica claimed that the list was worth $3 million.
- A California man was accused of connecting directly into his competitor's computer network, bypassing the computer security system and copying information as needed.

SABOTAGE   Computer sabotage poses a very serious danger to any information system. The destruction of a computer or software can result in the bankruptcy of a firm. Disgruntled employees, especially fired ones, are common perpetrators of sabotage.

In some cases, a defrauder may use sabotage to create confusion to cover up fraud. For example, an individual might alter the accounting databases and later try to cover up by sabotaging computer disks or other media.

There are many ways to cause serious damage to computers. Magnets can be used to erase magnetic disks simply by placing the magnet (a common magnet will suffice) near the media. A radar beam can have a similar effect if it is pointed at a building containing magnetic media. A hammer works well on many other types of media such as optical disks or flash drives.

- The head of a data center of a leading credit card company, angry at top management, erased computer files containing hundreds of thousands of dollars worth of accounts receivable.
- A Cleveland manufacturer was put out of business when a disgruntled employee, left alone a few minutes in a data storage vault, erased many data files with a simple hand magnet.
- A Dow Chemical Company employee aided a group of radicals in erasing a thousand of the company's computer files.
- An editor who had been fired from the Encyclopaedia Britannica Company sabotaged some of the company's computer files by rewriting history and substituting the names of Britannica employees for those of various historical figures.
- Some Internal Revenue Service (IRS) employees destroyed 27,000 tax returns and approximately 80,000 inquiry letters from taxpayers simply to avoid processing them.
- A programmer for USPA, a Fort Worth–based insurance company, was fired for alleged misconduct. Two days later, a logic bomb allegedly activated itself and erased approximately 160,000 vital records from the company's computers. Investigators concluded that the programmer had planted the logic bomb 2 years before he was fired.

MISAPPROPRIATION OR THEFT OF INFORMATION RESOURCES   One type of misappropriation of information resources exists when employees use company computers' resources for their own personal use or their own business:

- Five employees were accused of using their employer's mainframe computer during slack hours to operate their own data processing firm. The employees used the computer so heavily that their employer almost inadvertently upgraded the system to keep up with their demand.

The extent of this problem, like other types of computer fraud, is not well known. However, it is very likely that this problem occurs to some degree in many companies.

- Several employees stole their company's mainframe computer over a period of days, smuggling it out the back door a piece at a time!

The Information Security Management System

Controlling threats is accomplished by implementing security measures and contingency plans. Security measures focus on preventing and detecting threats; contingency plans focus on correcting the effects of threats. It is a well-accepted doctrine in information system security that some active threats cannot be prevented without making the system so secure that it is unusable. Furthermore, no security system is of much value without a general atmosphere of honesty and security consciousness.

It should be emphasized that the ISMS must be part of the company's overall ERM and internal control structure. This means that the basic elements of internal control (control environment, risk assessment, control activities, information and communication, and monitoring) are all important to the ISMS. Information systems security is simply a particular application of established internal control principles to particular problems in the information system. The following discussion focuses first on the control environment within the ISMS and then on specific control activities for active and passive threats.

The Control Environment

The control environment is basic to effectiveness of the overall control system. Establishing a good control environment depends on seven factors. Each of these factors is discussed as it pertains to the ISMS.

MANAGEMENT PHILOSOPHY AND OPERATING STYLE
The first and most important activity in systems security is creating high morale and an atmosphere conducive to security. No matter how sophisticated a system is, there is always a way around a systems's security measures. Therefore, the primary line of defense should be an overall atmosphere of security consciousness. This can be accomplished in many ways.

All employees should receive education in security. The objective of security education is to obtain security by consent. Security should be taken seriously. All violations should result in immediate apprehension of the guilty. Those in charge should set a good example.

Security rules should be monitored. Otherwise, the system will soon be forgotten. Good relations must be kept with employees. Low morale may result in a higher probability of fraud. Good communication with employees may mitigate problems. For example, files should contain a statement to the effect that they are the property of the company and that their inappropriate use may constitute a criminal offense or a cause for dismissal.

ORGANIZATIONAL STRUCTURE
In many organizations, accounting, computing, and data processing are all organized under one chief information officer (CIO). Such a division, therefore, performs not only the traditional record-keeping functions of accounting but also various information technology functions. This poses various problems for establishing and maintaining clearly defined patterns of authority and responsibility. For example, systems analysts and software engineers may be called on to design, program, and implement portions of an enterprise resource planning (ERP) system. An accountant might be called on to make configuration changes to an accounting package. The important thing is that clear organizational lines be drawn to designate who is responsible for making the decision directly pertaining to accounting software and accounting procedures. As was discussed, one individual must be in charge of the computer security system.

BOARD OF DIRECTORS AND ITS COMMITTEES
The Board of Directors must appoint an audit committee. The audit committee must, in turn, appoint or approve the appointment of an internal auditor. Ideally, the internal auditor should have a good background in information security and serve as the chief information security officer. In any case, this individual should report periodically to the audit committee on all phases of the information security system. The audit committee should consult periodically with the external auditors and top management as to the performance of the CSO and the information security system.

METHODS OF ASSIGNING AUTHORITY AND RESPONSIBILITY   The responsibilities of all positions should be carefully documented using organization charts, policy manuals, job descriptions, and so on.

MANAGEMENT CONTROL ACTIVITIES   It is important to establish controls relating to the use and accountability of all resources relating to the information systems. Budgets should be established for the acquisition of equipment and software, for operating costs, and for usage. In all three categories, actual costs should be compared with budgeted amounts, and significant discrepancies should be investigated.

Budgetary control is especially important in the information technology environment because there is often a tendency for companies to either overspend on information technology or spend on the wrong things. Employees often demand computing hardware, software, and services they really do not need. Buying the most recent model of a personal computer or the latest software package can be emotionally satisfying without producing any benefit to the company.

INTERNAL AUDIT FUNCTION   The information security system must be audited constantly and then modified to meet changing needs. The CSO should establish security policies relevant to the existing system and changes to the system. All modifications to the system, either hardware, software, or personnel, should be implemented in accordance with the established security policies.

Security policies and procedures should be tested for both compliance and effectiveness. Some companies actually hire computer hackers to look for security system vulnerabilities. In more than one case, a hacker's arrest and conviction have turned out to be good credentials in applying for a security job or developing a consultancy.

The system should be "challenged" periodically with hypothetical test transactions. Furthermore, changes to master files should be traced back to the relevant source documents or transactions. Such tracing is one way to detect unauthorized direct changes to master files. Another way to detect some such unauthorized changes is through batch control totals.

PERSONNEL POLICIES AND PRACTICES   Segregated duties, adequate supervision, job rotation, forced vacations, and double checks are all important personnel practices. Probably the most important rule is that the duties of information systems users and information systems personnel should be separated. This stems from the need to separate custody and record-keeping responsibilities. Users often have physical access to the company's assets, and information systems personnel often have privileged access to the software and data files containing the accounting records. Putting user privileges and system privileges in the same hands is an invitation to commit fraud.

There also should be, if possible, a separation of duties regarding access to key accounting files. In many information systems environments, having privileges to access a file for an asset account might be very close to having access to the asset itself. For example, it might be possible to transfer cash out of a cash account using electronic transfer if the cash account is linked directly to an account in a financial institution.

Job rotation and mandatory vacations should apply to all systems-related personnel who have access to sensitive files. Many fraudulent schemes require continued attention from the perpetrator. For example, an individual with access to both the cash and accounts receivable files might engage in electronic lapping. Such an activity would very likely be discovered by someone taking over the position either temporarily or permanently.

Personnel practices concerning hiring and firing are also important. Prospective employees should be screened carefully for the types of problems that might lead to fraud. Such problems include credit difficulties, various addictions (e.g., drugs, alcohol, and gambling), as well as previous employment problems. The more sensitive the position, the more extensive the background investigation should be. Remember, one deviant individual in a critical position might completely destroy the entire company.

Employees should be laid off and fired with the greatest care because terminated employees account for a significant portion of all sabotage incidents. When key employees are fired, all their access privileges to critical hardware, software, and data files should be revoked immediately.

EXTERNAL INFLUENCES   The company's information systems must be in compliance with all federal, state, and local laws and regulations. Among other things, these laws and regulations govern the security and privacy of many types of data, including those relating to customer and client credit, customer and client history, personnel, and government-classified records. They also govern the exportation of certain information to other countries. Failure to provide adequate security in any one of these areas could be a criminal offense.

It is also important to implement a well-documented internal policy to prevent **software piracy**—the illegal copying and distributing of copyrighted software. A company without such a policy might be subject to a variety of legal attacks.

Controls for Active Threats

The primary way to prevent active threats concerning hacker attacks, fraud, and sabotage is to implement successive layers of access controls. If all general organizational and data processing controls are in place and working, the primary consideration then becomes limiting unauthorized access to sensitive data and equipment. Just as it is impossible to start a fire without access to heat, it is impossible to commit information systems fraud without access to sensitive data or equipment. Access controls separate the perpetrator from his or her potential target.

The **layered approach to access control** involves erecting multiple layers of controls that separate the would-be perpetrator from his or her potential targets. Three such layers are site-access controls, system-access controls, and file-access controls.

The first step in establishing access controls is to classify all data and equipment according to their importance and vulnerability. Mission-critical equipment and data should be given the strictest controls. Of course, all controls must be applied on a cost–benefit basis within permissible legal constraints. Each group of controls is discussed below.

SITE-ACCESS CONTROLS   The objective of **site-access controls** is to physically separate unauthorized individuals from information systems resources. This physical separation must be applied especially to hardware, data entry areas, data output areas, data libraries, and communications wiring.

On site, all users should be required to wear security identification badges (with photographs). All rooms containing data processing devices or sensitive data should have locked doors. Preferably, the locks should be programmable so that they can reject the keys of those who have been transferred or fired. Many companies use card-key systems. Biometric hardware authentication systems are also available. These systems automatically identify individuals based on their fingerprints, hand sizes, retina patterns, voice patterns, and so on. Guards should patrol the premises. Operations should be monitored by closed-circuit television.

 CASE IN POINT

Data processing and data warehousing complexes should be located in isolated buildings surrounded by fences with gate access. No one except authorized employees should be permitted to enter the gate without having a prior appointment that is verified by security.

Walmart keeps its data warehouse so secure that the company has required local building inspectors to sign a nondisclosure agreement before entering the premises.

All concentrations of computer data (e.g., data libraries, network printers, data entry, and data output sites) and equipment should be located in hard-to-find places, behind doors with programmable locks. There should be no signs on how to find them, and their location should be kept as secret as possible, for there are many cases of highly visible data centers having been bombed.

Attacks on the data library and other mission-critical rooms can be minimized by a very strict entry system. One such system involves a double-door setup for a computer data storage vault, as shown in Figure 6.5. The person desiring admittance to the room must pass through two doors to gain entrance. The individual first uses the programmable lock to enter the outer door and then enters a small room where the intercom must be used to gain admittance to the vault. The vault may then call security, which checks the individual by way of the television monitor and informs the vault whether or not to admit the person. The room can also contain magnet and metal detectors.

Centralized data entry centers should be highly protected areas and strictly off-limits to all nonessential persons. Network printers or other central printers, plotters, and facsimile machines, as well as their output, must also be protected. Highly sensitive output can be printed on hooded printers. The distribution of output should be controlled by a formal, secure delivery system.

PCs, terminals, disks, tapes, and other storage media must also be protected. All these objects are subject to theft, malicious tampering, and destruction. Keeping everything under lock and key is the best protection. PCs should be physically locked to avoid internal tampering. PCs should boot only from internal devices or network devices, and they should be accessible only by password. POS terminals should be locked when not in use. Finally, when possible, all computer devices should be located behind locked doors, and the walls should be shielded to prevent intrusions of undesirable electromagnetic radiation.

No software should be installed on any computer without prior approval of security. This is a difficult problem because viruses can enter the computer in so many ways. All software purchases should be required to pass through central purchasing and receiving. Any access to the Internet should be limited to those who can be trusted to not download programs from outside without approval. Any programs received in the mail or on the network from unsolicited sources should be destroyed, erased, or referred immediately to security for inspection.

There are other ways to physically limit the intrusion of viruses. One is to assign employees disk-less workstations (i.e., that use network disks for storage). All software and data are stored on central file servers. This approach has the advantage of centralizing the installation of all software, as well as file backups. A second way to physically inhibit the intrusion of viruses is to use read-only memory (ROM)-based operating systems. Many viruses alter key operating system files and routines. Putting the operating system in ROM therefore will provide some protection from virus threats.

All physical wiring should be unobtrusive, both indoors and outdoors. In some areas, it might be advisable to add air shielding to the wiring that will sound an alarm if broken. Fiberoptic

FIGURE 6.5

Data Storage Vault

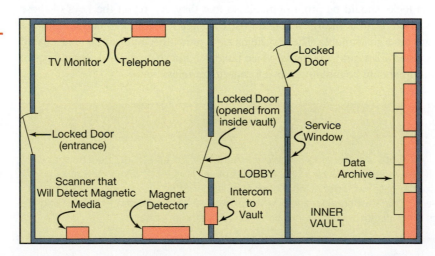

cable is generally considered reasonably safe from tapping and might be used. Wiring centers and communication devices should be located behind locked doors. Finally, all wireless access should be through secure, encrypted channels.

SYSTEM-ACCESS CONTROLS   System-access controls are software-oriented controls designed to keep unauthorized users from using the system. The objective of **system-access controls** is to authenticate users by using means such as user IDs, passwords, IP addresses, and hardware devices.

Each internal user can be assigned a user ID number and password at nine levels: at the level of the workstation or personal computer, the network, the host computer, the file server, the file catalog, the program, the data file or database, the record, and the data field. Each of these levels provides a successive layer of protection, separating a would-be intruder from sensitive data. The operating system(s) and accounting software should automatically record the time, date, and user number associated with all accesses. This information can be used to investigate any illegal accesses after they occur.

All entries to master files and critical databases should automatically include the user's identification credentials and the time of the transaction entry. This makes it possible to audit all of an individual's transactions.

All employees need to be educated in the proper handling of passwords. Passwords should be some minimum length, such as eight characters, and require both uppercase and lowercase letters. Password strength is an increasing function of password length and the number of characters that can be used. Passwords should expire and therefore have to be changed periodically. Users who do not change their passwords by their expiration dates cannot access the system again until their accounts are reset by security.

The procedures for changing passwords should be carefully controlled. Security can be enhanced by using some type of a sign–countersign system. The user initiates the password change procedure and the system responds with a sign, typically a question or code word. The user must respond correctly to the question or code word in order to proceed. A variant of this procedure is to require that the user input the characters shown in a graphic that has been included in the system's reply to the request to change a password. Figure 6.6 shows a password change request with a graphic containing the letters "pardes." The characters in the graphic cannot be read by a machine, thus ensuring that the password change request is being made by a human.

Under some operating systems, the account limits for user accounts can be assigned a maximum number of attempted security violations within a given time interval. After this limit is exceeded, the account must be reset by security before it can be used again. Under such systems, entering a wrong password may be considered a security violation. A related operating system feature is the ability to automatically disconnect or block any remote communication device from which several consecutively wrong passwords are received.

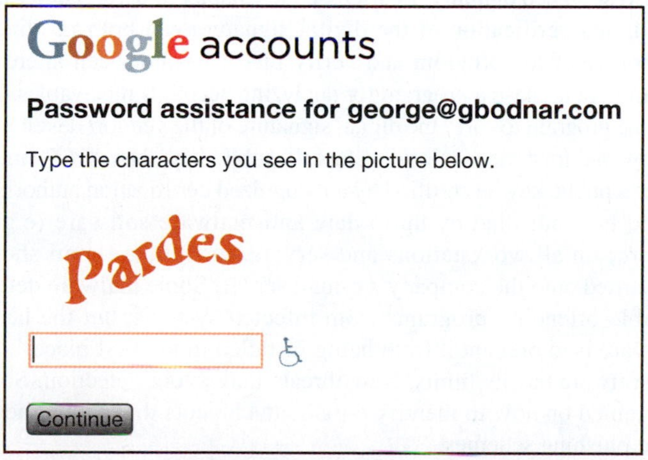

FIGURE 6.6

Password Change Control

Personnel should immediately notify security of any pending or actual termination or transfer of employees. Account access for these individuals should be cancelled immediately. Programmable locks should also be reprogrammed accordingly.

Hardware can also be combined with software to authenticate individuals requesting access to some part of the system. The biometric devices mentioned earlier can be used. An additional precaution is to authenticate the communication device requesting access. Some data terminals and network adapters in personal computers contain unique codes in ROM that are transmitted automatically to the host computer. The operating system or communication software can be programmed to analyze these codes and reject unrecognized devices.

Firewalls can be programmed to reject incoming packets of data that do not originate from preapproved IP addresses on the Internet. However, a determined hacker can spoof a valid IP address. Thus, firewalls represent more of a deterrent than a total solution. A stronger solution combines the use of firewalls with encryption techniques. Outsiders may be required to authenticate themselves with digital certificates or other credentials. All exchanges of information can then occur over encrypted channels. Firewalls can also block outgoing access or limit outgoing access to particular programs or servers. For example, the firewall might be set to allow outgoing access by an accounting program and the Web browser; any other program (such as a Trojan horse) would then be blocked automatically.

It is often desirable to withhold administrative rights from individual PC users. This can prevent users from installing software on their PCs, which can help prevent the PCs from becoming contaminated with malware.

FILE-ACCESS CONTROLS   **File-access controls** prevent unauthorized access to data and program files. The most fundamental file-access control is the establishment of authorization guidelines and procedures for accessing and altering files. Special restrictions should be placed on programmers who have the specific knowledge to make program changes. Program change controls aim to prevent unauthorized and potentially fraudulent changes from being introduced into previously tested and accepted programs. Elements of control include documentation of program change requests and a register of program changes with dates and appropriate approvals for authorization, programming the change, testing and certification of test results, and revision of the production program and its related documentation. Appropriate segregation of programmers, operations, and the program/data library is necessary in the process. Program maintenance is more subject to error than normal program development and represents a major loss exposure in terms of both fraud and access to sensitive programs. All important programs should be kept in locked files. This means that the program can be run but not looked at or altered. Security should keep a library of programs that are in operation. Security should periodically check the programs in operation to determine if they are bit-for-bit identical to authorized versions in the library.

Programs can also be signed digitally (as discussed in Chapter 3) in the same way that electronic messages are signed, and verification of the digital signature can both positively authenticate the identity of the source of the program and verify that it has not been altered. For example, the XYZ Company might purchase a program for analyzing accounts receivables. To protect itself, XYZ would require the program to carry the digital signature of the vendor/ developer. Furthermore, if XYZ does not know and trust the vendor/developer's public key, then XYZ can also require that the vendor/developer's public key be certified by a recognized certification authority.

Malware should be controlled by up-to-date anti-malware software (e.g., antivirus and antispyware software) on all workstations and servers. Incoming e-mail should be scanned before it is even admitted onto the company's e-mail server. Some malware detection programs eradicate recognizable offending programs from infected systems, but the best way to avoid problems with malware is to prevent it from being installed in the first place.

Anti-malware software has its limits. New threats may avoid detection. So, it is important that employees be trained on how to identify e-mail attachments that should not be opened and on how to recognize phishing schemes.

Finally, all software relating to servers, applications, and operating systems should be kept up to date, with security updates being applied in a timely manner. New software vulnerabilities constantly arise.

Controls for Passive Threats

Passive threats include such problems as power and hardware failures. Controls for such threats can be either preventative or corrective.

FAULT-TOLERANT SYSTEMS
Most methods of dealing with system component failures rely on monitoring and redundancy. If one part of the system fails, a redundant part immediately takes over, and the system continues operating with little or no interruption. Such systems are called fault-tolerant systems. Fault tolerance can be applied at five levels: to network communications, to CPU processors, to direct-access storage devices (DASDs), to the power supply, and to individual transactions. Many companies have a high degree of fault tolerance in their systems because computer failures can corrupt data and completely disrupt operations. Some companies could not survive a few days without a high degree of operational capability in their computers.

Networks can be made fault-tolerant by introducing duplicate communication paths and communications processors. There are two main approaches to redundant CPU processing. Systems with consensus-based protocols contain an odd number of processors; if one processor disagrees with the others, it is thereafter ignored. Other systems use a second watchdog processor that takes over processing if something happens to the first processor.

DASDs are made fault-tolerant by several methods, including read-after-write checks, bad-sector lockouts, and disk mirroring. With read-after-write checks, the disk drive rereads a sector after writing it to disk, confirming that it was written without error. If the confirmation fails, the offending sector on the disk can be flagged and locked out so that it will not be used again. The data can then be written to a good sector. If the software program does not support bad-sector error recovery, it will abort the write process and return an error message. A utility program can then be used to lock out the offending sector, and the application program can be tried again. Disk mirroring or disk shadowing involves writing all data in parallel to two or more disks. If one disk fails, the application program can automatically continue, using the good disk(s). There are also software programs helpful in recovering data from damaged files or disks.

Fault tolerance for power failures can be achieved with an uninterruptable power supply. If the power fails, the backup system, sometimes battery-powered, takes over so fast that no loss of continuity in the processing activities occurs. Then there is plenty of time to either switch the system to a generator or shut it down in an orderly manner. In brief power outages, the power is restored before either of these measures is necessary. Finally, some devices smooth out voltage drops and surges, which can cause severe damage to some electronic components.

Fault tolerance applied at the transaction level involves rollback processing and **database shadowing.** With rollback processing, transactions are never written to disk until they are complete. If the power fails or another fault occurs while a transaction is being written, at its first opportunity the database program automatically rolls itself back to its prefault state. Database shadowing is similar to disk shadowing, except a duplicate of all transactions is made and possibly sent via communications to a remote location.

CORRECTING FAULTS: FILE BACKUPS
Some studies have suggested that over 50% of PC owners do not properly back up their files. For this reason, a system that centralizes the backing up of files is essential. Such systems are commonly used to back up critical disks. For example, one major brokerage's system calls for files to be backed up every 2–5 minutes. Some companies constantly mirror all transactions to remote sites.

There are three types of backups: full backups, incremental backups, and differential backups. A **full backup** backs up all files on a given disk. In most systems, each file contains an **archive bit** that is set to 0 during the backup process. The operating system automatically sets this bit to 1 whenever a file is altered. An incremental backup backs up all files whose archive bit is set to 1. Each file's archive bit is then reset to 0 during the backup process. An incremental backup, therefore, backs up only those files that have been modified since the last full or incremental backup. Finally, a differential backup is the same as an incremental backup, and only the archive bits are not reset to 0 during the backup process.

The simplest backup scheme is to periodically make full backups. After such backups, the backup sets (e.g., tapes or optical disks) should be removed immediately to an off-site storage area. Alternatively, the backups can be made directly to remote locations. Ideally, all full backups should be made in duplicate as an extra precautionary measure.

In many cases, taking continual backups of the entire disk or computer system throughout the business day is not practical. Many such systems do incremental or differential backups between full backups, only backing up the altered files. This procedure can save both time and storage media costs and is useful in many situations. In general, incremental backups require less storage media and are faster than differential backups. One problem, however, comes in restoring incremental backups. The procedure to restore incremental backups involves first restoring the last full backup set and then restoring all incremental backup sets, one after the other, in chronological order. The problem with this procedure is that it can result in files being restored that were erased from the system sometime between the full backup and the last incremental backup. Of course, this is only a problem if files are erased. The differential backup, on the other hand, avoids this problem altogether.

Backing up files is not the same as archiving them. This is so because the media used for backup might not be reliable for long-term storage. For example, some optical disks are said to have an archival life of 10 years or less.

Internet Security—Special System and Configuration Considerations

This section provides additional discussion of Internet-related vulnerabilities.

OPERATING SYSTEM VULNERABILITIES   The Web server is essentially an extension of the operating system. Thus, any weakness in operating system security is also likely to create a related weakness in the Web server's security. For this reason, the security administrator must, first and foremost, secure the operating system.

Every operating system is subject to attack, and hackers continually find new weaknesses in operating systems. Therefore, the security administrator must constantly monitor security bulletins published by the operating system vendor and by third-party advisory services. For example, Microsoft keeps up-to-date security information for Windows on its Web site at www.microsoft.com/.

Even a correctly maintained operating system will fail if it is not configured properly. For example, by default, one version of Windows came preconfigured to include a "guest user" in its database of users authorized to access the system. The problem is, however, that this merely opened an unnecessary door for hackers. System administrators should set local and network security policies applicable to the configuration of the operating systems on individual workstations.

One way to minimize some of the risks associated with operating systems is to run different software programs in different virtual machines, using virtualization. **Virtualization** involves running multiple operating systems, or multiple copies of the same operating system, all on the same machine. The individual operating system instances run under the control of a "master program" called a **hypervisor.** For example, the Microsoft Windows[a] hypervisor (Hyper-V[a]) will simultaneously run Windows, Linux, and other operating systems on the same machine.

The security advantage of virtualization is that each operating system instance is isolated from all other operating system instances running on the same computer. This means that each virtual machine has access only to data, software, and memory allocated to it by the hypervisor. The result is that if a hacker compromises one virtual machine he will not have access to the data, software, and memory of other virtual machines running on the same computer.

One practical security use of virtualization might be to run, say, the e-mail and/or server and the accounting application on the same computer but in two different virtual machines. This way, if a hacker compromised the e-mail server, the accounting application would remain out of their reach. Of course, such a strategy is not without risk, because a hacker who compromises the hypervisor might thereby compromise both the e-mail server and the accounting application. The traditional approach would play it safer by running the e-mail server on one machine and the accounting application on another. But this safer approach is much more expensive in terms of the required hardware and energy consumption.

WEB SERVER VULNERABILITIES   Web servers are similar to operating systems in that it is necessary to constantly monitor advisory bulletins for security updates and information on configuration issues. Such monitoring is especially important for Web servers because Web servers and Web browsers tend to be updated more frequently than operating systems, and updates always come with the possibility of new security weaknesses. Web servers are often the front line of security because they are the portals through which outsiders frequently pass.

Web server security can be degraded seriously by configuration problems. One of the most common configuration problems is in the area of configuring permissions for directories and files relating to executable script programs. Executable script programs are a necessary component of almost any commercial Web site. For example, an executable program called a *forms handler* must be run anytime a customer enters a sales order into the company's Web site. Moreover, the forms handler must have write access to the disk to save the order information. Therefore, the anonymous customer must have both execute and write access, two privileges that together can form a very dangerous combination if applicable to the same file directory. This is so because a hacker could use the write privilege to upload a malicious program to a particular directory and then run the program in this directory using the execute privilege.

Therefore, write and execute access should never be granted to the same directory. In practice, however, this lethal combination of privileges is often granted by accident. For example, sometimes the administrator places the script files in the wrong directory, a directory that already has user-write privileges attached to it. Also, many Web administrators use Web authoring and design tools that automatically place files in particular directories unknown to the administrator and also automatically alter file permissions without any indication or warning. The file permission can get especially confused if more than one developer is working on the same Web site at the same time.

PRIVATE NETWORK VULNERABILITIES   Special risks are created when a Web server is placed on a host computer connected to other various users' computers via a local area network, and hackers may attack one computer through another. If the users' computers have access to the computer hosting the Web server, then the hacker can first break into one of the user's computers and then rely on the user's access rights to invade the host computer for the Web server.

This problem is very difficult because it may be virtually impossible for a server administrator to ensure adequate security on all users' machines. This is so because in many companies users typically access the Internet, run all kinds of strange and insecure programs, and improperly configure their operating systems.

One way hackers attack one computer through an alternate computer is by e-mailing (in the form of an attachment) a Trojan horse program to the alternate computer. The hacker typically tricks the recipient at the alternate computer into opening the e-mail attachment by spoofing a return address from someone familiar. The Trojan horse program is automatically and secretly installed when the user/victim on the alternate computer opens the e-mail message. One such Trojan horse program, Back Orifice, permits the hacker to remotely take control of the victim's computer via the Internet and from there access the host computer for the Web server. The user of the alternate computer never sees or hears anything; the Trojan horse program runs quietly in the background.

VULNERABILITIES FROM VARIOUS SERVER AND COMMUNICATIONS PROGRAMS   Many Web server host computers run not only the Web server but other servers as well, including FTP servers, e-mail servers, and remote control servers that permit legitimate remote computers to take control of the host computer. Each additional server poses additional security risks, and a security flaw relating to any one server can open a door for hackers to attack all the other servers and all the files on the computer, even other computers on the same local area network.

FTP servers are sometimes much more vulnerable than Web servers. This is so because basic FTP sends passwords in the clear with no encryption. Despite this weakness, many organizations rely on FTP as a means of transferring sensitive files over the Internet. Encryption-based versions of FTP exist and should be used whenever possible.

In general, almost all server programs have the built-in capabilities to grant access privileges to remote users. This makes server programs very dangerous, for many server programs are based on extremely weak security models. For this reason, the administrator should not run any server programs that are not absolutely necessary.

Various other types of programs present special threats. These include programs that work both as client and server: voice-over-IP (VOIP) programs, remote access programs, Web conferencing programs, chat programs, and peer-to-peer file sharing programs. All such programs potentially open doors for outsiders to attack. The risk can be minimized by running such software only on noncritical machines or at least on virtual machines.

CLOUD COMPUTING   *Cloud* is a synonym for the Internet, and the use of cloud-based services and data storage is referred to as *cloud computing*. The trend toward providing IT capabilities as a service via the Internet has led to **Software as a Service (SaaS).** SaaS is a cloud-computing platform in which software and its data are stored remotely from the user and accessed over the Internet using a Web browser. SaaS has become a common platform for business process applications, such as accounting and customer relationship management (CRM). Intuit's Quickbase™, for example, gives subscribers the capability of developing their own SaaS accounting applications. Salesforce.com is a cloud-based CRM provider that asserts "No Hardware. No Software. No Headaches." on its homepage. The distinguishing feature of SaaS is that end users only need a Web browser. All the software and data are stored by the SaaS provider in the "cloud."

Cloud computing raises security issues. On one hand, by shifting the computing into the cloud, security issues on the local computer are somewhat simplified. All that is really needed on the local computer is a Web browser to access the SaaS. On the other hand, cloud computing requires that the remote user place a tremendous amount of confidence in SaaS provider. Thus extreme care must be exercised when choosing a SaaS provider.

GRID COMPUTING   **Grid computing** involves clusters of interlinked computers that share common workloads. Individual computers can be linked locally or across different locations within the Internet. There are several types of computer clusters. High-availability clusters link physical or virtual computers together so that if one fails one or more of the others take over. High-availability clusters are also called fail-over clusters. Load balancing clusters link physical or virtual computers together so that computing jobs (e.g., page-view requests to web servers) are automatically distributed to computers in the cluster in order to balance out the workload. Performance clusters link physical or virtual computers together so that computing jobs are broken up into pieces and distributed to computers in the cluster in order to process the pieces in parallel. Performance clusters can greatly speed up the processing of complex tasks, such as converting videos from one format to another.

Grid computing poses an additional security risk. Grid computing can involve many different computers located in many different places and the lack of security in any one computer has the potential to result in a major security leak.

 CASE IN POINT

Various options exist for creating and using clusters in either private or public clouds. For example, RightScale (www.RightScale.com) provides software that makes it very easy to set up and deploy clusters with the public Amazon Elastic Cloud Computer (aws.amazon.com/ec2) infrastructure. VMware's (www.vshpere.com) vSphere product supports creating private clusters with only a few mouse clicks.

GENERAL SECURITY PROCEDURES   A good overall security atmosphere is essential. The best security software in the world will not help if the system administrators do not enforce the policies. Further, all errors and exceptions must be logged to secure files, and these logs must be constantly monitored.

Securing log files is an especially important issue because hackers often try to "cover their tracks" by altering log files. One way to secure logs is to write them to a remote computer or a virtual machine, where the file permissions on the remote or virtual machine are set so that new information can only be appended.

Disaster Risk Management

Disasters happen. The destruction of the World Trade Center in New York City by terrorists is just one example of an unexpected disaster that quickly and seriously interrupted normal business activity. Many organizations are critically dependent on computer systems to support daily operations. Consequently, if computer systems processing is delayed or interrupted, the organization may incur significant losses. Disaster risk management is essential to ensure continuity of operations in the event of a catastrophe.

Disaster **risk management** concerns prevention and contingency planning. In some cases, insurance might help control risks, but most insurers are reluctant to underwrite the costs of business interruptions for large companies, especially for those companies without disaster recovery plans. Both prevention and contingency planning are discussed in what follows.

Preventing Disasters

Disaster prevention is the first step in managing disaster risk. Studies have shown the following frequencies of disaster causes:

Natural disasters	30%
Deliberate actions	45%
Human error	25%

These data imply that a large percentage of disasters can be mitigated or avoided by good overall security policy.

Many disasters resulting from sabotage and errors can be prevented by good security policy and planning. Careful consideration should be given to natural-disaster risks associated with prospective building sites. Concentrations of computer equipment and data should be located in parts of buildings least exposed to storms, earthquakes, floods, and fire, as well as deliberate acts of sabotage.

Adequate electronic and mechanical systems for fire, flood, and intrusion are important. Water-based sprinkler systems can be harmful to electronic components. Many companies use fire-extinguishing systems that rely on something besides water, such as gas, foam, or powder.

Contingency Planning for Disasters

A disaster recovery plan must be implemented at the highest levels in the company. Ideally, it should be approved by a committee of the Board of Directors as part of the general computer security plan.

The first step in developing a disaster recovery plan should be obtaining the support of senior management and setting up a planning committee. When completed, the disaster recovery plan should be thoroughly documented and approved by these same individuals. Overall, a life-cycle approach should be used to design, implement, operate, and evaluate the plan. Estimates suggest that the initial costs of implementing a disaster recovery plan can range from 2 to 10% of the overall information systems budget. The design of the plan should include three major components: an evaluation of the company's needs, a list of priorities for recovery based on these needs, and a set of recovery strategies and procedures.

ASSESS THE COMPANY'S CRITICAL NEEDS   All mission-critical resources should be identified. These include hardware, software, power and maintenance requirements, building space, vital records, and human resources.

LIST PRIORITIES FOR RECOVERY   Even with a good plan, fully recovering from a major disaster can take a long time. Therefore, priorities should be established that correspond to the company's critical needs. The priority list might indicate that certain mission-critical activities and services are to be reestablished within minutes or hours after the disaster. On the other hand, the plan might indicate that other activities and services are to be reestablished days, weeks, or months later.

RECOVERY STRATEGIES AND PROCEDURES   A complete set of recovery strategies and procedures is essential. The plan should include such detail so that when disaster strikes, the company immediately knows what to do, who should do it, how to do it, and how long it should take. These considerations are discussed in detail in what follows.

Emergency Response Center   When disaster strikes, all authority for data processing and computer operations is transferred to the **emergency response team,** headed by the emergency operations director. These individuals direct the execution of the recovery plan from the emergency operations center, a predesignated site.

Escalation Procedures   The escalation procedures state the conditions under which a disaster should be declared, who should declare it, and who that person should notify when executing the declaration.

Alternate Processing Arrangements   The most important part of a disaster recovery plan is the specification of a backup site to be used if the primary computing site is destroyed or unusable. Three types of backup sites are possible: cold sites, hot sites, and flying-start sites. A **cold site** is an alternate computing site that contains the wiring for computers but no equipment. A **hot site** is an alternate site that contains the wiring and the equipment as well. A **flying-start site** is an alternate site that contains the wiring, the equipment, and also very up-to-date backup data and software. A cold site is capable of assuming full operation in a matter of days, a hot site in a matter of hours, and a flying-start site in a matter of seconds or minutes. In practice, the type of backup site used must be determined for each company on a cost–benefit basis, although few companies find the high cost of owning a flying-start site justifiable.

One way to maintain up-to-date data at a flying-start site is to mirror all transactions at the primary site and then immediately transmit them via communications to the backup site. Such data could be transmitted at high speed through the use of fiberoptic channel extenders. In some cases, a nearby backup site might be acceptable.

There are, however, alternatives besides actually purchasing an alternate site. Three such alternatives involve contracting with a computing service bureau, a commercial vendor of disaster services, or with another ordinary company, one possibly in the same industry.

A **service bureau** specializes in providing data processing services to companies who choose not to process their own data. In some cases, it may be useful to establish a contingency plan based on a contract with a service bureau. This option may be viable for relatively small companies with simple data processing needs. However, the service bureau is unlikely to be a workable solution for a company with complex computing needs. The computing needs of most large companies are too complex to be satisfied by the limited data processing services offered by typical service bureaus. Further, most service bureaus will not put computers on employees' desks, something that might be needed.

Several vendors, including Comdisco, IBM, and Sungard, provide disaster recovery services. Comdisco, for example, specializes in leasing hot sites for a monthly fee. This company supports an international disaster recovery network of hot sites linked together by satellite.

The third type of arrangement is a contract with another ordinary company. Some companies have enough excess computing power to temporarily assume the needs of others. A shared contingency agreement or **reciprocal disaster agreement** is an agreement between two companies in which each company agrees to help the other if the need arises. In a variation on this agreement, the two companies share a common hot site through joint ownership.

The Personnel Relocation Plan Contingency plans need to be made for the possibility of having to suddenly relocate employees to a backup site. Careful planning is needed in this regard, because many employees might have difficulty in relocating on short notice.

The Personnel Replacement Plan The possibility of losing employees to the disaster must be considered. Replacing highly skilled employees can be difficult, and the replacement employees may require extensive training.

The Salvage Plan In some disasters, it is possible to recover equipment and valuable records if quick action is taken. For example, a building that loses its roof in a hurricane will be exposed to rain. Losses in such a situation might be minimized if salvage efforts get under way immediately.

The Plan for Testing and Maintaining the System Computing needs often change rapidly. For this reason, any disaster recovery plan should be tested every six months. Outdated or untested plans might not work in a crisis.

Compliance Standards

Business is being increasingly pressed to comply with various standards relating to internal control and information security.

Information Security Standards

The main group of international standards for information security is the ISO/IEC 27000 series published by the ISO and the International Electrotechnical Commission (IEC). At the heart of this group of standards is ISO/IEC 27002, entitled *Information technology—Security techniques—Code of practice for Information Security Management.* This standard sets an auditable code of practices by which companies can seek voluntary certification.

ISO/IEC 27002 sets forth over 5,000 controls (to be implemented on an "as applicable" basis) under 12 general categories. Any organization considering information security should use these 12 categories as a general guide.

1. Risk Assessment
2. Security Policies
3. Organization and Governance of Information Security
4. Asset Management
5. Human Resources
6. Physical and Environmental Security
7. Communications and Operations Management—Management of Technical Security Controls in Systems and Networks
8. Access Control
9. Information Systems Acquisition, Development, and Maintenance
10. Information Security Incident Management
11. Business Continuity Management
12. Compliance

COBIT is another standard that defines a set, or code, of best practices. The COBIT framework is divided into four domains.

1. Plan and Organize
2. Acquire and Implement
3. Deliver and Support
4. Monitor and Evaluate

COBIT breaks down each of its domains into high-level objectives, resulting in a total of 34 high-level objectives. The high-level objectives are further broken down into individual control objectives.

ISO/IEC 27002 and COBIT are similar in that they both target IT professionals. COSO's *Internal Control—Integrated Framework: Guidance on Monitoring Internal Control*, on the other hand, is a more abstract, general framework targeted more toward management in general. As discussed in the previous chapter, the COSO report sets the basic structure for internal control processes: Control Environment, Risk Assessment, Control Activities, Information and Communication, Monitoring. The COSO report complements both the ISO/IEC series and COBIT.

Regarding Sarbanes–Oxley compliance, especially in relation to the sections that deal with internal control, the U.S. Securities and Exchange Commission (SEC) has recommended the COSO report. But in practice, implementation of multiple frameworks is often required in order to ensure compliance.

Business Continuity Planning and Disaster Recovery Standards

A **business continuity plan** is a strategy to mitigate disruption to business operations in the event of a disaster. The terms *business continuity planning* and *disaster recovery* are generally used interchangeably.

In the United States, various economic sectors and industries are subject to compliance standards for continuity planning. The U.S. Office of Management and Budget (OMB) provide various continuity planning directives. For example, OMB Circular A-130, Appendix III, *Security of Federal Automated Information Resources* requires continuity plans for systems within the federal government.

There are also various presidential orders and directives that require compliance. Presidential Decision Directive 67 requires all federal agencies to have continuity plans in place. Executive Order 12656 [Section 202] specifically directs heads of federal agencies to implement plans for national emergencies that include providing for emergency operations and protecting valuable records and resources. Finally, Presidential Decision Directive 63 orders a national plan aimed at ensuring security for the basic infrastructure that supports the federal government and the economy.

In the financial sector, the Gramm–Leach–Bliley Act (Section 501(b)), *Financial Institutions Safeguards*, requires federal agencies that oversee the financial sector to implement regulatory standards aimed at protecting the security of critical information resources. The Expedited Funds Availability Act requires all federally chartered financial institutions to have business continuity plans in place. The Basel II *Sound Practices for Management and Supervision*, issued by the Basel Committee on Banking Supervision, requires many major banks to maintain business continuity plans and appears to have developed into a general audit standard for banks.

Within the health-care sector, the Health Insurance Portability and Accountability Act (HIPAA) requires that health-care providers, insurance companies, and payment clearing-houses adopt standardized processes for processing electronic payments and claims. This mere standardization alone tends to promote de facto compliance standards through accreditation by organizations like the Joint Commission on Accreditation of Health Care Organizations, which audits for compliance.

In the utilities industry, Governmental Accounting Standards Board (GASB) Statement No. 34 requires utility companies to maintain business continuity plans. Similarly, the Federal Energy Regulatory Commission RM01-12-00 (Appendix G), 2003, requires many utility companies to maintain functional recovery plans.

With respect to international standards, BSI British Standards promulgates its Business Continuity Management Code of Practice as BS 25999-1. Similarly, BS 25999-2 (*Specification for Business Continuity Management*) provides specifications for implementing, operating, and improving a documented BCMS.

Summary

Information security seeks to provide for confidentiality, integrity, and availability. The information security management system (ISMS) is the subsystem of the organization that controls the special risks associated with information systems. Security systems are developed by applying the traditional life-cycle approach of systems analysis, design, implementation and operation, evaluation, and control. This approach also appears in the ISO/IEC 27000 series of international information security standards. However, instead of using the terms *systems analysis*, *design*, *implementation*, *operation*, *evaluation*, and *control*, ISO/ IEC 27001 uses the terms *planning*, *doing*, *checking*, and *acting*.

There are two major approaches to analyzing system vulnerabilities and threats in computer security planning. In the quantitative approach to risk assessment, each loss exposure is computed as the product of the cost of an individual loss times the likelihood of its occurrence. In the qualitative approach to risk assessment, the system's vulnerabilities and threats are listed and subjectively ranked in order of their contribution to the company's total loss exposures.

A vulnerability is a weakness in an information system, and a threat is a potential exploitation of a vulnerability. Various laws, regulations, and pronouncements address the problem of crimes against information systems. A successful attack on an information system requires some sort of access to the hardware, sensitive data files, or critical programs.

Anyone who accesses equipment, electronic data, or files, or any kind of privileged information without proper authorization is an intruder. Intruders who use electronic and other means to break into or attack information systems for fun, challenge, profit, revenge, or other nefarious motives are generically referred to as hackers.

Hacker methods can be grouped into several broad categories: social engineering, direct observation, electronic interception, and exploits. Electronic interception represents another category of possible attacks. Hackers may wiretap or piggyback wired connection, though such methods can normally be defeated by encryption. Exploits take advantage of security weaknesses in hardware or software. Some exploit techniques include buffer overflows, code injection, and port scanning. Browser exploits take advantage of vulnerabilities in Web browsers.

Employees and administrative personnel can also attack systems from the inside. We discussed six methods of attack that information systems personnel and users might use to perpetrate an information systems fraud. These methods are input manipulation (the most common method), program alteration (the least common method), direct file alteration, data theft, sabotage, and misappropriation or theft of information resources.

The ISMS seeks to achieve its objectives by controlling threats. This is accomplished by implementing security measures and contingency plans. Security measures focus on preventing and detecting threats; contingency plans focus on correcting the effects of threats. It is a well-accepted doctrine in information system security that some active threats cannot be prevented without making the system so secure that it is unusable. Furthermore, no security system is of much value without a general atmosphere of honesty and security consciousness.

Threats to the ISMS can be classified as active or passive. The primary way to prevent active threats is to implement successive layers of access controls. The successive layers include access controls at the site, system, and file levels. Passive threats are controlled through measures such as fault tolerance, disk mirroring, rollback processing, and database shadowing. Backups can be helpful in restoring data when preventive methods fail.

Business continuity and disaster recovery are important areas of information security. Organized plans must be in place and practiced ahead of time.

Glossary

active threats   computer fraud and computer sabotage.

adware   a type of spyware the displays advertisements, typically in pop-up windows.

archive bit   a bit used to determine whether or not a file has been altered.

backdoor   a method of covertly eluding normal authentication procedures while accessing a computer system.

black hat hackers   hackers tha t attack systems for illegitimate reasons.

botnets   collections of tens or hundreds of thousands of zombie computers that are often used to engage in malicious conduct, such as DoS attacks against Web sites, e-mail servers, and distributed name servers.

business continuity plan   a strategy to mitigate disruption to business operations in the event of a disaster.

code injection   a type of exploit that involves tricking a computer program to accept and run software supplied by a user.

cold site   an alternate computing site that contains the wiring for computers but no equipment.

cloned cell phone   a copy of a cell phone. The copy permits the holder to make and receive phone calls and text messages, just as if the copy were the original phone.

database shadowing a duplicate of all transactions is automatically recorded.

denial-of-service (DoS) attacks involve flooding victims with such enormous amounts of illegitimate network traffic that the victims can no longer process legitimate traffic.

distributed DoS attack a DoS attack that is distributed over many different nodes on the Internet or other network. The attack is typically coordinated through a botnet.

dumpster diving sifting through garbage to find confidential information such as discarded bank statements, department store bills, utility bills, and tax returns.

emergency response team individuals who direct the execution of a disaster recovery plan.

exploit occurs when a hacker takes advantage of a bug, glitch, or other software or hardware vulnerability to obtain unauthorized access to computer resources.

file-access controls prevent unauthorized access to both data and program files.

flying-start site an alternate processing site that contains the necessary wiring and equipment, and also up-to-date backup data and software.

full backup all files on a given disk are backed up.

gray hat hackers white hat hackers who skirt along the edges of the law.

grid computing involves clusters of interlinked computers that share common workloads. Individual computers can be linked locally or across different locations within the Internet.

hackers individuals who attack computer systems for fun, challenge, profit, revenge, or other nefarious motives.

hot site an alternate computer processing site that contains the wiring and the equipment as well.

hypervisor in software environments involving virtualization, the master program that controls the individual instances of operating systems running in the virtual machine.

information security protecting information to provide confidentiality, integrity, and availability.

information security management system (ISMS) the subsystem of the organization that controls risks relating to information security.

keyboard loggers secretly record and transmit to the hacker all the victim's keystrokes.

layered approach to access control erecting multiple layers of access control that separate a would-be perpetrator from potential targets.

malware any type of malicious software.

passive threats system faults and natural disasters.

phishing a form of social engineering that is aimed at tricking its victims into giving information (e.g., passwords), money, or other valuable assets to the perpetrator.

pretexting a form of social engineering in which the perpetrator impersonates another person, typically in a phone call or electronic communication.

qualitative approach to risk assessment a system's vulnerabilities and threats are listed and subjectively ranked in order of their contribution to the company's total loss exposures.

quantitative approach to risk assessment each loss exposure is computed as the product of the cost of an individual loss times the likelihood of its occurrence.

reciprocal disaster agreement synonym for shared contingency agreement.

risk management the process of assessing and controlling computer system risks.

service bureau provides data processing services to companies who choose not to process their own data.

shoulder surfing the surreptitious direct observation of confidential information.

site-access controls controls that physically separate unauthorized individuals from information system resources.

social engineering involves manipulating victims in order to trick them into divulging privileged information.

software as a service (SaaS) IT-related capabilities provided as a service via the Internet.

software piracy the copying and distributing of copyrighted software without permission.

spyware Trojans that seek to gain the victim's personal information or modify the victim's interaction with his or her computer in a way that provides some financial or other gain to the perpetrator.

system-access controls software-oriented controls designed to keep unauthorized users from using the system by such means as account numbers, passwords, and hardware devices.

system faults system component failures, such as disk failures or power outages.

threat a potential exploitation of a system vulnerability.

Trojan horse a malicious program masquerading as a legitimate one or that appears to come from a legitimate source.

virtualization involves running multiple operating systems or multiple copies of the same operating system, all on the same machine.

virus malware that replicates itself and thus spread throughout a computer or a network.

vulnerability a weakness in a system.

vulnerability scanner the same thing as a port scanner

white hat hackers legitimately probe systems for weaknesses in order to help with security.

worm a type of malware program that spreads itself over a computer network.

Webliography

www.wikipedia.org/wiki/Information_security
This article does a good job covering the basic concepts associated with information security.

www.iso.org
Home page of the ISO 27000 series of standards and other important international standards.

www.cos o.org
Home page of the COSO reports relating to internal control and ERM.

www.isaca.org
Home page of the COBIT framework. See also www.itgi.org, the ITGI.

www.itsecurity.com
A Web site rich in articles and resources relating to information security.

www. .org
Carnegie Mellon University's Computer Emergency Response Team. This site helps information security professionals keep up on the latest threats. It also contains a wide range of resources relating to information security.

www.microsoft.com/security
Microsoft's Security Central Web. This Web contains many important resources and links, including a link to Microsoft's Security TechCenter. TechCenter provides links to technical bulletins, advisories, updates, tools, and prescriptive guidance designed to help IT pros keep Microsoft servers, desktops, and applications up to date and secure.

www.bsigroup.com
Home page of BSI British Standards, the National Standards Body of the United Kingdom. This organization promulgates BS 25999-1 and BS 25999-2, which define best practices in business continuity planning.

www.isc2.org
Home page of (ISC)[2], a worldwide organization that provides certification to information security professionals.

www.redhat.com/security
Web devoted to Linux security. Most Web servers run on Linux operating systems.

Chapter Quiz

Answers to the Chapter Quiz appear on page 226.

1. Collusion appears to be (_____) in a computerized versus a manual system.
   a. less likely
   b. more likely
   c. equally likely

2. Which of the following is an active threat to computer security?
   a. computer sabotage
   b. earthquake
   c. equipment failures
   d. power outages

3. Individuals who attack computer systems for fun, challenge, and gain are sometimes called (_____).
   a. duffers
   b. geeks
   c. hackers
   d. flaggers

4. The interception of legitimate information and substitution of fraudulent information in its place is called (_____).
   a. EMI eavesdropping
   b. flagging
   c. hacking
   d. piggybacking

5. In most cases of computer fraud, (_____) is the method used.
   a. program alteration
   b. input manipulation
   c. direct file alteration
   d. misappropriation or theft of computer resources

6. A destructive computer program masquerading as a legitimate one is called a (_____).
   a. backdoor
   b. logic bomb
   c. Trojan horse
   d. worm

7. An alternate computer processing site that contains the necessary wiring and computer equipment for operation but not data files is called a (_____).
   a. hot site
   b. cold site
   c. flying-start site
   d. fault-tolerant site

8. A dormant piece of code placed in a computer program for later activation by a specific event is a (_____).
   a. backdoor
   b. logic bomb
   c. Trojan horse
   d. worm

9. Which of the following defines a code of best practices in IT security?
   a. ISO 27001
   b. ISO 27002
   c. ISO 27003
   d. ISO 27004

10. In the following, which source of information security frameworks or standards targets managers rather than IP professionals?
    a. COSO
    b. COBIT
    c. ISO
    d. none of the above

Review Problem

Hart Manufacturing has a large centralized data processing department. Barbara May is in charge of the internal audit staff. A routine investigation revealed that several customer accounts are phony and that several accounts with balances in excess of $1,000 each could not be traced to the names and addresses listed on the accounts. For example, one account was listed as belonging to an individual named John Day. When she tried to contact this individual, she found that the address was that of her local cemetery. In addition, the telephone number was not a working number. Furthermore, there was no individual in the telephone directory listed as John Day. Additional investigations revealed that there was no credit application on file for this individual.

To make things more complicated, it was found that all these accounts were 12 months overdue. For some reason that had not yet been ascertained, none of these accounts appeared on the accounts receivable aging reports.

Required

What type of fraud has probably been committed here? Which individuals are the ones most likely to have been involved?

Solution to Review Problem

Program alteration is the most likely cause of this problem:

A. It is very likely that someone has altered the accounts receivables program to allow transactions by individuals not on the approved credit list. This individual has covered up by fixing the aging program to omit these accounts. There is also the possibility of collusion between a programmer and someone in the credit department. This would explain the fact that there was not adequate supporting documentation on file supporting credit approval. Of course, the programmer might have put a backdoor in the program that would allow credit to certain individuals, even though they were not in the approved customers' database. This could have been done without the help of someone in the credit department.

   1. It should be noted that the program alteration might have been done by a system operator. System operators sometimes have access to all files on the computer system.

The operator might have replaced the legitimate version of the accounts receivables program with an altered one.

B. The solution to this type of problem is to have a formal system for installing and maintaining software.

   1. All changes to software should be supported by documentation, including complete review and approval.

   2. Programmers should not have access to the working versions of software. They should be restricted to making changes, on an approved basis, to copies of working software. The modified copies should be reviewed before formal installation.

   3. Master copies of software should be kept in a secure place. These master copies should be periodically compared, using readily available file comparison utilities, to the operating versions. Another option is to have the master copy digitally signed and to check the digital signature.

Review Questions

1. Identify several unique problems and risks associated with computerized information networks.
2. What elements are included in an ISMS system?
3. Does the development of an ISMS require application of the life cycle approach? Discuss.
4. What is risk management?
5. Distinguish between the qualitative and the quantitative approaches to analyzing system vulnerabilities and threats.
6. Identify some of the general types of threats that affect information systems.
7. Is it possible to rigorously identify characteristics of the white-collar criminal?
8. What types of individuals pose a threat to an information system?
9. Identify several different types of intruders.
10. Identify and discuss six different methods that an individual might use to perpetrate a computer fraud.
11. How might computer programs be used to commit acts of sabotage?
12. What is a virus program? Give several examples.

13. What role does an organization's control environment play in information systems security? Give several specific examples.
14. Describe the layered approach to access control. What specific layers of access control might be implemented?
15. What are fault-tolerant systems? Illustrate the application of fault tolerance to the following areas:
    a. network communications
    b. CPU processors
    c. DASDs
    d. power supply
    e. individual transactions
16. Distinguish between full backups, incremental backups, and differential backups of files.
17. What steps should be taken in the development of a disaster recovery plan?
18. Identify several recovery strategies and procedures that might be included in a disaster recovery plan.
19. Identify several alternate processing arrangements that might be included in a disaster recovery plan.

Discussion Questions and Problems

20. XYZ Hardware Retailing Company runs a batch system for accounts receivable. On the first Monday of each month, the operations specialist runs an accounts receivable update. The procedure is as follows: The accountant prepares a list of all updates on a disk file; this disk file is then transferred to the account of a systems specialist; the operations specialist then carefully edits the data and then generates the batch job.

Required

Evaluate this procedure from a control standpoint.

21. The Randell Company is a medium-sized toy manufacturer. The information services division of this company is composed of user services, systems programming, and systems maintenance. In addition, the company has a batch-oriented accounts receivable system. All the databases related to accounts receivable are maintained by the systems programmer. Recently, a minor bug was detected in the accounts receivable program. The procedure to correct the bug was as follows: First, it was reported to the systems programmer by a member of the accounting staff; next, the systems programmer discussed the problem with the head of systems programming and agreed to an appropriate change; then the individual who reported the problem was notified that appropriate corrective action was being taken.

Required

Evaluate the procedures used in the Randell Company for program modification.

22. Barbara Carson is a high-ranking officer in the Marines. She has recently been placed in charge of computer-assisted design and manufacturing for a highly classified project relating to a new high-technology aircraft. The project is so secret that she has been assigned to develop it in an abandoned base high in the mountains of California. Project resources included are a private super-cluster grid computing network, 100 military personnel (including programmers, operations specialists, and so on), and 50 nonmilitary support staff. Most of the support staff do not have security clearances. The problem is that their skills lie primarily in programming, computer operations, and hardware maintenance.

Required

Develop an overall security system that maintains appropriate security regarding outsiders and effectively uses the nonmilitary support staff without violating security.

23. Renco Manufacturing has had a problem with unauthorized access to its accounts receivable database. The chief accountant suspects that one of the systems administrators is somehow making changes to the accounts receivable database in an unauthorized manner. The accountant, however, is uncertain about the methods being used. It is possible that a systems administrator has made changes to the accounting program. Another possibility is that the operator is accessing the accounting program without proper authorization.

Required

Discuss appropriate methods for resolving this problem.

24. Rauls Retailing has a high turnover rate among its employees. It maintains a very large distributed computer network that supports approximately 200 networked PCs. The company maintains fairly extensive databases regarding its customers. These include customer profiles, past purchasing patterns, and prices charged.

Recently, the company has been having major problems with competitors. It appears that one competitor seems to be very effective at taking away Rauls' customers. Most of the company's customers have been visited by this competitor, and identical products have been offered at lower prices in every case.

Required

What is the possible security problem? What can be done about it?

25. Green Manufacturing maintains a large IT division. Recently, the company has faced a major problem with its software. It seems that ever since one of the computer programmers has been fired, disk files are mysteriously being erased. The chief analyst suspects that the fired programmer had placed a logic bomb somewhere so that disk files would be erased in the event that his Social Security Number was no longer in the accounting database.

Required

Discuss the methods for the detection of this logic bomb. What methods could be used to prevent this type of problem?

26. Finco Merchandising specializes in purchasing bankrupt firms and disposing of their assets by direct mail. It maintains about 30 sales offices around the United States. Each of these sales offices does the actual direct-mail work within its own region. The central office in Atlanta maintains the customer database, and customers' names are transferred from this office to the individual sales offices on a weekly basis. The transfer is presently being done through one of the major public packet-switched networks. It is suspected that customers' names are somehow leaking out to competitors as a result of their being transmitted through the public network.

Required

Discuss at least two alternatives that might be used to ensure greater security.

27. Hart Manufacturing Company is relatively small, with approximately 100 employees. The company's accounting server is run by two individuals. One individual is responsible for the physical operation of the computer. This includes maintaining the company's data library. At present, the library includes copies of master files for most of the important accounting systems databases, as well as copies of historical reports and documents that are no longer stored on the server. Although the company has plenty of online storage space, the data library keeps copies of the accounting master files and other files on optical disks. The archiving system is primarily batch-oriented, and updates are run only once a month. Currently, the library is adjacent to the room that houses the accounting server and can be entered either through the server room or via another outside door. Because this individual is very busy, most employees enter the library room and log optical disks in and out as needed.

Required

Given the limited resources of this company, discuss an appropriate security system for the data library.

28. Bundy Retailing sells building supply materials. It is located in a medium-sized Midwestern town and has four sales offices there. Each sales office has its own POS terminal that is hardwired to the company's main server through a dedicated line. These terminals are used to authorize sales transactions. Given that an appropriate credit check has been made, the salesperson simply types in the sales order on one of the POS terminals, and authorization to release the goods is immediately printed out at the company's central warehouse. Recently, however, the company has detected a security problem. There are several salespeople working in each office and sharing the same terminal. It appears that one of the salespeople has been entering sales transactions and charging them to Brown Contracting Company. The problem is that Brown Contracting has never received any of these goods. In fact, all the goods have been released to an impostor. This is a very serious problem because the total amount of goods released cost the company approximately $20,000. The chief of security is perplexed because she does not know which salesperson is responsible. There is even some discussion about the possibility that an unauthorized intruder may have accessed the terminal.

Required

Discuss appropriate security measures that could have been taken to prevent this problem from occurring.

29. Waldo Company has had a problem with one of its employees using the computer network to play games. In the past the company has not been very strict about controlling the use of the company's network because employees often have slack time during the off-season. Recently, however, a serious problem has occurred. It appears that one of the game programs run on the network server contained a virus. The virus is a special type of computer program that can cause considerable damage to a network when run with other computer programs in the system concurrently. The virus "looks around" the network and checks to see if other computer programs in the network are infected with the virus. If not, the virus program will then infect them. Part of the infection process involves making certain random changes to the other programs. These random changes are such that the infected program will produce unpredictable or invalid results at some specified date subsequent to the infection. For example, an accounting program might be modified so that it will scramble all the accounting databases exactly 6 months after its infection. The nature of the virus is particularly bad because a program, once infected, has the ability to spread the infection to other programs. Therefore, once a virus is introduced into a computer network, all programs in the network might be infected in a matter of a couple of weeks. To make things worse, the infection process may carry to all the company's backup copies as well. This is particularly true if the virus program lies dormant for a long period of time before producing its disastrous results.

On June 15, this company went into a major state of disaster. The virus had evidently invaded all major portions of the computer network. The network database manager looked with great horror to find that all the databases were completely scrambled. To make things worse, backup copies were scrambled as well. Inspection of the backup copies of databases revealed that they were completely worthless. As a result, the company was unable to do its accounts receivable billing. Two months later, it filed for Chapter 11 bankruptcy.

Required

Discuss the means by which this problem should have been prevented.

30. The Mid City Sales Company manages a discount store that sells most department store items at a discount. The entire accounting system is computerized. Barbara West is in charge of computer operations and oversees a medium-sized computer cluster with 10 support personnel. The present system is based on online input and online accounting

processing. All accounting updates are keyed directly into the system and processed immediately.

The company's accounts payable program works as follows: Customer invoices are matched with purchase orders and receiving reports. Assuming that these documents are in order, the chief accountant enters the appropriate information into the accounts payable program. Entering this information results in a computer-generated check (to pay the supplier) and updates the accounts payable. The check is processed by the finance manager, who signs it and then mails it out. To ensure against unauthorized access to the system, both an identification number and a password are required before the accountant can request the computer to make a payment on an account.

The company's computer system is such that the operator can access any account from the network operator's workstation. Over a period of several months, the operator has been accessing the accounts payable system and ordering the computer to make payments to fictitious vendors.

Required

What security measures can be taken to prevent and detect this type of problem?

31. A programmer in the Ace Bottle Company installs a patch in one of the computer's billing routines that skips over the billing of a friend's account. The program allows the account balance to increase without bounds. Another patch was put into the program to ensure that the friend's account balance never appeared in an aging report.

Required

Discuss the appropriate security measures that could detect and prevent this problem.

32. Manchester Sales Company is a medium-sized retail operation with an IT staff of 10 employees. The IT staff effectively maintains all accounting functions as well as computer operations. The overall internal control and security system is quite good. However, there are a number of problems. First, all the IT employees know the passwords to each other's accounts. Although this is a breach of the security system, most employees feel that the other employees are basically honest and that there is no need to worry. Second, employees are lax about document distribution procedures. Almost anybody can come into the server and pick up a printout without an entry being logged into the records. Security has repeatedly complained to these employees about the problem but to no avail.

Required

Discuss the problem of lax security in this company. What are its implications? What can be done about it?

33. Beard Manufacturing is extremely security conscious, especially in the area of its information system. Because of this, the director of the computer center has installed a sophisticated computer security system costing the company over $1 million. The system is so sophisticated that all

communications terminals require positive voice identification. In addition, each user is assigned a security-level clearance by the network operating system. All systems application and data files require specific levels of security for access. For example, individuals running accounting reports are assigned a low-level classification that will allow them to access the data files that they need but will not allow them to make any changes to these files. In addition, a large number of other measures are part of the system, including security guards and closed-circuit television.

Despite this sophisticated system, a very intelligent systems programmer managed to break through the company's security and alter the accounts receivable files. He managed to find a backdoor in the operating system that allowed him to operate with a level 8 security clearance. In addition, he was able to access the system update log to instruct the target computer to completely forget that he accessed the data files. In other words, he was able to make changes to the data files without any trace being left of the transaction.

In this case, the company was very lucky because the systems programmer was honest and took his scheme to the director of computer security. Needless to say, the director of security was flabbergasted. As a result of what the programmer did, the director of security is considering replacing the entire security system with a more sophisticated $2 million system.

Required

What response should the director of security make regarding the systems programmer? What measures could have been taken to prevent the problem from occurring? Is a more expensive security system a good idea?

34. Equity Financing Life Insurance Company is headquartered in Miami, Florida. The company is very large, so it operates an enormous mainframe computer system. Recently, a group of political radicals threw a small bomb through the window (breaking the glass) in the main computer room. Because this happened late at night, there were no human injuries. However, the damage was extensive, and the central processing unit and three major disk arrays were completely destroyed.

Required

Is what happened in any way the company's fault? Why or why not?

35. Eagle Airlines is headquartered in Chicago. The corporate administrative offices consist of 10 buildings in a complex that spreads over four square miles. The main data center is centrally located. All the buildings in the complex contain computer users and, therefore, are connected to the main computer center by way of Ethernet cables.

Recently, the company's computer network was violated by the following scheme: A couple of college students from a nearby university purchased an inexpensive line analyzer and packet sniffer. Using this device and a notebook PC, the two students recorded everything that came across the Ethernet cable.

To their amazement, the captured data included various employee sign-on IDs and passwords for access to all the company's major databases, including accounts payable and accounts receivable. To exploit this information, it was necessary for the students to obtain access to the company's computer through a data terminal. This posed a problem, however, because most of the company's data terminals were carefully guarded. To get around this, one of the students suggested that the company might have a telephone dial-in port. The biggest problem, however, was finding the correct telephone number of the port. They reasoned that the company's computer dial-in telephone number was probably very similar to the telephone number for the administrative offices. Therefore, they wrote a computer program that simply dialed one telephone number after another looking for a computer modem carrier signal. The program was set to try all numbers that matched administrative telephone numbers in the first four digits. Therefore, the program was set to test 999 different telephone numbers. This procedure worked out very well, and the company's dial-in port was discovered on about the twentieth try. As it turned out, the computer's number differed from the administrative number in only the last two digits.

Once into the company's network, it then became necessary to try a scheme to try to defraud the company. After much discussion, they finally decided to order the computer's accounts payable program to issue checks to a post office box registered under a fictitious name. Finally, the illegally obtained checks were deposited to the bank account registered to the fictitious name.

The students might have gotten away with their scheme if they had not gotten greedy. They had requested a large number of small checks totaling $100,000. This would have gone unnoticed; however, the checks requested bounced because there was not enough money in the company's bank account to pay them. Once the checks bounced, the accountant immediately figured out that the checks were not supported by adequate documentation. The authorities were notified, and the students were caught while checking their post office box for mail.

Required

Discuss the specific security measures that could have been taken to prevent this scheme.

36. Grand Bank Corporation (GBC)—Case A

Grand Bank Corporation (GBC) operates a communications network that supports data processing for its subsidiary banks and their branches. The corporate database is centralized at the GBC Network Communication Command Center (NCCC). About 300,000 transactions are processed against the database each day.

GBC's NCCC consists of two coupled mainframe processors, 32 disk arrays, and other equipment. The communication network uses dedicated lines leased from a PBX (private branch exchange). The system supports processing for demand deposit (checking), savings, commercial and personal loans, and general ledger.

Processing Controls

Control procedures exist to prevent unauthorized access to the communication network and unauthorized use of files. Transactions are entered by tellers using intelligent data terminals. In the case of communication interruptions, the terminals can do limited off-line processing. At the end of each day, the terminals print transaction totals for balancing the cash drawer. A log of all transactions received during the day is reprocessed off-line that evening and reconciled to the day's online processing. These totals along with an updated general ledger are transmitted to the network members each morning.

Each terminal's identification code is hardwired. Each transaction is identified by the terminal identification code, along with the employee identification code and time of day. The central computers recognize only authorized terminal identifications and requests to use the system.

Software controls are used to ensure that users access only their own data files and the application programs authorized for them. All files and programs are protected by frequently changed codes and passwords.

Access Controls

All visitors sign in and out in a log indicating the time of day, whom they represent, and whom they are visiting. Visitors are issued badges and are required to wear them in plain view while on the premises.

Access to the data processing area is restricted to authorized management and operating personnel. Access is controlled by doors activated with magnetic card readers attached online to a separate computer security system. Codes in the magnetic cards issued to each authorized employee designate which doors are available for access. A log is maintained of the card number and all access attempts.

Access to the data center is restricted to the operations staff and equipment vendors only. A building security guard is on duty at all times.

Environmental Controls

An electronic heat, fire, and smoke detection alarm system has been installed at NCCC. A halon gas fire extinguishing system is incorporated into the system to put out any fire in the computer area. The fire alarm system is connected to an automatic power-off trip switch and to the building's manned engineer console.

Portable carbon dioxide fire extinguishers are readily accessible in and around the computer facility. These are periodically weighed and kept charged, and IT support personnel are trained to use them. All electrical equipment is approved by Underwriters' Laboratories (UL).

Flammable material in or around the data processing center is removed daily to avoid potential fire hazards. Waste containers are designed to retain and smother fires. Paper and other combustible supplies are not stored in the data center. The data center's physical room construction material is noncombustible. Exterior walls have a 2-hour fire rating. A no-smoking rule is strictly enforced. There are several independently controlled air-conditioning modules distributed between two independently fused power panels. The failure of any module can be compensated for by the other modules. All air-conditioning modules are inspected monthly when filters are changed. There is a backup system for pumping water to the air-conditioning system. If one motor fails, that motor will be bypassed and pumping capacity maintained by a second motor and pump. The water softening system utilizes a dual filter to prevent clogging of water intake systems. A separate electrical power supply for the air-conditioning systems is maintained.

Maintenance Procedures

Proper maintenance procedures concerning hardware help NCCC prevent failures. The maintenance technicians perform preventative maintenance on the equipment daily, and on every Sunday, they thoroughly check the mainframe processors.

The operations manager, in order to locate problems, reviews the engineer's weekly report of preventative and remedial maintenance. The operations manager also closely supervises the work being done to ensure a prompt and proper solution.

File Security

The library of data files is physically controlled by a librarian who maintains the file usage records for removable media. Periodically, file media are checked and their operating condition certified. The librarian is the only person authorized to erase file media.

The librarian controls all files in the library and in the off-site storage location. Each removable media container has retention instructions printed on it. All file media that are necessary for recovery and restart are stored in a heat-resistant, fireproof, locked vault.

The locked computer center vault holds the first-generation backup files, which can be used for immediate backup. The files in the vault include program object files, transaction backup files, and account master files. Operating system backup is ensured by periodically copying the object code and related data files from the system residence device directly to optical disk. A copy of the source code for each application is also kept on optical disk.

Each day, two copies of the daily transactions are prepared and put on optical disk. One disk is placed in the data center vault and the other one is sent to an off-site storage location. Online and off-line month-end master files, month-to-date history, and object and source programs are sent to off-site storage twice a week and after each end-of-month processing.

Hardware Controls

Either of the two coupled processors can be used individually for running all online and off-line processing. If hardware problems should develop in one machine, the other is available for backup. All peripheral equipment, which includes disk drives, solid state storage devices, printers, and communication equipment, can be switched to either computer.

Backup telephone lines connect the telephone center to the data center. If a restart is needed, the online system files from the beginning of the day can be processed against the network transactions entered during the day.

Recovery and Restart

Procedures that are necessary for computer operators to restart and recover from a business interruption are fully documented. The run manual documents all necessary recovery and restart procedures for the network communications system together with their priorities.

The data library retains all necessary system files and transaction files so that the network communications processing for any of the last 30 days can be recreated.

In the event of the destruction of files at NCCC, the present system provides the capability to be operational with up-to-date files in 24 hours. To achieve this type of recovery, files would be removed from off-site storage and the most recent master files would be processed off-line with the 1–3 days of daily transactions required to recreate current master files.

There is a 20-page set of detailed procedures and guidelines to be followed in the case of a disaster. These procedures indicate who is to be notified, what tasks they are to perform, and in what order.

NCCC has letters of support from suppliers of the center's equipment and related elements that indicate that in case of a disaster, support will be offered on a timely basis. These letters are from the suppliers of business forms, the air-conditioning company, the computer manufacturer, the suppliers of the peripheral equipment, and the PBX company.

Required

a. Identify major areas that should be considered in a security review to determine the potential for loss of data or the ability to process it. Identify some controls in each of these areas.

b. Evaluate the general security and recovery procedures as described at NCCC. What other areas might warrant consideration in a review of security and recovery procedures?

37. Grand Bank Corporation (GBC)—Case B

Management of GBC commissioned a security review task force to review compliance with corporate security policies and procedures at NCCC. The following observations were made during several on-site visits to NCCC and the off-site file backup storage location.

1. Frequent visitors, such as equipment technicians or important management personnel, often do not have to sign the visitor's log.

2. The data center room door is often left unlocked by employees who are "running out for something and will be right back."

3. The back door to the data center room is sometimes opened on very hot days to help reduce the load placed on the air conditioners.
4. Several holiday banners were noticed hanging from a fire detector and a halon gas register.
5. Several computer programmers were observed playing video games on the data terminals at their desks.
6. Several unlabeled data files were observed in the data center. Several files that should have been destroyed several days previous were found in the library.
7. Several persons have "extra" keys to the file storage vault.
8. An outside vendor provides cleaning services on Sundays during off-hours. Often no NCCC employees are at the center during this weekly cleaning.
9. The company that picks up and transports data files to the remote storage location is often late picking up the files for off-site storage.
10. Several programmers were observed walking directly into the file library and picking up removable media for usage.
11. The off-site file storage location, a very old warehouse building, lacks adequate temperature and humidity controls and also has inadequate fire detection and prevention systems.
12. Records maintained at the off-site storage location—which is used by several different companies as well as GBC—were inadequate and not up-to-date. The physical storage of the backup files was in locked closets labeled only by numbers.
13. Letters sent to confirm the backup support promised to NCCC in letters obtained before equipment was actually purchased received lukewarm and sometimes contradictory responses from vendors. In several cases, the claim was made that existing NCCC equipment is quite different and somewhat incompatible with the products now offered and supported by the vendor.

Required

1. Discuss the security problems indicated by the items noted.
2. What do these data suggest about the evaluation of general security and recovery procedures such as those in effect at GBC's NCCC?

38. The ABC Company has suffered from repeated attacks on its Web site. In the most recent attack, the server was suddenly bombarded by requests to view Web pages. The number of requests was so large that it caused an overflow in the activity log after the first hour. The Web manager estimated that the total number of requests exceeded 4 million, but she would never know for sure because the entire Web server crashed after 45 minutes.

One of the analysts inspected the remains of the activity log and quickly discovered that all the requests came from a small group of IP addresses.

Required

Describe what types of measures might be taken to protect the ABC Company against subsequent attacks of this nature.

39. Ace Pencil, the Web manager of the XYZ Company, was horrified when he received a call one night around midnight from Bob Drake, one of the salespersons.

"Our entire Web site has been replaced by cartoon characters," said Bob Drake. Ace jumped out of bed and stepped into his home office, where he nervously viewed the company Web pages. Sure enough, the story was true. There, in front of him, he was staring at all the cartoon characters that his children watched on Saturday mornings.

Further investigation revealed that in fact there was absolutely nothing wrong with his Web site. All the files on the server were exactly as they were supposed to be. Yet, when he went to the Web site, he only saw cartoon characters.

Required

a. Describe what has happened to the XYZ Company.
b. What can be done to correct the problem?

40. The Greenwood Worm Company sells earthworms over the Web. You have been hired as a consultant to help Greenwood set up a completely new Web site, and the owner of the company tells you that she wants all the best in security.

Required

a. What would be your top priorities in developing a secure Web site?

41. The Nelm Company has discovered through experience that somehow Erm, its major competitor, seems to discover its every secret. For example, when Nelm launches a new advertising campaign, Erm always immediately launches an advertising campaign that appears to be specifically designed to nullify the effects of Nelm's advertisements.

Barbara Woods, the head of Nelm's security department, is convinced that somehow Erm is invading its computer network and browsing secret files at will.

Nelm's network is set up as follows:

a. One large Web server machine that also supports applications for 15 users in the sales department.
b. The Web server is on a local area network, and the files for the 15 users in the sales department are shared with users in engineering and production.
c. Nelm supports Internet-based e-mail services for all its employees.

Required

a. Describe security flaws in Nelm's system.
b. Make suggestions for improving Nelm's security system.
c. How might Erm be invading Nelm's network?

42. The RWD company has three Web servers, A, B, and C, connected together over a local area network. Server A is the "sacrificial lamb," the only server outside the firewall. In other words, from outside the company it is only possible to reach server A and not servers B and C.

There has been a debate among the company's IS security staff about the desirability of local area network links between the three servers. Jane Doe argues that there should be no links between server A and the other two servers. "It's just too dangerous," she said.

The other employees feel that there is no need to worry about the other two computers, as they are safe behind the firewall.

Required

a. Do you agree with Jane Doe? Why or why not?
b. What risks, if any, would be caused by connecting server A to the other two servers via the local area network?

43. The GGY company is debating the issue of who should be in charge of managing its private keys that it uses for its digital signatures. Some argue that the keys should fall under control of management, others argue that the job should belong to finance, and still others feel that it should belong to accounting.

Required

a. In general, which of the above-mentioned groups is in the best position, from a control standpoint, to manage the company's private keys?
b. Does your answer depend on which particular keys are in question? Explain.

44. The North Palm Company sells its own brand of shoes via its Web site. The company is owned and operated by a small family consisting of Maria and Henry Rodriguez, the husband and wife, and their 25-year-old son Jeremy Rodriguez.

Jeremy has some understanding of Web development but not enough to do things himself. So the Rodriguez family contracted with a local company who provides turnkey Web-based storefronts.

The Web site had been working well for several months, and every week the number of orders continued to grow. Both Maria and Henry were ecstatic with all the money they were making. They were continually amazed how with a tiny office and an inexpensive computer they make enough money to live comfortably.

Things changed, however, one Monday morning when Maria tried to access the orders that had arrived over the weekend. The problem was that there was not one single order in the system.

Jeremy Rodriguez investigated, and by noon he had to come to realize that their home page had been replaced by a picture of a crazy-looking stuffed duck and a banner message that said "Hackers Unite. Free the Web."

Desperate, Maria Rodriguez called their Web developer, who was out of the office for unexplained reasons. She left a message for him to return the call and that it was very urgent.

The whole afternoon went by, and still no more orders, and no call back from the Web developer. Henry called the developer 6 times, until the developer's secretary became angry. Finally, Henry Rodriguez became so agitated that he drove to the developer's office and caused a minor scene, but the developer was still nowhere to be found.

At 9:00 A.M. the next morning the developer returned the call and said, "I'll give it my highest priority this morning."

The whole morning went by without word from the developer. So Henry called the man's office again, and to his surprise the developer himself answered on the first ring.

"Have you figured out the problem?" asked Henry Rodriguez.

"To make a long story short, no," said the developer.

Henry was mortified. "This is killing us," he said. "We'll lose all our customers, and we have not one penny in sales now."

"I understand," said the developer. "The only problem is that about 30 of my customers have the same problem as you. I've been trying to repair some of their sites today, but it seems that the hackers managed to infect the Web servers with some terrible new virus. It is going to take 2–4 weeks to get everyone going again."

Things got even worse, and by Wednesday several other merchants had filed lawsuits against the developer. Maria Rodriguez heard about the lawsuits late that day from a friend who worked at the newspaper office, and she called the developer the first thing Thursday morning, only to find that the telephone was disconnected.

In a panic she went to another Web developer, who promptly told her that she had been the victim of a sophisticated multilevel marketing scam. The people involved had all been selling the same prepackaged Web storefront, which they had actually stolen from a legitimate company. To make things worse, they had installed every customer's Web site on an insecure server, with almost no access restrictions. Anyone could modify anyone else's Web site without even entering any account and password information.

Reluctantly, Maria wrote the new developer a check for $5,000 for him to get started on creating a new Web site, but the developer cautioned them it would take at least 2 days because he had to transfer North Palm's domain name to his server.

Maria and Henry signed a contract with the new developer and went home feeling better. "That took every penny from our bank account," said Maria. "Now I don't even have enough cash to pay the mortgage on our house or any of the bills this month."

"Don't worry," said Henry, "the money will start coming in again in a couple of days, as soon as we get our new site up and running."

Two days later they got a call from the new developer. "Bad news," he said. "I can't transfer your domain name because it is registered in the name of your previous developer. So, technically, the name belongs to him and not to you."

"What can we do?" asked Maria.

The developer sighed. "There's only one thing you can do to get things moving quickly. Start over. You can e-mail all your old customers about your Web site."

Henry and Maria thought for a few seconds. Then Maria realized that all the customer files were stored on the server. The developer had convinced them that the server was the safest place to keep all the files, because the developer did backups of the server several times a day.

The Rodriguez family ended up in personal bankruptcy and lost everything, including their house and car. In the end, they were forced to move in with Maria's parents in Miami.

Required

    a. Could the Rodriguez family have prevented all their problems? How?

    b. Prepare a list of all the mistakes that the Rodriguez family made.

    c. For each mistake, make a positive suggestion as to what should have been done instead.

45. The Wilting Tree Company (WTC) sells shrubs and trees to the general public in the entire West Texas area. WTC has nurseries in many cities and a corporate office in Houston with over 100 clerical employees. All clerical employees use personal computers as part of their work, and many freely share files with each other via e-mail. They also routinely exchange instant messages with each other using chat software.

In recent weeks, the IT department has become increasingly frustrated because many of the employee workstations have become infected with malware. Some computers have refused to boot, others run slowly, and still others are corrupted so badly that the Web browser freezes and needs frequent restarting.

What really frustrated the IT department is that all workstations have the best malware protection software suites on the market, and regular vendor updates take place in real time. Still, despite malware protection, the problems of malware keep getting worse, and overall operations have begun to slow down considerably.

Required

    a. How do you recommend solving the problem?

Web Research Assignments

46. You are the controller for a medium-sized electronic parts manufacturer. Your company already has ISO 9001 certification, which has immensely helped in impressing new customers. Your CEO now wants ISO/IEC 27000 series certification.

Required

    a. Write a report to the CEO that explains the costs versus benefits of certification under the ISO/IEC 27000 series.

    b. The report should explain how to go about getting the certification. What will the steps be? How long will it take? Will the company's existing ISO 9001 certification help it get the additional certification?

47. You are the controller for the WhatsTheMatta furniture company. You have decided to use COBIT to benchmark the security of your information system. But before proceeding, you need to explain your decision to the Board of Directors. The board is especially interested in something called the *maturity model*.

Required

    a. Write a memo to the Board of Directors explaining to them how the CMM works, how it relates to COBIT, and how it might help your company.

48. You are the IT security director for the Weezle Pretzle Company. You have convinced top management the need to implement ISO 27002. You don't intend to seek formal certification, so the CFO wants you to provide some measure of the gain that you expect in security effectiveness. So she has asked you to provide her a report on how to evaluate security effectiveness.

Required

    a. Write a report to your CFO explaining various options for evaluating information security effectiveness. [Hint: Consider Part 3 of ISO 15408 (The Common Criteria for IT Security Evaluations), especially the parts related to Evaluation Assurance Levels (EALs). Also consider ISO/IEC 15443.]

49. You are the assistant to the information security director. Your director is interested in hiring a new group of IT staff professionals.

Required

    a. Write a report to your director explaining the benefits of hiring Certified Information Systems Security Professionals (CISSPs).

Answers to Chapter Quiz

1. b   **2.** a   **3.** c   **4.** d   **5.** b   **6.** c   **7.** a   **8.** b   **9.** b   **10.** a

Electronic Data Processing Systems

Learning Objectives

Careful study of this chapter will enable you to:

- Describe how application controls are used in data processing systems to ensure accuracy and integrity of input, processing, and output.
- Characterize the various types of electronic systems used for transaction processing.
- Describe the basic functions and operation of a computerized accounting application.

The Input System

Manual Input Systems

In some computerized accounting systems, inputs are based on handwritten or typed paper documents. These manually prepared documents are collected and forwarded to the data processing department for error checking and processing.

PREPARATION AND COMPLETION OF THE SOURCE DOCUMENT **Source documents**, such as customer orders, sales slips, invoices, purchase orders, and employee time cards, are the physical evidence of inputs into the transaction processing system. They serve several purposes:

- Capture data;
- Facilitate operations by communicating data and authorizing another operation in the process;
- Standardize operations by indicating what data require recording and what actions need to be taken; and
- Provide a permanent file for future analysis, if the documents are retained.

Source documents should be standardized forms that are carefully designed for ease of use and accurate data capture. Errors that might occur during manual preparation can be minimized if the source document is well designed and easy to understand. Completed source documents are collected periodically and transferred to the data processing department for entry into the computer system.

TRANSFER OF SOURCE DOCUMENTS TO DATA PROCESSING Batch control totals and data transfer registers are fundamental controls over data transfer between user departments and data processing. The absence or inadequacy of procedures for the control of data transmitted between user departments and the data processing department is a significant control weakness as it presents an opportunity for unauthorized and/or fraudulet transactions to be introduced into the processing system.

CASE IN POINT

Many small businesses use Intuit's Quickbooks™ (www.quickbooks.com) to batch-process payroll. Quickbooks™ provides a guided three-step workflow for batch processing of payroll: (1) Enter payroll data into a single screen, (2) review a summary of payroll transactions, and (3) print paychecks and paystubs. In Step 1, payroll data is typically entered based on manually or electronically prepared employee time cards or worksheets.

The use of batch control over the entire data processing input–process–output sequence is fundamental to organizational independence. Proof and control functions should be performed outside the data processing department. Original source documents should be retained for a period of time sufficient to facilitate error correction. Procedures should be designed to ensure that source documents are not processed more than once.

Submission of input data should be accompanied by the completion of an **input document control form** similar to the one shown in Figure 7.1. Document counts are a simple form of batch control. One simply totals the number of documents to be processed. The term "record" is synonymous with document. Thus, a record count is the same as a document count. In addition to document and/or record counts, batch totals may be taken for all or several numeric fields in the original data file. These totals may be used throughout the data processing cycle to monitor the completeness of processing.

The data processing department should not accept data unless an input document control form is present to evidence and reference the transfer of these data. The input document control form may be dated and time-stamped, and the batch should be checked to ensure that it is complete and consistent with control procedures. Information in the input document control form typically is entered in a *data transfer log* (register) to provide a control over the disposition and use of these data. Batch control totals are fundamental to this process.

Figure 7.2 illustrates the development and use of batch control totals in a data processing application. User departments develop control totals over batches of input and then forward the batches of documents along with an input document control form to the data processing department. The input document control form is logged in the data processing department and then balanced to the output control totals that are developed during the processing of the batch of input.

FIGURE 7.1

Input Document Control Form

[Prenumbered]
150

Batch Control Form

Originating Department _____

Date   _____

Preparer's Signature   _____

Control Totals

Batch Number ⌞⌸⌸⌸⌸⌸⌸⌟

Number of Documents ⌞⌸⌸⌸⌟

Field Totals (list):

Field Number	Name	Total

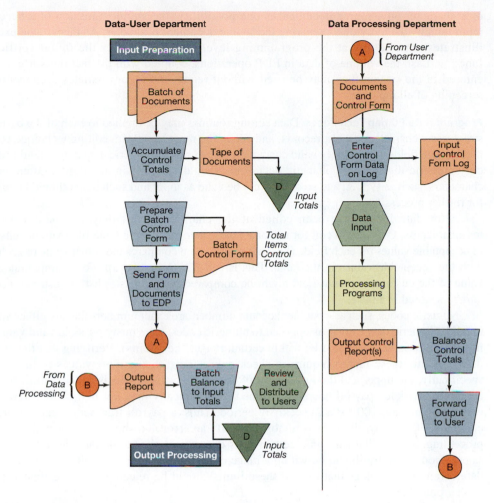

FIGURE 7.2

Use of Batch Control Totals

The output is returned to the user department, where it is batch-balanced to the batch totals on the input document control form.

Data Entry After the source documents such as invoices are received by data processing, they are manually key-transcribed or keyed (i.e., typed) using a data terminal or personal computer and then stored on disk. Next, the input file is key-verified. **Key verification** is a control procedure that detects errors in the keying operation. An error might occur, for example, when a customer account number is mistyped because the data entry clerk presses the wrong key or misinterprets a character on a source document. In key verification, each source document is key-transcribed a second time. The key verification software compares the retranscribed data as they are being entered, key-by-key, with the input data already on the disk file. If these are the same, nothing happens, and the operator proceeds with the next character of data. In the case of a mismatch, the operator is notified and he or she may then correct the error. To reduce the costs associated with key verifying input data, nonessential fields, such as a customer's name and street address (as opposed to account number or ZIP code), are often not verified. A second but less effective way to detect data entry error is *visual verification*. With this approach, someone compares the source documents with a printout or screen image of the key-transcribed file.

Program Data Editing Since verification does not edit data, it is essential that data be thoroughly edited after entry to ensure valid content. **Program data editing** is a software technique used to screen data for errors prior to processing. It should be used in addition to verification for several reasons. First, input errors can occur that will pass verification. Incorrect recognition of a character on a source document is one possibility; the simple omission of a necessary input item by the individual preparing the source document is another. As this second example illustrates, data editing at the programming level is a control over the initial verification function. Last, the volume of data in EDP operations, coupled with the fact that once data are entered in the system they may be used without reconversion, necessitates a methodologic screening of all input data.

Program Data Editing Techniques Data editing routines may be applied to each of the basic data structures—characters, fields, records, and files. The most basic data editing technique ensures that all data fields contain only valid characters. For example, numeric data items should contain only numeric digits, and alphabetic data items should not contain any digits. Often, certain characters, such as #, *, &, and so on may not be valid as input and such items should be rejected for further processing.

After data items have been edited at the character level, they can be checked for reasonableness. One way to edit for reasonableness is to establish a table file that contains a list of acceptable values for each field. The edit program then compares the actual value of each field with the acceptable values in the table. This is called a **table lookup**. For example, an actual value of the customer account field might be compared with a master list of customer account numbers stored in a table.

Numeric codes, such as customer account number, are exact numbers that are either valid or invalid. Numeric data values, as opposed to numeric codes, have many possible valid values but in general these values should be within certain ranges (i.e., limits). Verifying that the numeric data is within these ranges requires a check only against the extreme values of the range—specifically, the upper and the lower limit of acceptable values. This is called a **limit test**. For example, the field "payroll hours" in a time record typically may not be less than zero hours or more than, say, 100 for a 2-week pay period. Thus, a payroll transaction data record that contains 150 for payroll hours is almost certainly an error and should be rejected for further processing. Total dollar sales in a certain sales department or total dollar sales by a particular salesperson generally should be within a range of zero to some upper limit based on historical data. Transaction values that exceed these limits should be rejected and investigated before further processing.

 CASE IN POINT

Casino employees such as card dealers often receive tips from happy customers at gaming tables. These tips are often given in "chips" and these chips must be cashed in by the employee. Data editing of these transactions (i.e., cashing in of chips by employees) revealed unusually large amounts being collected by a particular employee. Further investigation revealed that this employee had devised a clever method of stealing chips while operating a gaming table.

As just discussed, it is possible to edit numeric data with respect to being outside of acceptable ranges; in such cases, the data are rejected. At times, it may be desirable to discriminate further among acceptable items as well. For example, a payroll field may contain a value that is acceptable but also unusually high or low as to warrant investigation. This item may be accepted for processing but flagged for a subsequent audit. Alternatively, such items may be held in suspense of processing until the data are reverified. The use of programmed edit tests to discriminate among acceptable data so that some items are either held in suspense of processing until audited or collected for audit after processing is called **continuous operations auditing**.

CASE IN POINT

Continuous operations auditing of credit card transactions enables financial institutions to reduce credit card fraud. Stolen credit cards are usually immediately used for multiple purchases. Typically, this activity results in excessive usage when it is compared to the customer's normal activity. Flagging such activity and immediately contacting the lawful owner regarding apparently unusual usage of the card can result in immediate cancellation of the card number when the card has been stolen.

Numeric codes can be verified by using a check digit. A **check digit** is an extra, redundant digit added to a code number. The check digit is computed when a code is initially assigned to a data element. Check digits are computed by applying mathematical calculations to the individual digits in a code number in such a way as to generate a result that is a single digit. This digit becomes the check digit and is added to the original code. In subsequent processing, this same mathematical operation can be performed to ensure that the code has not been recorded incorrectly.

There are numerous check digit procedures. The following illustration is one version of a technique known as *Modulus 11*:

The use of check digits is very common because of the high reliability of this procedure. Commercial check digit packages catch 100% of transposition errors and a very high percentage of random errors. However, check digits do not guard against all possible input errors.

Account number:	1	2	4		0	
Multiply each digit separately by the corresponding digit in the sequence 5 4 3 2:	$\times$ 5	$\times$ 4	$\times$ 3		$\times$ 2	
Add results of digit multiplication digit by digit:	$5 + 8 + (1 + 2) + 0 = 16$					
Subtract results from next highest multiple of 11:	$22 - 16 = 6$					
Check digit = 6						
Complete account number:	1	2	4	0	6	

Data Editing Terminology The data edits just discussed, as well as several other types of data edits, are illustrated with examples in Table 7.1. The terminology illustrated in Table 7.1 is typical, but many other terms are used to describe the same type of data edit. A **valid code check**, for example, is a particular type of table lookup in which the table file consists of valid codes. Other authors use terms such as *validity check* or *existence check* in describing the same type of data edit.

CASE IN POINT

Complexities may exist that are difficult to anticipate when designing program data editing tests. An airline company automatically mailed letters of welcome into their frequent fliers rewards program to any customers who had flown on the airline for the first time. After an airplane crash, several families received letters of welcome for persons who had been killed in the airplane crash.

TABLE 7.1 Data Edit Illustration

Data Edit	Description	Example
Completeness check	Check that entries exist in fields that cannot be processed blank.	Each field in a record is checked to assure the presence of data.
Field format check	Check that each character in a field is in proper mode (e.g., alpha or numeric).	Each character of a vendor number field is checked to assure it is numeric.
Field length check	Check the entry in a field for a specific number of characters.	A date field in a month-day-year format is checked that it contains six digits.
Field sign check	Check the sign (positive/negative) of a numeric field for the correct value.	The amount due field of a bill is checked that the sign is positive.
Limit check	The value of a numeric field is checked against a predetermined upper and/or lower limit.	The value of the hours worked field in a time card record is checked that it does not exceed a predetermined limit of 60 hours.
Reasonableness check	The value of a numeric field is compared to another numeric field in the same record.	Overhead costs in a work-in-process record are checked that they do not exceed 200% of the labor cost field.
Valid code check	Match the value of a code to a table file of acceptable code values.	A vendor code field is validated by matching it to a table file of valid vendor codes.
Check digit	Validate a numeric code through the use of a check digit algorithm.	A credit card transaction is validated by re-computing the check digit in the customer's account number.
Combination field check	The value of one field is compared or related to another field to establish validity.	A transaction code field is compared to a department code field. Certain transaction codes are only valid for certain departments.
Internal label check	An internal file label is read to validate the characteristics of a file.	The file code on an internal label is checked by a payroll program to assure that it is the payroll file.
Sequence check	A field in a series of records is checked for ascending or descending sequence.	The sequence of invoice numbers is verified as the invoice file is processed.
Record count check	The number of records in a file is counted during processing and balanced to input controls.	The record count of time cards processed is balanced to input totals from the payroll department.
Hash total check	The hash total of a field in a file is computed during processing and balanced to input controls.	The hash total of employee numbers is computed during processing and balanced to input controls from the payroll department.
Financial total check	The financial total of a field in a file is computed during processing and balanced to input controls.	The total dollar amount of invoices processed is computed and balanced to a total from the billing department.

Electronic Input Systems

In *electronic input systems*, sometimes called *online input systems*, transactions are input directly into the computer system and the need for keying in of paper source documents is eliminated. Electronic input systems provide a higher degree of automation than do manual systems. There are various degrees of automation possible. Users might initiate transactions by manually keying them into the computer. This type of input has become very common because it occurs when users enter data into forms displayed as Web pages. For example, a plant manager might manually type a purchase requisition into a data terminal. The requisition is then forwarded automatically to purchasing for additional processing. Alternatively, a customer creates a sales order by entering data into a form displayed as a Web page.

Many systems support completely automated transaction processing. The typical gasoline pump is a good example. The customer inserts a credit or debit card into the gasoline pump. The pump then serves the gasoline, the store's inventory and sales records are updated, and the customer's credit card company is billed electronically. EDI, as discussed later in this chapter, provides completely automated transaction processing. For example, when inventories are low, a purchase order message can be automatically sent to a vendor using EDI.

One problem with electronic input systems is the possible loss of segregation of duties and audit trail. In manual input systems, source document preparation and data entry are normally segregated, as they are in a manual processing system. In electronic input systems, however, these functions are performed by the same person, or no person is involved directly. Therefore, the concentration of functions in electronic data entry eliminates controls associated with a segregation of duties. These controls—review and batch control of source documents and controls related to source document preparation, such as prenumbering, authorization, and review—are important to the integrity of the audit trail and must be compensated for in electronic systems.

The loss of manual internal controls can be compensated for by using transaction logs. *Transaction logs* or *transaction registers* are created by logging all inputs to a special file that automatically contains tags to identify transactions. **Tagging** means that additional audit-oriented information is included with original transaction data. Such information as date and user authorization codes can be included to provide an extensive audit trail. Transaction logs also provide an important backup, as well as a source for control totals.

In electronic input systems, complete program data editing is often performed when the transaction is entered. Once the transaction is accepted, it might be processed either immediately or at a later time. If it is processed at a later time, additional data editing may be performed.

The Processing System

Processing involves the manipulation of files. Files provide storage of data. A file is a collection of records that are related by some attributes. For example, an accounts receivable file is a collection of records pertaining to a firm's customers. All records in the accounts receivable file share the attribute of being a customer to the firm. A record is an organized collection of fields (also called *data items*) that are grouped for processing. Fields contain data such as numbers, amounts, or alphabetic characters such as a name. For example, each record in the accounts receivable file would contain fields that are relevant to processing accounts receivable information for the firm's customers. Customer account number, customer name, and amount due from the customer would be typical examples of fields in the records of an accounts receivable file. To summarize, a file is a collection of records, and records are a collection of fields.

Types of Files

There are several types of files. A **transaction file** is a collection of transaction input data. Transaction files usually contain data that are of temporary rather than permanent interest. By contrast, a **master file** contains data that are permanent or of continuing interest. To illustrate this difference, consider the posting of sales on account to the accounts receivable ledger. Because a sales journal is a chronological record of sales on account transactions, it may be called a *transaction file*. The transaction file consists of raw data concerning sales to customers. Although there may be several sales to the same customer, this will not be known until the transaction data are processed. The process of posting sales to the accounts receivable ledger summarizes sales to an individual customer. Processing converts data into information. Management is more interested in summary data such as total sales and total account balance than in the details of a particular sales transaction. Management thus has a permanent interest in the information that is contained in the accounts receivable master file. In contrast, management's interest in transaction files is temporary. Once the data have been processed to update master files, they are no longer of direct interest to management. Transaction files must be saved, of course, to maintain an audit trail.

A **reference file**, also known as a **table file**, contains data that are necessary to support data processing. Reference files are not transaction files, and they are not modified as a result of processing transactions. Common examples of reference files used in data processing are payroll tax tables and master price lists.

Generic File Processing Operations

There are several basic types of file processing that are common to many computer applications. Sorting is a processing operation that arranges items in a predetermined order. For example, a transaction file of sales orders may be sorted so that the records are in order by customer account number as opposed to sales order number. Sorting is often desirable or necessary to facilitate further processing of a file. Merging is a processing operation that combines two or more files that are already arranged in the same order into a single file that contains all of the records from these files. The merged file remains arranged in the same order as the files that were merged. Extraction is a processing operation that copies selected records in a file into a new file for further processing.

Updating is a processing operation that applies changes pertaining to the records in a file to the file itself, producing a new file that reflects all of the changes. Updating includes making additions of records to a file, deleting records in a file, and making changes to items or amounts in the fields of a file. For example, an inventory file might be updated to reflect the addition of new items, the deletion of items no longer kept in stock, the changes to the prices of items, and the quantity of items on hand. Updating a file is necessary before producing outputs such as reports, to ensure the accuracy and completeness of the output. Updates are usually conducted on a regular schedule that corresponds with the required frequency of the output. For example, updates to the inventory file may be carried out weekly to correspond to the preparation of a weekly inventory status report.

Batch-Processing Systems

In **batch-processing** systems, transactions are processed periodically in batches. Manually prepared input forms are usually processed in batches. Processing weekly time reports to produce paychecks and processing groups of checks to update accounts payable master files are examples of batch processing.

CASE IN POINT

Adobe® Photoshop® uses batch processing to simplify the task of making the same corrections to a large number of photos. Using commands in the software, corrections to a group of images can be made automatically as a batch process.

Batch processing is economical when large numbers of transactions must be processed. It is best suited to situations in which files do not need to be updated immediately to reflect transactions, and reports are required only periodically. Payroll is a good example. Payroll is prepared periodically. It is not calculated every day. Batch processing is inherent in end-of-cycle business processes such as sending end-of-month statements of account to customers. The major disadvantage of batch processing is that files and reports might be out of date between periodic processing. A good example of this is an inventory file. If the inventory file must be used frequently to determine the availability of product for sale, the file often will be out of date if sales are processed only periodically in batches. It is primarily for this reason that many companies use real-time processing systems. Batch processing is still used widely, however, because there are still many situations in which it is a very efficient method of processing data.

Batch processing can be performed with either sequential- or random-access (i.e., direct or indexed) file updating. Both approaches are discussed below.

BATCH PROCESSING WITH SEQUENTIAL FILE UPDATING   Many manual batch-oriented systems use *sequential file processing* to update the master file. Processing in such a system usually involves the following steps:

- *Preparing the transaction file.* First, any additional data editing and validation are performed. Then the records in the transaction file are sorted into the same sequence as the master file.
- *Updating the master file.* The records in both the transaction and master files (i.e., subsidiary ledgers) are read one by one, matched, and written to a new master file that reflects the desired updates.
- *Updating the general ledger.* The general ledger is updated to reflect changes in the master files.
- *Preparing general ledger reports.* Trial balances and other reports are produced.

Figure 7.3 outlines the processing of transaction data in a typical manual batch-processing accounting system. Each business process generates batches of transactions for processing. Examples are sales transactions generated by the customer order management business

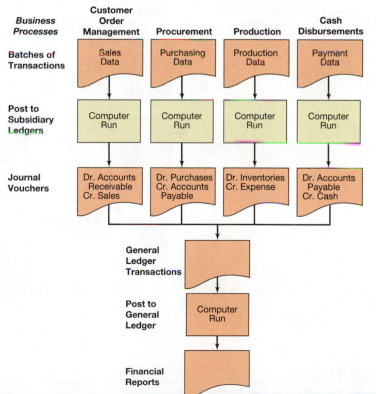

FIGURE 7.3

Overview of Batch Processing of Accounting Data

process and purchase transactions generated by the procurement business process. Batches of transactions from each business process are processed against the relevant application files in separate computer runs. The computer runs post the transactions to subsidiary ledgers and also generates the information necessary to prepare journal entries (journal vouchers) for posting to the general ledger. The journal vouchers are accumulated and processed as a batch against the general ledger in a separate computer run.

As indicated earlier, batch processing often involves maintaining a sequentially organized master file. This file—an accounts receivable master file for illustration—commonly resides on a direct-access storage device. Sales transactions affect the information on the accounts receivable file. These transactions and others—such as new accounts and payments on account—must be reflected in the master file. Figure 7.4 outlines the procedural steps in manual batch processing with sequentially organized files, beginning with data input. The numbers in this figure are keyed to the following discussion.

Preparing the Transaction File As Figure 7.4 illustrates, batches of documents are input (1), processed to build a transaction file (2), and subjected to batch balancing procedures (3) to ensure that all documents are accounted for prior to computer processing. The batch control totals would normally be supplied by the user along with the input data and reconciled by the data entry function prior to further processing. The resulting file of transactions is on disk (4). This file is processed with an edit program (5) to screen the data before further processing. Data editing of the source documents prior to input is essential to ensure the reliability of the data processed.

In addition to screening data, the edit program (5) must accumulate revised batch control totals for the input data. This is necessary, as the figure shows, because the input data have

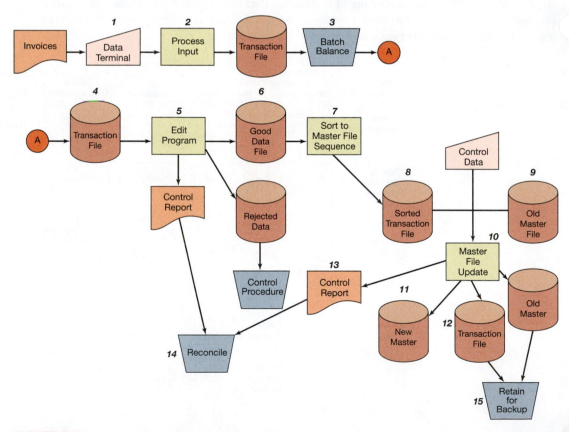

FIGURE 7.4

Systems Flowchart of Sequential File Processing

been divided into good data—those that have passed the edit program—and rejected data. The rejected data must be held in suspense until they are corrected. To facilitate processing, the rejected data usually are reentered for processing as a separate batch at a later date. The control report that is output by the edit program provides the data necessary to reconcile the results of the edit program to user-supplied batch control totals.

The file of edited transactional data (6) is sorted to master file sequence (7) to facilitate the matching process necessary for efficient sequential file processing. It should be noted that Figure 7.4 shows data editing performed at the earliest possible point in the flow of processing, that is, before the transactions are sorted. At times, however, depending on the particular circumstances, data editing may be performed after the transactional data have been sorted to master file sequence. This allows input editing to detect duplicate transactions or to check the sequence of records to be processed. Therefore, either sequence, "edit and sort" or "sort and edit," is possible, with the best sequence determined by the particular circumstances surrounding the application (Figure 7.5).

Updating the Master File Once the transaction data have been edited and sorted (8), they are processed against the old master file (9) in the accounts receivable application program(s) run (10). This master file update program (or set of programs) posts the detail of accounts receivable transactions to the accounts receivable master file. The new updated master file (11) is the basis for generating reports and other detailed information. This master file is a subsidiary ledger—the accounts receivable subsidiary ledger in this illustration. The transaction data (12) and the old master file are retained for backup control, as illustrated in Figure 7.4. The control report (13), which is printed at completion of the processing, is reconciled (14) with the batch totals/control report produced by the edit program. These control totals must be reconciled with user-supplied batch control totals before any output is returned to the user. Reconciliation must allow for any transactions that were rejected by data editing. This reconciliation of input to output control totals is performed by the user department, a special control unit or the internal audit function.

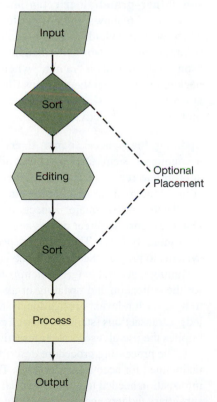

FIGURE 7.5

Placement of Editing in the Flow of Processing

FIGURE 7.6

Son–Father–
Grandfather Master
Files

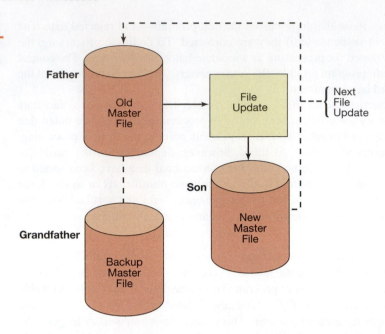

The control report (13) normally would include a detailed listing of transactions processed against the master file. This transaction register is the equivalent of a journal produced in a manual system.

As Figure 7.4 shows, the old master and the transaction files should be retained for backup (15). If the new master file is lost or found to be in error, the processing run may be repeated using the old master file and the transaction file. This concept is often referred to as **son–father–grandfather retention**, with each version of the master file being a *generation*. As Figure 7.6 shows, the old master file that is used as input to a file update is the "father." The processing yields a "son"—the new master file. The new master is another generation of information. The "son" file then becomes the input master for the next file update. Thus, the "son" file becomes a "father," when there is a new "son," and the old master file that is the backup master from the previous file update becomes a "grandfather" file, that is, a file that is at least two processing cycles old. Several generations of backup files may be kept, depending on the control objectives.

Updating the General Ledger Every organization must maintain some type of general ledger accounting system. Data must be collected, recorded, classified properly, and entered into the appropriate records for further financial report summations. A general ledger system is the cornerstone of an accounting system.

There are two major aspects to the operation of a computerized general ledger system. One concerns the direct processing of the general ledger programs, most of which takes place on a monthly basis. The second aspect concerns the processing in other computer application systems to prepare the inputs to the general ledger system. One of the tasks to be undertaken in designing a general ledger system is the creation of a pro forma set of journal entries providing for the collection and updating of all data needed for financial reports. The typical approach is to have each relevant application system (such as payroll or accounts payable) generate general ledger transactions (standard journal entry data) to be used as input at the proper time. Doing this implies the use of a separate transaction file in the general ledger system.

The processing procedure described in detail earlier posts transactions to subsidiary ledgers maintained for accounts receivable. The general ledger has not yet been updated. The summary information needed to prepare journal entries may be printed at the completion of processing the subsidiary ledgers and used to update a manual general ledger, or subsequently, this information

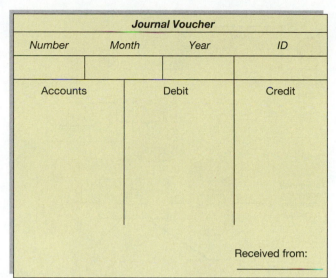

FIGURE 7.7

Journal Voucher Format

may be input for processing against a computerized general ledger system. Alternatively, the standard journal entries may be output initially in machine-readable form.

All entries into the general ledger should be documented with journal vouchers. Responsible departments originate the input data to the general ledger system. This may entail the manual preparation of journal vouchers or, in cases where these data are provided by other application programs, the review and adjustment (if required) of these data into journal voucher format.

The journal voucher format (Figure 7.7) is similar in most organizations and includes the journal voucher number and date, the control and subaccounts (as applicable), and the debit and credit amounts. One or several accounts may be entered on one journal voucher, depending on the complexity of the transaction and the system design. Journal voucher numbers are established to code the type of transaction (cash, receivables, sales, and the like). The column headed by ID designates that the journal is an original entry or the reversal of a prior entry. The account and debit–credit amounts are self-explanatory. This basic format may be expanded to include other information relevant to a particular system. Examples of such data are detailed cost ledger information (to support a subsidiary cost file) and details of expenses by organizational unit for responsibility reports. Either of these data items might be used in conjunction with a separate master budget file to produce reports showing "budget versus year-to-date" and so forth.

General Ledger File Update   Figure 7.8 provides a systems flowchart overview of a typical general ledger file update. As they are released by the general ledger department, journal vouchers are used to build a journal voucher file (the transaction file). This file is program data edited to check for the proper journal and account numbers and to determine whether the accounts are correctly associated with their related journals. Invalid data are reported as exceptions and returned to their originating sources for correction and reentry. The edited journal voucher file may be sorted and structured to produce a variety of reports. The current journal voucher transactions are processed against the previous month's general ledger master file (the old master) in order to update that file and produce the current period's general ledger register.

Computer processing of accounting data typically is a two-step procedure. The first step produces preliminary reports, which are forwarded to the accounting department for review and audit relative to the journal voucher listings and general ledger listing. After the audit and submission of corrections and any additional data, the second step is a run that produces the final listings and financial schedules. Numerous reports may be prepared.

Preparing reports requires a link between the general ledger accounts and the report(s) in which they appear. This process is called *line coding*. **Line coding** is a procedural step typically

FIGURE 7.8

Systems Flowchart Showing a General Ledger Update

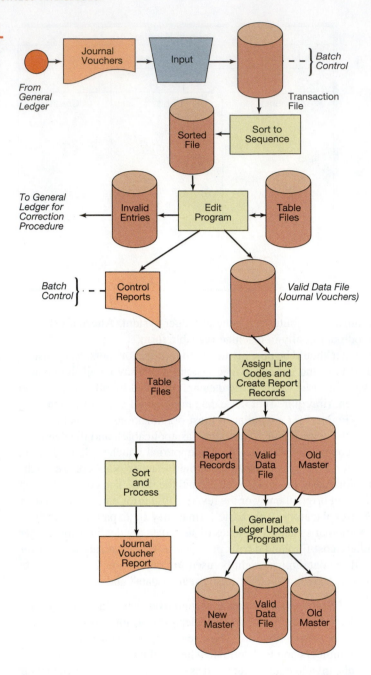

accomplished by a table-lookup (matching) process between the updated general ledger file and a line-coding table file. Table files function as reference files. Table files contain items or records that are not a part of data files but are an integral part of the processing function. Tax tables and line-coding assignments are examples of table files stored on direct-access storage devices in accounting applications. The result of the line-coding procedure is several report files that are ultimately printed and distributed to users.

Figure 7.9 illustrates a line-coding assignment. A specific general ledger account, such as "marketable securities," is located in the line-coding file. The line code is then used to structure the report. In Figure 7.9, the first field (one digit) indicates the type of schedule—a financial one in this illustration. The second field identifies the specific report—a balance sheet in our example. The third and fourth fields locate the item in the report structure. The third line item

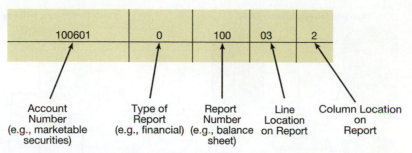

FIGURE 7.9

Example of a Line Code

on the balance sheet is marketable securities, and this account value is placed in Column 2. A balance sheet typically has four columns of data: (1) actual this period, (2) beginning-of-year balance, (3) budget, and (4) variance between (1) and (3). As an alternative to the procedure just described, line codes could be stored within the general ledger file itself. The line code for the marketable securities account could be stored as a separate field within the marketable securities record structure.

Common General Ledger Reports In addition to financial reports and schedules, common reports from a general ledger system would include the following five items:

- Journal voucher in sequence
- Journal voucher within general account
- General ledger by account
- General ledger summary
- Working trial balance

The general ledger by account is a summary of a particular month's activity in the general ledger; the general ledger summary is a year-to-date summary; and the working trial balance is a sort/summarization of the year-to-date general ledger in trial balance format. Typically, financial statements and trial balances contain details summarized from the general ledger rather than a listing of all the individual accounts. Detailed reports for lower levels of management may be prepared from the relevant subsidiary ledger files.

BATCH PROCESSING WITH RANDOM-ACCESS FILE UPDATING Although the updating in the preceding example is done with sequential file updating, random-access updating is also possible, even desirable, with batch processing. In many systems [especially database management system (DBMS)–oriented accounting systems as opposed to file-oriented accounting systems], indexes are maintained for both the subsidiary and general ledger files. Maintaining these indexes serves the primary need of allowing users to quickly access a particular account. For example, an interactive query program might use an index file to help the end user to quickly locate a customer's account. Given that an index is present, however, it can also be used for file updating.

Random-access file updating is simpler than sequential-access updating. With random-access updating, it is not necessary to sort the transaction file into the same order as the master file, and there is no need to generate a new master file. Instead, individual records are read one by one from the transaction file and used to update the related records in the master file *in place*. The following steps are followed:

- A record is read from the transaction file.
- The key value of the transaction record is used to randomly access (by using the index) the related record in the master file.
- The record in the master file is updated in memory and then rewritten back to the data file.

Of course, a backup of the master file should exist before the updating begins, and a transaction register must be generated as the update proceeds.

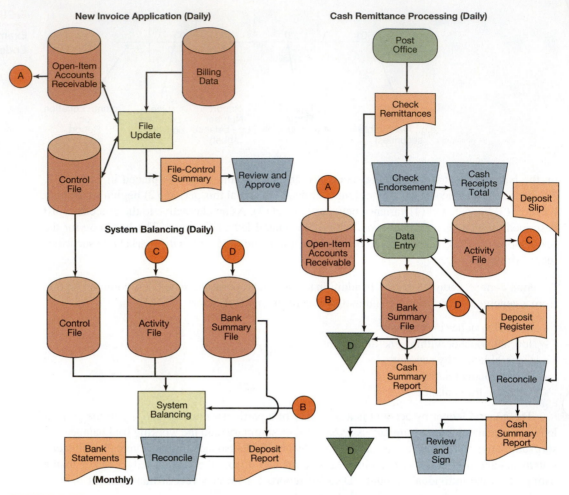

FIGURE 7.10

Cash Receipts Application

ILLUSTRATION OF BATCH PROCESSING WITH RANDOM-ACCESS FILE UPDATING   This section depicts an online cash receipts application. Batches of customer remittances on account are entered via data terminals and posted with random-access file updating directly to the accounts receivable file. Figure 7.10 presents a system flowchart of the online cash receipts application.

New Invoice Application   The application maintains an open-item accounts receivable file. New invoices are posted periodically to the open-item accounts receivable file. A control file is updated to reflect the addition of the new batch of invoices to the accounts receivable file. The control file is a summary of the accounts receivable file by type of account (such as installment or net 30 days). A file-control summary report is generated, reviewed, and approved by management prior to the processing of daily cash remittances. This procedure ensures that the accounts receivable file and the control file are in balance after the new billing data are added.

Cash Remittance Processing   Customer payments are remitted to a special post office box number. This approach separates the checks from other mail received by the organization, thus eliminating manual sorting of the checks and reducing the number of individuals handling them when they are received.

When the checks are brought from the post office, they are given to a control desk, where a clerk restrictively endorses them. This stamped endorsement prevents the deposit of the remittance to any unauthorized bank account. The clerk then totals all checks with the help of an adding machine and prepares a deposit slip. This ensures the accountability of checks received and their subsequent disposition. When the checks are deposited, the bank-validated deposit slip and adding machine tape are filed to be reconciled later to a cash summary report.

For ease of handling, controlling, and reconciling, the payments are batched into groups of 30 or fewer checks. When the checks are ready to be processed, a terminal operator requests access to the accounts receivable system through a network terminal or computer. The operator keys into the terminal a unique security code and employee number and identifies the type of transaction to be processed.

A security application, which controls access to all applications, verifies that the operator is an authorized user of the system and that his or her personal profile of clearances includes the transaction he or she has requested. Accounts receivable management may delegate or remove authority to process transactions, but the security application limits management to the delegation of transactions within the scope of its authority (as defined by a similar type of manager's security profile) and to transactions that will not compromise good separation of duties when processed in combination with existing transaction authorities.

The terminal operator enters from the remittance advice the invoice number and check amount as an individual line item for as many lines as the terminal is capable of displaying. The accounts receivable system then compares the individual line items against the records in the accounts receivable file. For those line items where an invoice number and check amount match a corresponding record in the file, the check amount is applied using random-access file updating. If there are line items that do not completely match an invoice number and check amount, or if the accounts receivable system notes that an entered invoice number was cleared previously, an error message is immediately transmitted back to the input terminal indicating the line item in error and the reason for rejection (e.g., no unpaid invoice number on file or the check amount entered is under or over the invoice amount of the file).

As payments are applied against the unpaid invoice records on the accounts receivable file, the invoice records are updated to reflect the payment date, activity code (e.g., check payment, invoice adjustment), and a sequential check number generated by the system. The paid customer invoice records are retained online for 1 year and are available for inquiries.

The terminal operator is restricted by application controls within the system to applying cash remittances to a single customer account. The terminal can access only one customer account for each check remittance. The entire check remittance amount must be applied to that customer account. The terminal operator cannot apply the remaining check amount of one customer's payment to another customer's account. If a terminal operator is unable to apply a customer remittance because the customer's account is not on the file (usually the result of a check misrouted by the customer), then accounts receivable management follows up with the customer. If it is appropriate to do so, the check amount is subtracted from the batch total, and the check is returned to the customer.

All check remittances within a batch must be applied except those that were sent erroneously to the company. If a check remittance for some reason is not entered into the system and not subtracted from the batch control totals, the discrepancy will be highlighted by the cash-balancing procedure employed at the end of the daily application of remittances.

System Balancing All cash remittance activity is logged on an activity file to provide an audit trail of all cash transactions processed. The activity file is used in the daily balancing of the accounts receivable system and for preparing, on request, listings that assist data processing personnel in tracing any lost activity that may have resulted from a system error.

After a batch of checks has been applied, the system updates a bank summary file for the dollar amount of the batch of checks. Also, a deposit register detailing and totaling the invoice numbers and invoice amounts in the batch is printed.

Daily, on completion of the application of cash remittances, the accounts receivable system prints a cash summary report from the bank summary file. This report lists the total number of checks and total dollars applied during that day. The deposit register is compared with the cash summary report to ensure that the cash applied to the system is in balance. In addition, the bank-validated deposit slip is reconciled with the cash summary report. This reconciliation ensures that the cash deposited was applied by the accounts receivable system. After the deposit register and the cash summary report are balanced, the cash summary report is given to management for review and signature and is filed for future reference. The deposit register is filed with the day's customer remittance advices for future reference or reconciliation.

Daily, the activity file is summarized and compared with the totals in the bank summary file. Also, the activity file totals by type of accounts receivable are subtracted from the control file totals, which reflect the previous day's accounts receivable file data by type of accounts. Finally, the current accounts receivable file is accumulated by type of account. These accounts receivable system processing steps are made daily before the accounts receivable file is updated with new billing data or invoice adjustment data.

Comparing the activity file and the bank summary file ensures that all cash that has been deposited has been applied and recorded on the activity file. The total derived from subtracting the activity file from the control file should equal the sum of the totals by type of the current accounts receivable file. This system balancing imposes a three-way check to ensure that each file within the accounts receivable system is in balance. As a result, any out-of-balance condition is readily identified, and appropriate corrective action is initiated prior to proceeding with the next day's accounts receivable processing procedures.

Bank statements are received each month and reconciled with reports prepared from the bank summary file. Also, at the end of each month, the total amount of cash activity on the activity file is summarized and forwarded to the general ledger application system. This information, which is used as a standard journal entry, is output in machine-readable form and as such is directly entered into the month's journal voucher file for posting to the general ledger.

Real-time Processing Systems

With **real-time processing**, transactions are processed immediately. **Online, real-time systems (OLRS)** process transactions immediately after they are input and can provide immediate output to users. Transactions are not accumulated into batches, but rather, on input, they are applied immediately to update the master file using random-access file updating. *Immediate processing* and *direct processing* are synonyms for real-time processing. Immediate processing is the primary characteristic of OLRS. Master files are always up to date because they are updated as soon as transaction data are input. Responses to user inquiries are immediate because information in randomly accessible files can be retrieved quickly.

Types of Real-Time Processing
Many types of real-time processing are possible in OLRS. In *inquiry/response systems*, users do not input data for processing; rather, they only request information. Inquiry/response systems are designed to provide users with quick responses to their requests for information. A common example is when a bank clerk wishes to find out if a customer has a sufficient balance to cover the check he or she wishes to cash.

In *data entry systems*, users interactively input data. The data are stored by the OLRS but are periodically processed in batches. For example, stores may capture sales transactions in real time during the day and then process them at night in batches.

In file processing systems, users also interactively input data as they do in data entry systems. However, *file processing systems* differ from data entry systems in that they go one step further and immediately process the data against the relevant master files. For example, a retail store might collect and process sales transactions immediately, charging the customer's account within moments of the sale. The transaction, however, would be incomplete until the customer is billed at the end of the month.

In *full processing systems*, or **transaction processing systems**, users also interactively input transactions. However, full processing systems differ from file processing systems in that they go even further and complete the entire transaction when it is input. For example, in the case of the retail store example in the preceding paragraph, the customer also would be billed immediately, thus completing the transaction. Sometimes in practice, however, the terms *file processing system* and *full processing system* are used interchangeably.

The Economics of Real-Time Processing   Most of the attributes of OLRS, such as immediate processing of transactions and quick response to inquiries, are relative advantages when compared with batch-processing systems. OLRS are desirable in many situations. Online reservation systems, inventory control in retail stores, and customer account files in a bank are some familiar examples. The relative disadvantages of OLRS stem from the increased costs and complexity of systems operation. In particular, OLRS are more sensitive to hardware and software errors and are much more susceptible to processing errors that arise from erroneous or fraudulent input. Whereas a hardware or software malfunction in a batch system might have little or no effect on users because they are not directly using the system, a hardware or software malfunction in an OLRS immediately affects users. An incorrect transaction in a batch-processing system might be corrected prior to processing or detected in a review of the results of processing. In an OLRS, however, an incorrect transaction is processed immediately and might contaminate several different files that are updated at the same time. In addition, the results of processing an incorrect transaction are available immediately to users of the OLRS.

Control of transaction processing is much more involved in OLRS than in batch-oriented systems. Application system files are integrated, and transactions are entered directly by users through remote network terminals or PCs for immediate processing. Application system interfaces are handled automatically; once a transaction has been input, it may be posted immediately to several different files. Printed output concerning transaction processing usually is not produced because transactions are processed individually in real time rather than as a batch. As a result, a transaction may generate no directly human-verifiable evidence of its processing. The audit trail must be considered carefully in the design of such systems. The high degree of concentration of functions characteristic of online systems necessitates the use of special control techniques to ensure that data are processed accurately and reliably.

Real-Time Sales Systems

Today's real-time sales systems use information technology to maximize system performance and extend the traditional supply chain. In such real-time sales systems, purchase orders for inventory items are made on a *demand-pull* basis rather than a fixed interval (e.g., monthly or weekly) push basis to restock inventory levels. New goods arrive when they are needed, that is to say, just in time (JIT). Orders to vendors are placed on the basis of actual sales to quickly replenish stocks of items that are selling. Current sales demand pulls (i.e., automatically generates) orders for inventory. Retailers order on the basis of current buying trends. This is critical in retailing, where fads (i.e., customer demand for certain products) can and do change rapidly. What sold last year, last month, or maybe even last week may no longer be what the customer wants.

Extended supply chain systems are central to the competitive strategy of mass retailers such as Sears, Walmart, and J.C. Penney. These systems are also central to the competitive strategy of major vendors to mass retailers, such as Levi, Haggar, and Wrangler (all brand-name suppliers of men's clothing for retail outlets). This is so because major vendors to mass retailers are themselves operating sales systems, and they face exactly the same problems. If Levi, for example, is out of stock of a popular item when it is ordered, the delay or inability to satisfy the order is lost revenue. In a competitive market, this revenue is lost forever. Sears will buy similar merchandise from a competitor who can fill the order when it is needed. The customer, in turn, will purchase a competitor's product.

CASE IN POINT

Microsoft Dynamics™ (www.microsoft.com/dynamics) is an accounting system that is widely used by small- and midsized businesses. This accounting system provides sophisticated supply chain management features and functions. For example, its business portal functionality provides employees, suppliers, and customers Web access to supply chain functions, documents, and information.

Levi, Haggar, and Wrangler in their turn must issue purchase orders to their vendors to stock the items that they in turn manufacture and/or resell to retailers. The suppliers face the same situation in their sales systems. If they are out of stock when items are ordered, the delay or inability to satisfy the order is lost revenue. And so, the situation repeats for each trading partner. If a major competitor participates in a real-time retail sales system, then one is likely to be in a position of competitive disadvantage unless one also participates.

A significant degree of cooperation among trading partners is required to implement real-time sales systems that extend supply chains. Companies, their suppliers, and buyers often enter into close, noncompetitive trade partnership agreements. In some cases, customers and suppliers coordinate their production schedules so that goods can be manufactured JIT. Prior to real-time systems, trading partners customarily have worked at arm's length from each other, sharing the minimum information required to make a deal. Reveal more information, and your trading partners might take advantage of you. The development of mutual trust among trading partners is essential to the operation of real-time retail sales systems. The retailer must trust the supplier to whom it provides transaction data. The retailer trusts that the supplier will use these data to ship the right product to the right store at the right time. The supplier must, in turn, trust that the retailer is providing accurate data and that the retailer will accept shipments when they arrive. All trading partners must trust that their data are being used solely for the intended purposes and are not being sold or supplied to direct competitors.

COMPONENTS OF EXTENDED SUPPLY CHAIN SYSTEMS   Three technologies make extended supply chain systems feasible: POS (point-of-sale) systems, bar coding for automatic identification, and the EDI (electronic data interchange) ordering system. Each of these technologies is discussed below.

CASE IN POINT

RFID tagging is an alternate to (or supplement to) Universal Product Code (UPC) labeling. RFID tags are small chips that transmit digital identifying information via radio waves. RFID tags can be used at various levels, to tag entire shipments, transportation vehicles, pallets, crates, cases, and individual items. Sam's Club, a division of Walmart, has implemented a phase-in policy, requiring all its suppliers to use RFID tags on pallets, cases, and individual consumer items. Some consumer groups have complained that RFID tags on individual items raise privacy issues, as shoppers carrying tagged store items can be tracked as they move about the store. Further, if the item tags are not deactivated, and have powerful enough internal radios, consumers might even be tracked after they leave the store.

POS (point-of-sale) Systems   **Point-of-Sale (POS) systems** input sales data into the computer system for processing immediately at the time and point of sale. Cash registers are the traditional point of sale in a retail firm. The enhancement of cash registers to allow them to function as a source data entry device is the essence of a POS system (Figure 7.11). The enhanced cash

FIGURE 7.11

Real-Time Point-of-Sale System

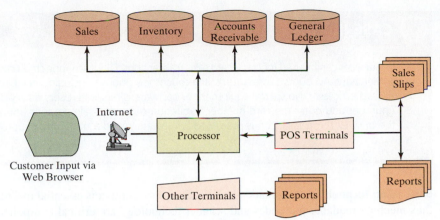

registers are called POS terminals. Data may be entered manually through a keying operation by the sales clerk or automatically using a variety of sensing devices. Card swipe devices for accepting credit and debit cards, bar-code readers for automatic identification of UPC codes, electronic signature pads, keypads to input personal identification numbers (PINs), and wireless sensing devices are common features of contemporary POS technology.

 CASE IN POINT

Quickbooks™ POS Pro is a POS software program that integrates with the Quickbooks™ accounting system. Quickbooks™ POS Pro not only handles debit and credit cards, it also rings up sales by scanning UPC bar codes.

POS terminals record both cash and charge sales. In a cash sale, the customer pays cash and receives the goods. In addition, a sales slip is printed by the terminal. Data relating to the transaction—such as the inventory codes for the items purchased, the number of items purchased, the cost of each item, the date, the total sales amount, and any sales taxes—are recorded via the terminal and made available to the store's computer network for immediate processing. Inventory records can be updated immediately in real time to reflect the goods purchased by the customer. The sales tax, cost of the items sold, and total sales price will be posted to daily sales records.

Sales on account require that a customer's charge account number and credit standing be verified prior to releasing the goods. The customer's charge account number is input to the POS terminal, allowing the computer system to access the customer's record, examine it, and determine the status of the account. If the charge sale is authorized, the system automatically completes the transaction. The sale on credit will be posted automatically against the appropriate records in the same manner as a cash sale. The status of the customer's charge account will also be updated to a new charge balance, and an update of the credit available to the customer and a record of the items purchased will be made.

The Internet has enhanced the real-time sales system by extending it to customers who are off-site. Using their Web browser, customers may input sales transaction data into the system to make purchases. The design of the browser interface guides the customer during input. The information that is collected can be identical to that which would have been collected had the customer physically been in the retailer's store and made the transaction at a POS terminal. Internet sales can be made 24/7, that is, 24 hours a day, 7 days a week. Cell phones and mobile handheld devices have further extended the capabilities of real-time systems. Customers can use such devices to make purchases almost anywhere at any time.

CASE IN POINT

Mobile devices can be used for credit card sales transactions. Dialpay phone credit card processing from Merchant Accounts Express turns any touchtone phone—including cell phones—into a credit card processor. No special equipment or software is required. Users simply dial a toll free 800 number and enter the card number, expiration date, and sale amount using the keypad on the phone. The transaction is processed immediately, and a transaction approval or denial is issued.

Bar-Coding Technology Automatic identification of sales input is essential to a real-time system; thus machine-readable bar codes and scanner technology are critical components of real-time retail sales systems. Maximum benefit is obtained when the standard, widely used UPC bar-code system is used. When UPC coding is used, all participants in the real-time system chain share and process the same basic data. Without code standardization, each agent in the chain uses his or her own codes, which must be cross-referenced to everyone else's codes. While cross-referencing codes is possible, it is both time-consuming and error-prone. Neither of these attributes facilitates real time.

Using UPC as a base, all agents use the same product code, eliminating cross-referencing problems. However, this is a relatively minor consideration when compared with the other benefits obtained from UPC standardization. The UPC product identification code can be scanned and used for automatic identification throughout the chain of real-time events. Cartons or other containers in transit or in inventory can be coded and scanned as well as individual items at the POS checkout counter. Cartons are UPC-coded when shipped by the vendor. Cartons are scanned when received by the retailer, and the data are input to the store information system. Cartons can be scanned when in inventory to easily identify the items contained within. UPC coding also lets the vendor code individual products for sale in the retailer's store. A retailer no longer has to code its own inventory; it arrives precoded with UPC.

The EDI Ordering System EDI (electronic data interchange) is the direct computer-to-computer exchange of business documents via a communications network. The EDI link between the retailer's computer system and the vendor's computer system allows near instantaneous placing and processing of the purchase order, facilitating quick shipment. The vendor could also invoice the retailer using EDI. In some cases, EFT payment might be made by the retailer to the vendor's account. All these events, including the picking of the order from the vendor's inventory, might take place without any human intervention.

Public EDI standards, in particular ANSI X.12 and ebXML, also provide maximum benefit when used in real-time systems. Without standardization, each agent in the chain must cross-reference everyone else's codes. Public EDI standards provide a common architecture for data interchange and thus eliminate costly and error-prone cross-referencing. Many early users of EDI started with their own proprietary codes for EDI and then switched to the ANSI X.12 or ebXML standard.

CASE IN POINT

TrueCommerce (www.truecommerce.com) provides EDI integration software that works with most accounting systems for small- and medium-sized businesses. Examples of accounting systems that it works with include Intuit Quickbooks, Microsoft Dynamics, SAP Business One, and Sage Pro ERP. The product works with Quickbooks™ by installing a transaction manager and plug-ins for each EDI partner.

In addition to purchase order and invoicing data, EDI also can be used to transmit retail sales data captured from the retail store to vendors. These data can then be analyzed by the vendor and input directly to purchasing and production applications to provide maximum inventory planning and control. This is feasible because both the retailer and vendor use the UPC. Actual retail sales data at the size and color level may be known instantaneously by the vendor due to the integration of UPC coding, POS technology, and EDI.

EDI also might be used by vendors to electronically transmit catalogs with current price information to retailers.

TRANSACTION PROCESSING IN EDI-BASED SALES SYSTEMS   Although the exact sequence of events will vary somewhat from system to system, the processing of an order typically will involve seven steps. These include sending the customer an electronic catalog, forecasting the customer's sales order, receiving and translating the incoming order, sending an acknowledgment, sending the order to inventory or production (as applicable), generating and transmitting an advance shipping notice, and shipping the goods (see Figure 7.12). Each of these events is discussed in turn.

Sending the Customer an Electronic Catalog   The customer is periodically sent (via EDI) an electronic catalog of the company's products. A special version of this catalog might be made for each customer to reflect any possible contract prices agreed on through competitive bidding.

Sending the catalog electronically has three major advantages over sending it in paper form. First, the information in the electronic catalog can be used by the customer to generate an EDI purchase order. This minimizes errors that might arise from the manual keying of data that

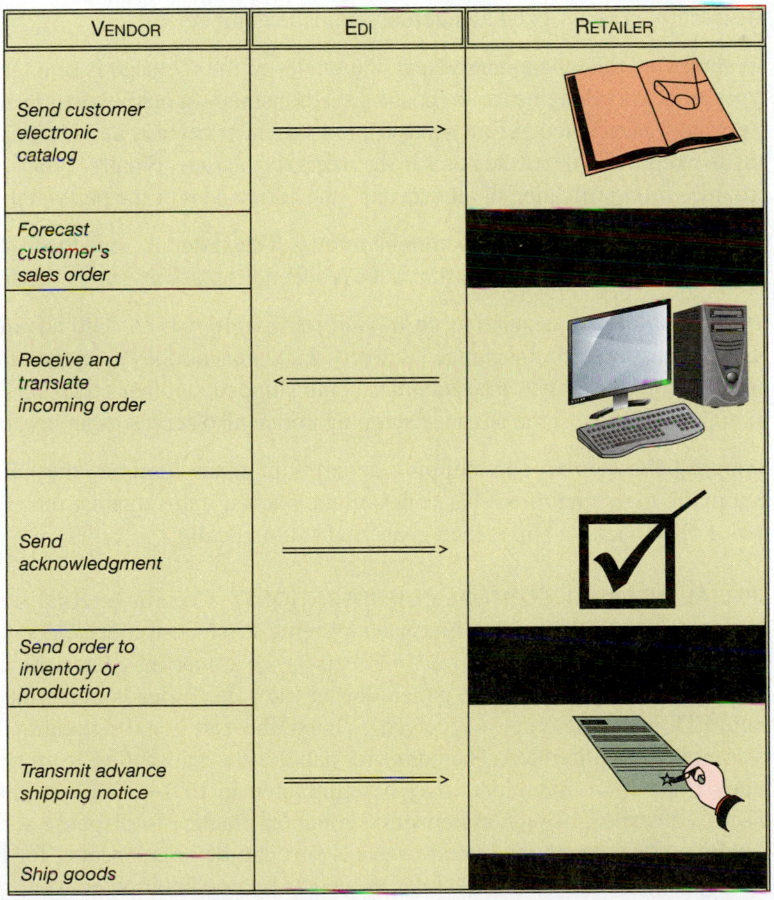

FIGURE 7.12

Transaction Processing in Real-Time Sales Systems

VENDOR	EDI	RETAILER
Send customer electronic catalog	===>	
Forecast customer's sales order		
Receive and translate incoming order	<===	
Send acknowledgment	===>	
Send order to inventory or production		
Transmit advance shipping notice	===>	
Ship goods		

would otherwise be required. Second, the catalog allows the company to almost instantly bring the customer up to date with new prices and other information order lead times. Third, the electronic catalog can contain UPC product codes that can be used subsequently by both companies for automatic identification and tracking.

Forecasting the Customer's Sales Order   In many cases, the company will analyze the customer's sales trends and predict future needs. Even in a JIT system, predicting demand can facilitate production planning.

Receiving and Translating the Incoming Order   The initial processing of the incoming EDI order involves several phases. These include the physical receipt of the order, validation and authentication, and decryption and translation.

There are several ways that an order may arrive, depending on the system. It can arrive as an e-mail message either in the company's internal mail system or in a third-party mail/EDI system. Alternatively, the company might have its own dedicated EDI communications server.

Regardless of how the incoming message physically arrives, it must be validated, decrypted, and authenticated. Even if the message itself is encrypted, its electronic envelope generally will not be. As an initial check, the return address in this envelope will be checked to see if the message originated from a recognized customer. Next, the message will be decrypted (if necessary) and authenticated. Authentication is accomplished through the use of authentication codes that ensure the message has not been altered in transit.

Once decrypted, the message is checked for internal consistency and completeness. EDI documents typically contain dual control numbers, one control number at the beginning of the message and another at the end. The correctness of internal passwords is also verified. Then the message is translated into a format recognized by the company's accounting system, and finally, the document is assigned an internal sequence number.

Sending an Acknowledgment   Next, the sender of the message is sent an acknowledgment. Three types of acknowledgments are possible. A transmission acknowledgment simply indicates that a message was received. A functional acknowledgment not only acknowledges receipt of the message but also reports in detail the items in the received message. Finally, a transactional acknowledgment provides full verification of all data (e.g., the correctness of the part numbers) in the message.

Sending the Order to Production/Inventory   The order is sent to production or inventory for processing. Transaction processing in the production and/or inventory department is discussed below.

Generating and Transmitting an Advance Shipping Notice   The advance shipping notice will alert the customer to the planned delivery date. This notice typically will include the customer's purchase order number, the quantities being shipped, and bar codes for automatic identification. In many companies, the advance shipping notice also serves as an invoice.

Shipping the Goods   The shipping department scans items as they are packed. This permits automatic matching of the bar codes on the packed items against those in the advance shipping notice. The packing slip is then generated automatically.

SPECIAL INTERNAL CONTROL CONSIDERATIONS   Certain internal control problems pertain particularly to EDI-type real-time sales systems. First, customer orders may be processed without human intervention or approval. In effect, the customer may have the ability to generate his or her own sales order because generation of the sales order is performed automatically when a valid EDI purchase order is received. Second, the traditional separation of duties in transactions is completely obliterated. The computer handles the transaction from beginning to end. Finally, many traditional documents may be eliminated in EDI-based systems. For example, as was discussed earlier, in such systems it is common practice to dispense with invoices. The various special control problems in real-time systems can be compensated for by careful program data editing checks and transaction logs, as well as by good computer security.

The Output System

The output system can be manual, electronic, or something in between. Most manual batch-oriented systems with sequential file processing produce very large volumes of output. Since such systems do not provide random-access user queries, they typically generate paper printouts or electronic log files that are used by employees as reference documents. For example, a printout of the accounts receivable file might be used to look up individual customer balances.

On the other hand, online, real-time electronic systems tend to produce very little reference-type output. Such systems are almost imperative in very large companies as it would be impractical to continually output what may be hundreds of thousands or even millions of records.

Output controls are designed to check that processing results in valid output and that outputs are distributed properly. Reports should be reviewed critically by supervisory personnel in user departments for general reasonableness and quality in relation to previous reports. Control totals should be balanced to control totals generated independently of the data processing operation, as discussed earlier. Further, program data editing checks should be performed on all outputs. This can prevent problems such as those that once occurred in the Social Security system when Social Security numbers were printed accidentally in the amount fields on Social Security benefits checks.

A separate *EDP control group* is often established to monitor EDP operations. The EDP control group is frequently part of the internal audit function. Procedures should be established to provide assurance that errors are reported to the EDP control group. These procedures must ensure that such errors are entered into controls, corrected, and reentered properly into the system for further processing. Corrections should be subject to the same testing as original data. The distribution of output should be controlled so as to minimize the danger of unauthorized access to confidential data. Output distribution is controlled through documentation and supervision. Typically, an **output distribution register** is maintained to control the disposition of reports. This register and its attendant documentation should be reviewed periodically in the internal audit function.

Summary

Data processing systems vary in the degree to which they are computerized. Some systems, although computerized, rely heavily on paper documents. Other systems can process transactions from beginning to end without a shred of paper. A number of application controls might be used in a data processing system, including batch controls, programmed data editing, and transaction logs.

Batch processing of transactions is a common approach to data processing. Representative examples of batch processing include processing weekly time reports to produce paychecks, processing groups of checks to update accounts payable files, and processing invoices to update an accounts receivable file. In a manual batch-processing accounting system, batches of transactions from each application system are processed against the relevant application files in separate computer runs. The computer runs post the transactions to subsidiary ledgers and also generate the information necessary to prepare journal entries (journal vouchers) for posting to the general ledger. The journal vouchers are accumulated and processed as a batch against the general ledger in a separate computer run. Computer processing of accounting data typically is a two-step procedure. The first step produces preliminary reports, which are forwarded to the accounting department for review and audit relative to the journal

voucher listings and general ledger listing. After the audit and submission of corrections or additional data, the second step is a run that produces the final listings and financial schedules.

Many systems maintain indexes for both subsidiary and general ledger files. These indexes allow users to quickly access particular accounts. When an index is present, it can also be used for random-access file updating. With random-access updating it is not necessary to sort the transaction file into the same order as the master file, and there is no need to generate a new master file. Individual records are read one by one from the transaction file and used to update the related records in the master file in place. Batch processing with random-access file updating was illustrated in the context of an online cash receipts application.

Online, real-time processing systems are transaction-oriented rather than file-oriented. Individual transactions may be input for processing by users through network terminals rather than being batched and submitted to a processing center as a group of source documents. Extensive control and audit trails may be implemented in such systems, but these features must be included within the design of the system during development. Standard application controls over system inputs and processing in an online, real-time processing system were discussed in the context of a purchasing application.

Glossary

batch processing   accumulating source documents into groups for processing on a periodic basis.

check digit   an extra digit added to a code number that is verified by applying mathematical calculations to the individual digits in the code number.

continuous operations auditing   the use of programmed edit tests to discriminate between acceptable and nonacceptable data values so that some items are either held in suspense of processing until audited or collected for audit after processing.

input document control form   documents batch control totals for batches of input data transmitted between user departments and the data processing department.

key verification   a control procedure to ensure the accuracy of key-transcribed input data.

limit test   an edit program checks the value of a numeric data field as being within a range of certain predefined limits.

line coding   assigning codes to items in the general ledger that indicate the item's use and placement in financial statements.

master file   contains data that are permanent or of continuing interest.

online, real-time systems (OLRS)   computer systems that process input data immediately after they are input and can provide immediate output to users.

output controls   designed to check that processing results in valid output and that outputs are distributed properly to users.

output distribution register   a log maintained to control the disposition of output and reports.

point-of-sale (POS) system   technology that enhances the traditional cash register to allow it to function as a source data entry device for sales transactions.

program data editing   a software technique used to screen data for errors prior to computer processing.

real-time processing   immediate or fast-response processing.

reference file   contains data that are necessary to support data processing.

son–father–grandfather retention   retaining the old master (i.e., father) and the transaction file for backup over the new master file (i.e., son).

source documents   the physical evidence of inputs into the transaction processing system.

table file   synonym for *reference file*.

table lookup   an edit program compares the value of a field with the acceptable values contained in a table file.

tagging   audit-oriented information that is included with original transaction data when they are recorded.

transaction file   a collection of transaction input data.

transaction processing system   a system that collects and processes transactions and provides immediate output concerning processing.

valid code check   a table-lookup procedure in which the table file consists of valid data codes.

Webliography

www.ebxml.org
The OASIS (Organization for the Advancement of Structured Information Standards, www.oasis-open.org)-hosted home page for XML-based EDI. OASIS is one of the most respected organizations dedicated to open standards for IT and communications. ebXML is becoming the universally accepted standard for EDI communications.

www.journalofaccountancy.com
The home page of the *Journal of Accountancy*, a publication of the American Institute of Public Accountants (AICPA) devoted to practical issues facing the accounting profession. Enter "ABCs of Batch Processing" in the search box to find a helpful article on batch processing published by Alan Vercio and Bill Shoemaker in the August 2007 issue.

www.x12.org
The home page of the ASC X12 (also called ANSI ASC X12), a standards committee accredited by the American National Standards Institute (ANSI). The committee has sponsored hundreds of EDI standards and many XML schemas relating to specific industries such as health care, insurance, transportation, and finance.

www.rfidjournal.com
The home page of the RFID Journal. Try entering "accounting" in the search box. This site has many interesting articles, including one entitled, "Can RFID Improve Sarbanes-Oxley Compliance."

Chapter Quiz

Answers to the chapter quiz appear on page 268.

1. Which of the following is (are) a typical example of batch processing?
   a. processing weekly time reports to produce paychecks
   b. processing groups of checks to update accounts payable files
   c. both a and b
   d. neither a nor b

2. Accumulating source documents into groups prior to processing is a characteristic of (_____).
   a. batch processing
   b. online, real-time processing
   c. both a and b
   d. neither a nor b

3. Which of the following errors probably would be corrected by key verification of data input?
   a. A salesperson manually enters an incorrect product number on a sales invoice, which is subsequently given to a data entry operator in the information systems department for key transcription to machine-readable format.
   b. A data entry operator in the information systems department mistypes a product number on a sales invoice while keying the document to machine-readable format.
   c. both a and b
   d. neither a nor b

4. Which of the following controls would prevent the following situation? A worker's paycheck was processed incorrectly because he had transposed letters in his department identification code, having entered *ABC*, an invalid code, instead of *CAB*.
   a. control total
   b. limit test
   c. internal label check
   d. table-lookup procedure

5. The son–father–grandfather concept of backing up master files can be used when master files are stored on (_____).
   a. magnetic tape
   b. magnetic disk
   c. both a and b
   d. neither a nor b

6. A review of an EDP system reveals the following items. Which of these is a potential internal control weakness?
   a. Backup master files are stored in a remote location.
   b. Users must verbally approve all changes to be made to application programs.

   c. Computer operators have restricted access to system programs and data files.
   d. Computer operators are required to take vacations.

7. For control purposes, data clerks total up the employee Social Security numbers in each batch of payroll transactions. Which of the following terms best describes the resulting total?
   a. hash total
   b. financial total
   c. parity total
   d. record count

8. In an online computer system, which of the following may be used to ensure that users have proper authorization to perform a task?
   a. check digits
   b. passwords
   c. control totals
   d. limit tests

9. For control purposes, data clerks total up the employee gross pay amounts in each batch of payroll transactions. Which of the following terms best describes the resulting total?
   a. hash total
   b. financial total
   c. parity total
   d. record count

10. A customer inadvertently orders part number 1234–8 instead of 1243–8. Which of the following controls would detect this error during processing?
    a. hash total
    b. financial total
    c. limit check
    d. check digit

Review Problem

The computer system most likely to be used by a large savings bank for customers' accounts would be (_____).

a. an online, real-time system
b. a batch-processing system
c. a generalized utility system
d. direct-access database system

Solution to Review Problem

Answer a.

a. An online, real-time system is characterized by data that are assembled from more than one location and records that are updated immediately. A large savings bank likely would have several different branches from which transactions on customer accounts are to be entered, and it is desirable that records be processed immediately in order that customer account data reflect their current financial positions.

b. A batch-processing system is characterized by data that are assembled at a centralized location and processed against records periodically as batches of sufficient size are accumulated. A large savings bank could use a batch-processing system to post transactions on customer accounts, but it is desirable that such records be processed immediately rather than periodically as a batch in order that customer account data reflect their current financial positions.

c. A *generalized utility system* is not a defined term in data processing.

d. A *direct-access database system* sounds good, but this is not a defined term in data processing, as is an online, real-time system.

Review Questions

1. Identify and describe several controls over data transfer between user departments and data processing. Why are such controls necessary?
2. Describe key verification of input data. What types of errors does key verification control?
3. Describe program data editing. Is program data editing necessary if input data have been key-verified? Explain.
4. Identify and describe several program data editing techniques.
5. Describe how the loss of manual internal controls can be compensated for in electronic input systems.
6. Give an example of automatic identification in an electronic input system that requires human intervention.
7. Give an example of an electronic input system that requires no human intervention.
8. Describe batch processing of transactions in a manual processing system. When is batch processing most economical?
9. Identify several points where reconciliation of control totals should occur in the batch processing of transactions against a master file.
10. Explain son–father–grandfather file retention.
11. What is a journal voucher? Describe how computer batch processing of journal vouchers may be used to update the general ledger.
12. Identify several general ledger reports that might be prepared after updating the general ledger with computer batch processing.
13. Explain how random-access file updating differs from sequential-access updating.
14. Characterize several different types of real-time processing in OLRS.
15. Identify and describe several output controls. Why are such controls necessary?

Discussion Questions and Problems

16. What type of EDP system is characterized by data that are assembled from more than one location and records that are updated immediately?
    a. personal computer system
    b. minicomputer system
    c. batch-processing system
    d. online, real-time system

    (CPA Adapted)

17. An EDP technique that collects data into groups to permit convenient and efficient processing is known as
    a. document-count processing.
    b. multiprogramming.
    c. batch processing.
    d. generalized-audit processing.

    (CPA)

18. Which of the following is not a characteristic of a batch-processed computer system?
    a. the collection of like transactions that are sorted and processed sequentially against a master file
    b. key transcription of transactions, followed by machine processing
    c. the production of numerous printouts
    d. the posting of a transaction, as it occurs, to several files without intermediate printouts

    (CPA)

19. What is the computer process called when data processing is performed concurrently with a particular activity, and the results are available soon enough to influence the particular course of action being taken or the decision being made?
    a. real-time processing
    b. batch processing
    c. random-access processing
    d. integrated data processing

    (CPA)

20. The real-time feature normally would be least useful when applied to accounting for a firm's.
    a. bank account balances.
    b. property and depreciation.
    c. customer accounts receivable.
    d. merchandise inventory.

    (CPA)

21. An EDP input control is designed to ensure that
    a. machine processing is accurate.
    b. only authorized personnel have access to the computer area.
    c. data received for processing are properly authorized and converted to machine-readable form.
    d. electronic data processing has been performed as intended for the particular application.

    (CPA)

22. When erroneous data are detected by computer program controls, such data may be excluded from processing and printed on an error report. This error report should be reviewed and followed up by the
    a. computer operator.
    b. systems analyst.
    c. EDP control group.
    d. computer programmer.

    (CPA)

23. Which of the following would lessen internal control in an EDP system?
    a. The computer librarian maintains custody of computer program instructions and detailed program listings.
    b. Computer operators have access to operator instructions and detailed program listings.
    c. The control group maintains sole custody of all computer output.
    d. Computer programmers write and debug programs that perform routines designed by the systems analyst.

    (CPA)

24. An internal administrative control sometimes used in connection with procedures to detect unauthorized or unexplained computer usage is
    a. maintenance of a computer tape library.
    b. use of file controls.
    c. maintenance of a computer console log.
    d. control over program tapes.

    (CPA)

25. A procedural control used in the management of a computer center to minimize the possibility of data or program file destruction through operator error includes
    a. control figures.
    b. crossfooting tests.
    c. limit checks.
    d. external labels.

    (CPA)

26. If a control total were to be computed on each of the following data items, which would best be identified as a hash total for a payroll EDP application?
    a. net pay
    b. department numbers
    c. hours worked
    d. total debits and total credits

    (CPA)

27. In designing a payroll system, it is known that no individual's paycheck can amount to more than $300 for a single week. As a result, the payroll program has been written to bypass writing a check and will print out an error message if any payroll calculation results in more than $300. This type of control is called
    a. a limit or reasonableness test.
    b. error review.
    c. a data validity test.
    d. a logic sequence test.

    (CPA)

28. Where disk files are used, the grandfather–father–son updating backup concept is relatively difficult to implement because the
    a. location of information points on disks is an extremely time-consuming task.
    b. magnetic fields and other environmental factors cause off-site storage to be impractical.
    c. information must be dumped in the form of hard copy if it is to be reviewed before being used in updating.
    d. process of updating old records is destructive.

    (CPA)

29. A customer inadvertently ordered part number 12368 rather than part number 12638. In processing this order, the error would be detected by the vendor with which of the following controls?
    a. batch total
    b. key verifying
    c. self-checking digit
    d. an internal consistency check

    (CPA)

30. In the weekly computer run to prepare payroll checks, a check was printed for an employee who had been terminated the previous week. Which of the following controls, if used properly, would have been most effective in preventing the error or ensuring its prompt detection?
    a. a control total for hours worked, prepared from time cards collected by the timekeeping department
    b. requiring the treasurer's office to account for the numbers of the prenumbered checks issued to the EDP department for the processing of the payroll
    c. use of a check digit for employee numbers
    d. use of a header label for the payroll input sheet

    (CPA)

31. Accounting functions that are normally considered incompatible in a manual system often are combined in an EDP system by using an EDP program or a series of programs. This necessitates an accounting control that prevents unapproved
    a. access to the magnetic tape library.
    b. revisions to existing computer programs.
    c. use of computer program tapes.
    d. testing of modified computer programs.

    (CPA)

32. Totals of amounts in computer-record data fields that are not usually added for other purposes but are used only for data processing control purposes are called
    a. record totals.
    b. hash totals.
    c. processing data totals.
    d. field totals.

    (CPA)

33. The use of a header label in conjunction with magnetic tape is most likely to prevent errors by the
    a. computer operator.
    b. data entry clerk.
    c. computer programmer.
    d. maintenance technician.

    (CPA)

34. Where computers are used, the effectiveness of internal accounting control depends in part on whether the organizational structure includes any incompatible combinations. Such a combination would exist when there is no separation of the duties between the
   a. documentation librarian and the manager of programming.
   b. programmer and the console operator.
   c. systems analyst and the programmer.
   d. processing control clerk and the data entry supervisor.
   (CPA)

35. The basic form of backup used in magnetic tape operations is called
   a. odd parity check.
   b. dual-head processing.
   c. file protection rings.
   d. the son–father–grandfather concept.
   (CPA)

36. When an online, real-time (OLRT) EDP system is in use, internal control can be strengthened by
   a. providing for the separation of duties between data entry and error-listing operations.
   b. attaching plastic file protection rings to reels of magnetic tape before new data can be entered on the file.
   c. preparing batch totals to provide assurance that file updates are made for the entire input.
   d. making a validity check of an identification number before a user can obtain access to the computer files.
   (CPA)

37. Which of the following most likely constitutes a weakness in the internal accounting control of an EDP system?
   a. The control clerk establishes control over data received by the EDP department and reconciles control totals after processing.
   b. The application programmer identifies programs required by the systems design and flowcharts the logic of these programs.
   c. The systems analyst reviews output and controls the distribution of output from the EDP department.
   d. The accounts payable clerk prepares data for computer processing and enters the data into the computer.
   (CPA)

38. An effective control designed to provide reasonable assurance that hourly payroll information has been entered accurately into the computer system is to
   a. establish the use of batch control totals for total hours to be processed.
   b. review the contents of the computer master file.
   c. limit access to the online terminals.
   d. circulate to user departments periodic reports containing the contents of the master file.
   (IIA)

39. Which of the following activities most likely would be performed in the EDP department?
   a. initiation of changes to master records
   b. conversion of information to machine-readable form

   c. correction of transactional errors
   d. initiation of changes to existing applications
   (CPA)

40. Carmela Department Stores has a fully integrated EDP accounting system and is planning to issue credit cards to creditworthy customers. To strengthen internal control by making it difficult for one to create a valid customer account number, the company's independent auditor has suggested the inclusion of a check digit that should be placed
   a. at the beginning of a valid account number only.
   b. in the middle of a valid account number only.
   c. at the end of a valid account number only.
   d. consistently in any position.
   (CPA)

41. One of the major problems in an EDP system is that incompatible functions may be performed by the same individual. One compensating control for this is use of
   a. a tape library.
   b. a self-checking digit system.
   c. computer-generated hash totals.
   d. a computer log.
   (CPA)

42. The primary documentation on which a company should rely for an explanation of how a particular program operates is the
   a. run manual.
   b. periodic memory dump.
   c. maintenance of three generations of master files.
   d. echo check printout.
   (CPA)

43. The use of external labels in conjunction with magnetic tape storage is most likely to prevent errors that might be made by which of the following?
   a. a computer programmer
   b. a systems analyst
   c. a data entry clerk
   d. a computer operator
   (CPA)

44. An online sales order processing system most likely would have an advantage over a batch sales order processing system by
   a. detecting errors in the data entry process more easily by the use of edit programs.
   b. enabling shipment of customer orders to be initiated as soon as the orders are received.
   c. recording more secure backup copies of the database on magnetic tape files.
   d. maintaining more accurate records of customer accounts and finished goods inventories.
   (CPA)

45. Which of the following is a general control that most likely would assist an entity whose systems analyst left in the middle of a major project?
   a. grandfather–father–son record retention
   b. input and output validation routines

c. systems documentation

d. check-digit verification

(CPA)

46. This question requires using the check digit formula presented in this chapter (page 231).

    a. Calculate check digits for the following hypothetical account numbers: 4388, 5100, and 9106.

    b. Verify the following codes (which include a check digit): 10307, 50008, and 22222.

47. Consider the following numerical input data used in an accounts receivable application:

Account Number, 4 digits	Invoice Number, 4 digits	Gross Amount, 7 digits	Discount, 5 digits	Net Amount, 7 digits
4012	1003	265000	15000	250000
4810	1007	321550	27130	294420
7188	1008	108010	11500	96510

Required

    a. For the preceding data, calculate an example of each of the following: hash total, financial total, record count.

    b. You are to design an edit program that will be used to screen the preceding data before they are processed against a sequentially organized accounts receivable master file. Assuming that the input data the edit program receives will be sorted in ascending order by account number, what detailed editing procedures would you include in the design of the edit program?

48. The Foxx Company is designing a standard postings file to be used in the editing of transactions to be posted to the general ledger. The file (relation) as designed has the following format:

```
<IPGM>STANDARD-ENTRIES (CODE#, DESCRIPTION,
DR-or-CR,
ACCOUNT#, ACCOUNT-NAME)</IPGM>
```

Is this relation a flat file? If not, how would you normalize this relation?

49. Indicate the objective of the following questions, which are abstracted from an EDP internal control questionnaire. What error or weakness might exist if the answer to a specific question is "No"?

    a. Do management and user departments review and approve all new systems design work?

    b. Have backup procedures been documented, and are the arrangements up to date?

    c. Is there an organizational chart of the EDP function?

    d. Are computer operators required to take vacations?

    e. Does more than one programmer or a supervisor have a working knowledge of each specific program?

    f. Are internal file labels tested by computer programs to validate file setup?

    g. Are check digits used where appropriate?

    h. Are changes to master files, such as pay rates or price changes, properly authorized, and is their posting to the file verified by the originating department?

    i. Are output reports reviewed critically by supervisory personnel in user departments for general reasonableness and quality in relation to prior periods?

50. What control or controls would you recommend in a computer processing system to prevent the following situations?

    a. Working through the main control console, the night-shift computer operator made a change in a payroll program to alter the rate of pay in his favor.

    b. A customer payment recorded on a remittance advice as $55.05 was entered into the computer from a data terminal as $550.50.

    c. A new program to process accounts receivable was unreliable and would not handle common exceptions. The programmer who wrote the program recently quit the organization because he was repeatedly asked to document this program (which he never did do).

    d. The payroll master file was loaded incorrectly on a disk drive that was supposed to hold the accounts receivable master file. The accounts receivable program was nevertheless run, destroying the payroll master file.

    e. A weekly payroll check issued to an hourly employee was based on 96 hours rather than 46.

    f. The master inventory file, contained on a removable magnetic disk, was destroyed by a small fire next to the area where it was stored. The company had to take a special complete inventory to reestablish the file.

    g. The magnetic tape containing accounts receivable transactions could not be located. A data processing supervisor said that it could have been put among the scratch tapes available for use in processing.

    h. In preparing payroll checks, the computer omitted 12 of a total of 1,570 checks that should have been processed. The error was not detected until the supervisors distributed the checks.

    i. A sales transaction document was coded with an invalid customer account code (seven digits rather than eight). The error was not detected until the updating run, when it was found that there was no such account to which the transaction could be posted.

    j. During data entry of customer payments, the digit 0 in a payment of $123.40 was mistakenly entered as the letter O. As a result, the transaction was not processed correctly.

    k. A systems analyst entered a special routine one evening after work. The next day she obtained the program that calculates interest payments on customer accounts and processed it to add her routine to the program's logic. Her routine adds the fraction of a cent of each customer's interest, which otherwise would be rounded off, to her own account at the bank.

    l. A salesman entering a customer order from a portable data entry terminal entered an incorrect but valid product number. As a result, the customer received a delivery of 100,000 kilograms of industrial salt rather than industrial sugar.

    m. A customer called to inquire as to why he received a bill for 5 cents amount due when postage cost much more than that amount.

51. The Western Savings and Loan Association, a client of yours, recently installed a new online, real-time computer system. Each teller in the association's main office and seven branch offices has an online input/output terminal. Customers' mortgage payments and savings account deposits and withdrawals are recorded in the accounts by the computer from data input by the teller at the time of the transaction. The teller keys the proper account by account number and enters the information in the terminal keyboard to record the transaction. The accounting department at the main office also has input/output devices. The computer is housed at the main office.

In addition to servicing its own mortgage loans, the association acts as a mortgage-servicing agency for three life insurance companies. In this latter activity, the association maintains mortgage records and serves as the collection and escrow agent for the mortgagees (the insurance companies), who pay a fee to the association for these services.

Required

You would expect the association to have certain internal controls in effect because an online, real-time computer system is employed. List the internal controls that should be in effect solely because this system is employed, classifying them as

a. those controls pertaining to input of information.

b. all other types of computer controls.

(CPA)

52. The inventory of Molly Company, a wholesaler of softgoods, is composed of approximately 3,500 different items. The company employs a computerized batch-processing system to maintain its perpetual inventory records. The system is run each weekend so that the inventory reports are available on Monday morning for management use. The system has been functioning satisfactorily for the past 15 months, providing the company with accurate records and timely reports.

The preparation of purchase orders has been automatic as a part of the inventory system to ensure that the company will maintain enough inventory to meet customer demand. When an item of inventory falls below a predetermined level, a record of the inventory item is written. This record is used in conjunction with the vendor file to prepare the purchase orders.

Exception reports are prepared during updating of the inventory and preparation of the purchase orders. These reports identify any errors or exceptions identified during the processing. In addition, the system provides for management approval of all purchase orders exceeding a specified amount. Any exceptions or items requiring management approval are handled by supplemental runs on Monday morning and combined with the weekend results.

Figure 7.13 presents a system flowchart of the inventory and purchase order procedure.

Required

a. The illustrated system flowchart of Molly's inventory and purchase order system was prepared before the system was fully operational. Several steps that are important to

successful operation of the system were omitted inadvertently from the chart. Now that the system is operating effectively, management wants the system documentation complete and would like the flowchart corrected. Describe steps that have been omitted, and indicate where the omissions have occurred. The flowchart does not need to be drawn.

b. In order for Molly Company's inventory purchase order system to function properly, control procedures would be included in the system. Describe the type of control procedures Molly Company would use in its system to ensure proper functioning, and indicate where these procedures would be placed in the system.

(CMA)

53. Music Now is a large wholesaler of sheet music, music books, musical instruments, and other music-related supplies. The company acquired a midrange computer system last year, and an inventory control system has already been implemented. Now the systems department is developing a new accounts receivable system.

Figure 7.14 is a diagram of the proposed accounts receivable system as designed by the systems department. The objectives of the new system are to produce current and timely information that can be used to control bad debts, to provide information to the sales department regarding customers whose accounts are delinquent, to produce monthly statements for customers, and to produce notices to customers regarding a change in the status of their charge privileges.

Input data for the system are taken from four source documents—approved credit applications, sales invoices, cash payment remittances, and credit memoranda. The accounts receivable file is maintained on magnetic disk by customer account number. The record for each customer contains identification information, last month's balance, current month's transactions (detailed), and current balance. Some of the output items generated from the system are identified and described briefly below.

1. Accounts receivable register (weekly)—a listing of all customers and account balances included on the accounts receivable file.

2. Aging schedule (monthly)—a schedule of all customers with outstanding balances, detailing the amount owed by age classifications—0–30 days, 30–60 days, 60–90 days, over 90 days old.

3. Delinquency and write-off registers (monthly)—(a) a listing of those accounts that are delinquent and (b) a listing of customers' accounts that have been closed and written off; related notices are prepared and sent to these customers.

Required

The systems department must develop the system controls for the new accounts receivable system. Identify and explain the system controls that should be instituted with the new system. When appropriate, describe the location in the flowchart where the control should be introduced.

(CMA)

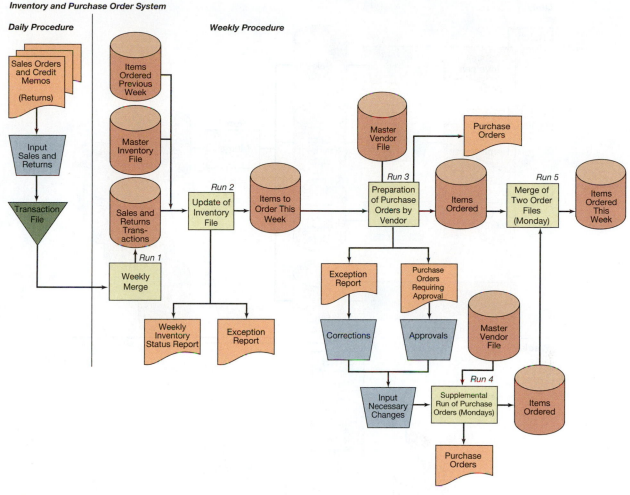

FIGURE 7.13

Flowchart for Problem 52

54. Consider the online cash receipts application discussed in this chapter. Modify the cash application procedure to allow the operator to process customer remittances with multiple payments or no payments (invoice numbers) referenced on them. Your comments should specify in detail the options that your procedure gives to the terminal operator.

55. Until recently, Amalgamated Gas employed a batch-processing system for recording the receipt of customer payments. The following narrative and Figure 7.15 describe the procedures involved in this system.

> The customer's payment and the remittance advice (an optically scanned turnaround document) are received in the treasurer's office. An accounts receivable clerk in the treasurer's office enters the cash receipt onto the remittance advice and forwards the document to the EDP department. The cash receipt is added to a control tape listing and then filed for deposit later in the day. When the deposit slips are received from EDP later in the day (approximately 2:30 P.M.

each day), the cash receipts are removed from the file and deposited with the original deposit slip. The second copy of the deposit slip and the control tape are compared for accuracy before the deposit is made and then filed together.

In the EDP department, the remittance advices received from the treasurer's office are held until 2:00 P.M. daily. At that time, the customer payments are processed to update the records on magnetic tape and to prepare a deposit slip in triplicate. During the update process, data are read, nondestructively, from the master accounts receivable tape, processed, and then recorded on a new master tape. The original and second copy of the deposit slip are forwarded to the treasurer's office. The old master tape (former accounts receivable file), the remittance advices (in customer-number order), and the third copy of the deposit slip are stored and filed in a secure place. The updated accounts receivable master tape is maintained in the system for processing the next day.

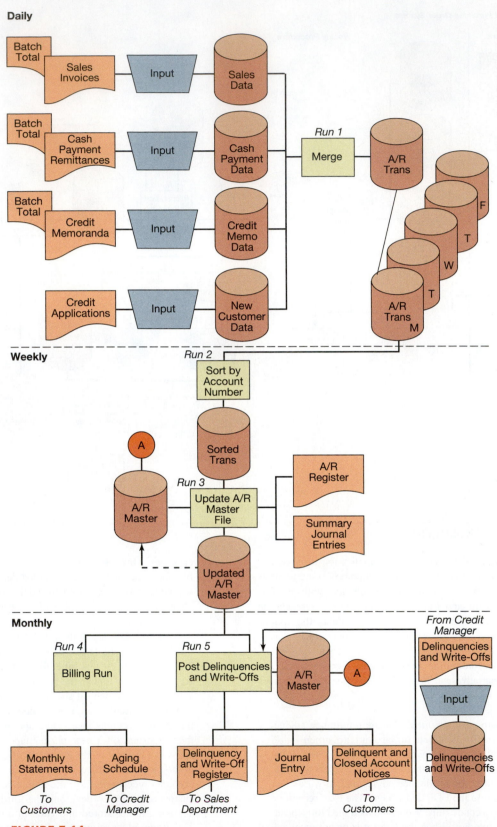

FIGURE 7.14

Flowchart for Problem 53

FIGURE 7.15

Flowchart for Problem 55

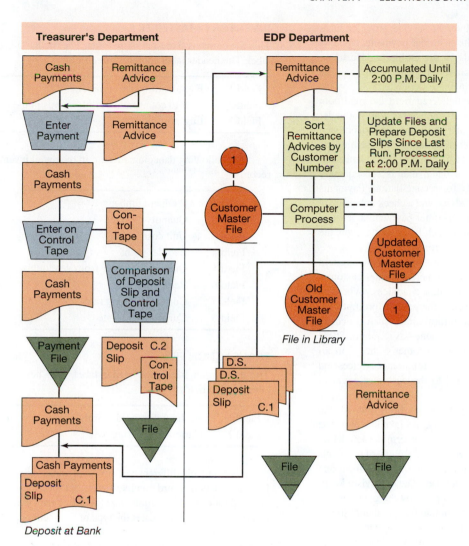

Treasurer's Department | EDP Department

Deposit at Bank

Amalgamated Gas has reviewed and redesigned its computer system so that it has online capabilities. The new cash receipts procedures, described below, are designed to take advantage of the new system.

The customer's payment and remittance advice are received in the treasurer's office as before. A terminal is located in the treasurer's office to enter the cash receipts. An operator keys in the customer's number and payment from the remittance advices and checks. The cash receipt is entered into the system once the operator has confirmed that the proper account and amount are displayed on the screen. The payment is then processed online against the accounts receivable file maintained on magnetic disk. The cash receipts are filed for deposit later in the day. The remittance advices are filed in the order in which they are processed; these documents will be kept until the next working day and then destroyed. The computer prints out a deposit slip in duplicate

at 2:00 P.M. for all cash receipts since the last deposit. The deposit slips are forwarded to the treasurer's office. The cash receipts are removed from the file and deposited with the original deposit slip; the duplicate deposit slip is filed for further reference. At the close of business hours (5:00 P.M.) each day, the EDP department prepares a record of the current day's cash receipts activity on a magnetic tape. This tape is then stored in a secure place in the event of a systems malfunction; after 10 working days, the tape is released for further use.

Required

a. Prepare a systems flowchart of Amalgamated Gas's new online cash receipt procedures.

b. Have the new cash receipt procedures as designed and implemented by Amalgamated Gas created any internal and systems control problems for the company? Explain your answer.

(CMA)

56. The With-It Company, an Internet service provider, uses direct, online processing in its customer payments business process. Data entry terminals in the cashier's department allow direct entry of customer payments data into the computer system for processing.

Customer payments are delivered from the mailroom to the cashier's office for processing. Clerks working under the supervision of the customer payment supervisor open the customer payments to ensure that both a remittance advice and a check are enclosed. If either of these is missing, the payment is set aside in a batch that is subsequently delivered to the chief cashier for reconciliation. Payments containing both a remittance advice and a check are grouped into batches of about 50. The customer payment supervisor attaches a batch control form to each batch and assigns the batches to the data entry operators for processing.

Data entry operators sign onto the computer system using their own unique password. Operators enter customer account numbers from the remittance advices. When an account number match is made, the system prompts the operator to key in the other information—such as check number and the amount of the payment—as required. These data are taken directly from the customer's check. In all cases where input is not possible, the remittance advices and customer payments are returned to the customer payment supervisor for resolution.

After each batch of payments has been entered, the operator terminates the session with a special command. The system then presents a summary report of terminal activity on the monitor. The operator copies the total amount of payments from the summary report onto the batch control form and then returns the batch to the supervisor. The supervisor keeps a cumulative total of payments applied by the operators; as each batch is returned, the total amount of payments shown on the batch control form is added to the running total. At the end of the shift, the customer payment supervisor prepares a payments received report (three copies). The customer payments and two copies of the payments received report are forwarded to the chief cashier for verification and deposit. The customer remittance advices, in batches, are filed with the payments received report by date.

Required

a. Identify deficiencies and/or weaknesses in the data entry procedures described here.

b. Suggest an improvement to remove each weakness/deficiency that you note in (a).

Use the following format to answer this question.

a. Deficiency/weakness

b. Improvement suggested

57. The Magic Rock Company of Houston, Texas, is implementing a computer-based inventory control system. The system will use a sequentially organized inventory master file and a transaction file. Transactions will be batched and processed at the end of each day. A description of the file structures and transaction processing logic follows.

INVENTORY MASTER FILE

This file contains fixed-length records. The file has a header label. The header label contains three fields:

Field 1	File identification number
Field 2	Record count (number of records in the file)
Field 3	Last posting date

The following data elements are in the detail inventory records:

Field 1	Product number
Field 2	Quantity on hand
Field 3	Unit cost
Field 4	Reorder point
Field 5	Quantity on order from vendor
Field 6	Reorder quantity
Field 7	Current shipping rate
Field 8	Current return rate

TRANSACTION FILE

The transaction file has a header label. The header label contains two fields:

Field 1	Hash total of field 3 of the transaction file
Field 2	Current processing date

There are four different types of detail transaction records. Each transaction record has five fields, but all five fields are not used for every transaction type. Field 1 of each transaction record is a code that indicates the type of transaction.

Transaction Code 1: Delivery from Vendor

Field 1	Transaction code
Field 2	Product number
Field 3	Quantity
Field 4	Vendor number
Field 5	Not used

Each delivery-from-vendor transaction causes an increase in the quantity-on-hand field in the associated inventory record and a reduction in the quantity-on-order-from-vendor field.

Transaction Code 2: Inventory Status Check

Field 1	Transaction code
Field 2	Product number
Field 3	Quantity
Field 4	Not used
Field 5	Not used

Each inventory status check transaction initiates a comparison of the actual quantity on hand and that which is recorded in the related inventory record. If a discrepancy is found, the inventory master record is changed to agree with the physical count quantity indicated on the transaction record.

Transaction Code 3: Customer Order

Field 1	Transaction code
Field 2	Product number
Field 3	Quantity
Field 4	Customer number
Field 5	Salesperson number

Each customer order transaction causes a check of the quantity on hand for the ordered product. If sufficient goods are on hand, a shipment notice is output, and the quantity-on-hand field is reduced in the associated inventory record. If insufficient product is on hand, a shipment notice is made for the amount of product available and the quantity-on-hand field is reduced by this amount. A notice is then output indicating the quantity still on order by the customer. The amount of the product ordered by the customer but not yet shipped (possibly zero) is then subtracted from the sum of the updated quantity-on-hand field plus the updated quantity-on-order-from-vendor field. If this result is less than the reorder-point field, a purchase notice is output for the product. The purchase amount is the reorder quantity field. The current shipment-rate field is then recalculated for each actual shipment made. The update formula is

New value = $0.99 \times$ old value $\times 0.01 \times$ shipment amount

The return-rate field also must be updated. The update formula is

New value = $0.99 \times$ old value

This inventory reorder policy is reasonably simple and effective. These formulas calculate an average shipment and return rate using a form of exponential smoothing.

Transaction Code 4: Sales return

Field 1	Transaction code
Field 2	Product number
Field 3	Quantity
Field 4	Customer number
Field 5	Not used

Each sales return transaction causes an update of the quantity-on-hand field in the associated inventory record and also causes an update of the return-rate field. The updated formula is

New value = old value $\times 0.01 \times$ return

The transaction file will be sorted into ascending sequence on product number prior to processing against the inventory master file. Output from the processing run will include an updated master inventory file and a printed transaction register.

Required

a. Identify data edits and application-processing controls that you would recommend be included in this system.

b. From a control viewpoint, do you see any significant differences among the fields of data contained in the master inventory file? Explain your answer.

58. Circle Company has asked you to submit a contract bid to render a professional opinion concerning the operation and control of the company's database system. A centralized database is maintained, and these data are shared by all users. Users access the database using remote data terminals. All access to the database is controlled by a database software system. The information technology (IT) department includes a manager of operations and a manager of computer programming. Both these managers report to the head of the IT department. The head of the IT department reports to the controller.

You visit the company to make a preliminary survey and review of the operation and control of the database system. During your visit to Circle, you review some of the database system documentation, observe some data terminal usage of the system, observe the operation of the IT department, and interview the head of the IT department. At the end of a very busy day, you return home with the following notes:

a. Access to online data terminals is not restricted. Any type of transaction may be input from any terminal.

b. Documentation of the database system is extensive. Complete system documentation is available to users and to IT personnel.

c. The database software maintains a user authorization table. User passwords and access codes are assigned by user management and approved by the manager of computer programming.

d. The database dictionary was established and is controlled by the manager of computer programming. Changes to data definitions are approved by users.

e. The database software maintains a transactions-conflict matrix. User requests for data are validated against this matrix to ensure that users receive only authorized data.

f. Users must enter their passwords when signing on the system. Terminal activity logs are maintained for backup and control purposes.

g. Terminal input is edited for reasonableness and completeness. Transaction control totals are developed, and transaction logs are maintained.

h. Processing control totals are developed and reconciled with changes in the database.

i. Output is reconciled with transaction and input control totals. Printed output is placed in a bin outside the IT room, where users pick it up at their convenience.

j. Backup copies of the database are made daily and stored in the file library area. Access to the file library area is restricted to IT personnel.

Required

Several days after your visit, you are reviewing your notes to prepare a written proposal to perform a controls review for Circle Company. What is your preliminary opinion concerning the operation of their database system?

Web Research Assignments

59. Many consumer groups have raised various privacy issues with respect to the use of RFID tags on store items.

Required

Write a brief report on "RFID privacy" as it relates to tagging consumer items.

a. Include in your report the pros and cons of implementing RFID tags on individual items in a supermarket.

b. Include in your report some discussion about integrating RFID data with accounting software.

60. Quite a bit is written in the literature about lean accounting.

Required

Write a brief report about lean accounting and how it relates to EDI and ebXML.

a. Include in your report a very brief summary of an article published in the accounting literature that explains lean accounting. Hint: visit www.journalofaccountancy.com and search for "lean accounting."

b. Include in your report a discussion about the relationship between the extended supply chain and lean accounting.

61. Quickbooks™ is a very popular accounting system used by many small businesses.

Required

Do some Web research about Quickbooks™ and its transaction-processing capabilities. Write a brief report that deals with at least the following elements:

a. Is it possible to make Quickbooks™ work over the Web, so that multiple employees can access it at the same time via the Web?

b. Is Quickbooks capable of performing real-time processing?

c. Is it possible to create a Quickbooks extranet, to share inventory and order data with suppliers and customers?

Answers to Chapter Quiz

1. c   **2.** a   **3.** b   **4.** d   **5.** c   **6.** b   **7.** a   **8.** b   **9.** b   **10.** d

Revenue Cycle Processes

Learning Objectives

Careful study of this chapter will enable you to:

- Describe the sales business process.
- Illustrate controls that apply to order processing.
- Describe the customer account management business process.
- Illustrate controls that apply to accounts receivable processing.

Sales Business Process

Overview

The sales business process is the primary revenue cycle application in many organizations. The sales business process includes the following activities (Figure 8.1):

- Inquiry (optional)
- Contract creation (optional)
- Order entry
- Shipping
- Billing

Inquiry and contract creation are optional activities. These sometimes may occur or even may be required in the sales business process of some organizations, but they are not necessary activities for many customers or organizations. Order entry, shipping, and billing activities are essential activities in all organizations.

Order fulfillment is the primary function of the sales business process. Orders are created when a customer—a *sold-to party*—requests goods or services from a firm. We shall describe a typical customer order business process in which customer orders are filled from an inventory of finished goods.

INQUIRY The sales business process often begins when a potential customer makes an inquiry or requests a quotation. Some companies make quotations mandatory as a matter of company policy. Others do not. A **quotation** is a document[1] that is prepared and sent to a potential customer to inform him or her of product prices, product availability, and delivery information. A quotation is prepared when a potential customer has made a fairly specific request for details concerning a potential order. An **inquiry** is similar to a quotation, but an inquiry does not contain delivery information.

---

[1]The term *document* is generally used to be inclusive of any electronic or physical medium used to store and transmit information pertaining to a specific business process activity. A document, such as a quotation or order, may be paper or electronic.

FIGURE 8.1

Sales Business
Process

```
┌──────────────────────┐
│     Optional         │
│      Steps           │
│   ┌──────────────┐   │
│   │   Inquiry    │   │
│   └──────┬───────┘   │
│          │           │           ┌──────────────┐
│          ▼           │           │    Order     │
│   ┌──────────────┐   │──────────▶│    Entry     │
│   │  Contract    │   │           └──────┬───────┘
│   │  Creation    │   │                  │
│   └──────────────┘   │                  ▼
└──────────────────────┘           ┌──────────────┐
                                   │   Shipping   │
                                   └──────┬───────┘
                                          │
                                          ▼
                                   ┌──────────────┐
                                   │   Billing    │
                                   └──────────────┘
```

Customer information that is entered into the order-entry system to prepare the inquiry or quotation document is stored and can be reused subsequently if the customer places an order. A sales business process captures customer information as early as possible and reuses this information in subsequent activities.

CONTRACT CREATION   Some companies require that contracts (legal agreements) be prepared before selling to customers as a matter of company policy. Frequently, contract agreements are neither mandatory nor required as a matter of company policy. If contracts are required, then this is the next activity in the sales business process.

A *contract* is an outline agreement to provide goods or services to a customer. A contract usually specifies quantities and a general time frame for deliveries. Specific order details, such as delivery dates and perhaps even prices, are specified later, when the customer places an actual order that will be fulfilled according to the general conditions specified in the contract. A contract to provide goods over a period of time is sometimes called a **blanket order**.

ORDER ENTRY   Order entry prepares the **sales order** document. The order-entry activity is essentially the same whether it is the first activity in the sales business process or occurs subsequent to inquiry, contract preparation, or both. A different but similar document may be prepared when a customer is requesting delivery of goods that are detailed in a contract. For example, a document called a *release order* or *call-off* may be prepared rather than a sales order, but the information in these documents would be similar.

Order entry usually involves pricing and availability checking. Pricing an order involves knowing the current prices of products or services, any surcharges that may apply, any discounts that may apply, and shipping costs. Enterprise resource planning (ERP) information systems enable the implementation of sophisticated and flexible customer-specific and material-specific pricing procedures in the order-entry business process. Customer-specific procedures can be a significant competitive advantage in that the company can offer customers highly customized service. This is an essential aspect of the customer orientation that is central to ERP systems. Many companies perform a credit limit check of the customer once pricing is complete and before the order is released for fulfillment. An order is usually blocked if it would cause the customer to exceed his or her credit limit. Blocked orders are listed for review by the credit department. The credit department is empowered to decide whether to release blocked orders for fulfillment.

If the customer's credit is satisfactory, then the availability of goods is checked to determine whether the items are either currently in stock or are expected to be in stock and available by the requested delivery date. Several options may exist in cases where the goods will not be available.

The customer may wish to cancel the order. Partial delivery of the order is a possibility when the customer is willing to accept partial shipment. Another option is to hold the order until all the goods are available if the customer is willing to extend the requested delivery date.

SHIPPING Shipping activity is initiated with the preparation of a shipping document called a *delivery*. A delivery document is created to arrange for the delivery of goods to the customer. All the information that is required to prepare and deliver the goods to the customer is contained in the delivery. The delivery is usually prepared at the production or distribution location.

The sales order contains much of the information that is necessary in a delivery. The ERP automatically copies this information into the delivery. The ERP might perform additional checks at this point to ensure quality. For example, the availability of goods may be rechecked to ensure that delivery is immediately possible.

Delivery documents are processed to prepare a schedule (i.e., work list) for shipping. The schedule is based on customers' requested delivery dates. Actual shipment of goods out of inventory requires picking the order, packing the order, and posting the shipment. Picking fills the order and involves the selection of goods from the plant or warehouse to be prepared for shipment. Packing involves packaging of the goods in the order for shipment and loading the shipment onto vehicles for transportation to the customer. The complexity of picking and packing differs significantly for different products. Some products are ready to pick and ship "as is," whereas others may require assembly or special equipment to be used during picking and packing.

Several other documents are prepared during shipping activities. A picking list is prepared to guide picking activities. A packing list is prepared for each shipment, and a copy is usually included in the shipment to document what has been shipped. A **bill of lading** is prepared to document the loading of goods onto vehicles for transportation to the customer. The ERP can copy much of the information contained in these documents from either the sales order document or the delivery document.

 CASE IN POINT

> A bill of lading is a legal document signed by a transporter of goods (i.e., a carrier) and issued to the shipper. The bill of lading provides the shipper a receipt for the goods and serves as a contract for shipment. Many U.S. and international shippers use the Bolero (www.bolero.net) Trusted Trade Platform to electronically exchange electronic bills of lading and other documents. Digital signatures are used in place of pen-and-ink signatures.

Shipping personnel post a **goods issue notice** when goods have been shipped. This posting updates the relevant delivery document. The ERP uses this information to update inventory as necessary based on the shipment. The posting of a goods issue notice also initiates the billing process. **Shipping advice** is a synonym for a goods issue notice.

BILLING Deliveries are included in the billing work schedule and are invoiced. The ERP copies much of the data used in billing from the customer's sales order or from the customer's delivery document. An **invoice** (Figure 8.2) for the shipment is prepared and issued to the customer. The issuing of the invoice is the end of the sales business process.

In many cases, the goods are shipped before the customer is invoiced. In some cases, it may be appropriate to invoice customers after the sales order has been prepared but before the goods have been shipped. Invoices are forwarded to accounts receivable processing to await payment by the customer.

FIGURE 8.2

Invoice

SOLD TO:	CITRUS SUPPLY CO. 1467 CLAY STREET PETERSBURG, WISCONSIN 44444					INVOICE **Burroughs** 🅱		
SHIP TO:	CITRUS SUPPLY CO. 1467 CLAY STREET PETERSBURG, WISCONSIN 44444							

TERMS	ORDER NO.	CUSTOMER NO.	SOLD BY	SHIP VIA	DATE	INVOICE NO.
2-10 NET 30	P87654	102,912	7	OUR TRUCK	NOV. 15	12,347

CODE	QUANTITY	DESCRIPTION	PRICE	UNIT	GROSS	DISCOUNT	NET
13414522	10	CUTTING TIP TT-3	2.80	EA	28.00	.00	28.00
12415710	10	SCREWDRIVER 6"	1.90	EA	19.00	.38	18.62
15611410	5	WELDING GLOVE #10	1.50	PR	7.50	.15	7.35
12488806	10	DSK	1.00	EA	10.00	.00	10.00
							63.97
					TAX	5.0%	3.20
					HANDLING		25.00
							92.17

SAP ERP Illustration

ERP systems are capable of storing and processing a vast amount of information pertaining to the sales business process. This section provides an overview of the data that are stored and processed in the sales business process by SAP ERP.[2] The sales business process is part of SAP ERP's sales and distribution module.

> ## ⬤ CASE IN POINT
>
> The SAP ERP application is an integrated ERP software manufactured by SAP AG that targets business software requirements of medium and large organizations in all industries and sectors. It is the successor product to SAP R/3. SAP ERP is a worldwide market share leader.

CUSTOMER MASTER RECORDS Customer master records contain all the information that pertains to a customer. Customer master records have to be created before processing sales orders in SAP ERP because the information in customer master records is used in sales order processing.

SAP ERP requires four types of master records:

- Sold-to-customer records
- Ship-to-customer records
- Bill-to-customer records
- Payee–customer records

When a new sold-to-customer master record is created, the other three master records are created automatically using the same information. When a customer has different locations for receiving, shipment, and/or payment, the information in these records can be changed as necessary.

---

[2]SAP ERP is a registered trademark of SAP Aktiengesellschaft, Systems, Applications, and Products in Data Processing, Neurottstrasse 16, 69190 Walldorf, Germany (www.sap.com).

Additional records can be created as necessary. For example, a customer may have several ship-to addresses. Such records must be linked to the sold-to-customer master records. This is known as *partnering*.

Customer master records should be unique. Thus, it is necessary to check that a customer is not already in the system before the creation of a new customer master record. SAP ERP requires that a customer's hierarchy assignment be known prior to the creation of a master record. The customer's hierarchy assignment is a representation of the customer's organization structure that determines pricing information used in SAP ERP. For example, a chain of stores inherits pricing agreements from its main office. Hierarchy assignment includes a distribution channel, type of industry, and geographic location. SAP ERP also requires that a customer has been approved for sales prior to the creation of master records.

DATA FIELDS   Customer master records are created by inputting information into SAP ERP, which guides the input process by displaying a series of screens on a video monitor that prompt the user to input the necessary data. Each screen collects a category of data pertaining to a customer. Most input is coded as numbers. The user hits the "Return" key when a screen is completed, which causes the next screen to display. The "Create Customer" input screens in SAP ERP facilitate input through the use of list boxes and search facilities. List boxes allow the user to choose an item from a list. The items are usually displayed as text, and the input is coded as a number by SAP ERP when the user selects an item in the list. Search facilities allow the user to enter a word or phrase, and SAP ERP finds the required code. The "Create Customer" screens and some of the data that are input into these screens are described below (Figure 8.3).

Create Customer: Initial Screen   The initial screen prompts for a customer number that is used to uniquely identify the customer master record. This number can be assigned externally or internally. Customer numbers are assigned externally when the person who is inputting the data selects the number. Internal assignment is performed automatically by SAP ERP, which assigns the next number in a sequence.

Additional input is required for a company code and organizational data that identify the sales area. A sales area is identified by three required fields: sales organization, distribution channel, and division. Sales organization is the company unit that is responsible for the sale. Distribution channel includes direct sales, retail sale, and wholesale. Division is a code that identifies a subgroup in the sales organization. These items can be selected from drop-down list boxes. An account group field is filled automatically by default.

Create Customer: Address Screen   This screen prompts for the customer's address information, which is primarily text. The company's name is entered into the name field. The search term *field* is used to input a phrase that can be used to search for the company when the company number is required for input. For example, the search term for Candy Maker Corporation might be *candymaker*.

Input fields are provided for street, post office box, city, region (or state), postal code (or ZIP code), and country. Input is required for the city, postal code, and country fields. A code indicating the language to be used must be entered in the communication section of the "Create Customer" address screen. For example, "E" indicates English. Optional fields are provided for telephone, telex, and fax numbers.

• Initial Screen	• Payment Transactions
• Customer Address	• Correspondence
• Control Data	• Insurance
• Marketing	• Sales
• Payment Transactions	• Shipping
• Unloading Points	• Billing
• Foreign Trade	• Taxes
• Contact Person	• Output
• Account Management	• Partner Functions

FIGURE 8.3

SAP ERP "Create Customer" Input Screens

Create Customer: Control Data Screen The fields entered in this screen depend on a company's specific needs. The transport zone field is the only required field. It identifies the regional zone where the ship-to party is located. Zone is coded and is entered by selecting from a list box. Some of the other fields that may be entered to provide transport information are location number, industry, train station, express station, and location code. The account control section provides fields for vendor, trading partner, authorization, and group key. The tax information section provides fields for tax code, fiscal address, county code, city code, equalization tax, sole proprietor, tax on sales/purchase, VAT registration number, and tax jurisdiction code. A company defines its own tax codes. For example, Tax Code Field 1 could be used to enter a taxpayer ID number for a customer who resides in the United States.

Create Customer: Marketing Screen The marketing screen is used to input statistical and demographic data concerning the customer. The Nielsen ID field (which may be required) specifies a regional division according to marketing categories created by the A. C. Nielsen Company and is used for marketing analysis. Other fields collect codes for customer classification, industry, and region. Customer classification is freely definable according to a company's needs. The Operating Figures section collects statistics such as the annual sales of the customer and its number of employees.

Create Customer: Payment Transactions Screen This screen is used to input the customer's banking information. Fields are provided for a bank country code, bank key, bank account number, reference details, and several other details. Data may be input for several different banks.

Create Customer: Unloading Points Screen This screen is used to input where the customer unloads received goods and the customer's *factory calendar*, which specifies what days and hours the customer accepts deliveries. Each unloading point has a factory calendar that is stored and available as a menu selection. If the customer has multiple unloading points, one can be designated as the default. Receiving hours by day of the week are entered for each unloading point. Specific hours (as start and stop times) can be entered, or one can choose from a list of predefined delivery times. The input can be extremely detailed as to hours and dates for each unloading point.

Create Customer: Foreign Trade Screen This screen is used to input data relating to export controls.

Create Customer: Contact Person Screen This screen is used to input data relating to a contact person or persons. Fields are provided for name, telephone number, form of address (e.g., "Mr."), and department code. The department code field is filled by choosing from a list that has entries such as "0001 managing director," "0002 purchasing," and "0003 sales." There is also a department function field, which is a code identifying the contact's function. This is selected from a list box that has entries such as "01 executive board" and "02 head of purchasing." Once a code is selected, the accompanying description is displayed next to the code on the input screen.

Create Customer: Account Management Screen This screen is used to specify account reconciliation data. A reconciliation account is a general ledger account that is updated parallel to accounts receivable postings. It is a control account used for reconciliation. The account is selected from a menu list. A sort key is selected to specify how line items will be sorted in the customer's account listing. For example, posting date, document date, local currency amount, or some other field may be selected as the sort key. Several other optional fields may be input, such as head office and planning group.

Create Customer: Payment Transactions Screen This screen collects data for payment transactions, including automatic payment transactions. The payment terms field specifies cash discount terms and the payment periods that comprise overall terms of payment. One can specify that a payment history should be maintained by checking a specific field. One can input a lock-box number. Several fields collect data concerning payment methods used for automatic payment transactions as necessary. The account number of an alternate payer, if any, can be specified. If open items are to be paid separately during automatic payment, this is specified by selecting (i.e., checking) a specific field.

Create Customer: Correspondence Screen This screen can be used to establish a dunning procedure and other correspondence with the customer. A *dunning procedure* is the action taken to collect payments from customers who are late in making payments on their accounts. A dunning procedure code is input by selecting from a list box. One can specify the customer's representative who will receive dunning notices, as well as the customer's accounting clerk who handles invoices and dunnings (if a dunning recipient is not specified in the dunning recipient field).

Additional input can specify how frequently account statements are mailed to the customer and whether a customer's payment notice should display cleared items or not. If the customer's payment notice must be created for the legal department, then the legal department field on the entry screen should be selected. The sales field or accounting field is selected if the customer's payment notice must be created for either of these departments.

Create Customer: Insurance Screen This screen can be used to input data relating to export credit insurance. Fields are provided for policy numbers, amounts insured, insurance company, lead months, and deductible percent.

Create Customer: Sales Screen This screen is used to identify areas within the company that are responsible to the customer. As necessary, data are entered for geographic sales region or district, sales office, sales group, and customer group (wholesale or retail). One must specify a currency for the settlement of accounts. One can specify a *pricing procedure,* which is a SAP ERP term for the type and sequence of pricing conditions used to price a sales order. One can also specify a price list type—wholesale or retail.

The product proposal number field is used for defaulting products into the customer's orders if the customer routinely orders the same products. One can enter the company's vendor account number—what the customer uses to identify the company in the customer's information system. One also can enter a code that identifies how to determine the currency exchange rate.

Create Customer: Shipping Screen This screen is used to specify shipping details. The order combination field is selected by default. It should be deselected if the customer does not accept partial shipments. A shipping conditions code is input to select a general shipping strategy from those that have been defined by the company. Fields are provided for a shipping plant code and a delivery priority (low, normal, or high). The complete delivery field is selected if deliveries to the customer must be delivered all together. If individual items can be delivered partially, this is indicated with the appropriate code in another field. The maximum number of partial deliveries (up to nine per item) is entered into another field.

Create Customer: Billing Screen This screen is used to input data concerning billing. The incoterms field identifies international trading terms. A corresponding text description is required. For example, if "freight on board" (FOB) is entered in the incoterms field, then San Francisco could be entered as the corresponding required text to indicate the shipping location. Fields specify whether manual invoicing is required and if the customer is eligible for rebates. Input specifies the billing schedule, which defines the dates on which customers are billed. An invoice list schedule is input. This is a calendar used to place the customer's invoice on a collection list. An input field collects the account assignment group, which is used for integration with the accounts receivable module of SAP ERP.

Create Customer: Taxes Screen This screen is used to input data concerning the customer's tax liability. The categories displayed will vary depending on the countries in which the company does business. Tax classification fields are completed for each tax category that is listed. Data that are entered include tax exemption certificates, license number, date valid from, and date valid to.

Create Customer: Output Screen This input screen is used to change the default output specifications for various documents that can be produced for the customer. Fields collect data concerning details such as output type (quote, invoice, etc.), language, transmission medium (paper, fax, electronic data interchange—EDI), send time (immediately or next batch run), and number of copies produced. Items can be changed, added, or deleted.

Create Customer: Partner Functions Screen When a sold-to-customer record is created, SAP ERP automatically creates bill-to, payer, and ship-to master records for the same customer using the same information. These master records are partnered on this input screen. If a sold-to customer has multiple or different partners for billing, paying, or shipping, then the customer numbers of those partners are entered. However, if these partners do not have master records, then such records must be created before the partners' numbers can be entered in this screen.

The customer master record can now be saved because this is the final "Create Customer" screen.

ONE-TIME CUSTOMERS   Due to complexity of this process for creating customer master records, SAP ERP allows for the creation of a single master record *dummy* for one-time or infrequent customers. All these customers are passed through this one-time record. The master record has minimal information. Only the Address, Sales, Shipping, Billing, Taxes, and Output Create Customer screens are completed. For these screens, only fields that will apply to all of the customers who use this record are input. Additional specific information for shipping is added when orders by specific customers are placed. This process saves the trouble of creating detailed records for one-time customers.

Standard Order Processing in SAP ERP

OVERVIEW   This section provides an overview of standard order processing in SAP ERP. *Standard order processing* is a term that describes the sales business process in which customer orders are filled from an inventory of finished goods. Standard orders are usually received by telephone, mail, fax, sales representative, or voice mail.

A quotation may first be issued to the customer. If there is no quotation, then an order is created when a customer requests delivery of goods or services. A standard sales order contains information about prices, quantities, and dates (requested delivery date, shipping date, etc.).

After an order has been created and processed, a delivery document is created. SAP ERP calculates the expected shipping date using the requested delivery date and the transit time to the customer. These data are available in the customer master record.

CREATING A SALES ORDER   A customer master record has to exist before a sales order can be created. SAP ERP can copy information from the master record into the sales order as necessary.

Create Sales Order: Initial Screen This screen is used to input information for the sales area. There are three mandatory fields. The sales organization field identifies the unit responsible for the sale. The distribution channel field classifies the order as direct sales, retail sale, or wholesale. The division code field is used to identify a subgroup in the sales organization. For every division, customer-specific agreements concerning partial deliveries, pricing, payments, and so on can be defined. Optionally, an area may also contain a sales office and a sales group. These are the personnel responsible for processing sales. Fields are available to input these items if they are used. The order type field differentiates orders as to their purpose. Some examples of the many codes provided are "CR," credit memo request; "DL," delivery (without order); "DR," debit memo request; and "OR," standard order.

CASE IN POINT

Standard order processing in SAP ERP includes checking customer credit limits.

Create Sales Order Screen This screen has two parts: a document header and an area for item data. The document header contains fields for items that describe the entire order. The sold-to-party field collects the customer's code. The customer's purchase order number is entered into the purchase order number field. The purchase order date field is used for the date the customer's purchase order was received. Usually this date is the same as the order date, but not always. The requested delivery date field is used to enter the delivery date requested by the customer or a date that is proposed automatically by SAP ERP. The pricing date field is used to price material and to calculate foreign exchange rates. The order field number is assigned externally, or SAP ERP will automatically enter an order number. For example, if the order-entry system is down (i.e., not operating online) and a customer needs an order confirmation number immediately, the user can give the customer an externally assigned order number and then later enter it as the order number.

The item data section contains the product numbers and order quantities. Search features help the user to find product numbers. SAP ERP does an automatic availability check as items are entered. If an item is not available, it proposes options, such as partial delivery. SAP ERP also enters some default data, such as parts descriptions. The total value of the order is calculated.

The preceding describes the minimum number of data-entry fields necessary for an order. Several optional screens allow detailed editing of an order.

The optional pricing screen allows editing of pricing conditions, such as gross price, discount, rebate, units (how an item is priced: each, dozen, etc.), and currencies. The optional scheduling screen allows editing of individual items in the order. One can edit when an item will be available and schedule it for delivery. One can also edit shipping dates by item. Individual dates for each step in the shipping process are available, such as loading and goods issue. These dates can differ for products that are complicated to pack and ship.

The optional business data header screen allows editing of shipping and billing data for the entire order. One can edit the order combination field, which indicates whether the customer allows orders to be combined into one shipment. One can edit the complete delivery field, which indicates whether the customer accepts partial orders. The default value in both these fields defaults from the customer master record.

The delivery block field is used to block an order from further processing. For example, SAP ERP automatically places a block order if the customer's credit limit is exceeded. The billing block field is used to block an order from being invoiced. For example, there may be a need to verify or change pricing on the order before billing. One can edit business data concerning material, sales, shipping, and billing for specific line items. For example, one could block billing of a specific item if pricing information for that item is incomplete.

DATABASE FEATURES Each activity in the sales business process—quotation, order, delivery, invoice, and so on—generates a document. SAP ERP's document flow feature allows one to track and view these documents.

A *query* is a request for information in a database. SAP ERP features powerful query capabilities. One can display an order by inputting the order number. One can display a list of documents according to a specific criterion. For example, one can list all the orders for a particular customer or for a particular product number. The system allows one to drill down to more detail, for example, to display more detailed information concerning a line item on an order.

SAP ERP provides a Standard Order: Overview screen. One can list and display all the documents related to a particular sales order. A "Status Overview" button provides a summary of the processing status of the order.

Transaction Cycle Controls in Order Processing

Figure 8.4 illustrates a business process model of a standard sales order business process where customer orders are filled from an inventory of finished goods. The model shows two pools: customer and company. The company pool has lanes which identify typical function groupings in a sales process. Transaction cycle controls are based on separation of functions within a business process. In a standard sales order business process, these functions are order entry, credit, inventory, shipping, billing and accounts receivable, and general ledger. The business process model shows an overview of flow of activities in the company from receiving a customer purchase order through to its impact on the financial statements prepared by the general ledger function. Additional details are provided in the following discussion.

Order Entry

Figure 8.5 details activities in the sales and credit operation functions in processing a customer purchase order. As Figure 8.5 illustrates, the order-entry function should be subject to the control of an independent credit function to maintain a separation of duties within the business process. Once credit has been approved, the order is released for processing. The figure uses message flows between pools to illustrate the effect of operations on databases maintained for customers, orders, and inventory.

The order-entry function initiates the processing of customer orders with the preparation of the sales order document. The sales order contains descriptions of the products ordered; their prices; and descriptive data concerning the customer, such as name, shipping address, and if necessary, billing address. If the time between receiving an order and actual shipment of the order is significant, an acknowledgment notice may be sent to the customer to inform the customer that the order has been received and is being processed. Prices entered on sales orders should

FIGURE 8.4

Sales Business Process

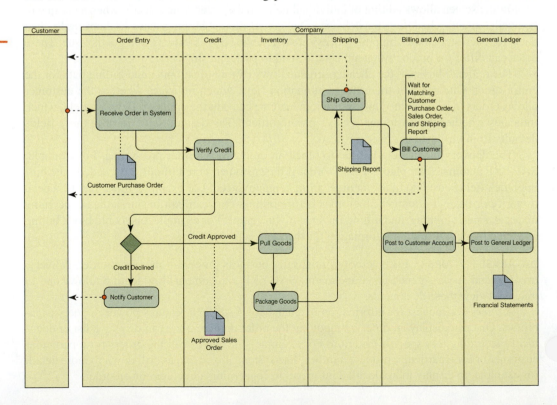

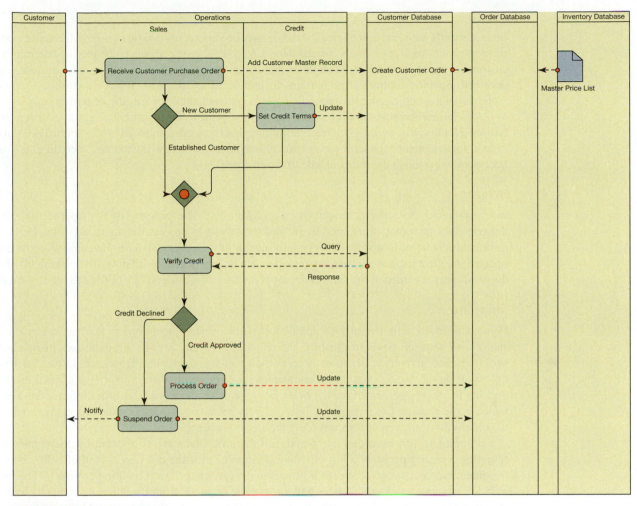

FIGURE 8.5

Sales and Credit

be approved by management or an organizational function that is independent of the sales order function. An independently prepared master price list contains the prices authorized by management and in effect at a particular date and should be the source of prices used in the preparation of sales orders. The master price list contained in the inventory database pool in Figure 8.5 emphasizes this control.

The sales order is primarily an internal document. The invoice, or bill, is a separate document that is usually prepared after the goods have been shipped and notice of shipment is forwarded to billing.

○ **CASE IN POINT**

Customer relationship management (CRM) systems are software solutions that help an organization manage customer relationships in an organized manner. The goal is to identify, acquire, and retain customers. Effective sales management is facilitated when sales personnel in the field have real-time access to customer data for inquiry and for entering orders and other transactions.

Credit

Management's authorization of credit standing may be general or specific in nature. General authorization applies to all customers. Establishment of general requirements to be met in determining customers' credit limits is an example of general authorization because no specific customer is involved. Specific authorization pertains to individual transactions for individual customers. Approval of a specific order for a specific customer is an example of specific authorization.

A customer's credit standing should be verified prior to the shipment of goods. For regular customers, the credit check involves determining that the total amount of credit granted does not exceed management's general or specific authorization. For new customers, a credit check is necessary to establish the terms of sale to the customer.

Inventory

Inventory picks the order as described on a picking list. The picking list is prepared from the delivery document that is prepared by the order database to process the approved order. Picking information is input to update delivery information in the order database. Inventory records are updated to reflect the actual quantities picked and to be forwarded to shipping. The picking list and the goods are forwarded to shipping. Shipping should acknowledge receipt of the goods transferred.

Shipping

Figure 8.6 details activities in the shipping function in processing an order. The figure uses message flows between pools to illustrate the effect of shipping activity on databases maintained for orders and inventory. Shipping accepts the order for shipment after matching the order as described on the picking list that accompanies the goods to the order as it is described on the packing list that is generated for the order from the order database. The order information contained in the packing list is prepared independently because it is based on the orders prepared by the order-entry function and approved by the credit function.

Shipping documentation is prepared, and the order database is updated for the shipment. Shipping typically prepares a bill of lading (Figure 8.7) for the delivery. A bill of lading is the documentation exchanged between a shipper and a carrier such as a trucking company. The bill of lading documents freight charges and the transfer of goods from the shipping company to the transportation company. Frequently, freight charges are paid by the shipper but billed to the customer on the sales invoice. Copies of the packing list and the bill of lading are usually included with the customer's order when it is shipped.

FIGURE 8.6

Shipping

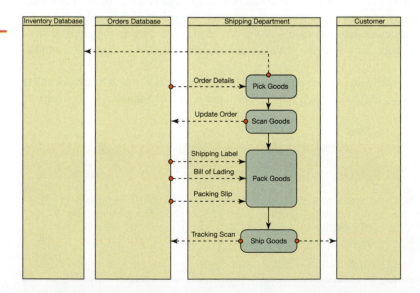

SHIPPER'S NO. | CARRIER'S NO.

STRAIGHT BILL OF LADING—SHORT FORM—ORIGINAL—Not Negotiable

RECEIVED, subject to the classifications and tariffs in effect on the date of the issue of this Bill of Lading

the property, described below, in apparent good order, except as noted (contents and condition of contents of packages unknown), marked, consigned, and destined as indicated below, which said carrier (the word carrier being understood throughout this contract as meaning any person or corporation in possession of the property under the contract) agrees to carry to its usual place of delivery at said destination, if on its route, otherwise to deliver to another carrier on the route to said destination, it is mutually agreed, as to each carrier of all or any of said property over all or any portion of said route to destination, and as to each party at any time interested in all or any of said property, that every service to be performed hereunder shall be subject to all the terms and conditions of the Uniform Domestic Straight Bill of Lading set forth (1) in Uniform Freight Classification in effect on the date hereof, if this is a rail or a rail-water shipment, or (2) in the applicable motor carrier classification or tariff if this is a motor carrier shipment.

Shipper hereby certifies that he is familiar with all the terms and conditions of the said bill of lading, including those on the back thereof, set forth in the classification or tariff which governs the transportation of this shipment, and the said terms and conditions are hereby agreed to by the shipper and accepted for himself and his assigns.

FROM:

NAME

ADDRESS:

CITY | STATE | ZIP CODE

CONSIGNED TO: | DATE SHIPPED

NAME

DELIVERY ADDRESS:

CITY | COUNTY | STATE

ZIP CODE

Number Packages	KIND OF PACKAGE, DESCRIPTION OF ARTICLES, SPECIAL MARKS, AND EXCEPTIONS	*WEIGHT (Subject to Correction)	Class or Rate	Ck. Col.

Subject to Section 7 of conditions, of applicable bill of lading, if this shipment is to be delivered to the consignee without recourse on the consigner, the consigner shall sign the following statement:
The carrier shall not make a delivery of this shipment without payment of freight and all other lawful charges.

(Signature of consigner.)

If charges are to be prepaid, write or stamp here, "To be Prepaid."

Rec'd $ to

apply in prepayment of the charges on the property described hereon.

Agent or Cashier.

Per

(The signature here acknowledges only the amount prepaid.)

Charges advanced:

$

*If the shipment moves between two ports by a carrier by water, the law requires that the bill of lading shall state whether it is "carrier's or shipper's weight." NOTE—Where the rate is dependent on value, shippers are required to state specifically in writing the agreed or declared value of the property.

The agreed or declared value of the property is hereby specifically stated by the shipper to be not exceeding per

Shipper, Per Agent

Permanent post office address of shipper. per

†"The fibre containers used for this shipment conform to the specifications set forth in the box maker's certificate thereon, and all other requirements of Rule 41 of the Uniform Freight Classification and Rule 5 of the National Meter Freight Classification."
†Shipper's imprint in lieu of stamp; not a part of bill of lading approved by the Interstate Commerce Commission.

FIGURE 8.7
Bill of Lading

Billing and Accounts Receivable

Figure 8.8 details activities in operations pertaining to billing. The figure uses message flows between pools to illustrate the effect of billing activity on databases maintained for accounts receivable and general ledger. The customer purchase order, the sales order, and the shipping report are necessary to process a completed sales transaction. Billing completes the order process by preparing invoices for orders that appear on the billing list. The billing list is prepared from the information concerning orders that have been shipped to customers. Billing verifies the order and then prepares the invoice. The invoice contains charges for the actual quantities shipped, freight charges (if any), and taxes (if any). Invoices are mailed to customers. Invoices are recorded in the order database, which contains the accounting information that serves as the sales journal, and notice is sent to accounts receivable in order that customer account balances may be updated. Periodically, a journal voucher is prepared to summarize sales, and this information is forwarded to the general ledger function for posting to the general ledger.

General Ledger

The distinction between billing and accounts receivable is important to maintain separation of functions. Billing is responsible for invoicing individual orders. Accounts receivable posts invoices prepared by billing to the accounts receivable ledger. The accounts receivable function maintains customer-accounts information and sends periodic statements of account to customers. Billing does not have access to the financial records (the accounts receivable ledger), and the financial records

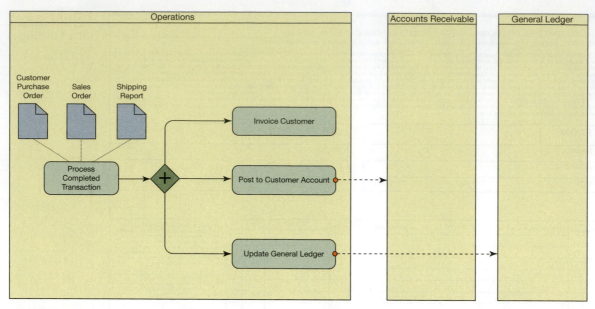

FIGURE 8.8

Accounting Operations

are independent of the invoicing operation. A common control procedure is to reconcile the total of postings to the accounts receivable ledger that is sent to the general ledger function by the accounts receivable function to the journal voucher total sent from the billing function to validate postings to the general ledger. In the same fashion, the distinction between shipping and inventory functions is important to the establishment of accountability for the release of goods from inventory. Shipping should only accept goods that are identified on the independently prepared packing list.

Sarbanes–Oxley Compliance: Sales Business Process

The Sarbanes–Oxley Act of 2002 (SOX) requires that companies maintain an adequate internal control structure over the business processes that support financial reporting. SEC Interpretive Guidance "Management's Report on Internal Control over Financial Reporting," approved by the Securities and Exchange Commission on May 23, 2007, focuses management on internal controls that best protect against risk of material misstatement in financial statements. Auditing Standard No. 5: "An Audit of Internal Control over Financial Reporting That Is Integrated with an Audit of Financial Statements," issued by the Public Company Accounting Oversight Board (PCAOB), establishes requirements and provides direction that applies when an auditor is engaged to perform an audit of management's assessment of the effectiveness of internal control over financial reporting that is integrated with an audit of the financial statements. Effective internal control over financial reporting provides reasonable assurance regarding the reliability of financial reporting and the preparation of financial statements for external purposes. If one or more material weaknesses exist, the company's internal control over financial reporting cannot be considered effective. Auditing Standard No. 5 describes a top-down approach to selecting controls to be tested. Auditors should understand risks related to the preparation of financial statements, focus on entity-level controls, and test controls that sufficiently address the assessed risk of misstatement. Risk assessment underlies the entire audit process described by this standard, including the determination of significant accounts and disclosures and relevant assertions.

The sales business process generates revenue amounts that are significant accounts, disclosures, and assertions on a company's income statement. The sales business process also generates accounts receivable amounts that are significant accounts, disclosures, and assertions on a company's balance sheet. Thus, risk assessment of the sales business process will be necessary for compliance with SOX. Rationale of assessed risks must be clearly documented and controls selected for testing and evaluation. Our discussion of transaction cycle controls in order processing has highlighted fundamental controls that are based on a separation of functions within this business process. Both management and auditors will be concerned with evaluating the existence and functioning of these controls as they are necessary to protect against risk of material misstatements in amounts reported in financial statements. Risk assessment should also evaluate whether the company's controls sufficiently address identified risks of material misstatement due to fraud and controls intended to address the risk of management override of these controls.

Customer Account Management Business Process

The customer account management business process includes accounts receivable processing through the collection of customer payments on account. We include a brief discussion of the cash-sales business process because it is often integrated with the process for the collection of customer payments on account.

CASE IN POINT

An iPhone® app from Germany-based company Sybase® allows users to interface to CRM software from SAP®. This enables sales representatives and field service employees to access customer data and enter updates online to the sales information stored by the CRM system while on-site with the customer.

Accounts Receivable

Accounts receivable represents the money owed by customers for merchandise sold or services rendered on account. Because most business is done on credit, accounts receivable often represents the majority of an organization's working capital. Accounts receivable also maintains customer credit and payment history information, which is essential in the sales business process.

Conceptually, the accounts receivable procedure is straightforward. A subsidiary ledger of individual accounts is maintained, with a control account in the general ledger. Remittance advices are routed from the cash receipts function; credit memos and other invoice adjustments are routed to the accounts receivable department from the billing department. Debits and credits are posted to the individual accounts. Periodically, statements that summarize amounts due are prepared and sent to customers. Accounts receivable processing also includes periodic preparation of aging schedules of outstanding customer account balances. An aging schedule, often referred to as an **aged trial balance**, reports outstanding customer account balances classified by their "age." Outstanding account balances are classified as to how long a time period the amounts have been due. Aging schedules are forwarded to the credit function in order that there will be follow-up on slow and doubtful accounts. Special credit reports also may be prepared if desired by management. Aging schedules are often referred to as aged trial balances.

There are two basic approaches to an accounts receivable application: open-item and balance-forward processing. In **open-item processing**, a separate record is maintained in the accounts receivable system for each of the customer's unpaid invoices. As customer remittances are received, they are matched to the unp aid invoices. In **balance-forward processing**, a customer's remittances are applied against the customer's total outstanding balance rather than against the customer's individual invoices.

Balance-forward processing has the advantage of operational simplicity. The total amount due from a customer is the total of all invoices due from the customer, and the payments are simply applied against this total. It does not matter which particular invoice (if any) that the customer is paying, and there is no need to match payments to specific invoices. The disadvantage of balance-forward processing is that its inherent simplicity may not be appropriate to the business process and thus, it might not support detailed reporting requirements. Open-item processing maintains a complete invoice history that supports inquiry into any invoice and supports detail or summary sales analysis. Customer reports such as average days to pay, average invoice balance, and sales by month are examples of reports that might be prepared. The disadvantage is that open-item processing is more complex. Payments, credits, and any other adjustments must be matched to specific invoices. Customers might identify their payments to specific invoices by returning copies of the invoices or by noting the invoice numbers in their payments. Numerous complexities can arise in processing. A customer may not identify their payments to specific invoices. Procedures for handling partial payments and overpayments must be specified. If a customer underpays, the invoice will remain open. If the customer overpays an invoice, the difference might be applied to some other invoice. Most commercial systems support both methods of processing customer payments, and many offer the option to use either method with specific customers.

 CASE IN POINT

A factor company purchases a company's accounts receivables by giving an advance payment on projected collections. This payment is typically 70–90% of the total value of the receivables. After charging a small fee of several percent, the remaining balance is released upon full receipt of payment for all the receivables/invoices. Factoring can help small companies finance larger sales by providing the necessary working capital to continue operations.

Data processing of accounts receivable can be complicated owing to the volume of transactions and number of accounts that may exist. Even with computer processing, mailing all statements at month's end may be impossible. Many businesses use a **cycle billing plan**, in which the accounts receivable file is subdivided by alphabet or account number. The idea is to distribute the preparation of statements over the working days of the month. For example, accounts A through H may be billed on the 10th, I through P on the 20th, and so on. Cycle billing plans often have a beneficial effect on a company's cash flow because consumers generally pay bills shortly after receiving them. Some companies sell their accounts receivable at a discount to collection agencies. This process, called **factoring**, avoids record-keeping costs. This alternative should be considered, but one should carefully consider the potential negative effects of factoring on customer relations. Some customers may be unhappy when they discover that their accounts are owed to a collection agency rather than to the company with which they did business.

Transaction Controls in the Accounts Receivable Business Process

Separation of Functions

Figure 8.9 illustrates a document flowchart of an accounts receivable business process. The main feature in the illustration is the separation of the following functions within the business process.

CASH RECEIPTS   Customer remittance slips are forwarded to accounts receivable for posting from cash receipts. Accounts receivable does not have access to the cash or checks that accompany customer remittances.

BILLING   Invoices, credit memos, and other invoice adjustments are routed to accounts receivable for posting to the customer accounts. This maintains a separation of functions. Billing does not have direct access to the accounts receivable records.

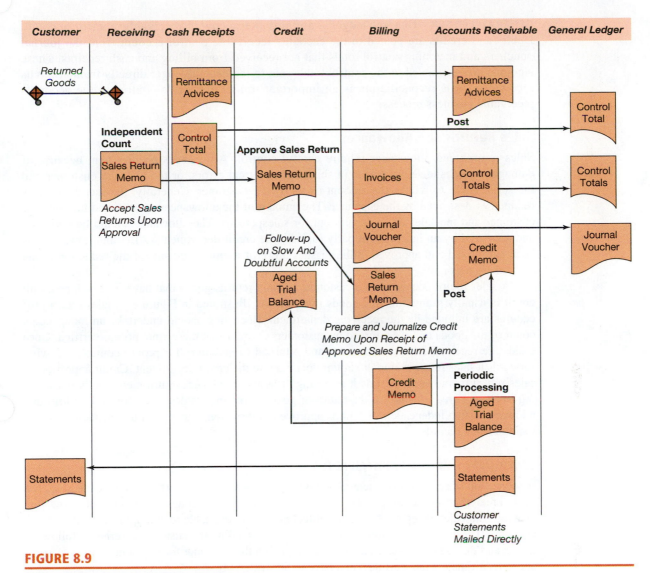

FIGURE 8.9

Accounts Receivable Business Process

ACCOUNTS RECEIVABLE Accounts receivable is responsible for maintaining the subsidiary accounts receivable ledger. A control account is maintained by the general ledger department. Debits and credits are posted to the customer accounts from the remittance advices, invoices, and other documents received from billing and cash receipts. This maintains a separation of functions. Periodically, customer statements are mailed directly to customers by the accounts receivable department. Periodic processing also includes the preparation of an aged trial balance of the accounts receivable subsidiary ledger for review by the credit department. Other types of customer credit reports may be prepared based on the needs of the company. Such reports are often prepared as a by-product of the processing required to send customers their statements.

CREDIT Credit department functions include the approval of sales returns and allowances and other adjustments to customer accounts, the review and approval of the aged trial balance to ascertain the creditworthiness of customers, and the initiation of write-off memos (documents) to charge accounts to bad-debt expense. These functions are discussed in what follows.

GENERAL LEDGER   General ledger maintains the accounts receivable control account. Debits and credits are posted to the accounts receivable control account from the journal vouchers and matching control totals that are received from billing and cash receipts. These amounts are reconciled to the control totals sent to the general ledger directly from accounts receivable. This reconciliation is an important transaction cycle control in the accounts receivable business process.

Sales Returns and Allowances

Sales returns and allowances require careful control. Allowances occur when, because of damaged merchandise, shortages in shipments, clerical errors, or the like, the customer and the seller agree to reduce the amount owed by the customer. Generally, the merchandise is retained or destroyed by the customer. The amount of the allowance is negotiated between the customer and the sales order department (or salesperson). The allowance should be reviewed and approved by an independent party (usually the credit department). After an allowance has been authorized and approved, billing issues a **credit memo** to document the reduction to the customer's account.

A sales return occurs when a customer actually returns goods that have been shipped. Full credit is usually granted for the goods returned. As illustrated in Figure 8.9, sales return procedures are initiated by the receiving department. Receiving should undertake an independent count of the goods that are returned by customers in order that these amounts are verified. Once goods are received from the customer and returned to inventory for proper control, receiving forwards a sales return memo or similar document to the credit department. Credit approves the sales return memo and forwards it to billing. The approved sales return memo authorizes billing to issue a credit memo for the return of goods. Note that as described for both returns and allowances, two independent functions approve a transaction, and a third independent function maintains the records.

Write-Off of Accounts Receivable

A separation of functions is essential in a business process to write off accounts receivable. The central feature in a write-off process is an analysis of past-due accounts. This is usually done with an aged trial balance report. A number of techniques are available to attempt to collect past-due accounts. These include dunning procedures such as sending the customer a series of follow-up letters and the use of collection agencies to approach the customer for payment. However, some accounts ultimately are worthless and have to be written off.

 CASE IN POINT

Several executives of Peregrine Systems were indicted in a federal case on charges of wire fraud, bank fraud, falsifying records, securities fraud, and conspiracy to commit securities fraud. As part of their manipulation of accounts receivable, the defendants allegedly caused the write-off of worthless or nonexistent accounts as uncollectible to be misidentified as "acquisition-related expenses" in order that they would not reduce regular operating income.

Figure 8.10 illustrates a separation of functions in a business process to write off accounts receivable. The credit department initiates a write-off by preparing a write-off memo (or similar document) that is approved by the treasurer or some other independent function. Accounts receivable is authorized to write off the account on receipt of the approved write-off memo. A copy of the

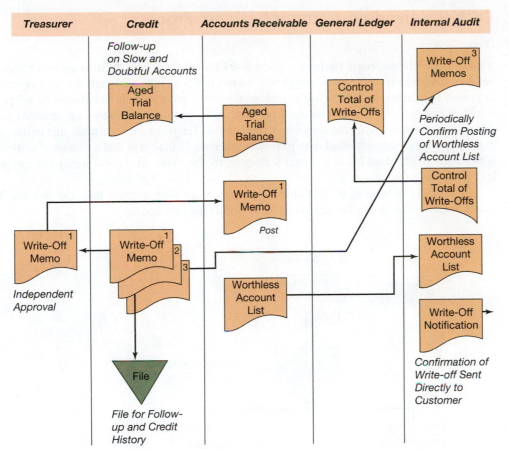

FIGURE 8.10

Write-Off of Accounts Receivable Business Process

approved write-off memo is also sent to an independent third party (internal audit in Figure 8.10) for purposes of record keeping. This is necessary because after the write-off, accounts receivable no longer has an active record of the account. Figure 8.10 details the role of the independent third party. Periodically, a worthless account list that summarizes write-offs is prepared by accounts receivable and forwarded to internal audit for review. Note that internal audit confirms write-offs directly with the customer to ensure that no collections have been made on written-off customer accounts. An employee might intercept a customer's payment on account and then arrange for the account to be written off so that the customer does not continue to be billed for the amount.

Sarbanes–Oxley Compliance: Accounts Receivable Business Process

The SOX requires that companies maintain an adequate internal control structure over the business processes that support financial reporting. The accounts receivable business process generates asset amounts that are significant accounts, disclosures, and assertions on a company's balance sheet and cash flow amounts that are significant accounts, disclosures, and assertions on a company's statement of cash flows. Thus, risk assessment of the accounts receivable business process will be necessary for compliance with SOX. Our discussion of transaction cycle controls over procurement has highlighted fundamental controls that are based on a separation of functions within this business process. Both management and auditors will be concerned with evaluating the existence and functioning of these controls as they are necessary to protect against risk of material misstatements in amounts reported in financial statements. Risk assessment should also evaluate whether the company's controls sufficiently address identified risks of material misstatement due to fraud and controls intended to address the risk of management override of these controls.

Cash-Received-on-Account Business Process

Overview

A cash-received-on-account business process is used when there is an existing customer account balance. Cash received on account typically comes into a business through the mail or is paid in person to a central cashier or cash window. Customer payments should always be acknowledged. Customers should receive receipts and monthly statements showing amounts paid. Acknowledgment of payments is an important control. The recorded receivable that exists prior to the payment enhances control over payments received. In the event that a customer's payment is not acknowledged on his or her next statement, the customer likely will notify the company and inquire as to the reason.

Figure 8.11 is an analytic flowchart of a cash-received-on-account business process. The major feature illustrated is the separation of the following functions.

FIGURE 8.11a

Cash-Received-on-Account Business Process

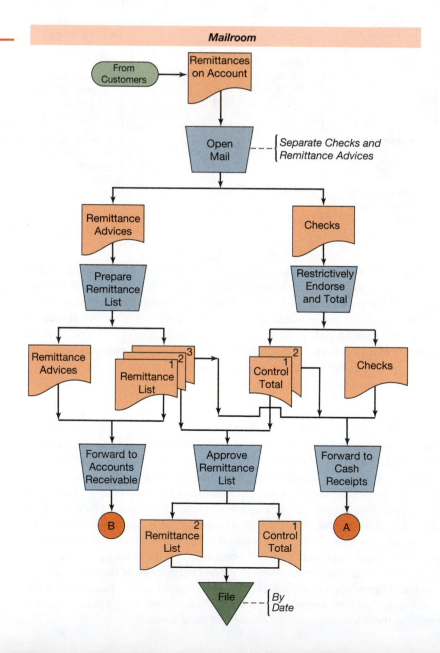

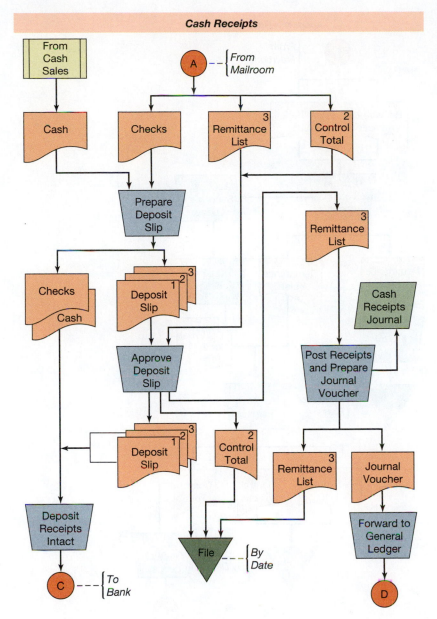

FIGURE 8.11b

Cash-Received-on-Account Business Process (continued)

MAILROOM   Customer remittances on account are received in the mailroom. The mail is opened, and the checks and remittance advices are separated. Checks are restrictively endorsed and totaled. A **remittance list** that documents the payments received is prepared. The remittance list is balanced to the total of the checks received, and the agreement of these amounts is approved. Copies of the remittance list and the remittance advices are forwarded to accounts receivable. The checks and a control total are forwarded to cash receipts for deposit. Copies of the remittance list and the control total are filed by date.

CASH RECEIPTS   Checks received from the mailroom are combined with cash receipts from cash sales (if any), and a deposit slip is prepared. The remittance list and control total received from the mailroom are balanced with the deposit slip, and the agreement of these amounts is approved. The remittance list is then used to post the amount of the payments received from the mailroom into the cash receipts journal. A journal voucher is prepared and forwarded to the

FIGURE 8.11c

Cash-Received-
on-Account Business
Process (continued)

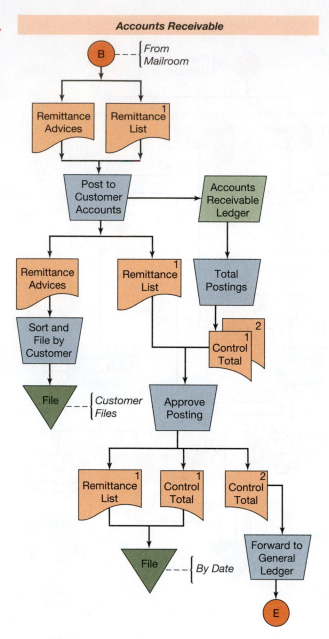

general ledger. The remittance list, control total, and a copy of the deposit slip are filed by date. The deposit is forwarded intact to the bank.

ACCOUNTS RECEIVABLE The remittance advices are posted to the accounts receivable ledger. The postings to the ledger are totaled. The control total is balanced to the remittance list. The agreement of these amounts is approved. The remittance advices are sorted and filed by customer. The remittance list and a copy of the control total of postings are filed by date. A copy of the control total is forwarded to the general ledger.

GENERAL LEDGER The journal voucher from cash receipts and the control total received from accounts receivable are compared. The amounts are then posted to the general ledger. The source of posting to the general ledger is the cashier's journal voucher notification of the amount of deposit of the payments received. This amount must reconcile with the total of items posted to the accounts receivable ledger. The journal voucher and the control total are filed by date.

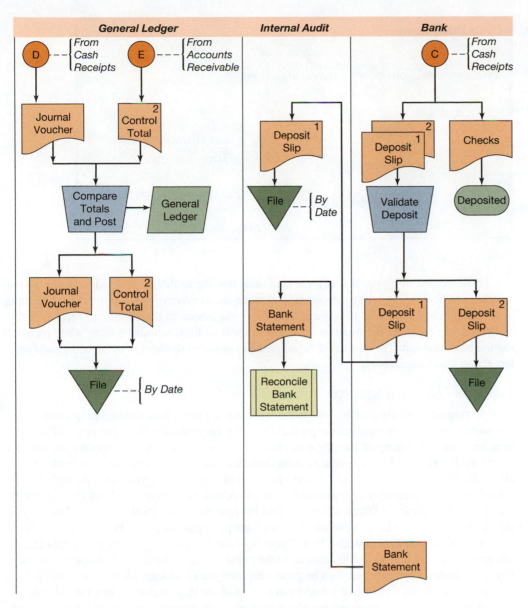

FIGURE 8.11d

Cash-Received-on-Account Business Process (continued)

BANK   The bank accepts the deposit and validates a copy of the deposit slip. The validated copy of the deposit slip is returned to internal audit. The validated deposit slip is filed by date.

INTERNAL AUDIT   Internal audit receives the periodic bank statement. An independent bank reconciliation is an important control in a cash-received-on-account business process.

SUMMARY   To control incoming cash received through the mail, it is important that no one in the mailroom (where the correspondence is opened), in cash receipts (where the money is summarized and a deposit prepared), or in accounts receivable (where the asset reduction is recorded) has complete control over the transaction. Often invoices or statements sent to customers are prepared such that the portion with the name and address of the customer is returned with the payment as a remittance advice. This is common with telephone, utility, and department store invoices and provides good documentation for the payment (Figure 8.12).

FIGURE 8.12

Remittance Advice

Circle Utility Company

NOV 28, 1999   123   _____ _____

PLEASE MAIL THIS ADVICE WITH YOUR PAYMENT
BRING ENTIRE BILL FOR RECEIPT IF PAYING IN PERSON   _____

CUSTOMER NAME

CUSTOMER ADDRESS

CIRCLE UTILITY COMPANY
BOX 1000
ANYWHERE, USA

4025170000005476

MAKE CHECKS PAYABLE TO "CIRCLE UTILITY"

TOTAL AMOUNT DUE   54.76

As illustrated in Figure 8.11(d), the source of posting to the general ledger is the journal voucher notification issued by the cashier indicating the amount of the deposit of cash receipts. This amount must reconcile with the total of the items posted to the subsidiary receivable file. Validated copies of the deposit slip go to the internal auditor, who uses them when reconciling the bank account. The control of actual cash (as opposed to checks) received by mail relies largely on direct supervision.

Lock-Box Collection Systems

In collecting accounts receivable, time is money. Even if a firm cannot persuade its customers to pay their accounts more rapidly, using a **lock-box deposit system** usually can reduce **float**—the time between the signing of the payment check by the customer and the moment the firm has use of the funds. A lock-box system reduces float that usually occurs because the bank does not allow the firm to have use of out-of-state checks until they have been cleared through the customer's bank. This process can take up to a week. A lock-box system reduces float by having the checks deposited to a firm's account before the firm processes them. A firm in Los Angeles might have its eastern U.S. customers forward their payments to a lock box in a post office in New York City and arrange with a New York City bank to pick up these checks; credit them to the firm's account; and advise the firm as to the names of customers, check amounts, and other payment details. Payments can then be processed after the checks are on their way through the clearing process. Savings of lost interest can be considerable, especially when interest rates are high. A bank will usually require a fee plus a compensating deposit—one on which the firm cannot draw—to provide lock-box services. However, the value of net funds freed by float reduction and additional benefits, such as learning of dishonored checks sooner, will generally justify one or more lock-box regional collection systems for a firm whose customers are geographically widespread. An illustrative calculation is shown below assuming average daily collections of $500,000, 7 days' float without a regional lock box, and 2 days' float in a regional lock-box collection system.

Float in central system	$3,500,000
Less: Float in regional system	$1,000,000
Gross funds freed	$2,500,000
Less: Required compensating balance	$500,000
Net funds freed	$2,000,000
Fees and expenses	$150,000

Cost of net funds freed = $150,000/$2,000,000 = 7.5%

Cash-Sales Business Process

The significant difference between a cash-sales business process and a cash-received-on-account business process is that there is no previous asset record (customer account balance) in a cash-sales business process. The generation of initial documentation of cash sales is thus the focal point of the control system. Once a record has been prepared, cash sales are subject to accounting control.

Cash sales are recorded in a cash register or other secure device to provide documentation. Sales receipts are prepared and issued to customers. Several techniques and devices are useful in establishing an initial record. **Customer audit** is a general term used to describe procedures in which the customer acts as a control over the initial documentation of a transaction. Pricing items at 99 cents rather than $1.00 is a customer audit technique as well as a marketing technique. This pricing forces the recording of a sale because the customer generally expects change. Techniques relating to sales invoices, such as awarding a customer a free gallon of ice cream if his or her receipt has a red star or other symbol, are intended to have the customer audit the recording of the sale. The possibility of receiving a prize increases the customer's interest in the invoice. Many cash registers sound a bell or buzzer when opened; it is hoped that the customer's attention is drawn to the amount actually being rung on the register. Sending monthly statements of accounts (to have the customer audit her or his own account) and providing customers with remittance advices (which they should return with their payments) are common examples of customer audit techniques.

CASE IN POINT

Mystery shopping services use professional shoppers to offer their clients a method of measuring customer satisfaction and employee performance. Professional shoppers visit stores or sales locations to engage in actual transactions based on a firm's marketing goals and operating standards and may focus on auditing operations to ensure that clients have consistent operational practice throughout their locations.

Supervision involves having someone observe the work performance of others. Direct supervision over clerical work is common, such as in a mailroom where cash receipts are opened. Supervision techniques include the use of **professional shoppers**, people hired to purchase goods in a retail environment for the specific purpose of observing the recording of transactions. Professional shopping services, also known as mystery shopping services, are also used as a method of measuring customer satisfaction and employee performance. Supervision also includes the use of test packages. For example, a precounted amount of cash may be given to a teller or cash counter (with or without that person's knowledge) to ascertain the validity or error rate of the person's work.

Imprest techniques are used to control cash receipts in the same manner (but usually with less accuracy) that they are used to control petty cash disbursements. A clerk is given a precounted number of tickets and must account either for their retail value or for the tickets themselves. Retail jobbers must account for the retail value of goods in their possession. Inventory control over sales that is applied through use of the gross profit method or retail sales analysis method of estimating inventory level is essentially an imprest technique. Although such controls cannot be effective enough to remove possibilities of manipulation completely, they can limit the size of potential defalcations.

Summary

The sales business process includes the following activities: inquiry, contract creation, order entry, shipping, and billing. SAP ERP systems are capable of storing and processing a vast amount of information pertaining to the sales business process. The chapter provided an overview of the data that are stored and processed in the sales business process by SAP ERP. Transaction cycle controls over the sales business process include a separation of the following functions: sales order processing, credit authorizations, custody of finished goods, shipping, billing, accounts receivable, and the general ledger.

The customer account management business process includes accounts receivable processing through the collection of customer payments on account. Transaction cycle controls include a separation of the following functions: cash receipts, credit authorizations, billing, accounts receivable, and the general ledger. Procedures that handle sales returns and allowances and procedures used to write off accounts receivable require careful design and control. The chapter included a brief discussion of the cash-sales business process because it is often integrated with the process for the collection of customer payments on account.

Glossary

aged trial balance   a report that classifies outstanding customer account balances as to how long a time period the amounts have been due.

balance-forward processing   a customer's remittances are applied against a customer's outstanding balance rather than against individual invoices.

bill of lading   the invoice received from a carrier for shipments.

blanket order   a single order that calls for several shipments to the same customer over a specific time period.

credit memo   a form used to document reductions to a customer's account due to sales returns or sales allowances.

customer audit   procedure in which the customer acts as a control over the initial documentation of a transaction.

cycle billing plan   the processing of accounts receivable is subdivided by alphabet or account number in order to distribute the preparation of statements over the working days of the month.

factoring   the selling of accounts receivable at a discount to a collection agency.

float   the time between the signing of the payment check by the customer and the moment the firm has use of the funds.

goods issue notice   documentation that is forwarded to the billing function to evidence a shipment to a customer.

imprest techniques   a control technique in which an item is held account to a specified total amount.

inquiry   A document similar to a quotation that does not contain delivery information.

invoice   the document that informs a customer of charges for goods or services rendered.

lock-box deposit system   customer remittances are sent directly to a bank and are credited to a company's account before they are posted to customer accounts.

open-item processing   a customer's remittances are applied against individual invoices rather than against the customer's outstanding balance.

professional shoppers   people hired to purchase goods in a retail environment for the specific purpose of observing the recording of transactions.

quotation   a document sent to a potential customer to inform him or her of product prices, product availability, and delivery information.

remittance list   a listing of customer remittances that is prepared for control purposes.

sales order   a document prepared to initiate the shipment of goods to a customer.

shipping advice   synonym for goods issue notice.

Webliography

www.bolero.net
The home page of Bolero. Bolero was founded with significant financial backing from the global banking and logistics industries. Bolero's Trusted Trading Platform supports electronic trading between buyers, sellers, and their logistics service and bank partners. Together, the Bolero Trusted Trading Platform, the Open Account Suite, and the Bolero Documentary Credit Suite provide an electronic solution to integrate the physical and financial supply chains.

www.salesforce.com
The home page of salesforce.com. Salesforce.com is a pioneer vendor in the SaaS (Software as a Service) delivery of CRM.

www.sap.com
Home page of SAP, a major vendor of ERP software.

Chapter Quiz

Answers to the chapter quiz appear on page 304.

1. Which of the following documents is used to post sales on account to customers in the accounts receivable ledger?
   a. purchase orders
   b. invoices
   c. remittance advices
   d. bills of lading

2. Which of the following departments should match shipping documents with open sales orders and prepare daily sales summaries?
   a. billing
   b. sales order
   c. accounts receivable
   d. shipping

3. The invoice is completed when (_____).
   a. payment is received from the customer
   b. the goods have been shipped
   c. the sales order is approved by the credit department
   d. the customer has acknowledged receipt of the shipment

4. The billing function normally should report to which of the following?
   a. controller
   b. treasurer
   c. director of internal auditing
   d. vice-president of sales

5. Which of the following departments normally should be responsible for the preparation and journalizing of credit memos on the receipt of approved sales return memos to authorize a reduction in customer account balances because of returned goods?
   a. receiving
   b. accounts receivable

   c. credit
   d. billing

6. Which of the following steps in the sales business process is optional?
   a. contract creation
   b. order entry
   c. shipping
   d. billing

7. Pricing usually occurs during which step in the sales business process?
   a. contract creation
   b. order entry
   c. shipping
   d. billing

8. What has to exist before a sales order can be created in SAP ERP?
   a. an invoice
   b. a delivery document
   c. a customer master record
   d. a vendor master record

9. The remittance list prepared in the mailroom to document cash receipts should be forwarded directly to (_____).
   a. finished goods
   b. billing
   c. accounts receivable
   d. general ledger

10. Cash remittances received in the mailroom should be forwarded directly to (_____).
    a. cash receipts
    b. billing
    c. accounts receivable
    d. general ledger

Review Problem

You are auditing the Alaska branch of Far Distributing Company. This branch has substantial annual sales, which are billed and collected locally. As a part of your audit, you find that the procedures for handling cash receipts are as follows:

Cash collections on over-the-counter sales and COD sales are received from the customer or delivery service by the cashier. On receipt of cash, the cashier stamps the sales ticket "paid" and files a copy for future reference. The only record of COD sales is a copy of the sales ticket, which is given to the cashier to hold until the cash is received from the delivery service.

Mail is opened by the secretary to the credit manager, and remittances are given to the credit manager for his review. The credit manager then places the remittances in a tray on the cashier's desk. At the daily deposit cutoff time, the cashier delivers the checks and cash on hand to the assistant credit manager, who

prepares remittance lists and makes up the bank deposit, which she also takes to the bank. The assistant credit manager also posts remittances to the accounts receivable ledger and verifies the cash discount allowable.

You also ascertain that the credit manager obtains approval from the executive office at Far Distributing, located in Chicago, to write off uncollectible accounts and that he has retained in his custody, as of the end of the fiscal year, some remittances that were received on various days during the last month.

Required

a. Describe the irregularities that might occur under the procedures now in effect for handling cash collections and remittances.

b. Give procedures that you would recommend to strengthen internal control over cash collections and remittances.

(CPA)

Solution to Review Problem

a. 1. The cashier could destroy cash or COD sales tickets and pocket the proceeds if sales tickets are not prenumbered or if accountability is not maintained for all sales ticket numbers.

2. Lapping might occur. This involves the withholding of cash receipts without an entry being made on the books. At a later date, cash is collected and an entry is made for the first cash collected. The latest collection is held and used by the dishonest person. In the situation described, any of the four Alaska employees could lap the collections of accounts receivable.

3. Since the assistant credit manager had been told of doubtful accounts previously written off as uncollectible, she could appropriate cash collections to the extent of the remittances received on accounts previously written off.

4. The credit department personnel could enter discounts not taken by the customer or enter discounts on remittances made after the discount date. Those entries could cover the appropriation of an equivalent amount of cash for personal use.

5. Since no record is made of mail receipts until they have been handled by four people, any of the four could abstract funds without any covering action. On discovery of the theft, there would be no records to identify the thief.

6. The assistant credit manager could cover abstractions of cash by adding or destroying accounts receivable ledger records, by falsifying subsidiary ledger trial balances, by sending statements that differ from the accounts, and so on.

b. The following procedures should be put into effect at the Alaska office to strengthen the internal control over cash receipts.

1. All sales tickets should be prenumbered, and all sales ticket numbers should be accounted for daily. All sales tickets stamped "paid" should be reconciled to the duplicate deposit slip receipted by the bank. This should be done by a responsible employee other than the cashier or a member of the credit department.

2. An employee other than the cashier or a member of the credit department should open the incoming mail and prepare daily a list in triplicate of remittances received that day. The original of the list should accompany the checks (and cash, if any) turned over directly to the cashier; one copy of the list of remittances should be routed to the responsible employee mentioned in Number 1 above; one copy should be routed to the person responsible for posting to the accounts receivable ledger.

3. The responsible employee who received the copy of the list of remittances should compare the remittances shown thereon with the duplicate deposit ticket at the same time the cash-sales tickets are reconciled to the deposit ticket. Any checks or cash not deposited the day received should be investigated.

4. Different forms (or colors) of sales tickets for cash, COD, and credit sales would facilitate the daily accounting for sales tickets used.

5. The cashier, who should have no duties connected with accounts receivable, should prepare bank deposits and forward the deposits to the bank. A responsible employee other than the cashier or a member of the credit department should establish agreement of the list of remittances and daily collections with the daily deposit ticket.

6. Remittances should not be held; those for each day or for each batch of mail, whichever is more practical, should be deposited intact. The credit department may make whatever record it needs for further follow-up on the remittances that are not in the correct amount.

7. The duty of posting remittances to the accounts receivable ledger may be left with the credit department. This operation normally should be performed subsequent to the receipt and control of cash; therefore, internal control over cash will not be weakened if credit department personnel perform the posting duty, provided they have no access to the cash represented by the remittance advices.

Review Questions

1. Identify the steps in the sales business process.
2. Identify several activities that usually occur during order entry.
3. Identify several documents that might be prepared during shipping activities.
4. List the four types of master records that are used in SAP ERP.
5. Describe some of the specifications that can be edited in the Create Customer: Output Screen section of the customer master record in SAP ERP.
6. What has to exist before a sales order can be created in SAP ERP?
7. Describe some of the basic database features available in SAP ERP for processing information pertaining to the sales business process.
8. Distinguish between the billing and accounts receivable functions in a sales order procedure.
9. What accounting journal entry or entries summarize the activities of a sales order procedure?
10. When is it desirable to use an acknowledgment copy of a sales order?
11. How does the use of a master price list enhance control of the billing function?
12. What should be verified prior to the shipment of goods to customers?
13. What is cycle billing?
14. State two advantages of using cycle billing.
15. What is a dunning procedure?

16. What functions are served by periodic statements of account that are sent to customers?
17. Distinguish between open-item processing and balance-forward processing of accounts receivable.
18. Outline the major features of internal control in a sales return and allowance business process.
19. Why should write-offs of receivables be confirmed with the customer?
20. Identify the basic objective in a cash receipts business process.
21. What is the most critical phase of a cash receipts business process? Identify several controls that may be used to control this phase.
22. What is a remittance advice? What function do remittance advices play in a cash receipts business process?
23. Identify the major features of control in a cash receipts business process.
24. What is the potential advantage of using a lock-box collection system for customer remittances?
25. What is a professional shopper?

Discussion Questions and Problems

26. The internal auditor is reviewing shipping procedures of a manufacturing company. The auditor should be greatly concerned when
    a. merchandise is shipped without an approved customer's order.
    b. invoiced prices on merchandise are not checked before orders are shipped.
    c. the sales department is not notified promptly when merchandise is shipped.
    d. only one quotation on transportation costs is obtained.
    e. transportation tariffs are not checked before merchandise is shipped.

    (*IIA*)

27. Which of the following is an effective internal accounting control over accounts receivable?
    a. Only people who handle cash receipts should be responsible for preparing documents that reduce accounts receivable balances.
    b. Responsibility for approval of the write-off of uncollectible accounts receivable should be assigned to the cashier.
    c. Balances in the subsidiary accounts receivable ledger should be reconciled to the general ledger control account once a year, preferably at year end.
    d. The billing function should be assigned to people other than those responsible for maintaining accounts receivable subsidiary records.

    (*CPA*)

28. Which of the following would be the *best* protection for a company that wishes to prevent the lapping of trade accounts receivable?
    a. Segregate duties so that the bookkeeper in charge of the general ledger has *no* access to incoming mail.
    b. Segregate duties so that *no* employee has access to both checks from customers and currency from daily cash receipts.
    c. Have customers send payments directly to the company's depository bank.
    d. Request that customers' payment checks be made payable to the company and addressed to the treasurer.

    (*CPA*)

29. To determine whether the system of internal accounting control operated effectively to minimize errors of failure to invoice a shipment, the auditor would select a sample of transactions from the population represented by the
    a. customer order file.
    b. bill of lading file.
    c. open invoice file.
    d. sales invoice file.

    (*CPA*)

30. For effective internal accounting control, employees maintaining the accounts receivable subsidiary ledger should *not* also approve
    a. employee overtime wages.
    b. credit granted to customers.
    c. write-offs of customer accounts.
    d. cash disbursements.

    (*CPA*)

31. Which of the following control procedures may prevent the failure to bill customers for some shipments?
    a. Each shipment should be supported by a prenumbered sales invoice that is accounted for.
    b. Each sales order should be approved by authorized personnel.
    c. Sales journal entries should be reconciled to daily sales summaries.
    d. Each sales invoice should be supported by a shipping document.

    (*CPA*)

32. To achieve good internal accounting control, which department should perform the activities of matching shipping documents with sales orders and preparing daily sales summaries?
    a. billing.
    b. shipping.
    c. credit.
    d. sales order.

    (*CPA*)

33. Shipping documents should be compared with sales records or invoices to
    a. determine whether payments are applied properly to customer accounts.

b. ensure that shipments are billed to customers.

c. determine whether unit prices billed are in accordance with sales contracts.

d. ascertain whether all sales are supported by shipping documents.

(IIA)

34. As payments are received, one mailroom employee is assigned the responsibility of prelisting receipts and preparing the deposit slip prior to forwarding the receipts, deposit slip, and remittance advices to accounts receivable for posting. Accounts receivable personnel refoot the deposit slip, stamp a restrictive endorsement on the back of each check, and then forward the receipts and deposit slip to the treasury department. Evaluate the internal control of the described process. Which of the following is a reasonable assessment of internal control in this process?

a. Adequate internal control.

b. Inadequate internal control because mailroom employees should *not* have access to cash.

c. Inadequate internal control because treasury employees should prepare the deposit slip.

d. Inadequate internal control because of a lack of segregation of duties.

(IIA)

35. Which of the following internal control procedures will *most likely* prevent the concealment of a cash shortage resulting from the improper write-off of a trade account receivable?

a. Write-offs must be approved by a responsible officer after review of credit department recommendations and supporting evidence.

b. Write-offs must be supported by an aging schedule showing that only receivables overdue several months have been written off.

c. Write-offs must be approved by the cashier who is in a position to know if the receivables have, in fact, been collected.

d. Write-offs must be authorized by company field sales employees who are in a position to determine the financial standing of the customers.

(CPA)

36. For the purpose of proper accounting control, postdated checks remitted by customers should be

a. restrictively endorsed.

b. returned to the customer.

c. recorded as a cash sale.

d. placed in the joint custody of two officers.

(CPA)

37. A company policy should clearly indicate that defective merchandise returned by customers is to be delivered to the

a. sales clerk.

b. receiving clerk.

c. inventory control clerk.

d. accounts receivable clerk.

(CPA)

38. To conceal defalcations involving receivables, the auditor would expect an experienced bookkeeper to charge which of the following accounts?

a. miscellaneous income.

b. petty cash.

c. miscellaneous expense.

d. sales returns.

(CPA)

39. The most likely result of ineffective internal control policies and procedures in the revenue cycle is that

a. irregularities in recording transactions in the subsidiary accounts could result in a delay in goods shipped.

b. omission of shipping documents could go undetected, causing an understatement of inventory.

c. final authorization of credit memos by personnel in the sales department could permit an employee defalcation scheme.

d. fictitious transactions could be recorded, causing an understatement of revenues and overstatement of receivables.

(CPA)

40. Proper authorization procedures in the revenue cycle usually provide for the approval of bad-debt write-offs by an employee in which of the following departments?

a. treasurer.

b. sales.

c. billing.

d. accounts receivable.

(CPA)

41. Tracing bills of lading to sales invoices provides evidence that

a. shipments to customers were invoiced.

b. shipments to customers were recorded as sales.

c. recorded sales were shipped.

d. invoiced sales were shipped.

(CPA)

42. A sales clerk at Schackne Company correctly prepared a sales invoice for $5,200, but the invoice was entered as $2,500 in the sales journal and similarly posted to the general ledger and accounts receivable ledger. The customer remitted only $2,500, the amount on his or her monthly statement. The most effective procedure for preventing this type of error is to

a. use predetermined totals to control posting routines.

b. have an independent check of sales invoice serial numbers, prices, discounts, extensions, and footings.

c. have the bookkeeper prepare monthly statements that are verified and mailed by a responsible person other than the bookkeeper.

d. have a responsible person, who is independent of the accounts receivable department, promptly investigate unauthorized remittance deductions made by customers or other matters in dispute.

(CPA)

43. For good internal control, the billing department should be under the direction of the

a. controller.

b. credit manager.

c. sales manager.

d. treasurer.

(CPA)

44. Which of the following controls *most likely* would be effective in offsetting the tendency of sales personnel to maximize sales volume at the expense of high bad-debt write-offs?

a. Employees responsible for authorizing sales and bad-debt write-offs are denied access to cash.

b. Shipping documents and sales invoices are matched by an employee who does *not* have authority to write off bad debts.

c. Employees involved in the credit-granting function are separated from the sales function.

d. Subsidiary accounts receivable records are reconciled to the control account by an employee independent of the authorization of credit.

(CPA)

45. Which of the following controls *most likely* would help ensure that all credit sales transactions of an entity are recorded?

a. The billing department supervisor sends copies of approved sales orders to the credit department for comparison with authorized credit limits and current customer account balances.

b. The accounting department supervisor independently reconciles the accounts receivable subsidiary ledger with the accounts receivable control account monthly.

c. The accounting department supervisor controls the mailing of monthly statements to customers and investigates any differences reported by customers.

d. The billing department supervisor matches prenumbered shipping documents with entries in the sales journal.

(CPA)

46. An entity with a large volume of customer remittances by mail most likely could reduce the risk of employee misappropriation of cash by using

a. employee fidelity bonds.

b. independently prepared mailroom prelists.

c. daily check summaries.

d. a bank lock-box system.

(CPA)

47. Which of the following would the auditor consider to be an incompatible operation if the cashier receives remittances from the mailroom?

a. The cashier prepares the daily deposit.

b. The cashier makes the daily deposit at a local bank.

c. The cashier posts the receipts to the accounts receivable subsidiary ledger cards.

d. The cashier endorses the checks.

(CPA)

48. The most effective way to prevent an employee from misappropriating cash and then altering the accounting records to conceal the shortage is to

a. perform bank reconciliations on a timely basis.

b. deposit promptly all cash receipts in the company's bank account.

c. prenumber all cash receipts documents.

d. enforce a segregation of duties between employees who have custody of cash receipts and those who account for them.

(IIA)

49. Which of the following is *not* a universal rule for achieving strong internal control over cash?

a. Separate the cash-handling and record-keeping functions.

b. Decentralize the receiving of cash as much as possible.

c. Deposit each day's cash receipts by the end of the day.

d. Have bank reconciliations performed by employees independent with respect to handling cash.

(CPA)

50. Cash receipts from sales on account have been misappropriated. Which of the following acts would conceal this defalcation and be *least likely* to be detected by an auditor?

a. Understating the sales journal.

b. Overstating the accounts receivable control account.

c. Overstating the accounts receivable subsidiary ledger.

d. Understating the cash-receipts journal.

(CPA)

51. Indicate the objective of each of the following controls.

a. Making surprise counts of imprest funds.

b. Having registers read and cleared by internal auditors rather than cashiers.

c. Comparing totals of mail receipts with duplicate bank deposit records (daily).

d. Providing multidrawer cash registers.

e. Offering bonuses to customers for "red stars" or other special symbols on sales tickets.

52. The customer billing and collection functions of the Misty Company, a small paint manufacturer, are attended to by a receptionist, an accounts receivable clerk, and a cashier who also serves as a secretary. The company's paint products are sold to wholesalers and retail stores.

The following describes *all* the procedures performed by the employees of the Misty Company pertaining to customer billings and collections:

a. The mail is opened by the receptionist, who gives the customers' purchase orders to the accounts receivable clerk. Fifteen to twenty orders are received each day. Under instructions to expedite the shipment of orders, the accounts receivable clerk at once prepares a five-copy sales invoice form, which is distributed as follows:

1. Copy 1 is the customer billing copy and is held by the accounts receivable clerk until notice of shipment is received.

2. Copy 2 is the accounts receivable department copy and is held for ultimate posting of the accounts receivable records.

3. Copies 3 and 4 are sent to the shipping department.

4. Copy 5 is sent to the storeroom as authority for release of the goods to the shipping department.

b. After the paint order has been moved from the storeroom to the shipping department, the shipping department prepares the bill of lading and labels the cartons. Sales Invoice Copy 4 is inserted in the carton as a packing slip.

After the trucker has picked up the shipment, the customer's copy of the bill of lading and Copy 3, on which any undershipments are noted, are returned to the accounts receivable clerk. The company does not back order in the event of undershipments; customers are expected to reorder the merchandise. The company's copy of the bill of lading is filed by the shipping department.

c. When Copy 3 and the customer's copy of the bill of lading are received by the accounts receivable clerk, Copies 1 and 2 are completed by numbering them and inserting quantities shipped, unit prices, extensions, discounts, and totals. The accounts receivable clerk then mails Copy 1 and the copy of the bill of lading to the customer. Copies 2 and 3 are stapled together.

d. The individual accounts receivable ledger cards are posted by the accounts receivable clerk using a one-write system, whereby the sales register is prepared as a carbon copy of the postings. Postings are made from Copy 2, which is then filed, along with staple-attached Copy 3, in numerical order. Monthly, the general ledger clerk summarizes the sales register for posting to the general ledger accounts.

e. Since the company is short of cash, the deposit of receipts is also expedited. The receptionist turns over all mail receipts and related correspondence to the accounts receivable clerk, who examines the checks and determines that the accompanying vouchers or correspondence contain enough detail to permit posting of the accounts. The accounts receivable clerk then endorses the checks and gives them to the cashier, who prepares the daily deposit. No currency is received in the mail, and no paint is sold over the counter at the factory.

f. The accounts receivable clerk uses the vouchers or correspondence that accompanied the checks to post the accounts receivable ledger cards. The one-write system prepares a cash receipts register as a carbon copy of the postings. Monthly, the general ledger clerk summarizes the cash receipts register for posting to the general ledger accounts. The accounts receivable clerk also corresponds with customers about unauthorized deductions for discounts, freight or advertising allowances, returns, and so on and prepares the appropriate credit memos. Disputed items of large amounts are turned over to the sales manager for settlement. Each month the accounts receivable clerk prepares a trial balance of the open accounts receivable and compares the resulting total with the general ledger control account for accounts receivable.

Required

a. Prepare a logical data flow diagram of the previous procedures.

b. Discuss the internal control weaknesses in the Misty Company's procedures related to customer billings and remittances and the accounting for these transactions. In your discussion, in addition to identifying the weaknesses, explain what could happen as a result of each weakness.

(CPA)

53. After a shipment is prepared, the shipping department prepares a shipping order form in three copies. The first copy is included with the goods sent to the customer as a packing slip. The second copy is forwarded to the billing department. The third copy is sent to the accountant. When the billing department receives the second copy of the shipping order, it uses the information thereon to prepare a two-part sales invoice. The second copy of the shipping order is then filed in the billing department. The first copy of the sales invoice is sent to the customer. The second copy of the sales invoice is forwarded to the accountant. Periodically, the accountant matches the copy of the shipping order with the copy of the sales invoice and files them alphabetically by customer name. Before doing so, however, the accountant uses the copy of the sales invoice to post the sales entry in the subsidiary accounts receivable ledger.

Required

a. For use in appraising internal control, prepare a flowchart covering the flow of documents reflected in the preceding situation.

b. List those deficiencies and/or omissions revealed by the flowchart that lead you to question the internal control.

(IIA)

54. In a large manufacturing organization supplying goods and services, several departments may be involved in the processing of customer complaints and the issuance of any resulting credit memos. Following is a list of such departments:

a. receiving.
b. sales.
c. production.
d. customer service.
e. accounts receivable.

Required

Explain briefly the control function each of these departments performs when processing complaints and issuing credit memos.

(IIA)

55. The flowchart in Figure 8.13 depicts the activities relating to the shipping, billing, and collecting processes used by Pittsburgh Wood, Inc.

Required

Identify weaknesses in the system of internal accounting control relating to the activities of the

a. warehouse clerk.
b. bookkeeper 1.
c. bookkeeper 2.
d. collection clerk.

(CPA)

56. The Happiness Corporation of Boston is considering using a lock-box system for its customers in California. At present, its credit sales to that area amount to about $21,600,000. Establishing a lock box in San Francisco would enable the company to reduce its collection float from 8 to 2 days. The bank in San Francisco will expect the company to maintain a minimum

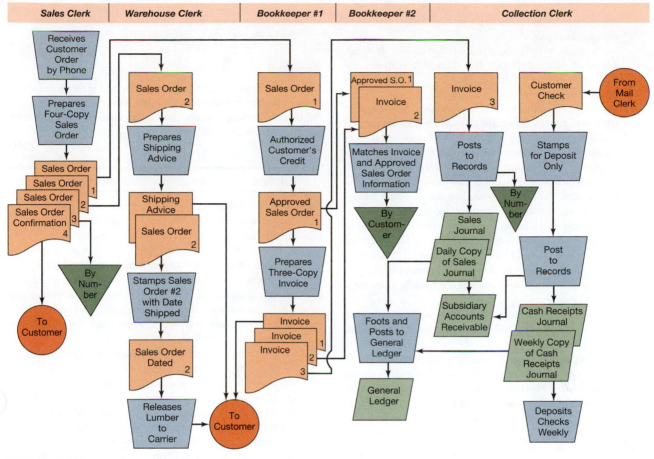

FIGURE 8.13

Flowchart for Problem 55

balance of $70,000. The net additional annual cost of adopting the system will be $1,200. Base calculations on a 360-day year.

   a. What is the net amount of cash that will be freed for use elsewhere in the business?

   b. What is the annual percentage cost of the funds released from the float?

57. Indicate the objective of the following questions taken from an internal control checklist.

   a. Are all disbursements, except petty cash, made by check?

   b. Are bank debit advices (such as NSF checks) delivered directly to a responsible employee (other than the cashier) for investigation?

   c. Is the credit department entirely independent of the sales department?

   d. Does the company record accruals of recurring income from rents, royalties, or other such items in advance of collection?

   e. Are requests for petty cash signed by the person who receives the cash?

58. A new audit client of yours processes its sales and cash receipts documents in the following manner:

   a. *Cash receipts.* The mail is opened each morning by a mail clerk in the sales department. The mail clerk

prepares a remittance advice (showing customer and amount paid) if one is not received. The checks and remittance advices are then forwarded to the sales department supervisor, who reviews each check and forwards the checks and remittance advices to the accounting department supervisor. The accounting department supervisor, who also functions as the credit manager, reviews all checks for payments of past due accounts and then forwards the checks and remittance advices to the accounts receivable clerk, who arranges the advices in alphabetical order. The remittance advices are posted directly to the accounts receivable ledger. The checks are endorsed by stamp and totaled. The total is posted to the cash receipts journal. The remittance advices are filed chronologically.

After receiving the cash from the preceding day's cash sales, the accounts receivable clerk prepares the daily deposit slip in triplicate. The third copy of the deposit slip is filed by date, and the second copy and the original accompany the bank deposit.

   b. *Sales.* Salesclerks prepare the sales invoices in triplicate. The original and the second copy are presented to the cashier. The third copy is retained by the salesclerk in the sales book. When the sale is for cash, the customer pays the salesclerk, who presents the money to the cashier with the invoice copies.

A credit sale is approved by the cashier from an approved credit list after the salesclerk prepares the three-part invoice. After receiving the cash or approved invoice, the cashier validates the original copy of the sales invoice and gives it to the customer. At the end of each day, the cashier recaps the sales and cash received and forwards the cash and the second copy of all sales invoices to the accounts receivable clerk. The accounts receivable clerk balances the cash received with cash sales invoices and prepares a daily sales summary. The credit sales invoices are posted to the accounts receivable ledger, and then all invoices are sent to the inventory control clerk in the sales department for posting to the inventory control ledger. After posting, the inventory control clerk files all invoices numerically. The accounts receivable clerk posts the daily sales summary to the cash receipts journal and sales journal and files the sales summaries by date.

The cash from cash sales is combined with the cash received on account, and this constitutes the daily bank deposit.

c. *Bank deposits.* The bank validates the deposit slip and returns the second copy to the accounting department, where it is filed by date by the accounts receivable clerk.

Monthly, bank statements are reconciled promptly by the accounting department supervisor and filed by date.

Required

a. Draw a flowchart for the sales and cash receipts application of your client.
b. Identify potential internal control weaknesses in the client's procedures.

(CPA)

59. The town of Bellevue operates a private parking lot near the railroad station for the benefit of town residents. The guard on duty issues annual prenumbered parking stickers to residents who submit an application form and show evidence of residency. The sticker is affixed to the auto and allows the resident to park anywhere in the lot for 12 hours if four quarters are placed in the parking meter. Applications are maintained in the guard office at the lot. The guard checks to see that only residents are using the lot and that no resident has parked without paying the required meter fee.

Once a week the guard on duty, who has a master key for all meters, takes the coins from the meters and places them in a locked steel box. The guard delivers the box to the town storage building, where it is opened and the coins manually counted by a storage department clerk who records the total cash counted on a weekly cash report. This report is sent to the town accounting department. The storage department clerk puts the cash in a safe, and on the following day, the cash is picked up by the town's treasurer, who manually recounts the cash, prepares the bank deposit slip, and delivers

the deposit to the bank. The deposit slip, authenticated by the bank teller, is sent to the accounting department, where it is filed with the weekly cash report.

Required

Describe weaknesses in the existing system, and recommend one or more improvements for each of the weaknesses to strengthen the internal control over the parking lot cash receipts. Organize your answer sheet as follows:

(CPA)

Weakness	Recommended Improvement

60. The Quill Electric Company has recently installed a new computer system that has online, real-time capability. Terminals are used for data entry and inquiry. A new cash receipts and accounts receivable file maintenance system has been designed and implemented for use with this new equipment. All programs have been written and tested, and the new system is being run in parallel with the old system. After 2 weeks of parallel operation, no differences have been observed between the two systems other than data-entry errors on the old system.

Al Brand, data processing manager, is enthusiastic about the new equipment and system. He reveals that the system was designed, coded, compiled, debugged, and tested by programmers using an online terminal installed specifically for around-the-clock use by the programming staff; he claimed that this access to the computer saved one-third in programming elapsed time. All files, including accounts receivable, are online at all times as the firm moves toward a full database mode. All programs, new and old, are available at all times for recall into memory for scheduled operating use or for program maintenance. Program documentation and actual tests confirm that data-entry edits in the new system include all conventional data error and validity checks appropriate to the system.

Inquiries have confirmed that the new system conforms precisely to the flowcharts. A turnaround copy of the invoice is used as a remittance advice by 99% of the customers; if the remittance advice is missing, the cashier applies the payment to a selected invoice. Sales terms are net 60 days, but payment patterns are sporadic. Statements are not mailed to customers. Late payments are commonplace and are not pursued vigorously. The company does not have a bad-debt problem because bad-debt losses average only 0.5% of sales.

Before authorizing the termination of the old system, Cal Darden, controller, has requested a review of the internal control features that have been designed for the new system. Security against unauthorized access and fraudulent actions, assurance of the integrity of the files, and protection of the firm's assets should be provided by the internal controls.

Required

a. Describe how fraud by lapping of accounts receivable could be committed in the new system, and discuss how it could be prevented.

b. Based on the description of the new system and the systems flowchart that has been presented in Figure 8.14,
  1. Describe any other defects that exist in the system.
  2. Suggest how each defect you identified could be corrected.

(CMA)

61. The flowchart in Figure 8.15 depicts part of a client's revenue cycle. Some of the flowchart symbols are labeled to indicate control procedures and records. For each symbol numbered 1 through 13, select one response from the answer lists below. Each response in the lists may be selected once or not at all.

Answer Lists

Operations and control procedures
a. Enter shipping data.
b. Verify agreement of sales order and shipping document.
c. Write off accounts receivable.
d. Send to warehouse and shipping department.
e. Authorize account receivable write-off.
f. Prepare aged trial balance.
g. Submit to sales department.
h. Release goods for shipment.
i. Submit to accounts receivable department.
j. Enter price data.
k. Determine that customer exists.
l. Match customer purchase order with sales order.
m. Perform customer credit check.
n. Prepare sales journal.
o. Prepare sales invoice.

Documents, journals, ledgers, and files
p. Shipping document
q. General ledger master file
r. General journal
s. Master price list
t. Sales journal
u. Sales invoice
v. Cash receipts journal
w. Uncollectible accounts file
x. Shipping file
y. Aged trial balance
z. Open order file

62. SAP ERP systems are designed to accommodate companies that conduct business internationally. International transactions are more complex than domestic transactions because a foreign currency and perhaps other factors are involved.

Consider the discussion of the SAP software for the sales business process in the text. Identify several order input data and/or customer master file fields that are necessary for international business transactions.

63. The process of creating customer master records in SAP ERP is complex but results in information that is useful in the sales business process. However, the process of creating customer master records is not practical for one-time or infrequent customers. How does SAP ERP accommodate the processing of sales to one-time or infrequent customers?

64. Figure 8.16 is an analytic flowchart of order-entry system.

Required

Match the following list of 10 items to the labels Q1 through Q10 that appear in the figure. Note that customer order is listed twice and is used for two of the 10 items.

  1. Master price list.
  2. Invoice.
  3. Approve credit.
  4. Customer order.
  5. Customer order.
  6. Prepare sales order.
  7. Credit files.
  8. Sales order.
  9. Bill of lading.
  10. File.

65. Match the following list of items to the letters A through F in Figure 8.17.

  1. Create Order.
  2. Master Price List.
  3. Customer Order.
  4. Order Database.
  5. Sales Order.
  6. Enter Order.

66. Excel® Assignment: Sales Projection Totals
A company has prepared a spreadsheet that contains 3 years of sales projections for its four sales groups: electronics, computers, appliances, and furniture. Several rows of this spreadsheet are illustrated.

Sales Projections by Group/Category

Group	Category	2012 (in dollars)	2013 (in dollars)	2014 (in dollars)
Electronics	Televisions	1,750,000	2,500,000	3,250,000
Computers	Laptop	1,500,000	2,100,000	2,850,000
Appliances	Kitchen	1,450,000	1,880,000	2,005,000
Furniture	Family Room	1,230,000	1,500,000	1,700,000

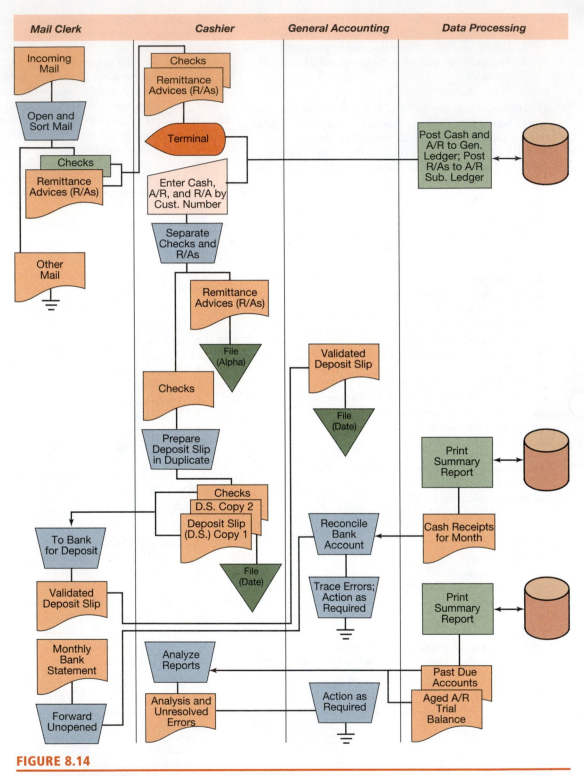

FIGURE 8.14

Flowchart for Problem 60

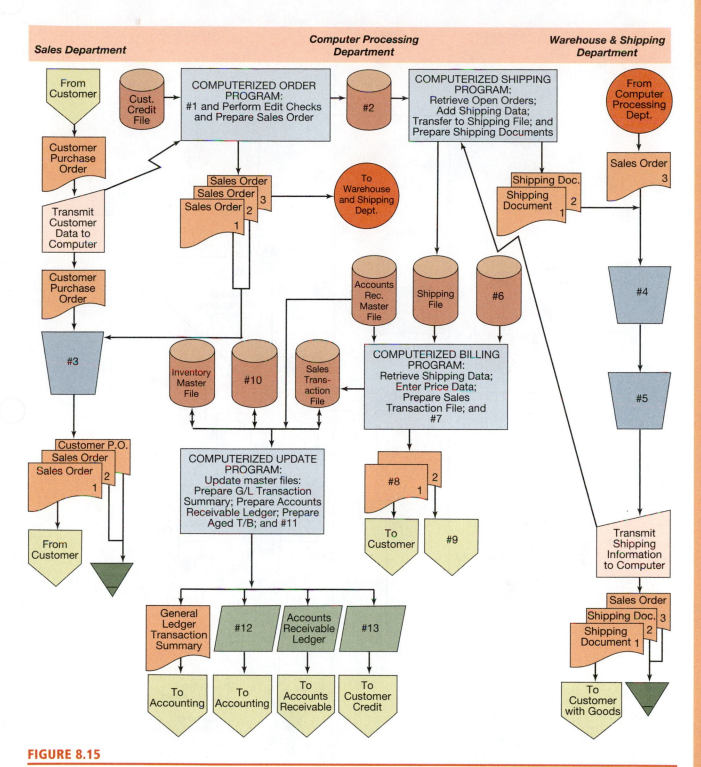

FIGURE 8.15

Flowchart for Problem 61

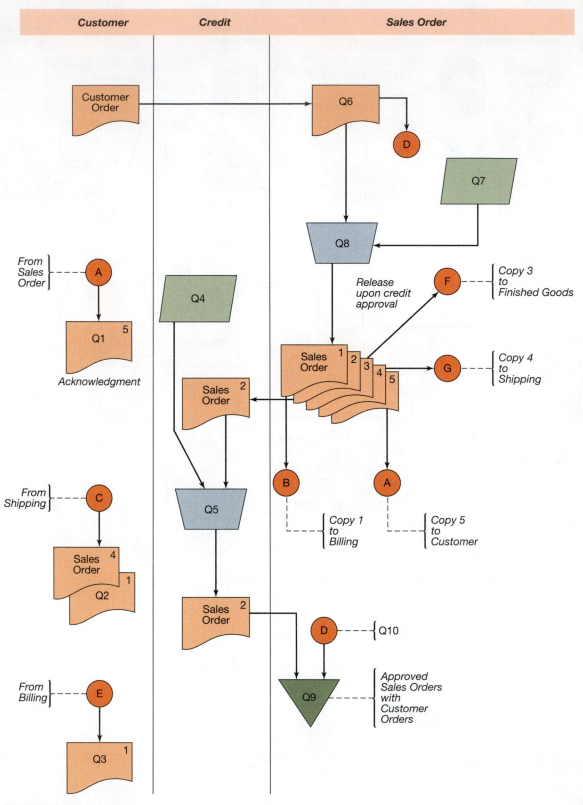

FIGURE 8.16

Flowchart for Problem 64

Order Entry

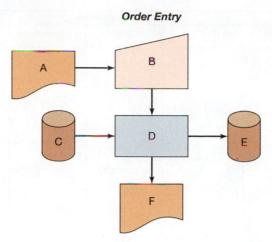

FIGURE 8.17

Flowchart for
Problem 65

Required

Download the spreadsheet file titled "chapter_8_66" from the textbook Web site and prepare a summary analysis of these projections by group for the 3 years in the following format:

Group	Sales Projections by Group			
	2012	2013	2014	3 Year Total
Appliances				
Computers				
Electronics				
Furniture				
Totals by Year				

This task can best be accomplished by using the SUMIF function.

67. Figure 8.18 is a portion of a business process diagram for an order-entry system.

Required

Match the following list of 9 items to the labels A through I that appear in the figure.

1. Pull Goods.
2. Verify credit.
3. Shipping report.
4. Customer purchase order.
5. Notify customer.
6. Approved sales order.
7. Package goods.
8. Receive order.
9. Ship goods.

68. Brian Wolf, controller for the Stiller division of International Amalgamated Incorporated, met with his new financial officer, Fred Gregory, to review the division's financial condition and to consider plans for the future. Brian stressed that it had been a good year. Sales had reached $210 million, slightly in excess of the division's goal of $200 million. Fred acknowledged this fine performance, but indicated that he was concerned about the future and that he desired to have more control over his reported sales and profits. He suggested several ways this could be achieved. He told Brian that when the division was having a good quarter he wanted to meet the assigned sales goals and then be very conservative in the accounting so as to have a good start on making the goals for the next period.

For example, if the division was near its quarterly target, a shipping moratorium could be declared for the last week or two of the quarter to shift some sales to the next quarter. These shipments could be sent to customers if absolutely necessary, but the paperwork could be delayed so that posting these shipments would not be recorded as sales until the next quarter. Fred told Brian that he should meet with Jim Ford of Sales to brainstorm for more ideas. He also told Brian that any discussions should be discreet. Even though none of this was illegal, he did not want to cause waves at the corporate headquarters.

Required

Should Brian have any ethical concerns after his meeting with Fred Gregory?

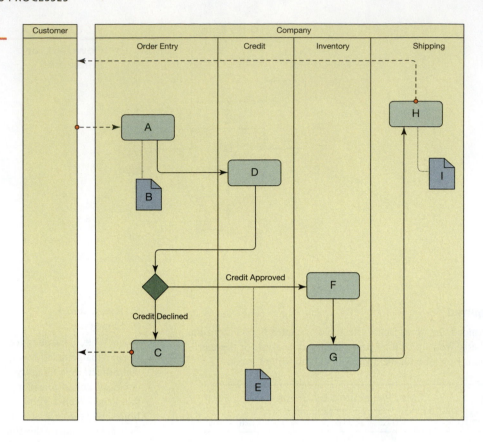

FIGURE 8.18

Business Process
Diagram for
Problem 67

Web Research Assignments

69. You are the controller for a growing national retail merchandise stores. You have begun to purchase large lots of goods directly from China, and several new suppliers are insisting that you point them to a registry where they can find your Collaboration Protocol Profile. You don't know much about these things, but you've heard that they have something to do with ebXML.

Required

Write a report to your CFO explaining what your suppliers are talking about, and what your company needs to know in order to do business with them.

70. You are a new hire for a small CPA firm. A client has asked you to explain some things about cash collections and the financial supply chain.

Required

Write a memo to your client that accomplishes the following:
1. Explains the financial supply chain.
2. Explains how the financial supply chain relates to cash collections.

3. Explains how ERP products like SAP help manage the financial supply chain.

71. You are the controller for a small manufacturing company that supplies small electronic parts to large manufacturers. Your company assembles many of its products from parts that it purchases from various large electronic manufacturers and suppliers.

At present, your company is using Intuit's Quick-Books™ accounting system. So far, you have been fairly happy with the system, but more recently, you have become interested in participating in new ebXML networks with your customers and suppliers. You hope that it will not only bring your company new business but also help you manage your supply chain.

Required

Write a memo to your CEO that covers the following topics:
1. The feasibility of integrating supply chain management software into your QuickBooks™ environment
2. Your ability to set up ebXML with QuickBooks™

Answers to Chapter Quiz

1. b   **2.** a   **3.** b   **4.** a   **5.** d   **6.** a   **7.** b   **8.** c   **9.** c   **10.** a

Procurement and Human Resource Business Processes

Learning Objectives

Careful study of this chapter will enable you to:

- Describe the procurement business process.
- Illustrate controls that apply to procurement.
- Describe the cash disbursements business process.
- Describe the human resource business process.
- Illustrate controls that apply to payroll processing.

The Procurement Business Process

Overview

Procurement is the business process of selecting a source, ordering, and acquiring goods or services. The goods or services might be obtained internally if the goods are produced by another entity in the company. *Purchasing* is a synonym for procurement.

The general steps in the procurement process are (Figure 9.1)

- Requirement determination
- Selection of source
- Request for quotation
- Selection of a vendor
- Issuing of a purchase order
- Receipt of the goods
- Invoice verification
- Vendor payment

Enterprise resource planning (ERP) systems are capable of storing and processing a vast amount of information pertaining to the procurement business process. This section provides an overview of the data that are stored and processed in the procurement process by SAP ERP.[1]

SAP ERP supports procurement in its materials management module. SAP ERP provides an online, fully integrated system for the creation and exchange of the documents that are required in the procurement business process. The fully integrated nature of the system reduces errors and speeds the business process.

Documents in SAP ERP are online documents; they are created online and may be processed entirely as electronic documents. They may also be printed and

---

[1] SAP ERP is a registered trademark of SAP Aktiengesellschaft, Systems, Applications, and Products in Data Processing, Neurottstrasse 16, 69190 Walldorf, Germany (www.sap.com).

FIGURE 9.1

Procurement
Business Process

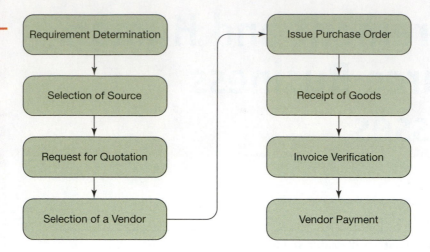

exchanged manually. Procurement documents that are available in SAP ERP include the following:

- Purchase requisition
- Request for quotation
- Quotation
- Purchase order
- Outline agreements
- Contracts
- Scheduling agreements
- Purchasing information records

Each of these documents will be discussed as they enter into the procurement process. In addition to the above-mentioned documents, there are other documents that are used in invoice verification and goods receipt. Each document type is not used every time an item is purchased.

All procurement documents are assigned a document type code. This code determines the fields that are displayed on video screens and controls the range of unique numbers that are assigned to particular document types. Each document has a header area and an item (detail) area. The header area contains information relevant to the entire document, such as vendor number. The item area specifies the details of the individual items in the document, such as the product numbers of items to be ordered. Each new document that is created must be assigned a unique number. The number is an alphanumeric code. Usually this number is assigned automatically by SAP ERP, but document numbers can be entered externally. Most documents can usually be prepared by referencing an existing document. SAP ERP can copy all relevant information from the existing document, thus speeding the process of creating the document and reducing error.

 CASE IN POINT

"Of all government activities, public procurement is most vulnerable to corruption."
    Excerpt from *"Integrity in Public Procurement; Good practice from A to Z,"* published by the Directorate for Public Governance and Territorial Development, Organization for Economic Co-Operation and Development (www.oecd.org).

Requirement Determination

A **purchase requisition** is an internal document created to request the procurement of something so that it is available at a certain point in time. Purchase requisitions can be prepared manually.

They might also be issued automatically by the materials requirements planning (MRP) system. The MRP system can perform sophisticated analyses to determine requirements based on customer demand for an item and the firm's production process. Purchase requisitions have an input field that indicates how they were created, that is, manually or automatically. A requisition tracking number is input when a large number of requisitions are issued for the same requirement. The requisition tracking number enables one to monitor progress of the group of requisitions. Purchase requisitions are processed line by line, so each line is, in effect, a separate requirement.

Once completed, the purchase requisition is forwarded electronically to a supervisor for approval. Approval typically involves determining that the purchase requisition is within cost limits. User profiles maintained in SAP ERP filter purchase requisitions and route them to the correct person for approval. A purchase requisition is an optional step in procurement in SAP ERP.

Selection of Source(s)

The next step in the business process is to assign a source of supply to the purchase requisition. SAP ERP can check whether a contract exists with a vendor to supply an item that is requisitioned. If a contract exists, SAP ERP appropriates the required amount. If there is no contract for an item, then a request for quotation document is prepared.

SAP ERP provides support for the selection process in several ways. SAP ERP monitors outline agreements that exist with vendors. Outline agreements are contracts that specify long-term arrangements with vendors. If quota arrangements for an item have been contracted with vendors, SAP ERP automatically assigns a source of supply to a purchase requisition based on the quotas defined in the contract. SAP ERP maintains records for the vendor, validity period of the contract, and the quota amounts.

SAP ERP maintains lists of approved and disapproved sources of supply. SAP ERP can also select vendors that will be invited to bid on the requisition, basing its recommendations on data that have been saved concerning previous sourcing for the item.

Request for Quotation

After vendors have been selected, SAP ERP is used to generate a **request for quotation** document. A request for quotation is created for high-cost items or services or for items or services for which bids are required as a matter of company policy. It is a document sent to vendors inviting them to confirm a price and payment terms for the supply of a product or service. The request for quotation might be sent as a paper document, as a fax, or electronically as an electronic data interchange (EDI). One can prepare a request for quotation document manually, but usually it can be prepared by referencing the purchase requisition. The request for quotation and the purchase requisition usually contain the same data except for the account assignments that are necessary on the purchase requisition. The request for quotation specifies closing dates for the application and bid-submission guidelines.

The issuing of a request for quotations results in one or more quotation documents being entered into SAP ERP. Potential vendors' quotes for pricing and terms are entered into quotation documents. Quotation documents are used in the selection of a vendor.

 CASE IN POINT

During a 2¹/2-year period, certain employees of the Wake County School Board in Raleigh, North Carolina, allegedly conspired with employees of Barnes Motor & Parts Co., based in Wilson, NC, to divert over $4.8 million through the use of fraudulent invoices in order to receive various kickbacks. Examples of items received included personal items such as automobiles, campers, golf carts, and plasma-screen televisions.

Selection of a Vendor

SAP ERP compares procurement needs with vendors' quotes as they have been recorded in quotation documents and identifies the most suitable quotation for the requisition. SAP ERP sends rejection letters to vendors whose bids were not accepted.

Vendor evaluation often requires expertise or experience. SAP ERP offers an automatic vendor evaluation function to assist an organization in the procurement business process. SAP ERP scores vendors on the basis of 100 points that are assigned on different criteria, such as delivery record on past orders, service, price, quality, and up to 99 user-defined criteria. There are also five system-defined subcriteria for each of the main criteria, and a user can define up to 20 subcriteria. The user can also weight each criterion. SAP ERP can display its vendor analysis sorted by total rank or sorted and ranked by a specific criterion. Quotes can be saved for future reference in purchase information records.

Issuing of a Purchase Order

A **purchase order** document identifies a vendor and confirms goods ordered, quantity, price, delivery date, terms of delivery, and payment terms. A purchase order can be created from scratch or by reference to an existing document. The purchase order can be sent as paper, as a fax, or electronically as an EDI document.

It is common for a company to configure its systems to issue a purchase order automatically for purchase requisitions that meet certain criteria. For example, a system might issue a purchase order automatically for purchase requisitions that do not exceed a specific price or amount.

SAP ERP processes several types of purchase orders. A standard purchase order is issued to order a good or service. A subcontract purchase order is issued when a vendor must receive parts (i.e., subassemblies) to produce an end product that will be delivered to the company. The subcontract purchase order specifies the end product and also the parts that the vendor must acquire. A consignment purchase order is issued for goods held in consignment. A third-party purchase order is issued when goods or services are to be delivered to a third party. Finally, a stock transport purchase order is issued to initiate a good movement between plants in the company.

Outline agreements are long-term arrangements with vendors. Terms and conditions are usually negotiated and maintained separately by each purchasing organization. An outline agreement has a header and items. The header specifies much the same data about terms and conditions as is done in a request for quotation and purchase order. Outline agreements also require specification of the time period to which the conditions apply. There are two types of outline agreements: contracts and scheduling agreements.

A *contract* is an outline agreement in which a vendor provides material for a period of time. A contract does not contain specific delivery dates or quantities. These are specified subsequently in release orders against the contract. A contract is either a value contract or quantity contract. A value contract is used when the total value of release orders is not to exceed a certain amount. A quantity contract is used when the total quantity to be ordered over a period of time is known.

Scheduling agreements are similar to contracts, but they also specify the price of items. A scheduling agreement has line items. A rolling delivery schedule is established for each scheduling agreement line item by creating a number of individual schedule times that are sent to the vendor in a scheduling agreement release document. Delivery dates and quantities are specified. Scheduling agreements reduce paperwork because a single schedule can replace many purchase orders or release orders. This helps reduce inventory because it enables just-in-time (JIT) delivery.

CASE IN POINT

SAP Mobile Procurement, a mySAP™ Mobile Business solution, enables users to enter procurement requests while in the field using handheld devices such as smartphones. Mobile requests are input to mySAP™ Supplier Relationship Management, where requests are then automatically approved or forwarded to a manager for sign-off.

Using SAP ERP, one can also set up a contract and/or a scheduling agreement at the same time that the purchase order is prepared. Because contracts are created in SAP ERP, they can be referenced by SAP ERP when subsequent purchase orders are to be entered. A purchase order that is prepared under an existing contract or scheduling agreement is called a *release order*.

A purchase order can be changed after it has been sent to a vendor. SAP ERP generates a change document that is sent to the vendor, identifying what has changed in the order. One can also cancel purchase orders, delete items, or block purchase orders to prevent receipt of the goods.

Receipt of the Goods

When the vendor makes delivery, a goods-receipt document is prepared in SAP ERP. This type of document is often called a **receiving report**. A goods-receipt document is issued whenever goods are inventoried, regardless of the source. Thus a goods receipt is prepared when an item is delivered from an in-house source as well as when an inventory transfer occurs that moves an item from one location to another.

If goods are damaged on delivery, they can be either entered as being returned or simply not accepted at delivery. If a vendor delivery is made in parts, then several goods-receipts entries must be made. SAP ERP monitors delivery and reports when an order has been fulfilled and may be closed. This ensures that payment for the goods occurs only after receipt. However, this feature can be overridden when necessary. For example, it would be necessary if a vendor could not fill an order completely but had made partial delivery.

A goods-receipt document can be prepared in three different ways. One way is by the inventory management (IM) system when the goods are assigned to temporary storage. After goods have been transferred and goods are checked and recorded, the goods receipt is complete. Another way that a goods-receipt document can be prepared is by reference to the purchase order. SAP ERP automatically fills the goods-receipt document using information in the purchase order and updates the purchase order for the goods receipt. A third way is that the goods receipt can be posted into quality inspection. Goods cannot be used until inspected and verified. If goods pass, a transfer posting is entered to move them from quality inspection to available inventory.

After a goods receipt is posted, SAP ERP makes an inventory document that documents the effect on inventory. It also produces an accounting document to show the general ledger transaction.

Invoice Verification

Invoices must be checked against goods-receipt documents and original purchase orders prior to payment. This business process—known as **invoice verification**—ensures that cost and quantity requirements have been met. SAP ERP has an invoice verification component. This component is not responsible for the actual payment of invoices. The accounts payable function pays invoices. Invoice verification links materials management and procurement with other SAP ERP modules such as financial accounting and controlling.

The purchase order number is entered along with other invoice details. SAP ERP copies information from the purchase order document into the invoice verification document. One must enter the amount of the invoice and the quantity of goods or service that actually was invoiced.

When an invoice is posted, SAP ERP performs a three-way match that compares the purchase order with the goods receipt and with the invoice. This check ensures against inconsistent charges or incorrect amounts being delivered. As a result of posting the invoice, the purchase order is updated, and SAP ERP produces an accounting document to indicate the general ledger transaction.

Vendor Payment

Once an invoice is posted, payment can take place. Payment is made according to the payment terms and conditions specified in the purchase order or the vendor master record. Payment is processed through accounts payable in the financial accounting module.

 CASE IN POINT

The Rockland County, NY, *Procurement Ethics Guide* requires that county employees, in the context of contracting may not:

Accept a gift worth $75 or more from any person or firm doing or intending to do business with any agency of the County. A gift includes cash, goods, meals, travel, sporting event tickets, entertainment, loans, services, or anything else of value; separate gifts within a 12-month period from the same person or firm or from related persons or firms—for example, from two employees of a single supplier—are grouped together.

Master Records

Master records are created in SAP ERP for the objects that reflect the organizational structure and business processes of the company. Objects are identified by a code. The coding system for objects incorporates fields that identify company, plant, storage location, purchasing organization, and purchasing group.

The company code identifies an accounting unit that has a balance sheet and income statement. A consolidated company consists of several different companies, each of which is legally responsible for creating and maintaining its own accounting documents for legal purposes. The plant code identifies a separate location, such as a plant or warehouse. The storage location code identifies an area where goods are stored. The purchasing organization code identifies the unit responsible for negotiating purchases for one or several plants. A firm's purchasing organization may be decentralized or centralized. A plant can have several purchasing organizations assigned to it. Finally, the purchasing group code identifies the individual or team that is responsible for the procurement of a material or class of materials. The purchasing group is the primary contact for the company's dealing with the vendor.

SAP ERP maintains a centralized database. Master records are created for each object. Each master record is accessible by every module in SAP ERP, but every module can only "see" different areas of each master record. Procurement accesses vendor master records and material master records.

Vendor master data are maintained in the materials management module of SAP ERP. Vendor master records are maintained centrally but are updated by users in many departments. There are three categories of information in vendor master records. General data consist of vendor number, name, address, telephone number, and similar items. Company code data (also called *accounting data*) are defined at the company code level and are linked to the financial accounting and general ledger modules in SAP ERP. Company code data define agreed payment terms and the subledger reconciliation account number. Every vendor master record must have a reconciliation account number that links the vendor to the accounts payable subledger. Finally, purchasing data describe purchasing needs and are defined at the purchasing organization level. For example, purchasing data include information used for quotations, invoice verification, or inventory control. Each vendor master record has an account group field that determines how the vendor record is numbered and also determines which fields display on the vendor master screens.

Material master records contain information about materials that a company might procure, produce, or sell to customers. Material master records are used and shared by many departments. Material master records have a hierarchical structure. The organizational or client level is the highest level. It contains data that are relevant to all users, such as item description, unit of measure, and material group. At the plant level, a material master record can contain production or sales requirements. Sales and warehouse data can be maintained at other levels. Material master records contain so much data that they are organized as "views": Each department accesses and maintains its own view of the master record. Engineering, purchasing, IM, MRP, and accounting all use material master records. Procurement uses several views, including purchasing, accounting, production planning, and warehouse.

The IM component of SAP ERP records both the value and quantity of inventory. This allows one to enter and check goods movement, manage inventory stocks, and take a physical inventory. A *goods movement* is an internal or external event that causes a change in stock level. The issue of stock to production is an example of an internal event. A sale to a customer or receipt from a vendor is an external event. Current stock level is tracked by considering items in stock, on order, reserved, and in quality inspection. Consignment inventory is accounted for separately. Several values are updated when stock level changes. The stock value is charged internally to a cost center or project. The corresponding general ledger accounts are also updated. The IM component supports cycle counting and inventory sampling. In addition to these basic features, IM can be extended to incorporate warehouse management. IM is part of the materials management module and is integrated with other modules.

Purchasing information master records are used only by purchasing. They are used for *source allocation*, which is the process of vendor evaluation. These records contain performance information, such as price and delivery times for the material from a vendor at a certain date, about a material, a vendor, and a plant. The vendor evaluation data include the planned delivery date and the corresponding actual delivery date for a material.

Contracts are transaction documents, but they function like master records for release orders.

Transaction Cycle Controls Over Procurement

Figure 9.2 illustrates a business process diagram of the activities in a procurement (purchasing) business process. The main feature illustrated in the diagram is the separation of the following functions: requisitioning (stores), purchasing, receiving, accounts payable, and general ledger. The diagram shows an overview of flow of activities in the company from the requisitioning of a purchase order through to its impact on the financial statements prepared by the general ledger function. Additional details are provided in the following discussion.

Requisitioning (Stores)

Requests for purchases originate outside the purchasing department. In Figure 9.2, purchase requisitions originate in the requisitioning (stores) department. "Stores" is a term that denotes an inventory of items that are to be used internally by a company. Often, the stores department maintains an inventory of raw materials and supplies that will be used in a firm's production process. Purchase requisitions might also originate in other departments within the firm. For example, the accounting department might make a purchase requisition for a PC that will be used in the accounting department. Thus, the business process diagram column heading of requisitioning (stores) is used to emphasize that the illustrated process pertains to both cases—the case where the requisitioned goods will be inventoried in stores and the other case where the requisitioned

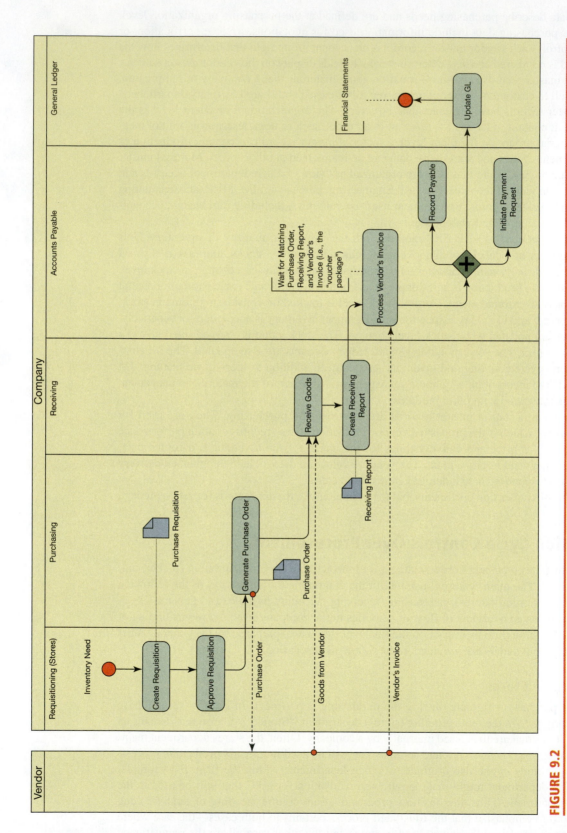

FIGURE 9.2

Procurement Business Process Diagram

goods will be sent to the requisitioning department. Note that in both of these cases the purchased goods are returned to the requisitioning department, whether it is the stores department or some other department like accounting. As illustrated in the diagram, purchase requisitions should always be approved in the originating department.

Purchasing

Regardless of how or where purchase requisitions originate, it is the function of the purchasing department to select a vendor and arrange for terms and delivery. How this is done depends on the relative degree of centralization in the company's purchasing function. Purchasing may at times override a purchase requisition due to insufficient budget, lack of authorization, or some other reason. Purchase requisitions might also be altered or returned to the originating department for modification.

As shown in Figure 9.3, purchasing verifies budget authority for the requisition, and then selects a vendor. Bids from vendors may or may not be required before a vendor is selected. Once a vendor has been selected, a purchase order for the requisition is prepared and approved. A copy is sent to the vendor. Accounts payable, the requesting department (stores), and the receiving department each will access the purchase order in subsequent processing of the order. The vendor may

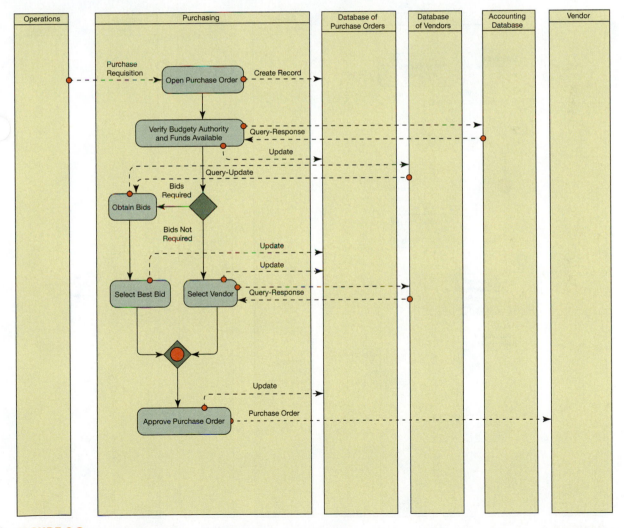

FIGURE 9.3

Purchasing Activities

return a copy of the purchase order to acknowledge receipt of the order. The requesting department should be notified that a purchase order has been issued, and it should review the order as necessary to verify its appropriateness for satisfying the needs identified in the purchase requisition. As noted, Figure 9.3 indicates that bids may be required before purchase orders are placed. The use of bidding procedures is discussed in the following section. Figure 9.3 uses message flows between pools to illustrate the use of online databases for purchase orders, vendors, and accounting.

Receiving

Figure 9.4 details activities in the receiving department, with message flows indicating the use of online databases for purchase orders and accounts payable. The receiving function should be separate from and independent of the requisitioning (stores) function. Receiving should access the purchase order and match it with the delivery from the vendor. The purchase order authorizes the receiving department to accept the delivery from the vendor when it is delivered. Any shipments that do not have a matching purchase order should be rejected. As shown in the figure, receiving procedures should call for an inspection and blind count of the delivery, the preparation of a receiving report, and then the transfer of the shipment to either stores or the requisitioning

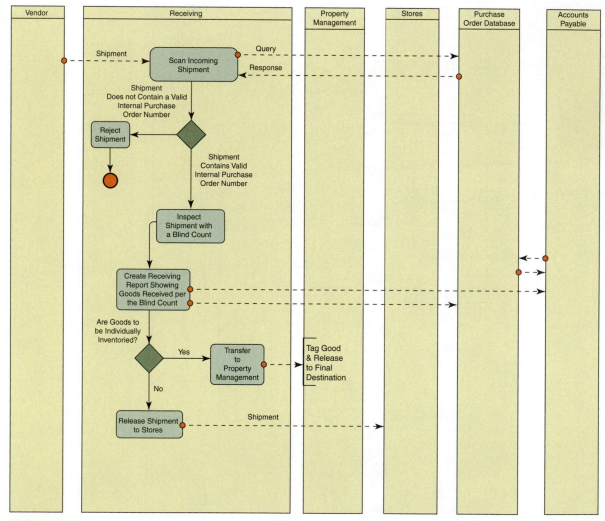

FIGURE 9.4

Receiving Activities

department, depending on the situation. Figure 9.4 shows the activity of transferring shipments directly to the requisitioning department (like the PC ordered by the accounting department in our example) first to a property management function in order that the item is physically tagged and recorded for internal control purposes.

An independent or **blind count** of a delivery may be obtained by not allowing the counters to have access to the quantities shown on the purchase order. This forces the counters to determine a quantity by counting, since it is not possible to simply copy the quantity number from the purchase order. A supervisor compares the quantities received as counted with those shown on the purchase order and then prepares a receiving report for the quantities received. A copy of the receiving report should accompany transfer of the delivery to the requisitioning department.

In many cases, only a person with technical ability can adequately inspect materials and give assurance to the requisitioning or using department. It may be desirable to have the quality of materials received tested before payment is made. An inspection function may be established for this purpose either as a part of the receiving department or as a separate department.

Stores

The stores department acknowledges receipt of the delivery from receiving by signing the receiving report and then forwarding it to accounts payable. If goods are delivered directly to the requisitioning department rather than to stores, a supervisor in the requesting department should acknowledge receipt on the receiving report and then forward the receiving report to account payable. This independent verification of receipt of the purchase is a central control feature in the procurement business process.

 CASE IN POINT

An accounts payable clerk for North Bay Health Care Group admitted to using her computer to access North Bay's accounting software without authorization, in turn issuing approximately 127 checks payable to herself and others. Several of the checks were cashed or deposited into her personal bank account, and some were deposited into the bank accounts of others. She attempted to conceal the fraud by altering the electronic check registers of North Bay to make it appear as if the checks had been payable to the company's vendors. The fraudulent scheme resulted in losses of at least $875,035 to North Bay.

Accounts Payable

Accounts payable is responsible for initiating payments to vendors. As Figure 9.5 details, three documents—purchase order, receiving report, and invoice—are available to document a purchase transaction. The collection of these three documents is referred to as a **voucher package**. The requirement that these three documents be reviewed and approved for payment before payment is made is the central feature of a voucher system. The use of a voucher system to support payment is a major transaction cycle control over procurement. A voucher system is essentially a review technique to ensure that all appropriate documentation is assembled, verified, and reviewed prior to actual payment of an invoice. Approved vouchers are forwarded to the cashier (i.e., cash disbursements function) for payment. Voucher systems are further discussed in the context of the cash disbursements business process, which is the next topic discussed in this chapter.

Additional Control Features

There are several additional control features worth noting.

- Purchasing does not control the actual goods; nor does purchasing have complete control over the documentation that is required for payment.

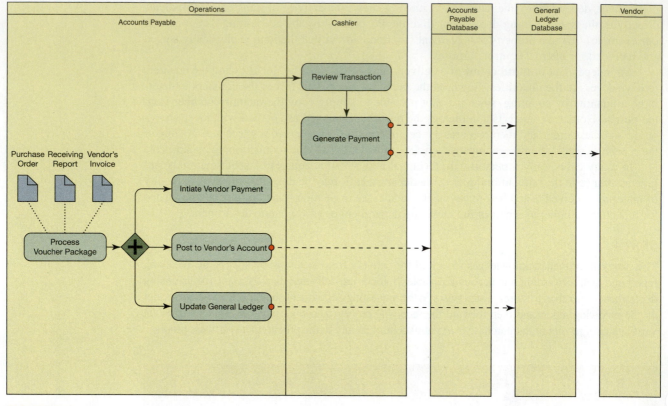

FIGURE 9.5

Voucher Processing by Accounts Payable

- Receiving is separate from final custody of the delivery, which is the requisitioning (stores) function. Acknowledgment from both receiving and final custody should be a requirement before payment is authorized.
- Accounts payable handles only documents and is not able to obtain merchandise or cash independently.
- Purchase requisitions should be reviewed independently outside purchasing. This is often done by accounts payable. This review could verify the accounting charges shown on the requisition and also ensures that requisitions do not originate in purchasing.
- Invoices should be routed to purchasing for review and approval prior to being sent to accounts payable. This is particularly important if purchasing expertise is necessary to evaluate the propriety of the invoice.
- Purchase terms should be reviewed for propriety outside the purchasing department. This review is often done by accounts payable.
- Inventory records should be updated to reflect the receipt of goods.

 CASE IN POINT

In a fraud survey conducted by KPMG, vendor-related and other third-party fraud was reported by 25% of the 75 firms experiencing fraud. Items reported included bid rigging, price fixing, duplicate billings, false invoices, and phantom vendors.

Integrity of the Procurement Business Process

Purchase documentation simply ensures that individual orders are received as expected. Purchase orders and receiving reports control individual purchases, but they do not exercise control directly over the procurement business process. Control of the procurement business process centers on the integrity of the buyer–vendor relationship. Bribery, kickbacks, and conflicts of interest (such as buying from a relative or friend) are examples of improper buyer–vendor relationships that the procurement business process must address. Buyer–vendor relationships are more a matter of policy than procedure. Most companies have found it desirable and often necessary to have formal written policy and procedure manuals covering the procurement business process. Purchasing policies may require competitive bidding, which is usually implemented through the use of request for quotation documents.

Buyers must request competitive bids through request for quotation documents. These documents are filed and reviewed by purchasing management. Selecting the lowest-cost bid is not always an acceptable basis for selecting a vendor. Methods of evaluating and selecting bids based on vendor attributes, which are known as *vendor rating plans*, often are formalized, with evaluation decisions subject to review by a higher authority. A policy of rotating a buyer's responsibilities weakens buyer–vendor relationships but reduces the potential for buyer specialization. **Approved vendor lists**, prepared by an independent function, may be used to restrict a buyer's options to those vendors who have been found reliable, financially sound, and free of conflicts of interest. These examples are not exhaustive, but they indicate the types of controls that may be used to ensure the integrity of procurement business process. SAP ERP, as discussed earlier in this chapter, provides extensive support for vendor selection and evaluation.

The Attribute Rating Approach to Vendor Selection

The **attribute rating** approach to vendor selection is appropriate whenever an objective evaluation of the opinions of several independent evaluators is desired, that is, an amalgamation of evaluations of the same system. The following steps are involved:

- Identify and list the attributes to be included in the evaluation.
- Assign a weight to each attribute based on relative importance and objectivity.
- Have individual evaluators rank each vendor on each attribute, giving a numerical score on a range of 1–10 or some other scale.
- Total the individual evaluations by multiplying each attribute's numerical ranking by its weight; then total all evaluations by adding the scores together.

Given that the relevant costs, such as a vendor's prices or a system's cost, have been identified, a benefit–cost ratio can be computed for comparisons. While this method appears to be objective, both assignment of weights and numerical ranking are very subjective processes. Accordingly, attribute evaluation techniques are most useful for screening proposals and identifying vendors or systems that should be subject to final consideration. SAP ERP, as discussed earlier in this chapter, provides extensive computational support for the attribute rating approach to vendor selection.

CASE IN POINT

Expert Choice (http://expertchoice.com) is one of many companies that offer software that is directed at vendor evaluation and selection. The software helps to overcome the limits of the human mind in its ability to synthesize qualitative and quantitative inputs from multiple participants in the vendor selection process.

Sarbanes–Oxley Compliance: Procurement Business Process

The Sarbanes–Oxley Act of 2002 (SOX) requires that companies maintain an adequate internal control structure over the business processes that support financial reporting. SEC Interpretive

Guidance "Management's Report on Internal Control Over Financial Reporting" focuses management on internal controls that best protect against risk of material misstatement in financial statements. Auditing Standard No. 5: "An Audit of Internal Control Over Financial Reporting That Is Integrated with an Audit of Financial Statements," issued by the Public Company Accounting Oversight Board (PCAOB), establishes requirements and provides direction that applies when an auditor is engaged to perform an audit of management's assessment of the effectiveness of internal control over financial reporting that is integrated with an audit of the financial statements. Effective internal control over financial reporting provides reasonable assurance regarding the reliability of financial reporting and the preparation of financial statements for external purposes. If one or more material weaknesses exist, the company's internal control over financial reporting cannot be considered effective. Auditing Standard No. 5 describes a top-down approach to selecting controls to be tested. Auditors should understand risks related to the preparation of financial statements, focus on entity-level controls, and test controls that sufficiently address the assessed risk of misstatement. Risk assessment underlies the entire audit process described by this standard, including the determination of significant accounts and disclosures and relevant assertions.

The procurement business process generates expense amounts that are significant accounts, disclosures and assertions on a company's income statement. The customer order management business process also generates asset amounts that are significant accounts, disclosures and assertions on a company's balance sheet. Thus, risk assessment of the procurement business process will be necessary for compliance with SOX. Rationale of assessed risks must be clearly documented and controls selected for testing and evaluation. Our discussion of transaction cycle controls over procurement has highlighted fundamental controls that are based on a separation of functions within this business process. Both management and auditors will be concerned with evaluating the existence and functioning of these controls as they are necessary to protect against risk of material misstatements in amounts reported in financial statements. Risk assessment should also evaluate whether the company's controls sufficiently address identified risks of material misstatement due to fraud, and controls intended to address the risk of management override of these controls.

Cash Disbursements Business Process

The cash disbursements business process controls check disbursements as well as actual cash disbursement. Typically, checks are used for the majority of disbursements, with currency disbursements restricted to small amounts drawn from and accountable to a petty cash imprest fund.

The imprest fund concept is not restricted to petty cash control. Imprest payroll funds and imprest charge or expense funds are common in systems design. An imprest fund is a fund maintained at a specified, predetermined amount. At all times, the amount of cash on hand plus documented expenditures should equal the specified amount of the fund. Periodically, an imprest fund is replenished; documented expenditures (petty cash vouchers) are reviewed and approved, and a check is drawn to the fund or custodian of the fund for the amount necessary to bring the fund back to its specified amount. Separate imprest checking accounts may be maintained for payroll and other expense categories, such as dividend payments.

The major control features of a cash disbursements business process are the use of a voucher system to support the drawing of checks, the separation of approval from actual payment, and independent bank reconciliation. These items are included in the following discussion.

Accounts Payable

The accounts payable department accesses the documents that are necessary to support a cash disbursement. As illustrated in Figure 9.5, these documents are a purchase order, a receiving report, and a vendor's invoice. These documents are reviewed, certified as to completeness, and processed to prepare a voucher. The voucher is typically prepared and processed for payment on the due date of the invoice.

Accounts payable initiates payment processing, which includes calculating the amount due, discount (if any), and other such items. A voucher check is prepared for each voucher. Voucher checks are posted to the voucher register. A total of these postings is prepared. Vouchers are posted to the accounts payable ledger. This posting is summarized on a journal voucher. Voucher processing includes processing the expense distribution. Vouchers are charged to the organizational units identified by the account number on the vouchers. The voucher checks and vouchers are approved and forwarded to the cash disbursements department. The journal voucher is forwarded to general ledger.

Cash Disbursements

Voucher checks and vouchers are received from the accounts payable department. After the voucher checks and vouchers are reviewed, the checks are signed, and the vouchers are canceled and filed by number. Vouchers, including the original documents, if possible, are canceled to avoid the possibility of duplicate payments. The voucher checks are posted to the check register. A control total of the amount posted is prepared and reconciled with the vouchers received from accounts payable. Voucher checks are forwarded directly to the payees. The control total is forwarded to the general ledger.

General Ledger

The journal voucher received from accounts payable and the control total from cash disbursements are reconciled, and the totals are posted to the general ledger. The journal voucher and the control total should be filed by date.

Internal Audit

The canceled checks are received from the bank along with the bank statement. An independent bank reconciliation is an important control in a cash disbursements business process.

Voucher Systems

A voucher system is essentially a review technique. The real control over disbursements is a final review of documents evidencing the entire transaction prior to authorization of payment. Authorization may take the form of physically signing off on a voucher package, preparing a document to authorize an entry in the voucher register, or directly entering data into a computer in response to a voucher which is displayed as a listing of documents on a computer screen. This final review process evidences that procedures have been duly authorized and completed according to system specifications. It is the review process, not the actual signing of checks, that is the control. This is particularly evident in computer applications where checks are "signed" with a signature imprinter at the rate of hundreds of checks per minute.

An accounts payable system typically maintains a subsidiary ledger of creditors' accounts, posting invoices and payments on account to each individual creditor's account. Accounts payable generally refers to trade accounts, whereas a voucher payable system encompasses *all* expenditures, including trade accounts, payroll, capital expenditures, and so on. In a strict voucher payable system, individual accounts for creditors need not be kept. The voucher system maintains a voucher register or, alternatively, files of voucher packages in numerical or any other order. Several vouchers may relate to the same creditor, as opposed to a single account in an accounts payable system. If information on individual creditors is desired, copies of vouchers may be used to generate this information. Numerous voucher payable files are maintained in most systems because payable information is essential to short-run financial planning.

A **voucher system** centers around vouchers. **Vouchers** themselves can take several forms, ranging from a simple form or envelope to a voucher–check combination (Figure 9.6). A voucher shows, among other things, the name and address of the vendor, a description of the invoice, total or net amount due, and the accounts to be charged (distribution). In a computer application, most of the documents included in the voucher are coded and processed by the computer. A voucher system may be implemented by rubber-stamping an invoice or purchase order with

FIGURE 9.6

Voucher Check

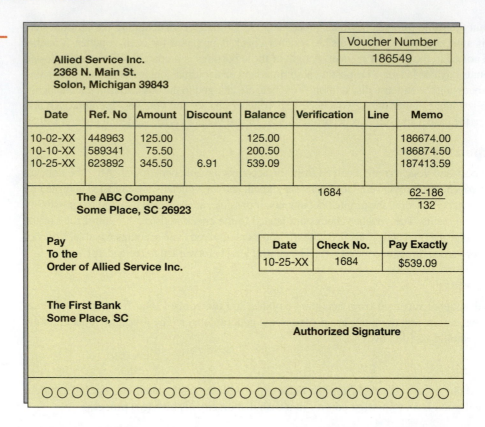

Date	Ref. No	Amount	Discount	Balance	Verification	Line	Memo
10-02-XX	448963	125.00		125.00			186674.00
10-10-XX	589341	75.50		200.50			186874.50
10-25-XX	623892	345.50	6.91	539.09			187413.59

Voucher Number
186549

Allied Service Inc.
2368 N. Main St.
Solon, Michigan 39843

The ABC Company
Some Place, SC 26923

1684

62-186
132

Pay
To the
Order of Allied Service Inc.

Date	Check No.	Pay Exactly
10-25-XX	1684	$539.09

The First Bank
Some Place, SC

_____
Authorized Signature

a voucher stamp and documenting the voucher on this original document. The voucher stamp creates an area on the document for authorizing signatures, document numbers, dates, and so on.

The form of the voucher itself is not significant. A voucher system may operate without a human-readable voucher. In this case, the "voucher" is an approved entry in the voucher register, some type of computer file. References to documents rather than the documents themselves are provided in the register, and voucher entries are under strict numerical control.

 CASE IN POINT

Businessdictionary.com defines a voucher as a written instrument that serves to confirm or witness (vouch) for some fact such as a transaction. Commonly, a voucher is a document that shows goods that have been bought or services that have been rendered, authorizes payment, and indicates the ledger account(s) in which these transactions have to be recorded.

Posting of Payables

A basic question in the design of a voucher system concerns when invoices are to be posted to vouchers payable. Specifically, when are liabilities "booked" (excluding end-of-period accruals)? After invoices have been approved for payment, they may be held until the due date and formally posted at that time; alternatively, they may be booked at the time of approval (which is generally different from the due date). Because most firms attempt to pay invoices on the due date to maximize working capital, this question relates to whether there is a formal record of amounts owed to creditors. If invoices are booked on the due date, there is no formal record of unpaid invoices because the liability is immediately canceled by payment. If invoices are booked on the date of approval, a formal record of liabilities exists. This advantage is gained at a cost: The voucher register (or file of vouchers) now must be searched or sorted by due date to facilitate payments. Typically, a voucher register is used for numerical control when invoices are booked at the time of approval.

Preparing vouchers for individual invoices when several invoices refer to the same vendor in the same time period would result in the drawing of several checks to the same vendor in the same month. This is generally inefficient. Accordingly, many firms use built-up voucher systems. **Built-up voucher systems** accumulate several invoices from the same vendor and pay these invoices with a single check.

A built-up voucher system functions essentially as an accounts payable system. After invoices are approved, they are sorted and accumulated by vendor or voucher number. Payments are made at month end or due date. A built-up voucher procedure as just described is a full accrual system; vouchers payable replace accounts payable in the general ledger.

Three files are necessary to maintain useful information: (1) a file of approved but unpaid invoices, with access to due date for payment, (2) a file of paid invoices, usually in numerical order, and (3) a vendor file showing both paid and unpaid amounts, ordered by vendor ID. In a manual system, these files are obtained by filing copies of vouchers. In a computer system, separate files may be maintained, or database processing may yield similar results without having three separate files.

The voucher concept is helpful in the disbursement procedure of any organization when a basic record is desired and proper authorization and control over disbursements are important. Knowledge and approval of the disbursement is documented by requiring signatures before the disbursement. Paid vouchers can be filed in strict numerical sequence to provide documentation for every amount paid. Such a procedure provides orderly records and good documentation and is advantageous in establishing good stewardship of cash.

Human Resource Management Business Process

The business process that involves management of human resources (HR) is concerned with establishing and maintaining an information system that processes HR information. The HR system should provide tools for the setup and maintenance of information pertaining to the organizational structure. A listing of jobs that exist in an organization, a listing of job descriptions, and a listing of any qualifications that are required for a job are examples of HR information pertaining to the organizational structure. The HR system should also provide tools for the processing of employee data, such as employee address, payroll, and employment history. Figure 9.7 illustrates basic

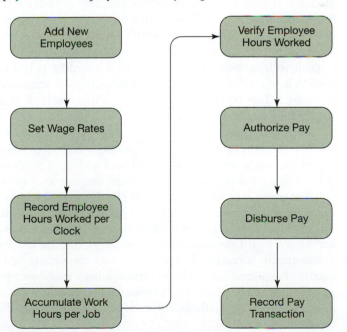

FIGURE 9.7

Payroll Activities

activities related to the payroll component of an HR system. We will illustrate these HR business process concepts by examining some of the basic features of the HR component of SAP ERP.

CASE IN POINT

Recording employee data for administrative, time reporting, and payroll purposes is central to human resources management. In SAP ERP, the information units used to enter master data are called *infotypes*. To the user, infotypes appear as data entry screens. Information such as last name, first name, and date of birth are entered as data fields.

HR Processing in SAP ERP

The HR module in SAP ERP includes components that address the objectives stated earlier in an integrated, online environment. HR data are immediately available to anyone who has authorization to use them because all HR data are online. The HR component can be implemented stand-alone or can be integrated with other modules, such as the production planning and control module or the plant maintenance module.

SAP ERP contains two HR modules. The personnel administration module (HR–PA) is concerned with the maintenance of employee data, such as personnel details, salary data, and performance appraisal data. The personnel planning and development module (HR–PD) provides tools for the setup and maintenance of organizational structure information. Organizational structure is represented as an administrative hierarchy in which each unit in a company reports to a parent organization unit. This type of hierarchy relationship is known as a *parent–child* or *parent–subordinate relationship*. A unit can be a subsidiary, a division, a department, a project team, and so on. Each unit is assigned a manager, and each unit is allocated positions to which individual employees are assigned. Other functions in HR–PD include workplace and job descriptions, career planning information, and shift planning.

The time management component is one of the most important and most often used HR modules. It performs time recording and time evaluation to record employee absences and attendance information. This module is usually implemented in a manufacturing or service environment where employees work in shifts and where attendance monitoring is critical to the management of operations. The component can be implemented to use either negative or positive time recording. Negative time recording is less complex because only exceptions need to be recorded. In positive time recording, all attendance and absence information must be entered. This requires a system such as time cards or electronic swipe cards to record the required information.

The payroll component can calculate pay based on attendance information accumulated in the time component or based on a fixed amount per pay period. Deductions for taxes, medical payments, and so on are made based on a variety of predefined wage types. The use of predefined data types or *blueprints* is an important characteristic of SAP ERP systems.

The travel expense component of HR–PA is used to process any employee expenses. One can enter and authorize expenses and pay the correct amount into employees' bank accounts. The module supports recruitment. It can track job vacancies and the applicants that are being considered to fill those vacancies. Any positions marked vacant in the HR–PD module are automatically accessible in the recruitment component of HR–PA. The module can record details of applicants and progress that has been made with processing their applications. The module can link applicants to the source that caused them to apply, such as advertisements in a newspaper. This allows HR management to evaluate the relative efficiency of different recruitment methods.

HR Data Structure

A data structure provides the basis for the storage and manipulation of data. The HR data structure contains three elements:

- HR master data
- HR data organization
- HR objects

MASTER DATA   Master data records in the HR–PA and HR–PD modules are created and maintained for organizational units, job profiles, employees, and training. In many business processes, the data in master records are often referenced but seldom changed. However, some HR master records are subject to frequent change. For example, employee master data change frequently as the lives and careers of the employees change. As this example illustrates, HR information systems are focused on maintaining master data records rather than processing transactions.

 CASE IN POINT

Smartphones and other mobile devices offer the possibility of mobile access to time reporting, payroll processing, and other aspects of the HR business process. An Aberdeen Group study reports that HR activities most affected by mobile devices, among companies who use them, were workforce management (53%), informal learning and development (39%), and talent acquisition/recruiting (38%).

DATA ORGANIZATION   Data are organized and presented to users in SAP ERP by *infotypes* and personnel *events*. An *infotype* is a SAP term that denotes a collection of data fields that are grouped together for display. In database terminology, an infotype is a segment. Employee personnel data, employee pay data, employee appraisal data, and a work schedule are common infotypes in HR. New or custom infotypes can be defined as necessary. SAP ERP offers a number of standard infotypes that are specific to the tax and benefit systems of different nations. These blueprint infotypes may be included in the implementation of the HR module as appropriate. Each of these nation-specific supplements adds a suite of infotypes to the employee management component of the HR–PA module.

Infotypes change over time, and it is usually important to retain old versions in order to track changes in HR organization and personnel records over time. Validity data are assigned to each infotype to make it unique and to prevent overwriting when an infotype is updated. Date fields are added to infotypes to indicate the beginning and end dates of the period for which the infotype is considered valid. Thus, several infotypes for the same object exist at the same time, but only one is valid. A *delimited* infotype is one whose validity end date is past.

The system has functions to create and manipulate infotypes as well as display them. The create function adds a new blank infotype with a default validity date from current date to "end of time." In SAP ERP terms, the end of time is December 31, 9999. If a current infotype already exists when one is being created, it is delimited automatically. Copy, delete, and list functions are supported.

A personnel *event* is a group of infotypes. Events are created to simplify HR transaction entry. Personnel events are specifically designed for use in a company and are easily customized in SAP ERP. For example, a hiring event would be recorded as a transaction by inputting all the infotypes necessary to create a new employee. The input screen would be designed to display and prompt for the infotypes. A "change of job" event would be input to a screen that displayed all the infotypes required to change an employee's job within the organization. The system can prompt for additional information and perform processing. For example, it might prompt for more information if a new employee is married. It might calculate the date of the end of a new employee's probationary period. It might also create a position vacancy if the employee in that position is transferred or leaves the organization.

HR OBJECTS   HR object types are identified with a one- or two-letter identifier. The code for the object employee is "P." Each employee also has a unique personnel number that identifies him or her throughout the information system. The code for the object job is "C." A job is a generic description. A job is not identical to the actual positions in the HR organization. The code for the object qualifications is "Q." A qualification is a skill required for a particular job, such as an educational degree, job experience, or capability. The code for organization unit is "O." An organization unit is a distinct area or section of the organization, such as the accounting department. The code for the object position is "S." A position is a specific work assignment within an organization unit. Each organization unit consists of one or more positions. Each position has a particular job and often one or more qualifications if these are needed to further define the job. The code for the object cost center is "K." Cost center data are used to capture and assign any HR costs that are incurred. For example, salary costs are often assigned to cost centers.

We illustrate the use of HR objects with an example. The organization unit marketing department has five positions. Each position has a job description. One of these positions is manager, one is supervisor, and three are sales associates. In addition, the manager position has the qualification "Japanese language skills" because the marketing department has frequent correspondence with a Japanese subsidiary.

Transaction Cycle Controls in Payroll Processing

Payroll processing is extremely complex. In a large organization, it is one of the most complex procedures in operation. All levels of government impose payroll taxes of one sort or another; regulations and rates are changed constantly, with the result that a payroll system usually requires constant modification. Payroll processing is one area in which the law imposes not only a fine but also a jail sentence for willful negligence in maintaining adequate records. As with any law, ignorance is no excuse. The responsibility is on the systems analyst to keep current in this area.

Figure 9.8 depicts the business process diagram of payroll processing. The most significant feature is a separation of the personnel, timekeeping, and payroll functions.

Personnel

The personnel (employment) office is responsible for placing people on the company's payroll, specifying rates of pay, and authorizing all deductions from pay. This is indicated in the activities "add new employee" and "set wage rates" in the personnel lane of Figure 9.8. All changes, such as adding or deleting employees, changing pay rates, or changing levels of deductions from pay must be authorized by the personnel office. The personnel function is distinct from timekeeping and from the payroll preparation function.

CASE IN POINT

SAP ERP checks for "collisions" when new time records are entered to ensure that there are no contradictory records for that particular employee and time period. It is not possible, for example, to enter an absence record if there is already an attendance record in the system for the same employee and time period.

Timekeeping

The timekeeping function is responsible for the preparation and control of time reports and job-time tickets (clock hours). In a production firm, an hourly employee typically clocks on and off the job. At the end of a pay period, the employee's time card (or time report) indicates the amount of time the employee was on the job and the time for which he or she expects to receive pay.

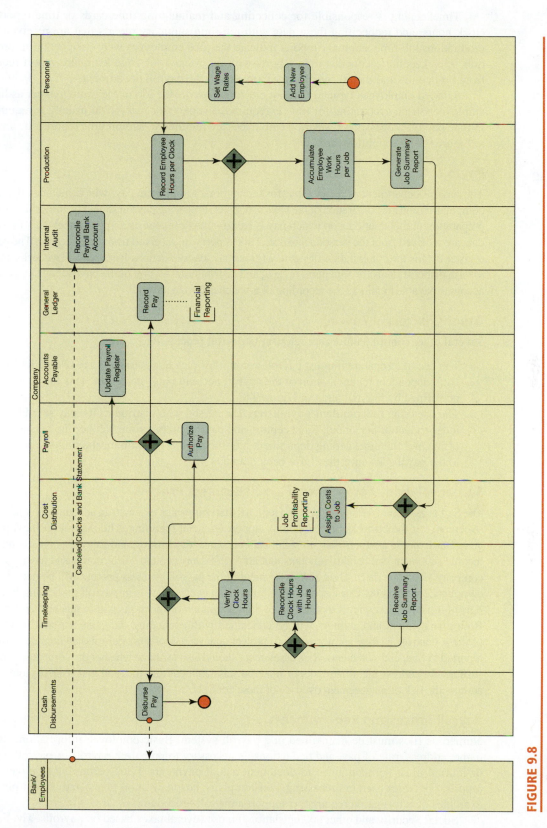

FIGURE 9.8

Payroll Business Process Diagram

Timekeeping is responsible for collecting and maintaining time cards or time reports for clock hours, and reconciling these data with job-time summary reports that are received from production. Job-time summary reports indicate the jobs employees were assigned to in production. Timekeeping reconciles time reports with the related job-time summary report received from production and then forwards time card data to the payroll department.

Salaried employees typically do not clock on and off the job in the same manner as hourly employees. If no accounting for time is required, a supervisor's approval usually is required to initiate payroll processing. If salaried employees are required to submit time reports, the analogy to Figure 9.8 is straightforward.

Payroll

The payroll department is responsible for the authorization of the pay, which includes the actual computation and the preparation of the payroll register. Preparing payroll should be independent of the preparation of the input data on which pay is based—the time reports and personnel data. Personnel data are received from the personnel office. Time reports are received from timekeeping. The payroll register details the computation of net pay (gross pay less deductions from pay). Paychecks are sent to cash disbursements for signature, review, and distribution. A copy of the payroll register is sent to accounts payable to initiate the recording of a voucher for the payroll.

Other Controls in Payroll

Several other control features are relevant to payroll processing.

- The use of a separate imprest payroll account for paychecks to facilitate reconciliations.
- An independent reconciliation of the payroll-account bank statement. This function is performed by internal audit in Figure 9.8.
- The use of an **independent paymaster**. The person who distributes the pay should be independent of personnel, timekeeping, and payroll preparation. Neither the personnel office, nor the timekeeping department, nor the payroll department should have access to the paychecks once they have been drawn.

Sarbanes–Oxley Compliance: Payroll Business Process

The Sarbanes–Oxley Act of 2002 (SOX) requires that companies maintain an adequate internal control structure over the business processes that support financial reporting. The payroll business process generates expense amounts that are significant accounts, disclosures, and assertions on a company's income statement and liability amounts that are significant accounts, disclosures, and assertions on a company's balance sheet. Thus, risk assessment of the payroll business process will be necessary for compliance with SOX. Our discussion of transaction cycle controls in payroll processing has highlighted fundamental controls that are based on a separation of functions within this business process. Both management and auditors will be concerned with evaluating the existence and functioning of these controls as they are necessary to protect against risk of material misstatements in amounts reported in financial statements. Risk assessment should also evaluate whether the company's controls sufficiently address identified risks of material misstatement due to fraud and controls intended to address the risk of management override of these controls.

Payroll Processing Requirements

Numerous files must be maintained in a payroll system. Basic employee information, such as name, address, rate of pay, and deductions, is necessary to prepare a payroll. A payroll register or journal must be maintained to document actual payments. Files pertaining to government reports, tax tables used in processing, pension plans, hospitalization plans, and similar plans are examples of information required to support a payroll procedure.

Social Security and other tax legislation impose several taxes based on payrolls. The Federal Insurance Contributions Act (FICA) provides that employees contribute equally to funds for old age, survivors, disability, and hospital insurance benefits for certain individuals and members of their families. The contribution is based on a tax rate applied to gross wages. The employer is required to deduct the amount of FICA tax from each employee's pay each pay period. The employer is then required to match these deductions and deposit the entire amount in a government depository. A penalty is levied for failure, without reasonable cause, to make required deposits when due. Taxpayers who willfully claim credit on the record of federal tax deposits for deposits not made are subject to fine and/or other criminal penalties. The employer is responsible for the full amount of the tax even when he or she fails to withhold contributions from employees.

The Federal Social Security Act and the Federal Unemployment Tax Act provide for the establishment of unemployment insurance plans. Employers with covered workers employed in each of 20 weeks during a calendar year are affected. Payment to the federal government is required quarterly. Unemployment benefits are provided by the systems created by the individual states. Revenues of the federal government under the acts are used to meet the cost of administering state and federal unemployment plans, as well as to provide supplemental unemployment benefits.

Unemployment compensation laws are not the same in all states, but all states participate in the federal–state unemployment insurance program. In most states, laws provide for taxes only on employers. The federal legislation applies to all employers of one or more employees. Tax payment is generally required on or before the last day of the month following each calendar quarter. Most states have a merit-rating plan that permits a reduction in the tax rate for employers who establish a record of stable employment.

CASE IN POINT

The Internal Revenue Service (IRS) maintains a list of companies that have passed the IRS Assurance Testing System (ATS) and/or Business Acceptance Testing (BATS) requirements for software developers, reporting agents, and transmitters of electronic business returns to the IRS.

Federal income taxes on wages of an individual are collected in the period in which the wages are paid. Our "pay-as-you-go" system requires employers to withhold a portion of the earnings of their employees. The amount withheld depends on the amount of the earnings and on the number of exemptions allowed to the employee. A withholding exemption certificate must be prepared by each employee. The certificate states the number of exemptions to which the employee is entitled. This certificate is given to the employer, who computes the proper amount of tax to be withheld. Current regulations provide a graduated system of withholding designed to make the amount of tax withheld closely approximate to the rates used in computing the individual's tax liability at the end of the year.

Employers engaged in interstate commerce are required by the Federal Fair Labor Standards Act (also known as the Wages and Hours Law) to pay overtime at a minimum rate of one and one-half times the regular rate for hours worked in excess of 40 hours per week. Many companies also pay overtime premium rates for night shifts and for work on Sundays and holidays.

Employers must take care to deduct payroll taxes from all employees. A distinction is drawn between employees and independent contractors. Public accountants, architects, attorneys, and other people who render services to a business for a fee but are not controlled or directed by the client are not employees but independent contractors, and the amounts paid to them are not subject to payroll taxes.

At the close of each quarter, an employer is required to file a quarterly return of Form 941 and pay the balance of any undeposited taxes. This return covers income tax withheld and FICA tax for all employees. On or before January 31, each employer is required to give each employee a completed Form W-2 Wage and Tax Statement. The employer is required to forward a copy of these W-2 forms with a Form W-3 on or before February 28 to the government. Also on or before January 31, employers must file Form 940, Employer's Annual Federal Unemployment Tax Return.

FIGURE 9.9

Sample Payroll
Events Timetable

Date	Event
January 31	Form W-2 (Wage and Tax Statement) to be furnished to employees
January 31	Form 941 (Employer's Quarterly Federal Tax Return) due for fourth quarter of preceding calendar year
January 31	Form 1099-Misc. (U.S. Information Return for Recipients of Miscellaneous Income) to be furnished to consultants paid directly
February 28	Form W-3 (Transmittal of Wage and Tax Statements) due with Copy A of each Form W-2; Form 1096 (Transmittal) with each 1099-Misc.
March 15	File Form 1120 or 1120-S (Federal Corporate Income Tax Return for calendar year)
April 30	Form 941 due for first quarter
July 31	Form 941 due for second quarter
October 31	Form 941 due for third quarter

The basic information about what the U.S. government requires with respect to payroll is outlined in the Department of Treasury Internal Revenue Service publication, *Circular E Employers Tax Guide*. This publication contains all the latest information on new laws and detailed information for employers. It tells how to fill out all the forms and reports required, how to compute employment taxes, and how and when to make deposits and payments, and it provides the invaluable tax tables. An employer who does not have this publication, or access to the information contained in it, will sooner or later make an error in payroll procedure that will cost a penalty.

Figure 9.9 contains a schedule of payroll-related deadlines that illustrates some of the processing and information that a typical payroll system must provide.

Summary

The procurement business process includes the following activities: requirement determination, selection of a source, request for quotation, selection of a vendor, issuing of a purchase order, receipt of the goods, invoice verification, and vendor payment. SAP ERP systems are capable of storing and processing a vast amount of information pertaining to the procurement business process. This chapter provided an overview of the data stored and processed in the procurement business process by SAP ERP. Transaction cycle controls over the procurement business process includes a separation of the following functions: requisitioning, purchasing, receiving, stores, accounts payable, and the general ledger. Adequate vendor-selection procedures are an important factor in the overall integrity of a purchasing application system.

The cash disbursements business process is designed to control check disbursements as well as actual cash disbursements.

Transaction cycle controls over cash disbursements include the use of a voucher system to support the drawing of checks, the separation of approval from actual payment, and an independent bank reconciliation. The design of the cash disbursements business process should include a separation of the following functions: cash disbursements, accounts payable, the expense ledger, and the general ledger.

The HR business process establishes an information system that processes HR information. The HR system should provide tools for the setup and maintenance of information pertaining to the organizational structure, as well as for the processing of employee data, such as employee address, payroll, and employment history data. Transaction cycle controls over payroll processing include a separation of the following functions: personnel, timekeeping, and payroll accounting.

Glossary

approved vendor list   a list of vendors approved for use by the purchasing function.

attribute rating   an approach to vendor selection that identifies, lists, and evaluates several different aspects concerning a vendor.

blind count   counters in receiving do not have access to quantities shown on purchase orders.

built-up voucher system   the accumulation of several invoices from the same vendor and the payment of these invoices with a single check.

independent paymaster   the person who distributes pay is independent of the payroll preparation process.

invoice verification   the review of purchasing documentation prior to authorizing payment to vendors.

procurement   the business process of selecting a source, ordering, and acquiring goods or services.

purchase order   document issued to a vendor to initiate a purchase.

purchase requisition   document used to request a purchase.

receiving report   prepared to document the receipt of deliveries from vendors.

request for quotation   documents used to request competitive bids from vendors.

voucher   synonym for voucher package.

voucher package   a collection of documents that are reviewed and approved to authorize a disbursement.

voucher system   a system in which every organizational expenditure must be documented with an approved voucher.

Webliography

www.adp.com
The home page of Automatic Data Processing, Inc (ADP), one of the world's largest outsourcing services for payroll, human resources, benefits, and other employer processes. ADP also provides services in the areas of insurance claims processing, automobile dealer management, and brokerage houses.

www.americanpayroll.org
The home page of the American Payroll Association. This organization provides professional certifications for payroll professionals. Certifications include the Fundamental Payroll Consultant (FPC) and the Certified Payroll Professional (CPP).

www.american-purchasing.com
The home page of the American Purchasing Society. It provides the Certified Purchasing Professional (CPP) and Certified Professional Purchasing Manager (CPPM) certificates.

www.amsup.com
The home page of the American Supplier Institute. This private organization focuses on research, training, and education in quality improvement techniques such as Six Sigma, robust engineering, lean manufacturing, and Taguchi methods.

www.benchmarkingnetwork.com
Home page of the Procurement and Supply-chain Benchmarking Association™, devoted to identifying and benchmarking best-practices supply chain business processes.

www.ism.ws
Home page of the Institute for Supply Management, the largest supply management association in the world. This institute offers the Certified Professional in Supply Management designation. The institute also focuses on ethics and social responsibility. Adherence to ethics, codes, and principles is of concern to internal control.

www.naspo.org
Home page of the National Association of State Procurement Officials. This is a nonprofit organization whose directors are the central purchasing directors for the state governments in all 50 states and the District of Colombia.

www.purchasing.com
Home page of *Purchasing* magazine, which is concerned with best practices and case studies in procurement and related topics.

www.sap.com
Home page of SAP, a major vendor of ERP software.

Chapter Quiz

Answers to the chapter quiz appear on page 348.

1. In procurement, which of the following departments should normally be responsible for the preparation of purchase requisitions?
   a. cash disbursements
   b. purchasing
   c. receiving
   d. stores

2. In procurement, which of the following departments should normally be responsible for the preparation of purchase orders?
   a. cash disbursements
   b. purchasing
   c. accounts payable
   d. stores

3. In order to provide accountability for purchasing, purchase requisitions should be available to (_____).
   a. the vendor
   b. cash disbursements
   c. accounts payable
   d. receiving

4. Which of the following documents in the procurement business process is optional in SAP ERP?
   a. purchase requisition
   b. purchase order
   c. both are optional
   d. neither document is optional

5. For adequate internal control, the department responsible for preparing checks for signature should be (_____).
   a. the department that signs the checks
   b. the accounts payable department
   c. the purchasing department
   d. the treasury department

6. In a cash disbursements business process, the voucher package should be canceled by (_____).
   a. cash disbursements
   b. accounts payable
   c. stores
   d. general ledger

7. Which of the following documents should normally be included in a voucher package?
   a. vendor invoice
   b. purchase order
   c. both a and b
   d. neither a nor b

8. Which of the following departments should directly forward to accounts payable the copy of the receiving report that is included in the voucher package?
   a. purchasing
   b. receiving
   c. cash disbursements
   d. stores

9. In payroll processing, which of the following should be responsible for preparation of the payroll register?
   a. personnel department
   b. payroll department
   c. cash disbursements department
   d. timekeeping department

10. In payroll processing, which of the following should be responsible for the authorization of pay rates for employees?
    a. personnel department
    b. payroll department
    c. cash disbursements department
    d. timekeeping department

Review Problem

You have been engaged by the management of Alden, Inc., to review its internal control over the purchase, receipt, storage, and issue of raw materials. You have prepared the following comments that describe Alden's procedures.

Raw materials, which consist mainly of high-cost electronic components, are kept in a locked storeroom. Storeroom personnel include a supervisor and four clerks. All are well trained, competent, and adequately bonded. Raw materials are removed from the storeroom only on written or oral authorization of one of the production foremen.

No perpetual inventory records are kept; hence the storeroom clerks do not keep records of goods received or issued. To compensate for the lack of perpetual records, a physical inventory count is taken monthly by the storeroom clerks, who are well supervised. Appropriate procedures are followed in taking the inventory count.

After the physical count, the storeroom supervisor matches quantities counted against a predetermined reorder level. If the count for a given part is below the reorder level, the supervisor enters the part number on a materials requisition list and sends this list to the accounts payable clerk. The accounts payable clerk prepares a purchase order for a predetermined reorder quantity for each part and mails the purchase order to the vendor from whom the part was last purchased.

When ordered materials arrive at Alden, they are received by the storeroom clerks. The clerks count the merchandise and reconcile the counts with the shipper's bill of lading. All vendors' bills of lading are initialed, dated, and filed in the storeroom to serve as receiving reports.

Required

a. Prepare a logical data flow diagram (DFD).
b. Prepare an analytic flowchart.
c. Describe the weaknesses in internal control, and recommend improvements of Alden's procedures for the purchase, receipt, storage, and issue of raw materials.

(CPA adapted)

Solution to Review Problem

a. See Figure 9.10.

b. See Figure 9.10.

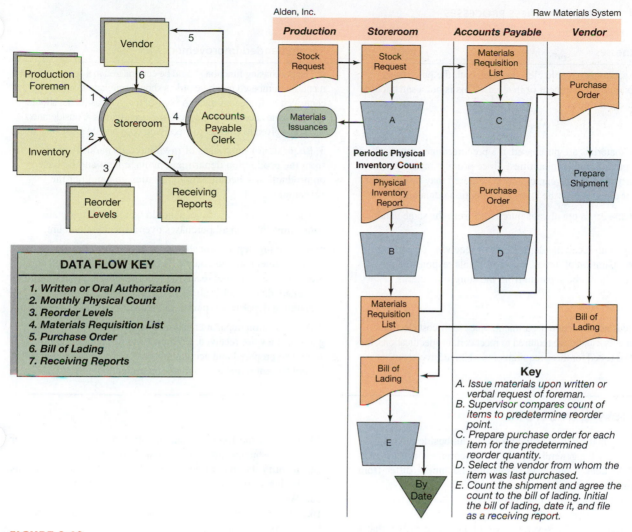

Alden, Inc.   Raw Materials System

DATA FLOW KEY

1. **Written or Oral Authorization**
2. **Monthly Physical Count**
3. **Reorder Levels**
4. **Materials Requisition List**
5. **Purchase Order**
6. **Bill of Lading**
7. **Receiving Reports**

Key

A. Issue materials upon written or verbal request of foreman.
B. Supervisor compares count of items to predetermine reorder point.
C. Prepare purchase order for each item for the predetermined reorder quantity.
D. Select the vendor from whom the item was last purchased.
E. Count the shipment and agree the count to the bill of lading. Initial the bill of lading, date it, and file as a receiving report.

FIGURE 9.10

Solution to Review Problem

c. Weaknesses and recommended improvements are as follows:

Weaknesses	Recommended Improvements
1. Raw materials may be removed from the storeroom on oral authorization from one of the production foremen.	1. Raw materials should be removed from the store room only on written authorization from an authorized production foreman. The authorization forms should be prenumbered and accounted for, with quantities and job or production numbers listed, and they should be signed and dated.
2. Alden's practice of monthly physical inventory counts does not compensate for the lack of a perpetual inventory system. Quantities on hand at the end of 1 month may not be sufficient to last until the next month's count. If the company has taken this into account in establishing reorder levels, then it is carrying too large an investment in inventory.	2. A perpetual inventory system should be established under the control of someone other than the store keepers. The system should include quantities and values for each item of raw material. Total inventory value per the perpetual records should be compared with the general ledger at reasonable intervals. When physical counts are taken, they should be compared with the perpetual records. Where differences occur, they should be investigated, and if the perpetual records are in error, they should be adjusted. Also, controls should be established over obsolescence of stored materials.

(continued)

Weaknesses	Recommended Improvements
4. The accounts payable clerk handles both the purchasing function and the payment of invoices. This is not a satisfactory separation of duties.	4. The purchasing function should be cen tralized in a separate depart-ment. Prenumbered purchase orders should originate from and be controlled by this department. A copy of the purchase order should be sent to the accounting and receiving departments. Consideration should be given to whether the receiving copy should show quantities.
3. Raw materials are purchased at a predetermined reorder level and in predetermined quantities. Since production levels often may vary during the year, quantities ordered may be either too small or too great for the current production demands.	3. Requests for purchases of raw materials should come from the production department management and be based on production schedules and quantities on hand per the perpetual records.
5. Raw materials are always purchased from the same vendor.	5. The purchasing department should be required to obtain competitive bids on all purchases over a specified amount.
6. There is no receiving department or receiving report. For proper separation of duties, the individuals responsible for receiving should be separate from the storeroom clerks.	6. A receiving department should be established. Personnel in this department should count or weigh all goods received and prepare a prenumbered receiving report. These reports should be signed, dated, and controlled. Copies should be sent to the accounting department, purchasing department, and store room.
7. There is no inspection department. Since high-cost electronic components usually are required to meet certain specifications, they should be tested for these requirements when received.	7. An inspection department should be established to inspect goods as they are received. Prenumbered inspection reports should be prepared and accounted for. A copy of these reports should be sent to the accounting department.

Review Questions

1. What is the nature of the procurement business process?
2. Identify the general steps in the procurement process.
3. How does a purchase requisition document differ from a purchase order document?
4. What accounting entry, if any, is necessitated by the issuance of a purchase order?
5. Briefly describe several types of purchase orders that are processed in SAP ERP.
6. Identify and describe three categories of information that SAP ERP maintains in vendor master records.
7. Identify the two major aspects of the procurement business process.
8. What is the function of a receiving report?
9. What is the invoice verification process?
10. Identify several controls directed at ensuring the integrity of the procurement business process.
11. How might budgetary control be exercised over the procure-ment business process? Give specific examples.
12. What factors or qualifications might be considered in the implementation of an approved vendors' list?

13. Criticize the following statement: "The major control over cash disbursements is the actual signing of the checks."
14. Identify the major control features in a cash disbursements business process.
15. What is a voucher system?
16. Identify several files that might be kept in a voucher system to provide useful information.
17. What is the major difference between booking invoices on date of approval and booking them on date of payment?
18. Identify several objectives of the HR business process.
19. Define the term *infotype* as it pertains to SAP ERP HR processing.
20. What is the meaning of the term *personnel event* in SAP ERP HR processing?
21. What is the basic source of information concerning federal requirements with respect to payroll processing?
22. Identify the major controls in a payroll business process.
23. Identify each of the following forms:
    a. Form 941   b. Form W-2
    c. Form W-3   d. Form 1099-Misc.
    e. Earnings statement

Discussion Questions and Problems

24. Which of the following procedures provides substantial assurance that invoices are paid for merchandise actually ordered and received in satisfactory condition?
    a. The purchasing department sends copies of the purchase requisition to the accounts payable department and the supplier.
    b. The receiving department counts all merchandise received.

    c. The accounts payable department sends purchase requisitions to the purchasing department and the stores department.
    d. The accounts payable department matches the purchase requisition, purchase order, receiving report, and invoice.
    e. The stores department sends copies of the invoices to the receiving department and the insurance department.

(IIA)

25. Which of the following in an internal control procedure would prevent a paid disbursement voucher from being presented for payment a second time?
    a. Vouchers should be prepared by individuals who are responsible for signing disbursement checks.
    b. Disbursement vouchers should be approved by at least two responsible management officials.
    c. The date on a disbursement voucher should be within a few days of the date the voucher is presented for payment.
    d. The official signing the check should compare the check with the voucher and should deface the voucher documents.
    (CPA)

26. An effective internal accounting control measure that protects against the preparation of improper or inaccurate disbursements would be to require that all checks be
    a. signed by an officer after necessary supporting evidence has been examined.
    b. reviewed by the treasurer before mailing.
    c. numbered sequentially and accounted for by internal auditors.
    d. perforated or otherwise effectively canceled when they are returned with the bank statement.
    (CPA)

27. Which of the following is an effective internal accounting control over cash payments?
    a. Signed checks should be mailed under the supervision of the check signer.
    b. Spoiled checks that have been voided should be disposed of immediately.
    c. Checks should be prepared only by people responsible for cash receipts and cash disbursements.
    d. A check-signing machine with two signatures should be used.
    (CPA)

28. In a properly designed accounts payable system, a voucher is prepared after the invoice, purchase order, requisition, and receiving report are verified. The next step in the system is to
    a. cancel the supporting documents.
    b. enter the check amount in the check register.
    c. approve the voucher for payment.
    d. post the voucher amount to the expense ledger.
    (CPA)

29. For the most effective internal accounting control, monthly bank statements should be received directly from the banks and reviewed by the
    a. controller.
    b. cash receipts accountant.
    c. cash disbursements accountant.
    d. internal auditor.
    (CPA)

30. In a properly designed internal accounting control system, the same employee may be permitted to
    a. receive and deposit checks and also approve write-offs of customer accounts.
    b. approve vouchers for payment and also sign checks.
    c. reconcile the bank statements and also receive and deposit cash.

    d. sign checks and also cancel supporting documents.
    (CPA)

31. In a properly designed internal accounting control system, the same employee should *not* be permitted to
    a. sign checks and cancel supporting documents.
    b. receive merchandise and prepare a receiving report.
    c. prepare disbursement vouchers and sign checks.
    d. initiate a request to order merchandise and approve merchandise received.
    (CPA)

32. For effective internal accounting control, the accounts payable department should compare the information on each vendor's invoice with the
    a. receiving report and the purchase order.
    b. receiving report and the voucher.
    c. vendor's packing slip and the purchase order.
    d. vendor's packing slip and the voucher.
    (CPA)

33. Which of the following is the most effective control procedure to detect vouchers that were prepared for the payment of goods that were *not* received?
    a. Count goods on receipt in the storeroom.
    b. Match purchase order, receiving report, and vendor's invoice for each voucher in the accounts payable department.
    c. Compare goods received with goods requisitioned in the receiving department.
    d. Verify vouchers for accuracy and approval in the internal audit department.
    (CPA)

34. The mailing of disbursement checks and remittance advices should be controlled by the employee who
    a. signed the checks last.
    b. approved the vouchers for payment.
    c. matched the receiving reports, purchase orders, and vendors' invoices.
    d. verified the mathematical accuracy of the vouchers and remittance advices.
    (CPA)

35. To determine whether accounts payable are complete, an auditor performs a test to verify that all merchandise received is recorded. The population of documents for this test consists of all
    a. vendors' invoices.
    b. purchase orders.
    c. receiving reports.
    d. canceled checks.
    (CPA)

36. Which of the following control procedures is *not* usually performed in the vouchers payable department?
    a. determining the mathematical accuracy of the vendor's invoice
    b. having an authorized person approve the voucher
    c. controlling the mailing of the check and remittance advice
    d. matching the receiving report with the purchase order
    (CPA)

37. For effective internal control purposes, the vouchers payable department should generally
    a. stamp, perforate, or otherwise cancel supporting documentation after payment is mailed.
    b. ascertain that each requisition is approved as to price, quantity, and quality of an authorized employee.
    c. obliterate the quantity ordered on the receiving department copy of the purchase order.
    d. establish the agreement of the vendor's invoice with the receiving report and purchase order.
    (CPA)

38. Which of the following procedures in the cash disbursements cycle should *not* be performed by the accounts payable department?
    a. comparing the vendor's invoice with the receiving report
    b. canceling supporting documentation after payment
    c. verifying the mathematical accuracy of the vendor's invoice
    d. signing the voucher for payment by an authorized person
    (CPA)

39. Mailing disbursement checks and remittance advices should be controlled by the employee who
    a. approves the vouchers for payment.
    b. matches the receiving reports, purchase orders, and vendors' invoices.
    c. maintains possession of the mechanical check-signing device.
    d. signs the checks last.
    (CPA)

40. Matching the supplier's invoice, the purchase order, and the receiving report normally should be the responsibility of the
    a. warehouse receiving function.
    b. purchasing function.
    c. general accounting function.
    d. treasury function.
    (CPA)

41. To avoid potential errors and irregularities, a well-designed system of internal accounting control in the accounts payable area should include a separation of which of the following functions?
    a. cash disbursements and vendor invoice verification
    b. vendor invoice verification and merchandise ordering
    c. physical handling of merchandise received and preparation of receiving reports
    d. check signing and cancelation of payment documentation
    (CPA)

42. It would be appropriate for the payroll accounting department to be responsible for which of the following functions?
    a. approving employee time records
    b. maintaining records of employment, discharges, and pay increases
    c. preparing periodic government reports as to employees' earnings and withholding taxes
    d. temporarily retaining unclaimed employee paychecks
    (CPA)

43. Jackson, the purchasing agent of Judd Hardware Wholesalers, has a relative who owns a retail hardware store. Jackson arranged for hardware to be delivered by manufacturers to the retail store on a COD basis, thereby enabling his relative to buy at Judd's wholesale prices. Jackson probably was able to accomplish this because of Judd's poor internal control over
    a. purchase orders.
    b. purchase requisitions.
    c. cash receipts.
    d. perpetual inventory records.
    (CPA)

44. Which of the following departments should have the responsibility for authorizing payroll rate changes?
    a. personnel
    b. payroll
    c. treasurer
    d. timekeeping
    (CPA)

45. Which of the following constitutes the most significant risk within the purchasing cycle?
    a. Receiving department personnel sign receiving documents without inspecting or counting the goods.
    b. Large quantities of relatively inexpensive parts are stored in open areas near workstations to reduce production slowdowns.
    c. Poor records of transfers between warehouses often result in unnecessary purchases and excess inventories.
    d. Warehouse personnel do not compare quantities received to quantities shown on transfer tickets.
    (IIA)

46. On receipt of a requisition, the stores manager initiates a three-part purchase order. Two copies go to the vendor, and one copy stays in the stores file. On receipt of goods, the stores manager matches the purchase order with the invoice and forwards them to accounts payable for payment. Which of the following statements best describes the internal control over purchasing?
    a. Adequate internal control exists.
    b. Inadequate separation of duties exists.
    c. Inadequate control over accounts payable exists.
    d. Inadequate control over the requisition process exists.
    (IIA)

47. An appropriate compliance test to confirm that only valid employees are on the payroll is to ensure that
    a. separate personnel folders are originated for each new employee.
    b. payroll checks are delivered directly to each supervisor by the payroll clerk.
    c. personnel places names on payroll only on the basis of written, prenumbered authorizations.
    d. payroll bank accounts are reconciled monthly to appropriate personnel.
    (IIA)

48. Which of the following would be the most appropriate test to determine whether purchase orders are being processed on a timely basis?
    a. Determine the dates of unpaid accounts payable invoices.
    b. Compare dates of selected purchase orders with those of purchase requisitions.
    c. Select a block of used purchase order numbers and account for all numbers in the block.
    d. Discuss processing procedures with operating personnel and observe actual processing of purchases.
    (IIA)

49. Which of the following procedures, noted by an auditor during a preliminary survey of the payroll function, indicates inadequate control?
    a. All changes to payroll data are documented by the personnel department on authorized change forms.
    b. Prior to distribution, payroll checks are verified to a computer-produced payroll register.
    c. A separate payroll bank account is used, and payroll checks are signed by the treasurer and distributed by personnel from the treasurer's office.
    d. All unclaimed payroll checks are returned to the payroll clerk for disposition.
    (IIA)

50. Proper internal control over the cash payroll function would mandate which of the following?
    a. The payroll clerk should fill the envelopes with cash and a computation of the net wages.
    b. Unclaimed pay envelopes should be retained by the paymaster.
    c. Each employee should be asked to sign a receipt.
    d. A separate checking account for payroll should be maintained.
    (CPA)

51. A CPA reviews a client's payroll procedures. The CPA would consider internal control to be less than effective if a payroll department supervisor was assigned the responsibility for
    a. reviewing and approving time reports for subordinate employees.
    b. distributing payroll checks to employees.
    c. hiring subordinate employees.
    d. initiating requests for salary adjustments for subordinate employees.
    (CPA)

52. Internal accounting control is strengthened when the quantity of merchandise ordered is omitted from the copy of the purchase order sent to the
    a. department that initiated the requisition.
    b. receiving department.
    c. purchasing agent.
    d. accounts payable department.
    (CPA)

53. Which of the following controls would be most effective in ensuring that recorded purchases are free of material errors?
    a. The receiving department compares the quantity ordered on purchase orders with the quantity received on receiving reports.
    b. Vendors' invoices are compared with purchase orders by an employee who is independent of the receiving department.
    c. Receiving reports require the signature of the individual who authorized the purchase.
    d. Purchase orders, receiving reports, and vendors' invoices are matched independently in preparing vouchers.
    (CPA)

54. The purpose of segregating the duties of hiring personnel and distributing payroll checks is to separate the
    a. administrative controls from the internal accounting controls.
    b. HR function from the controllership function.
    c. operational responsibility from the record-keeping responsibility.
    d. authorization of transactions from the custody of related assets.
    (CPA)

55. When goods are received, the receiving clerk should match the goods with the
    a. purchase order and the requisition form.
    b. vendor's invoice and the receiving report.
    c. vendor's shipping document and the purchase order.
    d. receiving report and the vendor's shipping document.
    (CPA)

56. Effective internal control procedures over the payroll function may include
    a. reconciliation of totals on job-time tickets with job reports by employees responsible for those specific jobs.
    b. verification of agreement of job-time tickets with employee clock card hours by a payroll department employee.
    c. preparation of payroll transaction journal entries by an employee who reports to the supervisor of the personnel department.
    d. custody of rate authorization records by the supervisor of the payroll department.
    (CPA)

57. For internal control purposes, which of the following individuals preferably should be responsible for the distribution of payroll checks?
    a. bookkeeper
    b. payroll clerk
    c. cashier
    d. receptionist
    (CPA)

58. The authority to accept incoming goods in receiving should be based on a(an)
    a. vendor's invoice.
    b. materials requisition.
    c. bill of lading.
    d. approved purchase order.
    (CPA)

59. Which of the following procedures most likely would be considered a weakness in an entity's internal controls over payroll?
    a. A voucher for the amount of the payroll is prepared in the general accounting department based on the payroll department's payroll summary?
    b. Payroll checks are prepared by the payroll department and signed by the treasurer.
    c. The employee who distributes payroll checks returns unclaimed payroll checks to the payroll department.
    d. The personnel department sends employees' termination notices to the payroll department.

    (CPA)

60. Indicate the objective of each of the following controls.
    a. canceling paid vouchers by perforating them at the time of payment
    b. simultaneously reconciling all bank accounts
    c. using prenumbered checks and carefully accounting for used and unused checks
    d. maintaining a record of numbers of all stock certificates and bonds
    e. periodically comparing personnel department rosters with payroll registers
    f. having checks mailed by people other than those causing them to be drawn

61. Indicate the objective of the following questions taken from an internal control checklist.
    a. Are voided checks mutilated properly and held available for subsequent inspection?
    b. Is the sequence of check numbers accounted for when reconciling bank accounts?
    c. Are payroll checks drawn against a separate payroll bank account?
    d. Are the names of employees hired reported in writing by the personnel office to the payroll department?
    e. Are payroll checks distributed to employees by someone other than the supervisor?
    f. Are salary payrolls approved by a responsible official prior to payment?

62. A treasurer insists that invoices be stamped "paid" prior to his actually signing the checks for payment. Discuss the merits of this policy.

63. Discuss the objectives of the following control procedures.
    a. purchasing policy manual
    b. approved vendors' list
    c. request for quotations form
    d. vendor rating plans (attribute evaluation)
    e. rotation of buyers

64. Identify the objective of distributing copies of a purchase order to the
    a. requisitioning department.
    b. receiving department.
    c. accounting department.

65. What are the differences between approving vendor invoices covering services rendered and those for physical goods sent to an organization? Illustrate with several examples.

66. You have completed an audit of activities within the purchasing department of your company. The department employs 30 buyers, seven supervisors, a manager, and clerical personnel. Purchases total about $500 million a year. Your audit disclosed the following conditions:
    a. The company has no formal rules on conflicts of interest. Your analysis produced evidence that one of the 30 buyers in the department owns a substantial interest in a major supplier and that she procures supplies averaging $50,000 a year from that supplier. The prices charged by the supplier are competitive.
    b. Buyers select proposed sources without submitting the lists of bidders for review. Your tests disclosed no evidence that higher costs were incurred as a result of that practice.
    c. Buyers who originate written requests for quotations from suppliers receive the suppliers' bids directly from the mailroom. In your test of 100 purchases based on competitive bids, you found that in 75 of the 100 cases, the low bidders were awarded the purchase orders.
    d. Requests to purchase (requisitions) received in the purchasing department from other departments in the company must be signed by persons authorized to do so. Your examination of 200 such requests disclosed that three, all for small amounts, were not signed properly. The buyer who had issued all three orders honored the requests because he misunderstood the applicable procedure. The clerical personnel charged with reviewing such requests had given them to the buyer in error.

Required

For each of the four conditions, state
    a. the risk, if any, incurred if each condition described above is permitted to continue.
    b. the control, if any, you would recommend to prevent continuation of the condition described.

    (IIA)

67. The flowchart in Figure 9.11 was prepared by a CPA to portray the raw materials purchasing function of one of her clients, a medium-sized manufacturing company, from preparing initial documents through vouching for invoices for payment in accounts payable. The flowchart was a portion of the work performed on the audit engagement to evaluate internal control.

Required

Identify and explain the systems and control weaknesses evident from the flowchart. Include the internal control weaknesses resulting from activities performed or not performed. All documents are prenumbered.

    (CPA)

68. A company employs about 50 production workers and has the following payroll procedures.

    The factory foreman interviews applicants and, on the basis of the interview, either hires or rejects the applicants. When the applicant is hired, he or she prepares a W-4 Form (Employee's Withholding Exemption Certificate) and gives it to the foreman. The foreman

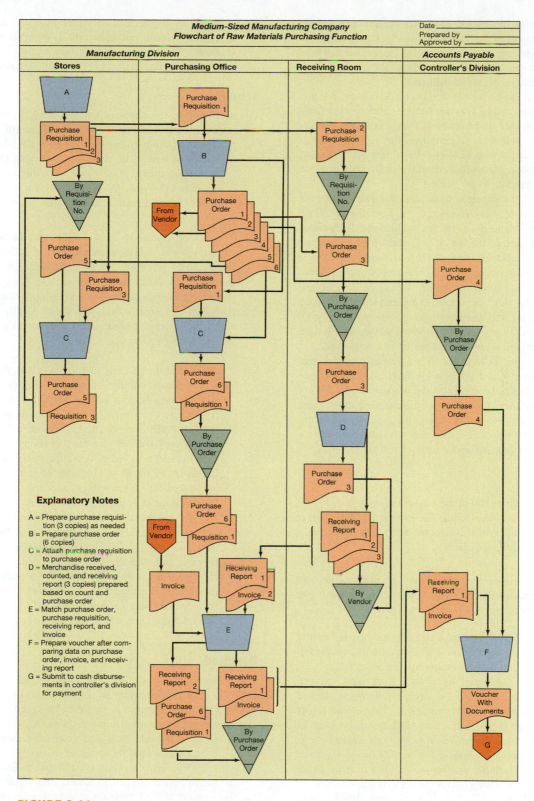

FIGURE 9.11

Flowchart for Problem 67

writes the hourly rate of pay for the new employee in the corner of the W-4 Form and then gives the form to a payroll clerk as notice that the worker has been employed. The foreman verbally advises the payroll department of rate adjustments.

A supply of blank time cards is kept in a box near the entrance to the factory. Each worker takes a time card on Monday morning, fills in his or her name, and notes in pencil on the time card his or her daily arrival and departure times. At the end of the week, the workers drop the time cards in a box near the door to the factory.

The completed time cards are taken from the box on Monday morning by a payroll clerk. Two payroll clerks divide the cards alphabetically between them, one taking the A to L section of the payroll and the other taking the M to Z section. Each clerk is fully responsible for his or her section of the payroll. He or she computes the gross pay, deductions, and net pay; posts the details to the employee's earnings records; and prepares and numbers the payroll checks. Employees are removed automatically from the payroll when they fail to turn in a time card.

Payroll checks are signed manually by the chief accountant and given to the foreman. The foreman distributes the checks to the workers in the factory and arranges for delivery of the checks to the workers who are absent. The payroll bank account is reconciled by the chief accountant, who also prepares the various quarterly and annual payroll tax reports.

Required

a. Draw a flowchart of these procedures.
b. List your suggestions for improving the company's system of internal control for the factory hiring practices and payroll procedures.

(CPA)

69. A CPA's audit working papers contain a narrative description of a segment of the Croyden Factory, Inc., payroll system and an accompanying flowchart as follows:

The internal control system with respect to the personnel department is well functioning and is *not* included in the accompanying flowchart.

At the beginning of each work week, payroll clerk no. 1 reviews the payroll department files to determine the employment status of factory employees and then prepares time cards and distributes them as each individual arrives at work. This payroll clerk, who is also responsible for custody of the signature stamp machine, verifies the identity of each payee before delivering signed checks to the foreman.

At the end of each work week, the foreman distributes payroll checks for the preceding work week. Concurrent with this activity, the foreman reviews the current week's employee time cards,

notes the regular and over time hours worked on a summary form, and initials the aforementioned time cards. The foreman then delivers all time cards and unclaimed payroll checks to payroll clerk no. 2.

Required

a. Based on the narrative and Figure 9.12, what are the weaknesses in the system of internal control?
b. Based on the narrative and Figure 9.12, what inquiries should be made with respect to clarifying the existence of *possible additional weaknesses* in the system of internal control? (*Note:* Do not discuss the internal control system of the personnel department.)

(CPA)

70. The Poster Company is a beauty and barber supplies and equipment distributorship servicing a five-state area. Management generally has been pleased with the overall operations of the company to date. However, the present purchasing system has evolved through practice rather than having been formally designed. Consequently, it is inadequate and needs to be redesigned. A description of the present purchasing system is as follows:

Whenever the quantity of an item is low, the inventory supervisor phones the purchasing department with the item description and quantity to be ordered. A purchase order is prepared in duplicate in the purchasing department. The original is sent to the vendor, and the copy is retained in the purchasing department filed in numerical order. When the shipment arrives, the inventory supervisor sees that each item received is checked off on the packing slip that accompanies the shipment. The packing slip is then forwarded to the accounts payable department. When the invoice arrives, the packing slip is compared with the invoice in the accounts payable department. Once any differences between the packing slip and the invoice are reconciled, a check is drawn for the appropriate amount and is mailed to the vendor with a copy of the invoice. The packing slip is attached to the invoice and filed alphabetically in the paid invoice file.

Required

The Poster Company intends to redesign its purchasing system from the point in time when an item needs to be ordered until payment is made. The system should be designed to ensure that all the proper controls are incorporated into the system.

a. Identify the internally and externally generated documents that would be required to satisfy the minimum requirements of a basic system, and indicate the number of copies of each document that would be needed.
b. Explain how all these documents should interrelate and flow among the various departments, including the final destination or file for each copy.

(CMA)

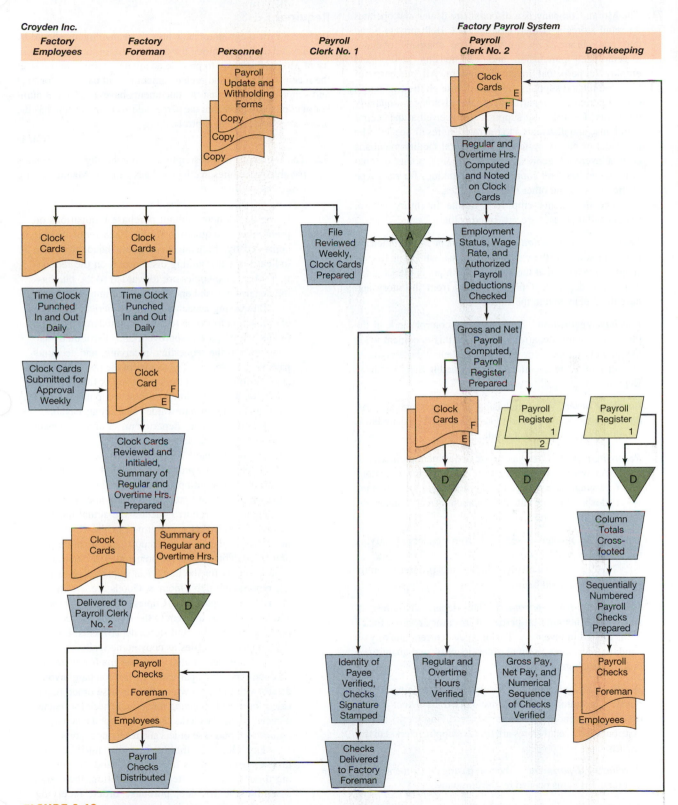

FIGURE 9.12

Flowchart for Problem 69

71. The Moran Company is a discount tire dealer that operates 25 retail stores in a metropolitan area. Both private-brand and name-brand tires are sold. The company operates a centralized purchasing and warehousing facility and employs a perpetual inventory system. All purchases of tires and related supplies are placed through the company's central purchasing department to take advantage of quantity discounts. The tires and supplies are received at the central warehouse and distributed to the retail stores as needed. The perpetual inventory system at the central facility maintains current inventory records, designated reorder points, optimal order quantities, and continuous stocktakings for each type of tire and size and other related supplies.

The documents employed in the inventory control system and their uses are presented below.

Retail stores requisition   This document is submitted by the retail stores to the central warehouse whenever tires or supplies are needed at the stores. The shipping clerks in the warehouse department fill the orders from inventory and have them delivered to the stores.

Purchase requisition   The inventory control clerk in the inventory control department prepares this document when the quantity on hand for an item falls below the designated reorder point. The document is forwarded to the Purchasing Department.

Purchase order   The purchasing department prepares this document when items need to be ordered. The document is submitted to an authorized vendor.

Receiving report   The warehouse department prepares this document when ordered items are received from vendors. The receiving clerk completes the document by indicating the vendor's name, the date the shipment is received, and the quantity of each item received.

Invoice   An invoice is received from vendors specifying the amounts owed by Moran.

The departments involved in Moran's inventory control system are described below.

Inventory control department   This department is responsible for maintaining all perpetual inventory records for all items carried in inventory. This includes current quantity on hand, reorder point, optimal order quantity, and quantity on order for each item carried.

Warehouse department   This department maintains the physical inventory of all items carried in inventory. All orders from vendors are received (receiving clerk) and all distributions to retail stores are filled (shipping clerks) in this department.

Purchasing department   The purchasing department places all orders for items needed by the company.

Accounts payable department   Accounts payable maintains all open accounts with vendors and other creditors. All payments are processed in this department.

Required

Prepare a flow diagram to show how these documents should be coordinated and used among the departments at the central facility of Moran Company to provide adequate internal control over the receipt, issuance, and replenishment of and payment for tires and supplies. Assume that the documents have a sufficient number of copies to ensure that the perpetual inventory system has the necessary basic internal controls.

(CMA)

72. The following is a description of purchasing and accounts payable procedures in effect at the Northwest Manufacturing Company:

Using departments submit purchase requisitions on prenumbered requisition forms. Each requisition is approved by the using department head, who also indicates the accounting distribution on the requisition form. Two copies are forwarded to the purchasing department, and one copy is filed numerically.

Purchasing accounts for the numerical sequence of requisition forms on receipt. Prenumbered purchase orders are prepared, approved, and distributed: one copy each to the requesting, receiving, and accounts payable departments. Two copies of the purchase order are sent to the vendor, and one copy is filed numerically with the requisition form attached to it. A copy of the requisition is also forwarded to accounts payable.

In the receiving department, counters inspect shipments and record their counts on tally sheets. The counters do not have access to purchase orders. The tally sheets are forwarded to the head of the receiving department. She compares the tally sheets with the purchase orders and prepares a prenumbered receiving report. This report indicates the actual quantity received. Items that are returned to the vendor are indicated on the receiving report, and separate prenumbered debit memos are prepared. The department head accounts for the numerical sequence of receiving reports and debit memos. Goods are transferred to the stores department. Copies of receiving reports and debit memos are sent to the requesting, accounts payable, purchasing, and stores departments. Each of these departments files its copy numerically.

Invoices are routed from the mailroom to the accounts payable department. Clerks compare invoice details with those shown on the purchase order, requisition form, and receiving report and check for mathematical errors. The clerks also account for the numerical sequence of purchase orders and receiving reports.

The clerks withhold invoices until all the preceding documents are received and the matching process is complete. On completion, the clerks assemble the invoice, purchase order, receiving report, and any related debit memos into a voucher package, initial the package, and forward the package to the accounts payable supervisor. The supervisor reviews the package, initials it to indicate approval for payment, indicates the date payment should be made, and forwards the package to the cash disbursements clerk, who then forwards it to data processing. After processing for input, the voucher packages are returned to the accounts payable department.

Checks prepared by data processing are returned to accounts payable, attached to the corresponding voucher package, and submitted to the accounts payable supervisor for a final review before submission to the controller for signature. The controller reviews each voucher package and manually signs the checks. The checks and voucher packages are then sent to the treasurer, who also manually signs the checks. Two signatures are required on all checks. The treasurer's secretary cancels all supporting documents and returns the canceled documents and the checks to the accounts payable supervisor. The voucher packages are filed by a clerk, who also prepares a data processing input sheet showing payee, check number, amount, and so on. The input sheets are processed to produce the cash disbursements records. The accounts payable supervisor forwards the signed checks to the mailroom.

Freight invoices, which are substantial in total amount, are routed from the mailroom to a clerk, who checks their mathematical accuracy. The freight invoices are then forwarded to the accounts payable supervisor for approval. The supervisor indicates the date payment should be made and then forwards the invoices for check preparation by data processing. At month's end, the cash disbursements book is totaled, and a journal entry is prepared by the cash disbursements clerk. It is approved by the accounts payable supervisor and given to the general ledger clerk for posting. The general ledger clerk is independent of all accounts payable and disbursement functions. Monthly bank statements are sent directly to the accounts payable supervisor, who performs the reconciliation.

Required

a. Design a flowchart of the present system.
b. Identify potential internal control weaknesses in the present procedures. Exclude the data processing department's operations in your review. Suggest modifications to present procedures to support your recommendations concerning potential weaknesses.

73. The accounting and internal control procedures relating to purchases of materials by the Branden Company, a medium-sized company that manufactures special machinery to order, have been described by your junior accountant in the following terms.

After approval by manufacturing department supervisors, materials purchase requisitions are forwarded to the purchasing department supervisor, who distributes such requisitions to the several employees under her control. These employees prepare prenumbered

purchase orders in triplicate, account for all numbers, and send the original purchase order to the vendor. One copy of the purchase order is sent to the receiving department, where it is used as a receiving report. The other copy is filed in the purchasing department.

When the materials are received, they are moved directly to the storeroom and issued to the supervisors on informal requests. The receiving department sends a receiving report (with its copy of the purchase order attached) to the purchasing department and forwards copies of the receiving report to the storeroom and to the accounting department.

Vendors' invoices for material purchases, received in duplicate in the mailroom, are sent to the purchasing department and directed to the employee who placed the related order. The employee then compares the invoice with the copy of the purchase order on file in the purchasing department for price and terms and compares the invoice quantity received as reported by the shipping and receiving department on its copy of the purchase order. The purchasing department employees also check discounts, footings, and extensions, after which they initial the invoice to indicate approval for payment. The invoice is then submitted to the voucher section of the accounting department, where it is coded for account distribution, assigned a voucher number, entered in the voucher register, and filed according to payment due date.

On payment dates, prenumbered checks are requisitioned by the voucher section from the cashier and prepared except for signature. After the checks are prepared, they are returned to the cashier, who puts them through a check-signing machine, accounts for the sequence of numbers, and passes them to the cash disbursements bookkeeper for entry in the cash disbursements book. The cash disbursements bookkeeper then returns the checks to the voucher section, which then notes payment dates in the voucher register, places the checks in envelopes, and sends them to the mailroom. The vouchers are then filed in numerical sequence. At the end of each month, one of the voucher clerks prepares an adding machine tape of unpaid items in the voucher register and compares the total thereof with the general ledger balance and investigates any difference disclosed by such comparison.

Required

Discuss the weaknesses, if any, in the internal control of Branden's purchasing and subsequent procedures, and suggest supplementary or revised procedures for remedying each weakness with regard to

a. requisition of materials.
b. receipt and storage of materials.
c. functions of the purchasing department.
d. functions of the accounting department.

(CPA)

74. The mail is opened by an accounting clerk. Vendor invoices are stamped with a voucher stamp and forwarded to the purchasing agent. The purchasing agent matches the receiving report, purchase order, and vendor invoices. He then forwards the combined voucher set to the controller, who reviews the documents, approves them, and records the account coding within the voucher stamp. She then forwards the voucher set to the accounts payable clerk.

The accounts payable clerk records the approved invoices onto an accounts payable vendor card and a purchases journal using a one-write system. The clerk then initials the invoice and files it alphabetically by vendor. At month's end, the clerk prepares an accounts payable aging report and totals the columns in the purchases journal, which is used by the controller for preparing a monthly journal voucher.

The controller uses the accounts payable aging report to indicate those vendors to be paid. In addition, the accounts payable clerk files invoices that contain cash discount terms in a calendar according to due date. The accounts payable clerk manually writes the checks, posts the amounts to the vendor cards, and records the amount in the cash disbursements journal using a one-write system. The clerk then runs the checks through a check protector and forwards them to the check signers.

Two signatures are required. Normally, the controller signs the checks first, followed by the office manager. The checks occasionally are signed in advance by the office manager. Normally, the supporting invoice vouchers are not given to the check signers. The checks are then returned to the accounts payable clerk, who mails them along with any requested remittance advices to the vendors. The clerk then files the vouchers alphabetically in a paid bills file.

Each month the accounts payable clerk receives the bank statement and canceled checks. Using the cash disbursements journal, the clerk prepares the bank reconciliation and forwards it to the controller for her review and approval.

Required

a. Prepare a DFD of these procedures.
b. Prepare an analytic flowchart of these procedures.
c. Identify potential internal control weaknesses in these procedures.

75. ConSport Corporation is a regional wholesaler of sporting goods. The systems flowchart in Figure 9.13 and the following description present ConSport's cash distribution system.

a. The accounts payable department approves payment of all invoices (I) for the purchase of inventory. Invoices are matched with the purchase requisitions (PR), purchase orders (PO), and receiving reports (RR). The accounts payable clerks focus on vendor name and skim the documents when they are combined.

b. When all the documents for an invoice are assembled, a two-copy disbursement voucher (DV) is prepared, and the transaction is recorded in the voucher register (VR). The DV and supporting documents are then filed alphabetically by vendor.

c. A two-copy journal voucher (JV) that summarizes each day's entries in the VR is prepared daily. The first copy is sent to the general ledger department, and the second copy is filed in the accounts payable department by date.

d. The vendor file is searched daily for the DVs of invoices that are due to be paid. Both copies of DVs that are due to be paid are sent to the treasury department along with the supporting documents. The cashier prepares a check for each vendor, signs the check, and records it in the check register (CR). Copy 1 of the DV is attached to the check copy and filed in check-number order in the treasury department. Copy 2 and the supporting documents are returned to the accounts payable department and filed alphabetically by vendor.

e. A two-copy JV that summarizes each day's checks is prepared. Copy 1 is sent to the general ledger department, and Copy 2 is filed in the treasury department by date.

f. The cashier receives the monthly bank statement with canceled checks and prepares the bank reconciliation (BR). If an adjustment is required as a consequence of the BR, a two-copy JV is prepared. Copy 1 is sent to the general ledger department. Copy 2 is attached to Copy 1 of the BR and filed by month in the treasury department. Copy 2 of the BR is sent to the internal audit department.

Required

ConSport's cash disbursement system has some weaknesses. Review the cash disbursement system, and for each weakness in the system,

a. identify where the weakness exists by using the reference number that appears to the left of each symbol.
b. describe the nature of the weakness.
c. make a recommendation on how to correct the weakness.
   Use a three-column format in preparing your answer:

Reference Number	Nature of Weakness	Recommendation to Correct Weakness

(CMA)

76. In 2001, XY Company purchased over $10 million of office equipment under its special ordering system, with individual orders ranging from $5,000 to $30,000. Special orders entail low-volume items that have been included in an authorized user's budget. Department heads include in their annual budget requests the types of equipment and their estimated cost. The budget, which limits the types and dollar amounts of office equipment a department head can requisition, is approved at the beginning of the year by the board of directors. Department heads prepare a purchase requisition form for equipment and forward the requisition to the purchasing department. XY's special ordering system functions as follows:

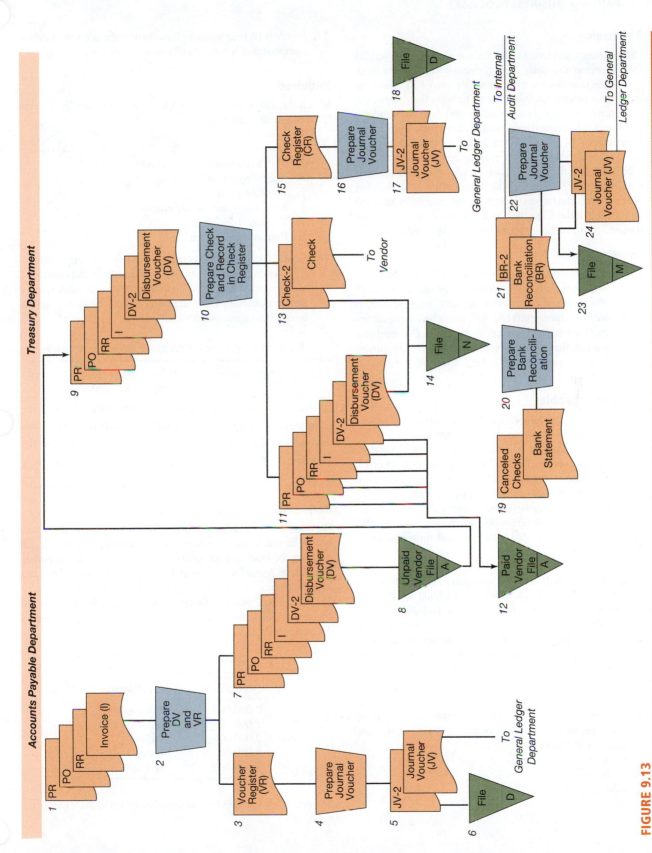

FIGURE 9.13

Flowchart for Problem 75

Purchasing

On receiving a purchase requisition, one of five buyers verifies that the person requesting the equipment is a department head. The buyer then selects the appropriate vendor by searching the various vendor catalogs on file. The buyer then phones the vendor, requesting a price quotation, and gives the vendor a verbal order. A prenumbered purchase order is then processed, with the original sent to the vendor, a copy to the department head, a copy to receiving, a copy to accounts payable, and a copy filed in the open requisition file. When the buyer is orally informed by the receiving department that the item has been received, the buyer transfers the purchase order from the unfilled file to the filled file. Once a month the buyer reviews the unfilled file to follow up and expedite open orders.

Receiving

The receiving department receives a copy of the purchase order. When equipment is received, the receiving clerk stamps the purchase order with the date received and, if applicable, in red pen prints any differences between quantity on the purchase order and quantity received. The receiving clerk forwards the stamped purchase order and equipment to the requisitioning department head and orally notifies the purchasing department.

Accounts Payable

On receipt of a purchase order, the accounts payable clerk files the purchase order in the open purchase order file. When a vendor invoice is received, the invoice is matched with the applicable purchase order, and a payable is set up by debiting the equipment account of the department requesting the items. Unpaid invoices are filed by due date, and at the due date a check is prepared. The invoice and purchase order are filed by purchase order number in a paid invoice file, and then the check is forwarded to the treasurer for signature.

Treasurer

Checks received daily from the accounts payable department are sorted into two groups: those over $10,000 and those of $10,000 and less. Checks for $10,000 or less are machine-signed. The cashier maintains the key and signature plate to the check-signing machine and maintains a record of use of the check-signing machine. All checks over $10,000 are signed by the treasurer or the controller.

Required

Describe the internal accounting control weaknesses relating to purchases and payments of special orders of XY Company for each of the following functions:

    a. purchasing
    b. receiving
    c. accounts payable
    d. treasurer

(CPA)

77. Figure 9.14 is an analytic flowchart of the accounts payable component of a procurement business process.

Required

Match the following list of eight items to the labels Q1 through Q8 that appear in the figure.

    1. File
    2. Invoice
    3. Match to requisition and purchase order
    4. Receiving report
    5. Purchase order
    6. Forward to cash disbursements
    7. Voucher
    8. Purchase requisition

78. Excel® Assignment: Procurement Expenditure Analysis.

    A company has prepared a spreadsheet that contains 3 years of procurement expenditures for its four sales groups: electronics, computers, appliances, and furniture. Several rows of this spreadsheet are illustrated.

Procurement Expenditures by Group/Category

Group	Category	2010 (in dollars)	2011 (in dollars)	2012 (in dollars)
Electronics	Televisions	1,750,000	2,500,000	3,250,000
Computers	Laptop	1,500,000	2,100,000	2,850,000
Appliances	Kitchen	1,450,000	1,880,000	2,005,000
Furniture	Family Room	1,230,000	1,500,000	1,700,000

Required

Download the spreadsheet file titled "chapter_9_78" from the textbook Web site. Compute column totals for each year and the 3-year summary totals for each group/category row. Then prepare an evaluation of these 3-year summary totals by comparing each to the amounts in the following table and entering the descriptive result (i.e., "average," "excellent," etc.) into the spreadsheet column that is next to the column containing the 3-year summary totals for each group/category that you calculated.

Amount (in dollars)	Evaluation
500,000	Unacceptable
1,000,000	Below Average
2,000,000	Average
5,000,000	Above Average
8,000,000	Excellent

The evaluation can best be accomplished by using the VLOOKUP function.

FIGURE 9.14

Flowchart for Problem 77

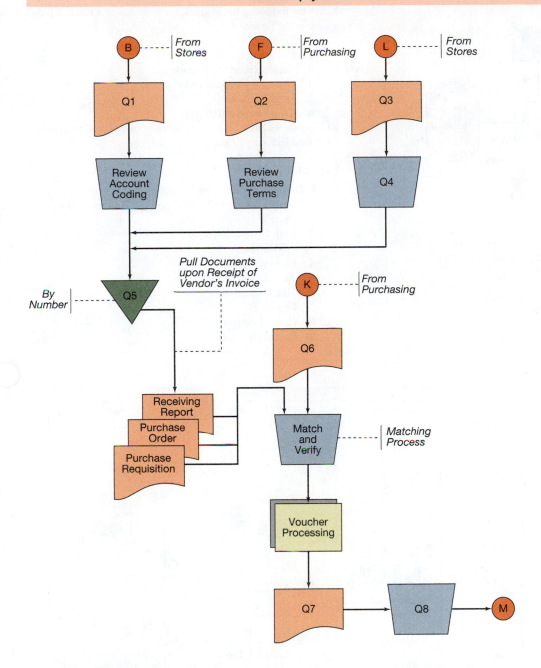

Accounts payable

79. Match the following list of seven items to the letters A through G in Figure 9.15.
    1. Purchase Database
    2. Purchase Order
    3. Prepare Order
    4. Vendor
    5. Purchase Requisition
    6. Select Vendor
    7. Order Processing
80. Figure 9.16 is a portion of a business process diagram for a procurement business process.

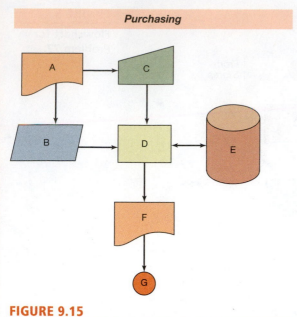

FIGURE 9.15

Flowchart for Problem 79.

Required

Match the following list of six items to the labels A through F that appear in the figure.

1. Purchase Requisition
2. Receiving Report
3. Create Receiving Report
4. Generate purchase order
5. Purchase order
6. Create Requisition

81. Figure 9.17 is a document flowchart of a payroll process in a manufacturing firm.

Required

Match the following list of nine functional processes to the labels A through I that appear in the figure a s the column headings.

1. Payroll
2. Cash Disbursement
3. Production
4. Internal Audit
5. Accounts Payable
6. Timekeeping
7. Personnel
8. General Ledger
9. Cost Distribution

FIGURE 9.16

Flowchart for Problem 80

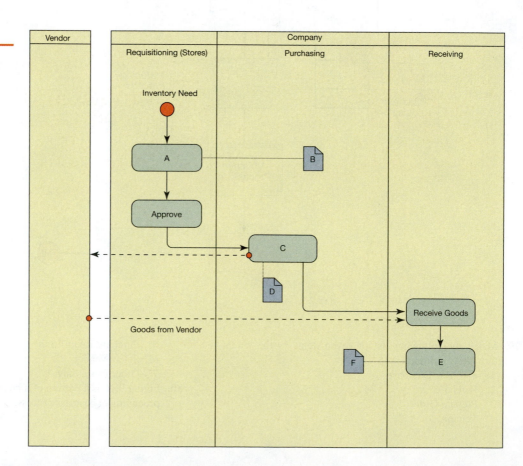

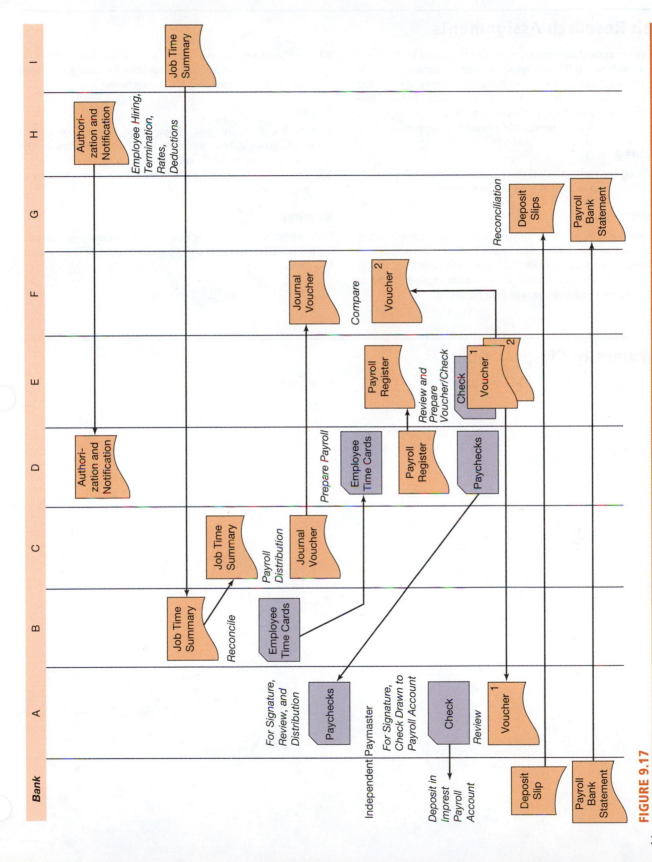

FIGURE 9.17

Flowchart for Problem 81

Web Research Assignments

82. eProcurement (electronic procurement) involves the business-to-business (B2B) and business-to-consumer purchase and sale of goods and services through electronic means. The value chain for B2B eProcurement includes Indent Management, eTendering, eAuctioning, Vendor Management, Catalogue Management, and Contract Management.

Required

Briefly explain each activity in the B2B eProcurement value chain.

83. Ethics is an important issue in procurement.

Required

Assume that you are a controller of a midsize manufacturing company. You have been asked by the CEO to write a memo to your purchasing managers, explaining to them basic good ethical practices in purchasing. Include at least one example of unethical conduct in the purchasing area in your memo.

84. SAP's (www.sap.com) application suites and ERP software include sophisticated capabilities for managing human resources and processing HR transactions.

Required

Visit SAP's Web site and review their support for human resources. Write a brief memo that explains the various HR processes included in SAP's software.

85. Paying payroll taxes is an important part of the overall payroll process.

Required

Write a brief memo outlining how a small business might process payroll and electronically pay its payroll taxes and file the related IRS forms.

Answers to Chapter Quiz

1. d   **2.** b   **3.** c   **4.** a   **5.** b   **6.** a   **7.** c   **8.** d   **9.** b   **10.** a

The Production Business Process

Learning Objectives

Careful study of this chapter will enable you to:

- Describe information flows and controls in the production business process.
- Describe the major features of a property accounting business process.
- Identify and describe key components of computer-integrated manufacturing (CIM) systems.
- Depict the flow of processing necessary to support manufacturing resource planning (MRP II) systems.
- Describe why activity-based costing is particularly relevant to CIM systems.

The Production Business Process

Production planning and control, inventory control, cost accounting, and property accounting are typical functions in the production business process of manufacturing firms. Few, if any, production activities exist as separate functions in nonmanufacturing firms, but to some extent most organizations hold some inventories and manage some type of productive activity, such as selling goods or services. Thus the principles of production control are relevant to most organizations.

This section provides an overview of the basic information flows and controls that support production planning and control, inventory control, and cost accounting within a manufacturing firm. The discussion includes an overview of controls relevant to the property accounting business process.

CASE IN POINT

SAP ERP has an operations component that supports operational processes in procurement and logistics execution, product development and manufacturing, and sales and service.

Production Planning and Control

Figure 10.1 provides an overview of the production business process. A sales order or sales forecast causes the creation of production orders, which specify items that should be produced. Materials are requisitioned and production is scheduled. Items are produced, inspected, transferred to finished goods inventory, and then transferred to shipping to complete the process.

Figure 10.2 is a business process diagram that details the functions involved in the production business process. Sales generate production requests based on sales orders or a sales forecast.

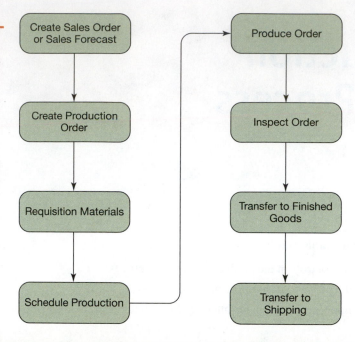

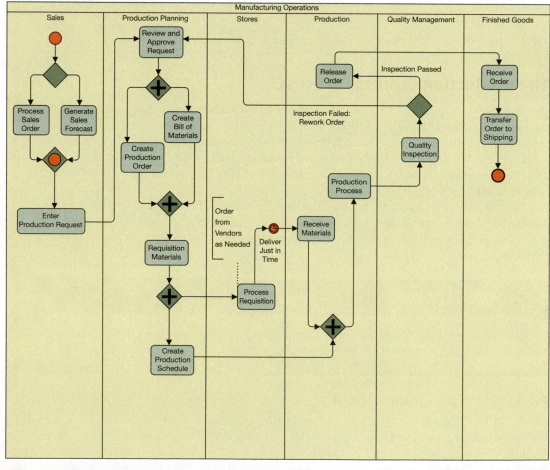

Production planning reviews and approves production requests. This requires the determination of which products to produce and scheduling production to make optimal use of resources. Basic production requirements are provided by the **bill-of-materials** and the **master operations list.** Detailed material specifications for a product are recorded on the bill of materials. The bill of materials lists all required parts and their descriptions in subassembly order. A master operations list is similar to a bill of materials: Detailed labor operations, their sequencing, and their related machine requirements are specified in the master operations list for a product. The bill-of-materials and the master operations list are used extensively in the production business process. In a standard cost system, the standard material and labor costs might be included on the bill-of-materials and master operations list.

Determining what products to manufacture requires an integration of the demand for a product, the product requirements, and the production resources available to the firm. Resources available for production are communicated to the production planning function through **inventory status reports** and **factor availability reports**. An inventory status report details the material resources in inventory that are available for production. A factor availability report communicates the availability of labor and machine resources. Demand requirements for a product depend on whether it is custom manufactured per customer order or manufactured routinely for inventory. If the product is manufactured for inventory, production requirements depend on a sales forecast. Sales forecasts must be related to the amount of a product held in inventory. This information is provided in a finished goods status report, which lists the quantities of products in inventory. The integration of all these factors results in a production plan for the organization. The production plan is embodied in a production schedule and production order(s).

A **production order** serves as authorization for the production departments to make certain products. **Materials requisitions** are issued for each production order to authorize the stores (i.e., materials inventory) function to release materials to the production departments. The items and quantities shown on a materials requisition are determined from the specifications in the product's bill of materials. Stores processes materials requisition requests and delivers items to production on a just-in-time (JIT) basis. Stores orders items from vendors as necessary.

Production receives materials from stores and produces goods. Labor operations are recorded on **job time cards**. These cards are posted to production orders to record labor costs. **Production status reports** are sent periodically from the production departments to the production planning function. A production status report details the work completed on individual production orders as they move through the production process. It is used to monitor the status of open production orders and to revise departmental production schedules as necessary.

As production is completed, a quality inspection is performed by the quality management function. Production that fails inspection is reworked as necessary. Production that passes inspection is released to finished goods inventory, where it is stored until it is transferred to shipping.

Figure 10.3 uses message flows between pools to illustrate the use of online databases for stores inventory and production orders. Production planning enters production order master records into the production orders database. These master records are updated with production order details and materials details from bills of material. The stores inventory database and the production orders database are also updated when materials are requisitioned.

COST ACCOUNTING CONTROLS   Cost accounting systems focus on the management of manufacturing inventories: materials, work in process (WIP), and finished goods. **Job costing** is a procedure in which costs are distributed to particular **jobs** or production orders. It requires a production order control system.

In **process costing**, costs are compiled in process or department accounts by periods (day, week, or month). At the end of each period, the cost of each process is divided by the units produced to determine the average cost per unit. Process costing is used where it is not possible or desirable to identify successive jobs or production lots. "Costs" in either job costing or process costing may be actual costs or standard costs.

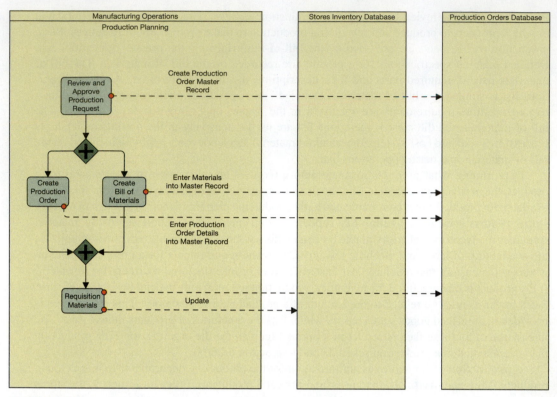

FIGURE 10.3

Business Process Diagram of Production Databases

Control over inventories and production is based on separation of functions and basic records and documentation, such as production orders, material requisition forms, and labor time cards. Protection of inventories from physical theft involves security and access provisions as well as periodic physical counts and tests against independent records. Overhead costs are often applied on the basis of direct labor hours or direct labor costs and are therefore posted at the same time as labor costs. Cost accounting initiates a journal voucher reflecting each batch of job time tickets posted that contains a debit to the WIP inventory and credits to payroll and manufacturing overhead. This journal voucher is transmitted and posted to the general ledger.

The cost accounting function receives a copy of the production order directly from production planning as well as a copy from the production departments when the production order is complete. In a similar fashion, cost accounting receives copies of materials requisitions from both the stores inventory and the production departments. This distribution of documents implements an adequate segregation of duties and provides accountability for the production departments. The comparison of these documents ensures that production has been authorized and that materials have been requisitioned in response to production requirements. The periodic reconciliation of time cards with production labor reports is another important control function.

As production orders are completed and inspected production is transferred to inventory, several documents must be updated. Production control removes the production order from its file of open production orders. Cost accounting closes the related WIP record, summarizes this activity, and communicates a completed production cost summary to various managers. The finished goods inventory records are updated to reflect availability of the product.

Control of production efficiency requires comparisons of actual production with scheduled production and an analysis of related variances. Production control also requires a comparison and analysis of other factors, including budgeted cost versus actual cost for individual production orders and/or departments and facility usage versus facility availability by department. The control of inventory loss and the maintenance of optimal inventory levels are also important to overall production control.

Inventory Control

The control of inventories is accomplished through a series of inventory records and reports that provide such information as inventory use, inventory balances, and minimum and maximum levels of stock. Reorder points and procedures are established. A **reorder point** is the level of inventory at which it is desirable to order or produce additional items to avoid an out-of-stock condition. The development of reorder points requires an analysis of product demand, ordering or production setup costs, vendor or production lead time, inventory holding costs, and the costs associated with an out-of-stock condition such as lost sales or inefficient use of production facilities.

CASE IN POINT

Wireless technology has extended real-time inventory control to the stand-alone vending machine. Cantaloupe Systems (www.cantaloupesystems.com), a leading provider of wireless, cloud-computing solutions for the vending industry, markets the Seed, a miniature device that is installed into vending machines and transmits sales data wirelessly to a remote server. The data generates online reports that facilitate inventory management and control. The system sends alerts to a PC or mobile phone when a machine is jammed, loses power, or is out of items such as soda or candies that it vends.

Because inventory control aims at minimizing total inventory costs, it is important to decide on the size of each purchase order quantity, that is, the most **economic order quantity (EOQ)**. The reorder quantity must balance two cost systems—total carrying costs and total ordering costs. A formula for calculating the EOQ is

$$EOQ = \sqrt{\frac{2RS}{PI}}$$

where

EOQ = economic order quantity (units)

R = requirements for the item this period (units)

S = purchasing cost per order

P = unit cost

I = inventory carrying cost per period, expressed as a percentage of the period inventory value

Once the EOQ has been calculated, the timing of the order must be decided; that is, the reorder point must be determined. If the order lead time and the inventory usage rate are known, determining the reorder point is straightforward. *Lead time* is the time between placing an order and the receipt of the goods. The *inventory usage rate* is the quantity of the goods used over a period of time. The reorder point is the point where the inventory level reaches the number of units that would be consumed during the lead time. Expressed as a formula,

Reorder point = lead time × average inventory usage rate

Perpetual inventory records are the best source of the inventory information necessary to calculate the EOQ. The units in the beginning inventory, on order, receipts, issues, and balance on hand should be included in these records. Appropriate control over inventories requires periodic verification of items on hand. This can be done on a rotational basis when perpetual inventory records exist, or it can be done with a periodic physical count.

An important part of inventory control is the evaluation of inventory turnover to determine the age, condition, and status of stock. Special controls should be established to write down obsolete and slow-moving inventory items and to compare the balance with an appropriately established inventory level. A stock status report showing detailed use by period is especially helpful in maintaining the inventory at a proper level and controlling slow-moving items.

Control over inventory includes methods of storing and handling. Items need to be classified and identified properly so that they can be located appropriately and so that proper verification and reporting are possible. The storage and handling of items must provide security against embezzlement, protection against damage or spoilage, avoidance of obsolescence, and assurance of proper control.

Inventory is a substantial investment. An inventory control system should provide status reports on each active product so that the company can reasonably meet customer demands. Because of the large number of inventory items and the variety of transactions affecting them, it is difficult to keep inventory and production information up to date with manual systems. A computerized inventory control system can result in a substantial reduction in inventory investment; these savings include a reduction in inventory without a corresponding decrease in service, determination of EOQ and order points, establishment of adequate safety stocks, and forecasts of future demand based on current and past information. Usage records, turnover and obsolescence analyses, reorder points and quantities, and other statistics relevant to inventory control are difficult to generate in purely manual systems.

Lean Production

Lean production is a production system in which parts are produced only as they are required in subsequent operations of a business process. The concept of lean production is based on the concept that inventory is waste. Lean production systems expose the hidden causes of maintaining inventory. Lean production systems differ from conventional production systems in that inventories of WIP, raw materials, and finished goods are minimized or totally eliminated. This concept is illustrated in Figure 10.4. The raw materials inventory, WIP inventory, and finished goods inventory are shown as dotted lines to indicate that they are eliminated to the extent possible in lean production. The term also describes this concept of minimizing inventories.

In a conventional production environment, batches of similar products are processed periodically to satisfy present and planned future needs. A batch production environment fosters a *push* concept of efficiency. Economic (i.e., efficient) batch size is derived by using formulas, such as those provided in EOQ models. Lean production operates under a *pull* concept of efficiency. Production of a product is not initiated until it has been ordered by a customer. Production flow occurs JIT (Just-in-Time) to satisfy demand. Demand "pulls" production and production pulls orders for materials. Inventories serve as a buffer between different operations. Inventories are eliminated by carefully analyzing operations to yield a constant production rate that will balance input and output at the various stages of production. Lean production also emphasizes quality control. Because inventories are minimized, defective production has to be corrected immediately if the constant flow of production is to be sustained. Vendors must guarantee timely delivery of defect-free parts that may be placed immediately into production rather than first being placed into raw materials inventory.

The financial benefits of lean production stem primarily from the overall reduction in inventory levels. This reduces a firm's total investment in inventories. Costs such as handling

FIGURE 10.4

Lean Production

and storing materials, obsolescence, storage space, and financing charges on total inventory cost are reduced, perhaps significantly. Other benefits include possible lower labor costs as operations are redesigned for constant-flow production, quantity discounts from vendors who in return receive long-term contracts, and increased emphasis on quality production and the corresponding reduction in the cost of waste and spoilage.

Property Accounting Applications

Property accounting applications concern an organization's fixed assets and investments. An important element of effective internal control is the accurate and timely processing of information relating to fixed assets and investments. Such processing is accomplished through the use of special accounting applications that provide for accounting, operational, and management information needs (see Figure 10.5).

FIXED ASSETS   There are four objectives of fixed asset or investment accounting applications:

- Maintain adequate records that identify assets with description, cost, and physical location
- Provide for appropriate depreciation and/or amortization calculations for book and tax purposes
- Provide for reevaluation for insurance and replacement-cost purposes
- Provide management with reports for planning and controlling the individual asset items

Fixed assets are tangible properties such as land, buildings, machinery, equipment, and furniture that are used in the normal conduct of a business. These items are relatively permanent and often represent the company's largest investment. Transactions that change the amount of investment in fixed assets tend to occur infrequently and usually involve relatively large amounts of money.

A company accumulates many assets over the life of the business, disposes of assets (by retirement, sale, or other means), moves assets from one location to another, and matches the costs (other than land) to revenues by means of periodic depreciation charges over the estimated useful life of the asset. To accomplish these tasks efficiently and to provide adequate control, an automated system is frequently required.

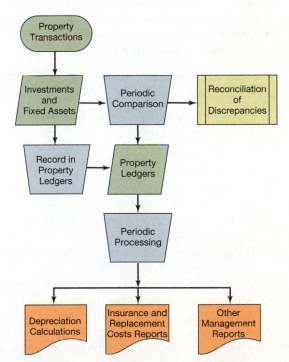

FIGURE 10.5

Property Accounting Application System

Every organization, including those that operate on a cash basis, should keep a ledger of fixed assets as an aid to effective control. A **fixed-asset register** is a systematic listing of an organization's fixed assets. A separate section of the fixed-asset register is usually kept for each major category of asset. This categorization should be consistent with the general ledger account descriptions. For example, an organization may have separate ledger accounts for buildings, furniture and fixtures, and automobiles. There would be a separate section for each of these categories. Assets themselves should be labeled with identifiers linked to the fixed-asset register.

When each asset is acquired, it should be tagged and entered in the fixed-asset register. The total dollar amount shown in the register should agree with the general ledger control accounts. For this reason, entries must be made in the fixed-asset register not only to record additions but also to record asset sales or other dispositions.

Several entries must be made when an asset is disposed of. The first entry records the date of disposal. The second entry removes the original cost of the asset in the current period. A third entry removes the accumulated depreciation taken to date. A fixed-asset register functions as a subsidiary ledger to the corresponding general ledger control accounts.

 CASE IN POINT

The Asset Sentry™ system by CISCOR (www.ciscor.com) provides anti-theft devices that are designed to prevent employee theft or unauthorized removal of assets. Typical anti-theft device and asset tracking applications include overhead projectors, lab equipment, computer equipment, furniture, fire extinguishers, and medical equipment. The asset tracking, anti-employee theft detection infrastructure uses totally wireless transceivers.

INVESTMENTS Investments, like fixed assets, require separate records; typically an investment register is used to provide accounting control over investments. As with all other assets, custody of investments should be separate and distinct from record keeping. The **investment register** should contain all relevant information, such as certificate numbers and the par value of securities, to facilitate identification and control. All investment transactions should be duly authorized and documented. A common control practice with respect to the physical handling of investment securities is to require two people to be present when the firm's safe deposit box or other depository is entered.

INTERNAL ACCOUNTING CONTROL PRACTICES The following questions suggest the internal accounting control procedures that would be expected in a property business process.

1. Do procedures require authorization by an official or committee for expenditures (possibly over certain amounts) for
   a. capital assets?
   b. repairs and maintenance?

2. Are actual expenditures compared with budgets and additional approvals required if budget authorization is exceeded?

3. Do written procedures exist that provide for distinguishing between capital additions and repair and maintenance?

4. Do procedures require formal authorization for the sale, retirement, or scrapping of capital assets?

5. Are property and equipment accounts supported by adequate detailed records?

6. Are these records maintained by people other than those who are responsible for the property?

7. Are the detailed records balanced at least annually with the general ledger controls?

8. Are physical inventories of property taken periodically under the supervision of employees who are not responsible for the custody or recording of such properties?

9. Are periodic appraisals of property made for insurance purposes?
10. Are significant discrepancies between book records and physical inventories reported to management?
11. With regard to small tools,
    a. Are these physically safeguarded, and is responsibility for them clearly defined?
    b. Are they issued only on written authorization?

Quick-Response Manufacturing Systems

A **computer-integrated manufacturing (CIM) system** integrates the physical manufacturing system and the MRP II systems. A **quick-response manufacturing system** is a CIM system in which the physical manufacturing system and the MRP II systems are integrated with advanced integration technologies (Figure 10.6). **Advanced integration technologies (AIT)** consist of electronic data interchange (EDI, possibly in the form of ANSI X.12 or ebXML) and automatic identification.

Components of Quick-Response Manufacturing Systems

THE PHYSICAL MANUFACTURING SYSTEM   Two subsystems directly support the physical manufacturing system. These are the **computer-aided design and drafting (CADD)** and the **computer-aided manufacturing (CAM)** systems.

Computer-Aided Design and Drafting (CADD)   CADD is the use of computer software to perform engineering functions, and it is intended principally to increase the design engineer's productivity. This productivity increase, in turn, allows the organization to be more responsive to market demands for new and improved product offerings. In addition, CADD systems allow the automation of repetitive design tasks, further increasing productivity, as well as accuracy.

Engineers, designers, and drafters work at CADD stations—electronic workstations dedicated to assisting in their jobs. A CADD station usually consists of a monitor with graphics

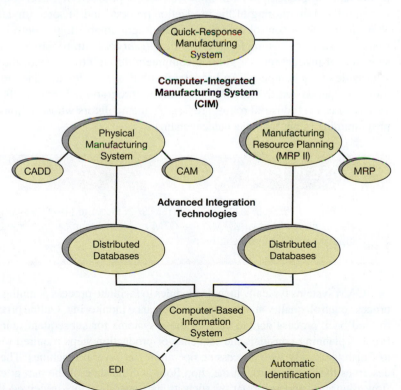

FIGURE 10.6

Quick-Response Manufacturing System

capability, a light pen or mouse for placing lines and other details on the screen, and a plotter or printer for hard copy. Details on the product design are stored by the computer and can be recalled and manipulated by the user.

CADD systems provide several different types of support functions. **Solids modeling** is the mathematical representation of a part as a solid object in computer memory. These models are represented as volumes enclosed by surfaces. Part models can be used to predict properties of finished products, such as weight, stability, or moments of inertia. **Finite element analysis** is a mathematical method used to determine mechanical characteristics, such as stresses of structures under load. The structure is reduced to a network of simple geometric elements, such as rods, shells, or cubes. Each of these elements has stress characteristics that are obtained easily from well-established theory. The behavior of the structure is predicted by having a computer solve a resulting set of simultaneous equations for all elements.

Automated drafting produces engineering drawings and other hard-copy documentation. Drawings are produced by plotting various views of the geometric model previously created and stored in computer memory.

CASE IN POINT

Solids modeling technology is incorporating sustainable design considerations as consumers demand more eco-friendly products. SolidWorks Sustainability (www.solidworks.com) software provides an assessment of the environmental impact of a product's design during the design process.

Computer-Aided Manufacturing (CAM) CAM systems include software for defining the manufacturing process, tools to improve process productivity, decision-support systems to aid in control and monitoring of the production process, and in some implementations elements of shop-floor process control such as robotics, programmable logic controllers, and machine vision systems. Such devices might be called *intelligent tools*. In robots or other intelligent tools, the sequence of instructions for guiding equipment through the steps of the manufacturing process is provided by a computer. An **industrial robot** is a device designed to move materials, parts, tools, or specialized devices through variable programmed motions for the performance of a variety of tasks. Industrial robots are flexible manipulators whose actions can be altered through programming rather than mechanical changes.

CASE IN POINT

INDUSTRIAL ROBOTS AND ROBOT SYSTEM SAFETY is the title of Section IV: Chapter 4 of the OSHA Technical Manual (OTM). The OTM provides technical information and guidance on occupational safety and health topics.

CAM systems typically include modules to facilitate process planning, line analysis, statistical process control, quality analysis, and maintenance monitoring. Online process controllers are used to feed back process data to each of these systems for subsequent manipulation and analysis. Process planning considers the sequence of production steps required to make a part from start to finish, generally with successive operations on several machines. The plan that is developed describes the routing through the shop floor and the state of the part at each work center. Logic flow diagrams and information such as part specifications received from a CADD system, tooling requirements, assembling, and machining conditions are used to develop a production sequence for fabricating the part in the fastest, most economical manner. Line analysis for existing manufacturing operations can be used to predict the work centers that require improvement tools.

CAM systems collect and process data from programmable manufacturing processes to provide decision support. The data are used to generate reports and to analyze the performance of the manufacturing process. The system monitors status conditions and processing parameters from production machines, quality gauges, and in-process materials handling systems. The information collected from these systems includes machine status, fault alarms, part counts, machine efficiency, float counts, cycle times, quality levels, and part characteristics. This information is input to production monitoring, quality analysis, and maintenance monitoring systems.

Many CAM systems use statistical process control. **Statistical process control** is used to determine whether a manufacturing process is under control. The process outputs are compared with the engineering specifications. Usually, an average variation value and range from highest to lowest variation are calculated. These values are plotted on control charts and compared with statistical control limits. The process is considered under control when the points fall within the limits and are randomly located around the desired average.

CASE IN POINT

Harley-Davidson, the motorcycle manufacturer, routinely trains its production line workers in statistical process control.

Some CAM systems, called **flexible manufacturing systems (FMS)**, incorporate programmable production processes that can be reconfigured quickly to produce different types of products. An FMS can contribute significantly to the overall speed in which a system responds, for it can greatly speed up time-consuming retooling.

THE MANUFACTURING RESOURCE PLANNING (MRP II) SYSTEM   The **manufacturing resource planning (MRP II) system** consists of the **materials requirements planning (MRP) system** and the related systems for sales, billing, and purchasing. However, the MRP system is the heart of the MRP II system.

Initial applications of computers in manufacturing concentrated on materials control systems. The term *MRP* was coined to describe the use of computers in production planning and control systems. MRP systems use the computational ability of computers to process the vast amount of detailed data necessary to plan and schedule materials usage requirements. The *M* in MRP is used to comprehensively include all inventories—raw materials, WIP, and finished goods. Since WIP inventory includes direct labor and overhead costs in addition to raw materials, all manufacturing elements are included in MRP systems. MRP systems integrate four subsystems (Figure 10.7): production planning, production scheduling, cost accounting, and reporting.

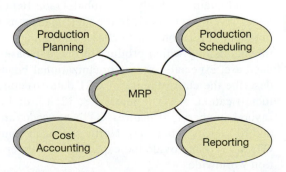

FIGURE 10.7

Materials Requirements Planning (MRP)

ADVANCED INTEGRATION TECHNOLOGIES   A manufacturing system's flexibility and speed of response depend largely on the degree to which its components are integrated. Automatic identification enhances integration because electronically tagging products and materials effectively makes them machine-readable and thus physically part of the organization's computer-based information system. EDI enhances integration because it effectively integrates the company's system with the systems of its suppliers and customers. Each of these integrating technologies is discussed below.

Automatic Identification   Automatic identification of production activities is essential to factory automation; thus machine-readable bar codes and scanner technology are indispensable elements. The information stored in a bar code is often represented by different widths and spacing of printed parallel lines; it can also be represented in patterns of dots, concentric circles, and text codes hidden within images called *matrix codes*. If you look under the hood of an automobile, you will see bar codes on many parts. Bar codes are as commonplace on factory goods as they are on consumer goods. Bar codes allow a computer or robot to identify materials, process information, and initiate whatever procedures are necessary.

Radio-frequency identification, or RFID, is an automatic identification technology that uses low power radio waves to send and receive data between RFID tags and readers. Bar code scanners require a direct line of sight in order to function. By using radio signals, RFID eliminates the need for a direct line of sight to the RFID tag in order to read it. RFID is not widely used for several reasons. RFID tags are much more costly than printed bar codes, and there is a much higher error rate in RFID than in scanning printed bar codes.

The Universal Product Code (UPC) is a bar code system that is widely used in the United States and Canada for tracking trade items. It is a 12-decimal digit code, also known as UPC-12. A manufacturer can obtain significant benefits by using the standard UPC bar code. UPC coding is as commonplace on commercial products as on consumer products. Products such as *UPC***Express*, an electronic listing of UPC bar codes, facilitate UPC bar code identification of products. Without UPC code standardization, one has supplier-assigned numbers for every product as well as customer-assigned numbers for every product. These codes must be cross-referenced during processing, which is both time-consuming and error-prone. With UPC coding, both customer and supplier use the same product code, eliminating cross-referencing problems. UPC coding is **vendor-based coding** that can be applied at any point. Problems with vendor-based coding usually result from different vendors using the same code for different items. UPC assigns a unique six-digit code to each vendor. Thus a duplication problem cannot occur as long as these six unique digits are included in the product code. Using UPC coding, one no longer has to code one's own inventory because it arrives precoded with UPC codes.

EAN-13 (European Article Number) is a bar coding standard, which is a superset of the original 12-digit UPC system. It is used worldwide to code items. The EAN-13 bar code is defined by the GS1. GS1 is a global organization dedicated to the design and implementation of global standards and solutions to improve the efficiency and visibility of supply and demand chains globally. A Global Trade Item Number (GTIN) is an identifier for trade items developed by GS1. In the same manner as UPC, GTIN is an identifier used to look up product information in a database. The uniqueness and universality of the identifier is useful in establishing which product in one database corresponds to which product in another database, especially across organizational boundaries. *GTIN* is an inclusive term used to describe the entire family of GS1 data structures for trade items (products and services) identification. A GTIN may be 8, 12, 13, or 14 digits long and can be constructed using several numbering structures. GTIN bar codes are commonplace as they are encoded in UPC and EAN-13 symbols. For North American companies, the UPC is an existing form of the GTIN. GTINs provide the capability to deliver automatically identified unique identification worldwide.

CASE IN POINT

UPC, EAN-13, and other GTIN identification symbols include a Check Digit—a calculated one-digit number used to ensure data integrity during processing.

EDI In manufacturing as in most environments, a typical EDI application links a vendor and a customer electronically. EDI thus is a continuation of the integration of computerized applications inherent in CIM. EDI has an impact on manufacturing and inventory efficiency by simplifying the logistical chain of events in placing and filling orders and by making such systems more responsive to current needs. Inventory levels can be reduced simply by using EDI to shorten order filling and placement times. Errors are also reduced. While useful in any type of manufacturing environment, EDI can be a critical component of a JIT manufacturing environment.

CASE IN POINT

Global Product Catalogue (GPC), a service mark of GXS, is a multi-industry electronic product catalogue and data synchronization services for GTINs. It supports various types of GTINs, including UPC-12 and EAN-13.

GTIN bar code identification of products and scanning technology are essential to obtain maximum benefit from EDI. Commerce is moving toward common pools of information, based on automatically identified GTIN bar codes that manufacturers, shippers, retailers, banks, and other trading partners can use to track goods and create the necessary documentation. Documents such as invoices will become superfluous as this type of open-flow intercompany exchange of information becomes commonplace.

Transaction Processing in Quick-Response Manufacturing Systems

The discussion in this section focuses on transaction flow through the manufacturing process. We concentrate on production planning, production scheduling, cost accounting, and reporting. Activity-based costing (ABC) and the relationships between JIT and CIM/MRP II are also discussed.

PRODUCTION PLANNING Production planning involves the determination of which products to produce and the scheduling of production to make optimal use of production resources. The determination of which products to manufacture requires an integration of the demand for a product, its production requirements, and the production resources that are available to the firm.

Figure 10.8 is a diagram of the data flows involved in production planning. Demand requirements for a product depend on whether the item is manufactured per customer order or manufactured routinely for inventory. If the item is manufactured for inventory, production requirements depend on a sales forecast. The sales forecast (data flow 1 in Figure 10.8) will generally be prepared by the sales or marketing department as part of the firm's budget preparation. On being authorized by management, the sales forecast is sent to the production planning function to indicate the expected demand for products.

The sales forecast must be related to the amount of each product that is currently held in inventory. Such information is provided in a finished goods status report (data flow 2 in Figure 10.8). A finished goods status report is sent to production planning from inventory control. The finished goods status report lists the quantities of finished product that are in inventory. The amount of resources available for production is communicated to production

FIGURE 10.8

Data Flow Diagram: Production Planning

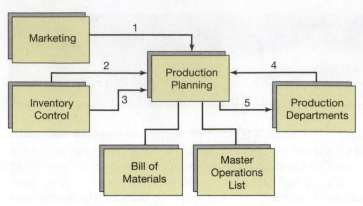

Data Flow Key

1 Sales Forecast
2 Finished Goods Status
3 Raw Materials Status
4 Factor Availability Report
5 Production Schedule

planning through raw materials status reports (data flow 3 in Figure 10.8) and factor availability reports (data flow 4 in Figure 10.8). A raw materials status report details the amount of raw materials available for production. A factor availability report communicates the availability of labor and machine resources.

The production requirements of products are specified in a bill-of-materials file and a master operations file. A bill of materials lists the raw materials necessary to produce a product and identifies the part number and quantity of each part used to make a product. A bill of materials provides a structured, level-by-level listing of the components of a product, including part number, part description, and quantity used and a linkage from each level of the assembly to subassemblies and components. In similar fashion, a master operations list identifies and specifies the sequencing of all labor operations and/or machine operations necessary to produce a product. The information contained in both the bill-of-materials file and the master operations file will generally be specified by the engineering or product planning department when a product is first designed.

The integration of all the preceding factors results in a master production plan for the firm. The master production plan is implemented through the issuance and subsequent accounting-for of production orders. Processing of production orders results in a master production schedule (data flow 5 in Figure 10.8). Generation of the master production schedule is the focal point of MRP systems.

Implementing the Production Plan   Figure 10.9 illustrates the processing required to implement the master production plan. The master production plan is processed against the production status, bill-of-materials, and master operations files. This processing generates production order files, materials requisitions, and routings and also updates the production status file. The *production status file* contains both accounting data and operational data pertaining to the status of production orders. This file integrates production order data pertinent to the stage of completion of projects; the production status file is a major input to the scheduling and cost accounting applications.

The *bill-of-materials file* contains a record for each product manufactured. Each record contains the detailed material requirements and standard material cost of the product identified by the record's key field value. The *master operations file* contains similar data related to each product's detailed labor and machine operation requirements and their sequencing through the production process. Standard times and costs are also contained in the master operations file.

The production planning application program integrates data from the master production plan, bill-of-materials file, and master operations file and generates the necessary production order documents—detailed production orders, materials requisition forms, and **routings (RTGs)** to guide the flow of production. RTGs indicate the sequence of operations required to manufacture

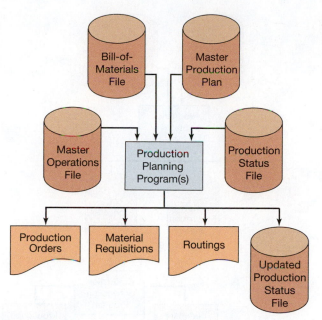

FIGURE 10.9

Production Planning

a product. RTGs contain information about the work center, length of time, and tooling required to perform each task. These documents are distributed to the factory departments along with up-to-date production schedules. The production planning application program also updates the production status file. This file contains information found on the production order and establishes a production status (WIP) record for each production order. This file is an essential input to the production scheduling and cost accounting applications discussed below.

PRODUCTION SCHEDULING   As Figure 10.9 illustrates, the production status file is updated by the production planning application. The production status file contains a record for each open production order. This file is also used to accumulate both cost and operational data pertinent to production status. It integrates functions relating to production order status and cost accounting. This integration results from use of the production status file in both the scheduling and cost accounting applications.

Production scheduling is detailed in Figure 10.10. RTG data concerning current production status are collected in the factory departments as work progresses. RTG data may be collected in different ways. RTGs may be output as turnaround documents by the production planning application. RTGs are filled in by the factory departments as work progresses on specific production orders. Each RTG contains a production order number and a format for specifying the work completed on an order. A separate RTG might be generated for each specific operation required on a production order. As each operation is completed, the corresponding RTG is completed by adding such information as units produced, scrap count, and actual time required. The RTGs are then forwarded to computer operations for input and processing. Alternatively, RTG data may be input directly from factory operations by having employees use data terminals to input RTG data at the completion of tasks. Employees might enter data such as production/work-order code, operation code, employee code, machine/department code, materials-used data, and time accumulated on the task.

CIM architectures provide the ability to tie factory floor machines directly to MRP systems. Automated data collection techniques may be used to electronically collect production data from the shop floor as production occurs. Sensors on production lines may be used to count production or identify completed operations, whereas data-entry stations are used by workers to manually enter codes indicating downtime and other production conditions.

FIGURE 10.10

Production
Scheduling

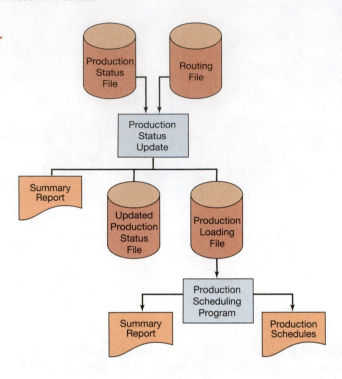

RTG data received from the factory are used to update the production status file. RTG data are posted to the corresponding production order record in the production status file. Outputs of this operation include a summary report, the updated production status file, and a production loading file that details the production requirements associated with open production orders.

The production loading file is the major input to the production-scheduling application. This file is processed by the scheduling application program to produce production schedules. The scheduling application program may simply accumulate and print reports showing total labor and machine operation requirements for each department/work center. In MRP systems, the scheduling application program would include the use of linear programming or other decision-support techniques to relate resource availabilities within each department or work center to overall production requirements to generate a schedule that represents an optimal assignment of available resources to production.

COST ACCOUNTING   Figure 10.11 presents a diagram of the cost accounting application within an MRP system. The central feature of the cost accounting application is the updating of the production status (WIP) file.

Materials requisitions data are transmitted from the inventory department for processing. Materials requisitions data document the issuance of materials to specific production orders. Job time data and machine time data are included in the RTGs forwarded from the production departments. RTG data show the distribution of labor and machine time to specific production orders within a production department or work center. Both materials requisitions data and RTG data are input to build a production data file. This transaction file is processed by the cost accounting application program, along with the production status file. This processing accumulates material and labor usage shown by materials requisitions data and RTG data and posts them to the WIP record maintained for each open production order. Overhead is applied to WIP on the basis of burden rates maintained in the cost accounting program. The program monitors the status of each production order and also prepares a file that summarizes the variances between standard cost and operational data maintained in the WIP record and the actual cost and operational data posted to each production order. As orders are completed, the related WIP record is closed,

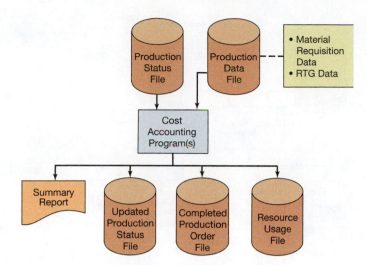

FIGURE 10.11

Cost Accounting

and a record is created to update the finished inventory file. The outputs of the cost accounting program include the following items:

- An updated production status file
- A completed production order file
- A resource usage file
- A summary report

The updated production status file contains current information on the status of all open production orders. This file is used in the next cycle of production planning and scheduling. The summary report includes batch and application control information, as well as the summary journal-entry data debiting WIP for standard material, labor, and overhead costs; crediting stores, accrued payroll, and applied overhead; and debiting or crediting the necessary variance accounts. The completed production order file and the resource usage file are described in the next section.

REPORTING   The completed production order file lists all cost data for completed production orders. This file is used to update the finished goods inventory file, as shown in Figure 10.12. Outputs of this processing include an updated finished goods inventory file, a finished goods stock status report, a completed production order cost summary, and a summary report that includes batch and application control information as well as the summary journal-entry data debiting finished goods and crediting WIP for the standard cost of goods completed.

The resource usage file that is output from the cost accounting application contains both the actual and standard material, labor, and operation costs for work completed, as shown by the materials requisitions data and RTG data. The standard quantities, time, and costs are copied to this file from the production status file. This file is input to a computer application program that accumulates material and operation costs by department or work center and prints resource usage reports. These reports detail variances between standard and actual cost data. Resource usage reports are distributed to department supervisors to assist in the overall production control function.

ACTIVITY-BASED COSTING   Traditional cost accounting techniques may be inadequate in a CIM environment. Three major elements enter into the cost of manufacturing a product. These are direct materials, direct labor, and overhead. Overhead is best described as the portion of manufacturing cost that is neither direct materials nor direct labor. Overhead costs cannot be identified readily with the manufacturing of specific products; rather, overhead costs are identifiable to the production process itself. In addition to indirect materials and indirect labor, overhead includes such items as factory rent or depreciation, heat, power, insurance, maintenance, supervision, machinery costs, and material handling costs.

FIGURE 10.12

Reporting

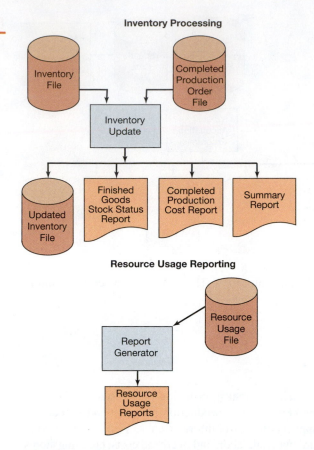

CIM Changes Cost-Behavior Patterns The term *applied overhead* describes the familiar cost accounting technique in which the overhead charge to a product is calculated using a predetermined overhead application rate. Predetermined overhead rates traditionally have been based on either total expected direct labor hours or total expected direct labor cost. A predetermined overhead rate is computed as follows:

$$\text{Predetermined rate} = \frac{\text{budgeted overhead cost}}{\text{budgeted activity}}$$

For example, if overhead is budgeted as $200,000 and activity is budgeted as 5,000 direct labor hours, the predetermined overhead rate would be $200,000 divided by 5,000 hours, a rate of $40 per hour. Predetermined overhead rates may be computed on either a plantwide or a departmental basis. A plantwide rate is a rate that is used throughout the firm. That is, the rate does not differ from one department or division to another. A plantwide rate is usually inappropriate in a large firm that produces a variety of products or services and that has several distinct departments or divisions. In such cases, better control is achieved when overhead costs and activity are budgeted on a departmental or divisional basis.

 CASE IN POINT

The Consortium for Advanced Manufacturing-International (www.cam-i.org) is largely responsible for the popularization and proliferation of ABC accounting. ABC accounting was originally introduced in the late 1980s by Professors William Bruns and Robert Kaplan.

CIM significantly alters a manufacturer's cost-behavior patterns by causing a substitution of capital equipment for direct labor. Direct labor is reduced, perhaps totally eliminated, as computer-controlled machinery manufactures products. Overhead costs increase, and direct labor costs decrease. The costs of computer-controlled machinery, like the costs of all other capital resources, are indirect rather than direct to production. They are primarily "fixed" relative to the volume of production. Thus CIM causes decreased variable costs by reducing direct labor cost and increasing the fixed costs of production (cost of CIM technology). In addition to equipment costs, many other overhead items may be increased significantly with CIM. Total supervision costs, for example, may increase even though there is less direct labor to supervise. The computer-controlled machinery that replaces workers needs to be "supervised" by skilled technicians, who likely earn significantly higher wages than the employee-oriented supervisors whom they replace.

Traditional cost accounting systems allocate overhead on a single base that all products have in common. This base typically has been direct labor hours or direct labor cost because direct labor was a critical manufacturing component common to all products. However, this method is deficient for a CIM environment because products manufactured with costly automated machinery, which contributes greatly to overhead costs, typically have the lowest number of direct labor hours associated with their production. If direct labor is used to allocate overhead, products that use relatively more manual labor will be unfairly charged more overhead than products that use relatively more automated, high-overhead machinery.

Activity-based costing (ABC) calculates several overhead rates, one for each manufacturing activity, and uses these rates to build product costs from the costs of the specific activities undertaken during production. Activities might be machine centers, materials handling, inspection stations, or any other type of manufacturing operation. A single department might contain several different activities. For example, an assembly department where some products are assembled using robotics equipment and other products are assembled manually might have two activities namely, robotics and manual assembly. Different overhead bases could then be used to more accurately assign these different activity costs to products.

Figures 10.13 and 10.14 provide an illustration. Figure 10.13 shows the costing of products A and B in a traditional cost accounting system where all overhead is allocated to products on the basis of direct labor hours. Note that product A, which requires five more hours of direct labor, costs more to produce than product B. Product B, however, requires more parts than product A, which means that product B requires relatively more use of high-overhead robotics equipment during assembly.

Traditional Cost Accounting (single overhead base)		
Overhead	$2,400,000	
Activity Base (labor hours)	100,000	
Rate per labor hour	$24	
	Product A	**Product B**
# Parts	50	100
# Labor Hours	25	20
Material cost	$800	$800
Labor cost ($20 per hour)	$500	$400
Overhead ($24 per hour)	$600	$480
Total cost	$1,900	$1,680

FIGURE 10.13

Traditional Cost Accounting

FIGURE 10.14

Activity-Based Cost Accounting

Activity-Based Cost Accounting (several overhead bases)		
	Robotic Assembly	All Other
Overhead	$400,000	$2,000,000
Activity	40,000 (parts)	100,000 (hours)
Rates	$10 per part	$20 per hour
	Product A	**Product B**
# Parts	50	100
# Labor Hours	25	20
Material cost	$800	$800
Labor cost ($20 per hour)	$500	$400
Overhead ($10 per part)	$500	$1,000
Overhead ($20 per hour)	$500	$400
Total cost	$2,300	$2,600

Figure 10.14 shows the costing of the two same products in an ABC accounting system where robotics equipment is identified as a separate activity. Several different overhead bases are used. Robotics equipment overhead is allocated to products on the basis of the number of parts in a product. All other overhead is allocated on the basis of direct labor hours. Note that product B, which requires 50 more parts, costs more to produce than product A according to the ABC accounting system.

Cost Drivers   A **cost driver** is an element that influences the total cost of an activity. Typically, several cost drivers influence the total cost of an activity. Materials handling costs are influenced by the total number of items handled, the types of items handled (i.e., small, big and heavy, hazardous, etc.), the type of equipment used, and worker efficiency, to name just a few examples. Cost drivers might be measured by production volume, number of employees, number of forms completed, or number of parts in a product. Time-in-process measures, such as direct labor hours, machine hours, or clock time, are used frequently as cost drivers.

The significance of ABC as a management tool depends largely on the accuracy of the cost drivers selected as the allocation bases for activity costs. The most benefit is obtained when the principal cost driver for an activity is selected as the overhead allocation base for that activity. This then links cost incurrence to product costing, and meaningful managerial decisions may be based on product cost information. Statistical regression analysis often is used as a means for identifying cost drivers.

MRP II VERSUS MRP   An MRP II system includes the major processing modules of MRP (Figure 10.15). The bill-of-materials module is used to communicate the structure of a product, as in MRP. Extensions to bill-of-materials processing in MRP II might include maintenance of engineering/product drawings from a CADD system. The routings file module indicates the sequence of operations required to manufacture a component or assembly, as in MRP. Extensions to RTGs file processing in MRP II might include expanded information concerning work center capacity data, maintenance of machine tooling data, and maintenance of numerical machine control data from the CADD system. The master production scheduling module maintains the assembly schedule for specific configurations, quantities, and dates based on product mix and material

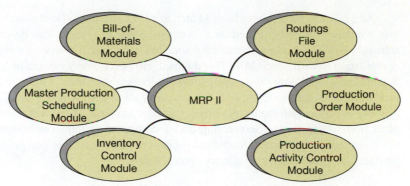

FIGURE 10.15

Major Processing Modules in MRP II

availability, much as in MRP. A production order module releases orders for manufacturing after evaluating materials, capacity, and tooling availability. If availability is adequate, a packet is prepared that contains the order, materials list, routing, and drawing information, much as in MRP. The packet is forwarded to the plant floor. Extensions to production order processing in MRP II might include the creation of transaction files and numerical machine control tapes for the plant floor. As in MRP, an inventory control module maintains accurate and timely status of on-hand balances. To maintain accuracy, techniques such as obsolescence analysis and cycle counting should be implemented to ensure accuracy on a continual basis. Finally, a production activity control module is used to implement the production plan developed in the master production scheduling module. As in MRP, this module reduces delays and waiting time by effective monitoring and feedback of production and shop-floor status data. Typical functions include attendance reporting, collecting direct labor and machine hours, and revising production status and priority data based on actual use of materials, labor, and machine resources.

ERP, ERP II, AND EAS   As was discussed in Chapter 1, MRP and MRP II have given way to ERP, ERP II (collaborative ERP), and the EAS (Enterprise Application Suite). These more advanced systems not only incorporate all the functionality of MRP and MRP II, but they also integrate all other major business processes (e.g., human resources) into a single system. The EAS differs from ERP and ERP II in that the EAS involves a suite of applications that work together to perform the same functions.

IMPLEMENTING LEAN PRODUCTION IN AN MRP II/CIM ENVIRONMENT   In a batch production environment, manufacture of specific products is sporadic. Batches of similar products are assembled periodically to satisfy present and planned future needs. Setup costs usually are incurred every time a batch is produced, and these costs are typically the same regardless of the proposed size of the batch production run. As the word *planned* indicates, a batch environment fosters a "push" concept of manufacturing efficiency. Economic (i.e., efficient) batch size is derived by using formulas (i.e., EOQ models) or is output from a computer simulation or computational model.

MRP II is directed at the synchronization and scheduling of the types of events that occur in batch environments. Batch size is determined from the production planning module. The scheduling module organizes and/or optimizes the timing of events necessary for production. The bill-of-materials module is used to forecast materials requirements and so on until the actual production orders are issued.

A lean production environment is a continuous-flow environment. A lean production environment requires economical production of small lots—essentially the operation of production on a continuous basis—to minimize or totally eliminate inventories. Lean production advocates the elimination of waste in the manufacturing process and stresses continuous improvement in operation. In a lean production environment, products are manufactured under a "pull" concept. Production occurs only when it is needed to fill a customer order. In contrast to a batch environment, there is no advance scheduling in a lean production environment. The customer order "pulls" product from the production line; in effect, demand schedules production. This type of operation requires rapid setups, high-quality production, continuous elimination of wasted motion, and inventory flow improvements.

As a manufacturer moves from a batch to a JIT continuous-flow manufacturing environment, less emphasis might be placed on a complete MRP II system. The de-emphasis on advanced scheduling in lean production and the associated reduction in inventories eliminate much data and computation toward which MRP II is directed. However, many aspects of MRP II might be used. Scheduling modules might generate level production schedules. MRP might generate estimated procurement quantities to support the demand-pull system. CADD and CAM applications can support quality requirements by allowing greater amounts of process control technology on the plant floor. Adaptive, self-correcting decision-support systems can become an integral part of the manufacturing process. Statistical process controls can monitor production to ensure that products are produced within quality control limits.

Special Internal Control Considerations

Quick-response manufacturing systems, similar to other totally computerized systems, intensify certain internal control problems. Transactions may be processed without human intervention or approval. This eliminates conventional controls associated with separation of duties in transactions. Thus a major consideration is to ensure that such controls, or their equivalents, are an integral part of a quick-response manufacturing system. Computer processing in general and EDI in particular eliminate human-oriented paper documents. However, challenging validation and authenticity problems are encountered in the operation of electronic processing systems, both within a firm (e.g., electronic production order) and in its exchanges with its trading partners (EDI and electronic fund transfer—EFT).

Extensive control and audit trails may be implemented in quick-response manufacturing systems, but these features must be included within the design and development of the system. It is neither feasible nor desirable to install controls in a computer-based information system after it has been implemented. Programmed controls and audit trails can be highly effective, but their integrity must be established during system development. A control may look good on paper, but it will be ineffectual if its operation is programmed incorrectly. Also, a programmer might deliberately code a program incorrectly. Thus internal controls over system operation must be complemented with increased control over the systems development process. Audit trail and control techniques such as transaction logs and programmed edit checks require extra developmental resources and extra processing. The costs of their use must be balanced against overall system objectives. Because audit trails and controls require direct and obvious expenditures, under usage is perhaps more likely than over usage.

Systems development is a major concern in any computer-based system, but systems development is mission-critical in quick-response manufacturing systems. A major deterrent to the proliferation of automation in factories is the same one that has plagued the application of computers to other application areas—programming and software. The lack of *turnkey systems*—robots or other automated tools that can be bought and immediately turned on and used—has constrained the application of hardware technology that has been available for years. The same types of systems development problems that occur in information systems development occur in the application of computers to production processes. The cost of programming an industrial robot, which frequently involves extensive engineering or systems development, can easily exceed the purchase cost of the robot system.

Summary

Production planning and control, inventory control, and property accounting are typical business processes in manufacturing firms. A sales order or sales forecast causes the creation of production orders, which specify items that should be produced. Materials are requisitioned and production is scheduled. Items are produced, inspected, transferred to finished goods inventory, and then transferred to shipping to complete the process. Materials requisition forms and job time cards are used to trace production costs to individual production orders.

Inventory control is accomplished through a series of records and reports that provide information concerning inventory use and inventory balances. Perpetual inventory records are the best source of inventory information. The storage and handling of inventory items must provide assurance of adequate control.

Property accounting business processes concern an organization's fixed assets and investments. Property accounting applications maintain records that identify an organization's fixed assets and investments, provide for appropriate depreciation and/or amortization for book and tax purposes, provide information for insurance purposes, and provide information to management concerning use and availability of an organization's fixed assets and investments.

CIM is an integrated approach to the use of information technology in manufacturing enterprises. Components of a CIM system typically include CADD workstations, real-time production monitoring and control systems, and order and inventory control systems. CIM components are connected by a network and equipped with software systems designed to support distributed operation. CIM can support product evolution from initial design and drafting through planning to manufacturing and assembly while also incorporating management accounting systems. CIM reduces information costs and, through EDI, brings the producer, the supplier, and the customer closer together.

Glossary

activity-based costing (ABC) a system that calculates several overhead rates, one for each manufacturing activity, and uses these rates to build product costs from the costs of the specific activities undertaken during production.

advanced integration technologies (AIT) consist of EDI and automatic identification.

bill-of-materials lists the raw materials necessary to produce a product.

computer-aided design and drafting (CADD) the use of computer software to perform engineering functions.

computer-aided manufacturing (CAM) includes software for defining the manufacturing process, tools to improve process productivity, and decision-support systems to aid in the control and monitoring of the production process.

computer-integrated manufacturing (CIM) system integrates the physical manufacturing system and the MRP II systems.

cost driver an element that influences the total cost of an activity.

economic order quantity (EOQ) the order quantity that minimizes total inventory cost.

factor availability reports reports that communicate the availability of labor and machine resources.

finite element analysis a mathematical method used to determine mechanical characteristics, such as stresses of structures under load.

fixed-asset register a systematic list of fixed assets maintained for control purposes.

flexible manufacturing system (FMS) a CAM system that incorporates programmable production processes that can be reconfigured quickly to produce different types of products.

industrial robot a device designed to move materials, parts, tools, or specialized devices through variable programmed motions for the performance of a variety of tasks.

inventory status reports reports that detail the resources available in inventory.

investment register a systematic list of investments maintained for control purposes.

job synonym for production order.

job costing production costs are assigned to production orders.

job time cards used to document the amount of labor time spent working on each production order (job).

lean production a system in which items are produced only as they are required in subsequent operations.

manufacturing resource planning (MRP II) system comprises the MRP system and the related systems for sales, billing, and purchasing.

master operations list identifies and specifies the sequencing of all labor operations and/or machine operations necessary to produce a product.

materials requirements planning (MRP) system the use of computers in production planning and control systems, particularly applications in materials control systems.

materials requisitions documents that authorize the release of raw materials to the production departments.

production status reports reports that detail the work completed on individual production orders as they move through the production process.

process costing production costs are compiled by department rather than by job.

production order document that authorizes the production departments to make certain products.

quick-response manufacturing system a CIM system in which the physical manufacturing system and the MRP II systems are integrated with AIT.

reorder point   the level of inventory at which it is desirable to order or produce additional items to avoid an out-of-stock condition.

routings (RTGs)   documents that indicate the sequence of operations required to manufacture a product.

solids modeling   the mathematical representation of a part as a solid object in computer memory.

statistical process control   procedures used to determine whether a manufacturing process is under control, which involve comparing process outputs to engineering specifications.

vendor-based coding   having a purchaser (i.e., retailer) use a vendor's product codes as its own product codes for the same products.

Webliography

www.apics.org
Home page of the APICS, the Association for Operations Management, which is a nonprofit educational society for resource management. This site provides many interesting technical papers relating to topics covered in this chapter.

www.asq.org
Home page of the American Society for Quality. This site contains links to various state-of-the-art manufacturing technologies and improvement methods. For example, it has an entire section devoted to Six Sigma and the lean enterprise.

www.journalofaccountancy.com
Home page of the *Journal of Accountancy*, a publication of the American Institute of Certified Public Accountants. Entering "Unleash the Power of Lean Accounting," into the search box leads to an interesting article published by Jan P. Brosnahan.

www.sme.org
Home page of the Society of Manufacturing Engineers. The Web site includes references relating to a wide range of technical materials relating to lean production, FMS, and so on. For example, entering "Lean Production" into the search box leads

to publications such as "Lean Production Simplified: A Plain Language Guide to the World's Most Powerful Production System."

www.robots.org
The home page of Robotics Online, sponsored by the Robotic Industries Association. This site provides many interesting technical papers relating to topics covered in this chapter. For example, entering "manufacturing" in to the search box, and then clicking on the Tech Papers tab leads to a free technical paper entitled "The Role of Robots in Lean Manufacturing."

www.igetleanaccounting.com
A general resource site for lean accounting, sponsored by Lean Accounting Summit, LLC

www.iienet2.org
The home page for the Institute of Industrial Engineers. Entering terms such as "lean" and "flexible manufacturing" into the search box yields many interesting resources. The Institute provides various educational programs, including one that leads to the Lean Enterprise Master Practitioner Certificate.

Chapter Quiz

Answers to the chapter quiz appear on page 380.

1. In a production control application system, which of the following documents serves as authorization to release raw materials to the production departments?
   a. production order
   b. job time card
   c. journal voucher
   d. material requisition

2. In a production control application system, which of the following departments should receive copies of production orders?
   a. inventory control
   b. cost accounting
   c. purchasing
   d. general ledger

3. In a production control application system, which of the following documents serves as authorization to the production departments to make certain products?
   a. production order
   b. job time card
   c. material requisition
   d. journal voucher

4. Which of the following is a characteristic associated with lean production?
   a. parts are produced only as they are required in subsequent operations
   b. a constant-flow production rate
   c. both a and b
   d. neither a nor b

5. Which of the following is an element of CADD technology?
   a. solids modeling
   b. statistical process control
   c. both a and b
   d. neither a nor b

6. (_____) integrates the physical manufacturing system and the manufacturing resource planning (MRP II) systems.
   a. MRP
   b. AIT
   c. CIM
   d. RTG

7. In a production planning system, the bill-of-materials file would be an input to which of the following?
   a. production planning program(s)
   b. cost accounting program(s)

c. both a and b
d. neither a nor b
8. In a production planning system, the production status file would be an input to which of the following?
   a. production planning program(s)
   b. inventory update program(s)
   c. both a and b
   d. neither a nor b
9. In a production planning system, the master operations file would be an input to which of the following?

a. cost accounting program(s)
b. inventory update program(s)
c. both a and b
d. neither a nor b
10. Cost drivers for ABC might be identified with (_____).
   a. solids modeling
   b. finite element analysis
   c. statistical regression
   d. statistical process control

Review Problem

CIM architectures provide the ability to tie factory-floor operations directly to computer-based information systems. Automated source data collection techniques may be used to electronically collect production data from the shop floor as production occurs. Sensors on production lines may be used to count production or identify completed operations, whereas data-entry stations are used by workers to manually enter data concerning completed operations.

Required

a. What types of data might be entered by production workers concerning completed operations?
b. Describe programmed edit checks that might be made on the data indicated in part a.
c. Assume that all necessary files are direct-access organization. What online processing might result from a worker entering data on completed operations?

Solution to Review Problem

a. Workers might enter the following types of data at the completion of an operation:
   1. production/work-order code
   2. operation code
   3. worker code
   4. machine/department code
   5. materials used data
   6. time accumulated on the task
b. Possible edit checks include
   1. label check on files
   2. data access matrix to verify worker authorization
   3. check-digit verification where appropriate

   4. valid code checks
   5. limit tests where appropriate
   6. validity check on operation code entered relative to the production order file
c. The following files might be updated to reflect the data entered:
   1. raw materials inventory file
   2. finished goods inventory file
   3. production order (WIP) file
   4. production scheduling file
   5. employee data file (a production scheduling file for workers)
   6. summary costing files

Review Questions

1. Distinguish between job-order costing and process costing.
2. Identify the accounting journal entries that summarize the activities involved in a manufacturing operation.
3. What is a bill of materials? A reorder point? A reorder quantity? A master operations list?
4. Identify the main features of control over inventories and production.
5. What information might be included on a production order? Identify the source(s) of this information. To whom should copies of production orders be distributed?
6. Identify the major features of lean production.
7. What are the objectives of a fixed-asset or investment accounting system?
8. Identify several controls relevant to fixed assets and investments.

9. What accounting entries are required when fixed assets are disposed of?
10. Identify and describe key components of CIM systems.
11. Distinguish between MRP and MRP II.
12. Describe several different types of support functions that typically are provided by CADD.
13. Describe support functions that typically are provided by CAM.
14. Describe several uses of automatic identification in production activities.
15. Describe the flow of processing necessary to support MRP II systems.
16. What is ABC? Why is ABC particularly relevant to CIM systems?

Discussion Questions and Problems

17. For several years, a client's physical inventory count has been lower than what was shown on the books at the time of the count, requiring downward adjustments to the inventory account. Contributing to the inventory problem could be weaknesses in internal control that led to the failure to record some
  a. purchases returned to vendors.
  b. sales returns received.
  c. sales discounts allowed.
  d. cash purchases.

  (CPA)

18. Ball Company, which has no perpetual inventory records, takes a monthly physical inventory and reorders any item that is less than its reorder point. On February 5, 20XX, Ball ordered 5,000 units of item A. On February 6, 20XX, Ball received 5,000 units of item A, which had been ordered on January 3, 20XX. To prevent this excess ordering, Ball should
  a. keep an adequate record of open purchase orders and review it before ordering.
  b. use perpetual inventory records that indicate goods received, issued, and amounts on hand.
  c. use prenumbered purchase orders.
  d. prepare purchase orders only on the basis of purchase requisitions.

  (CPA)

19. Sanbor Corporation has an inventory of parts consisting of thousands of different items of small value individually but significant in total. Sanbor could establish effective internal accounting control over the parts by requiring
  a. approval of requisitions for inventory parts by a company officer.
  b. maintenance of inventory records for all parts included in the inventory.
  c. physical counts of the parts on a cycle basis rather than at year-end.
  d. separation of the store-keeping function from the production and inventory record-keeping functions.

  (CPA)

20. To achieve effective internal accounting control over fixed-asset additions, a company should establish procedures that require
  a. capitalization of the cost of fixed-asset additions in excess of a specific dollar amount.
  b. performance of recurring fixed-asset maintenance work solely by maintenance department employees.
  c. classifying as investments those fixed-asset additions that are not used in the business.
  d. authorization and approval of major fixed-asset additions.

  (CPA)

21. Which of the following is the *most important* internal control over acquisitions of property, plant, and equipment?

  a. establishing a written company policy distinguishing between capital and revenue expenditures
  b. using a budget to forecast and control acquisitions and retirements
  c. analyzing monthly variances between authorized expenditures and actual costs
  d. requiring acquisitions to be made by user departments

  (CPA)

22. Which of the following is an internal accounting control weakness related to factory equipment?
  a. Checks issued in payment of purchases of equipment are *not* signed by the controller.
  b. All purchases of factory equipment are required to be made by the department in need of the equipment.
  c. Factory equipment replacements generally are made when estimated useful lives, as indicated in depreciation schedules, have expired.
  d. Proceeds from sales of fully depreciated equipment are credited to other income.

  (CPA)

23. Which of the following internal accounting control procedures could best prevent direct labor from being charged to manufacturing overhead?
  a. reconciliation of WIP inventory with cost records
  b. comparison of daily journal entries with the factory labor summary
  c. comparison of periodic cost budgets and time cards
  d. reconciliation of unfinished job summary and production cost records

  (CPA)

24. Which of the following is a question the auditor would expect to find on the production cycle section of an internal accounting control questionnaire?
  a. Are vendors' invoices for raw materials approved for payment by an employee who is independent of the cash disbursements function?
  b. Are signed checks for the purchase of raw materials mailed directly after signing without being returned to the person who authorized the invoice processing?
  c. Are all releases by storekeepers of raw materials from storage based on approved requisition documents?
  d. Are details of individual disbursements for raw materials balanced with the total to be posted to the appropriate general ledger account?

  (CPA)

25. Which of the following is the *most important* element of internal control relating to the raw materials inventory of a manufacturing company?
  a. The physical inventory count should be made by personnel independent of the inventory custodians.

b. Materials from vendors should be received directly by the production department that will be using the materials.

c. Shortages in shipments from vendors should be reported immediately to the production department that will be using the materials.

d. Issues from inventory should be supported by sales invoices.

(IIA)

26. A well-functioning system of internal control over the inventory/production functions would provide that finished goods are to be accepted for stock only after presentation of a completed production order and a(n)
    a. shipping order.
    b. materials requisition.
    c. bill of lading.
    d. inspection report.

(CPA)

27. If preparation of a periodic scrap report is essential in order to maintain adequate control over the manufacturing process, the data for this report should be accumulated in the
    a. accounting department.
    b. production department.
    c. warehousing department.
    d. budget department.

(CPA)

28. Which of the following control procedures would *most likely* be used to maintain accurate perpetual inventory records?
    a. independent storeroom count of goods received
    b. periodic independent reconciliation of control and subsidiary records
    c. periodic independent comparison of records with goods on hand
    d. independent matching of purchase orders, receiving reports, and vendors' invoices

(CPA)

29. Which of the following procedures is *most likely* to prevent the improper disposition of equipment?
    a. a separation of duties between those authorized to dispose of equipment and those authorized to approve removal work orders
    b. the use of serial numbers to identify equipment that could be sold
    c. periodic comparison of removal work orders to authorizing documentation
    d. a periodic analysis of the scrap sales and the repairs and maintenance accounts

(CPA)

30. Which of the following controls would be *most effective* in ensuring that the proper custody of assets in the investing cycle is maintained?
    a. Direct access to securities in the safety deposit box is limited to only one corporate officer.

b. Personnel who post investment transactions to the general ledger are *not* permitted to update the investment subsidiary ledger.

c. The purchase and sale of investments are executed on the specific authorization of the board of directors.

d. The recorded balances in the investment subsidiary ledger are compared periodically with the contents of the safety deposit box by independent personnel.

(CPA)

31. The objectives of the internal control structure for a production cycle are to provide assurance that transactions are executed and recorded properly and that
    a. independent internal verification of activity reports is established.
    b. transfers to finished goods are documented by a completed production report and a quality control report.
    c. production orders are prenumbered and signed by a supervisor.
    d. custody of WIP and of finished goods is properly maintained.

(CPA)

32. Independent internal verification of inventory occurs when employees who
    a. issue raw materials obtain materials requisitions for each issue and prepare daily totals of materials issued.
    b. compare records of goods on hand with physical quantities do *not* maintain the records or have custody of the inventory.
    c. obtain receipts for the transfer of completed work to finished goods prepare a completed production report.
    d. are independent of issuing production orders update records from completed job cost sheets and production cost reports on a timely basis.

(CPA)

33. Hermit Company manufactures a line of walnut office products. Hermit executives estimate the demand for the double walnut letter tray, one of the company's products, at 6,000 units. The letter tray sells for $80 per unit. The costs relating to the letter tray are estimated to be as follows for 20XX:
    a. Standard manufacturing cost per letter tray unit—$50
    b. Costs to initiate production run—$300
    c. Annual cost of carrying the letter tray in inventory—20% of standard manufacturing cost

    In prior years, Hermit Company has scheduled the production for the letter tray in two equal production runs. The company is aware that the EOQ model can be employed to determine optimal size for production runs. The EOQ formula as it applies to inventories for determining the optimal order quantity is as follows:

$$EOQ = \sqrt{\frac{2(\text{annual demand})(\text{cost per order})}{(\text{cost per unit})(\text{carrying cost})}}$$

Required

Calculate the expected annual cost savings Hermit Company could experience if it employed the EOQ model to determine the number of production runs that should be initiated during the year for the manufacture of the double walnut letter trays.

(CMA)

34. State why each of the following changes would affect (i) reorder point and (ii) EOQ, and state whether the effect would be an increase or a decrease in quantity.
    a. increase in demand for an inventory stock item
    b. decrease in the cost of capital to the firm holding the inventory
    c. increase in salaries in the purchasing and receiving departments

(IIA)

35. Valpaige Company is an industrial machinery and equipment manufacturer with several production departments. The company employs automated and heavy equipment in its production departments. Consequently, Valpaige has a large repair and maintenance (R&M) department for servicing this equipment.

   The operating efficiency of R&M has deteriorated over the past 2 years. Further, repair and maintenance costs seem to be climbing more rapidly than other department costs. The assistant controller has reviewed the operations of R&M and has concluded that the administrative procedures used since the early days of the department are outmoded due in part to the growth of the company. The two major causes for the deterioration, in the opinion of the assistant controller, are an antiquated scheduling system for repair/maintenance work and the actual cost system to distribute R&M's costs to the production departments. The actual costs of R&M are allocated monthly to the production departments on the basis of the number of service calls made during each month.

   The assistant controller has proposed that a formal work-order system be implemented for R&M. The production departments would submit a service request to R&M for the repairs and/or maintenance to be completed, including a suggested time for having the work done. The supervisor of R&M would prepare a cost estimate on the service request for the work required (labor and materials) and indicate a suggested time for completing the work on the service request. R&M's supervisor would return the request to the production department that initiated the request. Once the production department okays the work by returning a copy of the service request, R&M's supervisor would prepare a repair/maintenance work order and schedule the job. This work order provides the repair worker with the details of the work to be done and is used to record the actual repair/maintenance hours worked and the materials and supplies used.

   Producing departments would be charged for actual labor hours worked at a predetermined standard rate for the type of work required. The parts and supplies used would be charged to the production departments at cost.

   The assistant controller believes that only two documents would be required in this new system—a repair/maintenance service request initiated by the production departments and the repair/maintenance work order initiated by R&M.

Required

   a. For the repair/maintenance work-order document,
      1. Identify the data items that would be important to R&M and the production departments that should be incorporated into the work order.
      2. Indicate how many copies of the work order would be required, and explain how each copy would be distributed.
   b. Prepare a document flow diagram to show how the repair/maintenance service request and the repair/maintenance work order should be coordinated and used among the departments of Valpaige to request and complete the repair/ maintenance work, to provide the basis for charging the production departments for the cost of the completed work, and to evaluate the performance of R&M. Provide explanations to the flow diagram as appropriate.

(CMA)

36. The Wadswad Corporation manufactures both standard and customized electrical control boards for automated manufacturing machinery. The company was started by an electrical engineer and a salesman for a machinery company when they saw a demand for systems integration support by companies who were purchasing customized electrical control boards. Since neither of their former employers seemed interested in providing systems integration support for customized electrical control boards, they started manufacturing control boards and offered complete systems integration support to companies desiring this service.

   The firm was successful from the start and grew quickly. As the number of employees and sales increased, management began to computerize the firm's accounting system. First, payroll was computerized, and then accounts receivable and accounts payable were computerized. The company is now ready to implement a new computer system to control its WIP inventory. The firm uses a job costing system. WIP numbers are established to control the manufacture of both standard and customized control boards. Boards usually are produced in batches of 10 to several hundred units.

   Fred Beam, the controller of Wadswad, has just returned from a meeting with the programmer who is implementing the new computer system for WIP. The programmer explained the proposed structure of the master WIP file and the types of transactions that will be processed against the file. These structures are outlined below.

   Each record in the master WIP file will contain the following data:

   Field 1: WIP number
   Field 2: Units started
   Field 3: Units spoiled
   Field 4: Materials cost
   Field 5: Direct labor cost

Field 6: Total cost

Field 7: Expected completion date

The WIP number, number of units started, and expected completion date will be entered into the computer when a job is authorized to begin production. The following four types of transactions will be processed:

1. *Materials requisitions.* The cost of materials requisitioned for each job will be posted to field 4 of the master WIP file, which accumulates the total materials cost of a job. The cost of materials requisitioned for each job also will be posted to field 6 of the master WIP file, which is used to accumulate the total cost of each job.

2. *Job time tickets.* The direct labor cost for each job will be posted to field 5 of the master WIP file, which accumulates the total labor cost of a job. The direct labor cost for each job also will be posted to field 6 of the master WIP file, which is used to accumulate the total cost of each job.

   Applied overhead will be computed as a percentage of direct labor cost. Applied overhead will be posted to field 6 of the master WIP file, which is used to accumulate the total cost of each job.

3. *Spoiled-production reports.* Units spoiled in production for each job will be posted to field 3 of the master WIP file, which accumulates the total units spoiled in production for each job. Special messages will be printed during processing if the spoilage rate exceeds management's expectations.

4. *Completed-production reports.* When a job is complete, the computer system will report the total cost of the job and also the per-unit cost. The date of completion will be compared with the expected date of completion, field 7 in the master WIP file. Special messages will be printed during processing if a job is completed late.

Required

a. The new computer-based WIP system will provide summary accounting data that must be posted periodically to the firm's general ledger. Prepare the standard journal entries that Fred Beam, the controller of Wadswad, could use to document how the expected outputs of the new system will affect the general ledger.

b. Are accounting-related data the only type of output this system will provide? Discuss.

37. Deake Corporation is a medium-sized, diversified manufacturing company. Fred Richards has been promoted recently to manager, property accounting section. Richards has had difficulty responding to some of the requests from individuals in other departments of Deake for information about the company's fixed assets. Some of the requests and problems Richards has had to cope with are as follows:

a. The controller has requested schedules of individual fixed assets to support the balances in the general ledger. Richards has furnished the necessary information, but he has always been late. The manner in which the records are organized makes it difficult to obtain information easily.

b. The maintenance manager wished to verify the existence of a punch press that he thinks was repaired twice. He has asked Richards to confirm the asset number and location of the press.

c. The insurance department wants data on the cost and book values of assets to include in its review of current insurance coverage.

d. The tax department has requested data that can be used to determine when Deake should switch depreciation methods for tax purposes.

e. The company's internal auditors have spent a significant amount of time in the property accounting section recently attempting to confirm the annual depreciation expense.

The property account records that are at Richards' disposal consist of a set of manual books. These records show the date the asset was acquired, the account number to which the asset applies, the dollar amount capitalized, and the estimated useful life of the asset for depreciation purposes.

After many frustrations, Richards has realized that his records are inadequate and that he cannot supply the data easily when they are requested. He has decided that he should discuss the problems with the controller, Julie Castle.

RICHARDS: "Julie, something has got to give. My people are working overtime and can't keep up. You worked in property accounting before you became controller. You know I can't tell the tax, insurance, and maintenance people everything they need to know from my records. Also, that internal auditing team is living in my area, and that slows down the work pace. The requests of these people are reasonable, and we should be able to answer these questions and provide the needed data. I think we need an automated property accounting system. I would like to talk to the information systems people to see if they can help me."

CASTLE: "Fred, I think you have a good idea, but be sure you are personally involved in the design of any system so that you get all the information you need."

Required

a. Identify and justify four major objectives Deake Corporation's automated property accounting system should possess in order to provide the data necessary to respond to requests for information from company personnel.

b. Identify the data that should be included in the computer record for each asset included in the property account.

(CMA)

38. Yard Company is a family-owned medium-sized manufacturing company that has been in operation for more than 30 years. The company makes moldings and related parts for other manufacturing firms. Yard Company's manufacturing operations include machining, welding, and assembly. The company has always employed skilled artisans and has been able to maintain a reputation for high-quality production.

Moldings are made to order and sold through contract with the purchasing party. The uniqueness of its product had allowed the company to avoid automating its production processes until just last year. Realizing that labor costs were going to escalate steadily for the foreseeable future, management purchased three numerically controlled machines to automate some of its production processes. A numerically controlled machine is a computer-operated workstation that is programmed to operate tools and to perform a sequence of manufacturing operations in conjunction with one or more human operators. For example, the machine might be programmed to drill several holes of specific sizes in a certain sequence. The human operator manipulates the part, pressing a button to let the machine know when to drill a hole.

Programming the numerically controlled machines requires skills that are obtained most readily by studying computer science in college or a trade school. Because none of the artisans employed by the Yard Company had the necessary background, it was necessary to hire two recent college graduates to program the machines. The two programmers were much younger than most of the artisans and had very different backgrounds and career objectives. It was very difficult for the two groups to communicate.

Relations between the artisans and the programmers deteriorated quickly because the numerically controlled machines operated very inefficiently, mostly due to programming errors. For example, a drill bit would withdraw several feet into the air so that an artisan could rotate a part, when it was only necessary for the drill bit to withdraw several inches. In addition to the time delay, errors of this type lessened the artisans' confidence in the programmers' work. This situation has existed for more than a year. One of the original programmers quit the company, and another was hired to take his place. Rumor has it that both programmers are currently seeking other positions.

The management of Yard Company is aware that there is a problem but does not know how it should proceed. The numerically controlled machines were a sizable investment for the company and were expected to make production more efficient. Management expected some start-up problems, but the problems that have been encountered have been much more severe than expected. Total production costs have increased rather than decreased, and management is aware that both the programmers and the artisans are blaming each other for the company's problems.

Required

a. What factors have contributed to the problem Yard Company is experiencing in implementing numerically controlled machines in its production operations?

b. Suggest a solution to Yard Company's problem.

39. Molly Company manufactures both standard and customized electrical control boards for automated manufacturing machinery. The company recently completed installation of a robotic assembly unit. This automated unit completely eliminates direct labor in the production of several types of standard electrical control boards.

Molly uses a job costing system. Boards usually are produced in batches of 10 to several hundred units. Overhead is applied to products based on direct labor hours.

Sally Seed, the controller of Molly Company, recently met with Sam Nut, the production supervisor, concerning the cost of producing several of the firm's products. The following discussion took place:

SAM: "Sally, I'm perplexed by your most recent cost figures for products X, Y, and Z, our big sellers. Before we installed the robotic assembly unit, the following data applied. Products X and Y had identical unit costs, and product Z was the cheapest to produce."

SALLY: "That was correct, Sam. Our total budgeted overhead was $600,000. Given our expected

Product	X	Y	Z
Number of Parts	10	15	20
Labor Hours Costs	4	4	2
Material	$200	$200	$200
Labor ($30/hour)	120	120	60
Overhead	80	80	40
Total Cost	**$400**	**$400**	**$300**

30,000 hours of direct labor, we had an applied overhead rate of $20 per direct labor hour. You can see, then, how these costs were calculated, as our direct labor costs were $30 per hour."

SAM: "According to your latest report, the first since we installed the new automated equipment, the following data apply."

"Sally, I'm not so sure that these cost representations are believable. We purchased

Product	X	Y	Z
Number of Parts	10	15	20
Robot Hours	3	0	1
Labor Hours Costs	0	4	2
Material	$200	$200	$200
Labor ($30/hour)	0	120	60
Overhead	0	200	100
Total Cost	**$200**	**$520**	**$360**

expensive automated equipment and overall eliminated almost a third of our labor cost, yet product Y, which does not use the new equipment, has increased more than 25% in cost. On the other hand, product X, which does use the new equipment, has decreased 50% in cost."

SALLY: "Well Sam, our total budgeted overhead has increased to $1,000,000. But our expected hours of direct labor drop from 30,000 to 20,000. This gives an applied overhead rate of $50 per direct labor hour. You can see, then, how these costs were calculated, as our direct labor costs were $30 per hour."

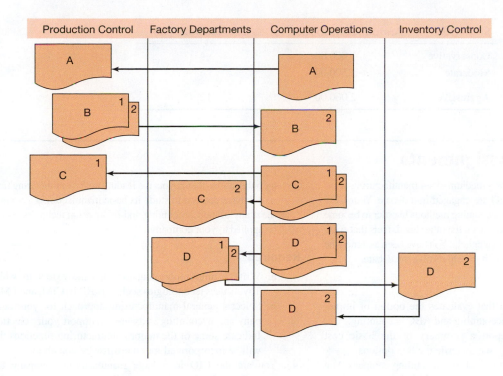

FIGURE 10.16

Flowchart for Problem 40

Production Control	Factory Departments	Computer Operations	Inventory Control

SAM: "Well, that may be, Sally, but something just doesn't make sense about using direct labor as the only allocation base for all overhead items. There are other things beside labor that increase production cost. Consider parts per product, for example. We spend a lot of effort in material handling, and it seems to me that more parts make more work, which means to me that it costs more."

SALLY: "Sam, you may be right. I wanted to investigate activity-based costing, and this conversation has convinced me to do so. I'm going to collect some data and recompute these cost figures using activity-based costing. I'll get back to you soon, and we can see if these new figures seem to make more sense."

Required

Sally collected the following data for ABC accounting.

	Activity		
	Material Handling	Robotic Assembly	All Other Overhead
Overhead	$200,000	$400,000	$400,000
Base	40,000 (parts)	5,000 (robot hours)	20,000 (labor hours)
Rate	$5	$80	$20

a. Compute product costs under ABC using the three activities and their associated allocation bases shown here.

b. How might allocation bases for activity costs be identified?

40. Figure 10.16 is a partial document flowchart of a production business process.

Required

Match the letters A through D in the flowchart to the following items.

1. Production orders
2. Production authorizations
3. Material requisitions
4. Inventory status reports

41. Excel® Assignment: Asset Retirement Scenarios

Molly Company plans to retire its primary production facility in 30 years. The company is considering the establishment of a retirement account that will be used to accumulate funds during the 30-year period. The retirement account will then be used to replace the retired production facility.

Required

Download the spreadsheet file titled "chapter_10_41" from the textbook Web site. Use scenario manager to create a scenario summary report of the total value of the retirement account for the following three scenarios concerning the value of the retirement account at the end of the 30-year period.

The annual contribution will be made at the beginning of each year, starting with the first year. This task can best be accomplished using the FV function.

Scenario	Annual Contribution ($)	Interest Rate (%)
Conservative	1,000.00	4
Moderate	1,500.00	6
Aggressive	2,000.00	12

Web Research Assignments

42. You are the controller for a medium-sized manufacturing company. Your CFO and CEO are engaged in a debate. Your CFO wants to implement lean accounting methods in order to become more competitive. Your CEO, on the other hand, feels that ABC accounting would be of greater help. You have been assigned the tasks of writing a brief report to help resolve the debate.

Required

    a. Write a brief report that evaluates the option of implementing both lean accounting and ABC accounting.

    b. Include in your report a summary of the basic cost accounting concepts that underlie the two options.

43. You are the controller of a small manufacturing company. You are considering adopting some sort of MRP-type software. You are considering various options, including the E-Z-MRP™ integrated manufacturing system (www.e-z-mrp.com) published by Beach Access Software.

Required

    a. Write a brief report to your CEO that explains the function that can be performed by E-Z-MRP™?

    b. Find, evaluate, and compare relative to E-Z-MRP,™ a second software option for your company.

44. You are the CIO in a small start-up automobile manufacturing company. You are interested in manufacturing small electric cars for use in urban commuting. You have already produced several working prototype models, and you have all the necessary safety and environment approvals to manufacture and sell your cars in the U.S. and European markets. Your main problem now is implementing the appropriate accounting and information technologies. You have already solved all the manufacturing issues: You will be retooling a robot-controlled manufacturing plant that was originally developed to manufacture recreational all-terrain vehicles (ATVs), which your company purchased when the seller abandoned the U.S. market. You know from reading industry publications that Toyota is a leading auto manufacturing firm, so you have decided to study its basic manufacturing system to see if any of their accounting and information technologies can be applied to your company.

Required

    a. Write a brief report that explains the extent to which Toyota uses technologies such as MRP II, CIM, and FMS?

    b. Select a general manufacturing approach for your company and accounting software to support your selection. Indicate some of the major manufacturing functions that will be incorporated into the software you choose.

45. You are the CIO in a large manufacturing company that specializes in low-cost upholstered living room furniture. You are very proud of your state-of-the-art system that involves nearly zero materials or finished goods inventories. Your CEO has just told you that a major European competitor has approached her regarding the creation of a virtual enterprise, dedicated to producing high-quality, expensive leather furniture. "You have to help me," your CEO said to you. "I have no idea what a virtual enterprise is. I didn't want to act ignorant, so I told the competitor that we were very interested and that we would schedule a video conference with them to further discuss the matter."

Required

    a. Write a brief report that explains the following:

        1. What a virtual enterprise is, and how it relates to a collaborative networked organization.

        2. How a virtual enterprise will work with your existing information technologies and information system. You currently use SAP.

        3. The possibility of setting up the virtual enterprise using an SOA that integrates with your existing system.

Answers to Chapter Quiz

1. d   **2.** b   **3.** a   **4.** c   **5.** a   **6.** c   **7.** a   **8.** a   **9.** d   **10.** c

Systems Planning, Analysis, and Design

Learning Objectives

Careful study of this chapter will enable you to:

- Describe the various stages of classical systems analysis.
- Describe the limitations of classical systems analysis and iterative alternatives.
- Discuss the major techniques for gathering and organizing data for systems analysis.
- Describe some of the human problems involved in systems analysis.
- Describe the various steps involved in specifying systems design alternatives.
- Discuss the various considerations relevant to preparing design specifications.
- Describe the content of a systems design proposal.
- Summarize several major design techniques.
- Discuss object-oriented analysis and design approaches and their advantages relative to classical approaches.
- Discuss the usefulness of systems design packages.

General Overview

Systems development is the process of modifying or replacing a portion or all of an information system. This process requires a substantial commitment of time and resources and is an ongoing activity in many organizations.

Systems development is normally undertaken by a project team composed of systems analysts, programmers, accountants, and other people in the organization who are knowledgeable about or affected by the project. IT projects are carried out within an IT governance framework, such as COBIT—Control Objectives for Information and related Technology—(discussed in Chapters 4 and 14). The governance structure not only oversees projects but also makes sure that they are selected and implemented in a way that ensures their congruence with the goals, objectives, and strategies of the organization, as well as with legal and regulatory structures.

Every systems development project goes through essentially the same **systems development life cycle:** planning and analysis, design, and implementation. Neglecting any portion of the life cycle may have serious consequences. The life-cycle concept provides a framework for planning and controlling the detailed developmental activities.

RIGID DEVELOPMENT The traditional systems development process follows a somewhat rigid top-down sequential approach: First, a plan is developed. Next, a design is developed to produce an architectural blueprint for implementing the plan. Finally, a working system that conforms to the architectural plan is developed and implemented.

The rigidity of the traditional approach to the systems development life cycle is reflected in names that are sometimes used to describe it. For example, it is sometimes referred to as the "**big-design-up-front**" approach because of its emphasis on the importance of an initial, unchanging plan. It is also referred to as the **waterfall approach,** because the sequential steps of analysis, planning, design, and implementation flow only in a single "downward" direction like water in a waterfall.

The traditional rigid approach is most appropriate in situations in which the plans and designs can be very clearly defined in such a way that it is unlikely that significant deviations from them will be desired or needed once they are set in place. Rigid development tends to be most appropriate in evolved, stable industries, especially in ones in which standardized systems exist. For example, many medical facilities adopt similar billing systems, so a given medical facility might be inclined to simply adopt one of the industry-leading billing systems and adapt its policies and procedures to those modeled by the industry-standard system. On the other hand, companies in emerging industries, complex companies, innovative companies, and companies with unique policies may find rigid up-front development impossible to work with.

The main reason that rigid up-front development is unworkable in many situations is because it's quite normal for deficiencies in a systems plan to only become obvious during the design and implementation phases. Similarly, no matter how carefully things are done in the design phase, previously-unthought-of problems can emerge during implementation. The more complicated, unfamiliar, or innovative the business and information environments, the more difficult it is to get everything right up front.

In a general sense, systems development means defining, shaping, and reshaping the four enterprise architectural domains (i.e., broad views of the enterprise) that were discussed in Chapter 3: the business architecture, the information architecture, the applications architecture, and the technical architecture. Recall that the enterprise architecture itself defines a development process that begins with the business architecture (i.e., company's goals and strategies and business processes), then proceeds to the information architecture (i.e., information requirements), and then the application (i.e., software) and technical architectures.

Although both systems development life cycle and enterprise architecture generally proceed in a top-down fashion, the two do not directly correspond to each other. In fact, each domain within the enterprise architecture is subject to analysis, planning, design, and implementation. For example, software within the application architecture must be designed (or selected) before it is implemented. Still, the systems development life cycle does roughly correspond to the top-down structure of the enterprise architecture, with the business and information architectures corresponding to analysis and planning, and the application and technology architectures corresponding to design and implementation.

FLEXIBLE DEVELOPMENT   The traditional rigid approach has been adapted in two ways to become flexible. First, it has become iterative. This means that the initial plan is rougher and more tentative so that it is more easily improved when its deficiencies become apparent in the design phase. Similarly, the initial design is rougher and more tentative so that it too can be easily modified when implementation problems appear. The result is that with so-called **iterative or agile approaches** to systems development, all phases of the life cycle are carried on simultaneously. These approaches require constant communication between analysts, planners, designers, implementers, and users so that each group can reshape its work as needed. The work between them iterates until their work in total converges to a workable system.

The second major adaptation of the rigid approach involves breaking up projects into smaller pieces. Working with smaller projects can greatly minimize the risk of project failure, since there is much less to go wrong if the costs of an individual project are kept to a minimum. Further, it is a lot easier to apply agile and iterative development methods to small projects than to large ones. In fact, smaller projects are in general easier to manage.

Service-oriented architecture (SOA) has greatly facilitated working in smaller projects, since the whole concept of SOA relies on small independent pieces of software called *services*. With SOA, project development teams can be assigned to developing individual services that can be orchestrated or reorchestrated as needed to function in enterprise application suites. If it turns out that some projects fail and produce unneeded or unusable services, then those services can quickly be repaired or replaced by new ones.

 CASE IN POINT

An important issue in systems development is how to define success and failure for a project. Consider these questions: Is a project a failure if the cost overrun is 20%? Is a project a failure if it takes 9 months to complete when it is supposed to take 6 months? What if a project goes as planned, but 25% of the employee-users hate the resulting system? What if a project has terrible cost overruns and is completed months later but then the resulting system works really well, saves the company an enormous amount of money, and makes all the employees very happy? How do you define success versus failure?

The discussion that follows presents the traditional top-down approach to systems development. This is because the elements of iterative development approaches and the traditional approach are very much the same. Both involve analysis, planning, design, and implementation. The main differences are likely to be a matter of the size of the particular project, flexibility in its administration, and the degree of teamwork and collaboration involved. In truth, even the rigid approach by necessity involves some iteration: It is nearly impossible to create a perfect plan or design, especially in a large project. Changes to the plan and design area are almost always necessary, and, as is discussed below, systems in practice require constant change, so that analysis, planning, design, and implementation tend to be never-ending iterative processes. The result is that project agility is always a matter of degree.

Overview of Systems Planning and Analysis

Systems planning involves identifying subsystems within the information system that need special attention for development. The objective of systems planning is to identify problem areas that need to be dealt with either immediately or sometime in the future. **Systems analysis** begins after the systems planning stage has identified subsystems for development. Its primary objectives (Figure 11.1) are to understand the existing system, to identify and understand problems, to describe information needs and system requirements, and to establish priorities for further systems work.

FIGURE 11.1

Objectives of Systems Analysis

Objectives
1. Gain an understanding of the existing system (if one exists).
2. Identify and understand problems.
3. Express identified problems in terms of information needs and system requirements.
4. Clearly identify subsystems to be given highest priority.
Focus
■ Identify critical success factors.
■ Give special attention to these factors.

FIGURE 11.2

Cost Patterns
at Varying
Development Stages

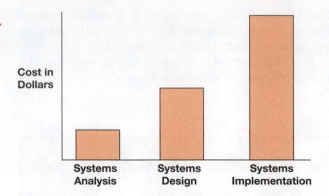

Once a particular subsystem is targeted for development, systems analysis focuses on defining the information needs and system requirements necessary for the system to implement management's objectives. Therefore, systems analysis emphasizes the study of managers' decisions and their associated information requirements. These requirements are then translated into specific applications during the design and implementation phases of the systems development life cycle.

The importance of the systems analysis process can be seen in Figure 11.2. Most development-cycle costs are incurred in the design and implementation phases. This means that major errors in the analysis phase can become quite costly later. It is therefore very important that the systems analyst gain a thorough understanding of the situation in terms of management's problems and information needs.

Systems Planning and Feasibility Analysis

It is essential that a top-down total systems approach be taken to systems development. Careful attention must be given to developing an overall systems plan and strategy. Such a plan must include the overall support and approval of top management. Without such an overall plan, the information system is likely to develop as a maze of patchwork. An overall plan seeks to ensure the following objectives:

- Resources will be targeted to the subsystems where the needs are greatest.
- Duplication and wasted effort will be minimized.
- Systems development will be consistent with the strategic plan of the organization.

Systems planning and feasibility analysis involve seven phases:

1. Discussing and planning on the part of top management
2. Establishing a systems planning steering committee
3. Establishing overall objectives and constraints
4. Developing a strategic information systems plan
5. Identifying and prioritizing specific areas within the organization for the systems development focus
6. Setting forth a systems proposal to serve as a basis of the analysis and preliminary design for a given subsystem
7. Assembling a team of individuals for purposes of the analysis and preliminary systems design

Notice that these seven steps operate in a top-down fashion. The planning effort begins with top management and ends with a specific team of individuals charged with the task of analyzing a particular system and coming up with a preliminary systems design. In the following sections, each of the seven phases is discussed individually.

Systems Planning and Top Management

It is crucial that all major systems development efforts have the support of top management. A major task of the systems developer is to discern the strategic plans, key success factors, and overall objectives of top management. The systems developer must do a lot more than simply ask top management what its problems are. The role of the systems developer is much like that of a doctor with regard to a patient. The patient is only able to describe symptoms of the problems; it is the doctor who must determine the underlying problem and its causes. Picture what a doctor would say if a patient said, "I have a bad headache, and I want you to give me a shot of penicillin." The doctor would take note of the patient's problems and suggested solution but would make an independent diagnosis and analysis of the underlying cause and the best treatment. The same approach must be taken by the systems developer.

Steering Committee

A useful approach to guiding the overall systems development effort is to have a **steering committee** representing top management and all major functional areas within the organization. A primary responsibility of this committee should be to focus on the overall current and future information needs of the company. Such a committee must have representation by top management because it is essential that the information system fit within the overall strategic plan of the corporation. This entails taking a long-run view. Failure to take a long-run view can be very costly to the company. For example, if it is known that the company plans to launch a new product within the next 5 years, the information systems plan should allow for growth of the existing system in such a way that it can easily accommodate the new product. In fact, it might prove cost-effective to include plans for the new product in the current systems development effort instead of adding them later.

The steering committee should be responsible for overall planning and control of the systems development effort of the company. An ideal person to be in charge of such a committee would be a vice president of information systems. The steering committee should not, however, become involved in the details of specific development projects. Individual projects should be supervised and managed by an individual who reports periodically to the steering committee.

Developing Objectives and System Constraints

Effective, overall sound planning calls for the development of general objectives for the company and specific objectives for individual subsystems within the company. General objectives include the overall strategic objectives relating to the company's long-run planning cycle. Subsidiary to the strategic objectives are tactical objectives. These correspond to tactical planning and typically relate to about a 1-year to 3-year time horizon.

Also important are the company's **key success factors.** These factors are the characteristics that distinguish a company from its competitors and are the keys to its success. For example, some companies emphasize speed of service; others emphasize product quality; still others emphasize low prices. Whatever the key success factors are, they must be incorporated into the objectives for systems design. A company that has an overall key objective relating to fast delivery times would want to make information relating to late deliveries an important part of its shipping/delivery system.

Developing a Strategic Systems Plan

A major output of the steering committee or individual in charge of systems development should be a **strategic systems plan.** This plan should take the form of a written document that incorporates both the short- and long-run goals of the company's systems development effort. Key elements of a strategic systems plan include

- An overall statement relating to key success factors of the company and overall objectives
- A description of systems within the company for which development efforts are needed

- A statement of priorities indicating which areas are to be given the highest priority
- An outline of required resources, including costs, personnel, and equipment
- Tentative timetables for developing specific systems

Identifying Individual Projects for Priority

As stated previously, the strategic plan should identify specific areas to be given the highest priority. Setting priorities is crucial because financial resources are always limited. Prioritizing projects should be done in the same way as in capital budgeting. Specific benefits should be defined for projects, and their costs should be estimated as closely as possible and set forth in financial budgets. These financial budgets should be as accurate as possible.

Because the benefits of systems development are often difficult to quantify, it is easy to lose sight of financial considerations when prioritizing systems development projects. However, it is almost always possible to quantify the costs, and this should be done before commissioning a project. In addition, even though benefits may be difficult to quantify, they should be stated in formal written terms. For example, a company might consider a sales order system that would allow its salespeople to check on the status of incomplete orders. Such a system would allow sales people to better deal with customers when there is a question about the status of a possibly over-due order. Such a system might allow a salesperson to immediately find the current or revised delivery date. This information could be conveyed to the customer, and the customer could plan accordingly. In this situation, it might be very easy to identify the costs. However, what are the financial benefits of being able to provide information to customers on short notice? There is an obvious benefit in terms of customer relations. This benefit might result in sales increases. If so, such increases should be estimated and incorporated into the formal system proposal.

Commissioning the Systems Project

In many respects, commissioning the systems project is like constructing a building. A building project requires carpenters, plumbers, bricklayers, electricians, and metalworkers. Similarly, a systems development project requires individuals from several disciplines. The actual personnel requirements will depend on the specific project; however, it is common to require management, accountants, systems users, computer programmers, and various types of technical support individuals.

The Steps in Systems Analysis

Figure 11.3 depicts the major steps or phases of the systems analysis effort.

Phase 1: Survey Current System

OBJECTIVES OF SURVEYING   The systems survey has four objectives:

- Gain a fundamental understanding of the operational aspects of the system.
- Establish a working relationship with the users of the system.
- Collect important data that are useful in developing the systems design.
- Identify specific problems that require focus in terms of subsequent design efforts.

FIGURE 11.3

Steps Involved in Systems Analysis

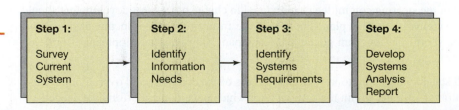

Step 1:	Step 2:	Step 3:	Step 4:
Survey Current System	Identify Information Needs	Identify Systems Requirements	Develop Systems Analysis Report

The systems development team must become very familiar with the workings of the system under consideration for change. It is dangerous to try to modify an existing system that you do not understand thoroughly. In addition, developers must become familiar with the people who work in the system on a daily basis. This familiarity allows developers to gain an understanding of problems that top management may be completely unaware of.

The objective of establishing a relationship with individuals who work within the system under development is especially critical. *The success or failure of a development project will depend to a large extent on the quality of the relationship between the development team and the individuals working in the system.* A poor relationship can result in misunderstandings and misplaced design efforts. The individuals working in the system must live with the development results on a long-term basis. More specifically, it is a very real possibility that the new system can be rejected by the individuals for whom it is designed. If these individuals do not respect the development team, they may resist implementation of the completed design. Such resistance can come in many forms, including complaints to top management, strikes, or sabotage.

BEHAVIORAL CONSIDERATIONS   The human element is a key factor in conducting the systems survey. The fact that systems development involves changing the existing system poses many problems. Most people do not like change. An individual may have been in a job routine that has not changed for many years. This individual is very likely to see you as a threat. Other individuals might be concerned about losing their jobs, possibly to a computer. Still other individuals might see you as a "front-office spy." Figure 11.4 depicts these problems in terms of a communication gap between the systems analyst and management. It is the responsibility of the systems analyst, not management, to bridge this communication gap. Therefore, the first task of the analyst conducting a systems survey should be to establish a good working relationship between the project team and management.

Certain approaches can help bridge this communication gap:

- Get to know as many people involved in the system as soon as possible.
- Communicate the benefits of the proposed system to the individuals involved.
- Provide assurances, to the degree possible, to all individuals that there will be no losses of jobs or major changes in job responsibilities.
- Provide assurances that you are genuinely concerned with making life better for those involved in the system.

SOURCES FOR GATHERING FACTS   A variety of techniques can be used to gather facts about the information subsystem under study. These include interviews, questionnaires, observations, and reviews of various types of documents such as corporate minutes, charts of accounts, organization

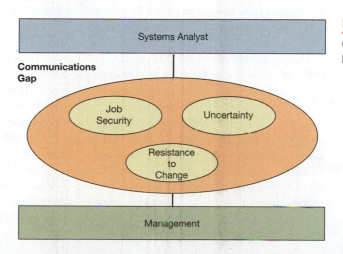

FIGURE 11.4

Communication Gap Problem

charts, financial statements, procedure manuals, policy statements, job descriptions, and so on. In addition, sources of information outside the company should not be overlooked. These include industry and trade publications as well as professional journals. Finally, the customer should be viewed as a vital component of the system and included in any analysis.

ANALYSIS OF SURVEY FINDINGS When the survey has been completed, the strengths and weaknesses of the subsystem under study should be thoroughly analyzed. The survey focuses on understanding the nature and operation of the system (with its associated problems), whereas the analysis of the survey findings focuses on strengths and weaknesses of the system. Some of the following questions might be asked in evaluating the present system:

- Is a given procedure necessary?
- Does the procedure involve unnecessary steps?
- Is the procedure cost-effective?
- Is a given report clear and easy to read?
- Are the source documents well designed?
- Are reports being generated that are not needed or used?
- What causes a particular problem?
- What additional reports might be useful to management?
- Is the system documentation adequate?

Overall, these questions should result in a report that summarizes the strengths and weaknesses of the existing system. In making such an evaluation, certain standards must be used as benchmarks. These standards relate to effectiveness and efficiency. *Effectiveness* here simply means that the system accomplishes the objectives set forth in the systems planning phase. *Efficiency* relates to whether these objectives are achieved at the lowest possible cost.

Evaluation of the effectiveness of the system's ability to achieve the overall planned objectives should focus on bottlenecks. **Bottlenecks** represent weaknesses in the system where small changes can result in major improvements. For example, a company may have difficulty delivering its goods to its customers within a reasonable time. An analysis of the situation might reveal that the job scheduling system is ineffective and that there are times when employees are idle, even though there is a backlog in the production schedule. In this case, the results of the analysis would indicate a need to focus on the production scheduling system.

Phase 2: Identify Information Needs

The second major phase of systems analysis involves identifying information requirements for managerial decision making. In identifying information needs, the analyst studies specific decisions made by managers in terms of the information inputs. This process is called **information needs analysis,** and the heart of it is the study of decisions made.

How do you identify the decisions made by managers? You might think that it is good enough simply to ask managers what decisions they make. Unfortunately, managers are often unable to answer this question specifically. One reason for this is that managers often think in terms of getting certain jobs done. For example, a product engineer might view her job responsibility as being the designer of a particular new product. If you ask her what decisions she makes, she might respond, "I simply design new products." Your responsibility as a systems developer would be to ask more detailed questions that would get at the nature of some of the decisions the engineer makes in the process. For example, you might ask her, "What are some of the design considerations you have to take into account?" and "How do you make these considerations?" Answers to these questions might reveal that safety considerations are an important factor. From all this, you might conclude that this particular individual might need certain product safety reports. In conclusion, you have to become intimately familiar with the problems of a particular manager in order to understand the decisions that he or she makes and the corresponding information needs.

Fortunately, some systematic techniques can be used to gain an understanding of decisions and information needs. Several basic approaches can be followed:

- Identify the manager's primary job responsibilities.
- Identify the means by which the manager is evaluated.
- Identify some of the major problems the manager faces.
- Identify the means by which the manager evaluates personal output.

The first two approaches suggest that you get an understanding of the manager's position and related responsibilities in a company. The means by which the manager is evaluated are especially important because they will determine, to a large extent, the approaches a manager takes in dealing with day-to-day problems. Another way of looking at this is that the criteria used to evaluate a manager should be based on a statement of the manager's performance goals. For example, an advertising manager might be evaluated on the responsiveness of customers to the company's advertising campaign. Therefore, such a manager would want specific reports relating to advertising expenditures and the associated customer responses.

While the approach of asking managers about their problems can often be very helpful, you cannot simply walk up to a manager and say, "What kind of problems do you have here?" First, managers are often reluctant to discuss their problems with someone they do not really know. Second, a given manager might feel that admitting a problem is somehow admitting failure. Therefore, it is often helpful to take an approach that involves asking the managers a lot of questions about what they do and then listening carefully. If you can get managers to talk long enough, their problems will come out. All this emphasizes the importance of establishing a good working relationship with the manager.

Phase 3: Identify the Systems Requirements

The third phase of the systems analysis project involves specifying systems requirements. Such requirements can be specified in terms of inputs and outputs. The input requirements for a given subsystem specify the specific needs that must be met in order for that subsystem to achieve its objectives.

For example, the information requirements of a production control system might include short-run sales forecasts, reports on the availability of materials, specifications of quality control and standard costs, and information needed to prioritize individual jobs. For the same system, the following might be considered as output requirements:

- Daily progress reports
- Daily finance reports
- Reports on defective units
- Reports on problems with raw materials

The input requirements for one subsystem will, in turn, specify output requirements for another subsystem. In this case, the input requirements of sales forecasts would be an output requirement for some other system within the company (such as marketing).

Phase 4: Develop a Systems Analysis Report

The final output of the systems analysis project is a report. This report is extremely important because it often serves as a basis for further decision making on the part of top management. In addition, this report organizes and documents all the findings of the three phases of the systems analysis project. Without such careful documentation, a lot of information would be lost in the long run. If the analysis is not documented carefully at the time it is conducted, when the time rolls around for doing the design and implementation work, a lot can be forgotten. Also, to develop a design report, all the analysis findings must be organized carefully within some consistent framework.

Some of the key elements of the systems analysis report include

- A summary of the scope and purpose of the analysis project
- A reiteration of the relationship of the project to the overall strategic information systems plan
- A description of any overall problems in the specific subsystem being studied
- A summary of the decisions being made and their specific information requirements
- Specification of system performance requirements
- An overall cost budget and timetable for the project to date
- Recommendations for improving the existing system or for designing new systems
- Recommendations relating to modifying objectives for the subsystem under study

The systems analysis report, when completed, is presented to the vice president of information systems, the information systems steering committee, or if appropriate, directly to top management. The report is then reviewed and discussed by the individuals who decide whether a preliminary systems design should be undertaken. The preliminary systems design, if undertaken, provides a complete budget for the design and implementation parts of the development project.

Fact-Gathering Techniques

A large portion of the systems analyst's job is to collect and organize facts. There are a number of techniques that help the analyst perform these difficult tasks. Table 11.1 summarizes some of the major tools used by analysts in fact gathering.

Techniques for Organizing Facts

The systems analyst needs formal techniques for organizing facts. Table 11.2 presents a number of techniques that are helpful in summarizing and organizing facts. Most of these techniques are discussed in Chapter 2. One additional technique, the Warnier–Orr methodology, is discussed here.

The **Warnier–Orr methodology** is based on analyzing the outputs of an application and factoring the application into a hierarchical structure of modules to accomplish the necessary processing. It uses a diagramming technique that is illustrated in Figure 11.5.

Warnier–Orr methodology uses brackets or braces to show hierarchy. The highest level is to the left of the figure, and the lowest level is to the right. The diagram is produced using

TABLE 11.1   **Techniques for Gathering Facts for Analysis**

Technique	Objective
Depth interview	Gain a fundamental understanding of the system.
Structured interview	Systematic follow-up based on depth interviews.
Open-ended questionnaire	Same as depth interview.
Closed-ended questionnaire	Same as structured interview.
Document reviews	Gain an understanding of the existing system.
Flowcharts	(*Caution*: Sometimes the system does not operate
Organization charts	as documented.) It is often helpful to review system
Procedure manuals	documents before conducting interviews and
Operations manuals	distributing questionnaires.
Reference manuals	
Historical records	
Observation	Familiarity with the system.

TABLE 11.2   Techniques for Fact Organization

Technique	Objective
Work measurement	Summarize resources required for various tasks.
Work distribution	Summarize employee time utilization for tasks.

Flow charting
   General
   Decision table
   Logical data flow
   Systems
   Detailed
	Graphically depict flows and relationships and process
	     requirements, with a focus on modularity.

Decision analysis	Summarize decisions and needed information.
Functional analysis	Summarize functions and related information.
Hierarchical function	
Matrix analysis	Summarize related data inputs/outputs.
Narratives	Written summarization.
File/report summaries	

only three basic constructs: sequence, selection, and repetition. The processes included in a sequence are enclosed in brackets and are executed from top to bottom. To compute the total amount due for a set of invoices, the following sequence is followed: First, determine the discount for an individual invoice, then determine the amount due as gross amount less discount, and then accumulate total amount due. Note that these three steps are enclosed in a single bracket. Selection is necessary when there are two or more alternatives. Mutually exclusive alternatives are enclosed in a bracket and separated by the exclusive symbol $\oplus$ (a plus sign enclosed in a circle). A discount is available if the due date is greater than or equal to today's date. There are two mutually exclusive alternatives, enclosed in a bracket and separated by the exclusive symbol. The discount calculation in either case is indicated by the next lower bracket in the hierarchy. If no processing is required, the word *null* or *skip* is used to indicate this in the diagram. Repetition is indicated by subscripts. If a process is to be repeated only once, the subscript 1 would be used. In our illustration, we have an unknown number of invoices, so the subscript n is used.

Warnier–Orr methodology is easy to understand and use. It can be used to document any type of system, from a top-level overview to detailed program logic. Most significant, the left-to-right pattern forces a structured, top-down approach to analysis.

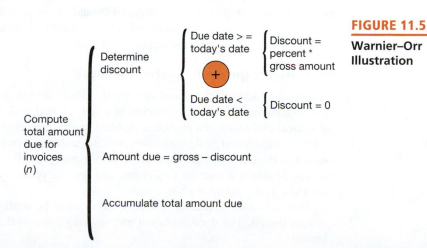

FIGURE 11.5

Warnier–Orr Illustration

Structured Systems Analysis and Design

Thus far, the discussion has focused on the general steps of systems analysis and the techniques for collecting and analyzing facts. In this section, the focus is on the analysis of specific systems. Together, **structured systems analysis and design** comprise a classical waterfall approach to systems development that begins with a very general description of a particular system and then proceeds through a logically related set of steps, each increasing in detail, and ends with computer program code (and other details). Perhaps the best way to view structured systems analysis is as a system of documentation. This includes several levels of documentation, where each level is a logical blowup or "explosion" of the previous level. At the first level, logical data flow diagrams (DFDs) describe the system. They are then supported by additional logical flow or business process diagrams that provide more detail. Other documentation describes the process logic and data components of these diagrams.

Logical Flow Diagrams and Business Process Diagrams versus Flowcharts

The preceding description of structured systems analysis and design incorporates physically abstract diagrams (i.e., logical data flow or business process) as opposed to document or analytic flowcharts. In practice, either type of diagram might be used. Each approach has its unique advantages. The primary difference between the two approaches is that the flowchart gives a physical description of a system, whereas the DFDs and business process diagrams give a logical description of a system. Specifically, an analytic flowchart specifies input/output devices such as a point-of-sale (POS) terminal or printer. It also specifies storage devices, such as optical or solid-state disks. The DFDs and business process diagrams incorporate these same elements but leave the exact physical description open.

In designing new systems, the DFDs and business process diagrams are especially helpful because they do not require a commitment to a particular physical implementation. In addition, it is often useful to analyze an existing system without referring to physical input/output and storage devices. For example, an analyst might have to decide whether an existing accounts receivable system should be online or batch. The DFDs and business process diagrams would be the same for either system, but the document flowcharts would vary considerably across the two situations. The DFDs and business process diagrams would help the analyst conceptually separate the two problems of data flow, business processes, and physical implementation.

Document and analytic flowcharts are indispensable tools. It is always necessary to document the physical implementation of a system. In addition, all other types of documentation, such as hierarchy plus input–process–output (HIPO) charts, file matrices, and so on, should be used as needed.

In summary, similar documentation is used for both design and analysis. In designing new systems or analyzing existing systems, DFDs and business process diagrams are especially helpful because they separate the problems of logical flow and physical implementation. On the other hand, document flowcharts are important in documenting physical implementation.

Systems Design versus Systems Analysis

Structured systems analysis and structured systems design are very similar processes. Strictly speaking, *design* refers to the creation of a new or modified system, whereas *analysis* involves the critical evaluation of a particular problem or existing system. However, practically speaking, systems analysis and design are often indistinguishable. For example, in order to better understand and document a particular problem, the analyst will often develop DFDs and business process diagrams, document flowcharts, and specific process logic. All this documentation can also serve as the basis for a new system.

In conclusion, structured systems analysis must be studied simultaneously with structured systems design. The documentation and working steps of the two problems involve common elements.

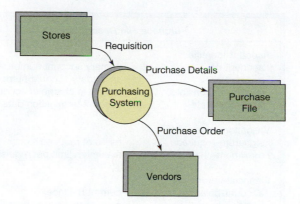

FIGURE 11.6

Purchasing System Context Diagram

The Steps in Structured Systems Analysis

DEVELOP LOGICAL DATA FLOW DIAGRAMS   The system is first described in general terms using a DFD or business process diagram. The example here will use a DFD. Figure 11.6 gives a context diagram for a purchasing system. This diagram does not show the details of the logical processes or any error conditions. These types of details should be given in supporting diagrams. For example, Figure 11.7 provides additional details, exploding the "Purchasing System" process in Figure 11.6 into two sub-processes, "Validate Requisition" and "Prepare Purchase Order." It should be possible to provide even more detail in support of the original purchasing system context diagram by exploding the sub-process in Figure 11.7 into lower-level sub-processes. This procedure should continue until the system is adequately described.

DEFINE DATA DICTIONARIES   The next step is to define data dictionaries corresponding to the data stores referenced in the DFDs. This involves giving a description of the data structure and data elements involved. For example, Figure 11.8 gives data dictionary details for the data store "Purchase File" in Figure 11.7. In this case, the data structure incorporates several categories, including "Account-Identifiers," "Validation-Information," "Financial-Information," and "Vendor-Information." Within each major category, individual data elements are listed. For example, the "Financial-Information" category includes the data items "account-balance" and "last-purchase."

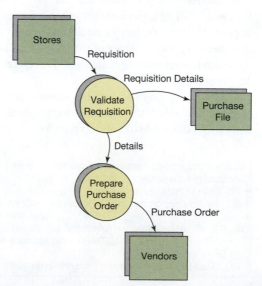

FIGURE 11.7

Expansion of Purchasing System Context Diagram

FIGURE 11.8

Data Dictionary for
Purchase File

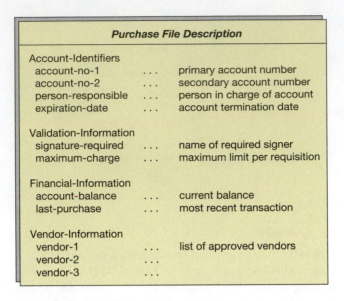

Purchase File Description

Account-Identifiers
- account-no-1 . . . primary account number
- account-no-2 . . . secondary account number
- person-responsible . . . person in charge of account
- expiration-date . . . account termination date

Validation-Information
- signature-required . . . name of required signer
- maximum-charge . . . maximum limit per requisition

Financial-Information
- account-balance . . . current balance
- last-purchase . . . most recent transaction

Vendor-Information
- vendor-1 . . . list of approved vendors
- vendor-2 . . .
- vendor-3 . . .

Note that no physical detail is given at this point. At a subsequent time (the design and implementation stages), it would be necessary to provide specifics on forms layout, storage media, and so on.

DEFINE ACCESS METHODS   It is also necessary to specify how the data stores will be accessed. This typically involves defining primary and secondary access keys. For example, the purchase file in Figure 11.8 might have "account-no-1" as the primary key and "person-responsible" as the secondary key.

DEFINE PROCESS LOGIC   There are many approaches to documenting the process logic. These include various types of decision trees and decision diagrams, as well as structured English. The latter approach is discussed here because it is particularly easy to understand, flexible, and useful in the development of computer programs.

Structured English is a special language for describing process logic that uses several key words, including *IF, THEN, ELSE IF*, and *SO*. Figure 11.9 gives an example of structured English describing account number validation in the "Validate Requisition" sub-process in Figure 11.7. The logic is structured in a format that a nontechnical person can understand. This approach, therefore, has the additional benefit that it can be read and modified by system users. Another very useful aspect of structured English is that it very closely resembles source code in structured programming languages. Therefore, structured English can greatly reduce the task of programming.

Structured English does not include provisions for error conditions and data file access. If these are added, the resulting documentation is sometimes referred to as **pseudocode.** It is sometimes desirable to develop pseudocode as a final step before program coding.

FIGURE 11.9

Structured English
for Account
Validation Related
to Purchase Routine

```
Access purchase file
For each purchase requisition
IF   account no. on requisition equals account-no-1
                    THEN   flag account-no-1 field
ELSE   IF   account no. on requisition equals account-no-2
                    THEN   flag account-no-2 field
ELSE   (none of the above)
SO   void the transaction and generate error code
```

Iterative Systems Development

The classical structured design approach, though still appropriate for some projects, has become less popular. In addition to suffering from problems associated with the waterfall approach, it is also often too slow. More in favor are iterative approaches. **Rapid application development (RAD)** represents a good example of an iterative approach. RAD involves a mixture of structured and iterative development. A key feature of RAD is the use of prototype designs, which form tentative designs relative to the finished system. Using structured methods, the analysts, designers, and programmers iterate back and forth, and each iteration results in the prototypes becoming more refined, until the project is complete.

Another example of an iterative approach is the **rational unified process (RUP)** developed by Rational Software and later published by IBM. RUP's creators developed the approach after analyzing failures in many software development projects. RUP now probably represents the most popular general development approach used in practice.

The RUP development framework breaks down project life cycles into four phases, which we roughly described here:

1. Inception phase. In this phase, the basic project is defined, described, and justified in terms of expected costs and benefits, risks, core requirements, and constraints.
2. Elaboration phase. The project is documented in further detail that includes unified modeling language (UML) diagrams, a working specification of the architecture, and prototypes that deal with the identified risks.
3. Construction phase. The actual software is coded.
4. Transition phase. The software is deployed to end users for testing and training.

The most salient aspect of RUP is that milestones corresponding to deliverables of each phase must be achieved before it is accepted by the management. Management must "sign off" and agree that the milestones have been met before the next phase begins. For example, at the end of the inception, management must sign off on the basic plan, its description, its justification, the risks involved, the core requirements, and the constraints.

The four RUP phases do not correspond to the traditional analysis, planning, design, and implementation life-cycle phases. This is largely due to the RUP's reliance on an iterative approach. For example, initially the inception phase primarily involves modeling business processes and specifying requirements (analysis and planning activities). However, since the approach is iterative, the initial business process models and project requirements are tentative. The result is that a considerable amount of time is likely to be spent again on modeling business processes and specifying requirements in the elaboration phase. Stated differently, the development does not proceed to the next RUP phase until management signs off on the current phase, but once the new phase begins, the previous phase still continues.

Obviously, if the project is going well, the need to rework previous phases should diminish as the project proceeds toward completion. For example, most of the business process modeling is likely to be done in the inception and elaboration phases, with possibly some reworking of these models in the construction phase and very little to no reworking of these models in the transition phase. The fact that the approach is iterative does not mitigate the need to produce a reasonable plan and design by the end of the elaboration phase. Having to rework previous phases still costs money, and completely changing the business process models after the construction phase could produce a financial catastrophe. So the iterative approach does not eliminate the failure risks associated with the waterfall approach; it merely tempers them and often results in completing projects more rapidly.

Object-Oriented Design and Analysis

Object-oriented (OO) analysis and design are strongly associated with iterative development approaches. The **object-oriented approach** differs radically from the classic approach that is based on DFDs, successive refinement, structured English, and related program coding.

The classic approach focuses on what functions are performed and the inputs and outputs for each function. The OO approach, on the other hand, focuses on the business problem domain. Specifically, it focuses on defining "objects," the actions that the objects perform, the data that they use, and how they collaborate (i.e., communicate) with each other. For example, in a bank system, objects might include User, ATM Machine, and Account.

Using OO terminology, **objects** are said to possess **methods** (things they do) and **attributes** (data related to objects). For example, the Methods for a User might be Make Deposit, Make Withdrawal, and Make Inquiry. Attributes for a User might be Name, Account Number, Card Number, PIN Number, and so on. Similarly, ATM Machine may have various methods such as Dispense Cash, Verify Daily Limits, Authenticate Users, and so on. Attributes of the ATM might be Machine ID Number, Available Cash, Network Connection Status, and so on. Finally, User and ATM Machine can collaborate by the exchange of messages. For example, User inputs and ATM receives User's pin number.

OO programming languages are constructed in terms of objects. The typical approach is to use UML diagrams to document the objects (and classes of objects that have similar characteristics) and how they communicate with each other. The UML diagrams can then be directly input into matching objects in computer programs. This greatly facilitates communications between the analysts, designers, and programmers, who essentially work in the same language of objects. Note that this is quite different from the classical approach in which there is a language gap between DFDs and programming code.

Older programming languages are not object oriented. Subsequently developed programming languages such as C++, Perl, and PHP are not "native" OO but are functional programming languages with OO features added. Still newer languages such as Ruby and Python are pure, native OO languages. Some Ruby developers have claimed that Ruby applications can be developed in 10% of the time that it takes to develop in a language such as Perl.

The Object Management Group (OMG, www.omg.org) has standardized and refined the process of OO, UML-documented development through **Model Driven Architecture**™ (MDA). The approach of MDA is to first develop (and document using UML case-use diagrams) a model of a given problem or project based on the object and business processes. Once developed, this model can be automatically transformed into computer software using a standard transformation language such as QVT (Query/View/Transformation), the transformation language under development by OMG.

MDA is the next major step in the evolution of systems development. The classical approach involves having to use pseudocode to translate the project design into computer software. The OO approach uses a single language for the design and software. But the MDA approach goes a step further and automatically generates the software from the design. This approach not only saves programming time but also makes it possible to deploy a given design to different types of hardware, networks, operating systems, and software languages. MDA is still in its early stages, with only limited QVT transformations available.

Diagrams in Process Orientation versus Object Orientation

As suggested above, the classical design approach—which relies on successive refinement of DFDs or business process diagrams—is process oriented. DFDs and business process diagrams describe business processes. As discussed in Chapter 2, Business Process Modeling Notation (BPMN) is the most widely accepted standard for diagramming business processes. Therefore, we can say that the classical top-down design approach is process oriented and relies on DFDs and BPMN diagrams.

On the other hand, OO design and analysis is object oriented and relies on OO UML diagrams. Specifically, OO analysis produces a conceptual model of what the system is functionally required to do. This conceptual model is typically represented in UML by use-case diagrams, class diagrams, and interaction diagrams. The conceptual model is then transformed into computer program code.

As has been discussed, trends in development have favored an OO approach, which seems to suggest that OO UML is more "important" than DFDs or BPMN diagrams. This, however, is not the case. First, accountants and auditors are typically interested in studying internal controls in terms of business processes rather than business objects. One reason for this is that auditors are typically concerned with tracing the flow of transactions through the accounting systems until they arrive in accounts that support the financial statements. Process-oriented diagrams are by definition flow oriented, so they are well suited for audit purposes. Second, BPMN is very popular in practice because it is very understandable by both managers and systems analysts. Third, the BPMN specification provides for the capability of transforming BPMN into Web Services Business Process Execution Languages (WS-BPEL, or abbreviated as BPEL). **BPEL** is an executable computer language that facilitates interactions between business processes and Web services. BPMN is capable of being transformed into **WS-BPEL,** the internationally recognized standard for business process execution languages, supported by the leading IT open standards organization, Organization for the Advancement of Structured Information Standards (OASIS) (www.oasis-open.org).

Overview of Systems Design

A systems design is very similar to the architectural layout of a house. In the planning phase, the architect determines the basic functions that the house should perform and formulates a general plan with regard to the overall layout. In the design stage, however, the architect prepares a specific blueprint of the house that can be used by electricians, plumbers, and carpenters. In a similar fashion, the systems designer prepares a blueprint that can be implemented by accountants, computer programmers, and management.

For a large project, small errors made at this stage can result in large amounts of wasted dollars and expenditures at later stages. Consider what would happen if, in building a house, an architect forgets to include plumbing in the kitchen. Further assume that such a house was built as designed. On discovering this error, the owners would have to pay to have the walls (and possibly the floors) ripped out to retrofit the omitted plumbing. Needless to say, this process would be quite painful and expensive. Similar problems can and often do occur in the design of accounting information systems. For example, a company might implement a systems design plan that calls for purchasing a particular computer and certain accounting software packages. After using this system for a year or two, the company might find that the software packages no longer meet the changing information needs of management. Furthermore, it might be impossible to modify these software packages, necessitating the replacement of the entire system after a short period of use.

There are other pitfalls. One of the most dangerous is user rejection of the system. Because of lack of adequate involvement of users in the design plan, the implemented system could become unpopular and ultimately be rejected by the individuals for whom the system was designed.

Steps in Systems Design

Systems design can be defined as the formulation of a blueprint for a completed system. Systems design proceeds from the general to the specific. This is the nature of the top-down approach. The general functions and objectives that a specific system will accomplish must be identified first. Given these objectives, it is then possible to prepare detailed specifications, such as database structures, record layouts, and specific report forms. Therefore, systems design can be viewed as either preliminary or detailed. In most cases, the design effort actually begins during the systems planning and analysis phases of the development cycle. The design effort should be viewed as a process of continuously increasing detail that begins during the analysis and planning phases and ends with the beginning of the implementation phase of the

FIGURE 11.10

Systems Design

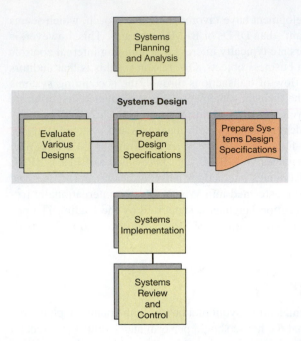

development cycle. Furthermore, the entire development cycle, including the design phase, is a never-ending process. During implementation, problems are often encountered with the design specifications. When this happens, it is necessary to go back to the design process and make the necessary changes. Furthermore, the business environment is always changing, and as new system requirements arise, the systems design must be restructured as needed.

Figure 11.10 defines these major steps in systems design. The first is evaluation of various design alternatives, the second is preparation of design specifications, and the third is preparation of systems design specifications.

Evaluating Design Alternatives

In every case, the systems design project arises out of a specific need, as determined by the systems planning and analysis phases of the development cycle. The systems design should provide a solution to a specific problem. Systems design problems are much like many other problems in life; there is usually no single solution that perfectly solves the problem. The systems designer is usually faced with a number of solutions, all of which may appear very attractive on superficial examination. Therefore, a very important aspect of systems design is enumeration and consideration of the various major design alternatives.

ENUMERATION OF DESIGN ALTERNATIVES   At the most general level, the designer is faced with two alternatives: develop a new system or modify the existing system. In designing a completely new system, there are two general approaches. One approach is to design the system completely from scratch. The other approach is to select a packaged (e.g., "off the shelf" software) system. For example, a given company might find it very economical to obtain a license for one of the major enterprise resource planning (ERP) systems that are available. However, some packaged systems may be inappropriate for a given application. In addition, most packaged systems (large or small) give the user a wide range of alternatives for data items, report formats, and so on. So it is still typically necessary to do a substantial amount of design work anyway, because even predesigned packages do not solve design problems completely. This is an important point because there is a tendency on the part of managers to feel that simply adopting a packaged system will solve their information needs.

Packaged systems can sometimes meet the specific needs of an individual situation with minimal design work. This is particularly true where a system has been written for a specific industry. For example, a number of **turnkey systems** are available for lawyers, doctors, contractors, and so on. Such systems can very closely meet the needs of management. However, as firms increase in complexity and in the number of their products, it becomes increasingly difficult to find a predesigned system that adequately meets the needs of management. Of course, the whole idea of ERP systems and enterprise application suites (EASs) is to meet the needs of a wide range of companies and industries. But remember, ERP systems and EASs typically require extensive customization and configuration before they can be used by an individual company. It is not uncommon for a large company to spend $100 or more to customize and implement an ERP system or EAS.

A second situation often faced in systems design is an existing system that is not functioning adequately. In this case, it is necessary to design changes into the existing system. As a general rule, it is more difficult to modify an existing system than to implement a new one. This is especially true because of a tendency for individuals to resist change.

In modifying an existing system, several basic approaches can be taken. The first of these is that of simply modifying the data collected and reports generated. This is the simplest approach because it involves little or no redefining of individual job responsibilities. A second approach to redesigning existing systems involves reorganizing job responsibilities. This approach is substantially more drastic than the first and is much more likely to be resisted by employees. Employees usually feel comfortable in a particular job after working at it for several months. The possibility of changing job responsibilities can introduce considerable uncertainty into an employee's life. This uncertainty alone can make an individual uncomfortable, and the result could be resistance to the change. Therefore, systems designers should be careful to recommend organizational changes only in situations where changes are really needed. Although organizational changes should be recommended with caution, it is often desirable to either completely reassign employees or make dramatic changes in their job responsibilities. Such changes occur when clear-cut costs/benefits or internal control considerations are involved. In these situations, every effort should be made to alleviate employee uncertainty and discomfort.

Finally, a number of design alternatives might apply either to a new system or to a modification of an existing system. One general alternative might involve considering whether or not a new system should be hosted internally or acquired as **software as a service (SaaS).** SaaS providers effectively lease the use of their software over the Internet. Further, if a company hosts its own software, it has the option to do so in its own data centers, on leased servers in outside data centers, or in the cloud using a service such as Amazon's Elastic Cloud Computing distributed network of computers (aws.amazon.com).

A company must very carefully consider the decision to use packaged software, SaaS, leased servers, or any approach that relies on outsourcing IT. Specifically, consideration should be given to the security of information placed into the hands of the outside source, the current and future reliability and financial stability of the outside source, and the vulnerability of the outside source to interruptions in communications and disasters. All these considerations and related issues should be considered as part of the company's disaster plan.

While there are many risks associated with outsourcing IT, one of the most dramatic and potentially devastating risk is the sudden financial failure of a SaaS provider. One can hardly imagine the horror that would result if one morning it is discovered that the company's SaaS accounting provider has shut down its servers, offices, phones, and so on. That would mean no access to any accounting records. Of course, the trend in SaaS is for the provider's service to continue to work when off-line, but even with off-line access, the company would be left stuck in a dead-end accounting system, one without updates or support. Further, even with up-to-date copies of all its databases, moving to a new SaaS provider could take more time and cost more than a company could afford to spend. This is because different accounting systems all organize and format their databases, input screens, and reports differently, so moving data from one accounting system to another is typically a long-drawn-out and expensive task. Further, any customizations in the old system would need to be recreated in the new system. Customizing can easily cost many more times than the software itself.

DESCRIBING THE ALTERNATIVES   Once a list of major alternatives has been made, each alternative should be documented and described. For example, a computer network for data collection and report distribution might be either centralized or decentralized. In a centralized design alternative, each division supplies accounting data to the central computer system. The central computer system then produces and distributes reports to each of the divisions. In a decentralized design alternative, each division has its own computer and collects its own data. The completed reports are transmitted to company headquarters. The description of each alternative should incorporate its relative advantages and disadvantages. Relevant cost information should also be provided so that cost-benefit comparisons can be made on design alternatives. For example, the centralized computer system might cost $1,000,000 and the decentralized computer system $1,250,000. On the surface, the centralized computer system appears cheaper. However, the decentralized system might provide a number of additional functions. Furthermore, the total capacity of the individual decentralized computers might exceed that of the centralized system substantially. This would be particularly important if there were a possibility that the capacity of the centralized system might be reached in the near future.

EVALUATING THE ALTERNATIVES   Once each alternative has been carefully laid out and documented, it is possible to compare alternatives. The primary criteria for selecting an alternative for implementation should be cost versus benefits. In addition, the selected alternative should satisfy all major systems objectives.

Another important factor that must be considered is **feasibility.** A given design proposal must be both technically and operationally feasible. It must be possible for a given company to actually implement the design specifications. For example, if a company is to acquire a sophisticated supercomputer, it must be prepared to administer it. This may involve upgrading the job responsibilities of existing individuals. When such an approach is to be taken, the company must ensure that the targeted individual is capable of managing the new system. *It is very easy to underestimate the requirements of maintaining, managing, and operating sophisticated information systems.*

 CASE IN POINT

Quite a few considerations can affect the feasibility of a project. Some of the considerations are the availability of adequate financial, human, and technological resources, the technological requirements of the project, behavioral considerations, legal issues, risks of failure, and the length of time required to complete the project.

The best major design alternative is normally selected by top management. Furthermore, the major designs presented to top management are typically not highly detailed. Once management selects a design, the design team prepares detailed design specifications.

Preparing Design Specifications

The primary rule in developing design specifications is that the designer should work backward from outputs to inputs. Working with the system objectives, the designer should design all management reports and operational output documents as a first step in the process. Once all these outputs are specified, the data inputs and processing steps are determined automatically. Once

FIGURE 11.11

Design of System Elements

Attribute

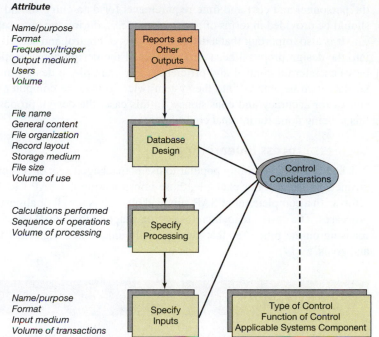

Name/purpose
Format
Frequency/trigger
Output medium
Users
Volume

Reports and Other Outputs

File name
General content
File organization
Record layout
Storage medium
File size
Volume of use

Database Design

Control Considerations

Calculations performed
Sequence of operations
Volume of processing

Specify Processing

Name/purpose
Format
Input medium
Volume of transactions

Specify Inputs

*Type of Control
Function of Control
Applicable Systems Component*

these decisions have been made, the designer then builds in the appropriate controls. Figure 11.11 shows this process. In each phase of the design sequence, specific considerations must be made. In designing the reports and other outputs, such factors as the reporting frequency, the output medium, and the actual report format must be considered. In developing a database, design considerations regarding file organization, record layout, storage media, and volume of usage must be made. For the processing phase, the exact calculations to be performed and the appropriate sequence of operations must be specified. Finally, in specifying the inputs, precise input formats, the input medium, and volume of transactions must be considered.

Preparing and Submitting the Systems Design Specifications

The completed design specifications should take the form of a proposal. If the project is large, the proposal should be reviewed by top management before approval. However, proposals that are relatively inexpensive might be approved by a department or division manager. The **detailed design proposal** should include everything necessary to actually implement the design project. In general, it will include specific timetables for completion, a budget, and a description of personnel requirements, as well as flowcharts and other diagrams that describe the systems to be implemented. A copy of all proposed system outputs would be incorporated, as well as specifics on any databases to be created or modified. The database specifications would include the exact contents of specific data items, as well as file organization and file access methods. In addition, details relating to storage requirements, file size, and updating frequency should be provided.

With regard to data processing, details regarding required hardware and software should be provided. Hardware normally includes the computer itself, as well as communications equipment, printers, and input/output devices. On the software side, specifications regarding processing operations should be included. Furthermore, specific processing cycles and times should be given.

Next, specific details relating to the input of data in the system should be provided. These should include the method of input, procedures for screening input data, and the content of data inputs.

Finally, in all cases, specific volume and cost information should be provided. For example, if the system calls for manual entry of sales orders into a computer system, details regarding the personnel and cost and time requirements for data entry should be given. This information should be provided in terms of peak volume (e.g., during the busy season) and average volume.

It is also important that a detailed analysis of control and security measures be incorporated into the design proposal because a number of the design considerations may involve trade-offs between internal control and efficiency. For example, a design might specify that a particular data item be entered into the system twice so that the computer can cross-compare the two entries for accuracy and consistency. In this case, the design proposal should clearly state that this is being done for internal control purposes.

Business Process Blueprinting

It is becoming increasingly popular to use prepackaged sets of blueprints for all of a company's business processes. For example, those implementing the SAP ERP™ system begin the design effort with a complete set of SAP-supplied blueprints for all or almost all the company's business processes. The design team then focuses on adapting this initial set of blueprints to its own needs, focusing on the processes that are especially unique and important to the company's strategies and goals.

 CASE IN POINT

Even small businesses use business process blueprinting. That is exactly what happens when a small company adopts an accounting system such as Intuit's Quickbooks™. After adopting Quickbooks™, small business may then customize forms (e.g., invoices) and reports.

Resources–Events–Agent (REA) Model

Information systems capture events and their related attributes. For example, in a sales event, the attributes might be the time, date, customer name, salesperson, the customer's apparent age (an attribute of the customer), the time spent with the customer, specific promotion codes applied, and so on. In the accounting literature, the **Resources–Events–Agent (REA) model** provides a very general model for capturing and recording events and their related attributes. The model stipulates that for each event there are two general categories of related attributes: resources and agents. Resources are the things of value or utility to the firm that are affected by the event. For example, in a sales transaction, both inventory and cash might be affected; however, other resources might also be affected, such as consumables (e.g., fuel to deliver the sale to the customer). Agents are those who participate in events. Events always generally involve two agents. In a sales transaction, the sales department is the first agent and the customer is the second.

The REA model can be generalized to include other event attributes besides resources and agents. For example, for purposes of supply chain management, Location has been added to the REA model, making it the REAL (Resources–Events–Agents–Location) model. The extra event attribute, location, can then be used to record the specific location of a resource (e.g., an item in raw materials or finished goods inventory) at the time of the event.

Implementing the REA model involves more than just capturing events. It is also necessary to specify how events relate to each other, and how the events and their interrelationships are stored and processed within some database system. While various types of implementations are possible, the typical implementation involves the entity-relation approach discussed in Chapter 3, with agents being defined as entities.

In a pure REA system there are no journals, ledgers, or accounts. All these things can be generated as reports or "views" from the basic recorded event data. REA has not been widely implemented, at least not in its pure form. For example, SAP ERP includes elements of both REA and the traditional accounting system. The development of REA has had an impact on the development of ebXML as REA events can readily be structured as XML data, since XML is an ideal carrier for multi-attribute data. XBRL, on the other hand, can be viewed as a somewhat competing standard, since it tends to focus on the traditional structure of accounts and financial statements.

Within the context of traditional accounting systems, event attributes may be included within hierarchical account or transaction codes. In other words, a single code can indicate the type of event and the resources and agents involved. So, viewed from this perspective, the traditional computerized accounting system is not too different from the REA system. Further, even though journals, ledgers, and accounts might not actually be stored objects in an REA system, they must still be at least created on demand in order to provide traditional financial statements. So the conceptual, if not mechanical, processing of transactions through journals, ledgers, and accounts remains relevant even in an REA system. In this sense, the REA approach provides a superior way to internally model accounting databases, but it does not supplant basic accounting concepts or principles. However, the superior data modeling provides for more efficient organization of internal data and promotes well-defined data schemas, which in turn can lead to more effective and cost-efficient data management, and greatly superior technologies for generating management reports and decision-relevant views of stored data and communicating data in XML-type formats. Another benefit of REA is that since it can provide a well-defined unit in which to record any type of arbitrary event in XML format, it serves as a good building block for the increasing number of information systems being built upon service-oriented architectures (SOA). This is because SOAs build on the standardized XML exchange of data information between services.

General Design Considerations

The preceding section focused on specific factors to consider in developing a systems design proposal. This section considers objectives pertinent to each phase of the design process. Table 11.3 summarizes these general considerations for each major system element in the design phase.

TABLE 11.3   Design Considerations for System Elements

System Element	Design Consideration
Outputs (report or document)	Cost-effectiveness
	Relevance
	Clarity
	Timeliness
Database	Cost-effectiveness
	Integration
	Standardization
	Flexibility
	Security
	Accuracy
	Efficiency
	Organization
Data processing	Cost-effectiveness
	Uniformity
	Integration
	Accuracy
Data input	Cost-effectiveness
	Accuracy
	Uniformity
Controls and security measures	Cost-effectiveness
	Comprehensiveness
	Appropriateness

Output Design

The first and foremost consideration for output design is **cost-effectiveness.** The principle of cost-effectiveness should be applied to all elements of the system because an investment in the information system is like any capital budgeting expenditure—it should be evaluated on a cost-benefit basis. The intent is to maximize the ratio of the benefits to cost while satisfying the objectives for a given system.

The properties of relevance, clarity, and timeliness are essential to managerial reports. Reports should include only information that is relevant to a particular decision maker. However, this principle cannot be strictly adhered to because some reports must be generated for more than one manager, and different managers have different preferences for information. Nevertheless, either unneeded or missing information can decrease the value of a report. A report that is cluttered with a lot of irrelevant information might be ignored by a manager who is unwilling to wade through a lot of useless data. The inclusion of irrelevant information in a report may also result in excessive information costs.

One very important factor relating to clarity involves including appropriate titles and captions within a report. Far too often, information systems produce reports that are not titled and captioned adequately. The justification that managers know the contents of the reports and do not need detailed explanations is offered often. The danger in this line of reasoning is that many companies have a high rate of turnover in their management staff, which means that a new manager might either misinterpret a report or ignore it altogether because of its lack of clarity.

Database Design

Several important principles apply to database design. Of particular importance is that a company's databases be integrated. **Integration** means the avoidance of collecting and maintaining the same data items in more than one place in the company. In an integrated system, various phases of business operations can share the same data. For example, the sales department, shipping department, and billing department might all need a customer's name and address. In a fully integrated system, this information might be entered into the system once in the credit department. It could then be accessed by the sales department for generating orders and by the shipping department for shipping to the correct address. In a system without integration, this information might have to be typed three separate times. This not only would produce higher costs but also would result in a higher error rate.

Another important consideration in database design is that of **standardization,** which means that all data items are entered in a standard format and assigned a common name when used in more than one place. For example, if a departmental expense budget shows the item "Automobile Expense," it should be defined to mean the same thing throughout the entire company. It therefore would be undesirable to have "Automobile Expense" include depreciation in one department but not in another. Flexibility and security are other important features of a database design. Databases should be designed in such a manner that users can structure a wide variety of queries. For example, one manager might want sales broken down by district and then by product, whereas another manager might want sales broken down by product and then by district. A flexible database design would allow for either type of report.

Data Processing

One important consideration in data processing relates to uniformity and integration. It is important that the company's overall data processing system develop according to some general plan. For example, it might be undesirable for a given department to acquire desktop computers that would be incompatible with other desktop computers in the same company.

Data Input

One often difficult consideration in designing the data input system is that of accuracy. The use of well-defined source documents can encourage employees to record data accurately without omissions. For example, if a customer's telephone number is a needed data input, the sales order document should have a specific line that is clearly labeled "Customer Telephone Number." A document that simply includes several lines with a label "Customer Information" would be less desirable because some employees would leave out the telephone number.

Controls and Security Measures

Implementing adequate controls is too often overlooked. Comprehensive, appropriate controls should be established for each phase of the system's design process. This is one area in which the accountant can play a critical role while working with a design team. In many cases, the design team primarily may involve information systems specialists who might have an appreciation for controls but not detailed expertise in this area. In this case, the accountant can review the overall plan and discuss inadequacies in controls with the individual team members.

Design Techniques

Designing a system is a creative activity. It is unlikely that two design teams will produce the same solution to a given problem. Therefore, systems design can be viewed somewhat as an art, although one in which various refined techniques have been developed. As an artist needs special tools for painting, the systems designer needs certain tools to assist in the design process. Many of these tools are also used in systems analysis. While all the systems analysis techniques pertain to systems design, certain special problems are more specific to information systems design. These are associated primarily with forms (document) and database design, which are discussed below.

Forms Design

The process of designing specific forms is called **forms design.** The area of forms design should be given very careful attention by the systems design team because forms are the interface between the users and the system itself. Therefore, forms design should focus on producing documents that provide effective interfaces between managers and the information system.

Database Design

A number of useful techniques are available for designing databases: data structure diagrams, record layouts, file analysis sheets, and file-related matrices. Data structure diagrams show the relationships between various kinds of records. For example, a manufacturing company may have several records in various databases relating to a given customer. One record contains sales order information, another record contains production status information, and another record contains information relating to billing. The data structure diagram defines the relationship among these different data records.

 CASE IN POINT

Database design software tools can be very helpful in designing databases. For example, Visual Paradigm's product DB Visual Architect (www.visual-paradigm.com) provides built-in support for entity relationship diagrams. The program can use these diagrams to output the instructions to actually create the database.

A record layout diagram shows the various data fields within a record. Both record layout and data structure diagrams are discussed in detail in Chapter 13, "File Processing and Data Management Concepts."

File analysis sheets provide the systems designer with all major points of relevant information regarding the contents of a particular file. Such information would include record layouts, the purpose of the file, the expected number of records, and so on.

File-related matrices show the interrelationships between files, their contents, and their uses. File-related matrices can be helpful in determining the effective and efficient use of data items within files, eliminating unneeded or redundant data items, and optimizing file structure in general. For example, one file-related matrix might show a list of data items on one side versus a list of files in which these data items are used on the other side. Another example of a file-related matrix would be one that lists data items on one side and reports on the other side. This type of matrix would be helpful in assessing the use of particular data items in reports. If a data item does not appear in any of the reports, the company might consider eliminating it from the file.

Systems Design Packages

A number of prepackaged design methodologies are available to assist in the systems development cycle. The purpose of these packages is to assist the designer in systematically approaching a given problem. These packages help the designer structure the design problem and can result in considerable time savings.

Computer-aided software engineering (CASE) is computer software technology that supports an automated engineering discipline for software development and maintenance. CASE can produce DFDs, narrative documentation, screen and report prototypes, and data dictionary descriptions. CASE can increase productivity, improve software quality though the introduction of rigorous standards and analysis, and decrease the cost of developing, documenting, and maintaining software. Most CASE products include some elements of prepackaged design methodologies.

Prepackaged design systems have the advantage of assisting the designer in structuring a particular problem; however, most design packages have certain shortcomings. In particular, the packages do not assist in specifying the desired outputs, nor do they deal adequately with the problem of system response time. The design packages may provide some assistance but not total solutions to all problems.

CASE IN POINT

Casewise (www.casewise.com) is a worldwide leader in CASE tools. The suite of Casewise products supports graphically modeling an entire enterprise. Their Corporate Modeler product links together organizational, process, IT architecture, and data modeling and enables employees to share project work through a common database. A related Casewise product, Automodeler, automatically generates diagrams from existing processes and diagrams. The Corporate Modeler product can even simulate virtually any kind of business situation.

Choosing Software and Hardware

At some point, the decision must be made as to whether the computer software is to be built from scratch or purchased. Although this seems to be a design decision, it should be made at the end of the analysis phase. Much of the design phase may be omitted if a purchase decision is made. Once the requirements of any new system have been specified, one can then look at available software packages to see which ones most closely fit a company's needs—all without actually "designing" that system.

On the other hand, nothing pleases computer professionals more than the freedom to design and build a new system from scratch. Since this is what they have been trained to do, they tend to ignore the multitude of good software packages already available on the market.

It is economically more feasible for many businesses, especially smaller ones, to buy rather than build software.

Purchased software packages have several advantages:

- They are cheaper. The cost of development is carried by many purchasers rather than just the creator.
- They are already debugged. If several other organizations have been using the package for some months, it is reasonably safe to assume that most of the bugs have been found and exterminated.
- The company can try the product before investing a great deal of money. With in-house software, it is possible to put months of development time into a program only to discover that it does not produce the desired results when it is done.

The main disadvantage to **canned software packages** (i.e., purchased software packages) is that they rarely exactly meet a company's needs. It may be necessary to modify the software (which can be expensive, if not impossible) or to modify the company's procedures to match what the package requires.

A **dedicated software package** is intended for a narrow audience, such as retail stores or accounting firms. To find a good dedicated software package, talk to people who work for other companies in the same industry. Someone who works for another manufacturing organization, for example, may know of a good production control package. Trade magazines and Web sites of an industry also tell what is available (e.g., software packages for florists are advertised in *Florist's Review*).

When evaluating purchased software, it is helpful to use a decision-table format to consider the following:

- How close is the fit to what is needed? Will the programs or our procedures or both have to be modified?
- How stable is the software vendor? Will it still be in business in a year or two when problems arise? Does it give prompt support when problems arise? A toll-free, 24-hour telephone line is a good indicator.
- Is there a trial period, during which everything can be returned for a full refund after a month or so?
- How many other installations have used the software? For how long? Who are they? Some people get a list of users' names from the vendor but do not ask those users for evaluations because they know the evaluation will be good or the vendor would not have supplied them. Instead, ask them for second-level references—other organizations that they know are using the package but whom the vendor failed to mention. Here is where the skeletons can be uncovered.
- How flexible is the software? Can it change along with the changing business environment? Are there any growth limits on file size, number of transactions, or embedded tables?
- Is it user friendly? Does the software guide the operator through each program, with adequate explanations and error messages? Is the documentation clear, complete, and easy to read?
- Are source programs supplied? If not, the company will be forever dependent on the vendor for modifications at whatever price is named.

Only after collecting data on the various software packages available is it time to worry about choosing the hardware. Since the software is what determines how well the computer meets the company's needs, it is usually fairly safe to be content with the hardware on which that software runs. There are a few constraints in hardware selection that are much the same as those detailed in the preceding points. In addition, try to get machinery that is **upwardly compatible**—easily upgradable to a larger or faster model in the future without losing existing data or programs.

One last note on purchasing any computer hardware or software: It is a mistake to put off a purchase in the belief that either the price will drop shortly or a new version will be available soon. In most cases, the price drop is negligible compared with the inconvenience caused by not having the product in the meantime. And the state-of-the-art methods of the newer version usually are not required; mere adequacy has its merits. It might be better to buy the system now, when it is needed, than to try to outguess the computer market, which is so unpredictable that no one has a very good batting average for forecasting.

Conventional Wisdom in Systems Development

Developing an information system is a creative and demanding task that can and should produce economic benefits for an organization. On the other hand, the systems development process can produce a disaster, with labor and financial resources being expended with no observable return and perhaps even a system that cannot be completed. In practice, the systems development process often has produced both these results. The history of systems development suggests that positive results are obtained more frequently if the systems development process is formally structured, documented, and subject to management control techniques. One of the most important control techniques is to actively involve the ultimate user in the development of information systems.

The nature of the problems that historically have plagued systems development is humorously summarized in Figure 11.12. This figure shows the phases in a "real" systems development life cycle. The cycle begins with wild enthusiasm in the analysis phase, when all things seem possible and "all systems are go." Disillusionment and total confusion set in during the design phase as serious problems develop as the project group tries to design unrealistic or hopelessly vague requirements specified during the analysis phase. The result is a system that does not work technically, or operationally, in the sense of doing what it was supposed to do, or economically, in the sense of its return on costs, or some combination of these possibilities. Accordingly, the major phases of implementation consist of the search for the guilty, punishment of the innocent, and promotion of nonparticipants.

While perhaps a lesson in "how to survive life in a systems group," the figure is, more importantly, a demonstration of the likely outcome of an inadequately structured systems development effort. Management abdication of its responsibilities for the control of systems development is frequently cited as a major reason for such system failures in the past. The need for active involvement of all levels of management in systems development is widely and generally recognized as a major deterrent to systems development failure. The best way to ensure this involvement is through use of the life-cycle concept.

Another type of problem that has plagued systems development concerns the quality of communication between the many parties in a systems development project. This problem can

| Wild Enthusiasm | Disillusionment | Total Confusion | Search for the Guilty | Punishment of the Innocent | Promotion of Nonparticipants |

FIGURE 11.12

"Real" Systems Development Life Cycle

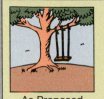 

| As Proposed by the User Manager | As Approved by the Steering Committee | As Structured by the Data Administrator | As Designed by the Lead Analyst | As Implemented by the Applications Programmers | What the User Actually Wanted |

FIGURE 11.13

Communication Problems in Systems Development

cause even a well-controlled project to generate a system that fails in the sense that the final user does not actually use it. The system works, is well documented, and is within budget and time controls, but it fails to provide the user with what he or she desires. This situation is shown pictorially in Figure 11.13, which illustrates a lack of communication between the many parties in the systems development process. Each party—user manager, steering committee, and so on—holds a different view of what is to be done. The lesson is that each party's perception of a system to be designed is influenced by his or her own functional specialty. Each functional specialty will see the project from its own viewpoint, preconceiving or assuming things based on its own knowledge. Great care must be taken to ensure that the chain of communication required in a project is effective and complete. Vagueness in communication leads to situations such as that shown in Figure 11.13. The solution to the communication problem is to actively involve the user in systems development.

Summary

Traditional (or classical) systems development involves a rigid, big-design-up-front, top-down approach that proceeds through the phases of systems planning, analysis, design, and implementation. This is called the *waterfall approach*. More recently, the shift has been toward iterative and more agile forms of systems development in which experiences in subsequent phases are fed back to make changes in previous phases. With this approach, no phase is complete until the entire project is complete. Another recent shift has been toward SOA, which favors small projects as opposed to classical ones, which tend to be large. Small projects have the potential advantage of lessening the overall risk of project failure.

Systems planning involves decisions on the part of top management with respect to prioritizing systems development needs. The output of systems planning is a written document that states the overall information systems objectives for the company. In addition, the document specifies general areas of need for systems development work. A general plan is given for implementing these needs. The systems analysis plan is dynamic and must be revised continuously. Systems development is a never-ending process because the business environment and corporate information needs are constantly changing.

Systems analysis begins with a system or systems specified in the overall company information systems plan. The systems analysis

effort involves three distinct phases: (1) surveying the current system, (2) identifying information needs, and (3) identifying systems requirements. After these steps are completed, a systems analysis report is written and conveyed to top management. This report should focus on particular problems discovered and should suggest general approaches to solving them. In addition, a specific proposal for developing a new system (or modifying an old system) should be included.

The systems planning and analysis portions of the development cycle are extremely crucial because mistakes made at these levels can be extremely costly. Design and implementation costs often can run into millions of dollars. Therefore, the analysis phase should give management a clear picture of where it needs to go.

Many techniques can aid in the systems analyst's work, including questionnaires, interviews, and direct observation. The analyst also uses work measurement and work distribution techniques. These analyses are accompanied by narratives, input/output matrices, DFDs, hierarchical function diagrams, and flowcharts.

The classical approach to systems development uses structured systems analysis. This approach begins with a general DFD, which is then supported with detailed DFDs, data dictionaries, access method descriptions, and specifics on process logic.

Systems design is an orderly process that begins at a very general level with the setting of objectives for a particular system. The process then proceeds to the more detailed level with the specification of file structures, processing operations, and forms design. The major steps in systems design include evaluating design alternatives, preparing design specifications, and submitting a completed systems design report. Once a particular design alternative has been selected, it can be presented to top management. Top management then reviews the proposed design, along with its budget, and decides whether the project should proceed in more detail. If management does decide in favor of selecting a particular design project, the design team can specify the design details. Detailed design considerations would include things such as output design, database design, data processing operations, data inputs, and controls and security measures. The preferred procedure is to first design the system outputs and then work backward to define the inputs.

The classical development approach uses DFDs or business process diagrams to represent the system. These diagrams are then used to produce structured English (pseudocode). The structured English is then used to produce program code.

One alternative to the classic approach is the RAD approach, which uses not only the structured approach but also iteration. Another alternative is the RUP, which defines its own four-phase (inception, elaboration, construction, and transition) iterative process in which milestones must be achieved at the end of each phase before beginning the next. However, when a new phase begins, the old phase continues, and no phase is complete until the project is complete.

Iterative development approaches generally rely on OO design and analysis. The OO approach focuses on indentifying objects (e.g., a User, ATM Machine, or Account). Objects possess methods (things the objects do) and attributes (data belonging to the objects). The system can then be described in terms of how objects communicate (or collaborate) with each other.

One advantage of object orientation is that it focuses on the business problem domain rather than on what functions are performed. A second advantage of the OO approach is that OO programming languages exist that greatly facilitate converting designs into computer programs. This is because systems designs and the computer programs can both be written in terms of objects, thus avoiding the need to use pseudocode to bridge a language gap between the two.

A number of systems design techniques are very helpful. These include standard systems design techniques, such as lowcharting, DFDs, and input/output analysis. There are, however, a number of techniques that are particularly useful in systems design. These include forms analysis sheets, data hierarchy diagrams, forms layout charts, data structure diagrams, record layouts, file analysis sheets, and file-related input/output matrices. The first three techniques assist the systems designer in preparing and analyzing forms. The latter techniques are useful in the design and layout of databases.

Systems design packages provide a structured approach to systems design. The more sophisticated packages allow the designer to specify the desired inputs, outputs, and processing operations. The design package then generates a working database system. Such packages save the designer a considerable amount of time. Many decisions must be made, however, that the design package cannot help with. For example, the design package cannot tell the designer what the desired outputs should be. In addition, the design package may be inadequate with regard to specifying the optimal database structure and file access methods.

In conclusion, systems analysis and design are processes that involve a considerable amount of creativity. Success comes with good communication between the systems design team and management. All feasible alternatives should be considered carefully. Special emphasis should be given to system integration and security measures.

Glossary

agile approach   an approach to systems development that is normally iterative and that focuses on keeping with certain best practices. See the related reference in Webliography.

attributes   data items related to objects.

big-design-up-front   an approach to systems development that focuses on producing initial plans and designs that are not subject to much change during the design and implementation phases.

bottlenecks   weaknesses in a system where small changes can result in major improvements in performance.

BPEL   short form of WS-BPEL.

canned software packages   software packages purchased from a vendor.

cost-effectiveness   the benefits of a design should exceed its costs.

dedicated software package   a commercially available software package that is intended for a narrow audience.

detailed design proposal   everything necessary to actually implement a design project, including timetables, a budget, personnel requirements, and design documentation.

feasibility   design criterion that it must be possible to actually implement the design specifications.

forms design   the process of designing specific forms.

information needs analysis   analysis of specific decisions made by managers in terms of the information inputs.

integration   design criterion that means the avoidance of collecting and maintaining the same data items in more than one place.

iterative approach   an approach to systems development in which the initial plans and designs are subject to revision as the project develops.

key success factors   characteristics that distinguish a company from its competitors and that are the keys to its success.

methods   things that objects do.

Model Driven Architecture   a trademarked approach to development based on modeling a given problem or project based on the object and business processes; it automatically transforms the model to computer software using a standard transformation language.

object   basic unit of analysis in object-oriented analysis and design methodologies. Objects possess methods (things that object do) and attributes (data related to objects).

object-oriented approach   an approach to development that is based on DFDs, successive refinement, structured English, and related program coding.

pseudocode   structured-English type of systems documentation that includes provisions for error conditions and data file access.

rapid application development   an approach to systems software development that combines iterative and structured approaches.

rational unified process (RUP)   a four-phase iterative development process and software product from IBM that focuses on achieving milestones at the end of each phase.

REA (Resources–Event–Agents) model   a model of the accounting system that focuses on recording events along with their impact on related resources and connection to related agents.

software as a service (SaaS)   a software application, suite of applications, or software services that are delivered over the Internet. Entire accounting systems are delivered as SaaS.

standardization   design criterion that all data items are to be entered in a standard format and assigned a common name when used in more than one place.

steering committee   committee representing top management and all major functional areas within the organization that is charged with guiding the overall systems development effort.

strategic systems plan   a written document that incorporates both short- and long-run goals relating to the company's systems development effort.

structured English   a special language for describing process logic that uses several key words, including *IF*, *THEN*, *ELSE IF*, and *SO*.

structured systems analysis and design   an approach to systems analysis that begins with a very general description of a particular system and then proceeds through a logically related set of steps, each increasing in detail.

systems analysis   the process of understanding existing systems and problems, describing information needs, and establishing priorities for further systems work.

systems development life cycle   the concept that every systems development project goes through essentially the same process or life cycle of systems analysis, systems design, and systems implementation.

systems planning   identifying subsystems within the information system that need special attention for development.

turnkey systems   computer packages that meet the specific needs of an individual situation with minimal design work.

upwardly compatible   computer hardware that is easily upgradable to a larger or faster model without losing existing data or programs.

waterfall approach   a synonym for the big-design-up-front approach to systems development.

Warnier–Orr methodology   a methodology and diagramming technique for analyzing the outputs of an application and factoring the application into a hierarchical structure of modules to accomplish the necessary processing.

WS-BPEL   Web Services Business Process Execution Languages (or as abbreviated, BPEL). WS-BPEL is an executable computer language that facilitates interactions between business processes and Web services.

Webliography

www.omg.org
Home page of the Object Management Group. This group supports standards for BPMN, Model Driven Architecture™, UML, and the QVT transformation language.

www.ibm.com
Home page of IBM® that publishes the RUP. The RUP is not only an approach to systems development, but it is also a computer software that can be used to guide IT managers through the RUP.

www.cms.hhs.gov
The home page for the U.S. Centers for Medicare and Medicaid Services. This site contains some helpful documents on systems

development. Enter "selecting a development approach" in the search box.

www.agilealliance.org
The home page of the Agile Alliance, an organization whose membership comprises thousands of organizations and individuals worldwide. Members subscribe to the Manifesto for Agile Software Development, which supports concepts like "individuals and interaction over processes and tools" and "customer collaboration over contract negotiation."

www.agilemodeling.com
The home page of Agile Modeling. This site contains an extensive amount of information relating to agile development.

www.aisnet.org
Home page of the Association for Information Systems. This site has an online virtual library and a bookstore that contain many development-related publications.

www.oasis-open.org
The home page of the Organization for the Advancement of Structured Information Standards (OASIS). OASIS is a

highly respected consortium devoted to open standards in IT. The organization has standing committees and sections devoted to a wide range of areas relating to IT and systems development.

Chapter Quiz

Answers to the chapter quiz appear on page 418.

1. It is crucial that all major systems development efforts have the support of (the) (_____).
   a. steering committee
   b. top management
   c. chief systems analyst
   d. controller

2. Which of the following should be responsible for the overall planning and control of the systems development effort of a company?
   a. steering committee
   b. top management
   c. chief systems analyst
   d. controller

3. Which of the following terms describes the analysis of specific decisions made by managers in terms of information inputs?
   a. HIPO charts
   b. work measurement
   c. functional analysis
   d. information needs analysis

4. The third phase of the systems analysis project involves specifying systems requirements. Such requirements are usually specified in terms of (_____).
   a. reports
   b. inputs and outputs
   c. decisions
   d. processes

5. Which of the following fact-gathering techniques best allows the systems analyst to establish a personal working relationship with a manager?
   a. depth interviews
   b. structured interviews
   c. open-ended questionnaires
   d. closed-ended questionnaires

6. Which of the following fact-gathering techniques will often provide the analyst with an insight into system activities that can be obtained in no other way?
   a. depth interviews
   b. structured interviews
   c. document reviews
   d. observation

7. An overview DFD, which shows only the basic entities and data flows in a system, is called a (_____).
   a. decision table
   b. sources and uses of information diagram

c. context diagram
   d. HIPO chart

8. In a DFD, which of the following symbols would be used to represent a file of data?
   a. terminator
   b. data flow
   c. data store
   d. process

9. In a DFD, which of the following symbols is drawn either as a circle or as a rectangle with curved edges?
   a. terminator
   b. data flow
   c. data store
   d. process

10. Which of the following is *not* one of the three basic constructs used in creating a Warnier–Orr diagram?
    a. redundancy
    b. sequence
    c. selection
    d. repetition

11. Which of the following design criteria holds that the benefits of a design should exceed its costs?
    a. feasibility
    b. cost-effectiveness
    c. standardization
    d. integration

12. Which of the following design criteria holds that it must be possible to actually implement the design specifications?
    a. feasibility
    b. cost-effectiveness
    c. standardization
    d. integration

13. In a certain company, the data item "Automobile Expense" includes depreciation in one department but not in another. This violates which of the following design criteria?
    a. flexibility
    b. security
    c. standardization
    d. integration

14. In a certain company, the data item "Customer Address" is entered and maintained in separate databases by both the billing and the sales departments. This violates which of the following design criteria?
    a. flexibility
    b. security

c. standardization

d. integration

15. Forms design should be given very careful attention by the systems design team because (_____).
    a. forms are expensive to produce in volume
    b. forms are the interface between users and the system
    c. forms are the first step in detailed systems design
    d. forms are the final step in detailed systems design

16. Computer packages that meet the specific needs of an individual situation with minimal design work are called (_____).
    a. turnkey systems
    b. CASE systems
    c. integrated systems
    d. database systems

17. Which of the following tools uses a grid on which each item in the grid corresponds to a particular location on a medium where a form is to be displayed?
    a. input/output matrix
    b. forms layout chart
    c. data hierarchy diagram
    d. forms analysis sheet

18. The main disadvantage to canned software packages is (_____).
    a. they rarely exactly meet a company's needs
    b. they are more expensive than developing software in-house
    c. they need to be debugged
    d. they cannot be tried without investing a great deal of money

19. When evaluating purchased software, a good indicator of vendor support for the package is (_____).
    a. a toll-free telephone number
    b. the relative price of the package
    c. the number of installations using the package
    d. how user-friendly the package is

20. Computer hardware that is easily upgradable to a larger or faster model without losing existing data or programs is said to be (_____).
    a. a superflexible system
    b. an upwardly compatible system
    c. a user-friendly system
    d. a turnkey system

Review Questions

1. Define and explain each of the following terms.
    a. systems planning
    b. systems analysis
    c. communications problem
    d. information needs analysis
    e. depth interview
    f. open-ended questionnaire
    g. closed-ended questionnaire
    h. structured interview
    i. work measurement
    j. work distribution
    k. hierarchical function diagram
    l. input/output matrix
    m. logical flow diagram

2. Is the systems analysis phase of systems development more expensive than the systems design phase?

3. Which individuals should be involved in systems planning?

4. What is the function of the systems steering committee?

5. What are the primary phases of systems analysis?

6. What are some of the major hurdles that the systems analyst must overcome?

7. Discuss the primary advantages of depth interviews.

8. Discuss the primary advantages of structured interviews.

9. Under what situations would a closed-ended questionnaire be appropriate?

10. What should be included in the contents of the systems analysis report?

11. What is the difference between work measurement analysis and work distribution analysis?

12. What is the primary advantage of hierarchical function analysis?

13. Where are the limitations of hierarchical function analysis?

14. What is a HIPO chart?

15. When would the use of a decision table be important?

16. What are the key elements of a DFD?

17. Give three examples of matrix-oriented analysis.

18. Why is systems analysis an important first step preceding systems design?

19. What are some of the key behavioral considerations that are important in systems analysis?

20. Define each of the following terms.
    a. design alternatives
    b. forms analysis sheet
    c. file-related matrices
    d. operational feasibility

21. What are the major steps in the systems design process?

22. What are some of the major considerations that must be incorporated into the systems design process?

23. Which step in the design process is the most important?

24. In what ways can an accountant contribute the most to the systems design team?

25. Discuss the purpose of systems design packages.

26. Discuss the limitations of systems design packages.

27. At what stage should the systems design proposal be reviewed by top management?

28. Describe the major components of the systems design report.

29. Describe several major considerations involved in database design.

30. Describe several major considerations involved in output document design.

Discussion Questions and Problems

31. Discuss some of the major problems often encountered in systems analysis. How can these problems be avoided?
32. Why is observation needed? Couldn't the analyst save a considerable amount of time simply by relying on the system as documented?
33. How do you deal with the situation in which a manager claims not to understand departmental information needs?
34. In a company too small for an information systems steering committee, which individual would be the most appropriate to oversee the systems development function?
35. For each of the following systems, develop a hierarchical function diagram.
    a. purchasing system
    b. production system
    c. inventory management system
36. Assume that you have been hired as a consultant for a small company that has problems with its payroll system. Describe the steps you would take in developing a solution.
37. Discuss the major goals of systems analysis.
38. Discuss the importance of the systems analysis report.
39. Below is a list of problem situations. In each case, discuss some of the major steps you would follow in systems analysis.
    a. A company has problems with raw material shortages.
    b. A company has production bottlenecks and is not able to manage production according to a preset schedule.
    c. A company has severe problems with credit losses.
    d. Overall production employee morale is low.
    e. Large quantities of units have been sitting in inventory for many years.
40. Describe several systems analysis techniques that would be helpful for purposes of gathering and organizing the facts needed in studying an accounts receivable system.
41. Which of the following systems analysis techniques—(i) work measurement analysis, (ii) work distribution analysis, (iii) questionnaire, (iv) logical data flow diagram, (v) interview, (vi) input/output diagram—would be the most appropriate for each case below?
    a. Analyzing the information needs of a production manager
    b. Analyzing the information flows within the sales department
    c. Analyzing an inventory management system
    d. Analyzing a purchase order system
42. Describe structured systems analysis.
43. Contrast and compare the waterfall approach to the iterative approach.
44. Why do accountants tend to prefer process-oriented flowcharts rather than object-oriented diagrams?
45. Herman Manufacturing has been having many difficulties. This company manufactures caps and gowns used for graduation ceremonies in both high schools and colleges. Most of the company's problems have revolved around its inability to generate sufficient sales to maintain overall profitability. The president of the company, Barbara Novel, feels that this situation has been caused by poor relations between the

company and its customers. Barbara has confided in some of the company's major customers about this matter, and they have advised her that they are very happy with the quality of the company's products. However, they mentioned a number of problems. Among the problems given were late deliveries and incomplete orders. Further discussion with some of the company's production employees has revealed that a wide range of production problems exist, including (i) low-quality raw materials, (ii) bottlenecks in production due to a general lack of coordination in job scheduling, and (iii) mix-ups in customer's orders.

You have been called in as an independent consultant and have been asked to advise Barbara Novel.

Required

a. Where do you begin dealing with this company's problem?
b. What type of systems analysis techniques would be useful in this situation?

46. Central Manufacturing produces custom-made kitchen cabinets. This is a medium-sized, family-owned corporation with approximately 150 employees. Joe Starr has been the president for the past 5 years. The company presently serves a wide range of customers in the Ft. Lauderdale–Miami area of south Florida. The organizational structure is reasonably simple. Under Joe Starr are three vice presidents (all of whom are major shareholders in the company): Mary Noddle (vice president of production), Ron Hill (vice president of sales), and Kim Debe (vice president of accounting).

Under Ron Hill are seven sales managers, each of whom represents a particular segment of the Dade–Broward County areas. As sales orders are received, the production department processes a custom manufacturing order, which specifies the exact materials to be used. In the next phase, the raw materials are pulled, and the job is assigned to a team of workers. The size of this team depends on the size of the job.

At present, Joe Starr is concerned with a number of problems but primarily with bad-debt losses. A superficial analysis of accounts receivable indicated that a large number of accounts are more than 90 days overdue. Mr. Starr is sure that these will be collected eventually; however, Central Manufacturing has had difficulty in paying its bills due to these late collections.

Joe Starr has asked the chief accountant, Jim Wdeve, for an explanation of the problem. Mr. Wdeve explained that he periodically reviews the accounts receivable records, making notes on overdue accounts, which he uses as a basis for telephoning customers and asking for explanations.

Mr. Wdeve recommended that the problem be solved by implementing a network of microcomputers throughout the company. He suggested that with a microcomputer on each employee's desk, everyone would have instant access to any information needed.

Required

Comment on Mr. Wdeve's suggestion for installing a network of microcomputers.

47. John Needles has been hired as a systems consultant for Arco Manufacturing. The company's president, Barbara Arco, has told John that the company has been having numerous problems with late deliveries on customers' orders. The problem has been very acute because the competition has taken away a lot of business by offering faster delivery times.

John sets up an interview with the production supervisor to discuss the problem. The interview goes as follows:

JOHN: I have been hired to help alleviate any bottlenecks leading to late deliveries.

SUPERVISOR: I appreciate your offer to help, but I'm afraid that our problems can only be solved by someone with a considerable amount of experience doing this type of work.

JOHN: I agree. That's why I hope I can rely on you and your experience.

SUPERVISOR: I'm still afraid there isn't much I can do for you. Perhaps it would be better if you work directly with Ms Arco. I have an awful lot of work to do and need to make a production deadline this afternoon.

JOHN: Perhaps I can come back later this afternoon?

SUPERVISOR: You're welcome to come back, but again, I don't think I can help you.

Required

John Needles seems to be having trouble communicating with the production supervisor. Discuss some possible causes of this problem, and make suggestions for overcoming it.

48. The General Company has an accounting staff of five employees: a supervisor and four clerks. The daily tasks of each clerk are as follows:

Supervisor (Mary Wild)
  Checking paperwork—5 hours
  Filing documents—5 hours
  Preparing invoices—4 hours
  Other activities—1 hour

Accounts payable clerk (Joe Freedmire)
  Preparing monthly statements—4 hours
  Preparing aging report—3 hours
  Checking invoices—4 hours

Helper clerk (Bob Stans)
  Checking invoices—3 hours
  Preparing aging report—2 hours
  Account posting—5 hours

Document verification clerk (Margaret Lee)
  Preparing disbursement vouchers—4 hours
  Checking invoices—2 hours
  Other activities—3 hours

Clerk-typist (Debbie Chase)
  Typing invoices—4 hours
  Assisting in verification of invoices—3 hours

Required

a. Prepare a work distribution chart using tasks such as aging of accounts receivable, voucher preparation, and so on.

b. Identify any weaknesses in the distribution of tasks. In addition, note any internal control problems.

49. Systems analyst Jack Blount has been hired as a consultant to a large national distributing company to develop a new system for inventory control. The company is extremely large and has manufacturing plants and offices throughout the country. Mr. Blount decided to focus his attention initially on the Chicago plant.

He first interviewed the plant manager. The discussion was very productive, and after several meetings, he felt that he was in a position to make suggestions for improving the system. Based on this, he prepared a systems analysis report for review by the company's chief accountant.

In his meeting with the chief accountant, a number of problems arose. The chief accountant told him that a number of employees had complained to him, "Mr. Blount said he was going to have a number of employees laid off." Several supervisors complained that they were being replaced by computers. The situation had got so out of hand that a number of employees were on the verge of striking. Such a strike could cost the company thousands of dollars in a very short time. For this reason, the chief accountant informed Mr. Blount that the company did not wish to proceed with systems design and implementation. Mr. Blount was very disappointed to hear this because he felt that a few simple changes to the existing system could be very helpful in terms of solving the company's problems.

Required

Has Mr. Blount made any mistakes? If so, what did he do wrong?

50. List several important data fields that would be found in a database design for accounts receivable.

51. In evaluating design alternatives, the costs versus the benefits of a particular design proposal should be weighed; however, it is often difficult to quantify the benefits associated with a particular proposal. Give several examples of systems design problems where the benefits would be difficult to quantify.

52. Consider a small manufacturing company that has taken on the project of designing databases for sales orders, inventory, and accounts receivable. List several data fields that these three databases might have in common.

53. A problem that sometimes can occur in systems design is that the final users of the system will fight its implementation. What can be done during the design phase to avoid this problem?

54. Assume that you have been assigned the job of designing a system for a medium-sized clothing manufacturing company.

This company maintains raw material inventories for about 19 different fabrics. These fabrics are dyed and cut according to prespecified patterns. The plant manager has been advocating the introduction of a standard cost control system. Your job as the systems designer is to help the plant manager describe the various reports that would be required from a new system. The plant manager is specifically interested in reports for production cost control and inventory management.

Required

Describe at least three reports that could be produced by the new system.

55. A systems design team is considering the development of a system for sales orders. What members of management should this team communicate with throughout the design project?

56. Does the size of a company have any impact on the approach taken to the systems design project? If your answer is "Yes," explain.

57. What would be some unique problems associated with systems design in the automobile manufacturing industry?

58. You are in the process of designing an accounts receivable system for your company. A local computer retailer hears that you are designing a system and calls on you. He tells you that he can sell you a computer and software package that will solve all your problems. What is your response to the computer salesman?

59. You have been charged with the responsibility of heading up a design team. The team's responsibility will be to design a production control system. The team consists of you and four other members, including two systems analysts, a database designer, and the production manager. To initiate the project, you call a meeting of all individuals on the design team. At the first meeting, however, you find that the two systems analysts and the database designer have already made up their minds regarding the structure of the system under consideration. As head of the team, you feel that several major design alternatives should be considered before selecting a particular system. How do you deal with this problem?

60. A medium-sized grocery store has point-of-sale cash registers. The cash registers automatically summarize sales of all items sold in the store. One major problem facing the store is that of keeping adequate amounts of all grocery items on the shelves. Therefore, the store is searching for a way to monitor inventories and place daily orders for new goods, as needed.

Required

Give two major alternatives for the design of a system that accounts for and controls inventory for this grocery store.

61. The *Daily Times* newspaper company serves a small community. A considerable portion of the newspaper's revenues come from advertising. At present, all advertising orders are taken by salespeople, usually at the customers' places of business. At the end of every 3 days, all advertising orders are processed in a batch. Therefore, it normally takes 4 days between the time the orders are taken and the time the ad appears in the newspaper. Recently, however, a competitive newspaper has offered faster service to its customers.

Required

Present two major design alternatives for processing sales orders for the *Daily Times*.

62. The Good Burger Company owns and operates a chain of fast-food restaurants located throughout the southeastern portion of the United States. The company's main headquarters is in Atlanta. A major problem of the company is that of delivering food products to all the individual company stores. This involves loading up warehouse trucks and then stopping at individual stores on a weekly basis. Each store has a large refrigerator room where a considerable amount of food supply inventory can be maintained. Charles Hill, the general manager of food distribution, has noted that the company should develop a formal system for determining the amount of food to be delivered to each store. In addition, he has questioned whether it is necessary to deliver food to each store on a weekly basis. His rough calculations indicate that some stores might be visited less often. The major problem is that of communication between individual stores and the central office. At present, there is no way for the central office to know how much food to deliver to the individual stores.

Required

Design a system that would collect data on a daily basis at the central office regarding the need for food supplies by the individual stores. Your system should incorporate a database that keeps track of the sales and inventories of food supplies at individual stores. Your answer should be expressed in general terms. It is not necessary to develop a detailed database design.

63. Green Hardware Manufacturing produces and sells hardware products throughout the western portion of the United States. The primary source of revenue for the company comes from sales to individual hardware stores. The company has divided its sales territory into seven districts, with a sales manager in charge of each district. The individual sales managers try to travel around from store to store and take sales orders directly from store owners. The sales orders are then sent to company headquarters in Los Angeles, where they are processed. The present procedure is for the sales manager to write his or her own name on the sales order. At the end of each month, the company's accountant prepares a summary of sales by each district and for each product. This process, however, is extremely difficult and usually takes the accountant about 4 days to complete.

Required

Compose a general design alternative for collecting sales data and producing sales reports in a timely fashion.

64. Assume that you are the information systems manager for a medium-sized department store. At present, your company does all its customer billing manually. Your responsibility is to design a computerized database for customer accounts receivable.

Required

What data fields are exactly needed for the accounts receivable database?

65. The Fund Travel Agency operates four offices in a medium-sized metropolitan area. Each office has several individuals who plan trips and make reservations for clients. In order to optimize the use of employee time, all reservationists are shifted from office to office as needed. The company's telephone system operates such that customers can dial a central number and then be connected to the office where a reservationist is then assigned to that particular customer. A problem in the system is that since the reservationists do not stay at one office, they do not always have the customer's records when a customer calls in to review or change a reservation.

Required

Design a centralized reservation system for the Fund Travel Agency. Create a computerized system such that a customer's file can be accessed from any location.

66. Brown Chemical Manufacturing produces a single product called *CRX*. The company's product is sold mainly to food processing manufacturers who use it as a preservative. The production process for CRX is quite complicated. The product goes through four different stages, and each stage is carefully controlled with regard to temperature and moisture. At the first stage, two basic chemicals are mixed together and heated to 1,500 degrees. At the second stage, the product is cooled, and an additional chemical is added when it reaches just the right temperature. At the third and fourth stages, the resulting chemical is refined successfully. Therefore, the company has to maintain raw materials inventory for three different chemicals. In addition, the finished-goods inventory for CRX has to be maintained. Almost all the cost of producing CRX is for raw materials and overhead. Since the process is fully automated, there is no direct labor cost. Another major cost, however, is that of storing the finished product. In order to increase the product's shelf life, the finished chemical is stored under specially controlled temperature conditions. These conditions require refrigeration to 0 degrees, with essentially no moisture. This refrigeration process is fairly expensive because the company manufactures a very large quantity of CRX.

Recently, management of the company has been evaluating the overall systems design. Several comments have been made with regard to the manufacturing and inventory systems:

a. It has been determined that a large number of production batches of CRX have to be discarded due to inadequate environmental conditions during processing. At present, there is no management reporting for the costs of the lost materials or time.

b. Management suspects that the company is incurring too high a cost in the refrigeration of finished goods. It would prefer that production batches be run as customer orders are placed. In this way, the finished CRX could be shipped directly to the customer without a need for refrigerated storage in inventory. However, the problem is that the company has never been able to successfully implement this type of system for several reasons: (1) delays in processing of customer orders, (2) difficulty with efficiently scheduling production, and (3) problems with distribution. It is often the case that when a production order is ready, the company's trucks are all out of state making deliveries. It would be disastrous if a production batch were completed and there was no truck to deliver it. This would result in the loss of the entire shipment.

Required

Present a systems design alternative for dealing with Brown Chemical's problems.

67. The Honest Law Firm is made up of five partners who specialize in various areas of law. The oldest partner, Bill Brown, founded the firm 30 years ago. His original practice consisted primarily of writing business contracts and helping businesses incorporate. In the early days, Mr. Brown had one secretary who did all the billing. Most of his work was done on a flat-fee basis, and there was no need to provide detailed accounting of time spent on individual clients. However, with the addition of the new partners, the business has become quite complicated. The newer partners specialize in areas such as criminal law, bankruptcy, real estate, and family law. The trend of the business has been such that most of the billing needs to be done on an hourly basis. At present, each partner submits a weekly billing report to the head partner's secretary. These reports are used as a basis for billing individual clients and providing weekly "salary" reports for the partnership.

The partnership's main problem is that most of the partners are having a difficult time recording all the necessary information to bill clients. As a result, it is estimated that only about 75% of the lawyers' actual time is billed to clients. Furthermore, it has been determined that a very weak area for collecting billing information is the telephone system. Several discussions among the partners revealed that the lawyers often spend a lot of time on the telephone with clients, but the information is not recorded into the system for appropriate measures of billing the client.

Required

Design a system that efficiently and effectively records and processes 100% of the firm's billing costs.

68. You are the partner in charge of management services for a medium-sized public accounting firm. You have contracted with a local manufacturing system to develop a specialized production control system. Several of your younger staff accountants have been involved in the actual systems design. A problem has arisen. They have reported to you that top management is very enthusiastic about the design of the new system. However, they are very confused about the response

of the production managers and other key employees. The major problem is that the production manager and other employees keep missing meetings with the design team.

On one occasion, the production manager told the design team that she liked what they were doing but just did not have time to work with them in detail.

Required

Discuss several possible causes for the problems encountered by the design team. What steps might have been taken to facilitate a better working relationship between the design team and management?

Web Research Assignments

69. The use-case diagram is an important part of UML diagramming. Use the Web search engines to learn about the use cases diagram. Prepare a use-cases diagram for the following situation. A bank customer performs the following activities in relation to a bank: deposits money, withdraws money, and inquires about account balance. The individual also performs the following activities with the xyz company: purchases supplies with credit, pays balance on account, and returns unused supplies.

70. Intuit's Quickbase™ (www.quickbase.com) is an online database system that operates as a Platform as a Service (PaaS). Write a brief report that explains in general terms the type of work that would be required to develop an accounts receivable program using Quickbase. How would developing the application in Quickbase™ differ from obtaining an accounts receivable application via SaaS?

71. Search the Web to find a complete SaaS accounting system for a midsized retail company. Write a brief report outlining why a midsized retail company would want to use the SaaS accounting system that you choose.

72. What is extreme programming? How does it differ from cowboy programming?

73. REA accounting is popular in the accounting literature.

Required

Write a brief report on the relationship between REA accounting and ebXML. What impact has REA had on ebXML? What do REA and ebXML have in common?

Answers to Chapter Quiz

| 1. b | 2. a | 3. d | 4. b | 5. a | 6. d | 7. c | 8. c | 9. d | 10. a | 11. b | 12. a | 13. c |
| 14. d | 15. b | 16. a | 17. b | 18. a | 19. a | 20. b | | | | | | |

Systems Project Management, Implementation, Operation, and Control

CHAPTER 2

Learning Objectives

Careful study of this chapter will enable you to:

- Describe the major phases of systems implementation.
- Recognize significant human factors involved in systems implementation.
- Detail the types of documentation involved in the implementation of a new system.
- Understand how to plan and control a systems project.
- Be aware of tools and technologies used in the project development environment.
- Describe several approaches for control over nonfinancial systems resources.

Overview

This chapter discusses implementation of the systems design plan. If the systems design process has been done carefully and thoughtfully, the systems implementation phase should proceed smoothly. However, it is impossible to anticipate all potential problems that might occur during the implementation phase. Accordingly, delays and problems with implementation are routine. For example, a design plan might call for the installation of a new cluster of networked computers. If the delivery of the new cluster is delayed beyond the delivery date specified in the general plan, the entire implementation project might be delayed.

Because of the many problems that can occur during systems implementation, formal plans and controls should be established. Figure 12.1 shows the three major steps in systems implementation: establish plans and controls, execute activities, and follow up and evaluate new system. Subsequent to implementation, the new system must be reviewed and controlled.

Systems Implementation

Establishing Plans and Controls for Implementation

Project management is a key concept in systems implementation. In order to manage the implementation project adequately, specific plans need to be developed. These plans should incorporate three major components: (1) a breakdown of the project into various phases, (2) specific budgets applicable to each phase, and (3) specific timetables applicable to each project phase. Various scheduling techniques might be used to control implementation.

FIGURE 12.1

**Systems
Implementation**

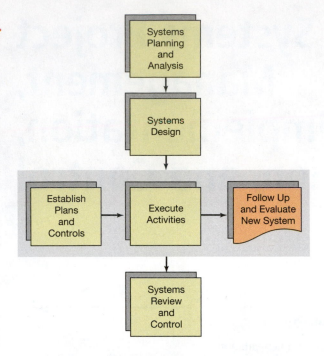

Figure 12.2 shows a **Gantt chart,** a tool which graphically depicts the planned and actual times for the major activities of a systems implementation project. The Gantt chart is a useful tool but becomes unwieldy where there are many activities. Gantt charts can be useful but they are limited in that they cannot show the relationships between various project activities. Gantt charts do not show the order in which the various activities must be performed.

CASE IN POINT

The Gantt chart was originally developed in Poland by Karol Adamiecki in the late 1800s. It was later popularized in the West by Henry Laurence Gantt during the early 1900s. In 1929, the American Society of Mechanical Engineers created the annual Henry Laurence Gantt Medal for "distinguished achievement in management and service to the community." The medal continues to be awarded to this day.

FIGURE 12.2

Gantt Chart Example

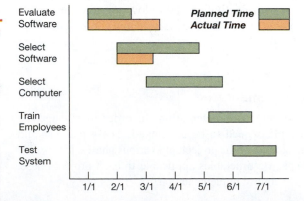

FIGURE 12.3

Simple Network Diagram

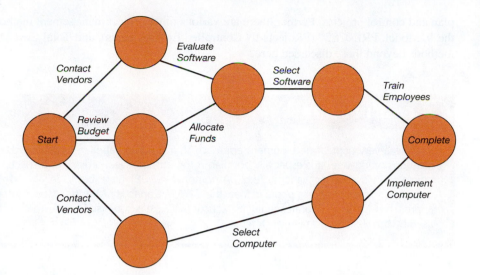

Figure 12.3 shows a **network diagram,** which depicts the order in which the activities must be performed. For example, notice that employees cannot be trained until the software is selected. The network diagram approach can be expanded to include estimated times for each of the individual activities. Given these times, it is possible to use the program evaluation and review technique (PERT) or the critical path method (CPM) to estimate the critical path for a project. The **critical path** is a list of activities that are critical to the project in the sense that if any one of them is delayed, the entire project will be delayed.

Focusing on completing activities on the critical path can help prevent project bottlenecks. However, well-defined critical paths may not exist in some projects, especially those that are developed iteratively. However, even in iteratively developed projects, critical paths may exist within given phases and iterations, if not for the project as a whole.

CASE IN POINT

PERT and CPM techniques help project managers prioritize activities that must be performed to complete a project. Using this information, the completion date of a project might be advanced by "fast tracking" (performing more activities in parallel) and/or by "crashing the critical path" (shortening the durations of critical path activities by focusing resources on their completion).

In general, the metrics used to plan and control a project will depend on the project development approach. Classical structured approaches best lend themselves to PERT type of analyses. Other approaches may instead lend themselves to other types of metrics, possibly in addition to PERT-type metrics. For example, **ISO 15504** (also called **SPICE,** Software Process Improvement and Capability dEtermination) is a process-based development approach that focuses on the "maturity" of the process being developed. Under the SPICE approach, processes are categorized into five broad areas (customer–supplier, engineering, supporting, management, and organization), with a process's "capability level" constantly being scored on a 6-point scale that ranges from 0 (incomplete) to 6 (optimized). In practice, multiple project development methods, such as rational unified process (RUP) (which was discussed in Chapter 11) and SPICE, might be used in combination, resulting in a wide variety of possible metrics used to plan and control projects. Further, there are various other project management methods, such as the V-Model, PRINCE2® (PRojects IN Controlled Environments), and Total Cost Management methods beyond those discussed here.

CASE IN POINT

SPICE is a very popular development approach that has been applied in thousands of organizations worldwide. It is especially popular in the automotive, medical, and space industry, where industry-specific variants (e.g., Automotive SPICE) have been developed. Overall, it as been somewhat less popular than the CMMI (Capability Maturity Model Integration) approach. CMMI incorporates many aspects of SPICE, has some similarities to COBIT, and is used by the U.S. Department of Defense.

Executing Implementation Activities

Executing implementation activities involves the actual carrying out of the design plan. Typical activities during execution include selecting and training personnel, installing new computer equipment, detailed systems design, writing and testing computer programs, system testing, standards development, documentation, and file conversion. Each of these activities is discussed in detail in this section.

In carrying out the implementation plan, certain measures should be taken to provide a smooth transition and to ensure acceptance on the part of company employees. It is normally desirable for the management and the systems team to make a formal announcement regarding execution of the project. Care should be taken to assure employees that the transition will be smooth, and when possible, employees should be assured that their jobs will be protected. A formal announcement process should have the benefit of minimizing rumors. This is important because rumors can generate a considerable amount of uncertainty and employee unrest.

Another important aspect of the execution phase is the organization of a special project team. Ideally, the team should consist of individuals who also participated in formulating the design specifications and plans for implementation. Affected managers should also participate.

EMPLOYEE TRAINING   Virtually any successful systems implementation requires that considerable attention be devoted to employee training. In some cases, new employees must be hired and trained. In other cases, existing employees must be taught to work with new forms, reports, and procedures.

The importance of adequate training cannot be overemphasized. You should never assume that employees will learn to use the system by themselves. If employees are not trained adequately, it is likely that they will simply ignore the new system. Therefore, the success of the entire systems development project is affected by the adequacy of training.

CASE IN POINT

Almost everything can be outsourced these days and that includes training—NIIT (www.niit.com). "NIIT's Corporate Learning Solutions offers integrated learning solutions, including strategic consulting, learning design, content development, delivery, technology, assessment and learning management to Fortune 500 companies, Universities, Technology companies."

The company typically will face a number of options relating to using and training employees. For example, management often has to decide whether the company should hire a new employee for a given position or retrain an existing employee. In many cases, it is best to retrain an existing employee. There are several reasons for this:

- Recruiting costs relating to hiring a new employee are avoided.
- Existing employees are already familiar with the firm's operations.
- Employee morale is often enhanced, especially in cases where the new position would be a promotion for an existing employee.

In addition, a number of training approaches are available to the company, including

- Hiring outside training consultants
- Using training manuals
- Using videotape presentations
- Using audiotape presentations
- Using training seminars
- Using individualized hands-on instruction
- Using computer-assisted training

ACQUIRING AND INSTALLING NEW COMPUTER EQUIPMENT   The installation of new computer equipment sometimes can be a monumental task. For installations of any appreciable size, engineers and other personnel may be required to assist in the installation. However, many problems can be encountered. First, adequate facilities must be available. Most large data centers require controlled environments that keep humidity and temperature within specified ranges. In addition, these installations require special provisions for complex wiring schemes. Other requirements typically include specialized security measures, such as special fire extinguishing systems, video monitoring systems, or specialized door locks.

DETAILED SYSTEMS DESIGN   During the implementation phase, it is almost always necessary to do some additional design work. This might include the design of various kinds of forms or reports. Also, it is not uncommon for the implementation phase to reveal that certain parts of the design plan are unworkable; therefore, it is always necessary to do some last minute fine-tuning of the systems design plan.

A very important part of detailed design execution during the implementation phase involves computer programming and/or customizations. Even if the design plan calls for prepackaged applications, such as ERP or SaaS, extensive customization is most likely required. In addition, more work may be required if the company is adding to or changing its data services. For example, the company may eliminate its own data center in favor of leasing data services in the cloud.

 CASE IN POINT

> Outsourcing data services has become increasingly popular. Rackspace (www.rackspace.com), a world leader in hosting services, provides cloud server services. "You'll be able to deploy one to hundreds of cloud servers instantly, for as long (or little) as you need them."
>
> With cloud services, it is literally possible to instantly create an entire virtual data center on demand.

The design specifications for a computer program are determined by the design team, not the programmer. The programmer's primary function is to implement a specific plan; however, it is important for the programmer to work in conjunction with the design team. Finally, computer applications should be tested very carefully before being put into operation. One powerful means of such testing involves processing test data. Test data either can be made up or can come from real data. In either case, the test data should include a large number of different kinds of errors. In addition, the test data should include a wide range of conditions, since a defective program will often work with no problems given that there are no errors in the input data file or where the test data represent the average operating conditions. Therefore, an attempt should be made to "break" the program; the individual doing the testing should do everything possible to find something wrong with the program.

Finally, all computer applications should be documented adequately, both internally and externally. Internal documentation includes various kinds of comments (embedded within the program) that describe different segments of the program code and define the various program variables. External documentation should be written both from the programmer's and users' point of view. Programmer's documentation would include such things as object descriptions, structured English, flowcharts of the program logic, definitions of various subprograms, functions, and program variables. The documentation should be usable by a different programmer, working several years later, to modify the application. Applications without adequate documentation may be worthless when the programmer who wrote them leaves the company.

In addition to testing programs (i.e., applications and services) individually, it is also important to test related programs as a group. For example, a given system may have four programs that access the same data file. In this case, all four programs should be tested together. This type of testing would uncover integration errors. Such errors might occur when one program makes faulty assumptions regarding the tasks performed by another program.

DOCUMENTING THE NEW SYSTEM   Documentation is one of the most important parts of systems implementation, but it is often overlooked. One reason for the neglect in documenting systems adequately is that programmers typically receive substantial amounts of training in programming languages but little or no training in documentation. Of course, some educational institutions do an excellent job in teaching documentation skills; however, the opposite is too often true.

It has been often said that a good computer programmer will write several lines of program code per day. One reason for the small number is that a good programmer will spend a substantial portion of time developing plans and documentation. The development of computer software without documentation is an almost worthless exercise. Good documentation can serve a wide range of useful purposes, including (1) training new employees, (2) providing programmers and analysts with useful information for future program evaluation and modification activities, (3) providing auditors with useful information for evaluating internal controls, and (4) assisting in ensuring that systems design specifications are met.

FILE CONVERSION   A typical problem involved in systems implementation is that of data conversion. In some cases, files maintained manually must be converted to computer format. In addition, it is often necessary to convert from one computer format to another. For example, a design plan might call for converting data in Intuit Quickbase™ format into data in Oracle database format.

Conversion can be an expensive, time-consuming process. This is especially true in the case of converting manual files to computerized files. In such cases, it is often necessary to do a lot of data screening after entering the information into the computer because errors are typically made in the data input process.

TEST OPERATIONS   Before the system is actually implemented, it must be thoroughly tested as a whole. There are three basic approaches to the final testing of the system: (1) the direct approach, (2) parallel operation, and (3) modular conversion. The **direct approach** involves switching to the new system and abandoning the old system at a fixed point in time called the **cutover point.** The direct approach, while relatively inexpensive, has the distinct disadvantage of allowing for the possibility of major system problems that impair actual operation of the company. For example, it could be disastrous to find that a new accounts receivable system bills all the company's customers for incorrect amounts. The second approach, **parallel operation,** involves running the new and old systems simultaneously. All transactions are processed by both systems. The results of operations based on the two systems are compared. Any discrepancies probably indicate a problem in the new system. Parallel operation has the advantage of being extremely safe; however, it is very expensive and may not be cost effective in all applications. The final approach, **modular conversion,** involves phasing in the new system in segments. For example, the new accounting system might include modules for accounts receivable, accounts payable, inventories, and general ledger. A modular conversion approach might implement the inventory module itself. After the company feels comfortable with this module, other modules could be brought online. A major drawback of the modular conversion process is that it can involve a greatly extended checkout period. This might delay final implementation of a new system far too long to be practical.

CASE IN POINT

Converting from one database system to another can be a daunting task if done one piece at a time. Ispirer (www.ispirer.com) publishes SQLWays™, a software tool that migrates databases from any one of the major database formats to any other. Some of the supported databases include Microsoft SQL Server, IBM DB2, MySQL, Oracle, and Teradata. SQLWays™ migrates not only the data but also the internal data structures and program scripts.

Evaluating the New System

Once the new system has been implemented, more work remains. Follow-up is necessary to ensure that the new system operates as planned. There are many approaches that can assist in follow-up and evaluation, including observation, questionnaires, performance measures, and benchmarks.

Planning and Organizing a Systems Project

Operationally, project management techniques are the heart of a well-controlled systems development life cycle. The term *project* refers to a specific application that has been approved for development. Once approval has been obtained, **project management** begins and is concerned with the detailed analysis, design, programming, testing, implementation, operation, and maintenance of the project.

Project Selection

If an organization's resources are limited, project development resources should be allocated to projects that yield the greatest benefits to the organization. Potential projects may be proposed directly by user departments or by a separate information system or corporate planning function or arise in response to an immediate problem—such as a change in federal reporting requirements. Typically, proposals arise in all these ways, and there are more project proposals that can be undertaken by the existing staff. Project selection is usually the responsibility of a steering committee or other organization-wide unit to ensure active user participation in the selection process. Project proposals are submitted to the steering committee in writing. A proposal should provide a statement of the expected benefits and costs, if possible. Frequently, costs and benefits can only be estimated subjectively owing to both the difficulties of costing information services and the difficulties of estimating the resources that will be necessary to complete the project. In large organizations, the project selection process may be highly formalized, with the project proposal document providing a detailed analysis of expected costs and benefits, both financial and nonfinancial. Expected return on investment (ROI) is frequently an important selection criterion in such cases. Once a project has been approved for development, a project team must be organized to begin work.

The Project Team

Labor is a basic resource in any systems project. One important task of project management is to assemble a suitable project team. For an applications systems project, analysts, programmers, and other technicians are necessary, but representatives of the user department(s) for which the application is being developed usually should be included as well. One member must be selected as the project leader in order to focus control responsibilities for the project. Whether this project leader should come from the user department or the information systems department is a question best answered in the context of the specific project environment. If the project leader comes from a user department, then the user likely will be deeply involved and committed to the project's success. However, the quality of technical leadership may be weaker than if an information systems person is selected as the project leader.

PROJECT LEADER RESPONSIBILITIES   A diagram of a project team organization appears in Figure 12.4. The project leader has direct responsibility to the steering committee for project progress and completion. A steering committee or other such organizational unit is used to ensure a high level of user involvement in the work of the information systems department. The project team consists of the project leader, analysts, and programmers from the information systems department and one or more user participants from the organizational unit(s) for which the project is being undertaken. Each member of a project team maintains line responsibility to the manager/supervisor of his or her department. However, for project activities, each project team member reports to the project leader. On a large project, one or more lead or chief analysts and/or programmers are assigned to assist the project leader in supervising the technical staff.

The project leader must maintain contact with the principal user department manager who has responsibility for the project. The user manager is typically the person who must formally approve the project at its completion. The project leader must also be in contact with technical specialists, such as the database administrator, as required to complete the project successfully. In addition to project team organization, the primary responsibilities of the project leader are planning, scheduling, and controlling the project. These responsibilities are detailed in Figure 12.5. Planning involves project breakdown and allocation of resources. Scheduling is a successive refinement to the project plan; activities are scheduled chronologically, and detailed project responsibilities are assigned to team members. Project scheduling is performed using techniques such as PERT and CPM. Project control involves time and progress reporting as well

FIGURE 12.4

Project Team Organization

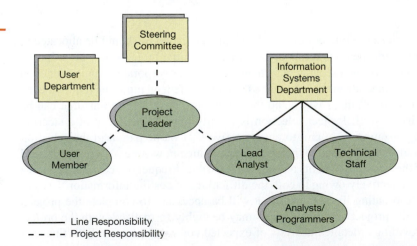

FIGURE 12.5

Project Leader Responsibilities

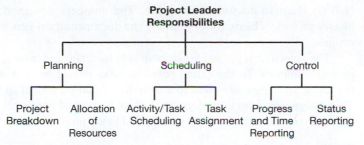

as periodic project status reporting to upper-level management. A project accounting system is the means by which the project leader fulfills her or his project control responsibilities.

PROJECT UNCERTAINTY   The major problem faced by any project team is the uncertainty associated with an application systems project. The technicians have to work with the users to elicit the system's data requirements. Users often are unaware of the problem creating the need for the new project and may, in fact, be unaware of the specific data they use in their decision-making responsibilities. For these reasons, the user–designer interface is characterized by a high degree of uncertainty. Uncertainty also exists in the development of the system. Once the systems design is set, programmers have to interpret the detailed specifications and write the necessary software. Software development is also uncertain. The total time required to code the software can only be estimated. Uncertainty also exists as to whether the resulting software will be reliable and as to whether it will conform to system specifications. The task of the project team is to reduce all these uncertainties, coordinate the activities of the diverse parties working on the project, and complete the project within a reasonable time and at a reasonable cost. The selection of an effective project leader is crucial to these tasks.

Project Breakdown into Tasks and Phases

To plan and control a project effectively, the required activities are broken down or factored into a detailed listing of tasks and phases. If a total project is suitably factored into the smaller components of a systems life cycle, the project becomes easier to control and understand. There is no standard method for factoring a project into detailed activities, just as there is no standard listing of phases in the systems development life cycle. There are several reasons for this, including different opinions, different commercial project management packages, and different requirements for particular projects. The guiding philosophy is iterative and/ or top-down design with successive refinement. The basic operational principle is that each specific task or phase should provide a *deliverable* at its completion, some type of tangible product (i.e., documentation) that can be reviewed and evaluated. The higher the degree of breakdown into specific tasks and phases, the higher is the certainty with which each task's or phase's requirements can be predicted. Figure 12.6 illustrates the concept of factoring a project into a set of phases and tasks and the use of a hierarchical plus input–process–output

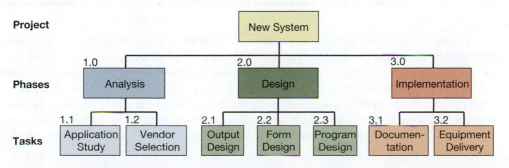

FIGURE 12.6

Factoring a Project into Phases and Tasks

(HIPO) chart to document this plan. The numbers assigned to the individual tasks and phases provide a basis for organizing the documentation generated during the course of the project.

The objective of project breakdown is to facilitate assignment and control of labor and other project resources. To the extent possible, tasks should be broken down to a level where task definition is sufficiently clear to enable individual personnel to be assigned to specific tasks. Task assignments should reflect the skills of individual personnel. Estimated time requirements for each specific task also must be included in the project breakdown.

Time Estimates

Estimating accurate task completion times for a systems project is difficult because of the uncertainties inherent in systems development. Poorly estimated task completion times severely limit the effectiveness of project management techniques. Accuracy depends partly on the previous project management experience within an organization. Experience from previous projects should increase the task time estimation skill of project personnel on each new project. However, estimates always will be inaccurate to some degree, and this fact must be accepted. Undue pressure to keep to unrealistic schedules may result in an unsatisfactory project outcome. The proper attitude toward time estimates is to accept them for what they are—estimates—and to be prepared to revise them frequently as a project is developed.

WORK MEASUREMENT TECHNIQUES   The simplest approach to estimation is to *guess*, meaning that no formal calculations are undertaken. The "guesstimate" is based on one's previous experience with similar projects or tasks. More rigorous approaches to estimation are based on the concept of work measurement, which was discussed in Chapter 2. Work measurement involves four basic steps:

- Identify the tasks to be estimated.
- For each task, estimate the total size or volume of the task in some suitable manner.
- Convert the size or volume estimate into a time estimate by multiplying the size or volume estimate by a standard or estimated processing rate.
- Adjust the estimated processing rate to include circumstantial considerations such as idle time, task complexity, or task newness.

CASE IN POINT

Projects can take too long to complete for a variety of reasons. One reason is called *scope creep.* Once projects commence, there is sometimes a strong temptation to keep adding new features to them, without adding corresponding amounts of resources to the project plan. The larger the project, the higher is the risk of scope creep. Almost all megaprojects suffer from some scope creep.

Figure 12.7 illustrates this general approach. Note the adjustment of the initial estimate of 50 standard man-days for the interviews to 65 man-days to reflect the complexity of the task as "somewhat above average." A further refinement involves adjusting the estimated time for a task as just calculated by experience or competency factors, increasing or decreasing the total estimated time to reflect the relative capabilities of the specific individuals to be assigned to each task. Figure 12.8 illustrates this type of adjustment. Extending the final time estimates by suitable costing or charging rates provides the method for estimating the total budgeted project cost.

FIGURE 12.7

**Sample Work
Measurement
Calculation**

Standard Man-Days for Interviews

People to Be Interviewed	Number to Be Interviewed	Standard Man-Day Allowance	Total Man-Days
Managers	4	0.5	2
Supervisors	17	1.0	17
Technical Staff	18	1.5	27
Clerical Staff	8	0.5	4
Total	47	—	50

Complexity Factors

Simple	0.50–0.75
Average	1.00–1.50
Complex	2.00–2.50

Complexity judgment for the case in point is "somewhat above average"

Assign a factor of 1.30

Adjusted man-days = standard man-days times complexity factor
= 50 x 1.30
= 65 adjusted man-days

Although estimation for each different task in a project, such as analysis or programming, requires different basic data to describe its size or volume, the principles of work measurement are the same in each case. Because applications development projects are a regular activity in many organizations, standard task times or processing rates can be estimated and refined based

FIGURE 12.8

**Competency
and Knowledge
Adjustments**

Personnel Factors

A. Competence and Experience

Experience	Competence Level	
	Low	High
Senior	1.0	0.7
Intermediate	1.8	1.1
Junior	2.8	1.9

B. Knowledge

Knowledge Available	Knowledge Required		
	Little	Average	Much
Much	0.0	0.1	0.3
Average	0.0	0.2	0.7
Little	0.1	0.5	1.0

Actual man-days = adjusted days x (personnel + knowledge)

Assume that a junior analyst of high competence will do the work. Average knowledge is available, and much knowledge is required.

Actual man-days = 65 x (1.9 + 0.7) = 169 man-days

on experience. Standards developed in house are likely to be more effective than standards or estimates available in the project management literature.

ACCURACY OF ESTIMATES   The literature on project management is a source of estimation techniques as well as of detailed time estimates or standard processing rates for performing various project tasks. There are no commonly accepted standards largely because there is no general agreement of standard project phases and tasks. However, there is general agreement on several points related to the estimation process. The first point is that estimates are only estimates, no matter how carefully prepared. A second point of agreement is that the accuracy of estimation improves considerably as a project proceeds through its course of activities. That is, estimates of, say, the 10th phase of a project that are made at the completion of, say, the fourth phase are likely to be more accurate than estimates for the 10th phase that were made at the beginning of the project. It is commonly held that estimation errors of 100% are not unreasonable for the latter phases of a project when these estimates are made at a project's conception. This reinforces the importance of frequently revising estimates contained in the project plan to reflect actual project experience. Estimates made during the early phase of a project can be expected to be considerably inaccurate even if they were prepared carefully. For this reason, "guesstimates" are used frequently in the initial phases of a project rather than detailed calculations. These original estimates are revised successively as the project proceeds through its course of activities. This approach reflects the practical fact that as a project proceeds, it takes shape, meaning that what is left to be done is now based on everything else that has been completed and is now more predictable and hence subject to greater control.

Lowballing   Another area of consensus is that initial estimates frequently are made too low. Estimates that are made by personnel such as computer programmers, who are subsequently the ones to perform the tasks for which they are providing time estimates, tend to be overly optimistic. In consulting or contracting businesses, this type of behavior is known as **lowballing**—purposely or inadvertently submitting unreasonably low time or cost estimates to obtain a contract, knowing that once the contract is obtained, the work likely will be completed regardless of the actual amount of time or cost that is required. While lowballing is a possibility for in-house personnel as well, more common reasons for task time underestimation reside in job performance measurement factors such as a natural desire to be perceived as efficient in one's duties by one's superior. Underestimation also occurs when work measurement techniques are used to estimate task times. Often estimates of "productive hours per day," "work days," or similar work units fail realistically to consider idle or nonproductive time due to sickness, vacations, coffee breaks, washroom breaks, and other such factors. There are also considerable differences in the productive capabilities of different people. One person's day of output might be equivalent to another person's week of output. This is the reason for suggesting in the earlier discussion that basic work measurements should be adjusted with factors that compensate for the relative capabilities of different people or groups of people (e.g., senior programmers versus junior programmers). There also may be significant variation in the output of a single person over time, even when the same person works on similar tasks. Again, the best strategy is to revise estimates successively based on actual project experience.

Cost Overruns   Cost overruns are a frequent problem in systems development, but to the extent that costs are higher than predicted by estimates made during the early phases of a project, analysis of the cost overrun should be tempered by the problems of estimation just discussed. This is particularly true because a relatively larger percentage of total systems development costs are incurred during the later phases of a project (design and implementation), and it is these later project phases for which initial estimates are likely to be optimistic. Typically, 30–40% of total project *time* is spent in the analysis phase of the systems development life cycle, but 75% or more of total project *costs* is incurred during the design and implementation phases. Project resources tend to be spent at an increasing rate as a project proceeds to completion. Thus, control of project costs in the early phases of the systems development life cycle is essential.

Project Accounting

Project control is established by setting measurable goals for each phase and task in the overall project, reporting actual performance against these goals, and evaluating any significant deviations from the project plan. Measurable goal analysis is facilitated by the documentation or deliverable that is required of each phase or task to evidence its completion, as well as major milestones or project checkpoints, at which times the overall status of the project to date is subject to review by upper-level management. Well-established, clearly defined responsibilities for project personnel (which is facilitated by a detailed project breakdown) and some form of project accounting system to measure and report actual performance against responsibility are essential elements of a project control system.

OPERATION OF THE SYSTEM   A project accounting system is a cost accounting system in which costs are assigned to individual projects as the projects proceed through their development. Regardless of whether project costs are assigned to users in the context of a responsibility accounting system, effective project control requires a project accounting system that can keep track of costs incurred to date on a project and provide a summary cost report at a project's completion. Timely cost data are essential to making rational decisions about resource usage. Historical cost data from previous projects are an important source of information to use in estimating the time and cost components of new projects.

The project accounting system might be batch or real time. A large firm that generally has several projects underway at the same time generally requires a fully automated system with real-time updates. On the other hand, a batch system would probably be run once a week. The important consideration is that status reports must be prepared on time. A weekly cost report that is available 2 weeks later is not likely to be effective for control purposes.

Figure 12.9 illustrates the components of a project accounting system. Projects must be numbered for identification purposes. The system operates much like a conventional cost accounting system: Materials, labor, and overhead charges are accumulated by project and compared periodically with budgeted costs, and reports are prepared. Materials in the case of application projects consist mostly of computer use charges for program development and testing. Labor costs are obtained from time sheets on which project personnel assign their chargeable hours to work in progress. Overhead consists of other charges that are only indirectly attributable to

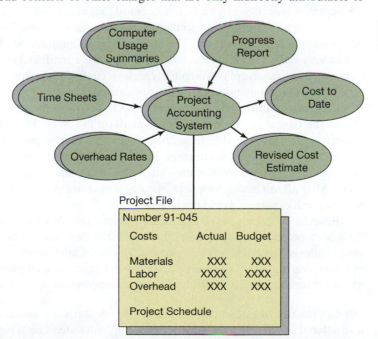

FIGURE 12.9

Project Accounting System

projects, such as the office space of personnel and the cost of running the project accounting system. Overhead charges usually are applied on the basis of an overhead rate. The final input that is needed on a regular basis is a report detailing the progress to date on each project. This is necessary if estimates of future costs to complete each project are to be revised successively. Progress is frequently measured in terms of earned hours—the equivalent of "standard earned hours" in a standard cost accounting system for manufactured products. Earned hours are used to represent the percentage of completion. For example, if a task time estimate is 40 hours and the task is estimated to be 30% complete, then the progress report would show 12 earned hours on the project task. Charging rates and the project budget are used in conjunction with the progress reports to provide revised cost estimates, project costs to date, and charges to users (if such charges are to be made). Periodically, special summary reports detailing the total cost of projects in process are prepared for supervisory management.

LEVEL OF DETAIL   As in any control system, if too much detail is required by the project accounting system, then the overhead cost of running the system will be too high, and project workers will be antagonized by the data required of them. If too little detail is provided, then the results will be ambiguous. The appropriate level of detail must be determined by project management. In most cases, weekly reports based on earned hours are sufficient for control purposes.

The Project Development Environment

We use the term **project development environment** to refer to the tools and technologies used to implement a given project. Aspects of the project development environment discussed here include the project collaboration platform, the software application framework, the integrated development environment, the software versioning system, and the development and deployment application solution stacks.

THE PROJECT COLLABORATION PLATFORM   Software development projects involve various groups of individuals that must effectively communicate with each other in order for the project to proceed smoothly and succeed. A typical project might involve a nontechnical end-user group or department, a project manager, one or more analysts, and one or more programmers. First, the end-user or department defines what is needed, often in the form of a project proposal. Such a proposal is typically written in nontechnical language. The project manager must then work with analysts to convert the project into technical specifications. These specifications must then be conveyed to the programmer. The result is a fairly complicated chain of communications that can be very difficult to maintain via telephone calls, e-mail, and other written communications. Consequently, because of its complexity, delays, confusion, and misunderstandings will certainly arise unless this communication chain is optimized.

Project collaboration platforms serve to optimize management of the communication chain. The typical project collaboration platform is a Web 2.0 application in which all of the project participants are able to access, create, and review project specifications, milestones, checklists, tasks, shared documents, work-time logs, and even software code. An important criterion for selecting a collaboration platform is that it should be simple enough for nontechnical users. After all, no matter how sophisticated a platform is, it is of not much value if those who need to use it cannot or would not use it.

BaseCamp® (www.basecamphq.com) is an example of a project collaboration platform. It supports project-communication functions, is simple to use for even those who are technologically challenged, and it is very inexpensive. The BaseCamp® platform has the particular advantage of integrating with a wide range of other development-oriented platforms, such as those relating to project accounting, flowcharting, and business process management.

THE SOFTWARE APPLICATION FRAMEWORK   A **software application framework** provides a structured environment in which to develop software. The typical framework may include specific programming languages, development tools and aids, and libraries of software than provide readymade functionality.

Specific frameworks typically exist to support software application development in specific domains, such as middleware, decision-support systems, financial modeling, and Web applications. Since most application development has shifted to the Web, the discussion in the remaining part of this section focuses on Web application frameworks.

In general, Web application frameworks can be divided into *client-side* and *server-side* frameworks. Client-side frameworks develop applications that run inside a user's Web browser and communicate with a Web server. Server-side frameworks lead to applications that run on an application server and communicate with the user through the user's Web browser. The general trend has been toward more client-side development, in which end-user software operates in Web browsers. Client-side software has the benefit that it can operate whether or not the end-user is connected to the Internet.

Almost all the major client-side Web application frameworks are built on the JavaScript language. One example is Microsoft's ASP.NET AJAX, which is part of Microsoft's general .NET Framework for developing Web applications. AJAX refers to Asynchronous JavaScript and XML, a combination that permits the developer to refresh parts of a Web user's Web page without refreshing the entire page. As part of Microsoft's .NET development environment, Microsoft provides its Visual Studio product, which integrates not only with AJAX but with other programming languages and development environments as well. The .NET framework also supports server-side development.

Despite the increasing importance of client-side Web applications, server-side applications are the mainstay of most Web 2.0 applications. So there are quite a few server-side Web application frameworks.

Individual server-side development frameworks tend to be related to specific programming languages, with those relating to PERL, PHP (personal home page), and Java being among the most popular. For example, Catalyst (www.catalystframework.org) is an open-source framework tied to the PERL Web scripting language. It includes a wide range of tools to simplify the development and deployment of Catalyst applications to Linux, Apple Macintosh™, and Windows™ systems.

While there are many platforms that support the Java server-side scripting language, Java itself refers to a group of products published by Sun Microsystems (www.sun.com) that were mostly made public under a GNU public license, making Java basically free to the public. Related to this platform are the Java Development Kit (JDK) and a wide variety of other products such as JavaFX available through java.sun.com.

One Web application framework that has received considerable attention has been the Rails framework for Ruby, often referred to as Ruby on Rails (rubyonrails.org). Ruby on Rails is an object-oriented (OO) programming language that is based on the Model–View–Controller structure. Models represent the data structures (e.g., relations), the views represent the Web pages, and the controllers represent the business process logic. What Rails does, among other things, is to provide the programmer with simple-command access to relational databases without having to write any SQL code. Rails has been used to develop several popular Web applications such as Twitter (www.twitter.com) and YellowPages (www.yellowpages.com). Supporters claim that Ruby on Rails is so simple that it is possible to develop a Web Rails application in 10% of the time that it takes to develop a PERL, PHP, or Java application.

In a service-oriented architecture (SOA), an important part of the application development framework is the Business Process Execution Language (BPEL) service engine. First, individual Web services are developed. Examples of services would be things like "charge credit card," "credit customer account," "withdraw funds from a bank account," or "produce a customer invoice." When used alone, services are like individual instruments in an orchestra. Individually, they don't make an application "symphony." They are developed according to industry standards that include WS-BPEL (Web Services Business Process Execution Language) and WSDL

(Web Services Description Language). Basically, services can be developed in any programming language and then "formatted" to conform to these standards.

The second step in the SOA development, after creating services, is stitching the services together—orchestrating them—so that they function as cohesive software applications. This stitching process is typically done using a BPEL service engine.

The BPEL service engine needs a roadmap to tell it how to orchestrate the individual services. In practice, the roadmap is a set of visual diagrams based on Unified Modeling Language (UML) and/or Business Process Modeling Notation (BPMN), a set of diagrams that contain the underlying business logic. Various visual modeling tools exist that directly work with BPEL service engines. Examples of such tools include the Visual Paradigm Suite (www.visual-paradigm.com) and the Sun (www.sun.com) BPEL designer. The Sun BPEL designer integrates directly with the Sun BPEL service engine. Another popular BPEL visual modeling tool is IBM WebSphere Business Modeler, which integrates with the IBM WebSphere BPEL service engine (www.ibm.com/websphere).

THE INTEGRATED DEVELOPMENT ENVIRONMENT   The **Integrated Development Environment (IDE)** is a software platform for actually writing program code. It provides various features to ease the task of programming, including specialized text-editors that automatically format program code as it is written, add indents as required, add different colors to different types of programming statements, and check the syntax of program commands as they are typed.

IDEs also provide specialized tools for testing and debugging programs and for deploying them to servers for testing or final release. Most of the major IDEs also support third-party plug-ins. The plug-ins permit the IDEs to support a wide range of different programming languages and environments. The result is that most major IDEs will work with the various popular Web scripting languages such as JavaScript, Java, PHP, PERL, and Ruby.

Some of the most popular IDEs are available free to use. These include NetBeans (www.netbeans.org), sponsored by Sun Microsystems, and Eclipse (www.eclipse.org), sponsored by the Eclipse open-source community. Another popular IDE is Microsoft's Visual Studio, a commercial product that is available in a collaborative team edition.

THE SOFTWARE VERSIONING SYSTEM   The **software versioning system** keeps current and historical versions of the software source code (i.e., the programs as they are written by programmers). Such version control permits programmers (and managers) to logically retain a complete updated copy of the software as often as every time it is saved by the programmer during development. This maintains a historical record and audit trail of the development. Version control also permits the software to be rolled back to an earlier version in case of a problem in the current version.

The two major software versioning systems are Subversion (SVN) and Concurrent Version System (CVS). SVN was developed by CollabNet Inc. and is released under a license that permits its use free of charge. It is now available through www.Tigris.org (subversion.tigris.org). CVS is a somewhat older system but still very popular. It is available through www.nongnu.org, a site dedicated to free software distribution and development.

Both SVN and CVS work with the major IDEs. For example, Netbeans supports plug-ins for both SVN and CVS. SVN and CVS both rely on a client–server model. The hosting environment runs the server version of the product, and the developer accesses the versioning system through a client plug-in that runs in the IDE product. There are also commercial Web 2.0 versioning platforms, such as BeanStalk (www.beanstalkapp.com), which rely on SVN. Services like BeanStalk can directly integrate with the project management platform, such as BaseCamp® (which was discussed above).

THE APPLICATION SOLUTION STACK   An **application solution stack** is a group of software components needed to deliver a workable application. The solution stack for a Web application typically includes the target operating system, the Web server, the database system, the programming language(s), and any other necessary components of the application software framework. For example, LAMP is a common Web application solution stack. LAMP is an acronym for the Linux operating system, the Apache Web server, the MySQL database management system, and the Perl, PHP, and/or Python server-side scripting languages.

The WISA stack is historically popular for Windows Applications. It includes the Windows operating system (typically the server version), Microsoft's Internet Information Services (theWeb server), Microsoft SQL server (the database system), and ASP.NET, which contains the supporting Web framework.

For a Ruby on Rails application, the Web stack might include one of several specialized Web servers that supports Ruby on Rails, such as Mongrel or Glassfish (which is tied to the Sun Microsystems Java development framework discussed earlier).

Regardless of the stack used, the database system is generally interchangeable. For example, in a Ruby on Rails application, the developer could easily switch between the MySQL and Microsoft SQL Server database. After Rails version 2, Ruby on Rails defaults to SQLite, a very simple but powerful file-oriented database published by the SQLite consortium (www.sqlite.org).

It is not uncommon for developers to develop applications with one stack optimized for ease of development and then deploy the applications using another stack, one that is optimized for deployment. For example, the target deployment system might be a cluster of 100 load-balanced servers running a distributed database system. The developer would probably use a simpler database system during development.

All-in-One and Integrated Platforms

There is a trend toward integrating IT governance, enterprise architecture, business process modeling, and management into application suites. For example, Casewise (www.casewise.com) provides a high-end set of integrated solutions targeted toward governance and development. Similarly, companies like SAP provide products like the Netweaver Developer Studio™ to facilitate development within the context of their SOA and enterprise application suites (EAS). In general, platforms such as those discussed here can work in conjunction with the above-discussed components of the development environment.

Control Over Nonfinancial Information
Systems Resources

A number of factors relating to information systems are important to management from a control point of view but are not measured in terms of dollars. These include performance measures for hardware, software, and personnel.

Measuring hardware performance involves systems utilization, systems downtime, and systems responsiveness. Measures of systems utilization typically include ratios such as server CPU time actually used to time available. Also, statistics can be derived for the individual components of the computer system, such as point-of-sale (POS) terminals, application servers, database servers, and so on. Utilization statistics are very important because they can indicate bottlenecks or needs for systems expansion. In addition, utilization statistics reported for various times of the day can assist management in planning load balancing.

In many systems, downtime is a major concern. **Downtime** is the percentage of time that the application is unavailable for use. Typically, the total number of hours in a given month that the application is not available is reported. In addition, the mean time between outages and the mean time to restore the system to working condition are also reported. Hardware downtime statistics are helpful in evaluating overall hardware effectiveness. A system that is down too much can cause a number of problems—including lost business.

A second major nonquantitative factor important to control is software performance. A very sound overall approach to evaluating software performance is to survey systems users, asking a large number of questions relating to ease of use, functionality, and user friendliness. Software performance must be monitored constantly because environmental changes can produce changes in the satisfaction of users.

Finally, it is necessary to apply controls relating to personnel. Therefore, reports need to be prepared for a large variety of factors. For example, programmers might be evaluated in terms of the quality of documentation written and the number of program lines written per day. Various other types of reports needed for evaluating personnel performance might include

- Performance reports for software technicians—These reports might include statistics such as the number of cases resolved and the time to resolve each case.
- Reports relating to the efficiency of hardware repair persons—Such reports might include statistics on the number of repair jobs and the average length of time required for each repair job, broken down by various types of repair categories.

Auditing the Information System

Most firms employ either internal or external auditors to audit the information system. The audit's focus should be on the information system itself and on the validity and accuracy of data as processed by the system. The accountants' interests in auditing the information system tend to focus on internal control. The general approach followed by the auditor is to first obtain a detailed description of the internal control system, typically using internal control questionnaires. Once a description of the internal control system has been obtained, the auditor then performs tests of compliance. During this process, the auditor ascertains the degree to which the company actually applies the internal controls as documented in the internal control evaluation. Finally, the auditor performs tests of specific transactions as they flow through the system. The amount of testing required depends on the degree to which an adequate set of internal controls exists and is in effective operation. In systems with a large number of internal controls, the auditor can rely on a statistical sampling of transactions.

Maintaining and Modifying the System

In all operational systems it becomes necessary to make changes. One reason for changes is that it is not possible to foresee all contingencies during the design phase. In addition, environmental conditions and information need change. Finally, almost any computer application contains some bugs or customization problems. **Bugs** are computer programming errors that might not be detected until the system actually begins operation.

For control purposes, it is very important that all modifications to the system's software and data schema be formally reviewed and approved. Ideally, users should have the opportunity to make requests for systems modifications. These requests should be reviewed by a committee of managers and systems specialists. On approval, they should be referred to the appropriate systems or applications programmers for implementation. Systems and applications programmers should work according to a preestablished set of priorities. In addition, these programmers should not have access to the operational copy of software being modified. Instead, programmers should apply the modifications to a copy of the original software. This software, after being modified, should be reviewed very carefully and then installed by an independent person. All modifications of the system should be carefully documented. The documentation should include the reason for changes, the exact changes made, and the person approving the changes. In addition, normal documentation standards should apply. This means that user manuals and systems programming documentation should be updated.

Summary

Critical to success in systems implementation is the need to establish a systems implementation plan. This plan should include a detailed timetable and budget showing all key activities in the implementation plan. The implementation plan must then be monitored continuously, and any discrepancies relating to the timetable or budget should be reported.

Many implementation activities are required. These include personnel training, physical preparation, detailed systems design, program testing, standards development, documentation, file conversion, and systems cutover. In addition, the implemented system must be evaluated for ongoing control purposes.

Key concepts in systems project management include establishing a project team, dividing responsibilities (and tasks), dividing the project into phases, establishing timetables, and maintaining an accounting for project costs and compliance with timetables. Collectively, these steps work to ensure that the overall development effort produces systems that are cost-effective and meet the needs of the organization.

A number of factors relating to information systems are important to management from a control point of view but are not measured in terms of dollars. These include performance measures for hardware, software, and personnel. Formal procedures should be developed for maintaining and modifying the existing system.

Glossary

application solution stack   a group of software components needed to deliver a workable application.

bug   a computer programming error that is not detected until the program is in use.

critical path   a list of activities that are critical in that if any one of them is delayed, the entire project will be delayed.

cutover point   the point in time under the direct approach to implementation where the switch to a new system is made.

direct approach   an approach to implementation that involves switching to a new system and abandoning the old system at a fixed point in time.

downtime   the percentage of time that equipment is unavailable for use.

Gantt chart   a scheduling technique that graphically depicts both the actual and the planned times for activities but does not show the relationships between various activities.

Integrated Development Environment (IDE)   a software platform for writing programming code.

ISO 15504   see SPICE.

lowballing   purposely or inadvertently submitting unreasonably low time or cost estimates to obtain a contract.

modular conversion   an approach to implementation that involves phasing in a new system in segments.

network diagram   a scheduling technique that depicts the order in which activities must be performed.

parallel operation   an approach to implementation that involves running the new and old systems simultaneously before final conversion.

project collaboration platform   a software platform that serves to optimize management of the communication chain in software development projects.

project development environment   the tools and technologies used to implement a given project.

project management   tools used to track progress and manage resources for a systems development project.

software application framework   set of software components that collectively provides a structured environment in which to develop software.

software versioning system   a software platform that keeps current and historical versions of the software source code (i.e., the programs as they are written by programmers).

SPICE   acronym for Software Process Improvement and Capability dEtermination, a process-based development approach that focuses on the "maturity" of the process being developed. A synonym for ISO 15504.

Webliography

www.ganttchart.com
This Web site has examples of Gantt charts.

www.automotivespice.com
The home page of the automotive industry SPICE. The complete SPICE model for the automotive industry is available for download.

www.ittoolkit.com
The home page of ITtoolkit.com, published by Right Track Associates Inc. The Web site contains interesting articles relating to project management. It also contains various for-sale templates and toolkits relating to project management.

www.cio.com
The home page of CIO, a Web site directed at chief information officers, published by CXO Media. It contains a wealth of articles and helpful links relating to project management. For example, entering "IT Project Management" into the search box leads to an article titled "ABC: An Introduction to IT Project Management."

The article explains that only 29% of IT projects are completed on time and on budget.

www.pmi.org
The home page of Project Management Institute (PMI), an international association, with over 250,000 members in over 170 countries, dedicated to project management professionals. PMI offers various professional certifications relating to project management. The PMI Web site contains links to various periodicals, white papers, virtual library, and to global standards relating to project management.

www.attask.com
The home page of AtTask's @task™ project management platform. The @task™ platform is a world-leading online, collaborative project management platform, used by many prominent companies, including Apple, Adobe International, Amazon.com, CBS, HBO, McDonalds, and the Walt Disney Company.

Chapter Quiz

Answers to the chapter quiz appear on page 440.

1. Which concept is the most important to systems implementation?
   a. Ashby's law of requisite variety
   b. Grosch's law
   c. project continuity
   d. project management

2. The Gantt chart shows (_____).
   a. planned activity times
   b. relationships between activities
   c. both a and b
   d. neither a nor b

3. The conversion approach that is most risky to a company's operations is (_____).
   a. the direct approach
   b. parallel operation
   c. modular conversion

4. The conversion approach that involves phasing in a new system in segments is (_____).
   a. the direct approach
   b. parallel operation
   c. modular conversion

5. The least expensive conversion approach is (_____).
   a. the direct approach
   b. parallel operation
   c. modular conversion

6. If a project activity on the (_____) is delayed, then the entire project will be delayed.
   a. Gantt path
   b. critical path
   c. cutover point
   d. flex point

7. A report specifying the events to occur in the implementation of a new system is called (_____).
   a. a conversion plan
   b. project acceptability
   c. a feasibility study
   d. information analysis

8. Time estimates should be (_____).
   a. revised occasionally over the life of a project
   b. revised frequently over the life of a project
   c. not revised at all

9. The project team leader for a systems development project should have direct responsibility to the (_____).
   a. user department
   b. information systems department
   c. steering committee
   d. project lead analysts

10. Computer programming errors that are not detected until the system actually begins operation are called (_____).
    a. nuts
    b. bugs
    c. moths
    d. crackers

11. A Web server is part of a (an) (_____).
    a. IDE
    b. database system
    c. application solution stack
    d. none of the above

12. Software project collaboration platforms focus on (_____).
    a. implementing IDEs
    b. getting bugs out of programs
    c. communications
    d. none of the above

13. Regarding the coding of Web applications, one could correctly say that (_____).
    a. server-side scripting is more popular than client-side scripting
    b. server-side scripting is less popular than client-side scripting
    c. server-side scripting and client-side scripting are equally popular
    d. none of the above

14. Which of the following is an example of client-side scripting?
    a. Java
    b. PHP
    c. Ruby
    d. none of the above

15. Which of the following is not true of versioning software?
    a. it can keep old copies of the application software.
    b. it can be used to rollback mistakes after they are made.
    c. it mainly works as stand-alone software.
    d. none of the above.

Review Questions

1. Define each of the following terms.
   a. PERT chart
   b. Gantt chart
   c. critical path
   d. parallel operation
   e. modular conversion
   f. test data
2. Identify the major steps in systems implementation.
3. Identify several key activities in systems operation. Briefly discuss the components of the systems implementation plan.
4. Why is detailed systems design work necessary during the systems implementation phase?
5. Contrast and compare the modular versus parallel operations approaches to conversion.
6. Discuss several functions of systems documentation.
7. What are some factors that should be considered when selecting a project leader?
8. What is the objective of project breakdown?
9. Identify several types of adjustments that might be made to basic time estimates in a project breakdown.
10. What is lowballing? What are some reasons that often make time estimates overly optimistic?
11. Identify the basic components of a project accounting system.
12. Do project costs always have to be charged to users? If not, why is a project accounting system necessary?

Discussion Questions and Problems

13. The productivity of programmers is typically of concern to project management. Identify some factors that may affect the productivity of a programmer. How would you measure or evaluate the productivity of programmers assigned to a project team? What means might be used to increase the productivity of programmers?
14. A specific project task has been estimated to require 100 work hours to complete. Using the adjustment factors in Figures 12.7 and 12.8, adjust this estimate to reflect the following.
    a. The complexity is judged to be quite simple.
    b. The task is assigned to a "junior" whose competency level is low.
    c. Average knowledge is available, and average knowledge is required.

Required

What is the adjusted time estimate? Are adjustments of these types worthwhile?

15. If it is estimated that five programmers can complete a task in 50 workdays, is it likely that 50 programmers can complete the same task—such as coding programs for an application system—in 5 days? Would you expect diminishing returns in the addition of labor to project tasks? Why or why not?
16. How might a project accounting system assign overhead to individual projects? Does the assignment of overhead to individual projects enhance management control?
17. The information system at Wright Company has been developed in stages over the past 5 years and has been fully operational for the last 12 months. When the system was being designed, all department heads were asked to specify the types of information and reports they would need for planning and controlling operations. The systems department attempted to meet the specifications of each department head. Company management specified that certain other reports should also be prepared for department heads. During the 5 years of systems development and operation, there have been several changes in the department head positions due to attrition and promotions. The new department heads often made requests for additional reports according to their specifications. The systems department complied with all these requests. Reports were discontinued only on request by a department head and then only if it was not a standard report required by top management. As a result, few reports were, in fact, discontinued. Consequently, the system is generating a large number of reports each reporting period.

Company management became concerned about the quantity of information that was being produced by the system. The internal audit department was asked to evaluate the effectiveness of the reports generated by the system. The audit staff determined early in the study that more information was being generated than could be used effectively. They noted the following reactions to this information overload:

i. Many department heads would not act on certain reports during periods of peak activity. The department head would let these reports accumulate with the hope of catching up during a subsequent lull.

ii. Some department heads had so many reports that they did not act at all on the information, or they made incorrect decisions because of misuse of the information.

iii. Frequently, action required by the nature of the report data was not taken until the department head was reminded by someone who needed the decision. These department heads did not appear to have developed a priority system for acting on the information produced by the data processing system.

iv. Department heads often would develop the information they needed from alternative, independent sources rather than using the reports generated by the system. This often was easier than trying to search among the reports for the needed data.

Required

a. For each of the observed reactions, indicate whether they are functional or dysfunctional behavioral responses. Explain your answer in each case.

b. Assuming that one or more of the preceding were dysfunctional, recommend procedures the company could employ to eliminate the dysfunctional behavior and to prevent its recurrence.

(CMA)

18. You are assigned to review the documentation of a data processing function.

Required

a. List three advantages of adequate documentation for a data processing function.

b. Following are two columns of information. The first column lists six categories of documentation, and the second column lists 18 elements of documentation related to the categories. Match each of the elements of documentation with the category in which it should be found. List letters *A* through *F* on your answer sheet. After each letter, list the numbers of the elements that best apply to that category. Use every element, but none more than once.

Categories

a. Systems documentation
b. Program documentation
c. Operations documentation
d. User documentation
e. Library documentation
f. Data entry documentation

Elements

1. Flowcharts showing the flow of information
2. Procedures needed to balance, reconcile, and maintain overall control
3. Storage instructions
4. Contents and format of data to be captured
5. Constants, codes, and tables
6. Verification procedures
7. Logic diagrams and/or decision tables
8. Report distribution instructions
9. Messages and programmed halts
10. Procedures for backup files
11. Retention cycle
12. Source statement listings
13. Instructions to show proper use of each transaction
14. A complete history from planning through installation
15. Restart and recovery procedures
16. Rules for handling blank spaces
17. Instructions to ensure the proper completion of all input forms
18. List of programs in a system

(IIA)

Web Research Assignments

19. AtTask's @task™ is an industry-leading collaborative project management platform.

Required

a. Visit the Web site for @task™ (www.attask.com) and write a report that details what would be required to integrate @task projects with SAP or SalesForce.com.

20. You are a newly appointed CIO for a large wholesale company. Your first major project will be installing a new inventory system, possibly using SAP.

Required

a. Write a report to your CEO explaining three major ERP projects that have failed in other companies. Give your opinion as to why they failed and what you can do to prevent a failure in your inventory project.

21. You are the controller for a mid-size manufacturing company. Your company is about to embark on a series of IT projects, and you are looking for appropriate project management software. As part of your search, you are considering Easy Projects.NET™ (www.easyprojects.net) and AtTask's @task™ (www.attask.com).

Required

a. Contrast and compare Easy Projects.NET™ (www.easyprojects.net) and @task™. Which product would you select for your company? Why?

22. Search the Web and find a complete software stack to install Ruby on Rails on a Windows computer. Write a brief report explaining your findings.

Answers to Chapter Quiz

1. d **2.** a **3.** a **4.** c **5.** a **6.** b **7.** a **8.** b **9.** c **10.** b
11. c **12.** c **13.** a **14.** d **15.** c

Data Management Concepts

Learning Objectives

Careful study of this chapter will enable you to:

- Define the basic terms used in database technology.
- Identify the three levels of database architecture.
- Compare and contrast the different logical models of databases.
- Explain the different methods of accessing files.
- Explain the benefits of database management systems.
- Describe the considerations that are appropriate to the design of databases.

Introductory Terminology

Databases

Data are stored in databases. A **database** is simply a structured collection of data stored in a computer system or network. The data in a database are manipulated and retrieved using **database software.** A database together with related database software is called a **database management system (DBMS),** or sometimes more simply, a database system.

All eBusiness software products, such as ERP and EAS, store data in databases. Further, databases are frequently connected to eBusiness software at the "back end," meaning that the DBMS is completely separate from the eBusiness software product. **Database agnostic** means that software can function with any DBMS. SAP is database agnostic. SAP works with major relational DBMSs, such as IBM's DB2, Microsoft's SQL Server, Oracle, and SAP DB, SAP's own product. Most companies have traditionally used Oracle rather than SAP DB as a back-end to their SAP installations.

 CASE IN POINT

Although the concept of databases dates back to the 1960s, the popularization of modern databases began with Edgar F. Codd publishing "A Relational Model of Data for Large Shared Data Banks" in 1970. Codd worked in IBM Research Labs, where much of the early research on databases was conducted.

Although not all eBusiness software products are database agnostic, many adhere to the principle of the DBMS being independent of the application software. This permits upgrading or modifying the eBusiness application without having to reorganize, restructure, or otherwise modify the data or database software. Database agnosticity also permits multiple applications to share the same database. Database agnosticism permits the data to be physically stored apart from the application, which facilitates a client–server, tiered-architecture environment in which multiple client users access a shared database.

Database concepts and technology are important to the design, operation, management, auditing, and security of information systems. This chapter discusses how databases are internally organized and used in practice.

Basic Database Elements: Fields, Data Items, Attributes, and Elements

The terms **field, data item, attribute,** and **element** are used interchangeably to denote the smallest block of data that will be stored and retrieved in an information system. If only some portion of the field may be needed by the users, then the field should be split into several separate data items. A field may be a single character or number, or it may be composed of many characters or numbers. Examples of fields include such items as

- Customer name
- Employee Social Security Number
- Purchase order number
- Customer account number

A field is usually logically associated with other fields; a logical grouping of fields is called a **record.** Records are groups of data items that concern a certain entity such as an employee, a customer, a vendor, and an invoice. We will denote a record structure as follows:

```
RECORD-NAME (FIELD 1, FIELD 2, ..., FIELD N)
```

RECORD-NAME is the name of the record, such as VENDOR or EMPLOYEE. The entries in parentheses are the names of individual fields in the record. The following examples explain:

```
CUSTOMER(ACCOUNT_NUMBER, NAME, ADDRESS, ACCOUNT_BALANCE)
EMPLOYEE(NAME, SSN, AGE)
PURCHASE_ORDER(PO_#, DATE, AMOUNT, VENDOR, QUANTITY, PRICE)
```

In the first example, CUSTOMER is the name of the record, and ACCOUNT_NUMBER, NAME, ADDRESS, and ACCOUNT_BALANCE are the names of the fields.

Data Occurrences

A record structure has **occurrences,** also called **instances.** A record occurrence is a specific set of data values for the record. For example, for the record

```
EMPLOYEE(NAME, NUMBER, AGE)
```

we might have the occurrence

```
EMPLOYEE(Brown, 111222333,33),
```

and an occurrence for the CUSTOMER record just described might be

```
CUSTOMER(12122, ABC Hardware, 222 West Street, $1,050)
```

Fixed- and Variable-Length Records

Records within a file may be of either fixed or variable length. In a **fixed-length record,** both the number of fields and the length (character size) of each field are fixed. Fixed-length records are easier to manipulate in computer applications than variable-length records because the size of fixed-length records is standardized. Most records stored on direct-access storage devices (DASDs) are fixed-length.

The drawback of fixed-length records is that each field must be large enough to contain the maximum expected entry into the field. This typically results in wasted space, as in leaving 25 or so spaces for a name, whereas many names have eight characters or fewer. In **variable-length records,**

FIGURE 13.1

**Variable-Length
Records**

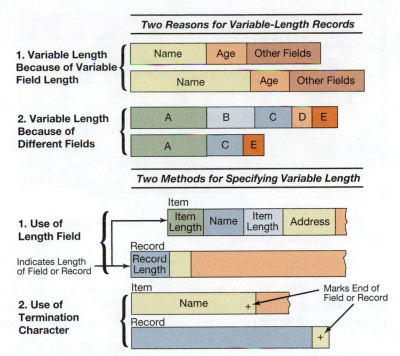

Two Reasons for Variable-Length Records

however, the width of the field can be adjusted for each data occurrence. Further, in variable-length records, the actual number of fields can vary from one data occurrence to another.

The end of a variable-length record must be indicated by a special symbol or a record-length field contained in the record itself. Variable-length records efficiently use available storage space, but manipulating such records is relatively difficult. Figure 13.1 illustrates several ways to implement variable-length records.

One approach to variable-length records that does not require programming system support for the variable-length structure is to use fixed-length trailer records. A **trailer record** is an extension of a master record. It is separate from the master record and written as required. Using an open-item accounts receivable file, for example, the master records contain information common to all accounts and the number of invoices sufficient for most of the accounts, whereas the trailer record contains more invoices. A master record may have as many trailer records associated with it as required. The trailer records may be written immediately after the associated master record.

Consider a hypothetical manufacturing company, Ace Tools, that maintains a raw materials inventory of hundreds of machine parts. Further, assume that Ace Tools purchases each part from one of several suppliers and then stores it in one of several warehouses. Any part can be purchased from any one or more of the suppliers and then stored in any one or more of the warehouses. The following data fields pertain to the parts inventory:

PART_NO	the part number
PNAME	the part name
TYPE	the type of part
COST	the standard cost per unit of the part
PVEND	the name of the vendor (supplier) from whom the part is purchased
WARHSE	the warehouse where the part is stored
LOC	the last two digits of the ZIP code of the warehouse where the part is stored

FIGURE 13.2

Repeated Groups as Part of Variable-Length Records

Variable-Length Record		
RECORD NAME	SUPPLIER (Repeated group 1)	LOCATION (Repeated group 2)
PART (PART_NO, PNAME, TYPE, COST,	PVEND # 01, PVEND # 02, PVEND # 03, PVEND # 04, • • • PVEND # 99,	WARHSE # 01, LOC # 01, WARHSE # 02, LOC # 02, WARHSE # 03, LOC # 03, WARHSE # 03, LOC # 03, • • • • • • WARHSE # 99, LOC # 99)

Note that it is not possible, in general, to store all information about a particular part in the following fixed-length record:

        PART(PART_NO, PNAME, TYPE, COST, PVEND, WARHSE, LOC)

This is not possible, for example, because there may be more than one supplier for each part and because the record has room for only one supplier. The two-supplier case would require the following record format (assuming that there is only one storage location):

        PART(PART_NO, PNAME, TYPE, COST, PVEND#1, WARHSE#1, LOC#1, PVEND#2,
        WARHSE#2, LOC#2)

where the suffix #1 applies to the part supplied by vendor number 1 and suffix #2 to the part supplied by vendor number 2. The record would need to be even longer if there were three suppliers, and in general, its length would depend on the number of vendors and storage locations associated with a given part. Therefore, such a record would be a variable-length record.

Note that the variable record length arises because both the supplier (PVEND) and the storage locations (WARHSE and LOC) can occur more than once per record. That is, they are repeating (or repeated) groups of fields. (WARHSE and LOC are grouped together because they both relate to the storage location.) **Repeated groups** are related groups of fields that repeat themselves in variable-length records. This is shown in Figure 13.2. The second column shows the SUPPLIER group, and the third column shows the LOCATION group. Both these repeating groups belong to PART. This relationship is depicted in Figure 13.3 in a diagram that looks like a family tree. PART is shown to be the **parent** of SUPPLIER and LOCATION because each instance of PART may give rise to more than one supplier or location. In general, the highest-level element in a tree diagram is the parent; lower-level elements in the tree diagram that are connected to (i.e., part of) the parent are called **children.**

PART itself might have a parent. For example, PART might be one of many children belonging to INVENTORY, with the other children being such things as SUPPLIES and EQUIPMENT. For this reason, we shall refer to all the nodes in the tree, including PART, as *repeated groups*. In some cases, we shall simply refer to them as **segments** or groups, or even **nodes.** Thus the terms *segment, group,* and *node* are shorthand for *repeated groups.* As we shall see in a later section of this chapter, segments are one of the fundamental building blocks used to construct databases.

FIGURE 13.3

Tree Diagram for PART, SUPPLIER, and LOCATION

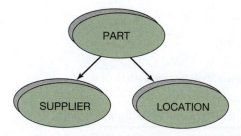

Segments can be summarized in the same shorthand that is used for records. For example, PART, SUPPLIER, and LOCATION can be written as follows:

```
PART (PART_NO, PNAME, TYPE, COST)
SUPPLIER (PVEND)
LOCATION (WARHSE, LOC)
```

Thus a record and a segment are in essence the same thing. Both are a collection of fields. In fact, there is nothing wrong with thinking of segments as records as long as it is remembered that segments, unlike simple records, have parents and children.

Record Key and File Sequence

A **key** or **record key** is a data item or combination of data items that uniquely identifies a particular record in a file. Consider a file containing records in the format

```
PART(PART_NO, WARHSE)
```

where PART_NO is the part number of the part, and WARHSE is the warehouse number associated with its location. Further, assume that the file contains the following four records:

```
PART(101,1)
PART(102,2)
PART(103,1)
PART(106,1)
```

In this example, PART_NO is an acceptable key because it can be used to uniquely identify any one of the four records. This is not true, however, for WARHSE. For example, specifying a value of 1 for WARHSE does not uniquely identify one particular record; rather, it identifies three records, the first, third, and fourth ones.

In some cases, it might be necessary to combine two fields to produce a key. Assume, for example, that one part can be stored in two warehouses. This would produce records such as

```
PART(101,2)
PART(101,1)
PART(102,1)
PART(103,1)
PART(103,2)
```

In this case, neither PART_NO nor WARHSE would in general uniquely identify an individual record. But both fields together would. Thus, combining the two fields into a single key would permit unique identification. For example, appending the value of WARHSE onto the value of PART_NO would work, giving key values of 1012, 1011, 1021, 1031, and 1032 for each of the five records, respectively.

It is sometimes useful to sort the records in a file so that they are either in ascending or in descending order, relative to the key. The four records in the first example are in ascending order by PART_NO. The five records in the second example could be ordered by the PART_NO + WARHSE key to produce the following:

```
PART(101,1)
PART(101,2)
PART(102,1)
PART(103,1)
PART(103,2)
```

In such cases, the first field (PART_NO) is called the **primary sort key** (or simply the **primary key**), and the second field (WARHSE) is called **secondary sort key** (or simply **secondary key**). Any additional fields required to uniquely identify and sort the records would be called **tertiary sort keys.** Therefore, a primary key is a field used to sort the records in a file, and a secondary key is used to determine relative position among a set of records when the primary key has the same value in each record of the set. In terms of the preceding example with five records, this means that when two records have the same value for PART_NO, the record with the smallest value for WARHSE will come first. In other words, the secondary key determines the order for records whose primary key values are all the same.

We shall denote key fields by underlining them. For example, VENDOR is a key field in the following record:

    PART(PART_NO, WARHSE, <u>VENDOR</u>)

The term **relative random order** applies to a field on which the file is not sorted. Before sorting the preceding five records, the file is in random order relative to the WARHSE field. In the first record, WARHSE = 2; in the second record, WARHSE = 1; and in the fifth record, WARHSE = 2. Therefore, the file is not ordered by WARHSE.

Keys are important because they are necessary to process and locate records in files. These topics are discussed below.

Database Management Systems and Their Architecture

As depicted in Figure 13.4, there are three levels of architecture relevant to databases and DBMS: the *conceptual level of architecture*, the *logical level of architecture*, and the *physical level of architecture*. At the conceptual level, databases are collections of various elements of information to be used for assorted purposes. Consider, for example, a sales-order database. Such a database might be defined at the conceptual level in terms of the kinds of information it includes (e.g., sales transactions, cash receipts, and customer information) and the purposes for which it is to be used (e.g., order entry and customer billing).

In order to implement a database defined at the conceptual level, specific data fields and records must be defined. It is also necessary to specify ways in which data records and fields will be viewed or reported, as well as related to each other. For example, it might be desirable to display the customer's account history with his or her open orders. This requires that the records and fields in the database be structured and organized in some logical manner, thus giving rise to **logical data structures.** Three basic types of logical data structures can be used to accomplish this objective: *hierarchical, network*, and *relational*. Each of these data structures is discussed below.

The physical level of database architecture deals with specific implementation techniques and issues relating to methods for accessing data. The three most important data access methods (sequential, indexed sequential, and direct) are discussed in detail below.

Conceptual Architecture

There is no one standard approach for developing a conceptual data model of a particular system. The **entity-relationship (E-R) data model** is one popular approach. The E-R model simply depicts the relationships between segments. In the E-R model, however, the term *entity* is used

FIGURE 13.4

Database Architecture

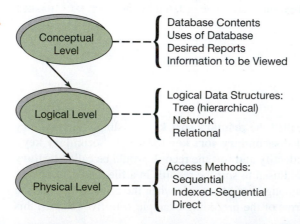

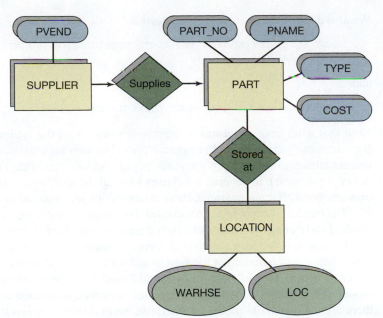

FIGURE 13.5

Entity-Relationship
Diagram for PART,
SUPPLIER, and
LOCATION

instead of segment, and the term *attribute* is used to refer to individual fields or data items. Graphically speaking, the E-R model uses square boxes for entities, ellipses for attributes, and diamond-shaped boxes for depicting relationships. Figure 13.5 shows an E-R diagram for the segments relating to the example record PART described previously. Note that two relationships are used: one indicating the relationship between the supplier and the part and the other indicating the relationship between the part and its storage location.

⬤ **CASE IN POINT**

Tools for creating E-R diagrams are quite common. For example, Microsoft Visio (www.microsoft. com) can produce E-R and many other types of diagrams. Further, products such as Embaradero Technologies' ER/Studio (www.embarcadero.com) provide predesigned E-R models (software templates) for a wide range of subject areas such as accounting and budgeting, human resources, and invoicing and billing.

Other conceptual methods exist, including the **object-oriented modeling technique (OMT),** originally developed for object-oriented programming and adapted for data modeling by Blaha, Premerlani, and Rumbaugh. This works by viewing the components of the system being modeled as object classes. In this method, an **object class** corresponds to a table or segment, and an **object** corresponds to a particular instance or data record. Like the E-R model, the OMT defines relationships between segments. The most fundamental of these relationships is called **inheritance.** An inheritance relationship is created when an object class is divided into subclasses. For example, a general or parent class might be plant equipment, which might have subclasses such as hand tools, heavy machinery, and repair equipment. The important thing is that the attributes of the general plant-equipment class are all inherited by each subclass. To further elaborate, we will define an object class as follows:

```
PLANT_EQUIPMENT(ACCOUNT_NO, COST, DEPRECIATION)
```

We also define the following two subclasses:

```
HEAVY_EQUIPMENT(ACCOUNT_NO, COST, DEPRECIATION, MAINTENANCE_FREQ,
DATE_PURCHASED)
```

and

```
HAND_TOOLS(ACCOUNT_NO, COST, DEPRECIATION, USAGE)
```

Note that `HAND_TOOLS` and `HEAVY_EQUIPMENT` inherit all the attributes of `PLANT_EQUIPMENT` (i.e., `ACCOUNT_NO`, `COST`, and `DEPRECIATION`). The two subclasses, however, have their own unique attributes (i.e., `USAGE` for `HAND_TOOLS` and `MAINTENANCE_FREQ`, `DATE_PURCHASED` for `HEAVY_EQUIPMENT`). In general, subclasses have all the attributes of their parent class plus their own attributes. For our example, these relationships are depicted in Figure 13.6.

The subclasses might be further divided. For example, `HEAVY_EQUIPMENT` might be divided into grinding and cutting equipment, with both these subclasses having their own unique attributes.

In summary, there are a number of ways to conceptually model a system. All methods seek to gain a better understanding of the system and document what is learned. Ideally, one would like to derive a logical model from the conceptual model and then a physical model from the logical model. All conceptual modeling techniques, however, share two common weaknesses. First, there are many ways to model an enterprise, so evaluating the results of a particular technique may be difficult. Second, there is a risk that the application of a particular technique might result in an incomplete picture of the system being modeled. The E-R model, however, can also lead directly to an implementable database. In fact, commercial software is available that takes the analyst's E-R model and automatically generates a working database system.

The OMT is perhaps the most promising modeling technique, at least in theory. It can be used with additional relationships besides inheritance (such as aggregation and association). Further, it can be implemented in successive levels of detail, leading directly to an implementable database.

Database Architecture at the Logical Level: Logical Data Structures

The major task an analyst faces in designing a database is to identify and design systematic relationships between its segments. The database must be structured so that it is able to provide users with the information they need to make effective decisions. The relationships that exist between the segments in the database are determined by the logical data structure, also called the **schema** or **database model.**

Three major models of logical data structures appear in the literature: (1) tree or hierarchical models, (2) network models, and (3) relational models. Some authorities define as many as eight additional models, but the ones discussed below are of special importance to practice.

TREE OR HIERARCHICAL STRUCTURES   Tree structures are a direct representation of the segmenting process described earlier. In a **tree structure,** each node represents a set of fields (i.e., a segment),

FIGURE 13.6

Example of Object-Oriented Data Modeling Technique

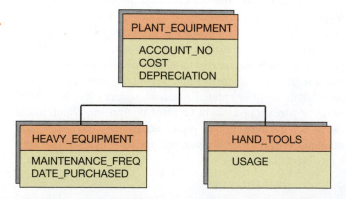

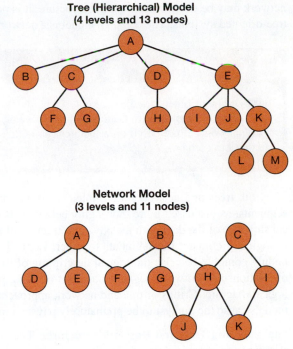

FIGURE 13.7

Tree and Network Models

and a node is related to another node at the next highest level of the tree. The latter is called the parent node. Every parent may have one or more children, and the connection between the children and parents is called a **branch.** The significant feature of the tree model is that a child node cannot have more than one parent. The tree model corresponds to the data structures supported by COBOL and other widely used programming languages and has been implemented in many commercial DBMSs such as Information Management System (IMS) and IDMS. Figure 13.3 is a simple example of a tree structure, and Figure 13.7 depicts both tree and network structures in general.

NETWORK STRUCTURES   A **network structure** is one that allows a child segment to have more than one parent. A network, therefore, is a more general data structure than a tree. As Figure 13.8 shows, any network structure can be transformed to one or more tree structures by introducing a redundancy of nodes. Some DBMSs do not directly support network structures, but because any

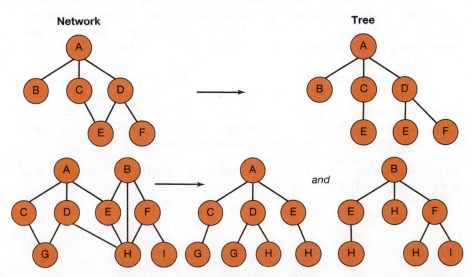

FIGURE 13.8

Transformation of Networks into Trees

network may be transformed to a tree structure, it is possible to implement network structures in tree-oriented systems. The CODASYL model is a network model.

CASE IN POINT

IBM's IMS was one of the first commercial dbmss. IBM first designed IMS beginning 1966 as part of a joint project with Caterpillar and Rockwell, for the Apollo space program. IMS was originally developed based on a hierarchical model. The product is still available to this day (www.ibm.com/ims).

Both trees and networks are implemented with embedded pointer fields, which cross-link segments, as discussed more thoroughly below. This creates a subtle intermingling of the logical structure of the data with the physical structure of pointers and chaining mechanisms needed to logically connect the segments together. Logical tree and network structures may become unduly complex because the logical description of the data tries to represent a complicated set of relationships between segments as a set of lines, physically representing the pointers in the logical diagram. Critics of tree and network approaches to database design have held that these models cause the analyst to be prematurely physical in database design.

Implementing Tree and Network Structures The topic of implementing tree and network structures is more a part of the physical architecture of databases than it is of the logical architecture. Still, we discuss physical implementation here because, as discussed earlier, it is intertwined with the logical structures of the tree and network models.

There are various ways to implement tree and network structures. These include using lists and pointers. In a list organization, each record contains one or more pointers (fields) indicating the address of the next logical record with the same attribute(s). An invoice record may contain a field that contains (points to) the key of another invoice from the same vendor. A record may be part of several lists. This list is called **multilist organization.** A customer record, for example, may contain pointers for geographic location and customer type (industrial, etc.). By including a pointer in a record to point to the next logical record, the logical and physical structure can be completely different. Figure 13.9 illustrates a simple **list structure** and a **ring structure.** A ring structure differs from a list in that the last record in the ring list points back to the first record. In addition, all records in a ring may point backward as well as forward through the use and maintenance of additional pointer fields. In a **multiple-ring structure,** several rings pass through individual records.

Designing and maintaining such structures are complicated, and pointers require additional disk space. Further, updating pointers is necessary every time a record is added or deleted. Nevertheless, using pointers in conjunction with hierarchical and tree structures is often a useful approach to data modeling, especially in cases when records are seldom added or deleted.

Hypertext systems are pointer-based systems that allow users to browse through databases in random fashion by selecting key words or objects. *Semantic data networks* are similar to hypertext systems. The only difference between the two is that in semantic networks the cross-linking of records is limited to text, whereas in hypertext systems the cross-linking can include multimedia objects such as photographs and other graphic forms.

RELATIONAL DATA STRUCTURES The **relational model** views the database as a collection of two-dimensional tables rather than a hierarchical or network type of structure. Recall the variable-length PART record used in the discussion on segments:

```
PART(PART_NO, PNAME, TYPE, COST, PVEND#1, WARHSE#1, LOC#1,
                               PVEND#2, WARHSE#2, LOC#2
                    ..         ..         ..
                             PVEND#n, WARHSE#n, LOC#n)
```

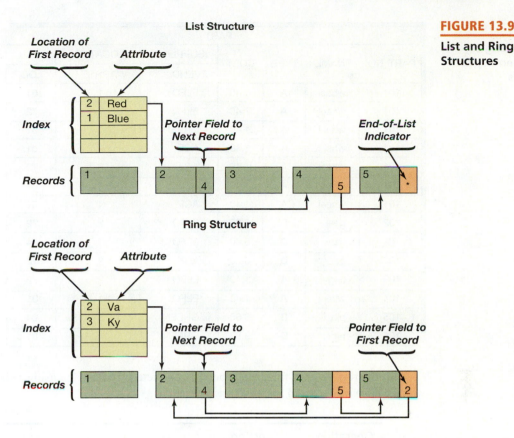

FIGURE 13.9

List and Ring Structures

This record can be segmented as follows:

```
PART (PART_NO, PNAME, TYPE, COST)
SUPPLIER (PART_NO, PVEND)
LOCATION (PART_NO, WARHSE, LOC)
```

Note that unlike in the preceding example, we now assume that PART_NO, PVEND, and WARHSE are key fields. We also have added PART_NO to the SUPPLIER and LOCATION segments so that it is possible to identify the supplier and the storage location for each product.

 CASE IN POINT

> When Edgar F. Codd invented the relational model in 1970, IBM originally resisted implementing his ideas in order to protect sales of its IMS product, which was based on a hierarchical model.

Data (instances) for each of these three segments can be stored in a table, as shown in Figure 13.10. This is the essence of the relational model—representing segments in tables. The advantage of this logical data structure over trees and networks is immediately obvious: There are no complicated pointers or lists. Further, any information that can be extracted from a tree or network structure also can be extracted from relational tables. For these reasons, the relational model is the most popular data structure in today's business environment. However, despite its popularity, it is less efficient than trees and networks when the database is seldom updated and the relationships between nodes can be reasonably defined.

FIGURE 13.10

Partial Listing of
Parts Inventory for
Ace Tools

PART						
PART_NO	PNAME	TYPE	COST	(SUPPLIER) PVEND	(LOCATION) WARHSE	LOC
101	wheel	A	1.40	ELFO	1	01
101	wheel	A	1.40	ELFO	2	72
101	wheel	A	1.40	GREEN	1	01
101	wheel	A	1.40	ACE	1	01
101	wheel	A	1.40	ACE	2	72
101	wheel	A	1.40	ACE	3	64
101	wheel	A	1.40	ACE	4	81
102	gear	D	6.60	ELFO	2	72
102	gear	D	6.60	ELFO	3	64
102	gear	D	6.60	ACE	2	72
103	cog	A	1.40	ELFO	2	72
104	wire	A	1.40	ELFO	1	01
105	pin	D	6.60	GREEN	3	64
105	pin	D	6.60	GREEN	4	81

Information (e.g., a financial report) is extracted from tables using **relational algebra,** which can be summarized as three basic operations:

Operation	Function
Selection	Creates a new table from selected rows of existing tables. The rows are selected on the basis of their data values.
Join	Creates a new table from the rows of two existing tables. The rows are selected on the basis of their data values.
Projection	Creates a new table by deleting columns from an existing table.

Other operations also exist, but they are not discussed here because Selection, Join, and Projection represent the essence of the relational algebra. Using these three basic operations, it is possible to create a new table that contains any single occurrence of a data element or combinations of data elements.

Certain rules called **normal forms** govern the creation of tables. The process of applying these rules is called **normalization.** Tables that satisfy these rules are said to be *normalized.* Tables that do not satisfy these rules are *unnormalized.* Normalization is important because without it, updating the entries in the tables can cause problems. We will show this with an example.

Normalization is simply the process of converting the record structure from a tree or network format into the appropriate tables. This is not a difficult process because it is always possible to collapse a tree diagram into a single table, as is demonstrated for PART in Figure 13.11. This table is completely unnormalized, so it will serve as a good example of why normalization is necessary.

Note that part number 101 (as well as its name and cost) appears in each of the first seven rows in Figure 13.10. This is unnecessary duplication that not only wastes storage space but also makes it possible for the same part to have two different names in different rows. Thus a primary purpose of normalization is to eliminate unnecessary duplication.

PART			
PART_NO	PNAME	TYPE	COST
101	wheel	A	1.40
102	gear	D	6.60
103	cog	A	1.40
104	wire	A	1.40
105	pin	D	6.60

SUPPLIER	
PROD_NO	PVEND
101	ELFO
101	GREEN
101	ACE
102	ELFO
102	ACE
103	ELFO
104	ELFO
105	GREEN

LOCATION		
PROD_NO	WARHSE	LOC
101	1	01
101	2	72
101	3	64
101	4	81
102	2	72
102	3	64
103	2	72
104	1	01
105	3	64
105	4	81

FIGURE 13.11

PART, SUPPLIER, and LOCATION Depicted as Relational Tables

The first step in normalization is to create a separate table for each repeating group. This is accomplished in Figure 13.11. Tables without repeating groups are said to be in **first normal form.** In the first normal form, no repeated groups (variable-length records) are allowed. There are also second and third normal forms, which can be obtained by eliminating redundancies from the tables in first normal form. The first of these additional redundancies can be seen in the LOCATION table. Note that LOC is always 01 when WARHSE is 1, 72 when WARHSE is 2, 64 when WARHSE is 3, and 81 when WARHSE is 4. It is therefore true that the value of WARHSE strictly determines the value of LOC. The value of LOC is therefore redundant. Again, as was the case with the first normal form, the redundancy not only wastes space but also makes it possible for the same warehouse (WARHSE) to have two different ZIP codes in two different rows. This problem occurs because the value of a key field (WARHSE) strictly determines the value of a nonkey field (LOC). In the **second normal form,** no key is allowed to determine the values of a nonkey field. The LOCATION table can be put in second normal form by dividing it into two tables, putting LOC in its own table away from PROD_NO:

```
LOCATION (PROD_NO, WARHSE)
WAREHOUSE (WARHSE, LOC)
```

In the **third normal form,** no nonkey field can determine the values on another nonkey field. This form is violated in the PART table. Both TYPE and COST are nonkey fields, and TYPE strictly determines COST. Again, this problem can be solved by splitting the table:

```
PART (PROD_NO, PNAME, TYPE)
COSTS (TYPE, COST)
```

In summary, the three normal forms are as follows:

Normal Form	Rule
First normal form	Divide tables to eliminate repeated groups.
Second normal form	Divide tables so that no key determines the values of a nonkey field.
Third normal form	Divide tables so that no nonkey field determines the values of another nonkey field.

Finally, we note that in the terminology of relational databases, the term **relation** is synonymous with *table*, and **tuple** refers to a row in a table.

Database Architecture: The Physical Level

In discussing the physical level of database architecture, we will focus on the three file-access methods: sequential, indexed, and direct. DASDs are capable of supporting all these methods, and the choice of the best one will depend on the particular application.

SEQUENTIALLY ACCESSED FILES   In a **sequential-access file,** records can only be accessed in their predefined sequence. For example, if there are 100 records in a file, one must access the first 99 records before accessing the last record. The predefined sequence is normally a result of the records having been sorted on some record key. For example, instances of the record PART (PROD_NO, PNAME) would be sorted by PART_NO, and the record for part number 101 would appear in the file before the record for part number 102. In general, however, the sorting can be in either ascending or descending order.

Sequential file organization is not a useful means of storing data when only a small number of records need to be accessed in a file containing a large number of records. For example, accessing the last record in a file containing 1 million records would require 999,999 records to be accessed before reaching the 1-millionth record. This would produce an intolerable delay (perhaps several minutes) on a disk storage unit.

 CASE IN POINT

A flat file database is typically a plain-text file with one record per line. A primary example of a flat file database is a CSV (comma separated value) file. CSV files separate individual data items with commas (e.g., "Jane Doe," "201-555-5555," "Washington DC."). Flat file databases systems are normally too inefficient and slow to be of use in most large applications. Berkley DB (BDB) is probably the most well-known flat file database system.

Sequential files are useful in batch processing, which normally accesses all the records in a file. The usual procedure is to first sort both the transaction and master files on the same key. A typical application might be updating customers' accounts receivable (in the master file) to reflect payments received (in the transaction file). First, the program sorts both files in ascending order by account number. Next, the program reads one record from each file. If the account numbers on these two records match each other, then the information on the payment record is used to update the balance field on the accounts receivable record. The updated account record is then written to a new master file. This procedure continues according to the logic in Figure 13.12 until all records in both files are processed.

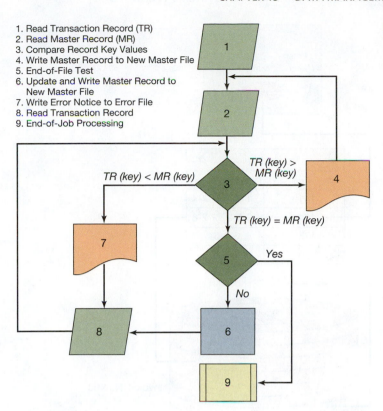

1. Read Transaction Record (TR)
2. Read Master Record (MR)
3. Compare Record Key Values
4. Write Master Record to New Master File
5. End-of-File Test
6. Update and Write Master Record to New Master File
7. Write Error Notice to Error File
8. Read Transaction Record
9. End-of-Job Processing

FIGURE 13.12

Sequential File Processing Logic

A careful study of Figure 13.12 will reveal that this sequential updating procedure will not work unless the files are sorted. For example, if the record in the transaction file with the highest key value is placed at the beginning of this file (instead of at the end, where it belongs if the file is sorted in ascending order), then the program will find and update the matching record at the end of the master file and then immediately terminate processing. In other words, the program will process only one transaction and quit. This happens because the program makes only one pass through each file and must go all the way to the end of the master file to find the record matching the first record in the transaction file. After that, there are no records left in the master file to process.

In conclusion, sequential file organization is useful when batch processing is required. Batch processing normally involves sorting and processing all the records in both the transaction and master files. In cases where only a small proportion of the records need to be accessed, one of the other file-access methods discussed below is more efficient.

INDEXED FILES   Any attribute can be extracted from the records in a primary file and used to build a new file whose purpose is to provide an index to the original file. Such a file is called an **indexed file** or an **inverted file.** For example, assume that a customer invoice file exists with the record format

    CUSTOMER(ACCOUNT_NO, INVOICE_NO)

and the following instances followed by their disk addresses:

Record	Record's Address on the Disk (Cylinder #–Surface #–Record #)
CUSTOMER(141, 901)	1-2-1
CUSTOMER(164, 902)	9-5-2
CUSTOMER(175, 903)	6-1-6
CUSTOMER(141, 904)	7-4-4
CUSTOMER(182, 905)	2-3-7
CUSTOMER(164, 906)	2-2-8

FIGURE 13.13

**Example of Using a
File Index**

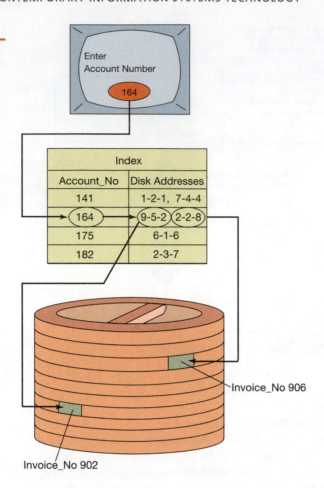

An index for ACCOUNT_NO is given in Figure 13.13. In this example, the account number, 164, is typed into the computer, located in the index along with two related disk addresses, 9-5-2 pointing to invoice number 902 and 2-2-8 pointing to invoice number 906.

This example shows that using the index to locate records on the disk is a two-step process. In the first step, the index is searched for the specified value of an attribute, and the desired disk addresses are retrieved. In the second step, the disk addresses are used to directly retrieve the desired records. This process can be considerably faster than sequentially searching every record in the file, especially when the entire index can be loaded into primary memory before it is searched, for searching in primary memory is fast relative to searching on a disk. Still, if the index is very long and will not fit into primary memory, it may take an undue length of time to complete the search. This problem can be solved by factoring a long index into subindexes, but even this technique is impractical if the file is large enough.

Of course, it is possible to have more than one index for a given file. A file is said to be **fully inverted** when indexes exist for all its fields. The processing time required to maintain a fully inverted file can be high because the indexes must be updated whenever records are added, deleted, or modified. Further, each index requires additional disk storage, and the indexes can end up requiring more storage space than the data file itself.

Indexed-Sequential Files One important type of indexed file is an indexed-sequential file. An **indexed-sequential file** is a sequential file that is stored on a DASD and is both indexed and physically sorted on the same field. Such files are commonly referred to as **ISAM** files, with ISAM being an acronym for *indexed-sequential access method*. ISAM is a powerful compromise between sequential and direct-access (discussed below) file organizations, providing the capabilities of both at a reasonable increase in cost.

Both the twin objectives of file usage—processing and inquiry—are addressed by ISAM organization. The processing of a batch of records may be done sequentially, whereas individual inquiries to the file may be handled using the index. The more detailed the index, the quicker is the access; the trade-off occurs in maintaining the index. Consider first a main file in sequence and an index (list of keys and record locations) to that file. If every record key is represented in the index (not normally necessary), then each time a main file record is added or deleted, the index must be changed. If, as is more likely, only every *n*th record or the first or last record in a major memory subdivision is represented in the index, then the index need not be changed so often, but it is always necessary to check to see whether this is the case. Most database programs automatically update the indexes as changes are made to the data file.

Structure of an ISAM File An ISAM file structurally consists of three distinct areas: the index, the prime area, and the overflow area. The index is a map that relates the key fields of records to their corresponding addresses in the prime area. Each entry in the index gives the range of key fields on a particular track of the disk on which the file is stored. By searching the index, a program can locate the track containing the desired record. Although the track must then be searched sequentially, this search is very rapid.

Figure 13.14 illustrates the process by which a computer would locate a file record whose key is 1002. The computer reads the first record in the master index, which refers to records with key values between 0001 and 0500. Since 1002 is greater than 0500, the computer looks at the next index record, but this refers to file records with key numbers between 0501 and 1000. Then the machine checks the next master index record, which contains information about file record keys 1001–1500 and therefore includes 1002, the record key for which it is searching. The computer reads in the index that the next level of the index associated with this record is on track 0300. The computer goes to track 0300 and starts to read the records on that track. The first record indicates that it has information pertaining to records 1001–1005. Since 1002 is within this range, the computer notes that the record being sought is on track 0301 in the prime area.

FIGURE 13.14

Structure of an ISAM File

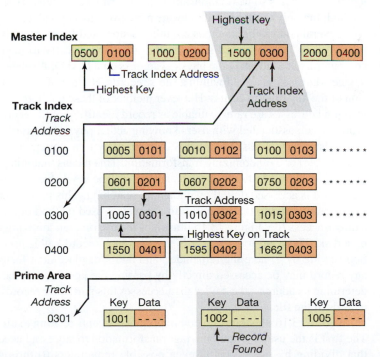

The computer goes to track 0301, searches sequentially until it finds record 1002, and retrieves the record called for. All this takes place in a fraction of a second.

The *prime area* is the portion of the disk on which the actual records are written. The *overflow area* is a separate section of the disk that is allocated to the file to allow additions to be made without extensive processing of the initial file. The overflow area is originally empty. When a new record is to be added to the file, it must be placed in its correct position in the prime area to maintain the sequential organization of the file. Existing records in the prime area must be bumped to make room for the new record. If space is available on the track where the record must be inserted, the record is inserted in position, and the other records on the track are moved. Space may be available for the new record because some empty prime space was left originally in the file to facilitate additions or because prime space was made available by the deletion of one or more records. At times, however, the addition of a new record will bump an existing record off the track being updated. In this case, the bumped record is moved to the overflow area. Although records in the overflow area are not physically in key sequence, they can be accessed in key sequence by using the index. As before, the index is used to identify the track on which the record should be located. If the record is not found on the track referenced in the index, the overflow area is automatically checked sequentially until the record is found. Overflow lengthens the time needed to process an ISAM file; accordingly, an ISAM file should be reorganized periodically to make access more efficient. Reorganization consists of merging all the records so that the file is once again in physical sequential order in the prime area.

The index may be factored into a hierarchical set of master and subindexes—usually a cylinder index and a track index—to facilitate retrieval. This is shown in Figure 13.14. At times, a single-level index will be sufficient. Record key fields are listed sequentially in the index. In an ISAM file, it is not normally possible for the record key field (e.g., account number or vendor number) to also serve as the address. The index links the record key to the address.

DIRECTLY ACCESSED FILES   **Direct-access files** allow individual records to be retrieved almost instantly without the use of an index. This is accomplished by assigning each record to a storage location that bears some relationship to the record's key values. Therefore, with the direct-access method, the only thing needed to locate a record is its key value.

Several addressing methods are used to store and locate records in a direct-access file. One method is to have a record's key field correspond directly to the coding scheme used by the computer itself to identify the physical address on a DASD. A related method is to store physical device addresses as a field within a file's records. Neither of these methods requires any conversion of the key prior to access. However, neither of these methods is used widely because storage location addresses are rarely suitable as record identifiers, and security and systems management problems are associated with users knowing actual physical storage locations.

Most direct-access file systems convert a key to a storage location address using either an index (table) or a randomizing transformation. This means that it is possible to access any record on the disk almost instantly given its key value. The key value is converted to a disk address, and the record is accessed directly without any searching. This process is depicted in Figure 13.15.

A **randomizing transformation** is a widely used method of storing and locating records in a direct-access file. Figure 13.16 illustrates the use of a randomizing transformation to load a file on a disk. There are four records in the file; each record key is used in a mathematical calculation (divide by 7, note the remainder, and add a displacement factor). Once the file is loaded, any record may be accessed directly by passing the key through the randomizing calculation to determine its address; the device then accesses this particular record directly, bypassing all other records in the file.

Figure 13.16 illustrates several important concepts relating to direct-access file organization. The first is the use of a randomizing transformation to store and access individual records. Note that dividing by seven yields seven possible remainders (0 through 6); dividing by a prime

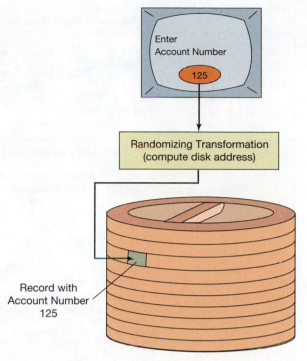

FIGURE 13.15

Example of Using the Direct-Access Method

number yields remainders that should tend to be uniformly and randomly distributed (thus the term **random access** is often used synonymously with *direct access*). In addition, it is very likely that several different records will randomize (*hash*) to the same physical address. Both these points are significant. The first point means that the storage space required for the file is largely determined by the range of the transformation results (0–7 in the example), even if the file is expected to be smaller than the range of the transformation. The second point is called *overflow* and means that some method of storing and retrieving overflow must be built into the system. In Figure 13.16, two records are hashed to the same address, requiring that one of them be stored in a different location. Overflow occurs when two or more records (called *synonyms*) yield the same address; in such cases, a special pointer field is used to indicate the addresses of the locations used to store overflow records. Note that overflow considerations require storage space in addition to that required by the randomizing transformation. The overall result is that storage efficiency typically is not high in direct-access files.

The drawbacks of vacant storage and overflow considerations typically are more than offset by the advantages of direct-access file organization. Direct access permits nonsequential updating—there is no need to sort and batch transactions. In fact, in a straight direct-access file update, nothing would be gained by batching and sorting transactions. Another major advantage of direct-access files is the speed of access to individual records. Records are accessed almost instantly. Often such speed is essential—as in an airline reservation system or a stock market quotation system. In addition, direct-access organization permits simultaneous updating of several related files. A sale affects both inventory and receivable files. If the inventory and receivable files are direct access, both may be updated in a single pass of an invoice by noting both inventory number and customer number, using each key to directly access and update the respective records. If both files were sequential, separate passes (and separate sorts) would be needed to accomplish this same task.

There is, however, a major limitation of the direct-access method. A record cannot be located if its key is not known. For example, it would not be possible to conveniently locate all sales transactions for product X with amounts greater than $1,000 because there is no common key to identify such transactions.

FIGURE 13.16

Use of a Direct-Access File

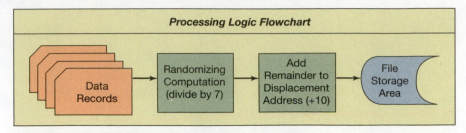

Processing Logic Flowchart

Data Records → Randomizing Computation (divide by 7) → Add Remainder to Displacement Address (+10) → File Storage Area

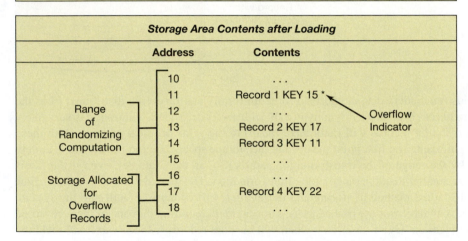

File Loading Illustration

Record	Key	Remainder after Division by Seven	+	Displacement Factor (Initial Address of File Area)	=	Record Storage Address	
1	15	1		10		11	*
2	17	3		10		13	Overflow
3	11	4		10		14	
4	22	1		10		11	*

Storage Area Contents after Loading

Address	Contents
10	. . .
11	Record 1 KEY 15 * → Overflow Indicator
12	. . .
13	Record 2 KEY 17
14	Record 3 KEY 11
15	. . .
16	. . .
17	Record 4 KEY 22
18	. . .

Range of Randomizing Computation (addresses 10–15)

Storage Allocated for Overflow Records (addresses 16–18)

Economic Relations between File Organization Techniques

The file-access techniques just discussed (sequential, indexed, and direct access) are appropriate in different circumstances. Figure 13.17 summarizes when to use each file organization technique. The basic economics of file processing are largely determined by the **activity ratio** (the number of accessed records divided by the number of records in the file) and the desired response time for processing and inquiries.

Figure 13.18 compares the average cost per transaction processed for these three techniques over a range of activity ratios. Sequential organization is a fixed-cost approach to file processing, as contrasted with direct-access organization, which is a variable-cost approach. In direct access, each record processed costs about the same amount, regardless of the number of records processed. For high activity, this is expensive relative to sequential processing. In sequential processing, the total costs are largely fixed (loading and passing the entire file); since these costs are spread over more and more transactions, the cost per transaction decreases rapidly. ISAM offers a middle ground: For low activity, records may be accessed through the index; for high activity, the index is ignored, and the file is processed sequentially. For either low or high activity, ISAM is less attractive than either direct or sequential processing; however, for a file with both low and high activity requirements, ISAM offers economic advantages over either of the other two methods.

The second economic consideration concerns response time. In relation to databases, *response time* is the length of time the user must wait for the system to complete an operation,

File Organization Techniques	When Best to Use	Limitations
Sequential	High activity ratio, as in batch processing	Not possible to access quickly a single record
Indexed	Low activity ratio, moderate to large file size	File updates require indexes to be updated
Indexed-Sequential	File needs to be processed both in batch (high activity ratio) and nonbatch (low activity ratio) modes	Same as with indexed and sequential
Direct	Low activity ratio, very large files, networks, and trees	Need keys to locate records

FIGURE 13.17

When to Use Each File Organization Technique.

such as a query. Direct-access files are necessary for very quick response times; longer response times (hours or more) can be handled economically by sequential files. When long response times can be tolerated, queries or file updates typically can be appended to batch processing runs. For example, a copy of customers' records can be obtained as a by-product of posting invoices to the accounts receivable file. ISAM again offers a middle ground. Short-response-time requests may be processed using the index; longer-response-time requests may be appended to any sequential processing runs against the file. Response times are also affected by hardware considerations, as discussed below.

Physical Architecture, Hardware, and Response Time

Response time can become a major problem with large databases that might be accessed by hundreds or even thousands of users at the same time. If the database system and computer hardware are not suited for the demands placed on them, then users might find themselves

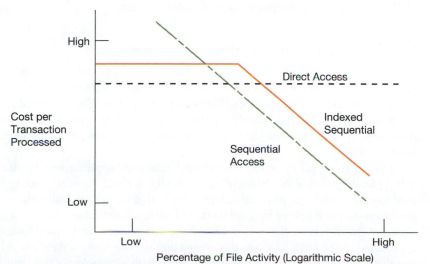

FIGURE 13.18

Unit Costs and File Activity

waiting a hopelessly long time for responses to their queries. Therefore, the database system must be designed properly for the use to which it will be put, and the hardware must be fast enough to get the job done.

On the hardware side, response time is affected by physical access time. This is typically the time required for the CPU to retrieve a single block of data from the disk, called the **disk access time.** One problem is that the CPU operates much faster than the disk does, requiring the CPU to wait while disk input/output operations are being executed. This means that minimizing disk input and output can in some cases result in considerable increases in response time.

Another factor that can affect response time is how data records are distributed physically on the disk. If a group of records is to be accessed in sequence, then the response time will be faster if these records are contiguous (physically next to each other) on the disk. If they are contiguous, the read/write head on the disk drive will need to move only a small distance each time it accesses the next record in the list. If, on the other hand, the records are strewn all over the disk, then the read/write head will have to move a relatively long distance to access each new record, thus slowing things down.

On a hard disk, data on the same track or cylinder can be accessed without moving the read/write head. This means that in some cases it is possible to considerably speed up a database application by storing the records of a particular data file contiguously on one or more disk cylinders.

It should be emphasized that many database systems rely on operating system routines for their input/output operations. This means that it may be the operating system that determines where data will be placed on the disk. This is important because many operating systems have no provision to ensure that data will be stored contiguously. In fact, many operating systems will deliberately break up files and spread them all over a disk, putting their pieces into small empty spaces so that all areas of the disk are used and no space is wasted.

The need to store a file contiguously depends on the physical architecture of the database and its corresponding file-access method. If the database uses the sequential-access method, then physically placing the records next to each other on the disk is desirable. For the indexed-access method, however, it is almost always desirable to place the indexes in contiguous storage because these files often are read sequentially and in their entirety. However, it may not be necessary to place the records in the related data files next to each other on the disk because records in these files are accessed randomly in the two-stage lookup process described earlier. Sometimes, however, it might be desirable to batch process all the records in an indexed file (as is often done with ISAM files), and in such cases, contiguous storage might be impossible due to the nature of the hashing approaches mentioned earlier.

Database Architecture and Database Development

The classical approach to database design for eBusiness applications is to use an E-R (conceptual) model that is translated into a relational database (logical model), which is then implemented using ISAM and/or other methods. Software tools such as those provided by Casewise (www.casewise.com) are used to visually represent the E-R models. Once the visual model is created, it can then be used as a template to automatically or semiautomatically generate the relational database.

In the case of off-the-shelf, prepackaged eBusiness applications, the eBusiness application will typically generate the database automatically, without the user needing to worry about the conceptual, logical, and physical models. Depending on the particular business application, the generated database may or may not work with different database systems. In many cases, a software **database driver,** also called a **database connector,** can be used to connect the business application to the DBMS. When this connection is done using a database driver, it is typically possible to make the business application work with a completely different DBMS by simply changing the database driver. For example, assume that a given accounting application resides on a Windows computer and uses an ODBC (Open DataBase Connection) database driver to connect to a Microsoft SQL Server software and database. Then this same accounting application might instead be able to switch to using a MySQL database management system simply by changing the ODBC database driver to one that supports MySQL instead of Microsoft SQL Server. Of course, changing to a different DBMS typically requires that the old database be migrated (i.e., converted) to the new database format, but there are plenty of database migration tools available on the market (e.g., see www.ispirer.com).

An alternate approach to database design is to use the object-modeling technique. As discussed in Chapter 11, object-oriented (OO) modeling is an alternative to procedure-type modeling. The advantage of OO modeling is that it can be readily transformed into OO program code, with the model-to-program-code transformation being much simpler and faster than with procedure-type modeling such as that which uses Business Process Modeling Notation (BPMN) or logical data flow diagrams (DFDs).

OO design and modeling are extremely popular. This raises the question as to why the E-R technique and not the object-modeling technique is the main approach used to model databases. Wouldn't it be much simpler to create an OO model, then the OO program code, and finally an OO database? In theory, the answer is "yes." But in practice, relational databases outperform (i.e., respond faster to inquires and updates) OO databases in a wide range of common tasks that are typically performed in a business environment. Further, since there are a lot more relational than OO databases in the world, there are many more development and administrative tools available for relational databases. Still, the interest in OO databases continues to grow.

Given the lack of popular OO database systems, the typical developer uses UML-based OO modeling, followed by OO programming for the application. The developer then uses object-relational mapping tools to convert the OO model into a relational database.

 CASE IN POINT

Object-relational mapping tools are available for most popular programming languages. For example, Ebean is an open source Java Object Relational Mapping tool available through www.avaje.com. Also, Ruby, the highly object-oriented language, supports object relational mapping through the ActiveRecord component of Ruby on Rails (www.rubyonrails.com).

Other Types of Logical Structures and Related Databases

OLAP   One of the most common alternative database types is **OLAP (OnLine Analytical Processing).** OLAP can be viewed as a multidimensional generalization of the two-dimensional relational table. The advantage of OLAP is that it provides lightning-fast responses, often 1,000 times faster than responses in standard relational system, to complicated queries. The increased speed is a result of OLAP using complicated multidimensional "indexes" called *aggregations.* OLAP is typically used in data mining applications.

IN-MEMORY DATABASES   In-memory databases are relatively new. They differ from conventional databases in that the entire database is loaded into computer-internal high-speed random access memory or other high-speed electronic storage device. The elimination of the relatively slow physical disk media results in enormous gains in speed. For example, SAP's in-memory database is capable of running a query against a billion records in less than one second. Further, using large memory arrays and efficient use of memory, it is possible to load petabyte-size databases into memory. (A petabyte is approximately 10^{15} bytes.)

ACID: Reliable Processing of Database Transactions

Regardless of the type of database architecture, certain fundamental requirements must be met in order to ensure the reliability of processing database transactions. These requirements are commonly described using the acronym **ACID** (Atomicity, Consistency, Isolation, and Durability).

Atomicity means that either the entire transaction is completed or no part of it is completed. This prevents problems like creating a debit without the corresponding credit. **Consistency** means that only valid data will be written to the database. All databases have consistency rules. For example, a database rule might be that phone numbers cannot contain letters. **Isolation** means that other operations cannot interfere with a transaction that is in the middle of being processed. For example, the database might "lock" a customer account record while a representative is manually making adjustments to it. This would prevent a second representative from inadvertently making duplicate or conflicting adjustments at the same time. **Durability** means that a transaction is not undone if the system fails after it is completed.

Database Management Systems and Databases in Practice

As discussed above, a DBMS comprises database software and an associated database. From the point of view of the typical eBusiness application, the database software inputs data to the database, retrieves data from the database, and manipulates data in the database. The database software may interact with more than one database.

More generally, all DBMSs contain the following three common attributes for managing and organizing data. These are discussed individually.

DATA DESCRIPTION LANGUAGE (DDL)   The **Data Description Language (DDL)** allows the database administrator (DBA) to define the logical structure of the database, called the *schema*. Defining the schema normally involves defining each of the following:

- The name of the data element
- The type of data (numeric, alphabetic, date, etc.) and the number of decimal positions if the data element is numeric
- The number of positions (e.g., nine positions for Social Security Numbers)

The DDL may also be used to define **subschema,** which are individual user views of the database. For example, the sales-order processing department might be able to view and edit the data elements DATE, CUSTOMER_NAME, ACCOUNT_NUMBER, QUANTITY, and PRICE. The production department might have a different view of the same database, seeing instead CUSTOMER_NAME, ACCOUNT_NUMBER, and SCHEDULED_DATE_OF_COMPLETION. Further, the production department might be restricted from editing CUSTOMER_NAME and ACCOUNT_NUMBER. Note that in this example the application program (i.e., the accounting system) automatically generates the DDL statements required to create the subschemas.

The DDL may also be used to create, modify, and delete tables in a relational setting.

DATA MANIPULATION LANGUAGE   The **Data Manipulation Language (DML)** consists of the commands for updating, editing, manipulating, and extracting data. In many cases, the user does not need to know or use the DML. Rather, the application program (e.g., the payroll program or interactive accounting system) automatically generates the DML statements to accomplish the user's requests. **Structured Query Language (SQL)** is a common DML in relational settings.

Name	Account Number	Account Balance
		>1000

FIGURE 13.19

Selecting Accounts >$1,000 Using Query By Example

DATA QUERY LANGUAGE   The **Data Query Language (DQL)** is a user-friendly language or interface that allows the user to request information from the database. One such friendly interface is **Query By Example (QBE),** a language which allows the user to request information simply by filling in blanks. For example, a user might fill in the blanks in a form such as that shown in Figure 13.19 to request all records with account balances greater than $1,000.

There also exist natural-language interfaces, which allow users to make requests for information using ordinary, everyday English—for example, "May I please have a sales report for the month of June?" Such systems are capable of recognizing a variety of phrasings for the requests, and if the user makes an unintelligible or incomplete request, the system will ask the necessary questions to resolve the problem.

Figure 13.20 depicts the processing of a user query as it relates to the schema, the subschema, the DDL, and the DML.

CASE IN POINT

SQL is both an ANSI and an ISO standard. However, major DBMS vendors typically add proprietary extensions to the SQL command set. The first version of SQL was developed in IBM by Donald D. Chamberlin and Raymond F. Boyce in the early 1970s.

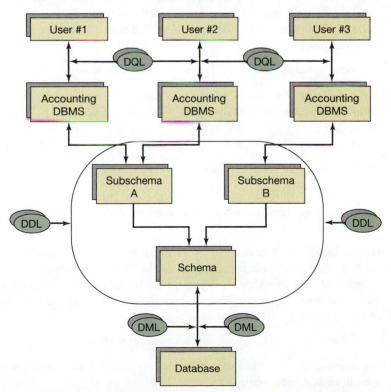

FIGURE 13.20

Logical Model for Processing User Queries

SQL Data Manipulation Language

SQL is the technology used to retrieve information from databases. SQL is a nonprocedural programming language. It allows the user to focus on specifying what data are desired rather than focusing on how to get those data.

Four basic statement types comprise the DML component of SQL. These are

SELECT	Retrieves rows from tables
UPDATE	Modifies the rows of tables
DELETE	Removes rows from tables
INSERT	Adds new rows to tables

This section will discuss and provide examples for the SELECT statement type. The examples will illustrate several of the basic data retrieval capabilities of the SELECT statement. The examples will also introduce several of the more general features of SQL, such as arithmetic and logical expressions, which are also applicable to the UPDATE, DELETE, and INSERT statements. These latter statement types will be described only briefly herein.

SELECT QUERIES   SELECT is usually the first word in an SQL statement that is intended to extract data from a database. SELECT specifies which fields (i.e., items in a database) or expressions based on fields that you want to retrieve. The FROM clause indicates which table(s) contain those items. FROM is required and follows SELECT.

SELECT Everything   The * is a special query character that represents "all fields." This query selects all fields from a table that is named *company*.

```
SELECT * FROM company
```

SELECT Fields   SELECT specific fields (i.e., items) by name. If you wish to include more than one item, separate the items with commas. List the items in the order in which you want them to be retrieved. This query selects three fields, titled *name, country, and currency* from a table that is titled *company*.

```
SELECT name, country, currency FROM company
```

Order By   ORDER BY sorts the displayed data in the order specified in the clause. ORDER BY is optional. If you do not include it, the data appear unsorted. The default sort order is ascending (A–Z, 0–9).

This query adds the ORDER BY field titled *name* clause to the previous query.

```
SELECT name, country, currency FROM company ORDER BY name
```

You may specify ascending sort order for a data item by including the ASC keyword at the end of the data item. To sort in reverse order (Z–A, 9–0), add DESC after each data item you want to sort in descending order.

WHERE Condition   You can use WHERE to determine which records from the tables listed in the FROM clause will appear in the results of the SELECT statement. WHERE is optional, but when it is included, it follows FROM. If you do not include WHERE, all records are selected. The SQL statement selects only companies where the *country* field contains the value "USA" from the *company* table.

```
SELECT * FROM Company WHERE Country = 'USA'
```

We note that character data such as the letters USA must be enclosed in quotes (e.g., 'USA') when used in an SQL statement.

Arithmetic Expressions SQL allows arithmetic expressions to be included in the SELECT clause. An arithmetic expression consists of a number of column names and values connected by any of the following operators:

+	Add
−	Subtract
*	Multiply
/	Divide

When included in the SELECT clause, the results of an expression are displayed as a calculated table column. The query selects three fields and forms a calculated table column titled *dif* that will contain the calculated amount *year1–year2*.

```
SELECT title, year1, year2, year1 - year2 as dif
FROM [budget report]
```

We note that when table names such as *budget report* contain a space, the name must be enclosed in brackets (e.g., [budget report]) when used in an SQL statement.

Comparison Operators Any of the following comparison operators may be used:

=	equal to
<>	not equal to
>	greater than
<	less than
>=	greater than or equal to
<=	less than or equal to

Compound Expressions with Boolean Operators Individual logical expressions may be combined in a WHERE clause with Boolean operators:

```
AND
OR
```

Aggregate Functions You can select amounts that are calculated with aggregate functions. The function COUNT(*) AS tally illustrates how to count the number of occurrences in a table and name the result (AS tally).

```
SELECT COUNT(*) AS tally FROM company
```

The AS tally clause gives the aggregate function the name "tally," which will be used in the report. The AS clause is optional with aggregate functions.

Additional functions include

AVG(*column-name*)	Returns the average value
MAX(*column-name*)	Returns highest value
MIN(*column-name*)	Returns the lowest value
SUM(*column-name*)	Calculates the total of values

Inner Join INNER JOIN combines fields from several tables in a query. The example selects the field *name* from the *company* table and the field *topic* from the *notes* table.

```
SELECT company.name, notes.topic
FROM company INNER JOIN notes
ON company.company = notes.company
```

We note that both the tables contain the same field titled *company*. Note that in this query the table names are appended with a period to each field name to fully identify the table location of the respective field. This can always be done in SQL but is necessary when more than a single table is used in the query, as here. Thus, *company.company* is the *company* field in the *company* table and *notes.company* is the *company* field in the *notes* table. The values of the *company* field are matched to form the result of the query.

CASE IN POINT

SQL was originally developed as a declarative as opposed to a procedural language. Procedural programming languages include commands that govern the flow of a program from one step to the next. SQL was originally developed without such commands. However, the 1999 specification of the standard included created procedural capabilities via SQL Persistent Stored Modules (SQL/PSM).

UPDATE, INSERT, AND DELETE QUERIES   These types of queries modify a database. We provide brief descriptions of their use.

The UPDATE statement consists of three clauses:

```
UPDATE tablename
SET column-assignment-list
WHERE conditional-expression
```

In SET, *column-assignment-list* lists the columns to be updated and the values they are to be set to and takes the general form column-name1 = value1, column-name2 = value2,...

The WHERE clause is optional. When it is used, the WHERE clause specifies a condition for UPDATE to test when processing each row of the table.

The general form of the DELETE statement is

```
DELETE from tablename
WHERE conditional-expression
```

The DELETE statement removes rows from *tablename* that satisfy the condition specified in the WHERE clause.

The INSERT statement has two general forms. The simplest form is used to insert a single row into a table.

```
INSERT INTO tablename
VALUES (constant-list);
```

The INSERT statement also may be used in conjunction with a SELECT statement query to copy the rows of one table to another.

High-Level Query Languages

Although SQL is an industry-standard query language for relational databases, it is a relatively low-level database language that is too verbose and complex to be used by many application programmers. Consequently, many developers prefer instead to use higher-level query languages when programming business applications. For example, a Ruby programmer would likely use ActiveRecord, a Ruby library that permits creating and manipulating relational database with simple commands. These commands are then automatically converted into SQL for execution.

End users are even less inclined to use SQL. They are instead likely to use a high-level graphical query language or natural language. QBE, discussed above, is one of the oldest graphical relational database query languages. With QBE, the end user simply fills in a form. The form data is then automatically translated into SQL. For example, a user might fill in a form as follows:

Name	State	Zip Code	Account Number
Jane Morris		33301	

This would produce the resulting SQL:

```
SELECT * FROM Customers WHERE Name = 'Jane Morris' AND ZipCode = '33301'
```

Relational Databases can also be accessed via **Natural Language Database Query,** which interfaces natural language processing and conversational analytics so that users can talk to database systems using everyday English. For example, a user might ask the question, "How many blue cars did we sell last month?" The database might then respond, "Do you want the sales broken down by week the same way you requested last time you made this query?"

CASE IN POINT

Semantra (www.semantra.com) uses a natural language interface and conversational analytics that make it possible "to have an intelligent conversation with your enterprise databases." Semantra interfaces with most major database systems, including Oracle, Microsoft SQL Server, IBM DB2, and MySQL.

For OO databases, there is the **Object Query Language,** modeled after SQL, developed by the Object Database Management Group and later "adopted" by the Object Management Group. However, it is very complex and has never been fully implemented by software vendors. But it has influenced newer query languages such as the **Java Data Objects Query Language,** which is Java-based and query-language agnostic. Thus, it is capable of converting queries into different underlying query languages. Java Data Objects Query Language was developed through the Java Community Process (www.jcp.org), a project sponsored by Sun Microsystems (www.sun.com).

Reporting Solutions

Since DBMSs are frequently independent of the eBusiness application, it is often possible to use a third-party reporting solutions to provide end users the ability to easily extract reports and queries from the application databases. Good examples of such reporting solutions include Crystal Reports (www.businessobjects.com) and Microstrategy (www.microstrategy. com). These types of solutions contain database drivers that permit them to directly access the eBusiness application database. Specialized reporting solutions such as these typically provide a much wider range of reporting features than are included in off-the-shelf eBusiness applications (including ERP systems).

Why Database Management Systems Are Needed

DBMSs *integrate*, *standardize*, and *provide security* for various accounting applications. In the absence of integration, each type of accounting application such as sales, payroll, and receivables will maintain its own separate, independent data files. Although maintaining independent files is simple, it has several disadvantages. First, the same data item may be used in several different application areas; with independent files, this data item has to be separately fed into each application file. A sale, for example, affects the inventory file, accounts receivable file, and various revenue and expense files. Inputting the same data element numerous times (once for each application it is used in) is time-consuming and potentially expensive; furthermore, there is a greater chance for errors and inconsistencies among the various representations of a piece of data in several independent files.

Second, because files must be rigidly defined early in the systems implementation process, procedures may be constrained by the existing file structure rather than the evolving needs of applications. Finally, independence among files often leads to different structures for the same data, different coding systems, different abbreviations, and different field lengths, to name a few examples. Comparison and reconciliation of supposedly identical data may be difficult under these conditions. The result of inconsistent data is that inconsistent reports are produced from the various application programs. Such problems call into question the integrity of an information system.

In addition to the data management and storage problems just discussed, independent files each require their own processing and maintenance instructions because neither the content nor the structure of the files is standardized. Inquiry capability concerning nonkey information is restricted because each individual application program must specify detailed instructions concerning the physical handling of data.

DATA INDEPENDENCE   The solution to the problems with maintaining independent files lies in separation of the physical handling of data from their logical use. This requires two fundamental changes: First, data storage is integrated into a single database, and second, all access to the integrated set of files (database) is through a single software system designed to manage the physical aspects of data handling and storage. These are the essential characteristics of the database approach to data processing.

In a sense, the word *file* loses meaning in a database environment. A single master file may be logically subdivided into numerous subsystem files, and these files may be combined and recombined into numerous other files. Database software separates the physical and logical aspects of file use and in doing so opens up a broad spectrum of information processing capabilities simply not feasible without such software.

Figure 13.21 illustrates these concepts with two independent application files, each containing four fields per record. Note that two data items, X and Y, are common to both files. Below these files is a database—a single file that contains all the nonredundant information previously found in the two physically independent files. This database file is structured and managed by a DBMS. On requests from user programs, the DBMS structures logical application files (subschema) through a database dictionary file. A **database dictionary** is a collection of all data item names in a database, along with a description of the standardized data representation form of these data items (e.g., their size, type of data—numeric, alphabetical, etc.). The database dictionary is defined and controlled by the DBA.

Logical files 1 and 2 (see Figure 13.21) are temporary files constructed by the DBMS for use by applications one and two. At completion of processing, the updated values in the logical files may be copied to the actual physical database. Logical file 3 is a new file created for a specific nonroutine use, such as a query (inquiry) or a special accounting data analysis. The ability to construct such special files quickly and efficiently is a major advantage of DBMSs. This ability is provided through the DBMS maintenance of inverted files, lists, rings, or other data structures designed to facilitate information retrieval by users.

SECURITY   Another advantage of DBMSs is their general ability to assign security codes to data items and their processing attributes. Part of the data dictionary file contains a list of authorized system users and their assigned security and access codes. Each of the six unique data elements in Figure 13.21 could be assigned a numerical priority code. These codes would specify which

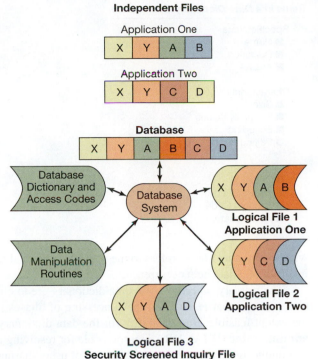

FIGURE 13.21

Database Management Concepts

data items may be retrieved by each user of the DBMS; furthermore, such codes may also be used to restrict and define the processing a user may do to any data item.

Application one in Figure 13.21 could have authority to request only items X, Y, A, and B and authority to modify/update only fields A and B. Application two could request X, Y, C, and D and modify only C and D. Similarly, application three may have authority to access but not to modify any data items, and so on through a hierarchy of security or privacy coding applied to data items in the database.

 CASE IN POINT

The Information Systems Audit and Control Association (ISACA, www.isaca.org) defines a DBA as an individual or department responsible for the security and information classification of the shared data stored on a database system. This responsibility includes the design, definition, and maintenance of the database.

Database Documentation and Administration

Database dictionaries are used both alone and with DBMSs to centralize, document, control, and coordinate the use of data within an organization. The data dictionary is simply another file, a sort of file of files, whose record occurrences consist of data item descriptions. Figure 13.22 illustrates some likely data items for a data dictionary occurrence of a field. Most of the items shown in Figure 13.22 are self-explanatory or have been discussed previously. An **alias** arises when different users call the same field different names. For example, the warehouse may call "Requisition Number" the data item that purchasing calls "Order Number." Aliases also arise because the same data item is called different things in different programs written in different languages or by different programmers. *Encoding* refers to the physical form that the data item

FIGURE 13.22

Data Dictionary Format

Items in a Data Dictionary Occurrence

Specifications
- Name
- Definition
- Aliases

Characteristics
- Size
- Range of Values
- Encoding
- Editing Data

Utilization
- Owner
- Where Used
- Security Code
- Last Update

will be stored in. *Owner* refers to the user who has final responsibility or primary interest in the integrity of a data item occurrence.

The primary objectives of a data dictionary are to eliminate or at least control inconsistencies in usage that result from the processing of aliases and to eliminate data redundancies to the extent feasible. Responsibility for the data dictionary should be centralized in a **database administrator (DBA).** DBA is responsible for resolving incompatibilities and coordination and communication problems between groups of users sharing a database. A major task of the DBA is to establish standards, conventions, and documentation of the data resource. Administration of the data dictionary is the major means by which the DBA accomplishes this task. Effective control of data is central to the database approach to data processing. Incompatibilities and redundancies abound in a traditional file-oriented system in which users maintain and process their own data files. It might be impossible to centralize all data usage. Users may be unwilling to give up responsibility for their data elements. Many of the problems the DBA faces are political. The DBA has to be a diplomat in coordinating usage among various users and in dealing with users who might not obtain significant benefits from centralization and standardization of data. Accordingly, the DBA function needs to be sufficiently high in the organization or at least directly responsible to someone sufficiently high to be able to deal effectively with problems that cross organizational units.

The data dictionary might be maintained manually, but usually it is computerized and processed like other computer files. If the dictionary is used in conjunction with a DBMS, it can be maintained by the DBMS. In either case, it is the procedures surrounding use of the dictionary, as well as the dictionary itself, which make the concept an important element of database administration.

Summary

The architecture of DBMSs consists of three levels: the conceptual level, the logical level, and the physical level. The conceptual architecture involves defining in general terms the contents of the database and the required uses of the data. The logical architecture involves defining the logical data structure, which can follow either a hierarchical, network or relational model. The physical architecture involves defining the file-access methods, which may be sequential, indexed, or direct. In practice, the overall architecture will be structured around the users' needs for information. In today's business environment, the relational model is dominant among the logical models and is often implemented with either an indexed or direct-access physical architecture. Still, all models are being used.

Two conceptual modeling methods were discussed. In the E-R model, segments (entities) are connected to each other by general relationships. In the OMT, segments (object classes) are related through the concept of inheritance.

Three logical models were discussed. In hierarchical models, logical records are chained to each other by embedded pointer fields. Accessing one record allows accessing of the next record in the chain. A hierarchical model is formed by chaining the records together in such a way that a graph depicting their interrelationships forms a tree. All records are ultimately interconnected to one common record that forms the top of the tree. Network models are similar to hierarchical models, but there is no constraint that the records be chained in such a way as to form a tree. Finally, the relational model interrelates records, sharing common attributes (fields) through the use of tables rather than embedded pointers.

Sequential file organization is the most basic physical architecture. In sequentially organized files, records are always accessed in the exact same sequence, from the first to the last. Such files are useful for batch processing, when a large percentage of the records need to be accessed. However, it is not an efficient file organization when, say, a single record needs to be accessed. A second type of physical architecture is an indexed file. An indexed, or inverted, file is used for faster access (relative to sequentially accessed files) to a single data record. To access an indexed file, the program first consults a directory (or index)

and looks up the address of the desired record; it then retrieves this record directly. One special type of an indexed file is an ISAM (indexed sequential-access method) file. An ISAM file is a sequential file that is indexed and ordered physically on one key. Such a file can be processed either sequentially or through use of the index. A third physical architecture is direct-access file organization. Direct access is accomplished by physically placing each record on disk in such a way that it can be located by one or more of its data values.

DBMSs are computer software programs that include a DDL, a DML, and a DQL. The DBA uses the DDL to define various fields and records and to create a data dictionary. Once data are input into the database, users can manipulate records and fields with a DML and then view data and extract reports with a DQL. DBMSs provide for standardization, integration, flexibility, and security.

Glossary

ACID   Atomicity, Consistency, Isolation, and Durability. Acronym for generally accepted requirements for the reliable processing of transaction in a database setting.

activity ratio   the number of active records divided by the number of records in the file.

alias   different users call the same field different names.

atomicity   the ACID rule that says that either the entire transaction is completed or no part of it is completed.

attribute   synonym for *field*.

branch   the connection between children and parent(s) in a tree structure.

children   lower-level elements in a tree diagram of a data structure that are connected to (i.e., part of) the parent element.

consistency   the ACID rule that requires that only valid data be written to the database.

database   a structured collection of data stored in a computer system or network.

Database agnostic   the capacity for software to function with any DBMS.

database administrator (DBA)   has overall responsibility for database administration.

database connector   another name for a database driver.

database dictionary   a collection of all data item names in a database, along with a description of the standardized data representation form of these data items.

database driver   software that connects a given application program to a particular DBMS.

database management system (DBMS)   computer software and related database that enable a user to create and update, select, and retrieve data, and to generate various outputs and reports.

database model   synonym for schema.

database software   software used to store, retrieve, and manipulate data in a database.

data description language (DDL)   the DDL is used to define the logical structure of the database (schema).

data item   synonym for field.

data manipulation language (DML)   the commands for updating, editing, manipulating, and extracting data from a database.

data query language (DQL)   a user-friendly language or interface that allows users to request information from a database.

direct-access file   each record has a storage location (address) that bears some relationship to the record's key field, allowing direct retrieval of each record in the file.

disk access time   the time required for the CPU to retrieve a single block of data from the disk.

durability   the ACID rule that requires that a transaction isn't undone if the system fails after it is completed.

element   synonym for field.

entity-relationship (E-R) data model   a conceptual model for depicting the relationships between segments in a database.

field   the smallest block of data that will be stored and retrieved in the information system.

first normal form   relational tables that do not contain any repeating groups.

fixed-length record   both the number of fields and the length (character size) of each field are fixed.

fully inverted   a file that is indexed for all its fields.

hypertext systems   systems that allow users to browse through databases in random fashion by selecting keywords or objects.

indexed file   one where an attribute has been extracted from the records and used to build a new file whose purpose is to provide an index to the original file.

indexed-sequential file a sequential file that is stored on a DASD and is both indexed and physically sorted on the same field.

inheritance a relationship created when an object class is divided into subclasses.

instance synonym for occurrence.

Isolation the ACID rule that that other operations cannot interfere with a transaction that is in the middle of being processed.

inverted file synonym for indexed file.

ISAM indexed-sequential access method; synonym for indexed-sequential file organization.

Java Data Objects Query Language a Java-based query-language capable of converting queries into different underlying query languages.

key synonym for record key.

list structure each record contains one or more pointers (fields) indicating the address of the next logical record with the same attribute(s).

logical data structure the logical manner in which records and fields in a database are structured and organized.

multilist organization a record may be part of several list organizations.

multiple-ring structure several ring organizations pass through individual records.

Natural Language Database Query a high-level database query approach that uses natural language processing and conversational analytics so that users can talk to database systems using everyday English.

network structure a logical data structure that allows a child segment to have more than one parent.

node synonym for repeated group.

normal forms rules that govern the creation of relational tables in the relational database model.

normalization the process of applying normal forms rules in the relational database model.

object corresponds to an instance in the object-oriented modeling technique (OMT).

object class corresponds to a segment in the object-oriented modeling technique (OMT).

object-oriented modeling technique (OMT) a conceptual model for depicting the relationships between segments in a database that views the components of the system being modeled as object classes.

Object Query Language a database query language structured after SQL but for object-oriented databases.

occurrence a specific set of data values for a record.

OLAP (OnLine Analytical Processing) a database approach that involves a multidimensional generalization of the two-dimensional relational table and is used primarily in data mining.

parent the highest level element in a tree diagram of a data structure.

primary key synonym for primary sort key.

primary sort key the first field used to sort the records in a file.

Query by Example (QBE) a high-level database query approach in which the end user fills in a form to initiate a query.

random access synonym for direct access.

randomizing transformation a widely used method of storing and locating records in a direct-access file.

record a logical grouping of fields (data items) that concern a certain entity.

record key a data item or combination of data items that uniquely identifies a particular record in a file.

relation synonym for table in the relational model.

relational algebra operations used to extract information from relational tables.

relational model a logical data structure that views the database as a collection of two-dimensional tables.

relative random order a field on which a file is not sorted.

repeated group related groups of fields that repeat themselves in variable-length records.

ring structure a list organization in which the last record in the ring list points back to the first record.

schema synonym for logical data structure of a database.

secondary key synonym for secondary sort key.

secondary sort key a field used to determine relative position among a set of records when the primary key has the same value in each record of the set.

second normal form no key in a relational table is allowed to determine the values of a nonkey field.

segment synonym for repeated group.

sequential-access file records in the file can only be accessed in their predefined sequence.

structured query language (SQL) nonprocedural programming language used to retrieve information from databases.

subschema individual, logical user views of the database.

tertiary sort keys additional fields beyond primary and secondary keys required to uniquely identify and sort records in a file.

third normal form no nonkey field in a relational table is allowed to determine the values on another nonkey field.

trailer record a fixed-length extension of a master record.

tree structure a logical data structure in which each node represents a segment, and each node is related to another node at the next-highest level of the tree.

tuple a row in a relational table.

variable-length record both the number of fields and the length (character size) of each field are variable.

Webliography

databases.about.com
This site provides a wealth of information about databases and links to many database topics such as learning SQL, database development, database security, database administration, and professional certifications in the database area.

www.sqlcourse.com
An SQL tutorial from Jupitermedia Corporation.

www.oracle.com
Home page of Oracle, a major vendor of database software.

www.databaseassociation.com
The home page of the Association of Database Developers. The resources section contains links to bibliographies on database research.

www.quickbase.com
The home page of Intuit's Quickbase™, an online product that delivers a Platform as a Service (PaaS) DBMS. Quickbase™ is an industry leader that is used by a large percentage of Fortune 500 companies.

www.ca.com
The home page of CA. CA is a global IT management software provider. CA publishes CA Erwin® Data Modeler, a data modeling software platform that supports creating and maintaining databases, data warehouses, and enterprise data resource models.

Chapter Quiz

Answers to the chapter quiz appear on page 481.

1. Which of the following is (are) "fixed" in a fixed-length record?
   a. the number of fields
   b. the length of each field
   c. both a and b
   d. neither a nor b
2. Which of the following types of files might be stored on a direct-access storage device (DASD)?
   a. a sequential-access file
   b. a direct-access file
   c. both a and b
   d. neither a nor b
3. Which of the following terms is *not* a synonym?
   a. field
   b. instance
   c. data item
   d. element
4. Which of the following terms is a synonym with repeated group?
   a. attribute
   b. segment
   c. field
   d. record key
5. In a(n) (_____) system, a user may browse a database by selecting key words to retrieve information in a random fashion.
   a. expert
   b. object-oriented
   c. segmented
   d. hypertext

6. Which of the following conceptual database models views the components of the system being modeled as object classes?
   a. object-oriented modeling technique
   b. entity-relationship (E-R) data model
   c. both a and b
   d. neither a nor b
7. The (_____) should have overall responsibility for documentation and control of an organization's database.
   a. database administrator
   b. manager of programming
   c. manager of operations
   d. manager of systems analysis
8. Which of the following types of queries does not modify a database?
   a. INSERT
   b. UPDATE
   c. SELECT
   d. DELETE
9. Which of the following refers to the overall logical structure of a database?
   a. alias
   b. virtual data
   c. schema
   d. network
10. Which of the following would the database administrator use to define the overall logical structure of a database?
    a. DBA
    b. DDL
    c. DML
    d. DQL

Review Problem

Consider the relation

    BOOK (ISBN, TITLE, AUTHOR, AUTHOR-AFFILIATION,
    PRICE)

The underlining of ISBN indicates that it is the record key.

a. Is this relation normalized? If so, is it in first normal form, second normal form, or third normal form?

b. If it is not already in third normal form, what is necessary to attain this?

Solution to Review Problem

a. Because the ISBN uniquely identifies each book, the relation is in first normal form. Since the key (ISBN) is a single key, the relation must be in second as well as first normal form. Is the relation in third normal form? That is, are all the nonkey fields mutually independent? No. AUTHOR-AFFILIATION clearly depends on AUTHOR.

b. To attain third normal form, we must separate this relation, giving two separate third normal form relations:

    BOOK (ISBN, TITLE, AUTHOR, PRICE)

and

    AUTHOR-AFFILIATION (AUTHOR, AUTHOR-
    AFFILIATION).

Review Questions

1. Distinguish between fixed- and variable-length records.
2. Distinguish between primary and secondary sort keys.
3. What is a hypertext system?
4. Distinguish between the conceptual level, the logical level, and the physical level of database architecture.
5. Characterize each of the three major models of logical data structures.
   a. Tree or hierarchical models
   b. Network models
   c. Relational models
6. What is list organization? How does it differ from a ring structure?
7. Identify the basic operations of relational algebra. What are they used for?
8. What is normalization? Distinguish between first, second, and third normal forms.
9. Distinguish between
   a. sequentially accessed files.
   b. indexed-sequential files.
   c. directly accessed files.
10. What factors affect response time in database systems?
11. What are database management systems?
12. Distinguish between
    a. data description language (DDL).
    b. data manipulation language (DML).
    c. data query language (DQL).
13. What is Structured Query Language?
14. What are the functions of the database administrator (DBA)?

Discussion Questions and Problems

15. Discuss some of the differences between the traditional approach to data processing and the database approach.
16. Discuss the advantages and disadvantages of having an industry-wide standard to which all database software systems conform.
17. For each of the following applications, specify a file organization method (sequential, direct access, indexed sequential). Briefly justify your selection in terms of the anticipated activity ratio, processing time frame, file size, and response time to inquiries about file status.
    a. General Motors stockholder file, updated weekly and used for mailing dividend checks, quarterly reports, and proxy requests.

    b. A salesperson commission file, updated at the time of sale from a point-of-sale data entry terminal.
    c. A bank's customer account file, updated daily for deposits and withdrawals and used for mailing monthly statements of account.
    d. An inventory file, updated daily, that is also used to ascertain product availability and other related inquiries during daily operations.
    e. A master payroll file, used biweekly to process payroll and also quarterly to process various tax reports.
    f. A master scheduling file, used by a large airline to reserve seats on all its flights. The file is used heavily every day for scheduling and ad hoc inquiries

concerning seat availability but is never processed to generate reports.

g. A file of authors for a publishing company, processed quarterly to prepare royalty checks and once at year-end to prepare tax reports.

h. A vendor file used by a large manufacturing company. The file is used heavily every day for ad hoc inquiries concerning orders and payments and is also processed once each week to generate payment checks for many of the company's 500 vendors.

i. A master file of fixed assets for a small manufacturing firm, processed quarterly to produce depreciation for tax and accounting reports and once each year for insurance purposes.

18. The West Company maintains a master accounts receivable disk file. Approved applications for new charge accounts are keyed to disk. The resulting file is sorted and processed against the master file.

   The current master disk file is strictly sequential. What are some advantages and disadvantages that might accrue from changing the file organization method to either a random or indexed-sequential structure?

19. For each of the following application files, discuss the relative merits of sequential, direct, and indexed-sequential file organization:

   a. open-order file in a large manufacturing firm
   b. accounts receivable file for a magazine publisher
   c. inventory file for a large automobile dealership
   d. accounts payable file for a retailing firm
   e. fixed-assets file in a manufacturing firm

20. Identify an inquiry for (i) a specific record and (ii) a group of related records that might be made for each of the following files. Discuss how these inquiries might be satisfied if the file organization method was sequential, direct, or indexed sequential.

   a. an employee master file
   b. an accounts receivable file
   c. a work-in-process file

21. Use the flowchart in Figure 13.12 to solve this problem. Assume that the master file and the transaction file are composed of the record numbers shown below in the sequence given.

| Master | 11, 15, 31, 84, 87, 99 |
| Transaction | 11, 12, 31, 31, 15, 84, 99 |

Record number 99 in each file is used to indicate the logical end of the file.

   Process these data, using the flowchart in Figure 13.12. Indicate

   a. which master records are updated.
   b. which master records are not updated.
   c. the disposition of each transaction record (i.e., posted to the master or an error condition).

22. Consider an open purchase order file in a manufacturing company. Identify several other files to which the purchase

order file might be linked (chained) through the use of pointer fields.

23. A personnel file contains a record for each employee in an organization. Each record contains four fields: (a) name, (b) division, (c) specialty, and (d) age. Below are four sample records:

Storage Location	Name	Division	Specialty	Age
22	Ash	New York	Audit	30
28	Fox	New York	Audit	25
64	Luh	Chicago	Marketing	29
106	Smith	Los Angeles	Personnel	40

   Each of the four fields is expected to be an important search parameter in the personnel application system. Design an index (directory) to invert the preceding file fully.

24. Discuss the relative advantages and disadvantages of inverted files and list or ring structures (pointer-field structures) in answering inquiries of the following types.

   a. Are there any records that have both attribute 1 and attribute 2 (sales greater than $5,000 and location equal to the state of New York)?
   b. How many records have attribute 1, attribute 2, ... attribute n?

25. Consider the following relation:

   CLASS-LIST (<u>STUDENT#</u>, <u>CLASS#</u>, STUDENT-NAME, STUDENT-MAJOR, CLASS-TIME, CLASSROOM)

Required

   a. Suppose that we wish to add a new class time and room (i.e., a new section) for a particular class number (#). Is this possible? If not, what is necessary before we can add a new class time and room to the file?
   b. Suppose that all students drop a particular class number (#) from their schedules. What effect would this have on the data stored in the CLASS-LIST relation?
   c. Is CLASS-LIST in first, second, or third normal form?

26. An automobile manufacturer maintains a cumulative sales file in the following relation:

   CUM-SALES (<u>MAKE</u>, <u>BODY-STYLE</u>, <u>COLOR</u>, <u>SALES-REGION</u>, SALES, OPEN-ORDERS)

   An example (tuple) would be

   CUM-SALES (Buick, Sedan, Red, West, 123 400, 4500)

   Is this relation in third normal form?

27. Consider the two-record hierarchy

   DEPARTMENT (<u>DEPT#</u>, DEPT-NAME, . . . , PROFESSOR)
   PROFESSOR (<u>PROF#</u>, PROF-NAME, . . . ,)

   in which professors are linked to their department by the field PROFESSOR in the DEPARTMENT record.

   Does this relation have a repeating group? If so, how would you normalize this relation?

28. Organizing and maintaining a database are more complicated than organizing and maintaining independent files because a database provides more data retrieval functions and performs more operations. A DBMS may have three different types of languages associated with its use: a data manipulation language (DML), a data definition language (DDL), and a data query language (DQL). For each of the illustrations below, indicate which of these three languages would probably be used.

    a. A programmer writes a COBOL program to update inventory records that are stored in the database.

    b. The database administrator (DBA) documents the content and structure of the database.

    c. A sales manager requests an ad hoc report on sales of a certain product over the past month.

    d. The field for customer address in the accounts receivable segment of the database is expanded to allow for a 10-digit ZIP code.

    e. The payroll manager requests a special report detailing those employees in the database who have college degrees.

    f. A programmer writes a COBOL program to prepare payroll checks for employees whose personnel records are stored in the database.

    g. A new field is added to employee personnel records in the database to allow for a new payroll deduction for health benefits.

    h. A programmer writes a COBOL program to update accounts receivable records that are stored in the database.

    i. The credit manager requests a special report detailing those customers in the database who have purchased more than $25,000 worth of goods in the past 3 months.

29. A data record is a collection of related fields or data elements. Record design is one of the fundamental problems of data management. A data record should include all the data elements that are essential to an application. In certain instances, however, a particular data element might be computed as needed on the basis of the other data elements stored in a record. In such cases, it is not really necessary to store this type of data element in a data record because its value can be computed readily as needed. This type of data element is called *virtual data*.

    For example, a payroll record might contain the following three data elements in addition to others:

    pay rate per hour

    hours worked

    gross pay

    In this case, gross pay would be a virtual data element. Gross pay could be computed as needed based on the pay rate per hour and hours worked data elements.

    Virtual data are an example of redundancy in data records. The elimination of virtual data has several advantages. One is to reduce the overall size of the data record and thus reduce the amount of storage space required. This would tend to reduce the total cost of storing a data record. Another advantage is that there are fewer data items in the data record that have to be maintained. This might lead to simpler application programs and

would tend to reduce the possibility of having errors occur when the data record is modified. This becomes more important when a data element is contained in more than one data record. In such cases, a data element might be updated in one record but not in others. This results in inconsistent data in an information system.

Required

Consider the following data record for a work-in-process application system:

> Work-in-process number
>
> Materials cost
>
> Direct labor cost
>
> Applied overhead cost
>
> Total cost
>
> Units started
>
> Units spoiled
>
> Good units in process

Which of these data items is (are) virtual data? What types of advantages might be gained if virtual data elements are removed from the work-in-process record? Explain.

30. Ernst and Anderson is a manufacturer of power tools and other products used in the construction industry. The company was founded in the early 1900s as a manufacturer of quality hand tools such as hammers and screwdrivers, but such products have represented a decreasing percentage of total company sales for more than a decade. The company has been very successful in industrial power tools, which is its primary line of business. Several small companies were acquired in the late 1980s to broaden the company's product line to include a variety of commercial products such as small appliances and household cleaning equipment such as vacuum cleaners. Because their products are consumer-oriented and thus do not compete with industrial power tools, these acquisitions generally have been allowed to operate as independent companies.

    The company operates several manufacturing facilities that produce power tools, but the largest and oldest plant, based in Pittsburgh, Pennsylvania, accounts for almost 80% of total production. The Pittsburgh plant employs more than 1,000 people and manufactures more than 250 different types of power tools. Much of the company's success in maintaining its position in the marketplace in the face of intense international competition can be attributed to its long-standing policies concerning good employee relations and adequate plant maintenance. Although old in years, the Pittsburgh plant has been well maintained, and the company has continuously invested in new manufacturing equipment.

    A computer-based information system for production control has been used at the Pittsburgh plant since the early 1970s. Management of Ernst and Anderson was an early believer in the view that adequate information is an essential ingredient in the successful operation of a complex manufacturing operation. The production control system is organized into five major applications: production scheduling, materials management, labor cost reporting, work-in-process inventory, and finished goods inventory. These applications were developed separately and have been modified constantly over the years. The five different applications all use their own separate files and programs. Applications are linked together through separate batch processing runs. For example, periodically the work-in-process application is processed to generate a file of completed jobs. This transaction file of completed jobs is then reformatted as necessary and processed by the finished goods inventory application to update the finished goods inventory records. The reformatting is necessary because each application has been developed independently. This has resulted in some inconsistencies between identical data elements in the different applications.

These inconsistencies have become more and more bothersome as the company has expanded the role of its computer-based production control system. Management is convinced that the effectiveness of the information system can be increased significantly if the five separate, stand-alone applications are integrated in a DBMS. To this end, the company has established a project team to study the feasibility of using a DBMS. The company hired a large public accounting firm to assist in this project. On the advice of the consultants, the project team has begun a study of the inputs, file structures, and outputs of the five separate applications to determine the data-definition ambiguities that exist in the present systems. These ambiguities will have to be eliminated if the production scheduling, materials management, labor cost reporting, work-in-process inventory, and finished goods inventory applications are to be integrated in a DBMS.

To date, the project team has studied three of the five applications, and this has taken three times as long as the team had originally expected. More than 400 different data names were discovered, but analysis of these data names indicated that only about 150 different data variables really existed. The difference is due to data redundancy. For example, the number of units being produced in a job is referred to by the data name "Units started" in the production scheduling application but by "Quantity" in the work-in-process application and by "Units" in the finished goods inventory application. These three different data names in the three different applications refer to the same real data element. As another example, the economic production quantity for a product is referred to by the data name "Lot size" in the production scheduling application but by "Minimum level" in the finished goods inventory application. These examples indicate one reason why data have to be reformatted when they are transferred from one application to another. The project team found many other similar instances of data redundancy in the three applications it has studied so far.

The problem of data redundancy is also complicated by the fact that the different data names for the same data element usually have different physical representations in the different applications. For example, "Units started" in the production scheduling application has a length of 8 characters, but "Quantity" in the work-in-process application has a length of 10 characters.

Inconsistency is another type of data ambiguity the project team discovered. Inconsistency occurs when the same data name is used to mean different things in different applications. For example, the data name "Code" in the production scheduling application means department code, but "Code" means transaction code in the work-in-process application and product number in the finished goods inventory application. This is yet another reason why data have to be reformatted when they are transferred from one application to another. The project team found several other similar instances of data inconsistency in the three applications it studied.

The five applications cannot be integrated while data ambiguities exist. Yet the project is taking considerably more time than expected. The status of the DBMS project is currently being reviewed by the management of Ernst and Anderson.

Required

a. If a user requested the data name "Lot size" in the production scheduling application, and the same user entered the data name "Minimum level" in the finished goods inventory application, what would be the result? If a user requested the data name "Units started" in the production scheduling application, then requested the data name "Quantity" in the work-in-process application, and then requested the data name "Units" in the finished goods inventory application, what would be the result? What additional consideration compounds this type of problem?

b. If a user requested the data name "Code" in the production scheduling application, then requested "Code" in the work-in-process application, and then requested "Code" in the finished goods inventory application, what would be the result?

c. Discuss the role of a data dictionary in analyzing data ambiguity. Indicate how specific sections of a data dictionary can help resolve data ambiguity.

d. What action should the management of Ernst and Anderson take concerning the status of the DBMS project? Should the project team complete its study of data ambiguity even though the project has taken considerably more time than expected? Should the DBMS project proceed in view of the large amount of data ambiguity that has been discovered? If so, what is the first database that should be implemented?

31. The database administrator (DBA) is not necessarily a single individual. In a large organization, several individuals may share overall responsibility for the DBA function. Discuss each of the following.

a. Why is the DBA function crucial to the concept of data management?

b. What administrative responsibilities should be vested in the DBA?

c. What responsibilities and duties should *not* be vested in or permitted to the DBA function?

d. Where should the DBA function be placed in the organizational structure of a firm?

32. Consider the following relation in first normal form:

ORDER (ORDER#, VENDOR#, PART#, DESCRIPTION, QUANTITY, PRICE, TOTAL_AMOUNT)

    The underlining indicates a combination key that consists of the concatenated fields ORDER#, VENDOR#, and PART#.

a. What is needed to attain second normal form?
b. What is needed to attain third normal form?

33. Consider the following relation:

CLASS-LIST (COURSE#, CLASS-ROOM, STUDENT#, STUDENT-MAJOR)

a. Assuming that each student can have only one major, is this relation normalized? If so, is it in first, second, or third normal form? If it is not already in third normal form, what is necessary to attain this?

b. Would your answer to part (a) be different if a student can have more than one major? Discuss.

34. At Bird Company, an order is recorded in two separate tables as follows. The table titled *orders* contains a single record of header information for each order in the following fields: order number (numeric data), customer number (character data), order type (character data), subtotal (numeric data), and shipping charges (numeric data). The items ordered and related amounts for each order (a "many-to-one" relationship) are recorded in the table titled *order details*. Each entry in the *order details* table contains the fields order number (numeric data), the vendor product number of the item (character data), quantity of the item (numeric data), and price of the item (numeric data). Sample records are illustrated below.

Orders (Sample Records)

Order Number (numeric)	Customer Number (character)	Order Type (character)	Subtotal (numeric)	Shipping Charges (numeric)
101	16822	Phone	145.00	12.25
102	10023	Email	224.00	15.66
103	12476	Fax	98.54	8.48
104	16822	Mail	210.44	24.00
105	14562	Fax	500.00	45.65

Order Details (Sample Records)

Order Number (numeric)	Vendor Product (character data)	Quantity (numeric)	Price (numeric)
101	16,822	2	22.50
101	10,023	5	10.00
101	12,476	2	25.00
102	15,822	2	112.00
103	10,023	5	10.00
103	11,476	2	20.00
103	10,099	1	8.54
104	15,822	3	168.00
104	15,444	2	21.22
105	12,476	20	25.00

Required

a. Write an SQL query that retrieves all of the fields for each record and all of the records from the *orders* table.
b. Write an SQL query that retrieves order number and vendor product number for all of the records from the *order details* table.
c. Write an SQL query that retrieves order number and order type for all of the records from the *orders* table. The query should sort the data ascending by order number.
d. Write an SQL query that retrieves order number and vendor product number for records from the *order details* table, selecting only records that have a price that is greater than 20.00.
e. Write an SQL query that retrieves order number and customer number for records from the *orders* table, selecting only records that have "fax" as the order type. The query should sort the data descending by customer number.
f. Write an SQL query that displays the total number of records in the *order details* table.
g. Write an SQL query that displays the average value of shipping charges for all of the records in the *orders* table.

h. Write an SQL query that displays the order number and the total amount of the subtotal and shipping charges for each record for all of the records in the *orders* table.

i. Write an SQL query that displays the order number and the customer number from the *orders* table and the corresponding vendor product number from the *order details* table for all of the orders in the *orders* table.

j. Write an SQL query that displays the order number and the shipping charges from the *orders* table and the corresponding vendor product number and quantity from the *order details* table for all of the orders that have an order type of either "fax" or "email."

Web Research Assignments

35. OpenOffice.org (www.openoffice.org) is both a project and a product. It is sponsored by Oracle, IBM, Google, and others. As a product, OpenOffice is an open source suite of software applications similar to Microsoft Office™. The database product associated with this suite is called *Base*.

Required

a. Write a report about OpenOffice Base. What type of database engine does it use? Is the product good enough to use for commercial applications? How does it compare to MySQL (www.mysql.com)?

36. Several of the most widely used database products are Oracle, DB2, MySQL, and MySQL Server.

Required

a. Write a report that contrasts and compares these database management systems.

b. Assume that you are developing a small business accounting application for a Linux-based computer running the Apache Web server. Further, you have decided to program your application using the Perl and PHP scripting languages. Which database system would be best to use with this project, MySQL or Oracle?

37. As discussed in this chapter, ACID rules are important for reliable transaction processing in a database setting.

Required

a. Write a brief report explaining the technologies that are used to ensure that the ACID rules are satisfied. (e.g., discuss the two-phase commit approach.)

38. As discussed in this chapter, object-oriented databases represent an emerging technology.

Required

a. Write a brief report explaining the commercial applicability of object-oriented databases. Do any commercial database products use an object-oriented database?

Answers to Chapter Quiz

1. c   **2.** c   **3.** b   **4.** b   **5.** d   **6.** a   **7.** a   **8.** c   **9.** c   **10.** b

Auditing Information Technology

Learning Objectives

Careful study of this chapter will enable you to:

- Distinguish between auditing through the computer and auditing with the computer.
- Describe and evaluate alternative information systems audit technologies.
- Characterize various types of information systems audits.
- Describe IT Governance and the COBIT standard for auditing information technology.

Information Systems Auditing Concepts

Generally speaking, auditing involves the process in which an individual or entity (the auditor) provides assurances to at least one other individual or entity regarding representations or assertions made by some third party (the auditee). In the typical corporate financial reporting situation, the auditor is a public accounting firm, auditee is the company being audited, the third party is the public, and the representations and assertions are financial statements of the company being audited.

In a broader sense, the subject matter of the audit (i.e., the assertions and representations) can be nearly anything. For example, in an income tax audit, the auditor provides assurances to the government regarding representations in the taxpayer's tax return. Similarly, in an election audit, the auditor may provide assurance to the public that the votes were collected and counted according to rules prescribed by law.

The term *information systems auditing* is commonly used to describe two different types of IT-related activity. One use of the term is to describe the process of reviewing and evaluating the internal controls in an electronic data processing (EDP) system. This type of activity is normally undertaken by auditors during compliance testing and might be described as **auditing through the computer**. The other general use of the term is to describe use of the computer by an auditor to perform some audit work that otherwise would have to be done manually. This type of activity is normally undertaken during substantive testing of account balances and might be described as **auditing with the computer**. Many audits involve both compliance testing and substantive testing. Both types of information systems auditing might be undertaken by both internal auditors and external auditors.

Structure of a Financial Statement Audit

The primary objective and responsibility of the external auditor is to attest to the fairness of a firm's financial reports. Whereas the internal auditor serves a firm's management, the external auditor serves a firm's stockholders, the government, and the general public. Despite this clear difference of purpose, internal and external auditors do similar things in the area of information systems auditing. This is not to say that much audit work is duplicated. Generally, the opposite is true, due to the large degree of cooperation and interaction that frequently exists between

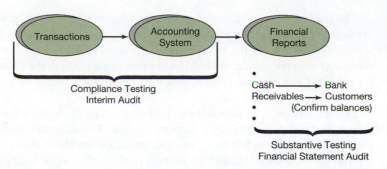

FIGURE 14.1

Structure of a Financial Statement Audit

a firm's internal and external auditors. Internal auditors commonly undertake audits that are reviewed and relied on by external auditors as they audit a firm's financial statements.

In an audit directed toward the attestation of financial statements, the auditor could, in theory, ignore the system of internal control and still obtain sufficient evidence to justify a professional opinion of the financial statements. This approach is generally impractical because the cost of obtaining enough substantive evidence to be sufficient without using the internal control system is prohibitive. Total audit cost usually can be reduced significantly if some audit resources are directed at reviewing and verifying the internal controls in the system that generated the financial statements. Then, relying on the client's internal control system, a lesser degree of assurance is necessary in direct substantive tests of financial statement figures. Further, legal requirements such as the Sarbanes–Oxley Act (SOX) may require the auditors to explicitly evaluate either internal controls or management's representations regarding internal controls, or both.

For this reason, an audit is almost universally divided into two basic components (Figure 14.1). The first component, usually called the **interim audit**, has the objective of establishing the degree to which the internal control system can be relied on. This usually requires some type of **compliance testing**. The purpose of compliance testing is to confirm the existence, assess the effectiveness, and check the continuity of operation of those internal controls on which reliance is to be placed. The second component of an audit, usually called the **financial statement audit**, involves **substantive testing**. Substantive testing is the direct verification of financial statement figures, placing such reliance on internal control as the results of the interim audit warrant. For example, as shown in Figure 14.1, substantive testing of cash would involve direct confirmation of bank balances. Substantive testing of receivables would involve direct confirmation of balances with customers. In an audit directed at the attestation of financial statements, the direct purpose of the audit is served by substantive testing in the financial statement audit phase, whereas an indirect purpose (achieving overall economy through permitting reliance on internal control) is served by compliance testing in the interim audit phase.

Auditing around the Computer

During the early years of information systems development, computerized accounting systems provided auditors with very little need to significantly alter audit approaches and technology used in manual systems. Batch processing was the dominant method used in computers, and an around-the-computer approach provided for an adequate audit.

 CASE IN POINT

The first widely known case of computer fraud occurred at Equity Funding Corporation of America. Beginning in 1964 and continuing on until 1973, managers for the company booked false insurance policies to show greater profits, thus boosting the price of the stock of the company. The scandal was so large that the story was made into a movie, *The Billion Dollar Bubble*.

In general terms, an accounting system is comprised of input, processing, and output. In the **around-the-computer approach**, the processing portion is ignored. Instead, source documents supplying the input to the system are selected and summarized manually so that they can be compared with the output. As batches are processed through the system, totals are accumulated for accepted and rejected records. Auditors emphasize control over rejected transactions, their correction, and then resubmission.

Given advances in information technology (IT), the around-the-computer approach is no longer used widely, especially in large companies. This approach implicitly ignores any computerized system as though it does not exist. Assumptions about the system are drawn by examining the source documents and the output, comprised of error listings, reports, and so on. This approach also assumes that a computer system cannot be used to falsify records without being detected by manual procedures.

Auditing through the Computer

Auditing through the computer may be defined as the verification of controls in a computerized system. Consideration of the nature of IT and internal control in an IT environment yields the framework shown in Figure 14.2. General controls are relevant to the information systems themselves, as well as to the systems development aspect of IT. Application controls are related to specific computer application systems. A thorough information systems audit involves verifying both general and application controls in a computerized system. More generally, an individual information systems audit would be directed at one of these areas, usually a specific application system such as accounts receivable.

Information systems audits to verify compliance with internal controls are performed by both internal and external auditors. The objectives of the external auditor are usually directed toward the attestation of financial statements. Internal auditors frequently embrace the same objectives; at other times, internal auditors perform compliance audits that are responsive to the desires of top management and the particular needs of the company. The general conduct of an information systems audit is subject to the same professional standards relevant to any audit. For the external auditor, these standards are specified in AICPA's (American Institute of Certified Public Accountants) Statements of Auditing Standards. Internal auditors have professional auditing standards promulgated by the Institute of Internal Auditors that are similar to the AICPA standards. Basic auditing standards are not altered by the technology employed in the system to be audited.

Auditing with the Computer

Auditing with the computer is the process of using IT in auditing. IT is used to perform some audit work that otherwise would have to be done manually. The use of IT by auditors is no longer optional. It is essential. Most of the data that auditors must evaluate are already in electronic

FIGURE 14.2

Control Framework in IT Environment

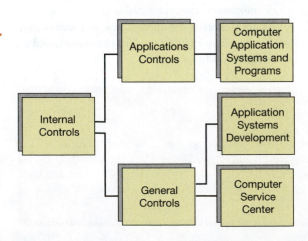

format. It is senseless to convert electronic data to a paper format strictly for audit purposes. Furthermore, auditing itself is not immune to competitive pressures to be more productive. The use of IT is essential to increase the effectiveness and efficiency of auditing.

The potential benefits of using information systems technology in an audit include the following:

- Computer-generated working papers generally are more legible and consistent. Such working papers may also be stored, accessed, and revised easily.
- Time may be saved by eliminating manual footing, cross-footing, and other routine calculations.
- Calculations, comparisons, and other data manipulations are performed more accurately.
- Analytical review calculations may be performed more efficiently, and their scope may be broadened.
- Project information such as time budgets and the monitoring of actual time versus budgeted amounts may be generated and analyzed more easily.
- Standardized audit correspondence such as questionnaires and checklists, proposal letters, and report formats may be stored and modified easily.
- Morale and productivity may be improved by reducing the time spent on clerical tasks.
- Increased cost-effectiveness is obtained by reusing and extending existing electronic audit applications to subsequent audits.
- Increased independence from information systems personnel is obtained.

The benefits identified in the first four points accrue primarily to the individual auditor who is actually performing the audit. Clear and obvious benefits are obtained from the calculating and data analysis capability provided by IT. Properly programmed, totals and the like should be accurate. More complicated calculations such as statistical regressions are performed easily. The other benefits may be realized by management of the internal audit function. Management of internal audit, like managers in other organizational functions, has much to gain from the efficient application of IT. The ability to analyze time budget and other types of project control information facilitates managerial control, a quality necessary to the internal audit function as well as to all other organizational functions. The ability to standardize work papers, questionnaires, and other such documents used in audits performed by the audit staff also enhances managerial control and helps to ensure uniform and consistent application of practice by the audit staff. The reusability of electronic audit technology increases overall cost-effectiveness. And the potential positive effects on staff morale and subsequent productivity gains should make the use of IT a goal of every audit manager.

Risk-Based Auditing

Risk-based auditing (RBA) provides assurances relating to the effectiveness of an organization's enterprise risk management (ERM) processes. Specifically, RBA provides assurance that risks are being managed within the organization's risk appetite. In effect, RBA involves an audit of an organization's ERM processes. It therefore deals with evaluating whether management has effective processes for identifying, classifying, scoring, and treating important risks with internal controls or other means.

In RBA, risks must generally be defined in the light of the organization's objectives. Potential events that are risks for one company may be of help to another. For example, a potential shortage of Middle East oil might be a threat to an airline company but a help to a company that specializes in alternative fuels.

RBA can be distinguished from the general use of a risk-based approach to auditing, although the two terms are sometimes used interchangeably. In RBA, the subject of the audit is how well the management manages risks. On the other hand, a risk-based approach can be applied to any type of audit, regardless of the subject. The goal of the risk-based approach to auditing is to apply audit efforts to areas in proportion to their likelihood to significantly impact the auditor's overall audit conclusions. For example, a risk-based approach might lead an auditor to pay relatively more attention to accounts receivable versus fixed assets in a company whose fixed assets have not changed in the previous 10 years but whose accounts receivable have tripled relative to the previous year.

The Public Company Accounting Oversight Board (PCAOB) has encouraged a risk-based approach to testing the effectiveness of internal controls as they related to financial audits. As applied, this approach involves a top-down, sequential identification of controls to be tested. The sequence in identifying controls to focus on is discussed below:

- **Company-level controls.** The auditor evaluates the design of the control environment, management's risk management processes, the internal audit function, training, and other control-related processes that have a pervasive effect throughout the organization.
- **Accounts.** The auditor identifies specific accounts of interest, specifically those that pose higher overall risk to the audit conclusions based on the magnitude of the account balance and the likelihood of error or fraud in the account.
- **Processes.** The auditor identifies processes and classes of transactions that relate to the accounts identified in the previous step.
- **Risks.** The auditor identifies points of possible fraud or error in the processes that were identified in the previous step.
- **Controls.** The auditor identifies controls that are designed to deal with the risks of frauds and errors identified in the previous step.

Information Systems Auditing Technology

Information systems auditing technology has evolved along with computer systems development. There is no one overall auditing technology (Table 14.1). Rather, there are a number of tools and techniques that may be used as appropriate to accomplish an audit's objectives. These technologies differ widely as to the amount of technical expertise required for their use. Several of the technologies entail significant costs to implement, whereas others may be implemented with relatively little cost.

Test Data

Test data are auditor-prepared input containing both valid and invalid data. Prior to processing the test data, the input is processed manually to determine what the output should look like. The auditor then compares the test output with the manually processed results (Figure 14.3). If the results are not as expected, the auditor attempts to determine the cause of the discrepancy.

Historically, test data represented the first attempt to audit through the computer. While it might be impractical for an auditor to be able to understand the detailed logic of a computer program, he or she can understand the general specifications of a system and use this knowledge to determine whether or not the system works.

The test data technique is widely used by auditors as well as computer programmers to verify the processing accuracy of computer programs. Test data may be used to verify input transaction validation routines, processing logic, and computational routines of computer programs and to verify the incorporation of program changes. The technique is particularly good for testing programs in which calculations such as interest or depreciation are involved. The technique requires minimal computer expertise and is usually inexpensive to implement because it requires no modification of existing computer applications.

With test data, regular live production programs are used, and it is essential to ensure that the test data do not affect the files maintained by the system. This requires coordination between the auditor and computer personnel. It would be ironic if an audit procedure designed to detect errors were to introduce its own errors. It is important to note that test data can only evaluate programs. Other tests of the integrity of input data and output files are usually needed as well.

TABLE 14.1 Information Systems Auditing Technologies

Technique	Description	Example
Test data	Test data are input containing both valid and invalid data.	Payroll transactions with both valid and invalid employee identification numbers.
Integrated test facility (ITF)	ITF involves both the use of test data and the creation of fictitious records (vendors, employees) on the master files of a computer system.	Payroll transactions for fictitious employees are processed concurrently with valid payroll transactions.
Parallel simulation	Processing real data through audit programs. The simulated output and the regular output are then compared.	Depreciation calculations are verified by processing the fixed-asset master file with an audit program.
Audit software	Computer programs that permit the computer to be used as an auditing tool.	An auditor uses a computer program to extract data records from a master file.
Generalized audit software (GAS)	GAS is audit software that has been specifically designed to allow auditors to perform audit-related data processing functions.	An auditor uses GAS to search computer files for unusual items.
PC software	Software that allows the auditor to use a PC to perform audit tasks.	A PC spreadsheet package is used to maintain audit working papers and audit schedules.
Embedded audit routines	Special auditing routines included in regular computer programs so that transaction data can be subjected to audit analysis.	Data items that are exceptions to auditor specified edit tests included in a program are written to a special audit file.
Extended records	Modification of programs to collect and store data of audit interest.	A payroll program is modified to collect data pertaining to overtime pay.
Snapshot	Modification of programs to output data of audit interest.	A payroll program is modified to output data pertaining to overtime pay.
Tracing	Tracing provides a detailed audit trail of the instructions executed during the program's operation.	A payroll program is traced to determine if certain edit tests are performed in the correct order.
Review of system documentation	Extending system documentation such as program flowcharts are reviewed for audit purposes.	An auditor desk checks the processing logic of a payroll program.
Control flowcharting	Analytic flowcharts or other graphic techniques are used to describe the controls in a system.	An auditor prepares an analytic flowchart to review controls in the payroll application system.
Mapping	Special software is used to monitor the execution of a program.	The execution of a program with test data as input is mapped to indicate how extensively the input tested individual program statements.

Test data are prepared after the system to be audited has been reviewed and transactions (test data) are designed to test selected aspects of the system. The test data might be generated by completing input forms to generate fictitious test transactions or, alternatively, by reviewing actual input data and selecting several real transactions for processing as test data. A less common technique is to create test data using test data generators—specially designed computer programs that create comprehensive test data based on input parameters that describe the nature of the program to be tested.

As an audit technology, test data have several limitations. A test can be run only on a specific program at a specific point in time. The test data may become obsolete because of program changes. The use of test data must be announced; the data are processed in a test run rather than concurrently with actual live transactions. Thus an auditor cannot always ensure that the program being tested is the one that is used regularly. Finally, test data generally cannot cover all combinations of conditions that a computer program might encounter in use.

FIGURE 14.3

Test Data Approach

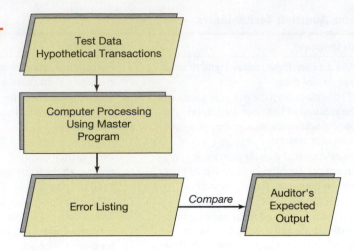

FIGURE 14.3

Test Data Approach

Integrated-Test-Facility Approach

Integrated test facility (ITF) involves the use of test data and also the creation of fictitious entities (e.g., vendors, employees, products, or accounts) on the master files of a computer system. The technique is integrated because the test data are processed concurrent with real transactions against live master files that contain the real as well as fictitious entities. Accordingly, audit checks are made as a part of the normal processing cycle, ensuring that the programs being checked are identical to the programs that process real data (Figure 14.4).

 CASE IN POINT

> The Internal Auditing Benchmarking Association™, a service of The Benchmarking Network, Inc., conducts benchmarking studies to help identify "best in class" internal auditing processes.

Test data are identified by special codes and must be excluded from the normal system outputs either manually or by modifying or initially designing the application programs to perform this function. The need to exclude the fictitious data from normal output reports is the major disadvantage of ITF, but this is an unavoidable consequence of the objective of the technique,

FIGURE 14.4

Integrated-Test-Facility Approach

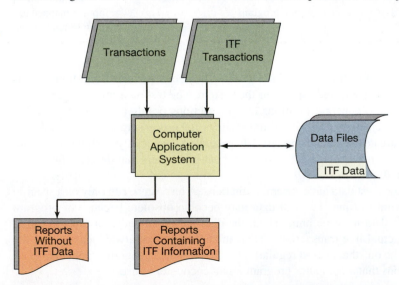

which is to process test data concurrent with real data. Careful planning is necessary to ensure that ITF data are segregated properly from the normal outputs.

ITF is a popular technique. If planned carefully, costs of using ITF are minimal. This is so because no special processing or other interruption of normal computer activity is involved. An ITF will normally be developed at the same time as the application system and will increase the normal cost of systems development. However, once implemented, operating costs are low. ITF is used commonly to audit large computer application systems that employ real-time processing technology. Concurrent testing is appropriate to concurrent real-time processing of transactions.

ITF is a powerful audit technology. Ironically, one of the earliest publicized computer fraud cases—the Equity Funding scandal—involved modification of computer programs to separately process thousands of bogus insurance policies, which is essentially the same concept used in ITF. The bogus policies were identified by a special code and were excluded routinely from reports provided to auditors but were included in all other reports. Similarly, test data differ from fraudulent data only in that test data are processed under controlled conditions by auditors.

Parallel Simulation

Both the test data and the ITF methods process test data through real programs. **Parallel simulation** processes real data through test or audit programs. The simulated output and the regular output are compared for control purposes. The amount of redundant processing undertaken by the test or audit program is usually limited to sections that are of major interest to the audit. For example, parallel simulation of a cost accounting program may be limited to the functions that update work-in-process (WIP) records. Other functions, such as scheduling or performance reporting, may not be included in the simulation program because they are not of direct interest to the audit. This is illustrated in Figure 14.5.

Parallel simulation—the redundant processing of all input data by a separate test program—permits comprehensive validation and is appropriate where transactions are sufficiently important to require a 100% audit. The audit program used in parallel simulation is typically some type of generalized audit program that processes data and produces output identical to the program being audited. The same actual data are processed by both programs and the results compared. This approach is expensive and time-consuming, but unlike the other approaches, it uses real data. Furthermore, it can be used off-site.

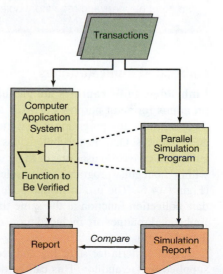

FIGURE 14.5

Parallel Simulation

Audit Software

Audit software includes computer programs that permit the computer to be used as an auditing tool. The computer is programmed to read, select, extract, and process sample data from computer files. There are many types of audit software that may be used to varying degrees. Conventional software such as system utility programs, information retrieval programs, or high-level languages might be used. More common is the use of specially designed audit software packages, known as *generalized audit software* (GAS). These are discussed separately.

GENERALIZED AUDIT SOFTWARE (GAS)   **Generalized audit software (GAS)** is software that has been specifically designed to facilitate the use of IT in auditing. GAS was originally developed by public accounting firms in the late 1960s and has a long history of use. GAS is designed specifically to allow auditors with little computer expertise to perform audit-related data processing functions. These packages can perform such tasks as selecting sample data from the files, checking computations, and searching the files for unusual items. They also incorporate many special features that are useful to auditors, such as the statistical selection of sample data and the preparation of confirmation requests.

The low cost of PCs, coupled with the availability of a wide variety of software packages, has made the PC an important tool in administrating an audit. General-purpose software packages such as word processing and spreadsheet software have many audit applications. In addition, special-purpose audit-oriented software packages have been developed specifically for use in audit administration.

ACL, published by ACL Software, is one example of PC audit software. It allows the field auditor to connect a PC to a client's accounting system and then extract and analyze data. For example, using ACL, an auditor can directly access SAP ERP data. ACL accesses files in their native format without any need to convert them. ACL provides a wide range of functions that allow the auditor to do such things as recalculate account balances for verification, age and analyze accounts receivable, and identify trends and exceptions.

 CASE IN POINT

ACL Services Ltd. (www.acl.com) is the publisher of widely used audit-related software solutions that enable comprehensive, independent testing and monitoring of transactional data, enabling organizations to validate the effectiveness of internal controls across the enterprise to meet business and regulatory objectives.

Embedded Audit Routines

Embedded audit routines are an audit technology that involves modification of computer programs for audit purposes. This is accomplished by building special auditing routines into regular production programs so that transaction data or some subset of them can be subjected to audit analysis. One such technique has been termed *embedded audit data collection*. Embedded audit data collection uses one or more specially programmed modules embedded as **in-line code** within the regular program code to select and record data for subsequent analysis and evaluation (Figure 14.6). The use of in-line code means that the application program performs the audit data collection function at the same time as it processes data for normal production purposes. Embedded routines are included more easily in a program as it is being developed than added as a modification later on.

Audit criteria for selecting and recording transactions by the embedded modules must be supplied by the auditor. This can be done in different ways. In an approach called the **system**

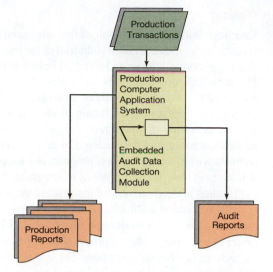

FIGURE 14.6

Embedded Audit Data Collection

control audit review file, auditor-determined programmed edit tests for limits or reasonableness (called *audit hooks*) are included in the program as it is developed initially. During normal operation of the program, data items that are exceptions to these edits are written to a log file. This file of exceptions may be reviewed by the auditor, and any appropriate actions may be undertaken. Values used in such limit or reasonableness tests may be set when the module is developed; alternatively, the module may be programmed so that the test limits may be altered by the auditor as desired. Transactions might be selected randomly rather than as exceptions to programmed edit tests. The objective of this approach is to generate a statistical sample of transactions for later audit. This approach has been termed **sample audit review file**.

Extended Records

Extended records involve the modification of computer programs to provide a comprehensive audit trail for selected transactions by collecting in one extended record additional data concerning processing that are normally not collected. Since many different processing steps may be combined within a single program, the intervening steps that make up the audit trail are often lost. Several different files might have to be reviewed to follow the processing of a specific transaction.

With the extended record technique, specific transactions are tagged, and the intervening processing steps that normally would not be saved are added to the extended record, permitting the audit trail to be reconstructed for these transactions. The extended record includes data from all the separate application programs that may process a transaction, thus providing a complete audit trail. Transactions might be identified by special codes, selected randomly, or selected as exceptions to edit tests.

Snapshot

Snapshot, as the name implies, attempts to provide a comprehensive picture of the working of a program at particular points in time. Snapshot is a common program-debugging technique. Snapshot involves the addition of program code to cause the program to print out the contents of selected memory areas at the time, during processing, that the snapshot code is executed. This provides a hard copy of the operation of the program that otherwise would not be available and is very useful in locating bugs in a program. As an audit tool, snapshot code may be added to areas of the program that are of interest to the audit and executed only for transactions that are exceptions to predetermined edit tests. Snapshot and extended records are very similar technology, with snapshot generating a printed audit trail and extended records incorporating snapshot data in the extended record rather than on hard copy.

Tracing

Tracing is another audit technique that originated as a program-debugging aid. Tracing a program's execution provides a detailed audit trail of the instructions executed during the program's operation. Tracing is normally executed using an option in the program source code language (such as C++). The audit trail provided by the trace depends on the particular trace package. High-level languages are traced at the source-statement level; lower-level languages are traced at a more detailed level. Tracing provides a detailed listing of the sequence of program statement execution. A trace can produce thousands of output records, and care must be exercised that an excessive number of transactions are not tagged for tracing. For audit purposes, tracing might be used to verify that internal controls within an application program are executed as the program processes live or test data. A trace may also indicate sections of unexecuted program code, a situation that in some instances has resulted in the discovery of incorrect or unauthorized modifications to a program.

All embedded audit routine techniques require a high level of technical expertise when they are first set up and a moderate to high level of knowledge to use them effectively. They are far easier to implement when a program and/or files for an application are designed rather than after the system has begun operation. The degree of independence that auditors can maintain while developing such systems will depend largely on the level of technical expertise they possess. Even when the auditor possesses a high level of technical expertise, development still requires a good deal of cooperation between the auditor and systems personnel.

Review-of-Systems Documentation

Review-of-systems documentation, such as narrative descriptions, flowcharts, and program listings, is probably the oldest information systems auditing technique and still a widely used one. This approach is particularly appropriate in the initial phases of an audit as preparation for the selection and use of other more direct audit technology.

Many types of reviews are possible. An auditor may request computer personnel to "dump" a computer file, that is, to provide the auditor with a complete listing of the file's contents. Alternatively, the auditor may request dumps of program source language listings. These listings may be reviewed manually by the auditor. Programs might be **desk checked** by the auditor. In desk checking, the auditor manually processes test or real data through the program logic. Program flowcharts might be reviewed in the same manner. A more sophisticated review of a program might be undertaken by requesting a dump of the object code, that is, machine-language version of a program. Review of this form of system documentation provides the greatest assurance that what is checked is actually what does the processing, but this form of review requires considerable technical expertise and patience. The auditor might review the manufacturer's blueprint of the software and compare it with the software in use. The auditor might verify a hash total of the object code of the software to detect modifications to the software.

Another type of documentation that may be examined is the operating documentation generated by many computer systems as a routine part of operations. Software that monitors the performance of computer operations is commonly available on large systems to provide technical statistics useful in tuning the system for efficient operation. While these statistics are oriented toward the operating functions of the system, such as channel and disk usage, they also might be used for specialized auditing purposes. Job accounting routines are frequently part of a computer's operating system. These routines collect and summarize statistics concerning program (job) resource use. Again, such statistics may be of interest to the auditor because they show who used the system, as well as when and which resources and programs were involved.

Control Flowcharting

In many cases, specific documentation for auditing purposes is reviewed and developed to show the nature of application controls in a system. This documentation has been termed **control flowcharting**. Analytic flowcharts, system flowcharts, and other graphic techniques are used to describe the controls in a system. A major advantage of flowcharts is that they are understandable to auditors, users, and computer personnel and thus facilitate communication between these different parties.

CASE IN POINT

Various software programs are available that will take an existing computer program and automatically generate flowcharts from it. For example, CyberMetrics® (www.usflowchart. com) publishes the PowerStructure® automatic flowcharting tool for COBOL and Visual Basic.

Mapping

More direct audit evidence concerning programs may be obtained by monitoring the running of a program with a special software measurement package. This audit technique is termed **mapping**. Special software is used to monitor the execution of a program; in doing so, the software counts the number of times each program statement in the program is executed and provides summary statistics concerning resource use. Mapping originated as a technique to assist program design and testing. Auditors can use the same software to determine whether specific program statements have been executed. Mapping can help to ensure that program application control statements that appear in the source language listing of a program actually execute when the program runs and that they have not inadvertently or otherwise been bypassed by a logic not readily apparent in the source-code listing of the program. Although software measurement packages can ensure that certain program steps have been executed, they do not ensure that execution was performed in the proper sequence. Counts of the number of times each program statement was executed do not imply that the total program executes in accordance with the intent of the programmer (i.e., that the program does the right thing).

Mapping can be used effectively in conjunction with a test data technique. The execution of a program with test data as input can be mapped. Evaluation of the output of the software monitor can indicate how extensively the input tested individual program statements. Statements that have not executed have not been tested.

Types of Information Systems Audits

General Approach to an Information Systems Audit

Most approaches to an information systems audit follow some variation of a three-phase structure. The first phase consists of an initial review and evaluation of the area to be audited and audit plan preparation. The second phase is a detailed review and evaluation of controls. The third phase involves compliance testing and is followed by analysis and reporting of results.

CASE IN POINT

The Information Systems Audit and Control Association (ISACA, www.isaca.org) is a global organization that publishes a variety of standards and other materials that are widely used by auditing and information systems professionals.

The initial review phase of an information systems audit determines the course of action the audit will take and includes decisions concerning specific areas to be investigated, the deployment of audit labor, the audit technology to be used, and the development of a time and/or cost budget for the audit. Documentation and review of performance are the primary control over the conduct of an information systems audit. Each general phase of an audit, as well as specific steps within each phase, should have the preparation of documentation as an objective. Such documentation provides a tangible output and goal for each audit step, allows effective supervision, and facilitates review.

Audit resources are usually limited, so it generally will not be possible to audit each application every year. Applications that are more subject to fraud or serious financial error are likely targets for audit. Frequently, a rotating system of selection is used to choose audit areas, with each application being audited according to some multiyear schedule.

Decisions concerning the deployment of auditing labor, the audit technology to be used, and the time/cost budget for the overall audit should also be made according to some systematic procedure. The outcome of all these decisions and the product of the initial review phase of an information systems audit is the audit program. An **audit program** is a detailed list of the audit procedures to be applied on a particular audit. Standardized audit programs for particular audit areas have been developed and are common in all types of auditing. The use of a standardized audit program is often possible, with modifications made to reflect the particular situation subject to audit.

The second general phase of an information systems audit is detailed review and evaluation. In this phase of the audit, effort is focused on fact finding in the area(s) selected for audit. Documentation of the application area is reviewed, and data concerning the operation of the system are collected by interviews, administration of internal control questionnaires, and direct observation. Transaction files, control logs, program listings, and other data are reviewed as necessary to confirm the scope of the audit set in the audit program and to design the test procedures to be used subsequently.

The third phase of the audit is testing. The testing phase of an audit produces evidence of compliance with procedures. Compliance tests are undertaken to provide reasonable assurance that internal controls exist and operate as prescribed in systems documentation. The nature of compliance tests that might be included in an information systems audit are discussed in the following sections.

Information Systems Application Audits

Application controls are divided into three general areas: input, processing, and output. An application audit generally involves reviewing the controls in each of these areas. In addition to the usual manual tracing and vouching techniques, all the audit technologies discussed earlier are relevant. The specific technology used will depend on the ingenuity and resources of the auditor. Test data, ITF, or parallel simulation might be used to test processing controls. Transactions to be selected for audit might be generated by an embedded audit module or by a separate audit program. GAS might be used to review transaction and/or output files. The nature of an application audit will be heavily influenced by the amount of audit involvement in the systems development process. ITF and embedded audit modules can be used only if they already exist in the application.

Application Systems Development Audits

Systems development audits are directed at the activities of systems analysts and programmers who develop and modify application programs, files, and related procedures. Controls governing the systems development process directly affect the reliability of the application programs that are developed. Three general areas of audit concern in the systems development process are systems development standards, project management, and program change control. The primary audit technique in each of these areas is a review and testing of the related documentation. This is accomplished by directly observing the documentation and by collecting relevant information through interviews and/or questionnaires.

Audits of the systems development process are more common to large organizations because many small organizations may not have a formal systems development process. The essence of a formal systems development process is documentation. If none exists, a potential audit is necessarily terminated because the audit consists primarily of review and testing of such documentation.

Computer Service Center Audits

Normally, an audit of the computer service center is undertaken before any application audits to ensure the general integrity of the environment in which the application will function. The general controls that govern computer service center operations complement application controls that are developed in specific application systems. The general controls that govern computer operations also help to ensure the uninterrupted availability of computer service center resources. Compliance tests would include review of documentary evidence; corroborating interviews with users, management, and systems personnel; direct observation; and inquiry. Audits of computer service center operations require a higher degree of technical training and familiarity with information systems operations than do audits of computerized applications.

Auditing Service-Oriented Architectures

Auditing a service-oriented architecture (SOA) involves special audit considerations. The typical SOA may be composed of hundreds or even thousands of individual services that can be connected together one way on one day and a different way on another day. Further, the different services will exchange messages (that contain privileged data) with each other. The result is no single clearly defined, fixed application that one can test, and the need for additional internal control.

Many SOA architectures externalize identity management (e.g., user password control) in the form of services that provide security to other services and applications composed of compositions of services. Security artifacts (e.g., user passwords and roles) are stored in centralized databases.

User security privileges are allocated through a centralized role provider, whose responsibilities include enforcing segregation of duties. The entire system of identity management and role management is supported by specialized services for authorization, authentication, provisioning of privileges, and audit and control. The audit and control services monitor the other services and messaging between them, constantly monitoring for security compliance and possible fraud.

In SOA environments, the auditor can still use many of the traditional audit techniques such as tracing test transactions, but he must also investigate the policies, procedures, and behaviors surrounding the specialized services unique to the SOA. In addition, special attention must be given to auditing samples of messages between services and to the security surrounding the deployment (i.e., orchestration) of services.

It Governance and COBIT

It is generally accepted that a strategic alignment of IT and enterprise objectives is a critical success factor. IT governance is an inclusive term that encompasses the variety of elements that interact to provide IT services within an organization. These elements include communication, business, legal and other issues, as well as management, IT users, IT staff, suppliers, auditors, and other parties. **IT governance** has the objective of enhancing and ensuring the efficient application of IT resources as a critical success factor that sustains and extends the organization's strategies and objectives.

 CASE IN POINT

The Computer Crime and Intellectual Property Section (CCIPS) of the U.S. Department of Justice is responsible for implementing the Department's national strategies in combating computer and intellectual property crimes worldwide. The Computer Crime Initiative is a comprehensive program designed to combat electronic penetrations, data thefts, and cyber attacks on critical information systems. CCIPS prevents, investigates, and prosecutes computer crimes by working with other government agencies, the private sector, academic institutions, and foreign counterparts.

Organizations must understand and manage the risks associated with implementing new technologies. There is a risk that IT strategy is not aligned with the business strategy of an organization. There is a risk that organizational structures that are necessary to facilitate the implementation of strategy and goals are not provided and sustained. There is a risk that a control framework for IT does not exist and thus IT is not subject to governance. There is a risk that IT performance is not measured and evaluated. Organizations must address these risks with an effective IT governance framework that addresses strategic alignment, performance measurement, risk management, value delivery, and resource management.

IT governance is an integral part of enterprise governance and consists of the leadership and organizational structures and processes that ensure that the organization's IT sustains and extends the organization's strategies and objectives. An IT governance framework such as Control Objectives for Information and related Technology (COBIT) can be a critical element in ensuring proper control and governance over information and the systems that create, store, manipulate, and retrieve it.

COBIT

COBIT is an open standard for control over IT. It is published by the IT Governance Institute. COBIT is directed at helping management discharge its responsibilities with respect to an organization's IT assets by "bridging the gaps" between business risks, control needs, and technical issues. COBIT provides good practices across a domain and process framework and presents activities in a manageable and logical structure. COBIT's "good practices" means that these practices represent a consensus of the experts. These practices will help management optimize the organization's information investments and will provide measures that may serve as benchmarks to be judged against when activities and events do not go according to plan. COBIT provides a generally applicable and accepted standard for IT security and control practices. It is designed to guide and assist management in determining and monitoring the appropriate level of IT security and control for their organization.

COBIT identifies 34 IT processes, a high-level approach to control over these processes, and several hundred detailed control objectives and audit guidelines to assess the IT processes. The 34 high-level COBIT objectives are organized into four domains. These domains are:

Plan and Organize. This domain deals with how the company as a whole uses its IT infrastructure to achieve its goals and objectives.

Acquire and Implement. This domain focuses on the company's overall strategies for identifying IT requirements and acquiring, implementing, and maintaining IT resources and projects.

Deliver and Support. This domain focuses on the processes involved in delivering, supporting, training, and security relating to IT applications.

Monitor and Evaluate. This domain deals with the company's strategies for assessing how effectively IT helps satisfy the company's objectives. The assessing process includes internal and external auditing.

The 34 high-level COBIT objectives organized by domain are shown in Table 14.2.

COBIT is designed for use by management, users, and auditors. Management can use COBIT to assist in balancing risk and control investment in the often unpredictable IT environment. Users of IT can use COBIT to obtain assurance concerning the security and associated controls of IT services that are provided by internal or third parties. Auditors can use COBIT to substantiate their opinions and/or provide advice to management on internal controls.

NAVIGATION DIAGRAM   COBIT contains a navigation diagram for each of the 34 IT processes. The diagram provides a description of the process, together with key goals and metrics in the form of a "waterfall" diagram. Each step in the framework is successively indented to give the diagram a waterfall-like appearance, as shown here.

Control over the IT process of
process name
> **that satisfies the business requirement for IT of**
> summary of most important IT goals
>> **by focusing on**
>> summary of most important process goals
>>> **is achieved by**
>>> activity goals
>>>> **and is measured by**
>>>> key metrics

TABLE 14.2   The 34 High-Level COBIT Objectives Organized by Domain

Plan and Organize
PO1 Define a Strategic IT Plan
PO2 Define the Information Architecture
PO3 Determine Technological Direction
PO4 Define the IT Processes, Organization, and Relationships
PO5 Manage the IT Investment
PO6 Communicate Management Aims and Direction
PO7 Manage IT Human Resources
PO8 Manage Quality
PO9 Assess and Manage IT Risks
PO10 Manage Projects

Acquire and Implement
AI1 Identify Automated Solutions
AI2 Acquire and Maintain Application Software
AI3 Acquire and Maintain Technology Infrastructure
AI4 Enable Operation and Use
AI5 Procure IT Resources
AI6 Manage Changes
AI7 Install and Accredit Solutions and Changes

Deliver and Support
DS1 Define and Manage Service Levels
DS2 Manage Third-party Services
DS3 Manage Performance and Capacity
DS4 Ensure Continuous Service
DS5 Ensure Systems Security
DS6 Identify and Allocate Costs
DS7 Educate and Train Users
DS8 Manage Service Desk and Incidents
DS9 Manage the Configuration
DS10 Manage Problems
DS11 Manage Data
DS12 Manage the Physical Environment
DS13 Manage Operations

Monitor and Evaluate
ME1 Monitor and Evaluate IT Performance
ME2 Monitor and Evaluate Internal Control
ME3 Ensure Regulatory Compliance
ME4 Provide IT Governance

Each of the corners in a navigation diagram contains a graphic that provides additional context. The context that is contained in each of the four corners in a COBIT navigation diagram is as follows.

Upper-left corner: A 3-D bar chart of information criteria with the following labels in individual bars: Effectiveness, Efficiency, Confidentiality, Integrity, Availability, Compliance, and Reliability. In each diagram, one of the above criteria is indicated as Primary and another as Secondary by including P or S on the bar that contains the criteria.

Upper-right corner: The four COBIT domains in button-like graphics: Plan and Organize, Acquire and Implement, Deliver and Support, and Monitor. The relevant domain is indicated with an enlarged button.

Lower-left corner: A pentangle figure of IT Governance focus areas with the following labels in individual segments: Strategic Alignment, Performance Measurement, Value Delivery, Risk Management, and Resource Management. One of these areas is indicated as Primary and another as Secondary by shading the appropriate segment P (dark) or S (gray).

Lower-right corner: A 3-D bar chart of IT resources with the following labels in individual bars: Applications, Information, Infrastructure, and People. Check marks indicate resources that are of concern to the process.

MATURITY MODELS   A maturity model component is used to evaluate an organization's relative level of achievement of IT governance. The defined levels in the scale are numbered 0–5, with 0 being the lowest level, and are as follows:

- 0: Nonexistent
- 1: Initial/Ad Hoc
- 2: Repeatable but Intuitive
- 3: Defined Process
- 4: Managed and Measurable
- 5: Optimized

The maturity model shows what has to be done to improve. Risk and controls in IT management processes are inherently subjective and imprecise topics that are not amenable to the more mechanistic approach that is found in the maturity models for software engineering. Scales need to be practical to apply and reasonably easy to understand. The advantage of a maturity model approach is that it is relatively easy for management to place themselves on the scale and appreciate what is involved if they need to improve performance. The 0–5 scale indicates how a process evolves from nonexistent to optimized. The scale includes 0 as it is quite possible that no process exists at all—a 0 measurement.

COBIT provides generic, qualitative descriptions of the six levels (0–5) in its maturity model (Table 14.3). An organization might use a similar but different maturity model. COBIT suggests that whatever model an organization decides to use, the scales should not be too granular. Too many levels would make the model difficult to use and, more important, suggest a precision that is not justifiable. Rather, management should concentrate on maturity levels based on a set of conditions that can be unambiguously met.

The maturity model offers a way of measuring how well-developed management processes are and how well-developed they should be. Management can map each of COBIT's 34 processes into the levels defined in the maturity model to determine:

- the organization's current status—where it is today
- the current status of the "best-in-class" in the industry—the benchmark
- the current status of international standards—an additional comparison
- the organization's strategy for improvement—where the organization wants to be

TABLE 14.3 COBIT's Generic Maturity Model

Level	Level Name	Level Definition
0	Nonexistent	Complete lack of any recognizable processes. The enterprise has not even recognized that there is an issue to be addressed.
1	Initial/Ad Hoc	There is evidence that the enterprise has recognized that issues exist and need to be addressed. There are, however, no standardized processes; instead, there are ad hoc approaches that are applied individually or on a case-by-case basis. The overall approach to management is disorganized.
2	Repeatable but Intuitive	Processes have developed to the stage where similar procedures are followed by different people undertaking the same task. There is no formal training or communication of standard procedures and responsibility is left to the individual. There is a high degree of reliance on the knowledge of individuals and, therefore, errors are likely.
3	Defined Process	Procedures have been standardized, documented, and communicated through training. It is mandated that these processes be followed; however, it is unlikely that deviations will be detected. The procedures themselves are not sophisticated but are the formalization of existing practices.
4	Managed and Measurable	Management monitors and measures compliance with procedures and takes action where processes appear not to be working effectively. Processes are under constant improvement and provide good practice. Automation and tools are used in a limited or fragmented way.
5	Optimized	Processes have been refined to a level of good practice, based on the results of continuous improvement and maturity modeling with other enterprises. IT is used in an integrated way to automate the workflow, providing tools to improve quality and effectiveness, making the enterprise quick to adapt.

The conceptual linkage of the maturity model to IT management processes is that increased maturity and capability is synonymous with increased risk management and increased efficiency.

The maturity model "scale" is used to quantify and make "graphic" what is inherently a subjective evaluation. Using the maturity model for a process, multiple parties share this quantification experience by using the same measurement scale. This should help professionals explain to managers where IT management shortcomings exist and set targets for where they need to be by comparing their organization's control practices to the best practice examples. The organization's business objectives and environment influence the appropriate maturity level for any process. The organization's dependence on IT, the level of technological sophistication, and the value of its information will determine the appropriate level of control maturity.

 CASE IN POINT

Val IT is a governance framework directed at the evaluation and selection of IT-enabled business investments, as well as benefit realization and delivery of value from those investments. The Val IT framework is based on the COBIT framework.

MANAGEMENT GUIDELINES   These consist of detailed inputs, outputs, activities, goals, and metrics for the 34 COBIT processes. Inputs and outputs illustrate what processes require from other processes and what the processes typically deliver. Activities and associated responsibilities are also provided. While this material is collected from hundreds of experts following rigorous research and review, the inputs, outputs, responsibilities, metrics, and goals are illustrative but not prescriptive or exhaustive. They provide a basis of expert knowledge from which each enterprise should select what efficiently and effectively applies to it based on enterprise strategy, goals, and policies.

Process inputs indicate what the process owner needs from other processes. Inputs are presented in a two-column table. The first column indicates the "From," or source of the input; the second column indicates the input. As an illustration, the first two of the eight inputs for process PO1 *"Define a Strategic IT Plan"* are Cost/benefits reports and Risk assessment. The process outputs are what the process owner has to deliver. This is also presented as a table. The first column indicates the output, while subsequent columns may vary in number and indicate the "To," or destination of the output. As an illustration, the first two of the six outputs for process PO1 *"Define a Strategic IT Plan"* are strategic IT plans and tactical IT plans.

Documentation and assignment of activities are shown in a RACI chart. A RACI chart identifies who is Responsible, Accountable, Consulted, and/or Informed. Activities are listed in the first column of the chart, while subsequent columns identify functions that receive assignments. The roles in the RACI chart include chief executive officer (CEO), chief financial officer (CFO), business executives, chief information officer (CIO), and business process owner, among others, and functions including compliance, audit, risk, and security—functions with control responsibilities but that do not have operational IT responsibilities. Assignments are indicted by placing an R (Responsible), A (Accountable), C (Consulted), and/or I (Informed) in the chart. For example, the first activity in the RACI chart for PO1 "Define a strategic IT Plan" is Link business goals to IT goals which is assigned as follows: CEO—C (consulted); CFO—I (informed); business executive—A/R (accountable/responsible); CIO—R (responsible); and business process owner—C (consulted).

PERFORMANCE MEASUREMENT   Goals and metrics are defined in COBIT at three levels:

- IT goals and metrics that define what the business expects from IT and how to measure it
- Process goals and metrics that define what the IT process must deliver to support IT objectives and how to measure it
- Activity goals and metrics that establish what needs to happen inside the process to achieve the required performance and how to measure it

Goals are defined top-down in that a business goal will determine a number of IT goals to support it. An IT goal is achieved by one process or the interaction of a number of processes.

Outcome measures are representations of the goals of an IT process. They are targets to be achieved. They are measurable indicators of the process that achieves the goals of an IT process. Outcome measures are lag indicators, as they can be measured only after the fact. They are usually expressed in positive terms but may be expressed negatively, that is, in terms of the impact of not attaining a goal. Outcome measures should be explicit. They should be measurable as a number or percentage. Management should set specific targets which need to be met, taking into account the past performance and future goals of an IT process. As an illustration, the following are the outcome measures for the Process PO1 *"Define a Strategic IT Plan"*:

- Percent of IT objectives in the IT strategic plan that support the strategic business plan
- Percent of IT initiatives in the IT tactical plan that support the tactical business plans
- Percent of IT projects in the IT project portfolio that can be directly traced back to the IT tactical plans

Performance indicators are measures that indicate that a process is achieving its business requirements by monitoring the performance of the enablers of the process. They are lead indicators of whether a goal will likely be reached or not. Performance indicators are process oriented and often express how well resources are utilized. Performance indicators are usually expressed as a number or percentage. A "good" performance indicator will accurately predict success or failure of attaining a process goal. As an illustration, the following are the performance indicators shown for Process PO1 *"Define a Strategic IT Plan"*:

- Delay between updates of business strategic/tactical plans and updates of IT strategic/tactical plans
- Percent of strategic/tactical IT plan meetings where business representatives have actively participated
- Delay between updates of IT strategic plan and updates of IT tactical plans
- Percent of tactical IT plans complying with the predefined structure/contents of those plans
- Percent of IT initiatives/projects championed by business owners

COBIT and Sarbanes–Oxley Compliance

While it is not specifically targeted at Sarbanes–Oxley compliance, COBIT may be used to address this issue. Indeed, one of the COBIT products is titled "IT Control Objectives for Sarbanes–Oxley." This product is of primary interest to governance, assurance, control, and security professionals. It provides guidance on how to ensure compliance with the IT environment based on the COBIT control objectives. It addresses the importance of IT in the design, implementation, and sustainability of internal control over disclosure and financial reporting.

Under the Securities and Exchange Commission's (SEC) rules for reporting Sarbanes–Oxley compliance, management's annual internal control report must contain, among other items, a statement identifying the framework used by management to evaluate the effectiveness of this internal control. The rules specifically refer to the COSO framework created by the Committee of the Sponsoring Organizations (COSO) of the Treadway Committee and suggest its use as a model framework. Technology is a vital component to any organization in assisting it to comply with the Sarbanes–Oxley Act. The importance of IT controls is implicit in the COSO internal control framework, but IT managers need detailed guidelines to establish, document, and evaluate their company's controls. COBIT is an IT control framework built in part upon the COSO framework. For Sarbanes–Oxley attestation, corporations must be sure that the IT systems that house, move, and transform data are secure. The COBIT framework was designed to address these IT concerns. Thus, COBIT can help IT managers address specific control objectives for Sarbanes–Oxley compliance.

 CASE IN POINT

U.S. Department of Defense (DoD) 8570.01-M *"Information Assurance Workforce Improvement Program"* manual identifies ISACA's Certified Information Systems Auditor (CISA) and Certified Information Security Manager (CISM) certifications among those approved for DoD information assurance (IA) professionals.

Professional Certifications Relating to IT Governance

ISACA sponsors three professional certifications relating to IT Governance. The *Certified Information Systems Auditor* (CISA) certification is for information systems audit, control, assurance and/or security professionals. The CISA certification program has been available since 1978 and has been renowned as the globally recognized achievement for those who control, monitor, and assess an organization's IT and business systems. The *Certified Information Security Manager* (CISM) certification is a management-focused certification that has been available since 2003. CISM is for the individuals who manage, design, oversee, and assess an enterprise's information security program. CISM defines the core competencies and international performance standards that those who have information security management responsibilities must master. CGEIT, *Certified in the Governance of Enterprise IT*, is the most recent certification program. The IT Governance certification is intended to recognize a wide range of professionals for their knowledge and application of IT governance principles and practices. It is designed for professionals who have management, advisory, or assurance responsibilities as defined by a "job practice" consisting of IT governance-related tasks and knowledge. Earning this designation will enable professionals to respond to the growing business demand for a comprehensive IT governance program that defines responsibility and accountability across the entire enterprise. Information on the CISA, CISM, and CGEIT certifications is available online at www.isaca.org.

Summary

The term *information systems auditing* is used commonly to describe two different types of computer-related activity. One use of the term is to describe the process of reviewing and evaluating the internal controls in an EDP system. This type of activity is described as auditing through the computer. The other general use of the term is to describe use of the computer by an auditor to perform some audit work that otherwise would have to be done manually. This type of activity is described as auditing with the computer.

Information systems audit technology has evolved along with computer system development. There is no one overall auditing technology. Rather, there are several technologies that may be used as appropriate to accomplish an audit's objectives. Technologies discussed include test data, ITF, parallel simulation, and generalized audit software, among others. Information systems audit technologies differ widely as to the amount of technical expertise required for their use. Several of the technologies entail significant costs to implement, whereas others may be implemented with relatively little cost.

Most approaches to an information systems audit follow some variation of a three-phase structure. These phases are initial review and evaluation of the area to be audited, detailed review and evaluation, and testing. Several general types of information systems audits might be undertaken. These are application audits, application systems development audits, computer service center audits, and audits of a service-oriented architecture (SOA).

IT governance is an integral part of enterprise governance and consists of the leadership and organizational structures and processes that ensure that the organization's IT sustains and extends the organization's strategies and objectives. An IT governance framework such as COBIT can be a critical element in ensuring proper control and governance over information systems that create, store, manipulate, and retrieve it.

Glossary

around-the-computer approach   information systems auditing approach in which the processing portion of a computer system is ignored.

auditing through the computer   the process of reviewing and evaluating the internal controls in an EDP system.

audit program   a detailed list of the audit procedures to be applied on a particular audit.

audit software   computer programs that permit the computer to be used as an auditing tool.

auditing with the computer   use of the computer by an auditor to perform some audit work that otherwise would have to be done manually.

COBIT   acronym for Control Objectives for Information and related Technology, an open standard for control over IT.

compliance testing   testing to confirm the existence, assess the effectiveness, and check the continuity of operation of internal controls.

control flowcharting   analytic flowcharts or other graphic techniques are used to describe the controls in a system.

desk checked   the auditor manually processes test or real data through the logic of a computer program.

embedded audit routines   special auditing routines included in regular computer programs so that transaction data can be subjected to audit analysis.

extended records   modification of programs to collect and store additional data of audit interest.

financial statement audit   the second stage of a financial statement audit that uses substantive testing for direct verification of financial statement figures.

generalized audit software (GAS)   audit software that has been specifically designed to allow auditors to perform audit-related data processing functions.

in-line code   an application program performs an embedded audit routine function such as data collection at the same time as it processes data for normal purposes.

integrated test facility (ITF)   concurrent information systems audit technology that involves the use of test data and also the creation of fictitious entities on the master files of a computer system.

interim audit   first stage of a financial statement audit that has the objective of establishing the degree to which the internal control system can be relied on.

IT governance   process that has the objective of enhancing and ensuring the efficient application of IT resources.

mapping   special software is used to monitor the execution of a program.

parallel simulation   the processing of real data through audit programs, with the simulated output and the regular output compared for control purposes.

review-of-systems documentation   existing systems documentation such as program flowcharts are reviewed for audit purposes.

sample audit review file   use of in-line code to randomly select transactions for audit analysis.

snapshot   modification of programs to output data of audit interest.

substantive testing   direct verification of balances contained in financial statements.

system control audit review file   auditor-determined programmed edit tests for audit transaction analysis are included in a program as it is initially developed.

test data   auditor-prepared input containing both valid and invalid data.

tracing   provides a detailed audit trail of the instructions executed during the program's operation.

Webliography

www.topcaats.com
The home page of the TopCAATs suite of computer-assisted audit tools (CAATs). TopCAATs includes over 100 audit tools and functions. TopCAATs is especially easy to use with minimal training.

www.audimation.com
The home page of Audimation Services, Inc., the provider of the IDEA Data Analysis Software, which is frequently used by auditors.

www.informationactive.com
The home page of InformationActive, Inc., the provider of ActiveData for Excel™, a suite of CAATs that work inside Microsoft Excel, and ActiveData for Office™, a similar suite of tools that works with a larger number of data records.

www.acl.com
The home page of ACL Services Ltd., the leading company in audit-analytic software. ACL provides a full suite of audit-related software, including for audit productivity, continuous auditing, fraud detection, regulatory compliance, secure data access, and team collaboration.

www.isaca.org
The home page of ISACA, a worldwide chapter-oriented organization devoted to information governance, control, security, and audit professionals. ISACA publishes information system auditing and control standards that are widely respected by accounting and IT professionals. The organization publishes a wide variety of materials and supports various professional certifications, including the Certified Information Systems Auditor (CISA).

www.theiia.org
The home page of the Institute of Internal Auditors. A chapter-based organization dedicated to internal auditing. The Institute provides the Certified Internal Auditor professional designation. It also supports research, education, and training, and the widely read *Internal Auditor* periodical (http://www.theiia.org/intauditor/).

Chapter Quiz

Answers to the chapter quiz appear on page 512.

1. Which of the following is a potential problem when using test data?
   a. testing a program that is not the actual program used for processing
   b. introducing errors into the program being tested
   c. both a and b
   d. neither a nor b

2. Which of the following is a potential problem when using ITF?
   a. testing a program that is not the actual program used for processing

   b. introducing errors into the program being tested
   c. both a and b
   d. neither a nor b

3. Which of the following is a concurrent auditing technology?
   a. test data
   b. ITF
   c. both a and b
   d. neither a nor b

4. Which of the following is a concurrent auditing technology?
   a. parallel simulation
   b. generalized audit software

    c. both a and b
    d. neither a nor b

5. Which of the following is a concurrent auditing technology?
    a. embedded audit routines
    b. control flowcharting
    c. both a and b
    d. neither a nor b

6. Which of the following is used to test the functioning of computer programs?
    a. test data
    b. parallel simulation
    c. both a and b
    d. neither a nor b

7. Which of the following is used to select data for audit analysis?
    a. generalized audit software
    b. embedded audit routines
    c. both a and b
    d. neither a nor b

8. Which of the following most likely would be implemented with generalized audit software?
    a. embedded audit routines
    b. parallel simulation
    c. both a and b
    d. neither a nor b

9. Mapping is a technology that provides the auditor (_____).
    a. assurance that program instructions are executing in proper sequence
    b. summary information regarding which program instructions are executed
    c. both a and b
    d. neither a nor b

10. Normally an audit of the computer service center is undertaken (_____) any application audits.
    a. during
    b. before
    c. after
    d. instead of

Review Problem

In the past, the records to be evaluated in an audit have been printed reports, listings, documents, and written papers, all of which are visible output. However, in fully computerized systems that employ daily updating of transaction files, output and files are frequently in machine-readable forms, such as tapes or disks. Thus they often present the auditor with an opportunity to use the computer in performing an audit.

Required

Discuss how the computer can be used to aid the auditor in examining accounts receivable in such a fully computerized system.

(CPA)

Solution to Review Problem

Testing Extension and Footings

The computer can be used to perform simple summations and other computations to test the correction of extensions and footings. The auditor may choose to perform tests on all records instead of just on samples because the speed and low cost per computation of the computer enable this at only a small extra amount of time and expense.

Selecting and Printing Confirmation Requests

The computer can select and print out confirmation requests on the basis of quantifiable selection criteria. The program can be written to select the accounts according to any set of criteria desired and using any sampling plan.

Examining Records for Quality (Completeness, Consistency, Valid Conditions, etc.)

The quality of visible records is readily apparent to the auditor. Sloppy record keeping, lack of completeness, and so on are observed by the auditor in the normal course of the audit. If machine-readable records are evaluated manually, however, a complete printout is needed to examine their quality. The auditor may choose to use the computer for examining these records for quality.

If the computer is to be used for the examination, a program is written to examine the record for completeness, consistency among different items, valid conditions, reasonable amounts, and so forth. For instance, customer file records might be examined to determine those for which no credit limit is specified, those for which account balances exceed credit limit, and those for which credit limits exceed a stipulated amount.

Summarizing Data and Performing Analyses Useful to the Auditor

The auditor frequently needs to have the client's data analyzed and/or summarized. Such procedures as aging accounts receivable or listing all credit balances in accounts receivable can be accomplished with a computer program.

Selecting and Printing Audit Samples

The computer may be programmed to select audit samples by the use of random numbers or by systematic selection techniques. The sample selection procedures may be programmed to use multiple criteria, such as the selection of a random sample of items under a certain dollar amount plus the selection of all items over a certain dollar amount. Other considerations can be included, such as unusual transactions, dormant accounts, and so forth.

(CPA)

Review Questions

1. What is meant by the expression *auditing around the computer*?
2. What are the two meanings of the term *information systems auditing*?
3. List and briefly describe the three phases of an information systems audit.
4. Distinguish between auditing through the computer and auditing with the computer.
5. What is a computer audit program?
6. What types of documents are examined in an information systems audit?
7. List five embedded audit routine techniques.
8. Compliance testing tests what?
9. How have PCs affected information systems auditing?
10. Identify the characteristics that are common to a typical information systems audit.
11. How would you select areas that should be audited in an information systems system?
12. Why do computer service center audits require the greatest expertise of an information systems auditor?

Discussion Questions and Problems

13. Auditors' initial response to computer systems was to audit around the computer. This strategy is *least* likely to be successful in an audit of
    a. a batch processing system for payroll.
    b. a card-based system for inventory.
    c. an online system for demand deposit accounts.
    d. a mark-sense document system for utility billing.

    (IIA)

14. Normally, auditors using the ITF technique enter immaterial transactions to minimize the effect on output. This is a disadvantage because
    a. certain limit tests cannot be attempted.
    b. the transaction will not appear normal.
    c. a special routine will be required in the application system.
    d. designing the test data can be difficult.

    (IIA)

    Use the following information to answer Questions 15, 16, and 17.

    Management has requested a special audit of the recently established electronic controls systems division because the last three quarterly profit reports seem to be inconsistent with the division's cash flow. The division sells customized control systems on a contract basis. A work-in-process (WIP) record is established for each contract on the WIP master file, which is kept on magnetic disk. Contract charges for materials, labor, and overhead are processed by the WIP computer program to maintain the WIP master file and to provide billing information.

    The preliminary audit has revealed that not all costs have been charged against the WIP records. Thus, when contracts are closed, reported profits have been overstated. It is now necessary to determine the reason(s) for this loss of control.

15. Which of the following information systems auditing techniques would be *most appropriate* to audit the processing accuracy of the WIP computer program in posting transactions to the WIP master file?

    a. control flowcharting
    b. test data
    c. review of program documentation
    d. embedded audit source code

16. Which of the following information systems auditing techniques would be *most appropriate* to audit the content of the WIP master file that is stored on magnetic disk?
    a. control flowcharting
    b. test data
    c. generalized audit software
    d. embedded audit source code

17. Which of the following information systems auditing techniques would be *most appropriate* to audit the overall business control context of the WIP computer processing system?
    a. control flowcharting
    b. test data
    c. generalized audit software
    d. embedded audit source code

    (IIA)

18. Smith Corporation has numerous customers. A customer file is kept on disk storage. Each customer file contains name, address, credit limit, and account balance. The auditor wishes to test this file to determine whether credit limits are being exceeded. The best procedure for the auditor to follow would be to
    a. develop test data that would cause some account balances to exceed the credit limit and determine if the system properly detects such situations.
    b. develop a program to compare credit limits with account balances and print out the details of any account with a balance exceeding its credit limit.
    c. request a printout of all account balances so that they can be checked manually against the credit limits.
    d. request a printout of a sample of account balances so that they can be checked individually against the credit limits.

    (CPA)

19. When an auditor tests a computerized accounting system, which of the following is true of the test data approach?
    a. Test data are processed by the client's computer programs under the auditor's control.
    b. Test data must consist of all possible valid and invalid conditions.
    c. Testing a program at year-end provides assurance that the client's processing was accurate for the full year.
    d. Several transactions of each type must be tested.

    (CPA)

20. An auditor's objective is to verify the processing accuracy of an application. An information systems audit approach for achieving this objective that avoids contaminating client master files or requiring substantial additional application programming is the
    a. embedded data collection technique.
    b. integrated test facility.
    c. test data method.
    d. snapshot method.

    (IIA)

21. Headquarters' auditors are reviewing a payroll application system via the ITF technique. Which of the following would be used by the auditors?
    a. Fictitious names processed with the normal payroll application of the corporation to a dummy entity
    b. Fictitious names processed in a separate run through the payroll application of the corporation
    c. A sample of last month's payroll reprocessed through the audit software package to a dummy entity
    d. Fictitious names processed through the generalized audit software package with the same company codes

    (IIA)

22. Which of the following is true of generalized audit software packages?
    a. They can be used only in auditing online computer systems.
    b. They can be used on any computer without modification.
    c. They each have their own characteristics, which the auditor must consider carefully before using in a given audit situation.
    d. They enable the auditor to perform all manual compliance test procedures less expensively.

    (CPA)

23. The most important function of generalized audit software is the capability to
    a. access information stored on computer files.
    b. select a sample of items for testing.
    c. evaluate sample test results.
    d. test the accuracy of the client's calculations.

    (CPA)

24. When auditing around the computer, the independent auditor focuses solely on the source documents and
    a. test data.
    b. computer processing.
    c. compliance techniques.
    d. computer output.

    (CPA)

25. In auditing through a computer, the test data method is used by auditors to test the
    a. accuracy of input data.
    b. validity of the output.
    c. procedures contained within the program.
    d. normalcy of distribution of test data.

    (CPA)

26. Which of the following methods of testing application controls uses a generalized audit software package prepared by the auditors?
    a. parallel simulation
    b. integrated-test-facility approach
    c. test data approach
    d. exception report tests

    (CPA)

27. A primary advantage of using generalized audit software packages in auditing the financial statements of a client that uses a computer system is that the auditor may
    a. substantiate the accuracy of data through self-checking digits and hash totals.
    b. access information stored on computer files without a complete understanding of the client's hardware and software features.
    c. reduce the level of required compliance testing to a relatively small amount.
    d. gather and permanently store large quantities of supportive evidential matter in machine-readable form.

    (CPA)

28. When testing a computerized accounting system, which of the following is *not* true of the test data approach?
    a. Test data are processed by the client's computer programs under the auditor's control.
    b. The test data must consist of all possible valid and invalid conditions.
    c. The test data must consist of only those valid and invalid conditions in which the auditor is interested.
    d. Only one transaction of each type need be tested.

    (CPA)

    Problem 29 is based on the flowchart in Figure 14.7.

29. The flowchart in Figure 14.7 depicts
    a. program code checking.
    b. parallel simulation.
    c. integrated test facility.
    d. controlled reprocessing.

    (CPA)

    Problem 30 is based on the flowchart in Figure 14.8.

30. In a credit sales and cash receipts system flowchart, the symbol X could represent
    a. auditor's test data.
    b. remittance advices.
    c. error reports.
    d. credit authorization forms.

    (CPA)

31. Which of the following computer-assisted auditing techniques allows fictitious and real transactions to be processed

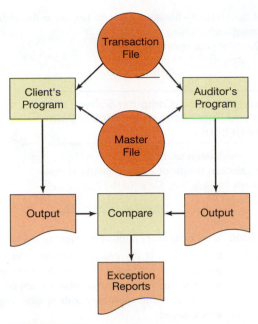

FIGURE 14.7

Flowchart for Problem 29

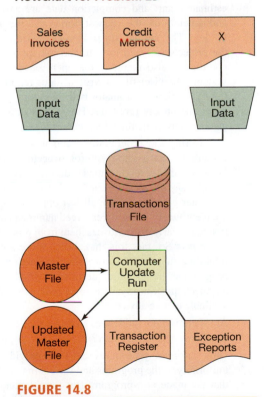

FIGURE 14.8

Flowchart for Problem 30

together without client operating personnel being aware of the testing process?

a. parallel simulation

b. generalized audit software programming

c. integrated test facility

d. test data approach

(CPA)

32. An auditor who is testing information systems controls in a payroll system most likely would use test data that contain conditions such as

a. deductions *not* authorized by employees.

b. overtime *not* approved by supervisors.

c. time tickets with invalid job numbers.

d. payroll checks with unauthorized signatures.

(CPA)

33. An auditor most likely would test for the presence of unauthorized systems program changes by running a

a. program with test data.

b. check-digit verification program.

c. source-code comparison program.

d. program that computes control totals.

(CPA)

34. You decided to use a newly acquired audit software package in auditing accounts payable. The accounts payable system has been computerized for several years, and the transaction records are recorded on magnetic disk.

Required

a. Briefly describe five of the major functions of the typical generalized audit software package.

b. List three important steps in auditing of accounts payable for which generalized audit software can be used.

c. Briefly describe how the generalized audit software should be used to perform these audit steps.

(IIA)

35. An auditor is conducting an examination of the financial statements of a wholesale cosmetics distributor with an inventory consisting of thousands of individual items. The distributor keeps its inventory in its own distribution center and in two public warehouses. An inventory computer file is maintained on a computer disk, and at the end of each business day, the file is updated. Each record of the inventory file contains the following data:

> Item number
>
> Location of item
>
> Description of item
>
> Quantity on hand
>
> Cost per item
>
> Date of last purchase
>
> Date of last sale
>
> Quantity sold during year

The auditor is planning to observe the distributor's physical count of inventories as of a given date. The auditor will have available a computer tape of the data on the inventory file on the date of the physical count and a general-purpose computer software package.

Required

The auditor is planning to perform basic inventory auditing procedures. Identify the basic inventory auditing procedures and describe how using the general-purpose software package and the tape of the inventory file data might be helpful to the auditor in performing such auditing procedures.

Organize your answer as follows:

(CPA)

Basic Inventory Auditing Procedure	How General-Purpose Computer Software Package and Tape of the Inventory File Data Might Be Helpful
1. Observe the physical count, making and recording test counts where applicable.	Determine which items are to be test counted by selecting a random sample of a representative number of items from the inventory file as of the date of the physical counts.

36. Rayo Corporation: Completion of Systems and Programming Questionnaire.[1]

Mike Kess, a senior auditor for the regional accounting firm Sanders and McDonald, was assigned to audit the Rayo Corporation. He was to conduct a preliminary review of the general controls over systems and programming. He has already identified the current applications and the equipment used in the data processing system (Figure 14.9) and is about to start on system maintenance.

Mike contacted Jim Stram, the manager of systems and programming in the EDP department. A summary of their conversation is presented below.

MIKE: How are system maintenance projects initiated and developed?

JIM: All potential projects are sent to a member of my staff called an applications coordinator for analysis. We do all our systems and programming work in-house. If a programming change is required for a project, the applications coordinator prepares a revision request form. These revision request forms must be approved by both the manager of operations and myself. The director of data processing and the internal auditor receive copies of each revision request form for information purposes.

MIKE: How does the applications coordinator keep track of the revision request form and any change that might be made to it?

JIM: The revision request forms are numbered in different series depending on the nature of the change requested. The applications coordinator assigns the next number in the sequence and records in a master log each request he prepares. Changes in revision requests, from whatever source, are prepared on request forms just as initial requests are. Each change request is given the same basic number with a suffix indicating that it is an amendment, and there is a place for recording amendments in the master log.

MIKE: What is the distribution of an approved request form?

JIM: It goes to one of my systems supervisors for design, programming, and testing. The primary effort is usually performed by a programmer who has responsibility over the area of the application or the specific programs to be changed.

MIKE: But how are projects controlled?

JIM: At the beginning of each programming project, an estimated start and completion date are assigned and entered on the request form and the master log. The system supervisor keeps on top of the projects assigned to him, and the applications coordinator also monitors the open requests. The system supervisor files a written status report with the applications coordinator twice a month, and he briefs me on any problems. However, I'm usually aware of any difficulties long before then.

During the programming and testing phase, I think we have good control over the project. None of the compiles made during this phase changes any production source code for the existing computer programs. Also, all test object programs are identified by a strictly enforced naming convention that clearly distinguishes them from production programs. So far, this has been successful in inhibiting their use in processing production. If a programmer has specific questions or problems on a project, his or her systems supervisor generally is available to give advice.

MIKE: Are there written guidelines to direct this activity? If so, how detailed are they?

JIM: Only informal procedures exist to provide any uniformity to the programs and the coding changes that are made to a program. But formal standards do exist that define what documentation should be present for a system and for the programs within a system. These apply to program changes as well and again are strictly enforced. There is a periodic management review to see that we comply. We just had one about a month ago and got a clean bill of health.

[1]Prepared by Frederick L. Neumann, Richard J. Boland, and Jeffrey Johnson; Funded by the Touche Ross Foundation Aid to Accounting Education Program.

Data Center Organization Chart

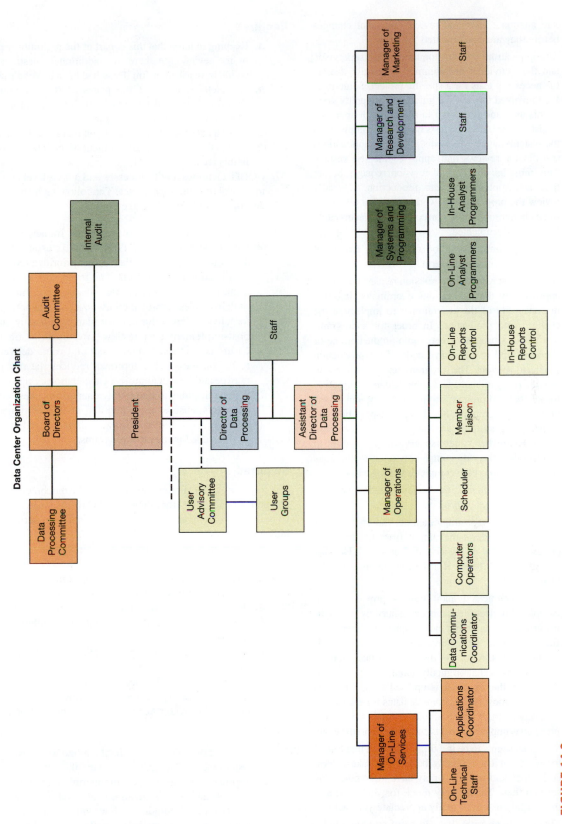

FIGURE 14.9

Chart for Problem 36

MIKE: Are adequate tests and reviews made of changes before they are implemented?

JIM: The applications coordinator, the systems supervisor, and the individual programmer informally discuss the necessary tests for a specific project. Sometimes I get involved too, but our guidelines are pretty good in this area and provide a fairly thorough approach to test design. After the tests have been completed to the systems supervisor's satisfaction, the applications coordinator reviews and approves the test results. This must be done on all revision requests before they are implemented into production. I usually review the programmer's work to see that all authorized changes are made correctly and are adequately tested and documented.

MIKE: How does implementation take place, and what controls are exercised over it?

JIM: After the test results for a revision request have been approved by the applications coordinator, it is the responsibility of the programmer to implement the changes into production. In order for a programmer to put a program change into production, he or she must update the source code of the production program version. The programmer is required to provide program name and compile date information for all changed programs to his or her system supervisor. The programmer also has the responsibility of updating the systems and programming documentation. His or her system supervisor is supposed to review this and certify completion to the applications coordinator, who then completes the log entry.

MIKE: Are postimplementation reviews undertaken on system maintenance projects?

JIM: Once the project is implemented, the applications coordinator reviews the output from the first few production runs of the changed program. He also questions users to see if any problem areas can be identified.

A documented audit trail is provided by a completed project file that is maintained by the applications coordinator for each request number. This file contains all the required documentation, including test results. A copy of the final summary goes to the department that originally submitted the request. A table in the computer is updated to provide listings of the most current compile dates for each set of production object code within the system. Before any program is implemented it is checked against the table.

MIKE: Well, that seems to be it. I think I have all that I need for now, but I'll probably be back to take a look at the files and records. I may have more questions for you then. Thanks very much for your time and thoughtful answers. I really appreciate your help.

JIM: That's quite all right. If I can be of any more help, just let me know.

Required

a. Keeping in mind that this is part of the preliminary phase of the review, are there any additional questions you would have asked of Jim if you had been in Mike's place?

b. Complete as much of the pages of the questionnaire shown in Figure 14.10 as you can from the information Mike did collect in the interview.

c. Make a list of weaknesses that you feel should be considered in the preliminary assessment of the internal control in this area.

37. COBIT identifies 34 IT processes and a high-level approach to control over these processes. The following is the process description of PO10 "Manage Projects."

> A program and project management framework for the management of all IT projects is established. The framework ensures the correct prioritization and coordination of all projects. The framework includes a master plan, assignment of resources, definition of deliverables, approval by users, a phased approach to delivery, QA, a formal test plan, and testing and post-implementation review after installation to ensure project risk management and value delivery to the business. This approach reduces the risk of unexpected costs and project cancellations, improves communications to and involvement of business and end users, ensures the value and quality of project deliverables, and maximizes their contribution to IT-enabled investment programs.

Required

The following items, in random order, are the outcome measures and performance indicators shown for PO10 "Manage Projects." Classify each item as an outcome measure or performance indicator.

1. Percent of projects following project management standards and practices
2. Percent of certified or trained project managers
3. Percent of projects on time and on budget
4. Percent of projects meeting stakeholder expectations
5. Percent of projects receiving postimplementation reviews
6. Percent of stakeholders participating in projects (involvement index)

38. COBIT identifies 34 IT processes and a high-level approach to control over these processes. The following is the process description of AI2 "Acquire and Maintain Application Software."

> Applications are made available in line with business requirements. This process covers the design of the applications, the proper inclusion of application controls and security requirements, and the development and configuration in line with standards. This allows organizations to properly support business operations with the correct automated applications.

Client _____	Audit Date _____		
Systems and Programming Questionnaire	*Yes*	*No*	*N/A*
1. Are there systems and programming standards in the following areas:			
a. Applications design?	___	___	___
b. Programming conventions and procedures?	___	___	___
c. Systems and program documentation?	___	___	___
d. Applications control?	___	___	___
e. Project planning and management?	___	___	___
2. Does the normal documentation for an application include the following:			
Application Documentation			
a. Narrative description?	___	___	___
b. Systems flowchart?	___	___	___
c. Definition of input data and source format?	___	___	___
d. Description of expected output data and format?	___	___	___
e. A listing of all valid transactions and other codes and abbreviations and master file fields affected?	___	___	___
f. File definition or layouts?	___	___	___
g. Instructions for preparing input?	___	___	___
h. Instructions for correcting errors?	___	___	___
i. Backup requirements?	___	___	___
j. Description of test data?	___	___	___
Program Documentation			
a. Program narrative?	___	___	___
b. Flowchart of each program?	___	___	___
c. Current source listing of each program?	___	___	___
Operations Documentation			
a. Data entry instructions, including verification?	___	___	___
b. Instructions for control personnel, including batching?	___	___	___
c. Instructions for the tape librarian?	___	___	___
d. Operator's run manual?	___	___	___
e. Reconstruction procedure?	___	___	___
3. Is there a periodic management review of documentation to ensure that it is current and accurate?	___	___	___
If yes, when and by whom was it last performed?_____			
4. Is all systems and programming work done in-house?	___	___	___
If not, is it done:			
a. By computer manufacturer's personnel?	___	___	___
b. By contract programming?	___	___	___
c. Other? Describe_____			
5. Are all changes programmed by persons other than those assigned to computer operations?	___	___	___
6. Are program changes documented in a manner that preserves an accurate chronological record of the applications?	___	___	___
If yes, describe _____			
7. Do the users participate in the development of new applications or modifications of existing applications through frequent reviews of work performed?			
If yes, are the results of reviews documented?	___	___	___
8. Are testing procedures and techniques standardized?	___	___	___
9. Are program revisions tested as stringently as new programs?	___	___	___
10. Are tests designed to uncover weaknesses in the links between programs, as well as within programs?	___	___	___
11. Are users involved in the testing process, i.e., do they use the application as it is intended during the testing process?	___	___	___
12. Do user departments perform the final review and sign off on projects before acceptance?	___	___	___
13. What departments and/or individuals have the authority to authorize an operator to put a new or modified program into production?_____			
14. What supervisory or management approval is necessary for the conversion of files? _____			

FIGURE 14.10

Questionnaire for Problem 36

Required

The following items, in random order, are the outcome measures and performance indicators shown for AI2 "Acquire and Maintain Application Software." Classify each item as an outcome measure or performance indicator.

1. Average time to deliver functionality based on measures such as function points or lines of code
2. Average programming effort to deliver functionality based on measures such as function points or lines of code
3. Number of production problems per application causing visible downtime
4. Reported defects per month (per function point)
5. Percent of application software projects with a software QA plan developed and executed
6. Percent of application software projects with appropriate review and approval of
7. Percent of development projects on time and on budget
8. Percent of development effort spent maintaining existing applications

Web Research Assignments

39. COBIT is based in part on the maturity model. Write a brief report on the maturity model and how it relates to COBIT.

40. Write a brief report that explains the overall COBIT framework (see www.isaca.org), how it implemented by managers, and how software can be of assistance in implementing COBIT.

Answers to Chapter Quiz

1. a **2.** d **3.** b **4.** d **5.** a **6.** c **7.** c **8.** b **9.** b **10.** b

Index